ATLAS

CONTENTS

HOW TO USE THE ATLAS.................... 4   AZEROTH WORLD MAP 6

REGION MAPS

Alterac Mountains 8	Eastern Plaguelands..................... 40	Stormwind 72
Arathi Highlands 10	Elwynn Forest............................... 42	Stranglethorn Vale 74
Ashenvale 12	Felwood 44	Swamp of Sorrows 76
Azshara 14	Feralas 46	Tanaris 78
Badlands 16	Hillsbrad Foothills 48	Teldrassil 80
Barrens 18	Hinterlands 50	Thousand Needles 82
Blasted Lands 20	Ironforge 52	Thunder Bluff 84
Burning Steppes 22	Loch Modan 54	Tirisfal Glades 86
Darkshore 24	Moonglade 56	Undercity 88
Darnassus 26	Mulgore 58	Un'Goro Crater 90
Deadwind Pass 28	Orgrimmar 60	Western Plaguelands 92
Desolace 30	Redridge Mountains 62	Westfall 94
Dun Morogh 32	Searing Gorge 64	Wetlands 96
Durotar 34	Silithus 66	Winterspring 98
Duskwood 36	Silverpine Forest 68	
Dustwallow Marsh 38	Stonetalon Mountains................... 70	

TOWN & CAMP MAPS

Aerie Peak.................................... 100	Gadgetzan................................... 113	Rut'theran Village 125
Agamand Mills............................. 100	Ghost Walker Post 113	Sen'jin Village.............................. 126
Astranaar 101	Goldshire 114	Sentinel Hill 126
Auberdine 101	Grom'Gol Base Camp 114	The Sepulcher.............................. 127
Bloodhoof Village 102	Hammerfall 115	Shadowglen 127
Bloodvenom Post 102	Hillsbrad Fields 115	Shadowprey Village 128
Booty Bay 103	Kargath 116	Silverwind Refuge 128
Brackenwall Village....................... 104	Kharanos 116	Southshore 129
Brill 104	Lakeshire 117	Splintertree Post 129
The Bulwark................................. 105	Light's Hope Chapel 118	Starfall Villlage 130
Camp Mojache 105	Marshal's Refuge 118	Steamwheedle Port 130
Camp Narache.............................. 105	Menethil Harbor 119	Stonard 131
Camp Taurajo 106	Mirage Raceway 119	Stonetalon Peak........................... 131
Cenarion Hold 106	Mudsprocket................................ 120	Stromgarde Keep 132
Chillwind Camp 107	Morgan's Vigil 120	Sun Rock Retreat 132
Coldridge Valley 107	Nethergarde Keep 120	Talonbranch Glade 133
The Crossroads............................. 107	Nighthaven 121	Tarren Mill 133
Darkshire 108	Nijel's Point 121	Thelsamar 134
Deathknell.................................... 109	Northshire Valley 122	Theramore Isle.............................. 135
Dolanaar 109	Ratchet 122	Thorium Point 136
Emerald Sanctuary 110	Raven Hill 123	Valley of Trials.............................. 136
Everlook 110	Raven Hill: Cemetery 123	Valor's Rest................................... 137
Farstrider Lodge 111	Razor Hill 124	Zoram'gar Outpost 137
Feathermoon Stronghold............... 111	Rebel Camp.................................. 124	Zoram Strand 137
Flame Crest 112	Refuge Pointe 124	
Freewind Post............................... 112	Revantusk Village 125	

INDICES

Main Index...138	Resource Index..187
Flight Masters, Innkeepers,	Rare Mobs...188
Mount Trainers and Weapon Masters......................183	Skill Trainers and Specialty Vendors 191
Class Trainers..184	
Profession Trainers..186	

HOW TO USE THE ATLAS

This project began when we rediscovered Azeroth through new eyes in **World of Warcraft**. The lush regions, vast population of players and the abundance of in-game characters provided the impetus to begin development.

This section explains how each section can be used, both alone and with other sections, and how best to tackle the massive amount of information in the indices.

AZEROTH WORLD MAP

Azeroth is a vast landmass currently broken apart into 40 playable regions. Each region has points of interest including flight points, cities and dungeons. The Azeroth world map shows all this and more. However, to see a more detailed map of the regions, you'll need to refer to those specific maps. The world map is meant to give you an overall view of the world and give you a better understanding about where regions are located in relation to the continents and other regions throughout Azeroth.

FLIGHT POINTS & PATHS

The available flight/travel paths are indicated by faction-specific colors. (See the Azeroth Map Legend.) The points themselves are numbered and correspond to the legends on either side of the map. These legends give you a specific city, town or camp in which the flight points are located. If you're trying to find the Alliance flight point in the Hinterlands (Page 50) for example, you'll see that it's #12 on the Alliance Travel Point legend and can be found at Aerie Peak (Page 100).

Every flight point connects to each other. The in-game flight system automatically finds the quickest path and sends you on your way. If, for example, there's no mage around to offer a port and your hearthstone's still got some cooldown, but you're trying to fly from Booty Bay to Light's Hope Chapel, just take off and the game plots the course for you.

WORLD DUNGEONS

World Dungeons (a.k.a. Instances) are some of the most sought after locations in Azeroth. Dungeons are scattered across both continents and they're marked on the world map with numbered triangles that refer to a corresponding list of dungeon names. (See the Azeroth Map and Continent Instance legends.) The best way to find out exactly where an instance dungeon is within a region is to refer to the region map itself, but the world map offers the perfect start to your search.

ZEPPELINS AND SHIPS

Both types of alternate (often intercontinental) travel are indicated on the map with dotted lines. (See Azeroth Map Legend.)

REGION MAPS

Maps make up the bulk of the atlas and the region maps are going to be used more often than any others. They have been modified from those that you see in game to a) mark all of the mini-regions and b) include a grid. The grid is a component to be used in conjunction with the various indices and serves as a tool to help people find NPCs, monsters, and bosses. (For more information, check out the **Indices** section farther along in this section.)

These maps are listed in alphabetical order. (See the Table of Contents [Page 3] for a complete list.) The major city maps aren't broken out in any special form and are listed alphabetically as well. Region-specific legends border the map and highlight any Flight Masters, Trainers, and Vendors in the region. For ease, Innkeepers are listed under the "Vendors" heading. This is the fastest option to use when trying to discover whether there's a flight point or inn in the region.

Quick reference lists appear at the bottom of the page. These show the corresponding page numbers of any connecting regions and/or associated town/camp maps in the atlas. If you're having a tough time finding a character in one of the towns or camps, take advantage of the quick reference list to pinpoint their location.

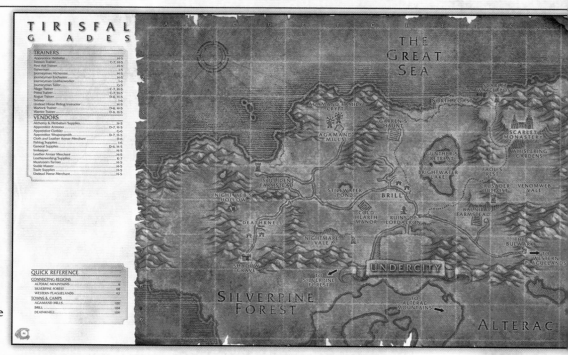

TOWN & CAMP MAPS

This section includes maps that detail some of the more interesting and/or complex areas that often include important NPCs. This section is organized in alphabetical order by the name of the town or encampment, **not** the region from which the maps are drawn.

The region in which the town or encampment can be found is indicated underneath the legend for that specific map, along with the page number of that region.

Callouts on each map correspond to the associated legend. All of the NPCs in the area are marked as are the mobs that may appear. (Some areas have various spawning points of the same type of mob and they're listed with the same number throughout the map.)

 In the legend, a mailbox icon shows whether the area has a mailbox and where it is located.

INDICES

These indices were created for use with the maps included in this atlas. They're cross-referenced with the regions, and the town/camp maps in some cases, and tie into the grids placed onto each region map.

THE MAIN INDEX

This is the exhaustive index in which all the NPCs, mobs (or creeps if you're a **Warcraft** player), and bosses appear. Here's the basic information that you'll find in a single entry.

Aayndia Floralwind
Ashenvale (12), Astranaar (101), E-5, Expert
Leatherworker, Left as you enter southwest building

Name: Aayndia Floralwind
Region: Ashenvale (Page 12)
Sub-Region: Astranaar (Page 101)
Grid: E-5 on the Ashenvale map
Title/Description: Expert Leatherworker
Note: A note on the location of the subject, what may be of interest about the subject, or the rarity of the subject

Here are a few things to keep in mind about the index entries.

- A subject may roam outside of the mentioned Grid, Sub-Region, and occasionally the Region. The information given in the listing only shows where it **spawns**.
- The page numbers in the Region and Sub-Region entries relate to pages in the Atlas where any associated maps are located. Many Sub-Regions don't have maps.
- Many entries don't have Sub-Regions or Titles/Descriptions. A few won't have Grid locations since they spawn throughout a Region (normally a city).

SUPPLEMENTAL INDICES

These indices were created to offer other ways to look up specific types of NPCs. For example, if you're looking for the enchanting trainers of the world, look in the table listing those trainers. The same rule applies for class trainers.

Class Trainer Listings

This is where to look to find trainers for your specific class. However, they're not broken down by faction, just region. If you're a Night Elf Priest, you can be sure that Aelthalyste (a Priest Trainer in the Undercity) won't be helping you any time soon.

Profession Trainer Listings

These lists show where all the trainers are for each profession and secondary skill and their level: Journeyman, Expert, Artisan, or Master.

Faction Flight Point Listings

This is a simple list for each faction showing all the flight points and in which Regions/Mini-Regions they appear.

Resource Listings

These tables are quick references to discover where to find specific resources. The Herb and Ore tables cross-reference each type of resource with each of the regions. To discover whether there's Tin Ore to be found in a region, just look across the table. Vice versa, if you want to discover which herbs are available in Felwood, that table shows all the available herbs in the region.

The Leather table explains which mobs to hunt for each type of leather. The general leather list is broken down by skill level, but the specialty leather list shows exactly which mobs to hunt for specific types of leather.

Vendor Listings

These lists break down each type of vendor and where to find them. General and Trade Goods vendors are excluded from this list since they appear all over the world and in almost every city or town. The vendors that many players are interested in are the unique and rare vendors scattered across the world of Azeroth.

Rare Spawn Listings

There are rare spawning mobs throughout the world and they often have better drops than regular mobs—that's why they're so sought after. This list shows all of the rare mobs, their levels, and their rarity. Use the corresponding table to decipher how often certain mobs spawn.

Many mobs and NPCs appear in multiple grids. The easiest type of grid entry is the simplest, a single vertical and horizontal coordinate: e.g. E-5. If an NPC appears in two adjacent grids, that would be listed in two ways. First, if it spawns in two horizontally adjacent grids, the grid locations are separated by a comma: e.g. E-5, F-5. If it's two vertically adjacent grids, it's shown with parenthesis: e.g. E:(5, 6). Lastly, if a mob appears in a few vertical grid locations, it's separated with a hyphen: e.g. E:(5-9).

There are many mobs that appear throughout a given map. The Angerclaw Grizzly in Felwood is a great example. Here's the grid entry for that mob: G:(2, 3), H:(1-3), I-2.

That mob is in the following grid locations: G-2, G-3, H-1, H-2, H-3, and I-2.

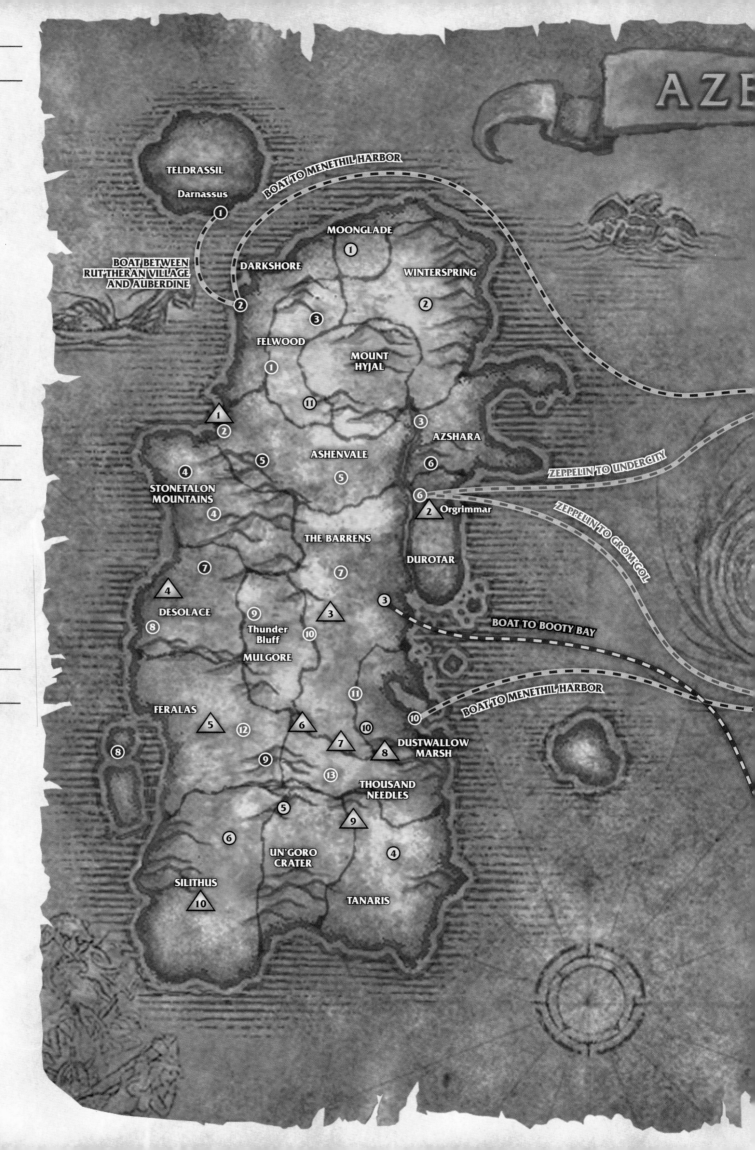

HORDE TRAVEL POINTS

1. Bloodvenom Post
2. Zoram'gar Outpost
3. Valormok
4. Sunrock Retreat
5. Splintertree Post
6. Orgrimmar
7. Crossroads
8. Shadowprey Village
9. Thunder Bluff
10. Camp Taurajo
11. Brackenwall Village
12. Camp Mojache
13. Freewind Post
14. Undercity
15. The Sepulcher
16. Tarren Mill
17. Hammerfall
18. Revantusk Village
19. Kargath
20. Flame Crest
21. Grom'Gol Base Camp
22. Stonard

NEUTRAL TRAVEL POINTS

1. Moonglade
2. Everlook
3. Ratchet
4. Gadgetzan
5. Marshall's Refuge
6. Cenarion Hold
7. Light's Hope Chapel
8. Thorium Point
9. Booty Bay
10. Mudsprocket
11. Emerald Sanctuary

KALIMDOR INSTANCES

1. Blackfathom Deeps
2. Ragefire Chasm
3. The Wailing Caverns
4. Maraudon
5. Dire Maul
6. Razorfen Kraul
7. Razorfen Downs
8. Onyxia's Lair
9. Zul'Farrak
10. Ahn'Qiraj

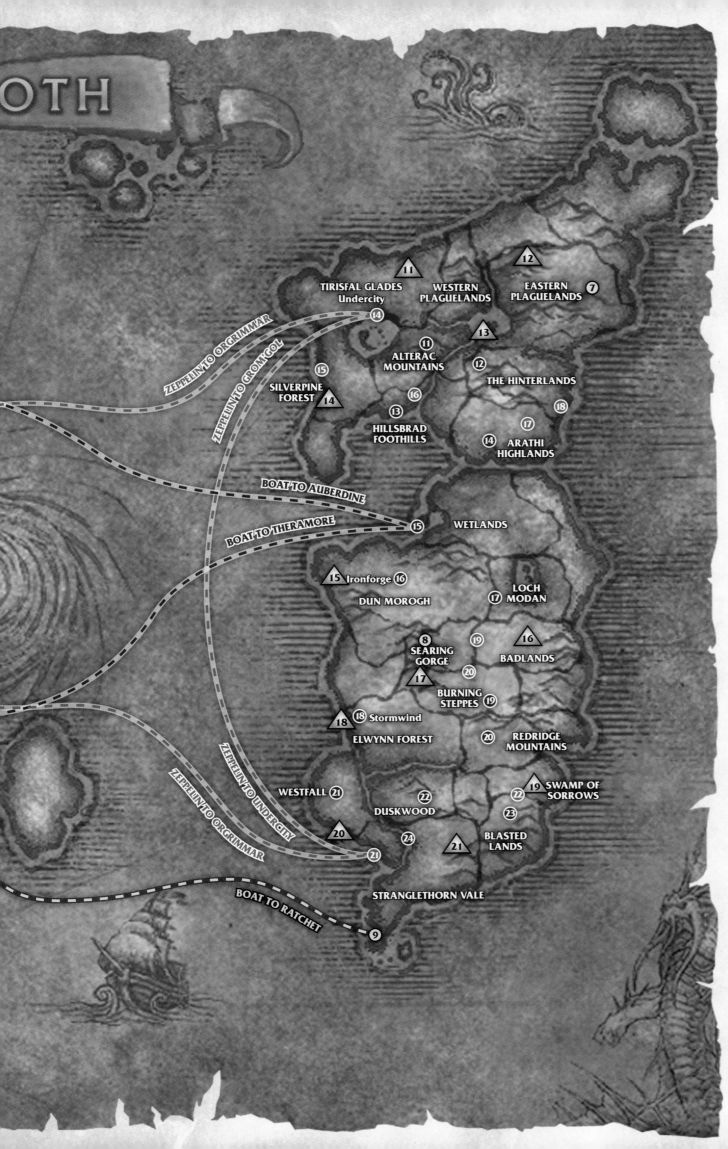

OTH

ALLIANCE TRAVEL POINTS

1 Rut'theran Village
2 Auberdine
3 Talonbranch Glade
4 Stonetalon Peak
5 Astranaar
6 Talrendls Point
7 Nijel's Point
8 Feathermoon Stronghold
9 Thalanaar
10 Theramore Isle
11 Chillwind Camp
12 Aerie Peak
13 Southshore
14 Refuge Pointe
15 Menethil Harbor
16 Ironforge
17 Thelsamar
18 Stormwind
19 Morgan's Vigil
20 Lakeshire
21 Sentinel Hill
22 Darkshire
23 Nethergarde Keep
24 Rebel Camp

EASTERN KINGDOMS INSTANCES

11 Scarlet Monastery
12 Stratholme
13 Scholomance
14 Shadowfang Keep
15 Gnomeregan
16 Uldaman
17 Blackrock Depths
   Blackrock Spire
   Blackwing Lair
   The Molten Core
18 The Stockade
19 The Temple of Atal'Hakkar
20 The Deadmines
21 Zul'Gurub

MAP LEGEND

 Instance
 Alliance Flight Point
- - - Alliance Boat Path
 Horde Travel Point
- - - Horde Zeppelin Path
○ Neutral Travel Point
▭▭ Neutral Boat Path

Map labels

TIRISFAL GLADES
Undercity
WESTERN PLAGUELANDS
EASTERN PLAGUELANDS
ALTERAC MOUNTAINS
THE HINTERLANDS
SILVERPINE FOREST
HILLSBRAD FOOTHILLS
ARATHI HIGHLANDS
ZEPPELIN TO ORGRIMMAR
ZEPPELIN TO GROMGOL
BOAT TO AUBERDINE
BOAT TO THERAMORE
WETLANDS
Ironforge
DUN MOROGH
LOCH MODAN
SEARING GORGE
BADLANDS
BURNING STEPPES
Stormwind
ELWYNN FOREST
REDRIDGE MOUNTAINS
ZEPPELIN TO UNDERCITY
ZEPPELIN TO ORGRIMMAR
WESTFALL
DUSKWOOD
SWAMP OF SORROWS
BLASTED LANDS
BOAT TO RATCHET
STRANGLETHORN VALE

VENDORS

Alchemy Supplies.. E-4
Engineering Supplies F-4
Rewards Vendor E-8, I-6

HERBALISM

Herb Name	Herbalism Skill Requirement
Bruiseweed	100
Fadeleaf	160
Goldthorn	170
Grave Moss	120
Khadgar's Whisker	185
Kingsblood	125
Liferoot	150
Stranglekelp	85
Wild Steelbloom	115
Wintersbite	195

MINING

Ore Name	Mining Skill Requirement
Copper	1
Gold	155
Iron	125
Mithril	175
Silver	75
Tin	65
Truesilver	230

QUICK REFERENCE

CONNECTING REGIONS

HILLSBRAD FOOTHILLS 48
SILVERPINE FOREST..68
WESTERN PLAGUELANDS...92

HILLSBRAD

TO
HILLSBRAD
FOOTHILLS

THORADIN'S
WALL

NORTHFOLD
MANOR

CIRCLE OF
WEST
BINDING

DABYRIE'S
FARMSTEAD

BOULDER'GOR &
BOULDERFIST
OUTPOST

REFUGE
POINTE

CIRCLE OF
OUTER BINDING

STROMGARDE
KEEP

CIRCLE OF
INNER BINDING

THE TOWER
OF ARATHOR

BOULDERFIST
HALL

FALDIR'S COVE

BLACKWATER
SHIPWRECK

TO
THE WETLANDS

THE DROWNED
REEF

THANDOL
SPAN

ARATHI HIGHLANDS

FLIGHT MASTERS

Gryphon Master...F-5
Wind Rider Master..J-3

TRAINERS

Superior Butcher...J-3
Trauma Surgeon (First Aid).................................J-4

VENDORS

Alchemy Supplies...F-5
Bowyer...J-3
Butcher...F-4, J-3
General Goods..F-5, J-3
Innkeeper...J-3
Leatherworking Supplies..................................F-5, J-3
Scrolls and Potions..C-6
Stable Master..J-3
Superior Macecrafter..F-5
Superior Tradesman F-5
Tailoring Supplies...J-4
Trade Goods J-3

HERBALISM

Herb Name	Herbalism Skill Requirement
Bruiseweed	100
Fadeleaf	160
Goldthorn	170
Grave Moss	120
Khadgar's Whisker	185
Kingsblood	125
Liferoot	150
Stranglekelp	85
Wild Steelbloom	115

MINING

Ore Name	Mining Skill Requirement
Gold	155
Iron	125
Lesser Bloodstone	75
Mithril	175
Silver	75
Tin	65
Truesilver	230

QUICK REFERENCE

CONNECTING REGIONS

HILLSBRAD FOOTHILLS 48
WETLANDS..96

CITY & CAMPS

HAMMERFALL 115
STROMGARDE KEEP..132
REFUGE POINT..124

ASHENVALE

FLIGHT MASTERS

Hippogryph Master E-5	Wind Rider Master B-4

TRAINERS

Expert Alchemist G-6	Hunter
Expert Leatherworker ... E-5	Trainer C-6, F-6, G-6
Fisherman B-4	Pet Trainer C-6, F-6
Herbalist G-6	Skinner F-6

VENDORS

Alchemy Supplies G-6	Leather Armor
Baker E-5	Merchant E-5
Bowyer G-6	Leatherworking
Clothier E-5	Supplies C-6, E-5
Fish Merchant	Reagent Supplies E-5
& Supplies B-4	Silverwing Supply
Food & Drink Vendor E-5	Officer H-8
General Goods E-5	Stable Master E-5
Heavy Armor	Tools & Supplies E-5
Merchant I-6	Trade Goods E-5, F-6
Innkeeper E-5, I-6	Weaponsmith E-5

HERBALISM

Herb Name	Herbalism Skill Requirement
Briarthorn	70
Bruiseweed	100
Kingsblood	125
Liferoot	150
Mageroyal	50
Purple Lotus	210
Stranglekelp	85
Wild Steelbloom	115

MINING

Ore Name	Mining Skill Requirement
Copper	1
Gold	155
Iron	125
Silver	75
Tin	65

QUICK REFERENCE

CONNECTING REGIONS

AZSHARA	14
BARRENS	18
DARKSHORE	24
DUROTAR	34
FELWOOD	44
STONETALON MOUNTAINS	70

TOWNS & CAMPS

ASTRANAAR	101
SILVERWIND REFUGE	128
SPLINTERTREE POST	129
ZORAM STRAND	137
ZORAM'GAR OUTPOST	137

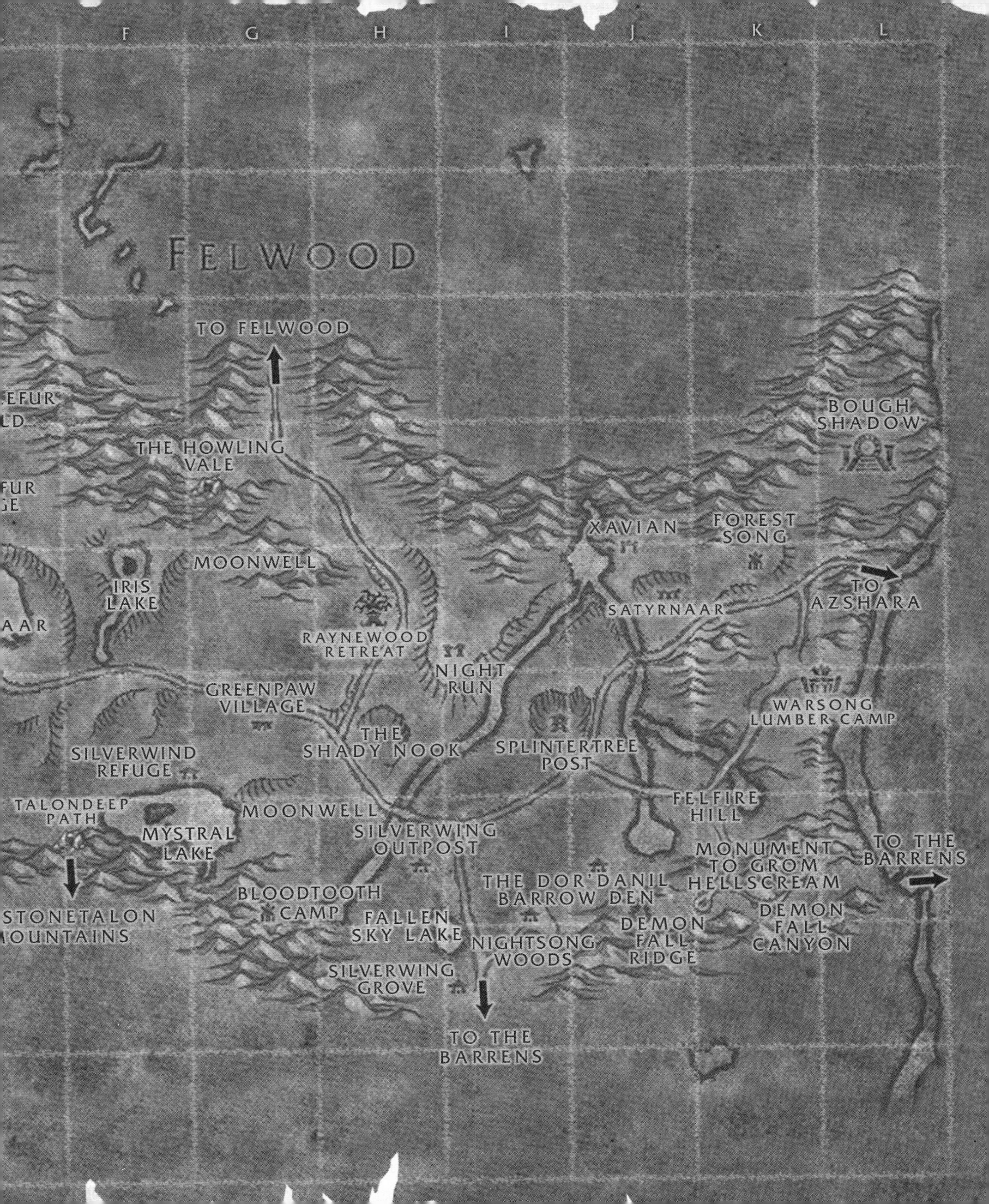

FELWOOD

TO FELWOOD

BOUGH
SHADOW

THE HOWLING
VALE

XAVIAN

FOREST
SONG

.EFUR
LD

MOONWELL

SATYRNAAR

TO
AZSHARA

FUR
GE

IRIS
LAKE

RAYNEWOOD
RETREAT

AAR

NIGHT
RUN

WARSONG
LUMBER CAMP

GREENPAW
VILLAGE

THE
SHADY NOOK

SPLINTERTREE
POST

SILVERWIND
REFUGE

FELFIRE
HILL

TALONDEEP
PATH

MOONWELL

MYSTRAL
LAKE

SILVERWING
OUTPOST

MONUMENT
TO GROM
HELLSCREAM

TO THE
BARRENS

STONETALON
MOUNTAINS

BLOODTOOTH
CAMP

FALLEN
SKY LAKE

THE DOR'DANIL
BARROW DEN

DEMON
FALL
RIDGE

DEMON
FALL
CANYON

NIGHTSONG
WOODS

SILVERWING
GROVE

TO THE
BARRENS

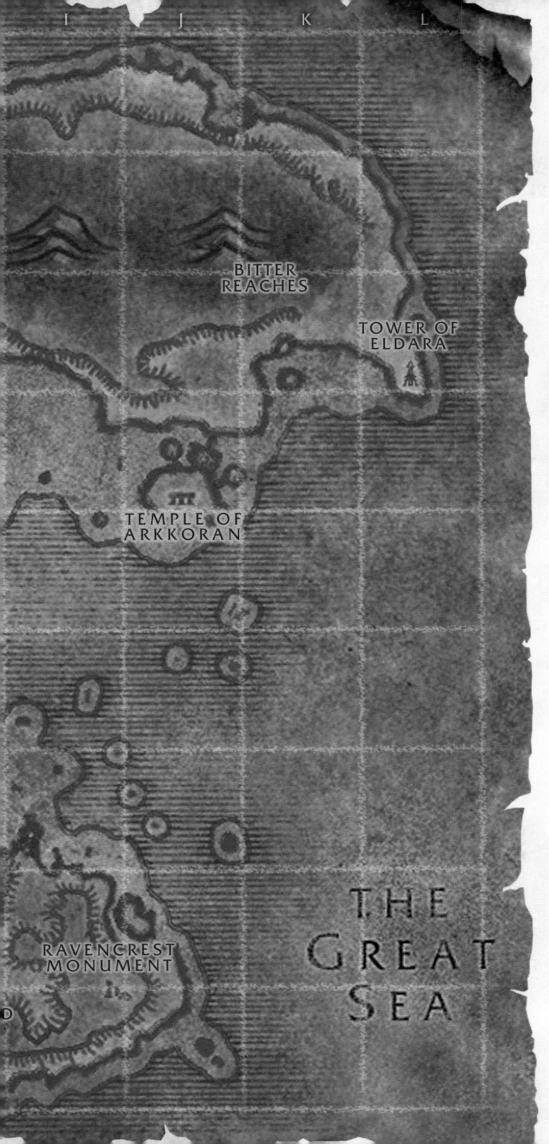

FLIGHT MASTERS

Hippogryph Master A-8
Wind Rider Master B-5

TRAINER

Master Dragonscale Leatherworker D-6

VENDORS

Bowyer A-8
Engineering Supplies E-9
Food & Drink B-5
Trade Supplies E-9
Weaponsmith B-5

HERBALISM

Herb Name	Herbalism Skill Requirement
Dreamfoil	270
Golden Sansam	260
Goldthorn	170
Khadgar's Whisker	185
Mountain Silversage	280
Purple Lotus	210
Stranglekelp	85
Sungrass	230

MINING

Ore Name	Mining Skill Requirement
Gold	155
Mithril	175
Rich Thorium	270
Truesilver	230

QUICK REFERENCE

CONNECTING REGIONS

ASHENVALE 12

BADLANDS

FLIGHT MASTER
Wind Rider Master A-5

VENDORS
Blacksmithing Supplies F-5
General Goods A-5
Innkeeper A-5
Light Armor & Weapons Merchant A-5
Master Dragonscale Trainer I-6
Stable Master A-5

HERBALISM

Herb Name	Herbalism Skill Requirement
Fadeleaf	160
Firebloom	205
Goldthorn	170
Khadgar's Whisker	185
Kingsblood	125
Purple Lotus	210
Wild Steelbloom	115

MINING

Ore Name	Mining Skill Requirement
Gold	155
Indurium	150
Iron	125
Mithril	175
Silver	75
Truesilver	230

QUICK REFERENCE
CONNECTING REGIONS
LOCH MODAN 54
SEARING GORGE 64
TOWNS & CAMPS
KARGATH 116

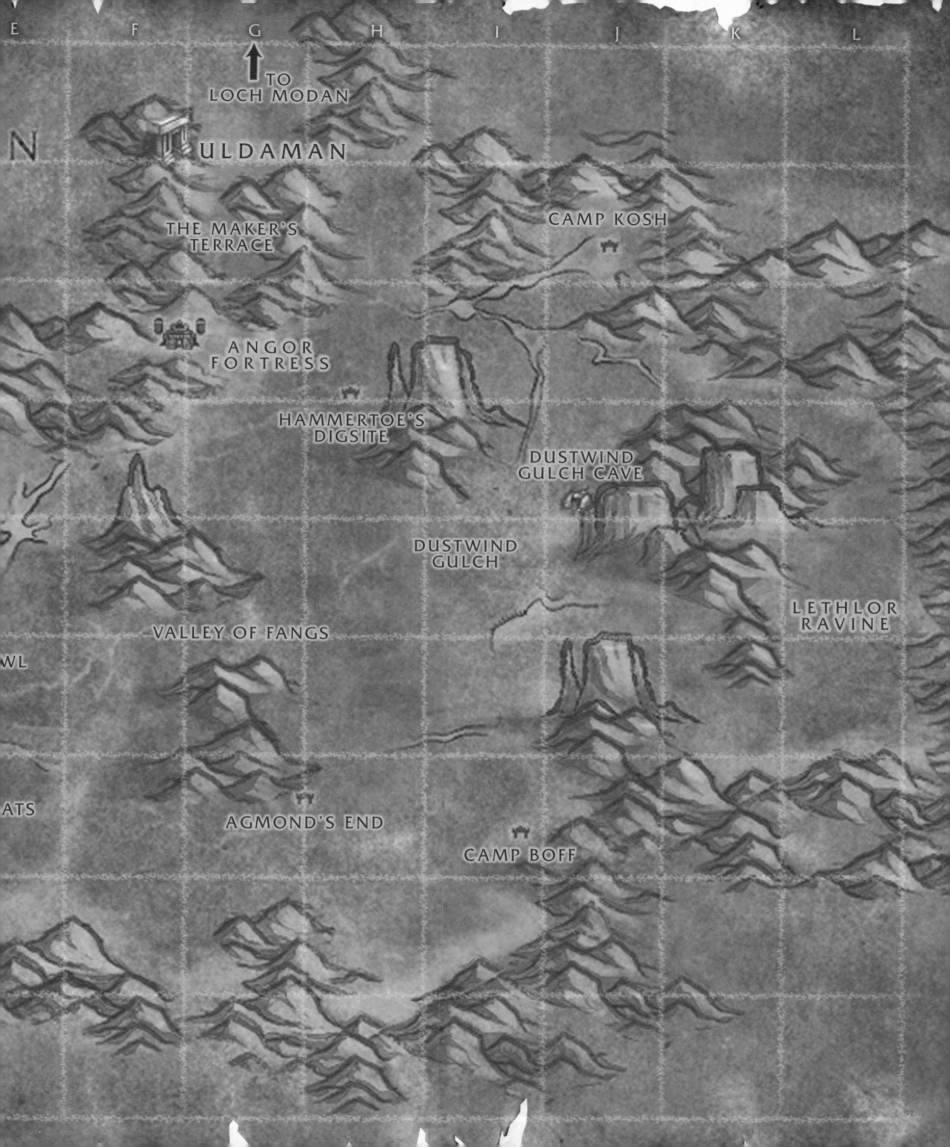

FLIGHT MASTER

Wind Rider Master F-3, E-6

TRAINERS

Cook G-3	Journeyman
Expert Blacksmith F-3	Leatherworker E-4
Expert Leatherworker ... E-6	Journeyman Tailor F-3
Expert Tailor.................. E-6	Master Goblin
Fisherman....................H-4	Engineer H-4
Journeyman Engineer....H-4	Skinner E-6

VENDORS

Armorer &	Leather Armor
Shieldcrafter................H-4	Merchant.............. E-4, E-6
Bael'dun Morale	Reagents and Herbs.......F-3
Officer F-8	Smokywood Pastures.... E-1
Bags & Sacks F-3	Specialist Leatherworking
Baker F-3, G-3	Supplies...................... E-4
Beverage Merchant F-3	Stable Master..F-3, E-6, H-4
Blacksmithing Supplies ..F-3	Stylish Clothier.............. E-4
Bowyer & Gunsmith F-3	Tailoring & Leatherworking
Butcher.................. F-3, E-6	Supplies...................... E-6
Cloth & Leather	Tailoring Supplies...........F-3
Armor Merchant.........H-4	Trade Supplies F-3, H-4
Clothier.........................F-3	Warsong Supply
Engineering Goods H-4	Officer E-1
General Supplies....F-3, H-4	Weapon Dealer.............G-4
Innkeeper F-3, E-6, H-4	Weaponsmith F-3, H-4
Leather & Mail Armor	Weaponsmith &
Merchant.....................F-3	Armorcrafter.............. E-1

HERBALISM

Herb Name	Herbalism Skill Requirement	Herb Name	Herbalism Skill Requirement
Briarthorn	70	Mageroyal	50
Bruiseweed	100	Peacebloom	1
Earthroot	15	Silverleaf	1
Grave Moss	120	Wild Steelbloom	115
Kingsblood	125		

MINING

Ore Name	Mining Skill Requirement
Copper	1
Silver	75
Tin	65

QUICK REFERENCE

CONNECTING REGIONS

ASHENVALE 12	MULGORE 58
DUROTAR.................... 34	STONETALON
DUSTWALLOW	MOUNTAINS............. 70
MARSH.................... 38	THOUSAND NEEDLES ... 82

TOWNS & CAMPS

CAMP TAURAJO 106	RATCHET 122
THE CROSSROADS 107	

BLASTED LANDS

FLIGHT MASTER
Gryphon Master...J-2

VENDORS
Alchemy Supplies...J-2
Armor Crafter J-2
Food & Drink I-2

HERBALISM

Herb Name	Herbalism Skill Requirement
Firebloom	205
Gromsblood	250
Sungrass	230

MINING

Ore Name	Mining Skill Requirement
Gold	155
Iron	125
Mithril	175
Small Thorium	250
Truesilver	230

QUICK REFERENCE

CONNECTING REGIONS
SWAMP OF SORROWS...................................76

CAMPS & TOWNS
NETHERGARDE KEEP...................................120

F   G   H   I   J   K   L

TO SWAMP OF
SORROWS

GARRISON
ARMORY

DREADMAUL
HOLD

NETHERGARDE
KEEP

RISE OF THE
DEFILER

ALTAR OF
STORMS

THE SERPENT'S
COIL

DREADMAUL
POST

THE
DARK PORTAL

THE
TAINTED SCAR

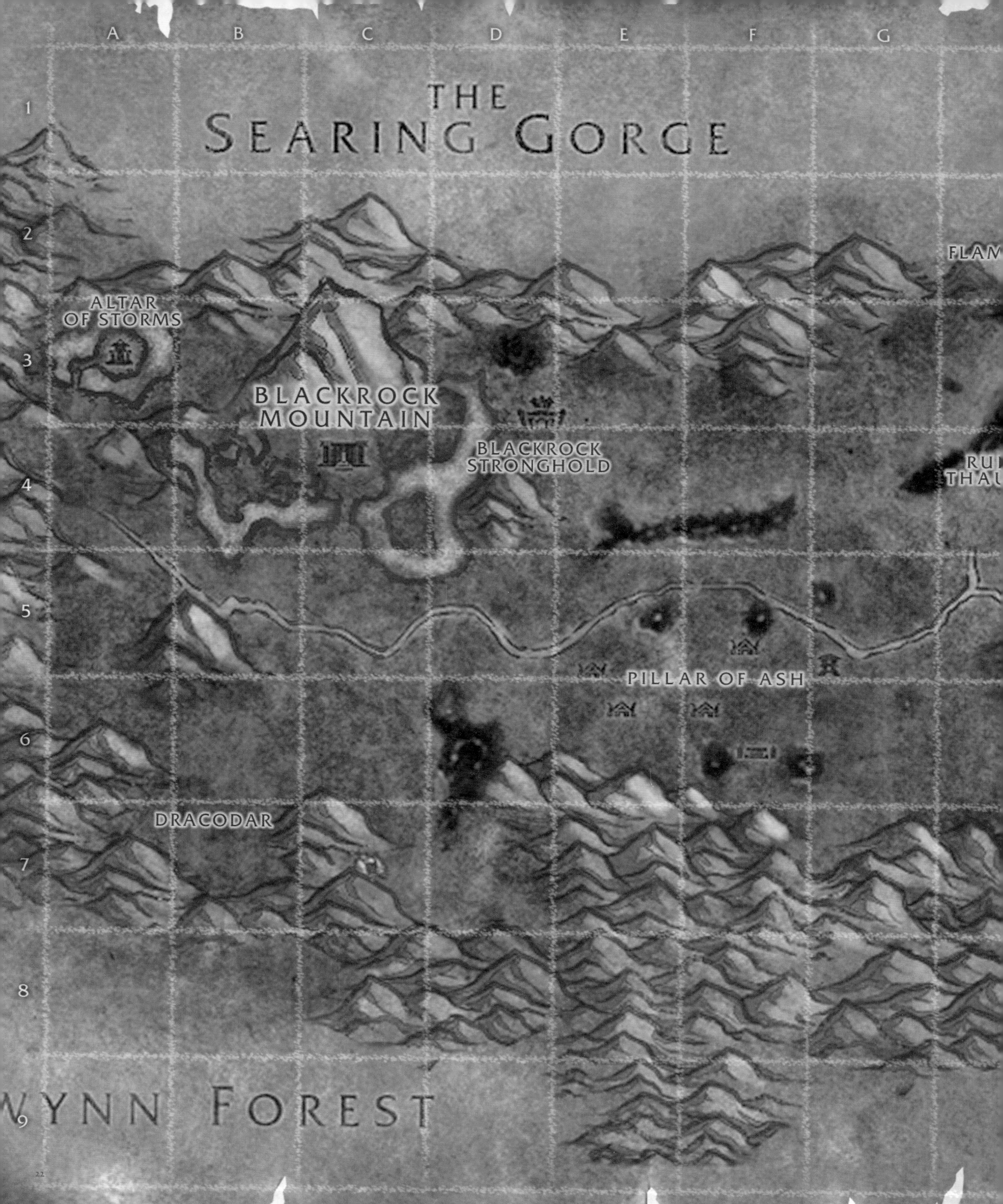
A
B
C
D
E
F
G
1
2
3
4
5
6
7
8
9
THE SEARING GORGE
ALTAR OF STORMS
BLACKROCK MOUNTAIN
BLACKROCK STRONGHOLD
FLAM
RU
THAU
PILLAR OF ASH
DRACODAR
WYNN FOREST

Map labels:

RIJKL

SLITHER ROCK

DREADMAUL ROCK

TERROR WING PATH

BLACKROCK PASS

MORGAN'S VIGIL

TO REDRIDGE MOUNTAINS

REDRIDGE MOUNTAINS

FLIGHT MASTERS

Gryphon Master...K-7
Wind Rider Master...H-2

VENDORS

Food & Drink Vendor H-2, K-7
Weaponsmith K-7

HERBALISM

Herb Name	Herbalism Skill Requirement
Black Lotus	300
Dreamfoil	270
Golden Sansam	260
Mountain Silversage	280
Sungrass	230

MINING

Ore Name	Mining Skill Requirement
Dark Iron	230
Gold	155
Iron	125
Mithril	175
Rich Thorium	270
Small Thorium	250
Truesilver	230

QUICK REFERENCE

CONNECTING REGIONS

REDRIDGE MOUNTAINS...62
SEARING GORGE 64

TOWNS & CAMPS

FLAME CREST...112
MORGAN'S VIGIL 120

DARKSHORE

FLIGHT MASTER

Hippogryph Master F-4

TRAINERS

Fisherman... E-6
Journeyman Blacksmith..F-4
Journeyman Engineer...F-4
Journeyman Tailor..F-4
Mining Trainer...F-4

VENDORS

Armorer & Shieldsmith..F-4
Baker..F-4
Blacksmithing Supplies F-4
Clothier..F-4
Drink Vendor..F-4
Fish Vendor..F-4
Food & Drink Vendor F-4, G-8
General Goods..F-4
General Trade Supplies F-4
Innkeeper F-4
Leather Armor & Leatherworking Supplies F-4
Mining Supplies...F-4
Stable Master..F-4
Tailoring Supplies..F-4
Trade Supplies G-8
Weaponsmith F-4

HERBALISM

Herb Name	Herbalism Skill Requirement
Briarthorn	70
Bruiseweed	100
Earthroot	15
Mageroyal	50
Peacebloom	1
Silverleaf	1
Stranglekelp	85

MINING

Ore Name	Mining Skill Requirement
Copper	1
Silver	75
Tin	65

QUICK REFERENCE

CONNECTING REGIONS

ASHENVALE..12
TELDRASSIL 80

TOWNS & CAMPS

AUBERDINE 101

MIST'S EDGE

RUINS OF MATHYSTRA

CLIFFSPRING RIVER

TOWER OF ALTHALAXX

BLACKWOOD VILLAGE

CLIFFSPRING FALLS (MUSHROOM CAVE)

BASHAL'ARAN

THISTLEBEAR DEN

AUBERDINE

AMETH'ARAN

TWILIGHT VALE

WILDBEND RIVER

GROVE OF THE ANCIENTS

REMTRAVEL'S EXCAVATION

BLACKWOOD DEN

THE MASTER'S GLAIVE

TO ASHENVALE

MOONG

FELWOOD

DARNASSUS

CITY OFFICIALS

Alliance Cloth Quartermaster	I-2
Alterac Valley Battlemaster	H-4
Arathi Basin Battlemaster	H-4
Auctioneer	G-5, H-5
Bankers	E-4
Commendations	E-4
Eye of the Storm Battlemaster	H-4
Guild Master	I-2
Warsong Gulch Battlemaster	H-3

TRAINERS

Artisan Alchemist	G-2
Artisan Leatherworker	I-2
Cooking Trainer	F-2
Druid Trainer	D-1
Expert Enchanter	H-1
Expert Leatherworker	I-2
Expert Tailor	H-2
First Aid Trainer	G-1
Fishing Trainer	F-5
Herbalism Trainer	F-7
Hunter Trainer	E-1
Journeyman Alchemist	G-2
Journeyman Enchanter	H-1
Journeyman Leatherworker	I-2
Journeyman Tailor	I-2
Nightsaber Riding Instructor	E-1
Pet Trainer	E-1
Portal Trainer	E-8
Priest Trainer	E:(8, 9)
Rogue Trainer	D-2, E-2
Skinning Trainer	I-2
Warrior Trainer	H:(3, 4)
Weapon Master	H-5

VENDORS

Alchemy Supplies	G-2
Axe Merchant	I-6
Bag Merchant	I-5
Blade Merchant	I-6
Bow Merchant	H-6
Cloth Armor Merchant	H-7
Cooking Supplies	F-2
Enchanting Supplies	H-1
Fish Vendor	F-5
Fishing Supplies	F-5
Food & Drink	D-1, F-2, K-4
General Goods Vendor	I-5, K-5
General Trade Supplies	H-2
Herbalism Supplies	F-7
Innkeeper	I:(1, 2)
Leather Armor Merchant	G-8
Leatherworking Supplies	I-2
Mace & Staff Merchant	I-6
Mail Armor Merchant	H-7
Meat Vendor	H-5
Night Elf Armorer	H-4
Owl Trainer	K-4
Poison Vendor	D-2
Reagent Vendor	D-1, F-7
Robe Vendor	G-9
Saber Handler	E-1
Shield Merchant	H-7
Stable Master	E-1
Staff Merchant	G-9
Tabard Vendor	I-2
Tailoring Supplies	I-2
Thrown Weapons Merchant	H-6
Two Handed Weapon Merchant	H-7
Weapon Merchant	H-4, I-6

QUICK REFERENCE

CONNECTING REGIONS

TELDRASSIL 80

LAVE

CRAFTSMEN'S
TERRACE

CITY
ENTRANCE

WARRIOR'S
TERRACE

ARDENS

TRADESMEN'S
TERRACE

THE MOON

DARNASSUS

SWAMP
OF
SORROWS

THE
LASTED LANDS

DESOLACE

FLIGHT MASTERS

Hippogryph Master H-1
Wind Rider Master..B-7

TRAINERS

Expert Leathercrafter G-6
Fisherman...B-7
Skinning Trainer B-7

VENDORS

Cooking Supplies...C-7
Fishing Supplies B-7
Food & Drink G-5, I-1
General Goods..C-7, I-1
Innkeeper C-7, I-1
Mail Armor Merchant I-1
Stable Master..C-7, I-1
Superior Macecrafter G-6
Trade Goods G-5
Trade Supplies B-7
Weapons Vendor C-7

HERBALISM

Herb Name	Herbalism Skill Requirement
Bruiseweed	100
Ghost Mushroom	245
Grave Moss	120
Gromsblood	250
Kingsblood	125
Liferoot	150
Wild Steelbloom	115

MINING

Ore Name	Mining Skill Requirement
Copper	1
Gold	155
Iron	125
Mithril	175
Silver	75
Tin	65
Truesilver	230

QUICK REFERENCE

CONNECTING REGIONS
FERALAS..46
STONETALON MOUNTAINS................................70

CAMPS & TOWNS
GHOST WALKER POST 113
NIJEL'S POINT 121
SHADOWPREY VILLAGE 128

DUN MOROGH

TRAINERS

Cooking Trainer	F-5, I-5
Demon Trainer	D-7, F-5
Fisherman	E-4
Hunter Trainer	D-7, F-5
Journeyman Blacksmith	F-5
Journeyman Engineer	G-5
Mage Trainer	D-7, F-5
Mechanostrider Pilot	G-5
Mining Trainer	G-5, J-6
Paladin Trainer	D-7, F-5
Pet Trainer	F-5
Physician	F-5
Priest Trainer	D-7, F-5
Ram Riding Instructor	I-5
Rogue Trainer	D-7, F-5
Warlock Trainer	D-7, F-5
Warrior Trainer	D-7, F-5

VENDORS

Ale & Wine	D-5
Apprentice Weaponsmith	I-6
Armorer	D-7, F-5
Blacksmithing Supplies	F-5
Cloth & Leather Armor Merchant	D-7, F-5
Dwarven Weaponsmith	I-5
Engineering Supplies	G-5
Fisherman Supplies	D-4
Food & Drink Merchant	I-5
General Supplies	D-7, F-5
Gunsmith	E-6
Innkeeper	F-5
Leather Armor Merchant	D-4
Mechanostrider Merchant	G-5
Pet Vendor	I-5
Ram Breeder	I-5
Stable Master	F-5
Tradesman	F-5
Weaponsmith	D-7, F-5

HERBALISM

Herb Name	Herbalism Skill Requirement
Earthroot	15
Peacebloom	1
Silverleaf	1

MINING

Ore Name	Mining Skill Requirement
Copper	1

QUICK REFERENCE

CONNECTING REGIONS

IRONFORGE	52
LOCH MODAN	54

TOWNS & CAMPS

COLDRIDGE VALLEY	107
KHARANOS	116

Map labels: GNOMEREGAN, ICEFLO LAKE, BREWNALL VILLAGE, FROSTMANE HOLD, ANVILMAR, COL, COLDRIDGE VALLEY

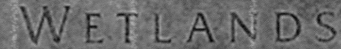

WETLANDS

IRONFORGE

AIRSTRIP

NORTH GATE
PASS

TO LOCH
MODAN

NORTH GATE
OUTPOST

SHIMMER
RIDGE

MISTY PINE
REFUGE

STEELGRILL'S
DEPOT

SOUTH GATE
OUTPOST

L BREEZE
ALLEY

KHARANOS

AMBERSTILL
RANCH

SOUTH GATE
PASS

HELM'S
BED LAKE

TO LOCH
MODAN

THE
GRIZZLED
DEN

GOL'BOLAR
QUARRY
AND MINE

IRONBAND'S
COMPOUND

THE
SEARING GORGE

DUROTAR

TRAINERS

Demon Trainer	F-7, H-4
First Aid Trainer	H-4
Fisherman	H-8
Herbalist	H-7
Hunter Trainer	F-7, H-4
Journeyman Alchemist	H-7
Journeyman Blacksmith	H-4
Journeyman Engineer	H-4
Mage Trainer	F-7, H-7
Miner	H-4
Pet Trainer	H-4
Priest Trainer	F-7, H-4
Raptor Riding Trainer	H-7
Rogue Trainer	F-7, H-4
Shaman Trainer	F-7, H-4
Warlock Trainer	F-7, H-4
Warrior Trainer	F-7, H-4

VENDORS

Armorer & Shieldcrafter	F-7, H-4
Bowyer	H-4
Butcher	F-7, H:(4, 7)
Cloth & Leather Armor Merchant	F-7, H-4
Fishing Supplies	H-7
General Goods	F-7, H:(4, 7)
Innkeeper	H-4
Raptor Handler	H-7
Stable Master	H-4
Trade Supplies	H:(4, 7)
Weapon Merchant	H-7
Weaponsmith	F-7, H-4

HERBALISM

Herb Name	Herbalism Skill Requirement
Earthroot	15
Peacebloom	1
Silverleaf	1

MINING

Ore Name	Mining Skill Requirement
Copper	1

QUICK REFERENCE

CONNECTING REGIONS

ASHENVALE 12
BARRENS 18
ORGRIMMAR 60

TOWNS & CAMPS

RAZOR HILL 124
SEN'JIN VILLAGE 126
VALLEY OF TRIALS 136

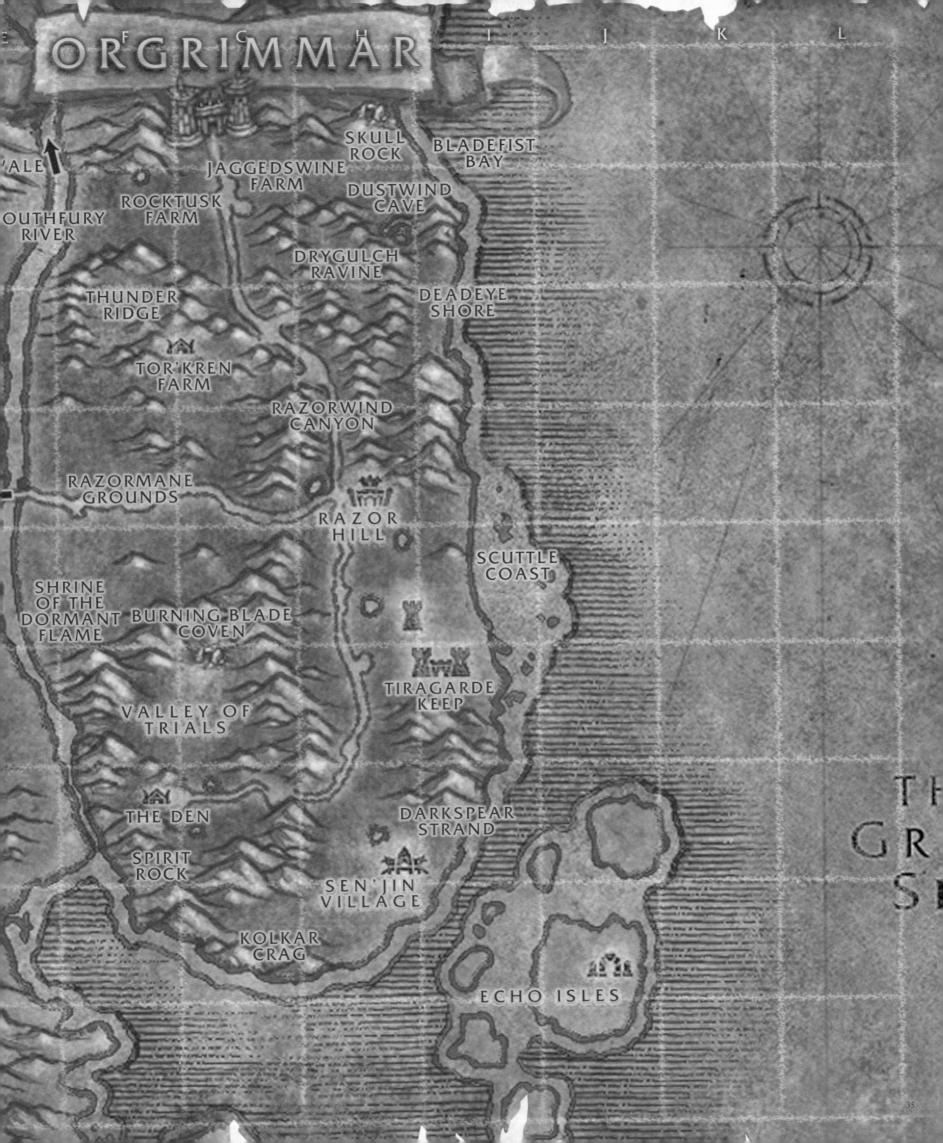

ORGRIMMAR

SKULL
ROCK

BLADEFIST
BAY

JAGGEDSWINE
FARM

DUSTWIND
CAVE

ROCKTUSK
FARM

DRYGULCH
RAVINE

'ALE

OUTHFURY
RIVER

DEADEYE
SHORE

THUNDER
RIDGE

TOR'KREN
FARM

RAZORWIND
CANYON

RAZORMANE
GROUNDS

RAZOR
HILL

SCUTTLE
COAST

SHRINE
OF THE
DORMANT
FLAME

BURNING BLADE
COVEN

TIRAGARDE
KEEP

VALLEY OF
TRIALS

THE DEN

DARKSPEAR
STRAND

SPIRIT
ROCK

SEN'JIN
VILLAGE

KOLKAR
CRAG

ECHO ISLES

DUSKWOOD

FLIGHT MASTER

Gryphon Master..K-4

TRAINERS

Expert Blacksmith J-5
Expert Engineer K-5
Mining Trainer...J-5

VENDORS

Alchemy Supplies Vendor....................................B-5
Armorer J-5
Bartender..J-4
Bowyer...J-4
Engineering and Mining Supplies........................K-5
General Goods Vendor.......................................J-4
Innkeeper J-4
Mushroom Seller K-5
Poison Supplies K-4
Rare Goods..K-2
Reagent Vendor K-4
Stable Master J-5
Tailoring Supplies..K:(4, 5)
Tradesman J-4
Weaponsmith J-5

HERBALISM

Herb Name	Herbalism Skill Requirement
Briarthorn	70
Bruiseweed	100
Grave Moss	120
Kingsblood	125
Mageroyal	50
Wild Steelbloom	115

MINING

Ore Name	Mining Skill Requirement
Copper	1
Gold	155
Iron	125
Silver	75
Tin	65

QUICK REFERENCE

CONNECTING REGIONS

DEADWIND PASS 28
ELWYNN FOREST 42
REDRIDGE MOUNTAINS...................................62
STRANGLETHORN VALE..................................74
WESTFALL...94

TOWNS & CAMPS

DARKSHIRE...108
RAVEN HILL 123
RAVEN HILL CEMETERY...................................123

DUSTWALLOW
M A R S H

FLIGHT MASTERS

Gryphon Master.............. I-5   Wind Rider Master .. E-3, F-7

TRAINERS

Artisan Fisherman ....H-6   Paladin Trainer I-5
Expert Alchemist ....H-5   Trauma Surgeon
Herbalist ....H-5   (First Aid)........................ I-5
Master Tailor .... I-5   Warrior Trainer I-5

VENDORS

Armorer .... E-3   Horse Breeder I-5
Armorer & Shieldsmith.. I-5   Innkeeper E-3, F-7, I-5
Barkeeper .... I-5   Potions, Scrolls and
Bowyer .... E-3, I-5   Reagent Vendor E-3
Butcher....................... E-3   Stable Master................ I-5
Chef............................. I-5   Tailoring Supplies.......... E-3
Cook............................ I-5   Trade Supplies I-5
Food & Drink Vendor .....F-7   Weaponsmith E-3, I-5
General Goods............... I-5   Weaponsmith &
Gunsmith .... I-5   Armorer F-7, I-5
Herbalism & Alchemy
Supplies......................H-5

HERBALISM

Herb Name	Herbalism Skill Requirement
Fadeleaf	160
Goldthorn	170
Khadgar's Whisker	185
Kingsblood	125
Liferoot	150
Stranglekelp	85

MINING

Ore Name	Mining Skill Requirement
Gold	155
Iron	125
Mithril	175
Silver	75
Truesilver	230

QUICK REFERENCE

CONNECTING REGIONS

BARRENS 18

TOWNS & CAMPS

BRACKENWALL VILLAGE..............................104
THERAMORE ISLE 135
MUDSPROCKET...120

EASTERN PLAGUELANDS

FLIGHT MASTERS

Bat Handler K-5
Gryphon Master K-6

VENDORS

The Argent Dawn K-6
Trade Supplies K-6

HERBALISM

Herb Name	Herbalism Skill Requirement
Arthas' Tears	220
Black Lotus	300
Dreamfoil	270
Golden Sansam	260
Mountain Silversage	280
Plaguebloom	285
Sungrass	230

MINING

Ore Name	Mining Skill Requirement
Gold	155
Mithril	175
Rich Thorium	270
Small Thorium	250
Truesilver	230

QUICK REFERENCE

CONNECTING REGIONS

HINTERLANDS 50
WESTERN PLAGUELANDS 92

TOWNS & CAMPS

LIGHT'S HOPE CHAPEL 118

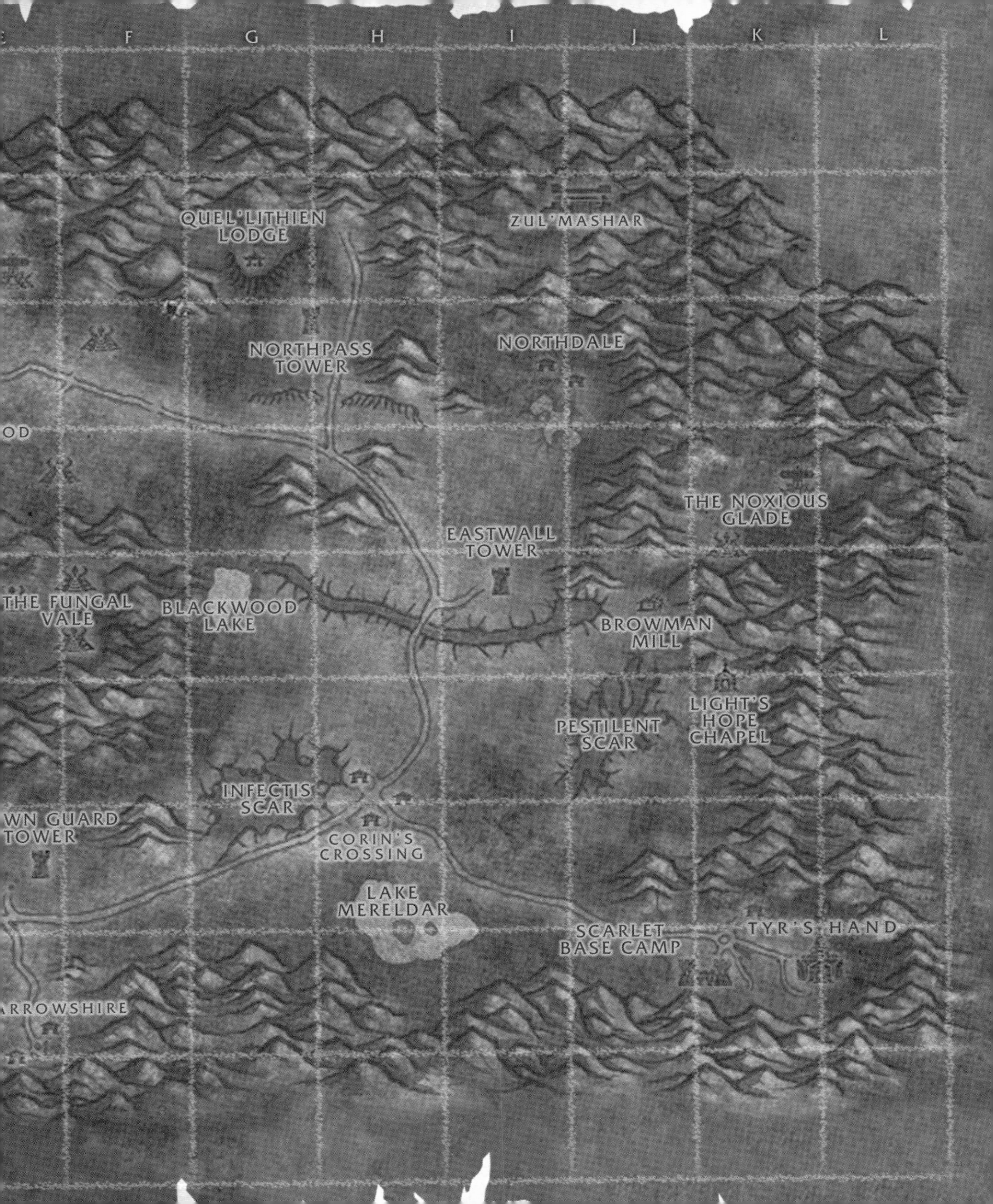

E
F
G
H
I
J
K
L
QUEL'LITHIEN LODGE
ZUL'MASHAR
NORTHPASS TOWER
NORTHDALE
OD
THE NOXIOUS GLADE
EASTWALL TOWER
THE FUNGAL VALE
BLACKWOOD LAKE
BROWMAN MILL
LIGHT'S HOPE CHAPEL
PESTILENT SCAR
INFECTIS SCAR
WN GUARD TOWER
CORIN'S CROSSING
LAKE MERELDAR
SCARLET BASE CAMP
TYR'S HAND
ARROWSHIRE

ELWYNN FOREST

TRAINERS

Artisan Enchanter............ I-7	Leatherworker F-6
Cook.....................F-7	Journeyman Tailor K-7
Demon Trainer F-7, G-4	Mage Trainer..........F-7, G-4
Fisherman.....................F-6	Paladin Trainer E-7, G-4
Herbalist Trainer............ E-5	Physician F-7
Horse Riding Instructor . L-6	Priest Trainer F-7, G-4
Journeyman Alchemist.. E-5	Rogue Trainer.........F-7, G-4
Journeyman	Skinner F-6
Blacksmith E-6	Warlock Trainer F-7, G-4
Journeyman	Warrior Trainer E-7, G-4

VENDORS

Arcane Goods................ I-7	General Supplies......F:(4, 7)
Armorer &	Horse Breeder L-6
Shieldcrafter.. C-7, E-7, F-4	Innkeeper F-7
Bartender......................F-7	Leather Armor
Bowyer.........................L-7	Merchant C-7
Butcher.........................F-7	Lumberjack................... L-6
Cloth & Leather Armor	Master Weaponsmith....C-7
Merchant............. E-6, F-4	Stable Master.................F-7
Clothier.........................I-7	Trade Supplies E-7
Crazy Cat Lady..............F-5	Traveling Baker F-7
Fishmonger....................F-6	Vinter F-9
Fruit Seller....................D-8	Weaponsmith E-7, F-4
General & Trade	
Supplies.....................K-7	

HERBALISM

Herb Name	Herbalism Skill Requirement
Earthroot	15
Peacebloom	1
Silverleaf	1

MINING

Ore Name	Mining Skill Requirement
Copper	1

QUICK REFERENCE

CONNECTING REGIONS

DUSKWOOD..36
REDRIDGE MOUNTAINS.....................................62
STORMWIND...72
WESTFALL..94

TOWNS & CAMPS

GOLDSHIRE 114
NORTHSHIRE VALLEY 122

FELWOOD

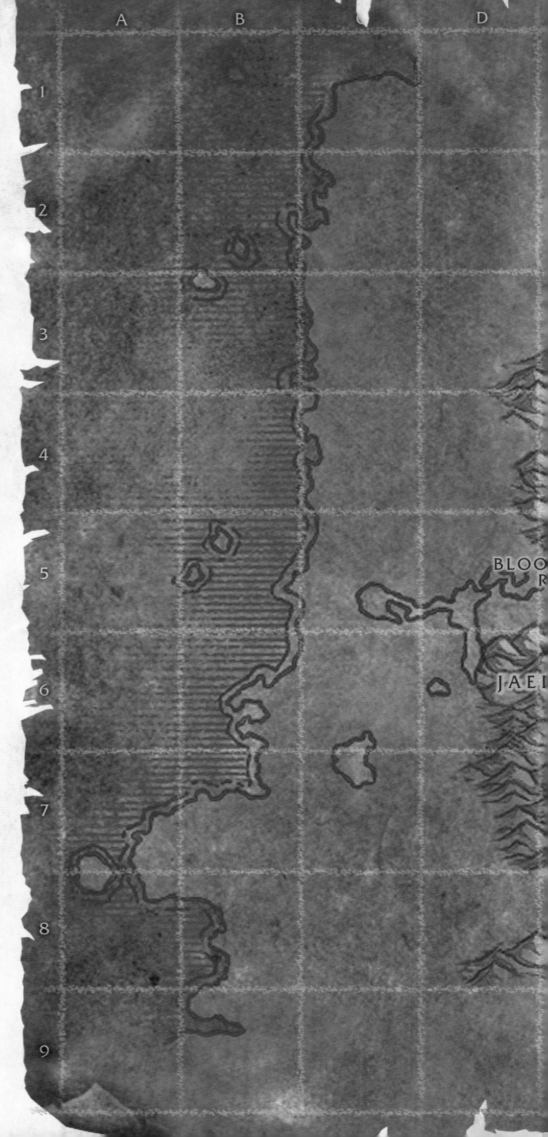

FLIGHT MASTERS

Flight Master...G-8
Hippogryph Master H-3
Wind Rider Master.......................................E-5

TRAINERS

Druid Trainer..H-3
Hunter Trainer..H-3
Pet Trainer..H-3

VENDORS

General Goods.....................................E-5, H-3
Weapon Merchant E-5

HERBALISM

Herb Name	Herbalism Skill Requirement
Arthas' Tears	220
Dreamfoil	270
Golden Sansam	260
Gromsblood	250
Mountain Silversage	280
Plaguebloom	285
Sungrass	230

MINING

Ore Name	Mining Skill Requirement
Gold	155
Mithril	175
Small Thorium	250
Truesilver	230

QUICK REFERENCE

CONNECTING REGIONS

ASHENVALE...12
MOONGLADE 56
WINTERSPRING 98

TOWNS & CAMPS

BLOODVENOM POST 102
EMERALD SANCTUARY.............................110
TALONBRANCH GLADE.............................133

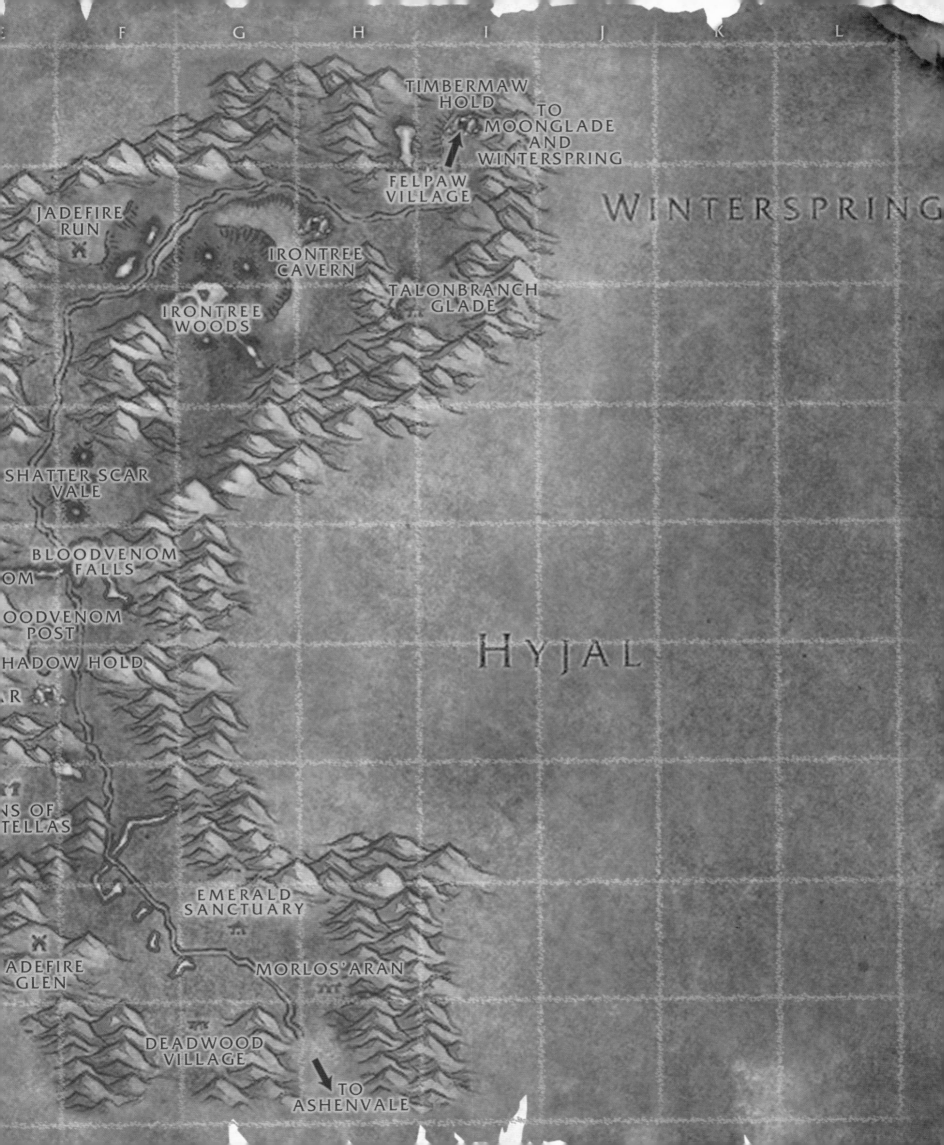

E F G H I J K L

TIMBERMAW
HOLD

TO
MOONGLADE
AND
WINTERSPRING

FELPAW
VILLAGE

WINTERSPRING

JADEFIRE
RUN

IRONTREE
CAVERN

IRONTREE
WOODS

TALONBRANCH
GLADE

SHATTER SCAR
VALE

BLOODVENOM
FALLS

OM

OODVENOM
POST

HADOW HOLD

AR

HYJAL

NS OF
TELLAS

EMERALD
SANCTUARY

ADEFIRE
GLEN

MORLOS'ARAN

DEADWOOD
VILLAGE

TO
ASHENVALE

FERALAS

FLIGHT MASTERS

Hippogryph Master	C-4, K-5
Wind Rider Master	I-4

TRAINERS

Druid Trainer I-4	Master Leatherworker.... I-4
Expert Enchanter C-4	Skinning Trainer I-4
Fisherman C-4	Tribal Leatherworking
Herbalism Trainer I-4	Trainer K-5
Master Alchemist C-4	

VENDORS

Alchemy Supplies ... C-4, I-4	Leatherworking
Cloth Armor Merchant .. C-4	Supplies C-4, I-4
Fish Vendor C-5	Light Armor Merchant ... I-4
Fishing Supplies C-5	Reagent Vendor C-4, I-4
Food & Drink C-4, I-4	Stable Master C-4, I-4
General Supplies C-4	Tailoring Supplies K-5
Gunsmith & Bowyer I-4	Trade Supplies C-4, I-4
Innkeeper C-4, I-4	

HERBALISM

Herb Name	Herbalism Skill Requirement
Golden Sansam	260
Goldthorn	170
Khadgar's Whisker	185
Liferoot	150
Purple Lotus	210
Sungrass	230

MINING

Ore Name	Mining Skill Requirement
Gold	155
Iron	125
Mithril	175
Silver	75
Small Thorium	250
Truesilver	230

QUICK REFERENCE

CONNECTING REGIONS

DESOLACE 30
THOUSAND NEEDLES 82

TOWNS & CAMPS

CAMP MOJACHE 105
FEATHERMOON STRONGHOLD 111

ALTERAC

TO ALTERAC
MOUNTAINS

TO ALTERAC
MOUNTAINS

TARREN MI

DARROW
HILL

HILLSBRAD FIELDS

YETI
CAVE

HILLSBRAD

TO
SILVERPINE
FOREST

SOUTHPOINT
TOWER

SOUTHSHORE

NETHAN
STEA

AZURELODE
MINE

WESTERN
STRAND

EASTERN
STRAND

PURGATION
ISLE

FLIGHT MASTERS

Bat Handler G-2	Gryphon Master.............F-5

TRAINERS

Expert Alchemist G-2	Herbalist G-2
Fisherman F-6	Master Tailor H-2
Grand Master Rogue K-2	

VENDORS

Alchemy Supplies..........F-6	Merchant Supreme G-3
Bartender.....................F-6	Mushroom Seller G-2
Butcher........................F-6	Poison Vendor K-2
Cook H-2	Poisons and Reagents F-6
Fish Merchant F-6	Speciality Engineer K-2
Freewheeling	Stable Master.........F-6, H-2
Tradeswoman J-4	Superior Armorsmith F-5
General Goods.......F-5, H-2	Tackle and Bait..............F-6
Hillsbrad Tailor D-4	Tailoring Supplies..........G-2
Horse Breeder F-6	Trade Goods F-5
Innkeeper F-6, H-2	Tradesman H-2
Leatherworking	Waitress F-6
Supplies.................... L-4	Weaponsmith G-3

HERBALISM

Herb Name	Herbalism Skill Requirement
Briarthorn	70
Bruiseweed	100
Khadgar's Whisker	185
Kingsblood	125
Liferoot	150
Mageroyal	50
Stranglekelp	85
Wild Steelbloom	115

MINING

Ore Name	Mining Skill Requirement
Copper	1
Gold	155
Iron	125
Mithril	175
Silver	75
Tin	65
Truesilver	230

QUICK REFERENCE

CONNECTING REGIONS

ALTERAC MOUNTAINS.. 8	SILVERPINE FOREST 68
ARATHI HIGHLANDS... 10	WESTERN
HINTERLANDS............ 50	PLAGUELANDS 92

TOWNS & CAMPS

HILLSBRAD FIELDS 115	TARREN MILL 133
SOUTHSHORE 129	

HINTERLANDS

FLIGHT MASTERS
Gryphon Master.. B-5
Wind Rider Master... L-8

TRAINERS
Fishing Trainer and Supplies................................ L-8
Master Leatherworking Trainer........................... B-4

VENDORS
Bartender... B-4
Blacksmithing Supplies B-4, L-8
Cooking Supplies L-8
Engineering Supplies E-4
Innkeeper B-4, L-8
Leatherworking Supplies..................................... B-4
Reagent Vendor L-8
Stable Master... B-5, L-8
Trade Goods Vendor E-4

HERBALISM

Herb Name	Herbalism Skill Requirement
Fadeleaf	160
Ghost Mushroom	245
Golden Sansam	260
Goldthorn	170
Khadgar's Whisker	185
Liferoot	150
Purple Lotus	210
Sungrass	230

MINING

Ore Name	Mining Skill Requirement
Gold	155
Mithril	175
Silver	75
Small Thorium	250
Truesilver	230

QUICK REFERENCE
CONNECTING REGIONS
EASTERN PLAGUELANDS 40
HILLSBRAD FOOTHILLS 48
WESTERN PLAGUELANDS...........................92
TOWNS & CAMPS
AERIE PEAK 100
REVANTUSK VILLAGE...............................125

WESTERN PLAGUELANDS

1

A   B   D

2

TO WESTERN
PLAGUELANDS

PLAGUEMIST
RAVINE

3

4

WILDHAMMER
KEEP

AERIE
PEAK

5

Q

TO
HILLSBRAD
FOOTHILLS

HIRI

6

7

8

9

IRONFORGE

CITY OFFICIALS

Alliance Cloth
  Quartermaster...... F-3, J-5
Alterac Valley
  Battlemaster................ J-9
Arathi Basin
  Battlemaster............... J-9
Auctioneers C-7
Bankers........................D-6

Gnomeregan
  Commendations...........I-5
Ironforge
  Commendations...........F-5
Eye of the Storm
  Battlemaster................ J-9
Guild Master................D-8
Warsong Gulch
  Battlemaster............... J-9

FLIGHT MASTER

Gryphon Master..G-5

TRAINERS

Artisan Blacksmith G-4
Artisan Engineer I-4
Cooking Trainer.............H-4
Demon Trainer G-1
Expert Alchemist I-5
Expert Blacksmith G-4
Expert Enchanter H-4
Expert Engineer I-4
Expert Leatherworker ... E-3
Expert Tailor.................F-3
First Aid Trainer.............G-6
Fishing Trainer...............F-1
Herbalism Trainer G-6
Hunter Trainer.... I-8, J:(8, 9)
Journeyman Alchemist... I-5
Journeyman
  Blacksmith.................G-4
Journeyman Enchanter ..H-4

Journeyman Engineer..... I-4
Journeyman
  Leatherworker E-3
Journeyman Tailor F-3
Mage Trainer.................C-1
Master Gnome
  Engineer....................J-5
Mining Trainer...............G-3
Paladin Trainer C-1
Pet Trainer.....................J-8
Portal Trainer.................C-1
Priest Trainer C-1
Rogue Trainer................G-1
Shaman Trainer G-3
Skinning Trainer E-3
Warlock Trainer G-1
Warrior Trainer I-9, J-9
Weapon Master H-9

VENDORS

Alchemy Supplies........... I-5
Armor Crafter F-4, G-4
Axe Merchant...............H-9
Bag Vendor................... E-7
Blacksmithing
  Supplies G-4
Blade Merchant F-1, H-9
Bow Merchant............... J-6
Bread Vendor........ C-6, D-8
Cloth Armor
  Merchant E-1
Cooking Supplies...........H-4
Enchanting Supplies......H-4
Engineering Supplies I-4
Fireworks Vendor J-5
Fishing Supplies.............F-1
Fruit Vendor E-1, C-3
General Good Vendor ... E-7
Guild Tabard Vendor D-8
Gun Merchant................ J-6
Heavy Armor
  Merchant D-6, G-9
Herbalism Supplies G-6

Innkeeper B-5
Leatherworking
  Supplies E-3
Light Armor
  Merchant D-5, G-9
Maces & Staves............H-9
Mail Armor Merchant ...G-9
Meat Vendor.......... H-8, I-7
Mining Supplies............G-3
Pie Vendor E-4
Reagent Vendor B-6, D-3
Robe Merchant E-1
Shady Dealer G-1
Special Weapon
  Crafter G-5, H-5
Speciality Tailoring
  Supplies F-3
Stable Master................ I-8
Tailoring Supplies...........F-3
Trade Supplies E-7, F-3
Wands Merchant C-2
Weapon Merchant C-2,
  E:(6, 7), H-9

QUICK REFERENCE

CONNECTING REGIONS

DUN MOROGH...32
STORMWIND 72

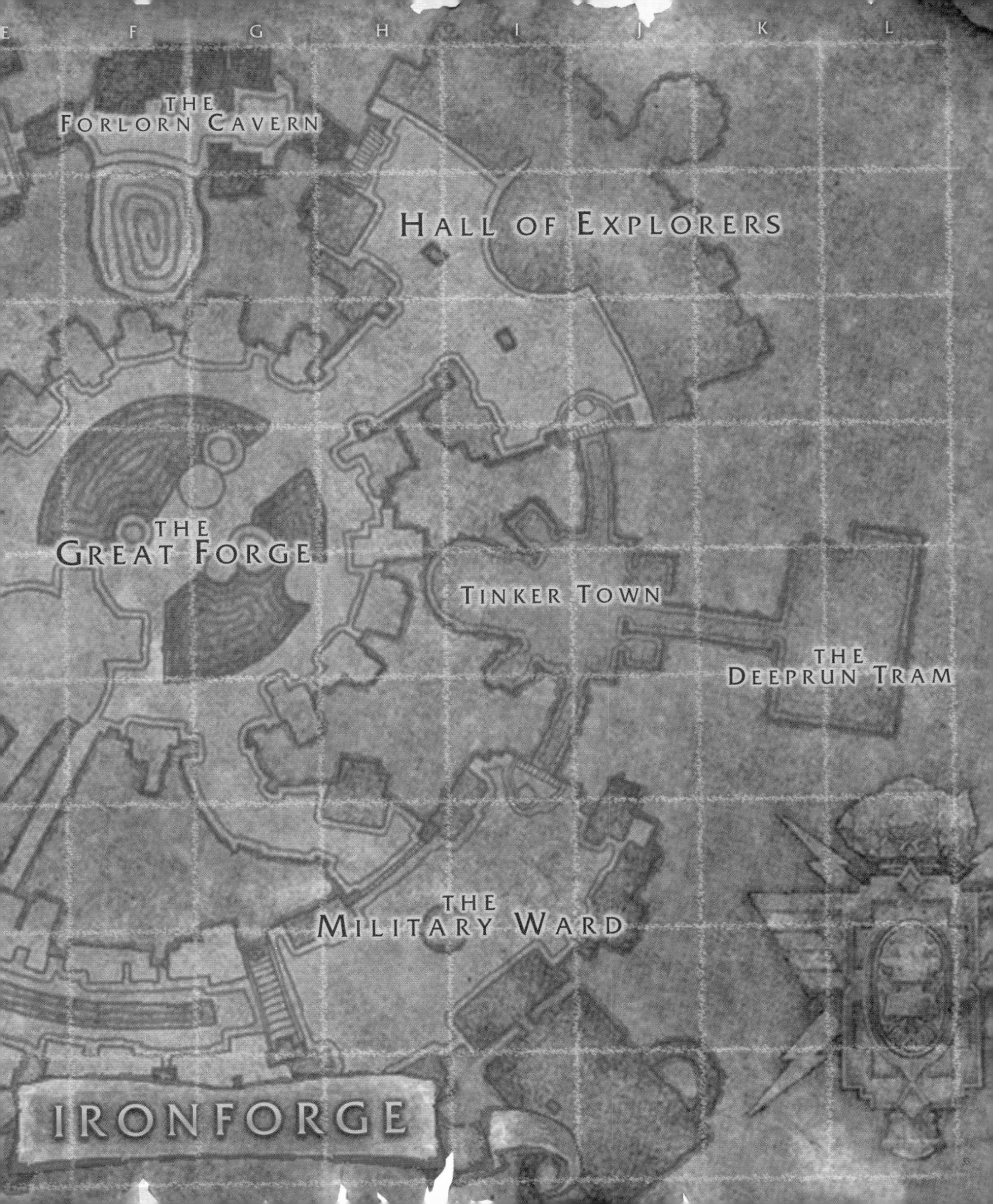

E F G H I J K L
THE FORLORN CAVERN
HALL OF EXPLORERS
THE GREAT FORGE
TINKER TOWN
THE DEEPRUN TRAM
THE MILITARY WARD
IRONFORGE

TO WETLANDS

ALGAZ GATE

NORTH GATE PASS

TO DUN MOROGH

ALGAZ STATION

STONEWROUGHT DAM

SILVER STREAM MINE

TUNNEL RAT CAVE

THE LOCH

THELSAMAR

GRIZZLEPAW RIDGE

TO DUN MOROGH

CARAVAN

SOUTH GATE PASS

VALLEY OF KINGS

STONESPLINTER VALLEY

TO SEARING GORGE

STONESPLINTER CAVES

TO BADLANDS

LOCH MODAN

FLIGHT MASTER
Gryphon Master..D-5

TRAINERS
Fisherman...E-4
Herbalist...D-5
Hunter Trainer..K-6
Journeyman Alchemist.......................................E-5
Journeyman Engineer...F-1
Mining Trainer..E-5
Pet Trainer..K-6

VENDORS
Armorer..C-2
Baker...D-5
Bowyer..K-6
Clothier...I-7
Fishing Supplies...E-4
General Supplies.......................................D-5, K-6
Gunsmith...D-4, K-6
Innkeeper..D-5
Leather Armor Merchant K-6
Macecrafter..E-1
Metalsmith D-5
Mining Supplies...E-5
Stable Master..D-5
Tailoring Supplies..D-5
Tradesman...D-5
Traveling Merchant C-1

HERBALISM

Herb Name	Herbalism Skill Requirement
Briarthorn	70
Bruiseweed	100
Earthroot	15
Mageroyal	50
Peacebloom	1
Silverleaf	1

MINING

Ore Name	Mining Skill Requirement
Copper	1
Silver	75
Tin	65

QUICK REFERENCE
CONNECTING REGIONS
BADLANDS...16
DUN MOROGH...32
SEARING GORGE 64
WETLANDS...96
TOWNS & MAPS
FARSTRIDER LODGE 111
THELSAMAR...134

MOONGLADE

FLIGHT MASTERS

Darnassus Flight Master F-4
Hippogryph Master G-7
Wind Rider Master D-7

TRAINERS

Druid Trainer G-4
Herbalist F-5

VENDORS

Bowyer G-4
Food & Drink Merchant F-3, G-4
General Goods F-3
Light Armor Merchant H-3
Speciality Dress Maker G-3
Tailoring Supplies G-3
Trade Supplies G-4
Weaponsmith G-4

QUICK REFERENCE

CONNECTING REGIONS

FELWOOD 44
WINTERSPRING 98

TOWNS & CAMPS

NIGHTHAVEN 121

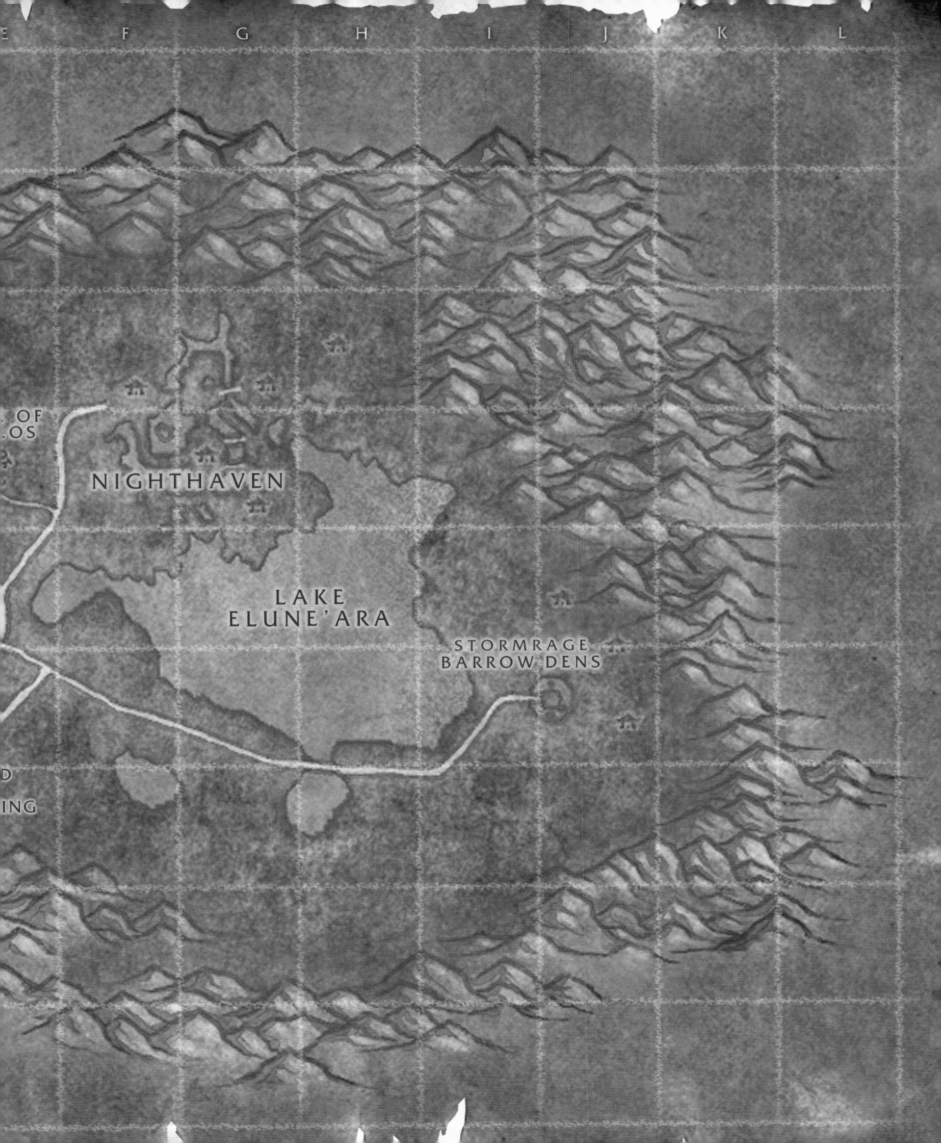

THE BARRENS

TO THE BARRENS

TRAINERS

Cook E-6
Druid Trainer E-8, F-6
First Aid Trainer E-6
Fisherman E-6
Hunter Trainer ....E:(6, 8)
Journeyman Engineer H-3
Journeyman Leatherworker E-6
Kodo Riding Instructor E-6
Pet Trainer.. E-6
Shaman Trainer E-8, F-6
Skinner E-6
Warrior Trainer E-8, F-6

VENDORS

Armor Merchant E-8
Armorer & Shieldcrafter............................E:(6, 8)
Baker ....E:(6, 8)
Fishing Supplies E-6
General Goods ....E:(6, 8)
Gunsmith E-6
Innkeeper E-6
Kodo Mounts... E-6
Leather Armor Merchant E-6
Stable Master... E-6
Trade Goods E-6
Weaponsmith ....E:(6, 8)

HERBALISM

Herb Name	Herbalism Skill Requirement
Earthroot	15
Peacebloom	1
Silverleaf	1

MINING

Ore Name	Mining Skill Requirement
Copper	1

QUICK REFERENCE

CONNECTING REGIONS

BARRENS 18
THUNDER BLUFF 84

TOWNS & CAMPS

BLOODHOOF VILLAGE 102
CAMP NARACHE 105

ORGRIMMAR

THE
VALLEY OF WISDOM

RAGEFIRE
CHASM

THE
CLEFT OF SHADOW

THE DRAG

THE
VALLEY OF STRENGTH

THE
VALLEY OF SPIRITS

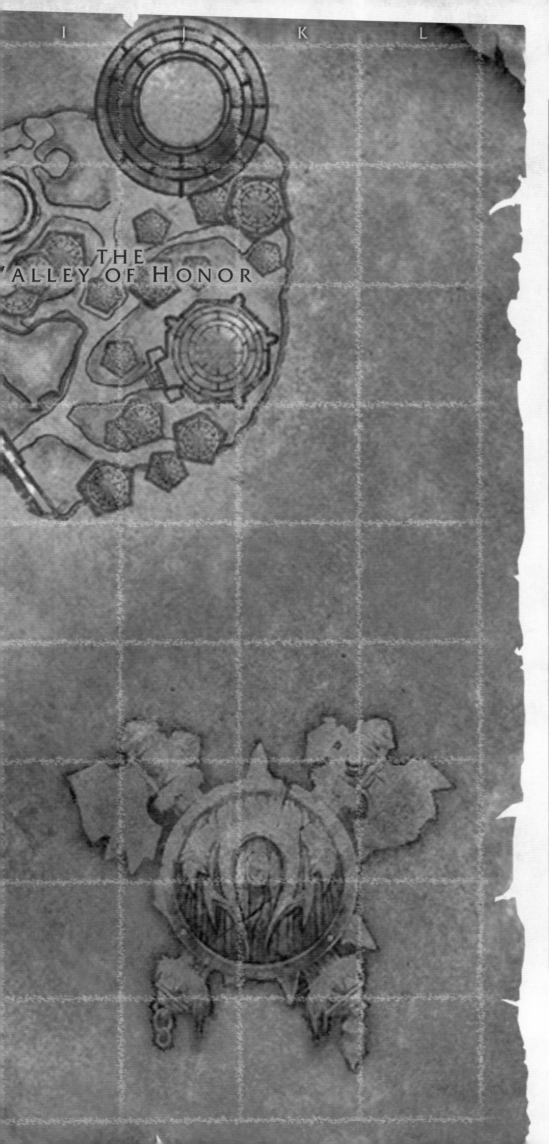

THE VALLEY OF HONOR

ORGRIMMAR

CITY OFFICIALS

Alterac Valley Battlemaster.................J-3	Darkspear Commendations.........E-4
Arathi Basin Battlemaster.................J-3	Eye of the Storm Battlemaster.................J-3
Arena Battlemaster........J-3	Guild Master.................E-7
Auctioneer....................G-6	Quartermaster..............D-9, H-5, E-7
Bankers.........................F-7	
Orgrimmar Commendations..........E-4	Warsong Gulch Battlemaster.................J-3

FLIGHT MASTER

Wind Rider Master....................................E-6

TRAINERS

Armorsmith....................J-2	Journeyman Engineer.................I-3, J-3
Artisan Blacksmith ..J-2, K-2	
Artisan Engineer I-3, J-3	Journeyman Leatherworker.............H-4
Cooking Trainer.............G-5	
Demon Trainer E-5, F-5	Journeyman Tailor.........H-5
Expert Alchemist G-3	Mage Trainer...........D:(8, 9)
Expert Blacksmith J-2	Mining Trainer.................I-3
Expert Enchanter F-4	Paladin Trainer D-4
Expert Engineer I-3, J-3	Pet Trainer................H:(1, 2)
Expert Leatherworker ...H-4	Portal Trainer...........D:(8, 9)
Expert Tailor...................H-5	Priest Trainer.................D-9
First Aid Trainer.............C-8	Rogue Trainer................ E-5
Fishing Trainer................I-3	Shaman Trainer D-4
Herbalism Trainer...F-4, G-4	Skinning Trainer H-4
Hunter Trainer...............H-2	Warlock Trainer E-5, F-5
Journeyman Alchemist...G-3	Warrior Trainer J-3
Journeyman Blacksmith.. J-2	Weapon Master J-2
Journeyman Enchanter...F-4	Weaponsmith J-2
	Wolf Riding Instructor I-1

VENDORS

Accessories Quartermaster............ E-7	Innkeeper G-7
Alchemy Supplies.........G-3	Leather Armor Merchant G-8
Armor Crafter J-2	Leatherworking Supplies H-4
Bag Vendor....................G-5	
Barkeep G-7	Light Armor Merchant..G-8
Blacksmithing Supplies J-2, K-2	Mace and Staff Vendor... J-2
	Mail Armor Merchant ...G-8
Blade Merchant E-5	Meat Vendor..........E-7, G-5
Bow Merchant J-4	Mining Supplies.............I-3
Cloth & Leather Armor Merchant ....H:(4, 5)	Mushroom Vendor........ E-5
	Poison Vendor E-5
Cooking Supplies...........G-5	Reagents Vendor......E:(4-6)
Enchanting Supplies.......F-4	Riding Wolf (Kennel Master)...........I-1
Engineering Supplies I-3, J-3	
	Snake Vendor........ A-6, C-8
Fishing Supplies.............I-3	Stable Master............I:(1-2)
Fruit Vendor D-5	Staff Merchant C-7, E-5
General Goods ....E:(4, 8), F-8	Sweet Treats E-7
	Tabard Vendor E-7
General Trade............E-8, F-8, G-5	Tailoring Supplies..........H-5
	Two-Handed Weapons Merchant J-2
Guns and Ammo Merchant F-7, G-7	
	Wand Merchant............ E-5
Heavy Armor Merchant J-2, K-2	War Harness Maker I-4
	Weapon Crafter..............J-2
Herbalism Supplies F-4, G-4	Weapon Merchant E-7
	Weapon Vendor............J-2

QUICK REFERENCE

CONNECTING REGIONS

DUROTAR 34

REDRIDGE
MOUNTAINS

FLIGHT MASTER
Gryphon Master..D-6

TRAINERS
Butcher..C-4
Cooking Trainer..B-4
Fishing Trainer..C-5
Herbalism Trainer...B-4
Skinning Trainer..L-7

VENDORS
Armorer D-5
Bait and Tackle Supplies.................................C-5
Cooking Supplies...C-4
Fletcher..C-4
Food and Drinks...C-4
Fruit Seller...B-5
General Supplies...C-5
Gunsmith...C-4
Innkeeper..C-4
Leather Armor Merchant L-7
Leatherworking Supplies.................................L-7
Mining and Smithing Supplies D-5
Poison Supplies..C-4
Shield Crafter...D-5
Specialist Tailoring Supplies J-8
Stable Master..C-5
Tailoring Supplies..C-4
Trade Goods Vendor C-5
Waitress B-4

HERBALISM

Herb Name	Herbalism Skill Requirement
Briarthorn	70
Bruiseweed	100
Mageroyal	50

MINING

Ore Name	Mining Skill Requirement
Copper	1
Silver	75
Tin	65

QUICK REFERENCE

CONNECTING REGIONS
BURNING STEPPES 22
DUSKWOOD...36
ELWYNN FOREST 42

TOWNS & CAMPS
LAKESHIRE 117

RENDER'S ROCK

RETHBAN CAVERNS

REDRIDGE CANYONS

LAKESHIRE

TO ELWYNN FOREST

THREE CORNERS

TO DUSKWOOD

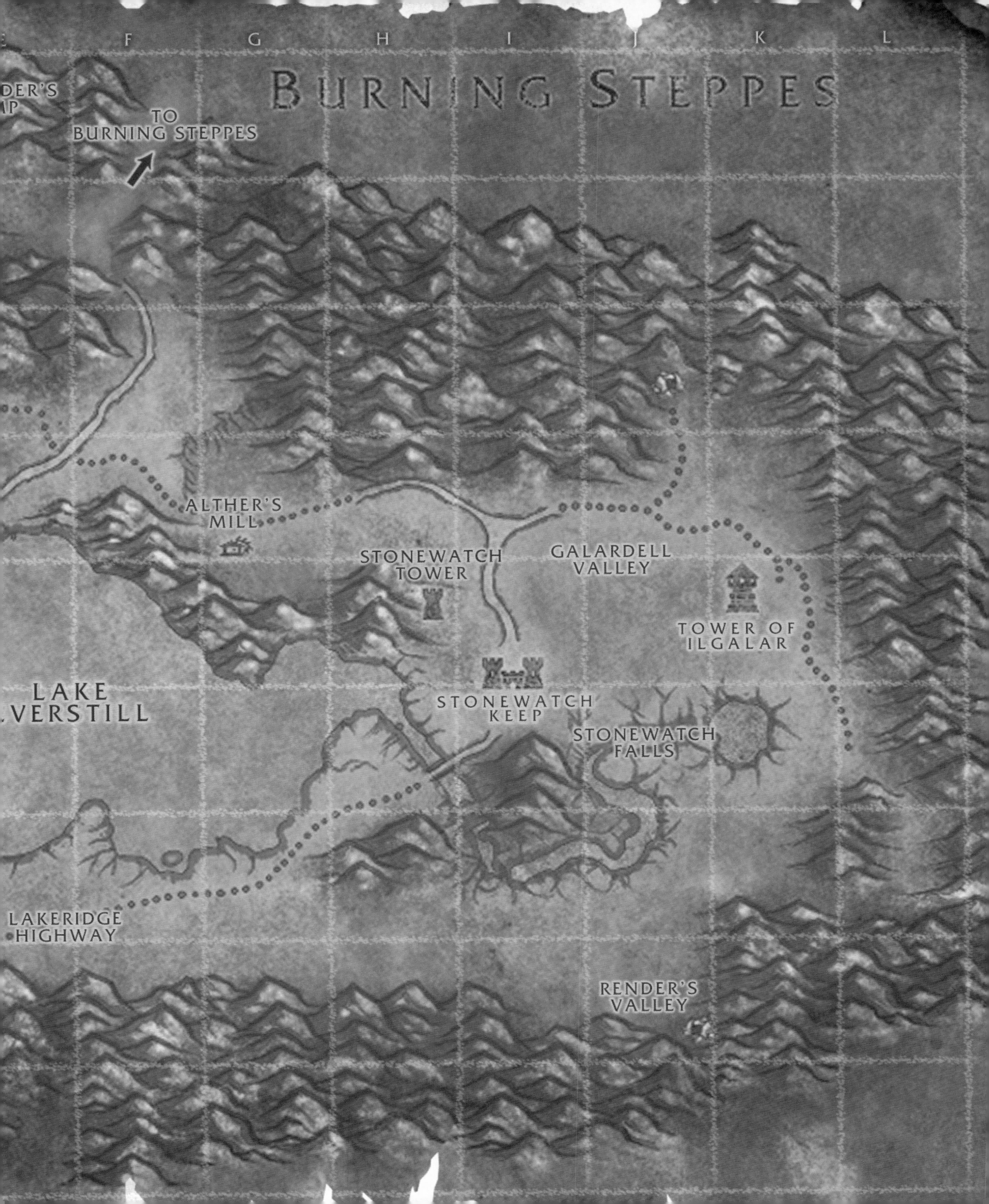

E F G H I J K L
BURNING STEPPES
DER'S
AP
TO
BURNING STEPPES
ALTHER'S
MILL
STONEWATCH
TOWER
GALARDELL
VALLEY
TOWER OF
ILGALAR
LAKE
VERSTILL
STONEWATCH
KEEP
STONEWATCH
FALLS
LAKERIDGE
HIGHWAY
RENDER'S
VALLEY

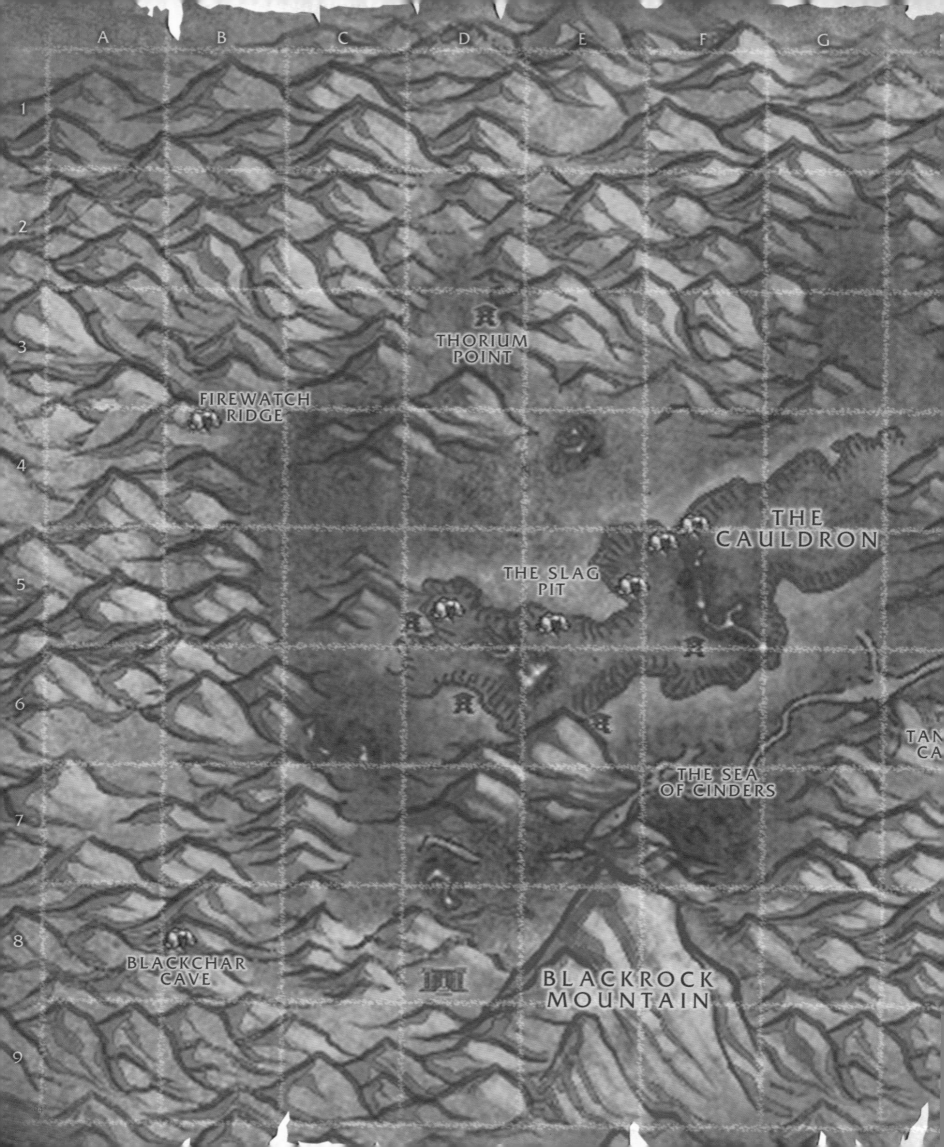

THORIUM
POINT

FIREWATCH
RIDGE

THE
CAULDRON

THE SLAG
PIT

TAN
CA

THE SEA
OF CINDERS

BLACKCHAR
CAVE

BLACKROCK
MOUNTAIN

I J K L

STONEWRAUGHT
PASS

TO
LOCH MODAN

FIRE
EY

GRIMSILT
DIG SITE

TO
BADLANDS

SEARING GORGE

FLIGHT MASTERS
Gryphon Master...D-3
Wind Rider Master..D-3

TRAINER
Master Elemental Leatherworker...................................H-7

VENDOR
Mail Armor Merchant E-7

HERBALISM

Herb Name	Herbalism Skill Requirement
Firebloom	205

MINING

Ore Name	Mining Skill Requirement
Dark Iron	230
Gold	155
Iron	125
Mithril	175
Silver	75
Small Thorium	250
Truesilver	230

QUICK REFERENCE
CONNECTING REGIONS

BADLANDS...16
BURNING STEPPES 22
LOCH MODAN..54

TOWNS & CAMPS

THORIUM POINT...136

SILITHUS

FLIGHT MASTERS

Hippogryph Master	G-3
Wind Rider Master	G-3

VENDOR

Enchanting Supplies	G-4
General Trade Goods	G-3
Innkeeper	G-4
Leatherworking Supplies	K-2, i-5
Reagent Vendor	G-4
Stable Master	G-4
Weaponsmith	G-4

MINING

Ore Name	Mining Skill Requirement
Gold	155
Mithril	175
Rich Thorium	270
Small Thorium	250
Truesilver	230

QUICK REFERENCE

CONNECTING REGIONS

UN'GORO CRATER	90

TOWNS & CAMPS

CENARION HOLD	106
VALOR'S REST	137

SILVERPINE FOREST

FLIGHT MASTER
Bat Handler G-4

TRAINERS
Journeyman Blacksmith F-4
Miner F-4

VENDORS
Armorer F-4
Bowyer G-4
Clothier G-4
Dalaran Brewmaster I-6
Dalaran Miner I-6
Enchanting Supplies F-5
Enchanting Supplies H-8
Fisherman E-2
General Supplies G-4
Innkeeper F-4
Leather Armor Merchant G-4
Mushroom Merchant G-4
Poison Supplies F-4
Pyrewood Armorer G-7
Pyrewood Leatherworker G-7
Pyrewood Tailor G-7
Stable Master F-4
Trade Goods F-4
Weaponsmith G-8

HERBALISM

Herb Name	Herbalism Skill Requirement
Briarthorn	70
Bruiseweed	100
Earthroot	15
Mageroyal	50
Peacebloom	1
Silverleaf	1
Stranglekelp	85

MINING

Ore Name	Mining Skill Requirement
Copper	1
Silver	75
Tin	65

QUICK REFERENCE

CONNECTING REGIONS
ALTERAC MOUNTAINS 8
HILLSBRAD FOOTHILLS 48
TIRISFAL GLADES 86

TOWNS & CAMPS
THE SEPULCHER 127

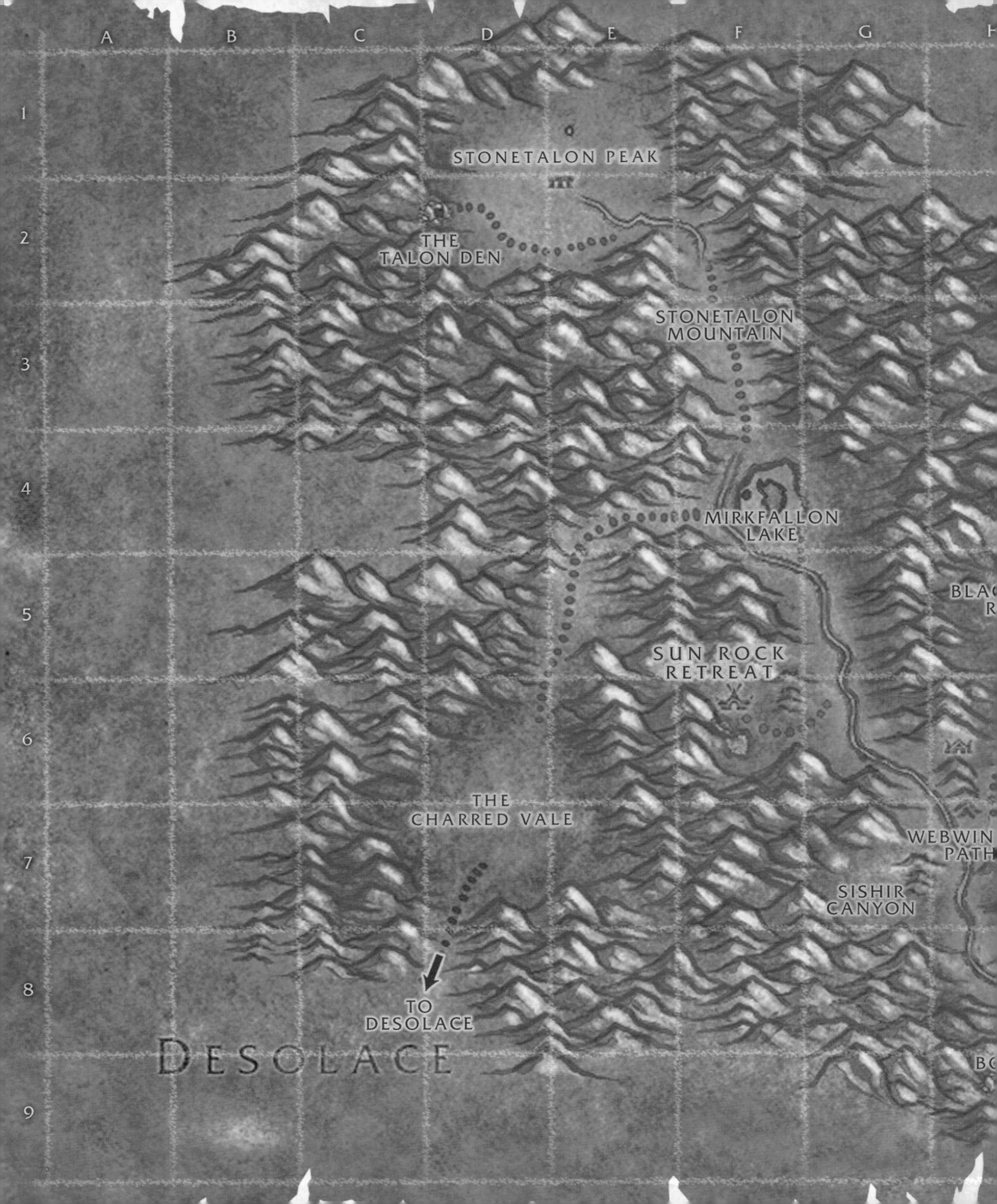

	A	B	C	D	E	F	G	H

STONETALON PEAK

THE
TALON DEN

STONETALON
MOUNTAIN

MIRKFALLON
LAKE

BLAC
R

SUN ROCK
RETREAT

THE
CHARRED VALE

WEBWIN
PATH

SISHIR
CANYON

TO
DESOLACE

DESOLACE

BO

STONETALON MOUNTAINS

FLIGHT MASTERS

Hippogryph Master D-1
Wind Rider Master E-6

TRAINER

Artisan Enchanter F-6

VENDORS

Apprentice Witch Doctor F-6
Bowyer E-6
Butcher E-6, I-9
Cloth Armor Merchant D-1
General Goods E-6
General Supplies D-1
Innkeeper F-6
Stable Master F-6
Trade Supplies E-6
Venture Armor Salesman H-4
Venture Co. Merchant G-5

HERBALISM

Herb Name	Herbalism Skill Requirement
Briarthorn	70
Bruiseweed	100
Kingsblood	125
Mageroyal	50
Wild Steelbloom	115

MINING

Ore Name	Mining Skill Requirement
Copper	1
Gold	155
Iron	125
Mithril	175
Silver	75
Tin	65
Truesilver	230

QUICK REFERENCE

CONNECTING REGIONS

ASHENVALE 12
BARRENS 18
DESOLACE 30

TOWNS & CAMPS

STONETALON PEAK 131
SUN ROCK RETREAT 132

STORMWIND

CITY OFFICIALS

Quartermaster G-7, K-6	Banker H-7
Alterac Valley	Commendations H-6
Battlemaster...............L-1	Eye of the Storm
Arathi Basin	Battlemaster................ L-1
Battlemaster...............L-1	Guild Master H-7, I-7
Arena	Warsong Gulch
Battlemaster...............L-1	Battlemaster............... L-1
Auctioneer...................H-6	

FLIGHT MASTER

Gryphon Master...J-6

TRAINERS

Artisan Tailor................G-7	Journeyman Enchanter...F-6
Cooking Trainer.............K-4	Journeyman Engineer....H-1
Demon Trainer D-8	Journeyman
Druid Trainer ....C:(5, 6)	Leatherworker J-5
Expert Alchemist G-8	Journeyman Tailor.........G-7
Expert Blacksmith H-2	Mage Trainer..................F-8
Expert Enchanter F-6	Master Shadoweave
Expert Engineer H-1	Tailor D-8
Expert Leatherworker J-5	Mining Trainer..............H-2
Expert Tailor...................F-8	Paladin Trainer F-3
First Aid Trainer.............F-3	Pet Trainer......................I-2
Fishing Trainer...............G-6	Portal Trainer.................F-8
Herbalism	Priest Trainer C-5, F-3
Trainer B-5, F-8, G-8	Rogue Trainer.........K-5, L-6
Hunter Trainer.....I:(1-3), J-2	Skinning Trainer J-5
Journeyman Alchemist..G-8	Warlock Trainer D-8
Journeyman	Warrior Trainer .... L:(4, 5)
Blacksmith.............I-2, J-2	Weapon Master H-6

VENDORS

Accessories	Innkeeper ....H:(6, 7)
Quartermaster............K-5	Leather Armor
Alchemy Supplies..........G-8	Merchant ...... H:(5, 6), J-5
Arcane Goods Vendor...H-6	Leatherworking
Arcane Trinkets	Supplies J-5
Vendor E-8	Light Armor Merchant..G-7
Axe Merchant...............H-1	Mail Armor Merchant ...F-4,
Bag Vendor....................J-5	H:(5, 6), K-5
Baker I-6	Master of Cooking
Blacksmithing	Recipes J-5
Supplies H-2	Merlot Connoisseur.......H-7
Blade Merchant K-4	Mining Supplies............H-2
Bow & Arrow	Poison Supplies K-6
Merchant H-6	Reagent
Bow & Gun Merchant...H-6	Vendor E-7, F-3, H-6
Cloth Armor	Robe Merchant F-8
Merchant ....H:(5, 6)	Robe Vendor..................F-4
Clothier...................G:(5, 6)	Shady Dealer L-6
Cobbler...........................J-4	Shield Merchant I-4, J-4
Cooking Supplies...........K-4	Stable Master... D-5, I-2, J-2
Enchanting Supplies.......F-6	Staff & Mace Merchant..F-3
Engineering Supplies H-1	Staves Merchant ......F:(6, 7)
Fireworks Vendor D-7	Tabard Vendor H-7, I-7
Fishing Supplies.............G-6	Tailoring Supplies..........G-7
Florist.............................J-6	Trade Supplies I-6
General Goods Vendor...I-6	Two Handed Weapon
Guns Vendor...........H:(1, 2)	Merchant J-4
Hatter F-8	Wand Merchant.......F:(6, 7)
Heavy Armor	Weapon Crafter.............H-1
Merchant K-5	Weapons Merchant.......H-6
Herbalism	Wine Vendor.................H-7
Supplies G-8, J-6	

QUICK REFERENCE

CONNECTING REGIONS

ELWYNN FOREST 42

IRONFORGE 52

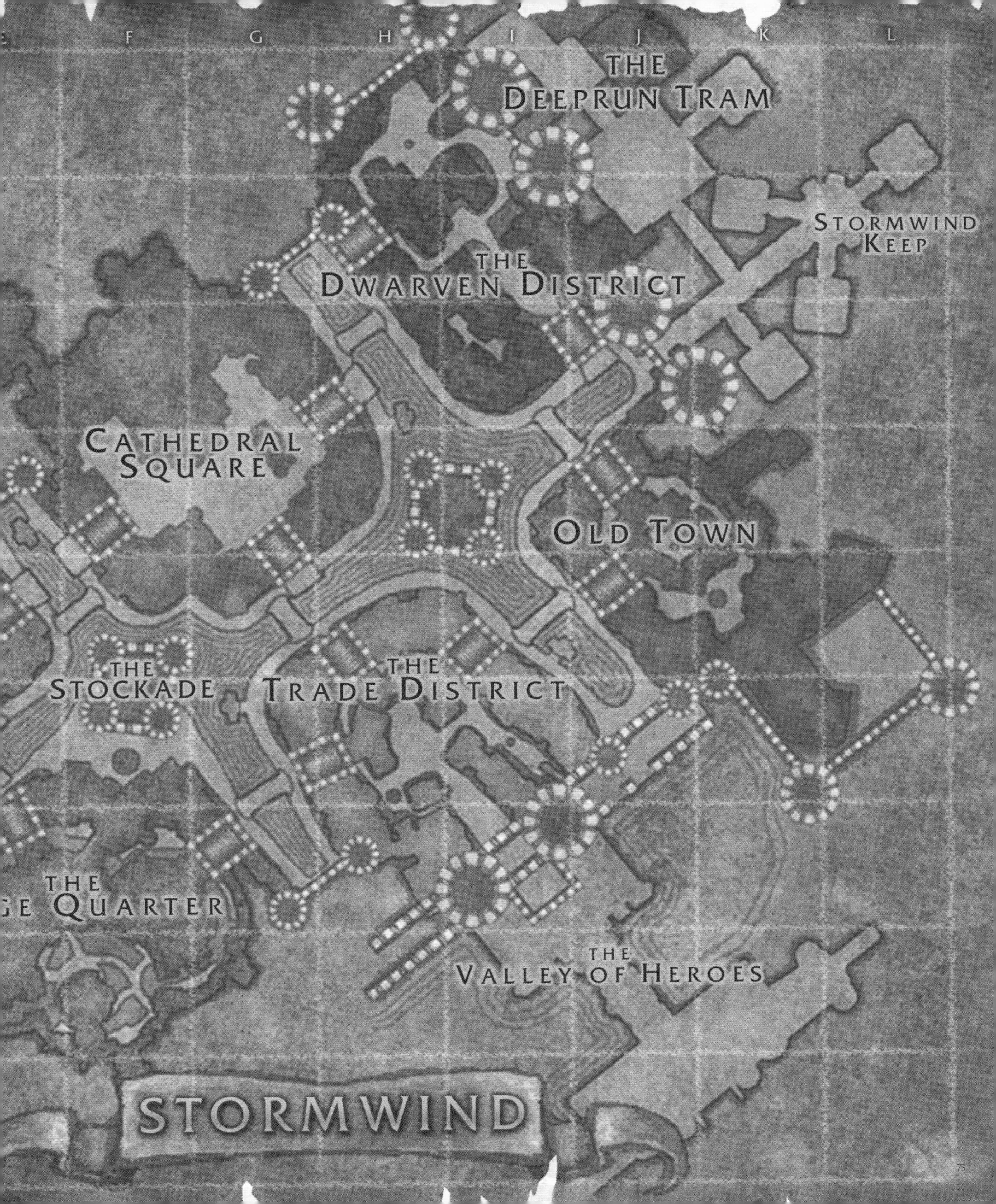

THE
DEEPRUN TRAM

STORMWIND
KEEP

THE
DWARVEN DISTRICT

CATHEDRAL
SQUARE

OLD TOWN

THE
STOCKADE

THE
TRADE DISTRICT

THE
ᴳᴱ QUARTER

THE
VALLEY OF HEROES

STORMWIND

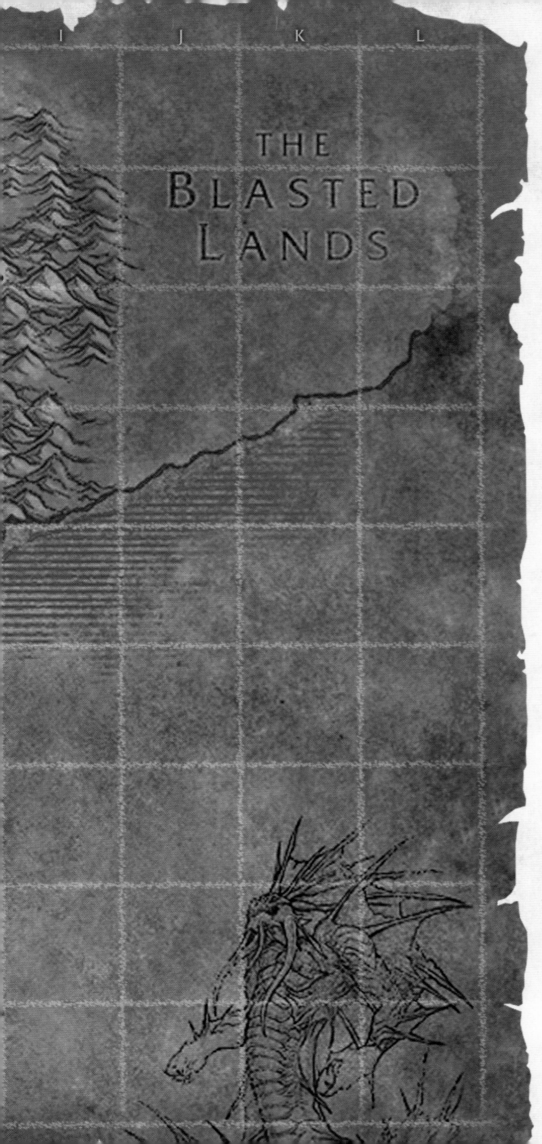

THE BLASTED LANDS

STRANGLETHORN VALE

FLIGHT MASTERS

Gryphon Master.....B-8, C-1 | Wind Rider Master........C-3
Wind Rider Master........B-8

TRAINERS

Artisan Blacksmith of the | Master Gnome
  Mithril Order (Quest) ...F-2 | Engineer B-8
Expert Alchemist ....B-8 | Master Tribal
Expert Leatherworker ...C-3 | Leatherworker D-4
Expert Tailor................B-8 | Pet Trainer....................C-3
Hunter Trainer..............C-3 | Rogue Trainer...............B-8
Master Blacksmith ....C-8 | Superior Fisherman B-8
 | Superior Herbalist ..B-8, C-3

VENDORS

Alchemy Supplies.........B-8 | Leatherworking
Blacksmithing | Supplies.....................B-8
  Supplies...............B-8, C-8 | Macecrafter..................B-8
Blade Trader.................B-8 | Pirate Supplies...............B-8
Camp Trader ....D-1 | Shady Goods B-8
Cloth and Leather Armor | Stable Master...............B-8
  Merchant....................C-3 | Superior Armorer ..B-8, C-3
Cloth Armor and | Superior Axecrafter.......C-1
  Accessories ....B-8 | Superior Bowyer B-8
Cook ....B-8 | Superior Cook C-3
Engineering | Superior Fisherman B-8
  Supplies............... B-8, F-4 | Superior
Fireworks Merchant ......B-8 | Weaponsmith B-8, C-3
Fisherman....................B-8 | Tailoring Supplies.... B:(8, 9)
Food & Drink ....B-8, C-3 | Trade Goods C-3
General Supplies...........C-3
Innkeeper B-8

HERBALISM

Herb Name	Herbalism Skill Requirement
Fadeleaf	160
Goldthorn	170
Khadgar's Whisker	185
Kingsblood	125
Liferoot	150
Purple Lotus	210
Stranglekelp	85
Wild Steelbloom	115

MINING

Ore Name	Mining Skill Requirement
Gold	155
Iron	125
Mithril	175
Silver	75
Tin	65
Truesilver	230

QUICK REFERENCE

CONNECTING REGIONS

   DUSKWOOD...36
   WESTFALL...94

TOWNS & CAMPS

   BOOTY BAY..103
   GROM'GOL BASE CAMP 114
   REBEL CAMP...124

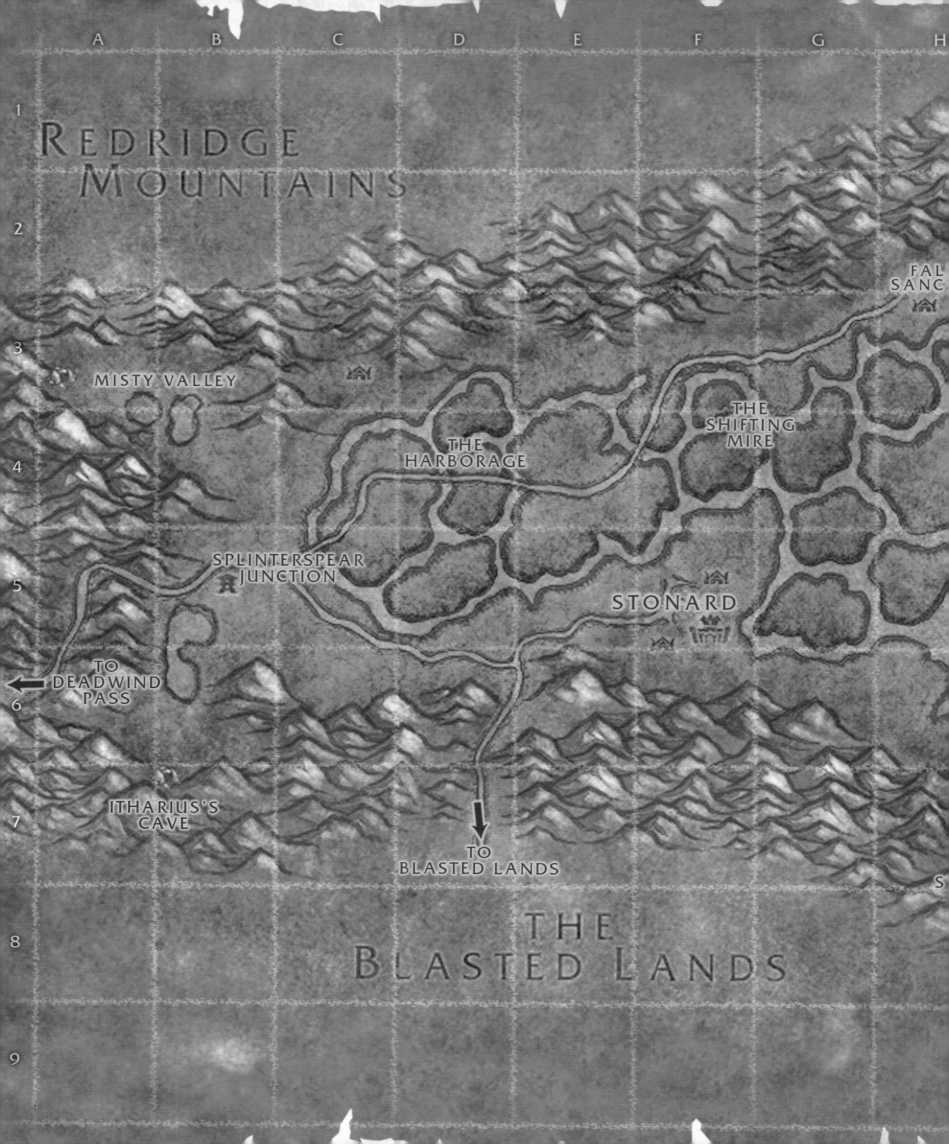

SWAMP OF SORROWS

MISTY REED
STRAND

TEMPLE OF
ATAL'HAKKAR

SORROWMURK

POOL OF
TEARS

STAGALBOG

LBOG
VE

MISTY REED
POST

FLIGHT MASTER

Wind Rider Master	F-5

TRAINERS

Demon Master	F-5
Hunter Trainer	F-5
Master Alchemist	F-5
Pet Trainer	F-5
Shaman Trainer	F-6
Warlock Trainer	F-5
Warrior Trainer	F-5

VENDORS

Alchemy Supplies	F-5
Arcane Goods Vendor	F-5
Blacksmithing Supplies	F-5
Cloth & Leather Armor Merchant	F-5
Food & Drink Vendor	F-5
Innkeeper	F-5
Mail and Plate Merchant	F-5
Stable Master	F-5
Superior Leatherworker	C-3
Trade Goods	F-5
Weapon Merchant	F-5

HERBALISM

Herb Name	Herbalism Skill Requirement
Blindweed	235
Fadeleaf	160
Goldthorn	170
Khadgar's Whisker	185
Kingsblood	125
Liferoot	150
Stranglekelp	85

MINING

Ore Name	Mining Skill Requirement
Gold	155
Iron	125
Mithril	175
Silver	75
Truesilver	230

QUICK REFERENCE

CONNECTING REGIONS

BLASTED LANDS 20

DEADWIND PASS 28

TOWNS & CAMPS

STONARD 131

TANARIS

FLIGHT MASTERS

Gryphon Master	H-3
Wind Rider Master	H-3

TRAINERS

Master Engineer	H-3
Master Goblin Engineer	H-3
Miner	G-3

VENDORS

Alchemy Supplies	G-3
Blacksmithing Supplies	H-3
Butcher (Cooking)	H-3
Fisherman	J-2
General Goods	J-2
Gunsmith	G-3
Innkeeper	H-3
Stable Master	H-3
Superior Armor Crafter	G-3
Tailoring Supplies	G-3

HERBALISM

Herb Name	Herbalism Skill Requirement
Firebloom	205
Purple Lotus	210

MINING

Ore Name	Mining Skill Requirement
Gold	155
Iron	125
Mithril	175
Silver	75
Small Thorium	250
Truesilver	230

QUICK REFERENCE

CONNECTING REGIONS

THOUSAND NEEDLES	82
UN'GORO CRATER	90

TOWNS & CAMPS

GADGETZAN	113
STEAMWHEEDLE PORT	130

TELDRASSIL

FLIGHT MASTER

Hippogryph Master G-9

TRAINERS

Cook...G-6
Druid Trainer ....G:(4, 6)
First Aid Trainer G-6
Fisherman G-9
Herbalist G-6
Hunter Trainer...G:(4, 6)
Journeyman Alchemist...G-6
Journeyman Enchanter...D-3
Journeyman Leatherworker E-5
Pet Trainer...G-6
Priest Trainer G-6, H-4
Rogue Trainer..G-6, H-4
Skinner E-5
Warrior Trainer G-6, H-4

VENDORS

Armorer & Shieldcrafter.................................G:(4, 6), H-4
Bowyer..G-6, H-4
Clothier...G-6, H-4
Cooking Supplies...G-6
Fishing Supplies G-9
Food & Drink Vendor G-6, H-4
General Supplies G-6, H-4
Innkeeper G-6
Leather Armor Merchant G-6, H-4
Stable Master..G-6
Trades Supplies...G-6
Weaponsmith ....G:(4, 6), H-4

HERBALISM

Herb Name	Herbalism Skill Requirement
Earthroot	15
Mageroyal	50
Peacebloom	1
Silverleaf	1

QUICK REFERENCE

CONNECTING REGIONS

DARKSHORE 24
DARNASSUS 26

TOWNS & CAMPS

DOLANAAR...109
RUT'THERAN VILLAGE 125
SHADOWGLEN...127

SHADOWTHREAD
CAVE

LSPRING
RIVER

ALDRASSIL

LSPRING
AKE

THE CLEFT

SHADOWGLEN

FEL ROCK

BAN'ETHIL

THIL BARROW

N'ETHIL
DEN

DOLANAAR

STARBREEZE
VILLAGE

OF
IEN

LAKE AL'AMETH

GNARLPINE
HOLD

THE
VEILED
SEA

RUT'THERAN
VILLAGE

THOUSAND
NEEDLES

FLIGHT MASTER

Wind Rider Master F-5

VENDORS

Butcher F-5
Drink Vendor ....K:(7-8)
Engineering Supplies K-8
Food & Drink Vendor B-3
General Goods F-5
Gun Merchant K-8
Gunsmith & Bowyer F-5
Ice Cream Vendor J-8
Innkeeper F-5
Stable Master F-5
Trade Supplies F-5

HERBALISM

Herb Name	Herbalism Skill Requirement
Bruiseweed	100
Kingsblood	125
Wild Steelbloom	115

MINING

Ore Name	Mining Skill Requirement
Copper	1
Gold	155
Iron	125
Mithril	175
Silver	75
Tin	65
Truesilver	230

QUICK REFERENCE

CONNECTING REGIONS

BARRENS 18
FERALAS 46
TANARIS 78

TOWNS & CAMPS

FREEWIND POST 112
MIRAGE RACEWAY 119

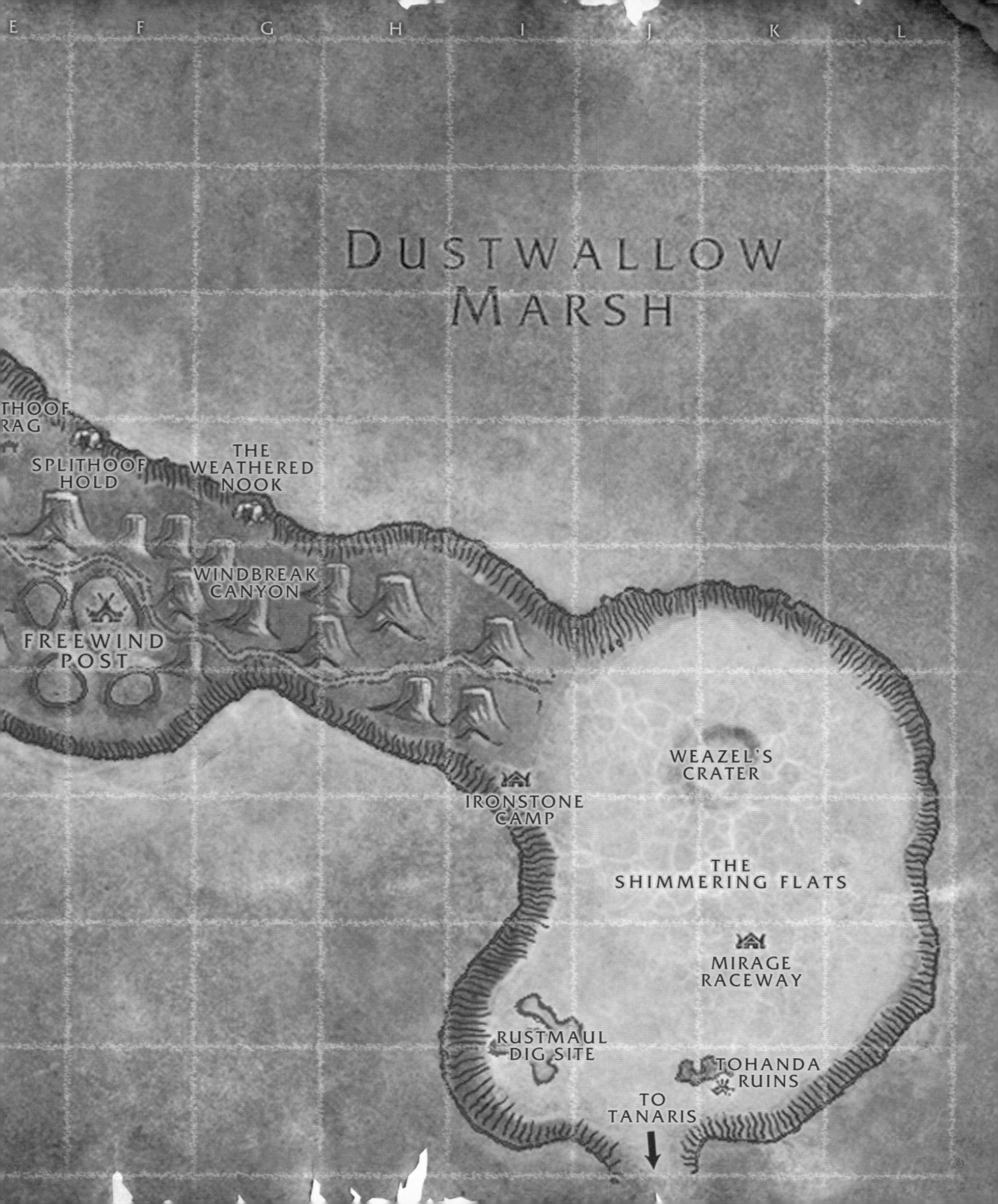
E
F
G
H
I
J
K
L
DUSTWALLOW MARSH
THOOF
RAG
SPLITHOOF HOLD
THE WEATHERED NOOK
WINDBREAK CANYON
FREEWIND POST
IRONSTONE CAMP
WEAZEL'S CRATER
THE SHIMMERING FLATS
MIRAGE RACEWAY
RUSTMAUL DIG SITE
TOHANDA RUINS
TO TANARIS

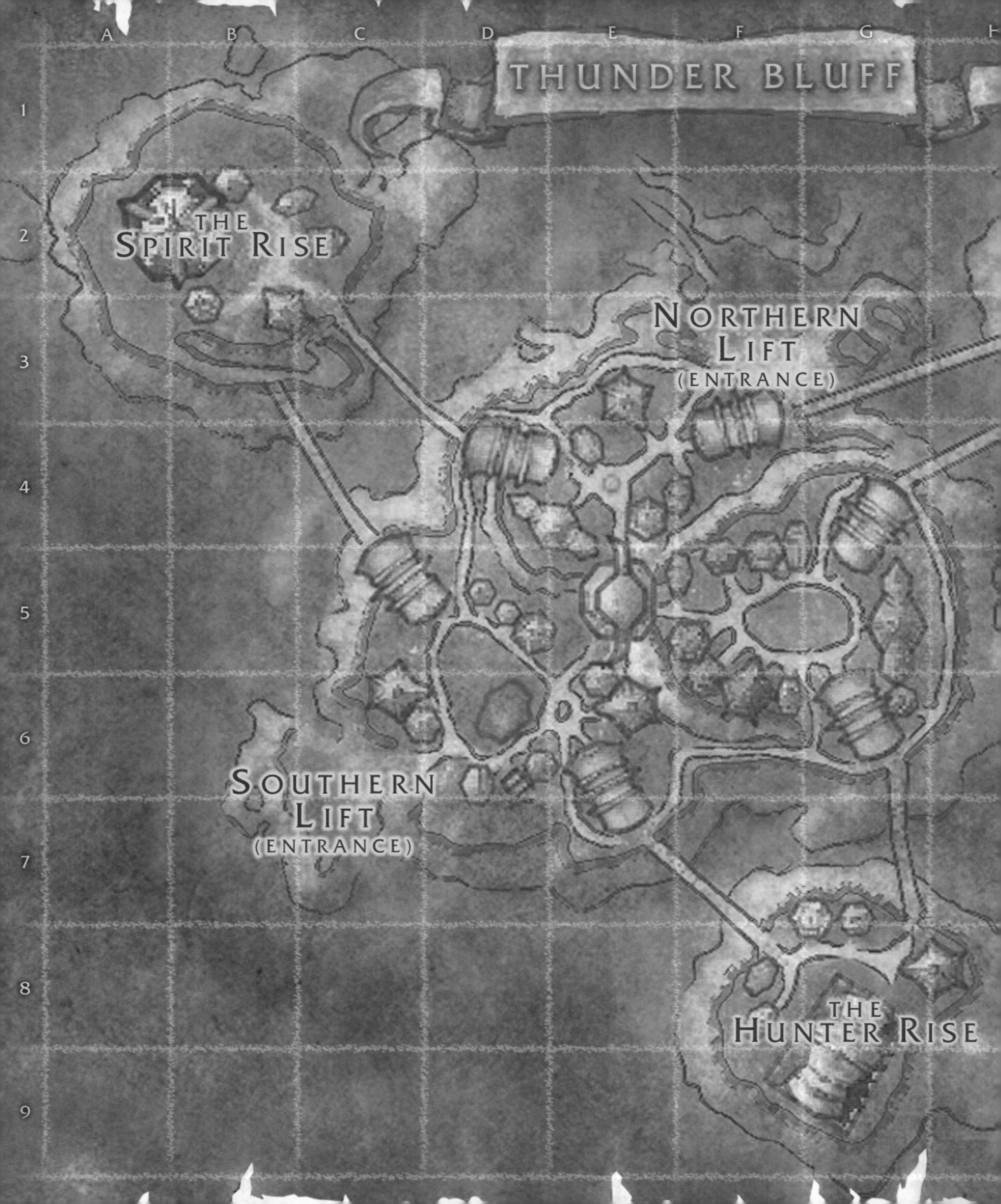
THUNDER BLUFF
A
B
C
D
E
F
G
H
1
2
3
4
5
6
7
8
9
THE
SPIRIT RISE
NORTHERN
LIFT
(ENTRANCE)
SOUTHERN
LIFT
(ENTRANCE)
THE
HUNTER RISE

THE
ELDER RISE

CITY OFFICIALS

Alterac Valley	Commendations D-6
Battlemaster G-8	Eye of the Storm
Arathi Basin	Battlemaster G-8
Battlemaster G-8	Guild Master.................D-6
Arena	Horde Cloth
Battlemaster G-8	Quartermaster............ E-4
Auctioneer...................D-5	Warsong Gulch
Banker E-6	Battlemaster..............G-8

FLIGHT MASTER

Wind Rider Master E-5

TRAINERS

Artisan Leatherworker...D-4	Journeyman Enchanter.. E-4
Cooking Trainer............F-5	Journeyman
Druid Trainer............I-3, J-3	Leatherworker D-4
Expert Alchemist E-3	Journeyman Tailor E-4
Expert Blacksmith D-6	Mage Trainer.................C-3
Expert Enchanter E-4	Mining Trainer...............C-6
Expert Leatherworker ... E-4	Pet Trainer....................F-8
Expert Tailor.................. E-4	Portal Trainer.................C-3
First Aid Trainer............C-2	Priest Trainer C-3
Fishing Trainer...............F-5	Shaman Trainer B-2
Herbalism Trainer..........F-4	Skinning Trainer E-4
Hunter Trainer...............G-9	Warrior Trainer ....G:(8, 9)
Journeyman Alchemist.. E-3	Weapon Master D-6
Journeyman	
Blacksmith.................D-6	

VENDORS

Alchemy Supplies......... E-3	Innkeeper E-6
Axe Merchant...............F-6	Leather Armor
Bag Vendor...................D-6	Merchant .... E:(4, 6)
Basket Weaver.............. E-3	Leatherworking &
Blacksmithing	Tailoring Supplies E-4
Supplies D-6	Mace & Staff Merchant..F-6
Bowyer & Fletching	Mail Armor Merchant ... E-6
Goods E-4	Meat Vendor................F-5
Bread..........................D-5	Mining Supplies............C-6
Cloth Armor	Reagent Vendor D-6
Merchant .... E:(4, 6)	Stable Master................ E-6
Cooking Supplies...........F-5	Staff Merchant E-5, F-5
Enchanting Supplies...... E-4	Sword and Dagger
Fishing Supplies............F-5	Merchant F-6
Fruit Vendor E-4	Tabard Vendor D-6
General Goods...............D-6	Trade Goods Supplies ...D-6
Guns Merchant F-6	Two Handed Weapon
Heavy Armor	Merchant F-6
Merchant D-4	War Harness Vendor F-5
Herbalism Supplies F-4	Weapon's Merchant......D-6

QUICK REFERENCE

CONNECTING REGIONS
MULGORE 58

TIRISFAL GLADES

TRAINERS

Apprentice Herbalist..H-5
Demon Trainer C-7, H-5
First Aid Trainer..H-5
Fisherman I-5
Journeyman Alchemist.......................................H-5
Journeyman Enchanter.......................................H-5
Journeyman Leatherworker I-6
Journeyman Tailor G-5
Mage Trainer C-7, H-5
Priest Trainer C-7, H-5
Rogue Trainer...D-6, H-5
Skinner I-6
Undead Horse Riding Instructor H-5
Warlock Trainer D-6, H-5
Warrior Trainer D-6, H-5

VENDORS

Alchemy & Herbalism Supplies.........................H-5
Apprentice Armorer D-7, H-5
Apprentice Clothier G-6
Apprentice Weaponsmith.............................D-7, H-5
Cloth and Leather Armor Merchant D-6
Fishing Supplies I-6
General Supplies...D-6, H-5
Innkeeper H-5
Leather Armor Merchant H-5
Leatherworking Supplies...................................K-7
Mushroom Farmer H-5
Stable Master...H-5
Trade Supplies H-5
Undead Horse Merchant...................................H-5

HERBALISM

Herb Name	Herbalism Skill Requirement
Earthroot	15
Peacebloom	1
Silverleaf	1

MINING

Ore Name	Mining Skill Requirement
Copper	1

QUICK REFERENCE

CONNECTING REGIONS

ALTERAC MOUNTAINS 8
SILVERPINE FOREST...68
UNDERCITY...88
WESTERN PLAGUELANDS..92

TOWNS & CAMPS

AGAMAND MILLS..100
BRILL 104
THE BULWARK 105
DEATHKNELL 109

THE GREAT SEA

SCARLET
WATCH POST

NORTH COAST

AGAMAND FAMILY
CRYPT

GARREN'S
HAUNT

SCARLET
MONASTERY

AGAMAND
MILLS

WHISPERING
GARDENS

GUNTHER'S
RETREAT

FAOL'S
REST

BRIGHTWATER
LAKE

STILLWATER
POND

CRUSADER
OUTPOST

VENOMWEB
VALE

BRILL

COLD
HEARTH
MANOR

RUINS OF
LORDAERON

BALNIR
FARMSTEAD

NIGHTMARE
VALE

THE
BULWARK

TO
WESTERN
PLAGUELANDS

UNDERCITY

TO
SILVERPINE
FOREST

TO
ALTERAC
MOUNTAINS

ALTERAC

UNDERCITY

A B C D

1

2

THE
SEWERS

3

4

5

6

7

8

9

CITY OFFICIALS

Alterac Valley Battlemaster H-8	Arena Battlemaster H-9
Arathi Basin Battlemaster H-9	Guild Master..................J-4
Auctioneers ....H:(4,5), I:(4,5), J:(4,5)	Horde Cloth Quartermaster.............J-3
Bankers........................I-4	Warsong Gulch Battlemaster.............G-9
Eye of the Storm Battlemaster H-9	

FLIGHT MASTER

Bat Handler I-5

TRAINERS

Artisan Alchemist F-7	Journeyman Engineer....K-7
Artisan Tailor..................J-3	Journeyman Leatherworker J-6
Cooking Trainer......H-4, I-4	Journeyman Tailor J-3
Demon Trainer ....L:(1, 2)	Mage Trainer.................L-1
Expert Alchemist G-7	Master Shadoweave Tailor L-2
Expert Blacksmith I-3	Mining Trainer...............H-4
Expert Enchanter I-6	Paladin Trainer H-9
Expert Engineer K-7	Portal Trainer.................L-1
Expert Leatherworker I-6	Priest Trainer F-2, G-2
Expert Tailor...................J-3	Rogue Trainer L-7
First Aid Trainer..............J-5	Skinning Trainer J-6
Fishing Trainer...............K-3	Warlock Trainer .... L:(1, 2)
Herbalism Trainer H-5	Warrior Trainer F-2, G-1
Journeyman Alchemist...F-7	Weapon Master H-3
Journeyman Blacksmith..................H-3	
Journeyman Enchanter... I-6	

VENDOR

Alchemy Supplies..........G-7	Innkeeper I-4, J-4
Bag Vendor....................J-6	Leather Armor Merchant J-6
Blacksmith Supplies I-3	Leatherworking Supplies J-6
Blade Merchant K-5	
Blue Moon Odds and Ends H-5	Light Armor Merchant... I-4
Bow Merchant H-4	Mining Supplies............H-4
Cloth Armor Merchant... J-3	Mushroom Vendor.........I-5
Cockroach Vendor.... I:(4, 5)	Poison Vendor K-5
Cooking Supplies I-4	Reagent Supplies L-2
Enchanting Supplies.......I-6	Reagent Vendor J-4
Engineer Supplies K-7	Robe Vendor..................J-3
Fishing Supplies K-3	Stable Master.................I-4
Fungus Vendor..............K-2	Staff Merchant J-3
General Goods Vendor... J-5	Tabard Vendor J-4
General Trade Goods Vendor I-5	Tailoring Supplies...........J-3
General Trade Supplies .. I-4	Thrown Weapons Merchant K-5
Gun Merchant...............I-3	Wand Vendor.................J-3
Heavy Armor Merchant ....I:(3, 4)	Weapon Merchant H-3
Herbalism Supplies H-5	Weapons Merchant H-4, I-4

QUICK REFERENCE

CONNECTING REGIONS

TIRISFAL GLADES...86

THE
RUINS OF LORDAERON

THE
WAR QUARTER

THE
MAGIC QUARTER

THE
APOTHECARIUM

THE
ROGUES' QUARTER

UNDERCITY

UN'GORO
CRATER

FLIGHT MASTER
Flight Master...F-1

VENDORS
General Goods Vendor....................................F-1
Weapon Merchant F-1

HERBALISM

Herb Name	Herbalism Skill Requirement
Blindweed	235
Dreamfoil	270
Golden Sansam	260
Mountain Silversage	280
Sungrass	230

MINING

Ore Name	Mining Skill Requirement
Rich Thorium	270
Small Thorium	250

QUICK REFERENCE

CONNECTING REGIONS
SILITHUS...66
TANARIS 78

TOWNS & CAMPS
MARSHAL'S REFUGE............................118

E
F
G
H
I
J
K
L
MARSHAL'S
REFUGE
FUNGAL
ROCK
LAKKARI
TAR PITS
IRONSTONE
PLATEAU
THE
MARSHLANDS
FIRE PLUME
RIDGE
ERROR RUN
TO
TANARIS
THE SLITHERING
SCAR

A
B
C
D
E
F
G
H
1
2
3
4
5
6
7
8
9
HEARTHGLEN
MARDENHOLDE KEEP
SCARLET TOWER
NORTHRIDGE LUMBER CAMP
DALSON'S TEARS
TO TIRISFAL GLADES
FELSTONE FIELD
THE BULWARK
THE WRITHING HAUNT
RUINS OF ANDORHAL
SORROW HILL
UTHER'S TOMB
CHILLWIND CAMP
SORROW HILL CRYPT
TO HILLSBRAD FOOTHILLS

WESTERN PLAGUELANDS

FLIGHT MASTER

Gryphon Master...F-8

VENDORS

Cooking Supplies...I-8
Leatherworking Supplies...F-8
Blacksmithing and Alchemy Vendor...............................I-8

HERBALISM

Herb Name	Herbalism Skill Requirement
Arthas' Tears	220
Dreamfoil	270
Mountain Silversage	280
Plaguebloom	285
Sungrass	230

MINING

Ore Name	Mining Skill Requirement
Gold	155
Iron	125
Mithril	175
Rich Thorium	270
Silver	75
Small Thorium	250
Truesilver	230

QUICK REFERENCE

CONNECTING REGIONS

EASTERN PLAGUELANDS 40
HILLSBRAD FOOTHILLS 48
TIRISFAL GLADES 86

TOWNS & CAMPS

CHILLWIND CAMP...107

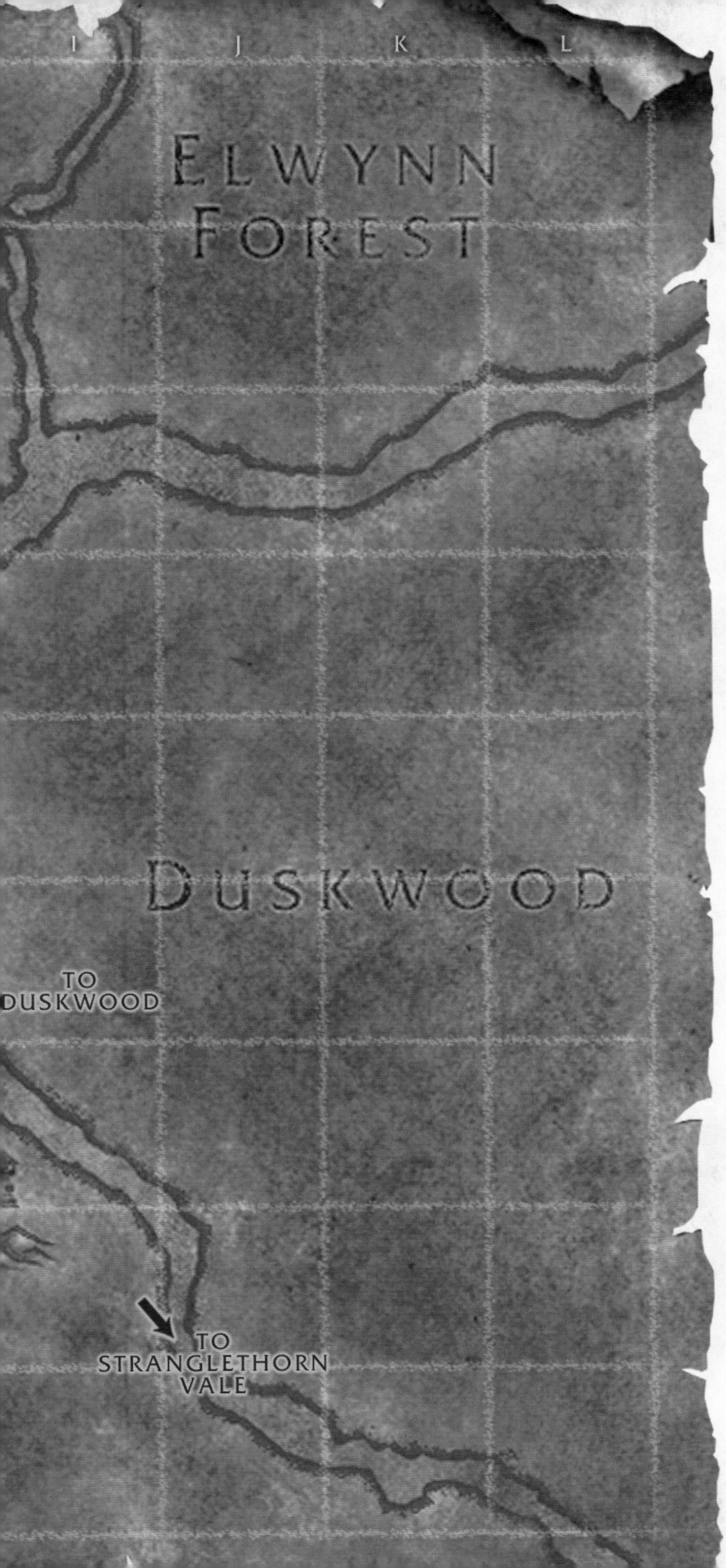

ELWYNN FOREST

DUSKWOOD

TO
DUSKWOOD

TO
STRANGLETHORN
VALE

FLIGHT MASTER

Gryphon Master...G-5

VENDORS

Bowyer..G-5
Bread Merchant..G-5
Fisherman..D-9
Freewheeling Merchant E-7
General Trade Goods Vendor.............................F-5
Innkeeper F-5
Quartermaster...G-5
Stable Master..F-5
Trade Supplies G-5
Traveling Salesman G-6

HERBALISM

Herb Name	Herbalism Skill Requirement
Briarthorn	70
Bruiseweed	100
Earthroot	15
Mageroyal	50
Peacebloom	1
Silverleaf	1
Stranglekelp	85

MINING

Ore Name	Mining Skill Requirement
Copper	1
Tin	65

QUICK REFERENCE

CONNECTING REGIONS

DUSKWOOD...36
ELWYNN FOREST 42
STRANGLETHORN VALE......................................74

TOWNS & CAMPS

SENTINEL HILL...126

WETLANDS

FLIGHT MASTER

Gryphon Master............A-6

TRAINERS

First Aid Trainer..............A-6   Herbalism Trainer..........A-6
Fishing Trainer...............A-6

VENDORS

Alchemy Supplies.........A-6   Potions & Herbs G-4
Armorer ....A-6   Reagent Vendor A-6
Bowyer..........................A-6   Shady Dealer A-6
Engineering & General   Special Goods Dealer....C-3
  Goods Supplies...........A-6   Specialty Goods............F-2
Engineering Supplies ....C-3   Stable Master................A-6
Fisherman.....................A-6   Tailoring Supplies &
Fletcher........................A-6   Specialty Goods..........A-6
General Supplies...........A-6   Tradesman A-6
Gunsmith......................A-6   Weaponsmith A-6
Horse Breeder A-5
Innkeeper A-6

HERBALISM

Herb Name	Herbalism Skill Requirement
Briarthorn	70
Bruiseweed	100
Grave Moss	120
Kingsblood	125
Liferoot	150
Mageroyal	50
Stranglekelp	85
Wild Steelbloom	115

MINING

Ore Name	Mining Skill Requirement
Copper	1
Gold	155
Incendicite	65
Iron	125
Silver	75
Tin	65

QUICK REFERENCE

CONNECTING REGIONS

ARATHI HIGHLANDS 10
LOCH MODAN 54

TOWNS & CAMPS

MENETHIL HARBOR...119

WINTERSPRING

FLIGHT MASTERS

Hippogryph Master I-4
Wind Rider Master I-4

TRAINER

Wintersaber Trainers G-1

VENDOR

Alchemy Supplies.. I-4
Engineering Supplies I-4
Food & Drink H-3, I-4
General Goods.. H-3
Heavy Armor Merchant I-4
Innkeeper I-4
Light Armor Merchant I-4
Mining Supplies.. I-4
Stable Master I-4
Trade Goods H-3, I-4
Weaponsmith & Gunsmith............................. I-4

HERBALISM

Herb Name	Herbalism Skill Requirement
Black Lotus	300
Icecap	290
Mountain Silversage	280

MINING

Ore Name	Mining Skill Requirement
Gold	155
Iron	125
Mithril	175
Rich Thorium	270
Silver	75
Small Thorium	250
Truesilver	230

QUICK REFERENCE

CONNECTING REGIONS

FELWOOD..44
MOONGLADE 56

TOWNS & CAMPS

EVERLOOK...110
STARFALL VILLAGE...130

FELWOOD

TO
FELWOOD
AND
MOONGLADE

FROSTSABER
ROCK

THE HIDDEN
GROVE

MOON HORROR
DEN

STARFALL
VILLAGE

WINTERFALL
VILLAGE

FROSTFIRE
HOT SPRINGS

EVERLOOK

TIMBERMAW
POST

LAKE
KEL'THERIL

ICE THISTLE
HILLS

THE RUINS OF
KEL'THERIL

MAZTHORIL

DUN
MANDARR

OWL WING
THICKET

FROSTWHISPER
GORGE

YJAL

DARKWHISPER
GORGE

E F G H I J K L

AERIE PEAK

1. Gryphon Master Talonaxe
2. Guthrum Thunderfist, Gryphon Master
3. Falstad Wildhammer
4. Forge
   Anvil
5. WILDHAMMER KEEP
   Mailbox
   Killium Bouldertoe, Stable Master
5a. Dorian Steelwing
    Drakk Stonehand, Master
      Leatherworking Trainer (Downstairs)
    Nioma, Leatherworking Supplies
      (Downstairs)
5b. Agnar Beastamer (Downstairs)
    Dwarven Fire
    Innkeeper Thulfram,
      Innkeeper (Upstairs)
5c. Truk Wildbeard, Bartender
5d. Fraggar Thundermantle
5e. Harggan, Blacksmithing
      Supplies (Upstairs)
6. Howin Kindfeather
   Claira Kindfeather
7. Kerr Ironsight
8. FEATHERBEARD'S HOVEL
   Dwarven Fire
9. Trained Razorbeak
   Mangy Silvermane
10. Ambassador Rualeth

HINTERLANDS page 50

AERIE PEAK

AGAMAND MILLS

AGAMAND MILLS

1. Nissa Agamand
2. Darkeye Bonecaster
   Rattlecage Soldier
3. Lost Soul
4. Cracked Skull Soldier
   Darkeye Bonecaster
5. Tormented Spirit
6. Cracked Skull Soldier
   Rattlecage Soldier
7. Gregor Agamand
8. Rotting Ancestor
9. Wailing Ancestor
10. AGAMAND FAMILY CRYPT
    Wailing Ancestor
    Rotting Ancestor
    Captain Dargol
11. Wailing Ancestor
    Rotting Ancestor

TIRISFAL GLADES page 86

ASTRANAAR

ASTRANAAR

1. Daelyshia, Hippogryph Master
2. Llana, Reagent Supplies
3. Faldreas Goeth'Shael
4. Fahran Silentblade, Tools & Supplies
   Raene Wolfrunner
5. Maliynn, Food & Drink Vendor
6. Nantar, Baker
7. Innkeeper Kimlya, Innkeeper
8. Mailbox
9. Maluressian, Stable Master
10. Pelturas Whitemoon
    Relara Whitemoon
11. Campfire
12. Aayndia Floralwind, Expert
    Leatherworker
    Xai'ander, Weaponsmith
13. Dalria, Trade Goods
14. Haljan Oakheart, General Goods
15. Sentinel Thenysil
    Vindicator Palanaar
16. Aeolynn, Clothier
17. Tandaan Lightmane, Leather Armor
    Merchant
18. Lardan, Leatherworking Supplies
19. Shindrell Swiftfire

ASHENVALE page 12

AUBERDINE

1. Caylais Moonfeather,
   Hippogryph Master
2. Gwennyth Bly'Leggonde
3. Kyndri, Baker
4. Laird, Fish Vendor
5. Innkeeper Shaussiy,
   Innkeeper
6. Taldan, Drink Vendor
7. Allyndia, Food & Drink
   Vendor
8. Wizbang Cranktoggle
   (Upstairs)
9. Cerellean Whiteclaw
10. Wanted Poster: Murkdeep!
11. Jaelysia, Stable Master
12. Yalda
13. Barithras Moonshade
    Mailbox
14. Archaeologist Hollee
    Campfire
15. Harlon Thornguard,
    Armorer & Shieldsmith
    Mavralyn, Leather Armor &
    Leatherworking Supplies
16. Thundris Windweaver
    Dalmond, General Goods
    Naram Longclaw,
    Weaponsmith

17. Allandarian Nightsong
18. Shaldyn, Clothier
    Grondal Moonbreeze,
    Journeyman Tailor
    Valdaron, Tailoring Supplies
19. Gorbold Steelhand, General
    Trade Supplies
    Elisa Steelhand,
    Blacksmithing Supplies
    Delfrum Flintbeard,
    Journeyman Blacksmith
    Kurdram Stonehammer,
    Mining Trainer
    Jenna Lemkenilli,
    Journeyman Engineer
    Thelgrum Stonehammer,
    Mining Supplies
    Forge
    Anvil
20. Thanarian Treetender
21. Gershala Nightwhisper
22. Terenthis
23. Sentinel Elissa Starbreeze
24. Gubber Blump
25. Buzzbox 827
26. Moonwell
27. Sentinel Glynda Nal'shea

DARKSHORE page 24

AUBERDINE

BLOODHOOF VILLAGE

1. Harant Ironbrace, Armorer and
    Shieldcrafter
   Varg Wind Whisper, Leather Armor
    Merchant
   Mahnott Roughwound, Weaponsmith
   Kennah Hawkseye, Gunsmith
2. Pyall Silentstride, Cook
   Chaw Stronghide, Journeyman
    Leatherworker
   Yonn Deepcut, Skinner
3. Moorat Longstride, General Goods
   Brave Cloudmane
   Wunna Darkmane, Trade Goods
4. Brave Ironhorn
5. Brave Wildrunner
6. Baine Bloodhoof
7. Mailbox
8. Skorn Whitecloud
   Seikwa, Stable Master
9. Vira Younghoof, First Aid Trainer
10. Magrin Rivermane
11. Innkeeper Kauth, Innkeeper
12. Var'jun
13. Jhawna Oatwind, Baker
14. Ruul Eagletalon
15. Brave Rainchaser
16. Mull Thunderhorn
17. Krang Stonehoof, Warrior Trainer
    Novice Warrior
    Hulfnar Stonetotem
    Thontek Rumblehoof
18. Gennia Runetotem, Druid Trainer
19. Harken Windtotem
20. Narm Skychaser, Shaman Trainer
21. Karm Stormsinger, Kodo Riding
    Instructor
    Harb Clawhoof, Kodo Mounts
22. Zarlman Two-Moons
    Tribal Fire
23. Maur Raincaller
24. Harn Longcast, Fishing Supplies
25. Reban Freerunner, Pet Trainer
    Yaw Sharpmane, Hunter Trainer
26. Brave Darksky
27. Brave Strongbash
28. Brave Swiftwind
29. Morin Cloudstalker
30. Brave Dawneagle
31. Uthan Stillwater, Fisherman
32. Ahab Wheathoof, The Old Rancher

MULGORE page 58

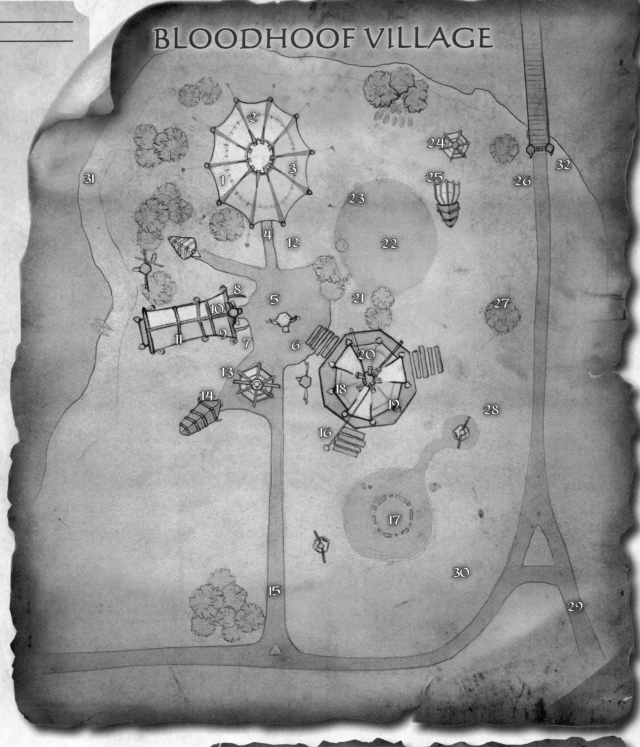

BLOODHOOF VILLAGE

BLOODVENOM POST

1. Brakkar, Wind Rider Master
2. Winna Hazzard
   Winna's Kitten
3. Dreka'Sur
4. Altsoba Ragetotem, Weapon Merchant
   Bale, General Goods
5. Trull Failbane
   Campfire

FELWOOD page 44

BLOODVENOM POST

BOOTY BAY

1. Grizzlowe, Shipmaster
2. Wharfmaster Lozgil
3. Sprogger
   Captain Hecklebury Smotts
   "Shaky" Phillipe
4. PLATE-N-CHAIN
   Hurklor, Blacksmithing Supplies
   Fargon Mortalak, Superior Armorer
5. BOOTY BAY BLACKSMITH
   McGavan
   Jansen Underwood, Blacksmithing Supplies
   Brikk Keencraft, Master Blacksmith
   Anvil
   Forge
6. Dizzy One-Eye

7. Rikqiz, Leatherworking Supplies
   Stove, Cooking Fire
8. Oglethorpe Obnoticus, Master Gnome
   Engineer
   Stove, Cooking Fire
9. A TAILOR TO CITIES
   Xizk Goodstitch, Tailoring Supplies
   Grarnik Goodstitch, Expert Tailor
   Stove, Cooking Fire
10. DEEP SOUTH TANNERY
    Stove, Cooking Fire
11. TAN-YOUR-HIDE-LEATHERWORKS
    Drizzlik
    Blixrez Goodstitch, Leatherworking
    Supplies

Qixdi Goodstitch, Cloth and Armor
   Accessories
12. OLD PORT AUTHORITY
    Markel Smythe
12a. CUTS-N-BRUISES INCORPORATED
    Zarena Cromwind, Superior Weaponsmith
    Kizz Bluntstrike, Macecrafter
12b. BOOMSTICK IMPORTS EAST
    Mazk Snipeshot, Engineering Supplies
12c. SWIFT FLIGHTS
    Haren Kanmae, Superior Bowyer
12d. NAUTICAL NEEDS
    Narkk, Pirate Supplies
12e. GOOD FOOD
    Kelsey Yance, Cook
13. Wigcik (Low Level), Superior Fisherman
    Stove, Cooking Fire
13a. Sly Garrett, Shady Goods
    Crazk Sparks, Fireworks Merchant
14. "Sea Wolf" MacKinley
    Book: The Sentinels and the Long Vigil
       (Top Level)
    Auctioneer Kresky
       (Lower Level)
15. BOUCHER'S CAULDRON
    Jaxin Chong, Expert Alchemist
    Glyx Brewright, Alchemy Supplies
    Stove, Cooking Fire
16. ALL THINGS FLORA
    Flora Silverwind, Superior Herbalist
17. Scooty, Chief Engineer
    Jutak, Blade Trader
    Teleporter to Gnomeregan
18. SOUTHERN SKIES PLATFORM
    Gyll, Gryphon Master
19a. THE SALTY SAILOR, LOW LEVEL
    Whiskey Slim
    Crank Fizzlebub
    Innkeeper Skindle, Innkeeper
    Nixxrax Fillamug, Food and Drink
19b. THE SALTY SAILOR, MID LEVEL
    Catelyn the Blade
    Ian Strom, Rogue Trainer
19c. THE SALTY SAILOR, TOP LEVEL
    Deeg
    Krazek
    Kebok
    Book: Beyond the Dark Portal
    Mailbox
20. Fin Fizracket
    Old Man Heming (Low Level) Fisherman
21. Fleet Master Seahorn
    Baron Revilgaz
22. Gringer, Wind Rider Master
23. BOOTY BAY BANK
    Privateer Bloads
    Viznik Goldgrubber, Banker
    Rickle Goldgrubber, Banker
    Mailbox/Auctioneer O'relly
24. Caravaneer Ruzzgot
25. Myizz Luckycatch, Superior Fisherman
26. Grimestack, Stable Master

    Zandalarian Emissary

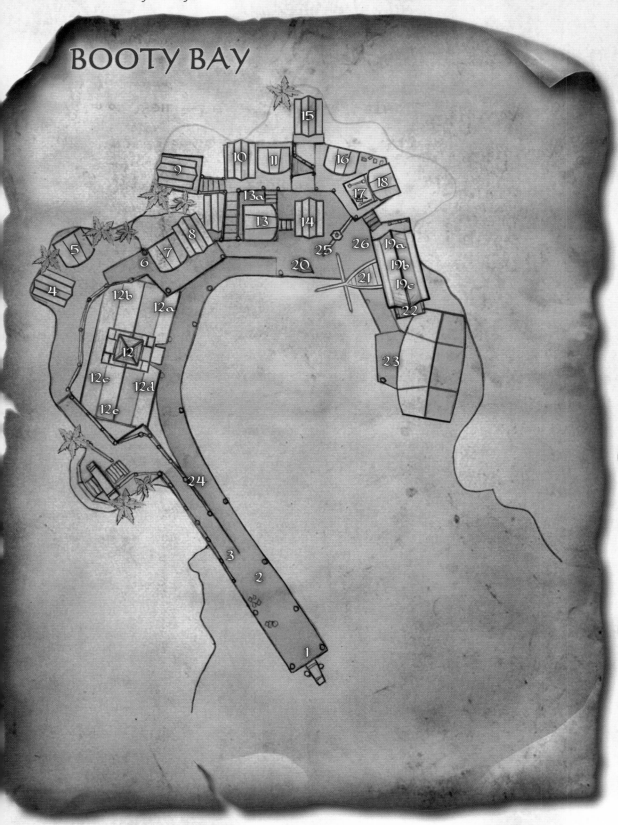

BOOTY BAY

STRANGLETHORN VALE page 74

BRACKENWALL VILLAGE

1. Tharg
2. Ogg'marr, Butcher
3. Do'gol
4. Krak, Armorer
5. Overlord Mok'Morokk
   Bonfire
6. Draz'Zilb
7. Krog
8. Zulrg, Weaponsmith
9. Shardi, Wind Rider Master
10. Ghok'kah, Tailoring Supplies
11. Nazeer Bloodpike
12. Zanara, Bowyer
13. Balai Lok'Wein, Potions, Scrolls &
    Reagents
14. Balandar Brightstar

DUSTWALLOW MARSH page 38

BRILL

1. Deathguard Terrence
2. Deathguard Mort
   Mailbox
3. GALLOW'S END TAVERN
   Nurse Nelia, First Aid Trainer
   Cain Firesong, Mage Trainer (Upstairs)
   Gretchen Dedmar
3a. Yvette Farthing
    Ageron Kargal (Upstairs)
    Gina Lang, Demon Trainer (Upstairs)
    Rupert Boch, Warlock Trainer (Upstairs)
3b. Austil De Mon, Warrior Trainer
    Coleman Farthing
    Ratslin Maime
    Innkeeper Renee, Innkeeper
    Dark Cleric Beryl, Priest Trainer (Upstairs)
    Marion Call, Rogue Trainer (Upstairs)
3c. Captured Scarlet Zealot (Downstairs)
    Captured Mountaineer (Downstairs)
    Deathguard Royann (Downstairs)
    Deathguard Gavin (Downstairs)
    Vance Undergloom, Journeyman Enchanter
     (Upstairs)
4. Mrs. Winters, General Supplies
5. Abigail Shiel, Trade Supplies
6. Deathguard Burgess
7. Deathguard Cyrus
   Executor Zygand
   Wanted Poster: Maggot Eye
8. BRILL TOWN HALL
   Jamie Nore
8a. Magistrate Sevren
9. Junior Apothecary Holland, Royal
   Apothecary Society
10. Deathguard Kel

11. Deathguard Barthomew
    Deathguard Lawrence
    Deathguard Dillinger
12. Hamlin Atkins, Mushroom Farmer
13. Deathguard Lundmark
14. Sahver Bloodshadow
15. Carolai Anise, Journeyman Alchemist
    Apothecary Johaan, Royal Apothecary
     Society
16. Faruza, Apprentice Herbalist

17. Morganus, Stable Master
    Thomas Arlento
    Zachariah Post, Undead Horse Merchant
    Velma Warnam,
     Undead Horse Riding Instructor
    Deathguard Morris
    Doreen Beltis
18. Eliza Callen, Leather Armor Merchant
19. Abe Winters, Apprentice Armorer
    Oliver Dwor, Apprentice Weaponsmith
    Forge
    Anvil
20. Selina Westor, Alchemy and Herbalism
    Supplies

TIRISFAL GLADES page 86

THE BULWARK

THE BULWARK

1. Argent Quartermaster Hasana, The Argent Dawn
2. Argent Officer Garush, The Argent Dawn
3. High Executor Derrington
4. Apothecary Dithers Cauldron

5. Werg Thickblade, Leatherworking Supplies
6. Mehlar Dawnblade
7. Alexi Barov, House of Barov
8. Bardu Sharpeye
9. Shadow Priestess Vandis
10. Mickey Levine Cauldron

TIRISFAL GLADES page 86

CAMP MOJACHE

CAMP MOJACHE

1. Shyn, Wind Rider Master
2. Loorana, Food & Drink Vendor
3. Sage Korolusk
4. Blaise Montgomery Mailbox
5. Tarhus, Reagent Vendor
   Innkeeper Greul, Innkeeper
6. Cawind Trueaim, Gunsmith & Bowyer
7. Rok Orhan
8. Witch Doctor Uzer'i
   Shyrka Wolfrunner, Stable master
9. Kulleg Stonehorn, Skinning Trainer
   Hahrana Ironhide, Master Leatherworker

   Jangdor Swiftstrider, Leatherworking Supplies
   Sheendra Tallgrass, Trade Supplies
   Worb Strongstitch, Light Armor Merchant
10. Hadoken Swiftstrider
11. Sage Palerunner
12. Ruw, Herbalism Trainer
    Bronk, Alchemy Supplies
13. Talo Thornhoof
14. Krueg Skullsplitter
15. Jannos Lighthoof, Druid Trainer
16. Orik'ando
17. Orwin Gizznick

FERALAS page 46

CAMP NARACHE

CAMP NARACHE

1. Brave Greathoof
2. Brave Proudsnout
3. Moodan Sungrain, Baker
4. Grull Hawkwind
   Brave Windfeather
5. Vorn Skyseer
6. Bronk Steelrage, Armorer and Shieldcrafter
   Marjak Keenblade, Weaponsmith
   Varia Hardhide, Leather Armor Merchant
7. Brave Running Wolf

8. Harutt Thunderhorn, Warrior Trainer
   Chief Hawkwind
   Lanka Farshot, Hunter Trainer
   Burning Embers
9. Seer Ravenfeather
10. Meela Dawnstrider, Shaman Trainer
    Gart Mistrunner, Druid Trainer
11. Kawnie Softbreeze, General Goods
12. Brave Lightninghorn

MULGORE page 58

CAMP TAURAJO

1. Kelsuwa, Stable Master
   Innkeeper Byula, Innkeeper
2. Sanuye Runetotem, Leather Armor
   Merchant
   Dranh, Skinner
3. Jorn Skyseer
   Krulmoo Fullmoon, Expert
   Leatherworker
   Gahroot, Butcher
   Ruga Ragetotem
   Mahani, Expert Tailor
   Yonada, Tailoring and Leatherworking
   Supplies
   Burning Embers, Cooking Fire
4. Mailbox
5. Kirge Strenhorn
6. Burning Embers, Cooking Fire
   Barrel of Milk, Spawn Point
7. Tatternack Steelforge
   Anvil
   Forge
8. Omusa Thunderhorn, Wind Rider
   Master
   Grunt Logmar
   Mangletooth

BARRENS page 18

CAMP TAURAJO

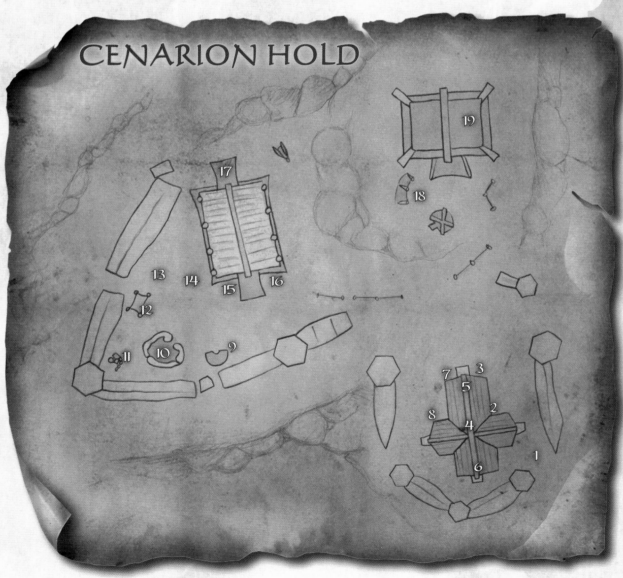

CENARION HOLD

CENARION HOLD

1. Garon Hutchins
2. Windcaller Yessendra
   Aurel Goldleaf
3. Mailbox
4. LOWER LEVEL
   Calandrath, Innkeeper
   J.D. Shadesong
   Dirk Thunderwood
   Keyl Swiftclaw
5. UPPER LEVEL
   Beetix Ficklespragg
   Noggle Ficklespragg
6. UPPER LEVEL
   Kania, Enchanting Supplies
7. Wanted Poster
   Windcaller Proudhorn
8. Vargus, Bladesmith
   Warden Haro
   Anvil, Forge
9. Geologist Larksbane
10. Moonwell
11. Huum Wildmane
    Bor Wildmane
12. Khur Hornstriker, Reagent Vendor
13. Runk Windtamer, Wind Rider Master
14. Scout Bloodfist
15. Squire Leoren Mal'derath, Stable
    Master
    Baristolth of the Shifting Sands
16. Mishta, General Trade Goods Vendor
    Windcaller Kaldon
17. Commander Mar'alith
18. Cloud Skydancer, Hippogryph Master
    Rifleman Torrig
19. UPPER LEVEL
    Vish Kozus, Captain of the Guard

SILITHUS page 66

CHILLWIND CAMP

CHILLWIND CAMP

1. Bibilfaz Featherwhistle, Gryphon Master
2. High Priestess Mac Donnell
   Anchorite Truuen
3. Leonard Porter, Leatherworking Supplies
4. Alexi Ironknife
5. Commander Ashlam Valorfist
6. Alchemist Arbington
7. Argent Quartermaster Lightspark, The
   Argent Dawn
   Argent Officer Pureheart, The Argent
   Dawn
8. Weldon Barov, House of Barov
9. Flint Shadowmore, SI:7
10. Nathaniel Dumah

WESTERN PLAGUELANDS page 92

COLDRIDGE VALLEY

COLDRIDGE VALLEY

1. ANVILMAR
   Solm Hargrin, Rogue Trainer
   Felix Whindlebolt
   Rybrad Coldbank, Weaponsmith
   Grundel Harkin, Armorer
   Bromos Grummner, Paladin
     Trainer
   Thorgas Grimson, Hunter Trainer
   Thran Khorman, Warrior Trainer
   Branstock Khalder, Priest Trainer
   Marryk Nurribit, Mage Trainer
   Durnan Furcutter, Cloth &
     Leather Armor Merchant
   Wren Darkspring, Demon Trainer

   Alamar Grimm, Warlock Trainer
2. Balir Frosthammer
   Sten Stoutarm
   Adlin Pridedrift, General Supplies
   Yori Crackhelm
3. Talin Keeneye
4. Grelin Whitebeard
   Apprentice Soren
   Nori Pridedrift
5. Mountaineer Thalos
6. Hands Springsprocket

DUN MOROGH page 32

THE CROSSROADS

THE CROSSROADS

1. Hraq Blacksmithing, Supplies
   Jahan Hawkwing, Leather and Mail
     Merchant/Anvil, Forge
   Uthrok, Bowyer and Gunsmith
   Nargal Deatheye, Weaponsmith
   Traugh, Expert Blacksmith
2. Korran
3. Devrak, Wind Rider Master
   Apothecary Helbrim
   Hula'mahi, Reagents and Herbs
4. Sikwa, Stable Master
   Grenthar
5. Barg, General Supplies
   Tarl'qa, Trade Supplies
6. Gazrog
   Mailbox
7. Boorand Plainswind, Innkeeper
   Larhka, Beverage Merchant
8. Zargh, Butcher
9. Moorane Hearthgrain, Baker
10. Sergra Darkthorn
11. Thork
    Darsok Swiftdagger
12. Mankrik
13. Kil'hala, Journeyman Tailor
    Wrahk, Tailoring Supplies
14. Halija Whitestrider, Clothier
    Tonga Runetotem
15. Kalyimah Stormcloud, Bags and
    Sacks

BARRENS page 18

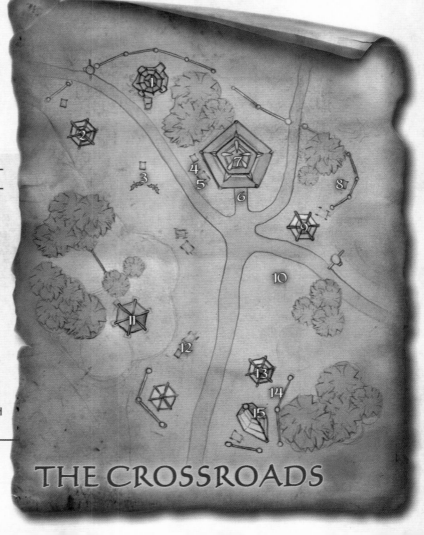

DARKSHIRE

1. **SCARLET RAVEN TAVERN**
   Mabel Solaj, General Goods Vendor

2. Tavernkeep Smitts
   Innkeeper Trelayne, Innkeeper
   Barkeep Han, Bartender

3. Chef Grual

4. Gunder Thornbush, Tradesman (Upstairs)

5. Farrin Daris (Upstairs)

6. Mailbox

7. Steven Black, Stable Master

8. Watcher Bukouris, The Night Watch

9. Commander Althea Ebonlocke, Leader of
   The Night Watch

10. **DARKSHIRE TOWN HALL, FOYER**
    Clerk Daltry

11. **DARKSHIRE TOWN HALL, ANTEROOM**
    Sirra Von'Indi, Historian of Darkshire

12. **DARKSHIRE TOWN HALL, MAIN HALL**
    Hogan Ference
    Councilman Millstripe, Council of Darkshire
    Ambassador Berrybuck, Council of Darkshire
    Role Dreuger, Deputy Mayor of Darkshire
    Lord Ello Ebonlocke, Mayor of Darkshire
    Anchorite Delan

13. Clarise Gnarltree, Expert Blacksmith
    Morg Gnarltree, Armorer
    Gavin Gnarltree, Weaponsmith
    Forge
    Anvil

14. Matt Johnson, Mining Trainer

15. Watcher Mokarski, The Night Watch

16. Watcher Frazier, The Night Watch

17. Watcher Keefer, The Night Watch

18. Watcher Ladimore, The Night Watch
    Town Crier

19. Calor

20. Elaine Carevin
    Jonathan Carevin

21. Scott Carevin, Mushroom Seller

22. Watchmaster Sorigal

23. Watcher Hartin, The Night Watch

24. Madame Eva
    Alyssa Eva, Reagent Vendor

25. Lohgan Eva, Tailoring Supplies

26. Danielle Zipstitch, Tailoring Supplies
    Sheri Zipstitch, Tailoring Supplies (Upstairs)

27. Watcher Brownell, The Night Watch

28. Watcher Jan, The Night Watch

29. Finbus Geargrind, Expert Engineer
    Cog Glitzspinner

30. Herble Baubbletump, Engineering & Mining
    Supplies

31. Watcher Wollpert, The Night Watch

32. Watcher Royce, The Night Watch

33. Watcher Keller, The Night Watch

34. Whit Wantmal

35. Vitori Prism'Antras

36. Felicia Melline, Gryphon Master

37. Malissa, Poison Supplies

38. Watcher Petras, The Night Watch

DUSKWOOD page 36

DARKSHIRE

DEATHKNELL

1.	Deathguard Oliver
2.	Claire Willower
3.	Executor Arren
4.	Harold Raims, Apprentice Weaponsmith
	Blacksmith Rand, Apprentice Armorer
	Cozy Fire
5.	Maquell Ebonwood
	Dark Cleric Duesten, Priest Trainer
	Isabella, Mage Trainer
	Novice Elreth
	Shadow Priest Sarvis
	Kayla Smithe, Demon Trainer
	Maximillion, Warlock Trainer
	Venya Marthand
6.	Deathguard Saltain
7.	Deathguard Randolph
8.	Deathguard Bartrand
9.	Deathguard Phillip
10.	Joshua Kien, General Supplies
	Archibald Kava, Cloth & Leather Armor Merchant
11.	David Trias, Rogue Trainer
	Dannal Stern, Warrior Trainer
12.	Young Scavenger
	Duskbat
13.	Mindless Zombie
	Wretched Zombie
14.	Rattlecage Skeleton
	Wretched Zombie
15.	Mangy Duskbat
	Ragged Scavenger

TIRISFAL GLADES page 86

DOLANAAR

1.	Zenn Foulhoof
2.	Ancient Protector
3.	Malorne Bladeleaf, Herbalist
	Cyndra Kindwhisper, Journeyman Alchemist
4.	Nyoma, Cooking Supplies
	Zarrin, Cook
	Cauldron
5.	Sentinel Shaya
6.	Corithras Moonrage
	Kal, Druid Trainer
	Moonwell
7.	Keldas, Pet Trainer
	Dazalar, Hunter Trainer
	Seriadne, Stable Master
8.	Jannok Breezesong, Rogue Trainer
9.	Brannol Eaglemoon, Clothier
10.	Sinda, Leather Armor Merchant
	Shaloman, Weaponsmith
	Meri Ironweave, Armorer & Shieldcrafter
11.	Sentinel Kyra Starsong
12.	Kyra Windblade, Warrior Trainer
13.	Jeena Featherbow, Bowyer
14.	Mailbox
15.	Innkeeper Keldamyr, Innkeeper Melarith
16.	Syral Bladeleaf
17.	Athridas Bearmantle
18.	Danlyia, Food & Drink Vendor (Bottom Floor)
	Byancie, First Aid Trainer (Bottom Floor)
	Laurna Morninglight, Priest Trainer (Bottom Floor)
	Narret Shadowgrove, Trade Supplies (Middle Floor)
	Aldia, General Supplies (Middle Floor)
	Tallonkai Swiftroot (Top Floor)
19.	Moon Priestess Amara
	Huntress Yaeliura
	Huntress Nhemai

TELDRASSIL page 80

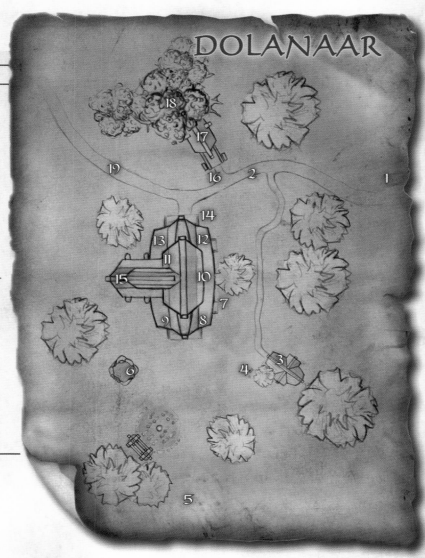

EMERALD SANCTUARY

EMERALD SANCTUARY

1. Tenell Leafrunner, Emerald Circle
2. Gorriam, Emerald Circle Flight Master
3. Greta Mosshoof, Emerald Circle
4. Jessir Moonbow
   Della, Jessir's Pet
5. Kelek Skykeeper, Emerald Circle
6. Eridan Bluewind, Emerald Circle
7. Taronn Redfeather, Emerald Circle
8. Ivy Leafrunner, Emerald Circle

FELWOOD page 44

EVERLOOK

1. Yugrek, Wind Rider Master
2. Azzleby, Stable Master
3. Evie Whirlbrew, Alchemy Supplies
4. Umi Rumplesnicker
5. Zap Farflinger, Unbalanced Engineer
6. Qia, Trade Goods Supplies
   Seril Scourgebane
   Lilith the Lithe
   Kilram
   Izzy Coppergrab, Banker
7. Nixxrak, Heavy Armor Merchant
   Blixxrak, Light Armor Merchant
   Wixxrak, Weaponsmith & Gunsmith
8. Jack Sterling

9. Umaron Stragarelm
   Witch Doctor Mav'ari
   Storm Shadowhoof
10. Lunnix Sprocketslip, Mining Supplies
11. Felnok Steelspring
    Legacki
12. Gogo
    Harlo Wigglesworth
    Mailbox
13. Innkeeper Vizzie, Innkeeper
    Jessica Redpath
    Gregor Greystone
    Himmik, Food & Drink Vendor
14. Malyfous' Darkhammer
    Forge/Anvil
    Malufous Catalogue
15. Xizzer Fizzbolt, Engineering Supplies
16. Meggi Peppinrocker
17. Maethrya, Hippogryph Master

WINTERSPRING page 98

EVERLOOK

FARSTRIDER LODGE

FARSTRIDER LODGE

1. Irene Sureshot, Gunsmith
2. Cliff Hadin, Bowyer
3. Xandar Goodbeard, General Supplies
4. Kat Sampson, Leather Armor Merchant
5. Vyrin Swiftwind
6. Kelt Thomasin
7. Claude Erksine, Pet Trainer
8. Dargh Trueaim, Hunter Trainer
9. Marek Ironheart
10. Daryl the Youngling

LOCH MODAN page 54

FEATHERMOON STRONGHOLD

1. Fyldren Moonfeather, Hippogryph Master
2. Pratt McGrubben, Leatherworking Supplies
3. Faralorn, General Supplies
4. Dulciea Frostmoon, Cloth Armor Merchant
5. Innkeeper Shyria, Innkeeper
6. Mardrack Greenwell, Food & Drink
7. Vivianna, Trade Supplies
8. Jadenvis Seawatcher, Reagent Vendor
9. Brannock, Fisherman
10. Antarius, Stable Master
11. Scholar Runethorn
    Mailbox
12. Xylinnia Starshine, Expert Enchanter
13. Vestia Moonspear
14. Shandris Feathermoon, General of the Sentinel
      Army
    Latronicus Moonspear
15. Savanne, Fishing Supplies
    Harklane, Fish Vendor
16. Kylanna Windwhisper, Master Alchemist
    Logannas, Alchemy Supplies
17. Bethan Bluewater
    Quintis Jonespyre
18. Troyas Moonbreeze
    Angelas Moonbreeze
19. Ginro Hearthkindle
20. Erik Felixe
    Paige Felixe
21. Campfire

FERALAS page 46

FEATHERMOON STRONGHOLD

FLAME CREST

FLAME CREST

1. Vahgruk, Wind Rider Master
2. Gruna, Food and Drink
3. Tinkee Steamboil
   Maxwort Uberglint
4. Ragged John
   Mathredis Firestar
   Cauldron
5. Kibler
   Opus
6. Yuka Screwspigot

BURNING STEPPES page 22

FREEWIND POST

1. Nyse, Wind Rider Master
2. Elu, Wind Rider Apprentice
3. Hagar Lightninghoof
4. Starn, Gunsmith and Bowyer
5. Montarr, Lorekeeper
   Dog, Sire
6. Guard Wachabe
7. Turhaw, Butcher
8. Cliffwatcher Longhorn
   Bonfire
9. Magistrix Elosai
10. Wanted Poster
11. Awenasa, Stable Master
    Mailbox
12. Innkeeper Abeqwa, Innkeeper
    Thalia Amberhide
    Jandia, Trade Supplies
    Jawn Highmesa, General Goods
    Rau Cliffrunner

THOUSAND NEEDLES page 82

FREEWIND POST

GADGETZAN

1. Bulkrek Ragefist, Wind Rider Master
2. Tran'rek
3. Jhordy Lapforge, Engineer
   Curgle Cranklehop/Egg-o-matic
4. Nixx Sprocketspring, Master Goblin
   Engineer
   Mux Manascrambler
5. Buzzek Bracketswing, Master
   Engineer
   Mailbox
6. Innkeeper Fizzgrimble, Innkeeper
   Dirge Quikcleave, Butcher
7. Laziphus, Stable Master
8. Spigot Operator Luglunket
   Chief Engineer Bilgewhizzle
9. Qizzik, Banker
   Gimblethorn, Banker
10. Auctioneer Beardo
11. Marin Noggenfogger
12. Forge/Anvil
    Krinkle Goodsteel, Blacksmithing
      Supplies
    Trenton Lighthammer
    Derotain Mudsipper
13. Pikkle, Miner
14. Quinn
15. Wrinkle Goodsteel, Superior Armor
      Crafter
    Blizrik Buckshot, Gunsmith
16. Vizzklick, Tailoring Supplies
    Shreev
17. Alchemist Pestlezugg, Alchemy
      Supplies
18. Sprinkle
19. Senior Surveyor Fizzledowser
20. Bera Stonehammer, Gryphon Master
21. Andi Lynn
22. Max Luna, Arena Battlemaster
    Wanted Poster
23. Katrina Turner
24. Bip Nigstrom, Arena Organizer
25. Rumsen Fizzlebrack

TANARIS page 78

GADGETZAN

GHOST WALKER POST

1. Gurda Wildmane
   Felgur Twocuts
2. Muuran, Superior Macecrafter
   Nataka Longhorn
   Narv Hidecrafter, Expert
      Leathercrafter
3. Takata Steelblade
4. Maurin Bonesplitter
5. Harnor, Food and Drink
   Kireena, Trade Goods
6. KODO GRAVEYARD
   Dying Kodos
   Ancient Kodos
   Aged Kodos
   Carrion Horrors

DESOLACE page 30

GHOST WALKER POST

GOLDSHIRE

1. Graveyard
2. Bo
   Joshua
   Mark
3. Lyria Du Lac, Warrior Trainer
   Brother Wilhelm, Paladin Trainer
   Corina Steele, Weaponsmith
   Andrew Krighton, Armorer and
      Shieldcrafter

Smith Argus, Journeyman Blacksmith
Kurran Steele, Cloth and Leather Armor
   Merchant
Anvil
Forge

4. Marshal Dughan
5. Remy "Two Times"
   Tharynn Bouden, Trade Supplies
   Food Crate Spawn Point

6. LION'S PRIDE INN
   Erma, Stable Master
   William Pestle
   Melika Isenstrider, Assistant Innkeeper
   Innkeeper Farley, Innkeeper
   Brog Hamfist, General Supplies
   Barkeep Dobbins, Bartender
   Toddrick, Butcher
   Tomas, Cook
   Cozy Fire
   Mailbox

6a. LION'S PRIDE, BASEMENT
    Cylina Darkheart, Demon Trainer
    Maximillian Crowe, Warlock Trainer
    Remen Marcot

6b. LION'S PRIDE, TOP LEVEL
    Zaldimar Wefhellt, Mage Trainer
    Priestess Josetta, Priest Trainer
    Michelle Belle, Physician
    Keryn Sylvius, Rogue Trainer
    Chest: Stalvan's Quest

7. Adele Fielder, Journeyman Leatherworker
   Helene Peltskinner, Skinner
   Dana
   Lisa
   Aaron
   John
   Cameron
   Jose
   Cozy Fire

8. CRYSTAL LAKE
   Jason Mathers, Fishmonger
   Lee Brown, Fisherman
   Matt

ELWYNN FOREST page 42

GROM'GOL BASE CAMP

1. Nez'raz, Zeppelin Master
   Squibby Overspeck, Zeppelin
      Master
2. Zudd, Pet Trainer
3. Kragg, Hunter Trainer
4. Hragran, Cloth & Leather Armor
      Merchant
5. Brawn, Expert Leatherworker
6. Mudduk, Superior Cook
7. Uthok, General Supplies
8. Nimboya
   Angrun, Superior Herbalist
   Kin'weelay

9. Vharr, Superior Weaponsmith
   Krakk, Superior Armorer
   Forge
10. Mailbox
11. Nerrist, Trade Goods
12. Thysta, Wind Rider Master
13. Commander Aggro'gosh
14. Nargatt, Food & Drink Vendor
    Far Seer Mok'thardin

STRANGLETHORN VALE page 74

HAMMERFALL

1.	Urda, Wind Rider Master	8.	Mu'uta, Bowyer
2.	Tharlidun, Stable Master		Forge
	Korin Fel		Anvil
	Mailbox	9.	Gor'mul
3.	Zengu	10.	Jun'ha, Tailoring Supplies
4.	Slagg, Superior Butcher	11.	Doctor Gregory Victor, Trauma
	Uttnar, Butcher		Surgeon
	Drum Fel	12.	Tor'gan
5.	Innkeeper Adegwa, Innkeeper	13.	Zaruk
6.	Graud, General Goods	14.	Tunkk, Leatherworking Supplies
7.	Keena, Trade Goods		

ARATHI HIGHLANDS page 10

HILLSBRAD FIELDS

1. Hillsbrad Farmer
   Hillsbrad Peasant

2. Farmer Kalaba

3. Hillsbrad Footman

4. Hillsbrad Tailor

5. Hillsbrad Farmer
   Hillsbrad Farmhand

6. Hillsbrad Farmer
   Hillsbrad Farmhand
   Farmer Getz

7. Stanley

8. Hillsbrad Farmer
   Hillsbrad Farmhand
   Farmer Ray (Upstairs)

9. Hillsbrad Footman
   Hillsbrad Councilman

10. Hillsbrad Footman
    Hillsbrad Councilman
    Hillsbrad Peasant

11. HILLSBRAD
    Hillsbrad Footman
    Hillsbrad Councilman
    Clerk Horrace Whitesteed
    Magistrate Burnside
    Hillsbrad Peasant

12. Citizen Wilkes

13. Blacksmith Verringtan
    Hillsbrad Apprentice Blacksmith
    Hillsbrad Councilman
    Hillsbrad Footman

14. Hillsbrad Apprentice Blacksmith
    Shipment of Iron
    Forge
    Anvil

HILLSBRAD FOOTHILLS page 48

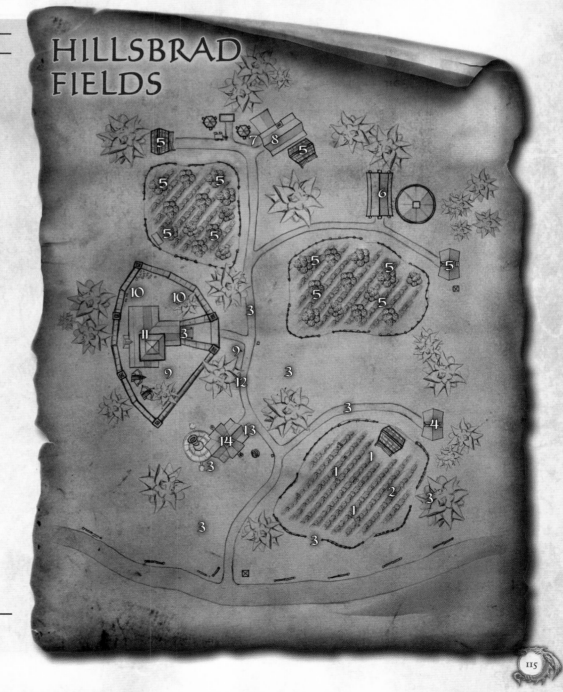

KARGATH

1. Gorrik, Wind Rider Master
2. Greth, Stable Master
   Mailbox
   Kill on Sight Poster: Dark Iron
   Dwarves
   Kill on Sight Poster: High Ranking
   Dark Iron Officials
3. Grunt Gargal, Kargath Expeditionary
   Force
   Thunderheart, Kargath Expeditionary
   Force
   Initiate Amakkar, Kargath
   Expeditionary Force
   Thal'trak Proudtusk, Kargath
   Expeditionary Force
   Razal'blade, Kargath Expeditionary
   Force

4. Hierophant Theodora Mulvadania,
   Kargath Expeditionary Force
   Shadowmage Vivian Lagrave,
   Kargath Expeditionary Force
   Bonfire
5. Sranda, Light Armor & Weapons
   Merchant
   Forge
6. Jarkol Mossmeld
7. Innkeeper Shul'kar, Innkeeper
   Gorn
   Grawl, General Goods
   Burning Embers
8. Warlord Goretooth, Kargath
   Expeditionary Force
   Lexlort, Kargath Expeditionary Force
   Galamav the Marksman, Kargath
   Expeditionary Force

BADLANDS page 16

KARGATH

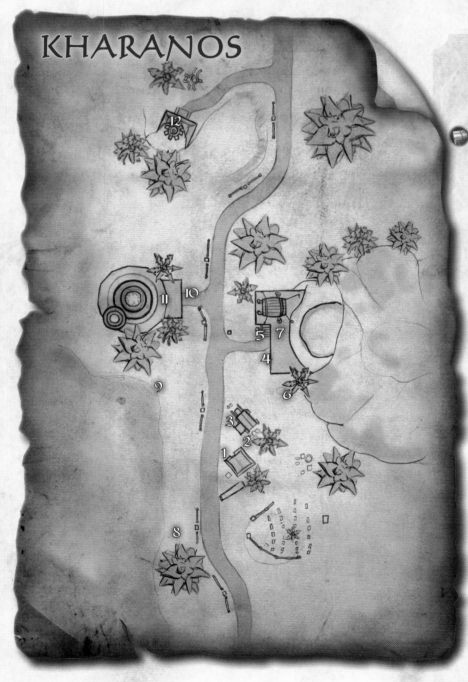

KHARANOS

KHARANOS

1. Peria Lamenur, Pet Trainer
2. Senir Whitebeard
3. Golorn Frostbeard, Tradesman
4. Shelby Stoneflint, Stable Master
   Mailbox
5. Ragnar Thunderbrew
6. Dannie Fizzwizzle, Demon Trainer
   Gimrizz Shadowcog, Warlock Trainer
   Tog Rustsprocket
7. THUNDERBREW DISTILLERY

   Azar Stronghammer, Paladin Trainer
   Magis Sparkmantle, Mage Trainer
   Maxan Anvol, Priest Trainer
   Tannok Frosthammer, Innkeeper Assistant
   Kreg Bilmn, General Supplies
   Thamner Pol, Physician
   Granis Swiftaxe, Warrior Trainer
   Innkeeper Belm, Innkeeper
   Gremlock Pilsnor, Cooking Trainer
   Hogral Bokkan, Rogue Trainer
   Jarven Thunderbrew
8. Mountaineer Dolf
9. Grif Wildheart, Hunter Trainer
10. Tharek Blackstone
11. Grawn Thromwyn, Weaponsmith
    Tognus Flintfire, Journeyman Blacksmith
    Gamili Frosthide, Cloth & Leather Armor Merchant
    Boran Ironclink, Armorer
    Kogan Forgestone
    Thrawn Boltar, Blacksmithing Supplies
12. Ozzie Togglevolt
    Razzle Sprysprocket

DUN MOROGH page 32

LAKESHIRE

LAKESHIRE

1. Deputy Feldon
   Ariena Stormfeather, Gryphon Master

2. Guard Howe

3. Guard Ashlock

4. Guard Pearce
   Guard Hiett

5. Marshal Marris

6. Foreman Oslow

7. Verner Osgood

8. Kara Adams, Shieldcrafter
   Dorin Songblade, Armorer

9. Karen Taylor, Mining and Smithing Supplies
   Forge

10. Wanted Poster: Gath'Ilzogg

11. LAKESHIRE TOWN HALL
    Baliff Conacher
    Magistrate Solomon

12. Amy Davenport, Tradeswoman
    Lindsay Ashlock, General Supplies

13. Dockmaster Baren

14. Penny, Stable Master
    Wanted Poster: Lieutenant Fangore
    Missing Poster: Corporal Keeshan
    Guard Berton
    Mailbox

15. LAKESHIRE INN
    Kimberly Hiett, Fletcher
    Darcy, Waitress
    Innkeeper Brianna
    Yorus Barleybrew
    Barkeep Daniels
    Bartender Wental, Food & Drinks
    Gloria Femmel, Cooking Supplies
    Sherman Femmel, Butcher

15a. LAKESHIRE INN, UPPER LEVEL
    Franklin Hamar, Tailoring Supplies
    Wiley the Black

16. Gerald Crawley, Poison Supplies

17. Erin
    Madison
    Guard Adams

18. Henry Chapal, Gunsmith

19. Chef Breanna
    Crystal Boughman, Cooking Trainer

19a. UPPER LEVEL
    Gretchen Vogel, Waitress

20. Alma Jainrose, Herbalism Trainer
    Hannah

21. Martie Jainrose

22. Bellygrub

23. Vernon Hale, Bait and Tackle Supplies

24. Matthew Hooper, Fishing Trainer
    Zem Leeward

25. Shawn
    Hilary

26. Jamin
    Roger

27. Arantir
    Lucius

28. Rachel
    Nathan

29. Submerged Tool Box

REDRIDGE MOUNTAINS page 62

LIGHT'S HOPE CHAPEL

1. Georgia, Bat Handler
2. Jase Farlane, Trade Supplies
3. Smokie LaRue
   Campfire
4. Lord Maxwell Tyrosus, The
   Argent Dawn
   Jessica Chambers, Innkeeper
   Leonid Barthalomew the
   Revered, The Argent Dawn
   Korfax, Champion of the Light
   Brotherhood of the Light
5. Khaelyn Steelwing, Gryphon
   Master
6. Betina Bigglezink, The Argent
   Dawn
   Duke Nicholas Zverenhoff, The
   Argent Dawn
   Carlin Redpath, The Argent Dawn
7. Quartermaster Miranda
   Breechlock, The Argent Dawn
8. Emissay Gormok
9. Dispatch Commander Metz,
   The Argent Dawn

10. Packmaster Stonebruiser,
    Brotherhood of the Light
11. Craftsman Wilhelm, Brotherhood
    of the Light
    Anvil/Forge
12. Rayne, Genarion Circle
    Rimblat Earthshatterer, The
    Earthen Ring
13. Father Indigo Mantoy,
    Brotherhood of the Light
    Commander Eligor Dawnbringer,
    Brotherhood of the Light
    Archmage Angela Dosantos,
    Brotherhood of the Light
    Scarlet Commander Marjhan, The
    Scarlet Crusade
14. Huntsman Leopold, The Scarlet
    Crusade
    Mataus the Wrathcaster, The
    Scarlet Crusade
    Rohan the Assassin, The Scarlet
    Crusade
15. Mailbox
16. Caretaker Alen, The Argent
    Dawn

EASTERN PLAGUELANDS page 40

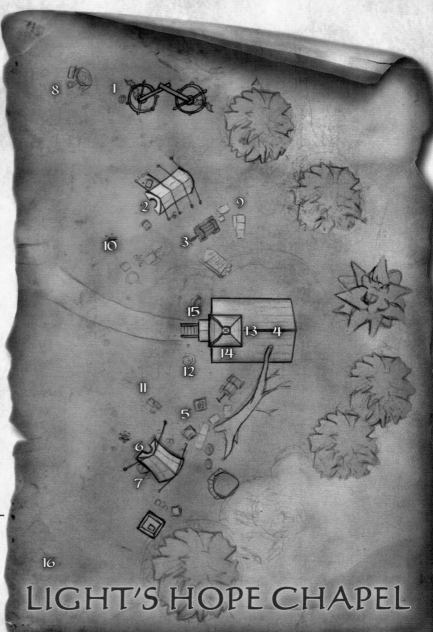

LIGHT'S HOPE CHAPEL

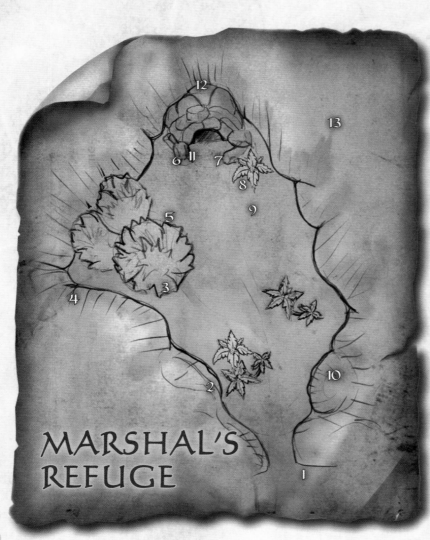

MARSHAL'S REFUGE

MARSHAL'S REFUGE

1. Karna Remtravel
2. Shizzle
3. Quixxil
4. Muigin
5. Spraggle Frock, Wanted Poster
6. Nergal, General Goods Vendor
7. Dadanga
   Petra Grossen
8. Williden Marshal
   Gibbert, Weapon Merchant
   Hol'anyee Marshall
9. Linken
10. Larion
11. Spark Nilminer
12. J.D. Collie
13. Gryfe, Flight Master

UN'GORO CRATER page 90

MENETHIL HARBOR

MENETHIL HARBOR

1. Shellei Brondir, Grpyhon Master
2. Adam Lind
3. Bart Tidewater
4. Karl Boran
   Harold Riggs, Fishing Trainer
   Stuart Fleming, Fisherman
5. Don Pompa
6. Falkan Armonis, Reagent Vendor
7. Telurinon Moonshadow, Herbalism
   Trainer
8. Dewin Shimmerdawn, Alchemy
   Supplies
9. Jennabink Powerseam, Tailoring
   Supplies & Specialty Goods
   (Upstairs)
10. James Halloran
11. Andrea Halloran
    Regina Halloran
    Jesse Halloran
12. Thomas Booker
    Unger Statford, Horse Breeder
13. MENETHIL KEEP
    Valstag Ironjaw
13a. Neal Allen, Engineering & General
    Goods Supplies
13b. Red Jack Flint
    Murphy West
    Timothy Clark (Upstairs)
    Captain Stoutfist (Upstairs)
14. Harlo Barnaby
15. Tarrel Rockweaver

16. Naela Trance, Bowyer
    Edwina Monzor, Fletcher
17. Gruham Rumdnul, General Supplies
    Derina Rumdnul
    Gimlok Rumdnul
18. Sida
19. Caitlin Grassman
20. Brahnmar, Armorer
    Brak Durnad, Weaponsmith
    Murndan Derth, Gunsmith
    Forge
    Anvil
21. First Mate Fitzsimmons
    Mailbox
22. Bethaine Flinthammer, Stable Master
23. DEEPWATER TAVERN
    Tapoke "Slim" Jahn
    Junder Brokk
    Vincent Hyal
    Glorin Steelbrow
    Hargin Mundar
    Kersok Prond, Tradesman
    Mikhail, Bartender
    Innkeeper Helbrek, Innkeeper
    Cozy Fire
    Samor Festivus, Shady Dealer
    (Upstairs)
    Archaeologist Flagongut, Explorer's
    League (Upstairs)
    Fremal Doohickey, First Aid Trainer
    (Upstairs)
24. Camerick Jongleur, Wandering Minstrel
25. Potbelly Stove

WETLANDS page 96

MIRAGE RACEWAY

1. Trackmaster Zherin
2. Zuzebee, Race Announcer
3. Drag Master Miglen
4. Riznek, Drink Vendor
5. Synge, Gun Merchant
6. Razzeric
   Pozzic
7. Zamek
   Daisy, Race Starter Girl
8. Fobeed, Race Announcer
   Race Master Kronkrider
9. Quentin
10. Magus Tirth
11. Wizzle Brassbolts
    Fizzle Brassbolts
12. Jinky Twizzlefixxit, Engineering
    Supplies
13. Kravel Koalbeard
14. Brivelthwerp, Ice Cream Vendor
15. Rizzle Brassbolts, Rizzle's Guarded
    Plans
16. "Plucky" Johnson

THOUSAND NEEDLES page 82

MIRAGE RACEWAY

MUDSPROCKET

1. Drazzit Dripvalve
2. Campfire
3. Gizzix Grimegurgle
4. Krixil Slogswitch, Food and Drink
   Wanted Poster
5. Mailbox
6. Razbo Rustgear, Weapon and Armor
   Merchant
   Anvil, Forge
7. Dyslix Silvergrub, Flight Master
8. Brogg, Stonemaul Survivor
   Axle, Innkeeper

DUSTWALLOW MARSH page 38

MORGAN'S VIGIL

1. Gabrielle Chase, Food & Drink	6. Marshal Maxwell
2. Borgus Stoutarm, Gryphon Master	Mayara Brightwing
3. Campfire	7. Helendis Riverhorn
4. Felder Stover, Weaponsmith	8. Jalinda Sprig
5. Oralius	

BURNING STEPPES page 22

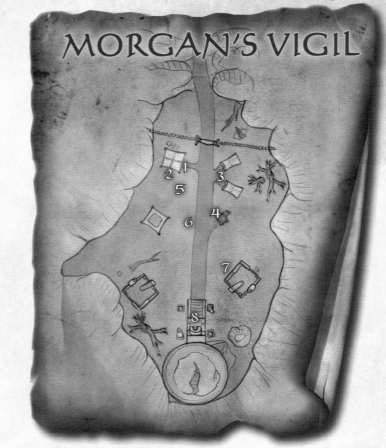

NETHERGARDE KEEP

1. Nethergarde Soldier
   Nethergarde Cleric
   Nethergarde Riftwatcher
2. Mailbox
3. Enohar Thunderbrew
4. Nethergarde Elite
5. Potbelly Stove
6. Nethergarde Officer
7. Quartermaster Lungertz
8. Nethergarde Analyst
9. Alexandra Constantine, Gryphon
   Master
10. Nethergarde Elite
    Watcher Mahar Ba (Upstairs)
    Ambassador Ardalan (Upstairs)
    Thadius Grimshade (Upstairs)
    Nina Lightbrew, Alchemy Supplies
    (Upstairs)
11. Strumner Flintheel, Armor Crafter
    Forge
    Anvil
12. Bernie Heisten, Food & Drink

BLASTED LANDS page 20

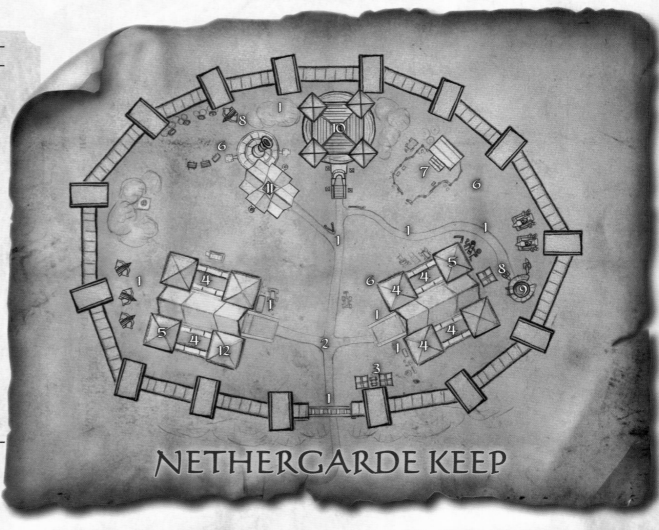

NIGHTHAVEN

NIGHTHAVEN

1. SHRINE OF REMULOS
   Keeper Remulos

2. My'lanna, Food and Drink Merchant
   Daeolyn Summerleaf, General Goods
   Umber

3. Bessany Plainswind

4. Darnall, Tailoring Supplies
   Geenia Sunshadow, Specialty Dress
     Maker
   Mylentha Riverbend

5. Celes Earthborne

6. Kharedon, Light Armor Merchant
   Dendrite Starblaze

7. Dargon, Food and Drink Merchant
   Lorelae Wintersong, Trade Supplies

8. Loganaar, Druid Trainer, Moonwell

9. Meliri, Weaponsmith
   Narianna, Bowyer
   Moren Riverbend
   Rabine Saturna

10. Malvor, Herbalist

11. Bunthen Plainswind, Thunder Bluff
      Flight Master
    Silva Fil'naveth, Darnassus Flight
      Master

12. Tajarri

13. Great Bear Spirit

14. Moonwell

MOONGLADE page 56

NIJEL'S POINT

1. Mailbox

2. Shelgrayn, Stable Master

3. Janet Hommers, Food & Drink
   Innkeeper Lyshaerva, Innkeeper

4. Christi Galvanis, General Goods

5. Brother Anton, Scarlet Crusade
     Emissary

6. Keeper Marandis

7. Baritanas Skyriver, Hippogryph
     Master

8. Kreldig Ungor, Reclaimers Inc.

9. Maxton Strang, Mail Armor Merchant
   Forge
   Anvil

10. Talendria
    Cooking Brazier

11. Moonwell

12. Captain Pentigast
    Corporal Melkins

13. Vahlarriel Demonslayer

DESOLACE page 30

NIJEL'S POINT

NORTHSHIRE VALLEY

1. Deputy Willem
2. Janos Hammerknuckle, Weaponsmith
   Merissa Stilwell
3. Brother Danil, General Supplies
   Dermot Johns, Cloth & Leather
     Armor Merchant
   Godric Rothgar, Armorer &
     Shieldcrafter
4. NORTHSHIRE ABBEY
   Marshall McBride
4a. HALL OF ARMS
   Llane Beshere, Warrior Trainer
   Brother Sammuel, Paladin Trainer
4b. LIBRARY WING
   Brother Paxton, Librarian
   Priestess Anetta, Priest Trainer
   Khelden Bremen, Mage Trainer
     (Upstairs)
4c. MAIN HALL
   Brother Neals (Upstairs)
5. Young Wolf
6. Eagan Peltskinner

7. ECHO RIDGE MINE
   Kobold Worker
   Kobold Laborer
8. Kobold Worker
9. Kobold Worker
   Kobold Vermin
   Timber Wolf
   Campfire
10. Milly Osworth
11. Timber Wolf
12. Falkhaan Isenstrider
13. Defias Thug
14. NORTHSHIRE VINYARDS
   Defias Thug
   Milly's Harvest
14a. Defias Thug
   Garrick Padfoot
15. Drusilla La Salle,
     Warlock Trainer
   Dane Winslow,
     Demon Trainer
   Imp Minion

ELWYNN FOREST page 42

NORTHSHIRE VALLEY

RATCHET

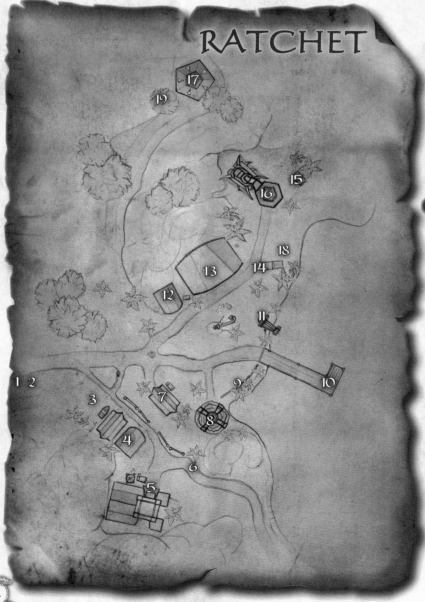

RATCHET

1. Graveyard
2. Anvil and Forge
3. Jorb, Lizzarik's Bodyguard
   Lizzarik, Weapon Dealer
4. JAZZIK'S GENERAL GOODS
   Ranik, Trade Supplies
   Jazzik, General Supplies
5. BROKEN KEEL INN
   Reggifuz, Stable Master
   Zizzek, Fisherman
   Innkeeper Wiley, Innkeeper
   Stoves, Cooking Fire
   Mailbox
6. Captain Thalo'thas Brightsun
7. PLATE-N-CHAIN
   Brewmaster Drohn
   Grazlix, Armorer and Shieldcrafter
   Vexspindle, Cloth and Leather
     Merchant
8. Liv Rizzlefix, Workshop Assistant
   Archimonde's Return and the
     Flight to Kalimdor, Book
9. Klixx, Fisherman
10. Wharfmaster Dizzywig
    Grimble, Shipmaster
11. Crane Operator Bigglefuzz

12. IRONZAR'S IMPORTED
     WEAPONRY
    Ironzar
    Mebok Mizzyrix
    Anvil
    Forge
13. BANK
    Fuzruckle, Banker
    Zikkel, Banker
    Wanted Poster: Baron Longshore
14. Sputtervalve
15. Wrenix the Wretched
    Wrenix's Gizmotronic Apparatus
16. Vazario Linkgrease, Master Goblin
      Engineer
    Tinkerwiz, Journeyman Engineer
    Gagsprocket, Engineering Goods
    Gazlowe
    Charge of the Dragonflights, Book
17. Strahad Farsan
    Menara Voidrender
    Acolyte Fenrick
    Acolyte Wytula
    Acolyte Magaz
18. Bragok, Flight Master
19. Babagaya Shadowcleft, Warlock
      Trainer
    Matero Zeshowal, Demon Trainer
    Nagulon

BARRENS page 18

RAVEN HILL

1. Jitters
2. Bliztik, Alchemy Supplies
3. Destroyed Inn
4. Food Crate Spawn Point
5. Empty Household

DUSKWOOD page 36

RAVEN HILL CEMETERY

RAVEN HILL CEMETERY

1. Skeletal Horrors
2. Carrion Recluses
3. Grave Robbers
4. DAWNING WOODS CATACOMBS, WESTERN
   Skeletal Raiders
   Skeletal Healers
   Skeletal Warriors
   Skeletal Warders
5. FORLORN ROWE
   Morbent Fel
   Plague Spreaders
   Skeletal Raiders
   Skeletal Waders
   Brain Eaters
   Anvil
6. Gravesite, Mor'Ladim
7. Rotten Ones
   Flesh Eaters
8. DAWNING WOODS CATACOMBS, EASTERN
   Plague Spreaders
   Brain Eaters
   Bone Chewers
9. Abercrombie, The Hermit
10. Gravesite, Embalmer's Wife
11. Mor'Ladim Patrol Area

DUSKWOOD page 36

RAZOR HILL

RAZOR HILL

1. Takrin Pathseeker
2. Furl Scornbrow
3. Grimtak, Butcher
   Cook Torka
4. Innkeeper Grosk, Innkeeper
   Yelnagi Blackarm
   Blazing Fire
5. Orgnil Soulscar
   Kaplak, Rogue Trainer
   Harruk, Pet Trainer
   Thotar, Hunter Trainer
   Gar'Thok
6. Wuark, Armorer and Shieldcrafter
   Krunn, Miner
   Dwukk, Journeyman Blacksmith
   Mukdrak, Journeyman Engineer
   Uhgar, Weaponsmith
   Anvil
   Forge

7. Ghrawt, Bowyer
   Cutac, Cloth and Leather Armor
      Merchant
8. Dhugru Gorelust, Warlock Trainer
   Ophek
   Kitha, Demon Trainer
9. RAZOR HILL BARRACKS
   Rawrk, First Aid Trainer
   Jark, General Goods
   Swart, Shaman Trainer
   Tai'jin, Priest Trainer
   Tarshaw Jaggedscar, Warrior
      Trainer
   Fierce Blaze
10. Mailbox
    Shoja'my, Stable Master
11. Flakk, Trade Supplies

DUROTAR page 34

REBEL CAMP

REBEL CAMP

1. Lieutenant Doren
2. Corporal Bluth, Camp Trader
3. Sergeant Yohwa
   Private Thorsen
   Campfire
4. Corporal Kaleb
5. Corporal Sethman
6. Brother Nimetz
7. Nizzle, Gryphon Master

STRANGLETHORN VALE page 74

REFUGE POINTE

REFUGE POINTE

1. Androd Fadren,
      Leatherworking Supplies
2. Commander Amaren
3. Cedrik Prose, Gryphon Master
4. Field Marshal Oslight
5. Sergeant Maclear
   Samuel Hawke, League of
      Arathor Supply Officer
6. Sir Maximus Adam,
      Arathi Basin Battlemaster
7. Targot Jinglepocket,
      Smokywood Pastures
8. Anvil, Forge

9. Skuerto
   Drovnar Strongbrew,
      Alchemy Supplies
10. Hammon Karwn,
      Superior Tradesman
    Vikki Lonsav, General Goods
11. Apprentice Kryten
    Wanted Board
12. Jannos Ironwill, Superior
       Macecrafter
    Captain Nials
13. Narj Deepslice, Butcher

ARATHI HIGHLANDS page 10

REVANTUSK VILLAGE

REVANTUSK VILLAGE

1. Gorkas, Wind Rider Master
2. Katoom the Angler, Fishing Trainer
   and Supplies
3. Mailbox
4. LOWER LEVEL
   Lard, Innkeeper
   UPPER LEVEL
   Primal Torntusk
5. Smith Slagtree, Blacksmithing
   Supplies
6. Forge, Anvil
7. Renn'az, Ammunition Vendor
8. Huntsman Markhor, Stable Master
9. Wanted Poster
10. Otho Moji'ko, Cooking Supplies
11. Mystic Yayo'jin, Reagent Vendor

HINTERLANDS page 50

RUT'THERAN VILLAGE

RUT'THERAN VILLAGE

1. Vesprystus, Hippogryph Master
2. Nessa Shadowsong, Fishing Supplies
3. Androl Oakhand, Fishing Trainer
4. Erelas Ambersky
5. UPPER LEVEL
   Daryn Lightwind, Cenarion Lore
   Keeper

TELDRASSIL page 80

SEN'JIN VILLAGE

1. Miao'zan, Journeyman Alchemist
2. Hai'zan, Butcher
   Smoking Rack
3. Vel'rin Fang
4. Master Vornal
   Master Gadrin
5. Ula'elek
   Kali Remik
   Anvil
6. Tal'tasi, Trade Supplies
   K'wail, General Goods
   Trayexir, Weapon Merchant
   Zansoa, Fishing Supplies
7. Un'Thuwa, Mage Trainer
8. Bom'bay, Witch Doctor in Training
9. Mishiki, Herbalist
10. Zjolnir, Raptor Handler
    Xar'Ti, Raptor Riding Trainer
11. Lar Prowltusk, Patroller

DUROTAR page 34

SEN'JIN VILLAGE

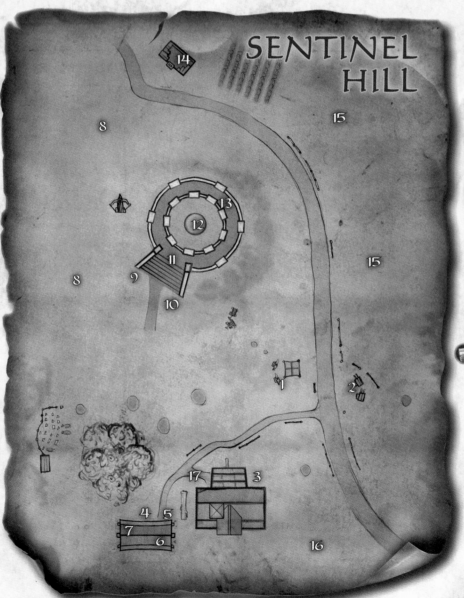

SENTINEL HILL

SENTINEL HILL

1. Thor, Gryphon Master
2. Mike Miller, Bread Merchant
   William MacGregor, Bowyer
   Gina MacGregor, Trade
   Supplies
   Campfire
3. Protector Deni, The People's
   Militia
   Protector Leick, The People's
   Militia
   Forge
   Anvil
4. Kirk Maxwell, Stable Master
5. Mailbox
6. Innkeeper Heather,
   Innkeeper
7. Christopher Hewen, General
   Trade Goods Vendor
8. Young Goretusk
9. Protector Bialon, The
   People's Militia
   The Defias Traitor

10. Protector Gariel, The
    People's Militia
11. Gryan Stoutmantle, The
    People's Militia
    Captain Danuvin, The
    People's Militia
12. SENTINEL TOWER
    Quartermaster Lewis,
    Quartermaster
    Scout Riell, The People's
    Milita (Upstairs)
    Protector Weaver, The
    People's Militia (Upstairs)
13. Protector Dutfield, The
    People's Militia
14. Fleshripper
15. Great Goretusk
    Greater Fleshripper
16. Goretusk
17. Scout Galiaan, The People's
    Militia

WESTFALL page 94

THE SEPULCHER

1. Karos Razok, Bat Handler
2. Nadia Vernon, Bowyer
3. Andrea Boynton, Clothier
   Alexandre Lefevre, Leather Armor Merchant
4. Dalar Dawnweaver
   Gwyn Farrow, Mushroom Merchant
   Edwin Harly, General Supplies
5. Shadow Priest Allister
6. Apothecary Renferrel
7. Sarah Goode, Stable Master
   Innkeeper Bates
   Deathguard Podrig
   Mailbox
8. Andrew Hilbert, Trade Goods
   Johan Focht, Miner
   High Executor Hadrec
   Sebastian Meloche, Armorer
   Guillaume Sorouy, Journeyman Blacksmith
   Advisor Sorrelon
9. Mura Runetotem
   Patrice Dwyer, Poison Supplies
10. Yuriv's Tombstone

SILVERPINE FOREST page 68

THE SEPULCHER

SHADOWGLEN

1. Conservator Ilthalaine
   Orenthil Whisperwind
2. Tarindrella
3. Young Nightsabre
   Young Thistle Boar

4. ALDRASSIL
   Melithar Staghelm
4a. Keina, Bowyer
4b. Dellylah, Food & Drink Vendor

4c. Andiss, Armorer & Shieldcrafter
   (Bottom Floor)
   Khardan Proudblade, Weaponsmith
   (Bottom Floor)
   Freja Nightwing, Leather Armor Merchant
   (Bottom Floor)
   Mardant Strongoak, Druid Trainer
   (Middle Floor)
   Ayanna Everstride, Hunter Trainer
   (Middle Floor)
   Tenaron Stormgrip (Top Floor)
4d. Alyissia, Warrior Trainer
   Frahun Shadewhisper, Rogue Trainer
4e. Gilshalan Windwalker
4f. Janna Brightmoon, Clothier (Second Floor)
   Lyrai, General Supplies (Second Floor)
   Shanda, Priest Trainer (Third Floor)

5. Thistle Boar
   Mangy Nightsabre
6. Dirania Silvershine
   Cauldron
7. Moonwell
8. Webwood Spider
9. Iverron
10. Githyiss the Vile
    Webwood Spider
11. Thistle Boar
    Grellkin
12. Grell
13. Porthannius

SHADOWGLEN

TELDRASSIL page 80

SHADOWPREY VILLAGE

SHADOWPREY VILLAGE

1. Thalon, Wind Rider Master
2. Jinar'Zillen
3. Lui'Mala, Fisherman
   Mai'Lahii, Fishing Supplies
4. Lah'Mawhani, Trade Supplies
5. Drulzegar Skraghook
   Meat Smoker
6. Malux, Skinning Trainer
   Vark Battlescar (Top Level)
7. Roon Wildmane
   Tukk, General Goods Vendor
8. Anvil
   Forge
9. Hae'Wilani, Axecrafter
10. Wulan, Cooking Supplies
11. Aboda, Stable Master
    Mailbox
12. Innkeeper Sikewa, Innkeeper
13. Taiga Wiseman
14. Rokaro, Champion of the Horde

DESOLACE page 30

SILVERWIND REFUGE

SILVERWIND REFUGE

1. Ulthaan, Butcher
2. Caelyb, Pet Trainer
3. Shandrina, Trade Goods
4. Sentinel Velene Starstrike
5. Jayla, Skinning Trainer
6. Danlaar Nightstride, Hunter Trainer
7. Bhaldaran Ravenshade, Bowyer
8. Cylania Rootstalker, Herbalism Trainer
9. Kylanna, Expert Alchemist
10. Harklan Moongrove, Alchemy
    Supplies

ASHENVALE page 12

SOUTHSHORE

1. Darla Harris, Gryphon Master
2. Caretaker Smithers
3. Hecular's Grave
4. Darren Malvew, Stablehand
5. Merideth Carlson, Horse Breeder
6. Farmer Kent
7. Robert Aebischer, Superior Armorsmith
   Forge, Anvil
8. Nandar Branson, Alchemy Supplies
   Apprentice Honeywell
9. Loremaster Dibbs
10. Phin Odelic
    Wesley, Stable Master
    Mailbox
11. Neema, Waitress
    Innkeeper Anderson
    Jaysen Lanyda (Upstairs)
12. Lieutenant Farren Orinelle
    Barkeep Kelly, Bartender
    Hemmit Armstrong (Upstairs)
    Tamara Armstrong (Upstairs)
13. Chef Jessen
    Brewmeister Bilger (Basement)
    Raleigh the Devout (Upstairs)
14. Donald Rabonne, Fisherman
    Lindea Rabonne, Tackle and Bait
15. Hal McAllister, Fish Merchant
16. Torn Fin Tidehunter
    Torn Fin Oracle
17. Daggerspine Siren
    Daggerspine Shorehunter
18. Marshal Redpath
19. Kundric Zanden, Town Historian
20. Magistrate Henry Maleb
21. Bront Coldcleave, Butcher
22. Bartollo Ginsetti
23. Micha Yance, Trade Goods
    Cozy Fire
24. Sarah Raycroft, General Goods
    (Upstairs)

HILLSBRAD FOOTHILLS page 48

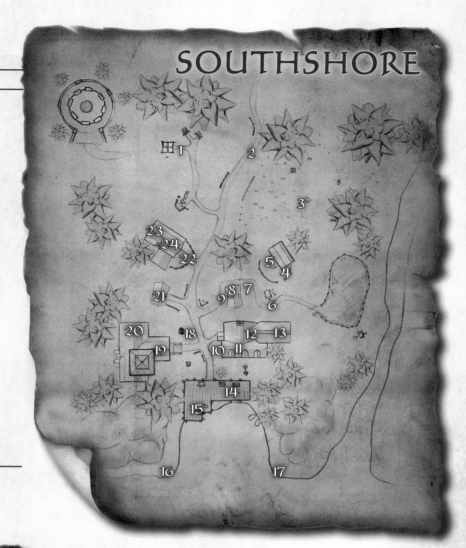

SOUTHSHORE

SPLINTERTREE POST

1. Ertog Ragetusk
2. Framnali
3. Vhulgra, Wind Rider Master
4. Pixel
5. Fahrak
6. Har'alen
7. Loruk Foreststrider
8. Mastok Wrilehiss
9. Burkrum, Heavy Armor Merchant
10. Innkeeper Kaylisk
11. Vera Nightshade
12. Yama Snowhoof
13. Mailbox
14. Senani Thunderheart
15. Valusha
16. Qeeju, Stable Master

ASHENVALE page 12

STARFALL VILLAGE

1. Syurana, Trade Goods
2. Lyranne Feathersong, Food and Drink
3. Natheril Raincaller, General Goods
4. Wynd Nightchaser
5. Jaron Stoneshaper, Explorers' League

WINTERSPRING page 98

STARFALL VILLAGE

STEAMWHEEDLE PORT

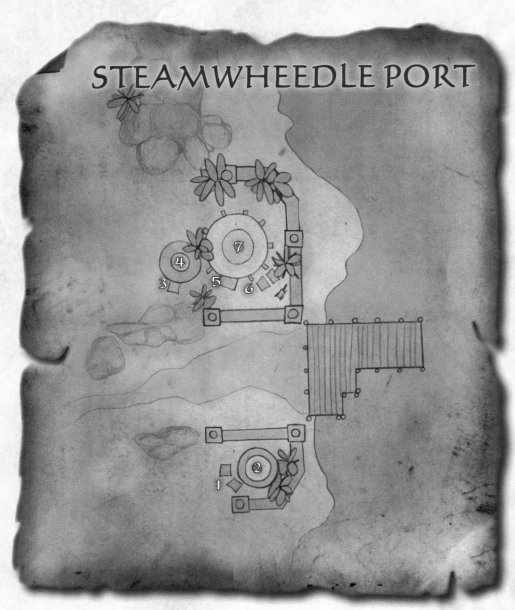

STEAMWHEEDLE PORT

1. Prospector Ironboot
2. Security Chief Bilgewhizzle, Water Co. Security
    Stoley
    Yorba Screwspigot
3. Haughty Modiste, Fashion Designer
4. Gikkix, Fisherman
5. Wanted Poster
6. Yeh'kinya
7. Jabbey, General Goods

TANARIS page 78

STONARD

1. Breyk, Wind Rider Master
2. Hekkru, Stable Master
   Mailbox
3. Innkeeper Karakul
   Bengor
   Malosh, Warrior Trainer
   Dar
   Rartar, Alchemy Supplies
   Banalash, Trade Goods
4. Zun'dartha
5. Grunt Zuul
   Grunt Tharlak
   Infiltrator Marksen
6. Thultazor, Arcane Goods Vendor
7. Thralosh, Cloth & Leather Armor
     Merchant
   Gharash, Blacksmithing Supplies
   Grimnal, Mail & Plate Merchant
   Hartash, Weapon Merchant
   Forge

8. Ogromm, Hunter Trainer
   Grokor, Pet Trainer
9. Greshka, Demon Master
   Kartosh, Warlock Trainer
   Rogvar, Master Alchemist
   Cersei Dusksinger

9a. UPPER LEVEL
    Helgrum the Swift
    Dispatch Commander Ruag
    Fel'zerul
10. Haromm, Shaman Trainer
11. Thultash, Food & Drink Vendor

SWAMP OF SORROWS page 76

STONETALON PEAK

1. Teloren, Hippogryph Master
2. Moonwell
3. Keeper Albagorm
4. Mailbox
5. Illyanie, Cloth Armor Merchant
6. Chylina, General Supplies
7. Innkeeper Faralia, Innkeeper

STONETALON MOUNTAINS page 70

STROMGARDE KEEP

STROMGARDE KEEP

1. Syndicate Conjuror
   Voidwalker Minion
   Syndicate Prowler
   Syndicate Magus

2. Marez Cowl

3. Stromgarde Defender

4. Boulderfist Mauler

5. Stromgarde Troll Hunter
   Stromgarde Vindicator

6. Stromgarde Vindicator

7. Deneb Walker, Scrolls & Potions

8. CRYPT
   Caretaker Nevlin
   Caretaker Alaric
   Caretaker Weston

9. Witherbark Berserker

10. Boulderfist Shaman
    Boulderfist Mauler
    Boulderfist Lord

11. Or'Kalar
    Boulderfist Shaman

12. TOWER OF ARATHOR
    Boulderfist Shaman
    Boulderfist Lord

13. Syndicate Prowler
    Syndicate Conjuror
    Voidwalker Minion

14. Syndicate Prowler
    Syndicate Conjuror
    Voidwalker Minion
    Otto (Upstairs)
    Lord Falconcrest (Upstairs)

ARATHI HIGHLANDS page 10

SUN ROCK RETREAT

SUN ROCK RETREAT

1. Tharm, Wind Rider Master

2. Borand, Bowyer
   Kulwia, Trade Supplies

3. Grawnal, General Goods
   Krond, Butcher
   Forge/Anvil

4. Tammra Windfield

5. Hgarth, Artisan Enchanter

6. Braelyn Firehand

7. Maggran Earthbinder

8. Gereck, Stable Master
   Mailbox

9. Innkeeper Jayka, Innkeeper
   Jeeda, Apprentice Witch Doctor

STONETALON MOUNTAINS page 70

TALONBRANCH GLADE

1. Malygen, General Goods
2. Mylini Frostmoon, Weapon Merchant
3. Golhine the Hooded, Druid Trainer
4. Kaerbrus, Hunter Trainer
   Shi'alune, Kaerbrus' Pet
5. Mishellena, Hippogryph Master
6. Nalesette Wildbringer, Pet Trainer

FELWOOD page 44

TALONBRANCH GLADE

TARREN MILL

TARREN MILL

1. Zarise, Bat Handler
2. Apothecary Lydon, Royal Apothecary Society
   Serge Hinott, Expert Alchemist Umpi
3. Aranae Venomblood, Herbalist Tallow
4. Deathguard Samsa
5. Theodore Mont Clair, Stable Master
   Mailbox
6. Kayren Soothallow, General Goods
   Wanted Poster: Dangerous
7. Delia Verana
8. Monika Sengutz
   Innkeeper Shay
   Captured Farmer (Upstairs)
9. Christoph Jeffcoat, Tradesman
10. Deathguard Humbert
11. Derak Nightfall, Cook
12. Vinna Wayne
13. Novice Thaivand
14. High Executor Darthalia
15. Melisara
    Wanted Poster: Syndicate Personnel
    Wanted Poster: Baron Vardus
    Advisor Duskingdawn
16. Krusk
17. Daryl Stack, Master Tailor
    Shara Blazen
18. Mallen Swain, Tailoring Supplies
19. Magus Wordeen Voidglare
    Keeper Bel'varil
20. Jason Lemieux, Mushroom Vendor
21. Hans Zandin
22. Tara Coldgaze
23. Craig Hewitt
24. Ott, Weaponsmith
25. Gray Bear
    Forest Moss Creeper

HILLSBRAD FOOTHILLS page 48

THELSAMAR

1. Thorgrum Borrelson, Gryphon Master
2. Mountaineer Roghan
3. Mountaineer Stenn/ Mountaineer Droken
4. Mountaineer Kadrell
5. Lina Hearthstove, Stable Master
   Mailbox
6. STOUTLAGER INN
   Innkeeper Hearthstove, Innkeeper
   Drac Roughcut, Tradesman
   Yanni Stoutheart, General Supplies
   Vidra Hearthstove
   Dwarven Fire
   Honni Goldenoat, Baker

7. Mountaineer Ozmok
8. Morhan Coppertongue, Metalsmith
9. Forge
   Anvil
10. Mountaineer Langarr
11. Magistrate Bluntnose
12. Mountaineer Kamdar
13. Mountaineer Gwarth
14. Vrok Blunderblast, Gunsmith
15. Dakk Blunderblast
16. Mountaineer Modax

17. Wanted Poster: Chok'sul
18. Karm Ironquill, Mining Supplies
    Jern Ironhelm, Explorer's League
    Brock Stoneseeker, Mining Trainer
    Torren Squarejaw, Explorer's League
19. Rann Flamespinner, Tailoring Supplies
20. Bailor Stonehand
21. Kali Healtouch, Herbalist
22. Ghak Healtouch, Journeyman Alchemist
23. Mountaineer Harn

LOCH MODAN page 54

THELSAMAR

THERAMORE ISLE

1. Decedra Willham
2. Privateer Groy
3. Theramore Lieutenant
4. Charity Mipsy, General Goods
5. Baldruc, Gryphon Master
6. Jensen Farran, Bowyer
7. Guard Lasiter
8. Helenia Olden, Trade Supplies
9. Timothy Worthington, Master Tailor
10. Gregor MacVince, Horse Breeder
11. Caz Twosprocket
    Hans Weston, Armorer & Shieldsmith
    Marie Holdston, Weaponsmith
12. Alchemist Narett, Expert Alchemist
    Brant Jasperbloom, Herbalist
    Uma Bartulm, Herbalism & Alchemy
       Supplies

13. Pained
    Lady Jaina Proudmoore, Ruler of Theramore
    Archmage Tervosh
14. Michael, Stable Master
    Mailbox
15. Guard Byron
    Smiling Jim
16. Fiora Longears
    Morgan Stern
    Innkeeper Janene, Innkeeper
    Bartender Lillian, Bartender
    Craig Nollword, Cook
    Cozy Fire
17. Ingo Woolybush, Explorers' League
    Sara Pierce
    Amie Pierce
    Dahne Pierce
    Mikal Pierce
18. Brother Karman, Paladin Trainer

19. Spot
20. FOOTHOLD CITADEL
    Dwane Wertle, Chef
21. FOOTHOLD CITADEL
    Potbelly Stove
22. FOOTHOLD CITADEL
    Doctor Gustaf VanHowzen, Trauma Surgeon
23. FOOTHOLD CITADEL
    Piter Verance, Weaponsmith & Armorer
    Torq Ironblast, Gunsmith
24. FOOTHOLD CITADEL
    Theramore Lieutenant
    Adjutant Tesoran
    Captain Garran Vimes
    Commander Samaul
    Captain Evencane, Warrior Trainer
    Clerk Lendry

DUSTWALLOW MARSH page 38

THERAMORE ISLE

THORIUM POINT

THORIUM POINT

1. Grisha, Wind Rider Master
2. Lookout Captain Lolo Longstriker, The Thorium Brotherhood
   Wanted Poster
3. Lanie Reed, Gryphon Master
4. Master Smith Burninate, The Thorium Brotherhood
   Anvil, Forge
5. Taskmaster Scrange, The Thorium Brotherhood
6. Hansel Heavyhands, The Thorium Brotherhood
   Evonice Sootsmoker, The Thorium Brotherhood
7. UPPER LEVEL
   Overseer Oilfist, The Thorium Brotherhood

SEARING GORGE page 64

VALLEY OF TRIALS

VALLEY OF TRIALS

1. Foreman Thazz'nil
2. Lazy Peon
3. Kaltunk
   Fire
4. Graveyard
5. Magga
   Frang, Warrior Trainer
   Jen'shan, Hunter Trainer
   Zureetha Fargaze
6. Ruzan
   Mai'ah, Mage Trainer
   Shikrik, Shaman Trainer
   Ken'jai, Priest Trainer
   Canaga Earthcaller

7. THE DEN
   Gornek
   Rwag, Rogue Trainer
   Huklah, Cloth and Leather Armor Merchant
   Rarc, Armorer and Shieldcrafter
   Kzan Thornslash, Weaponsmith
   Hraug, Demon Trainer
   Nartok, Warlock Trainer
   Crude Brazier
8. Duokna, General Goods
   Ziagk, Butcher
   Galgar
   Cooking Table

DUROTAR page 34

VALOR'S REST

VALOR'S REST

1. Zannok Hidepiercer, Leatherworking Supplies
2. Jarund Stoutstrider, The Cenarion Circle
3. Layo Starstrike, The Cenarion Circle
4. Bonfire

SILITHUS page 66

ZORAM'GAR OUTPOST

ZORAM'GAR OUTPOST

1. Talen
2. Andruk, Wind Rider Master
3. Warsong Rider
4. Muglash
5. Karang Amakkar
6. Marukai
   Mitsuwa
7. Je'neu Sancrea
8. Wik'Tar, Fish Merchant and Supplies
9. Kil'Hiwana, Fisherman

ASHENVALE page 12

ZORAM STRAND

ZORAM STRAND

1. Blackfathom Deeps Entrance
2. Hydra Island
3. Statue (Near Boat)
4. Talen
5. Zoram'gar Outpost
   Andruk, Wind Rider Master

Muglash
Karang Amakkar
Marukai
Mitsuwa
Je'neu Sancrea
Wik'Tar, Fish Merchant and Supplies
Kil'Hiwana, Fisherman

ASHENVALE page 12

#

7:XT
Rare Spawn, Badlands (16), A-8, B-7, C-8, D:(5, 7), H-8, I-7, Camp Boff, Camp Cagg, The Dustbowl, Mirage Flats, Lvl 41 Very Rare; Roams small area around spawn point

A

A TORMENTED VOICE
Burning Steppes (22), H-2, On top of hill along northern border

AAYNDIA FLORALWIND
Leatherworking Trainer, Ashenvale (12), E-5, Astranaar (101), Left as you enter southwest building

ABE WINTERS
Apprentice Armorer, Tirisfal Glades (86), H-5, Brill (104), Smithy

ABERCROMBIE
Duskwood (36), C-3, Raven Hill Cemetery (123), Shed northeast of Cemetery

ABIGAIL SAWYER
Bow Merchant, Undercity (88), G-4, The War Quarter

ABIGAIL SHIEL
Trade Supplies, Tirisfal Glades (86), H-5, Brill (104), Caravan between inn and town hall

ABODA
Stable Master, Desolace (30), C-7, Shadowprey Village (128), Front of inn

ABOMINATION
Eastern Plaguelands (40), D-6, E:(5, 6), F-5, K-4, The Fungal Vale

ACCURSED SLITHERBLADE
Rare Spawn, Desolace (30), C-2, D:(1-2), E-1, Sar'theris Strand, Lvl 35 Average Rare; Swims area between Ranzajar Isle and shore

ACHELLIOS THE BANISHED
Rare Spawn, Thousand Needles (82), B:(3-4), C-4, Whitereach Post, Lvl 34 Uncommon; Circles a couple plateaus in southwestern region

ACIDIC SWAMP OOZE
Dustwallow Marsh (38), F:(4-6), G:(5, 6), Beezil's Wreck, The Quagmire

ACOLYTE DELLIS
Stormwind (72), F-6, The Canals, Building South of Stockade

ACOLYTE FENRICK
Barrens (18), H-3, Ratchet (122), Tower in eastern hills

ACOLYTE MAGAZ
Barrens (18), H-3, Ratchet (122), Tower in eastern hills

ACOLYTE PORENA
Stormwind (72), D-8, Mage Quarter, The Slaughtered Lamb

ACOLYTE WYTULA
Barrens (18), H-3, Ratchet (122), Tower in eastern hills

ADAIR GILROY
Librarian, Stormwind (72), F-6, The Canals, Building South of Stockade

ADAM
Stormwind (72), Roams city

ADAM LIND
Wetlands (96), A-6, Baradin Bay, Southern dock

ADDLED LEPER
Dun Morogh (32), C-4, Gnomeregan

ADELE FIELDER
Journeyman Leatherworker, Elwynn Forest (42), F-6,Goldshire (114), House facing Crystal Lake

ADJUTANT TESORAN
Dustwallow Marsh (38), I-5, Theramore Isle (135), 2nd floor of Foothold Citadel

ADLIN PRIDEDRIFT
General Supplies, Dun Morogh (32), D-7, Coldridge Valley (107), By caravan

ADOLESCENT WHELP
Swamp of Sorrows (76), A:(5, 6), B:(5, 6), Itharius's Cave, Southwest lake

ADON
Eastern Plaguelands (40), H-2, At roadblock

ADRIAN BARTLETT
Undercity (88), K-1, The Magic Quarter, Green circle west of Skull Building

ADULT PLAINSTRIDER
Mulgore (58), C-3, D:(3-8), E:(3-7), F:(3-7), G:(4-7), H:(5, 6)

ADVISOR BELGRUM
Ironforge (52), K-1, Hall of Explorers, Library

ADVISOR DUSKINGDAWN
Hillsbrad Foothills (48), H-2, Tarren Mill (133)

ADVISOR SARPHAS
Badlands (16), A-5, Kargath (116)

ADVISOR SORRELON
Silverpine Forest (68), F-4, The Sepulcher (127)

AEAN SWIFTRIVER
Alliance Outrunner, Barrens (18), F-8, Southern Barrens, Spawns at border to Dustwallow Marsh and travels north to Lushwater Oasis

AEDIS BROM
Stormwind (72), K-4, Old Town, Roamer - Stops at Pig and Whistle Tavern

AELTHALYSTE
Priest Trainer, Undercity (88), F-2, The War Quarter, Outside Skull Building

AEOLYNN
Clothier, Ashenvale (12), E-5, Astranaar (101), Building to northwest of town

AETHALAS
Warsong Gulch Battlemaster, Darnassus (26), H-4, Warrior's Terrace, Lower northwest platform

AFFRAY CHALLENGER
Barrens (18), H-5, I-5, Fray Island

AFFRAY SPECTATOR
Barrens (18), H-5, I-5, Fray Island

AGAL
Teldrassil (80), F-5, Ban'ethil Hollow, Den south of the road

AGAM'AR
Barrens (18), E-9, Razorfen Kraul

AGATHELOS THE RAGING
Barrens (18), E-9, Razorfen Kraul

AGED KODO
Desolace (30), F:(1, 2, 5, 6), G:(1, 6, 9), H-9, J-6

AGENT KEARNEN
Westfall (94), H-7, The Dust Plains, Stealthed in the shade

AGERON KARGAL
Tirisfal Glades (86), H-5, Brill (104), Second floor of Gallows' End Tavern

AGGEM THORNCURSE
Barrens (18), E-9, Razorfen Kraul

AGNAR BEASTAMER
The Hinterlands (50), B-4, Aerie Peak (100), Wildhammer Keep

AG'TOR BLOODFIST
Azshara (14), B-5, Valormok

AGUSTUS MOULAINE
Mail Armor Merchant, Stormwind (72), G-4, Cathedral Square, Righteous Plates

AHAB WHEATHOOF (THE OLD RANCHER)
Mulgore (58), F-5, Bloodhoof Village (102)

AHANU
Leather Armor Merchant, Thunder Bluff (84), E-6, Lower rise, in Hewa's Armory

AINETHIL
Alchemist Trainer, Darnassus (26), G-2, Craftsmen's Terrace, Alchemy shop

AIR SPIRIT
Thousand Needles (82), H-5, Windbreak Canyon

AJECK ROUACK
Stranglethorn Vale (74), C-1, Nesingwary's Expedition, Camp

AKKRILUS
Rare Spawn, Ashenvale (12), C-6, D-6, Fire Scar Shrine, Lvl 26 Average Rare; Close to northern entrance to Fire Scar Shrine

AKUBAR THE SEER
Rare Spawn, Blasted Lands (20), G-5, H-5, I-5, Dark Portal, Lvl 54 Uncommon; Roams small area around spawn point

AKU'MAI
Ashenvale (12), B-2, Blackfathom Deeps

AKU'MAI FISHER
Ashenvale (12), B-2, Blackfathom Deeps

AKU'MAI SERVANT
Ashenvale (12), B-2, Blackfathom Deeps

AKU'MAI SNAPJAW
Ashenvale (12), B-2, Blackfathom Deeps

AK'ZELOTH
Barrens (18), H-2, Far Watch Post, Foot of Tower

ALAINDIA
Reagent Vendor, Darnassus (26), C-7, The Temple Gardens

ALAMAR GRIMM
Warlock Trainer, Dun Morogh (32), D-7, Coldridge Valley (107), Anvilmar

ALANNA RAVENEYE
Journeyman Enchanter, Teldrassil (80), D-3, The Oracle Glade, Hill at end of road

ALANNDARIAN NIGHTSONG
Darkshore (24), F-4, Auberdine (101), Center of northern building

ALARM-A-BOMB 2600
Dun Morogh (32), C-4, Gnomeregan

ALASSIN
Stable Master, Darnassus (26), E-1, Cenarion Enclave, Northeast structure

ALCHEMIST ARBINGTON
Western Plaguelands (92), E-8, Chillwind Camp (107), In front of crate in camp

ALCHEMIST MALLORY
Alchemist Trainer, Elwynn Forest (42), E-5, Secluded house on hill

ALCHEMIST NARETT
Alchemist Trainer, Dustwallow Marsh (38), H-5, Theramore Isle (135), Hut in west corner

ALCHEMIST PESTLEZUGG
Alchemy Supplies, Tanaris (78), G-3, Gadgetzan (113), Northwestern hut

ALDIA
General Supplies, Teldrassil (80), G-6, Dolanaar (109), Middle floor inside building north of road

ALDREN CORDON
Clothier, Loch Modan (54), I-7, Ironband's Excavation Site, Camp outside of excavation site

ALDRIC MOORE
Mail Armor Merchant, Stormwind (72), H-6, Trade District, Lionheart Armory

ALDWIN LAUGHLIN
Guild Master, Stormwind (72), I-7, Trade District, Stormwind Visitor's Center

ALEGORN
Cooking Trainer, Darnassus (26), F-2, Craftsmen's Terrace, Cooking shop

ALENNDAAR LAPIDAAR
Hunter Trainer, Ashenvale (12), C-6, Shrine of Aessina, Hidden in a camp near mountains in far southwest of region

ALEXANDER CALDER
Warlock Trainer, Ironforge (52), G-1, The Forlorn Cavern, Building to the right of Traveling Fisherman

ALEXANDRA BLAZEN
Azshara (14), H-9, The Ruined Reaches, Inlet

ALEXANDRA BOLERO
Tailoring Supplies, Stormwind (72), G-7, Mage Quarter, Duncan's Textiles

ALEXANDRA CONSTANTINE
Gryphon Master, Blasted Lands (20), J-2, Nethergarde Keep (120), Rear right of keep

ALEXANDRE LEFEVRE
Leather Armor Merchant, Silverpine Forest (68), G-4, The Sepulcher (127), House on right side of sepulcher

ALEXI BAROV
House of Barov, Tirisfal Glades (86), K-7, The Bulwark (105) (105), Camp on right side of road

ALEXI IRONKNIFE
Western Plaguelands (93), E-8, Chillwind Camp (107) (107)

ALEXIA IRONKNIFE
Western Plaguelands (92), E-8, Chillwind Camp (107), By fire in camp

ALGERNON
Alchemy Supplies, Undercity (88), G-7, The Apothecarium, Near Royal Quarter entry

ALIGAR THE TORMENTOR
Ashenvale (12), D-2, Spawns on road near Darkshore border

ALINA
Alterac Mountains (8), B-8, Lordamere Internment Camp, Building inside camp walls

ALLAN HAFGAN
Staves Merchant, Stormwind (72), F:(6, 7), Mage Quarter, Stormwind Staves

ALLESANDRO LUCA
Blue Moon Odds and Ends, Undercity (88), H-5, The Apothecarium

ALLYNDIA
Food & Drink Vendor, Darkshore (24), F-4, Auberdine (101), First floor of inn

ALMA JAINROSE
Herbalism Trainer, Redridge Mountains (62), B-4, Lakeshire (117), Roams inside small house on southwestern side of town

ALOWICIOUS CZERVIK
Sweet Treats, Orgrimmar (60), E-7, Valley of Strength

ALSHIRR BANEBREATH
Rare Spawn, Felwood (44), F-8, Jadefire Glen, Lvl 54 Uncommon; Roams Jadefire Glen

AL'TABIM THE ALL-SEEING
Stranglethorn Vale (74), A-2, Yojamba Isle

ALTAR OF SUNTARA
Searing Gorge (64), E-3, The Slag Pit, Lower level of the northernmost region of pit

ALTHALLEN BRIGHTBLADE
Eye of the Storm BM, Thunder Bluff (85), G-8

ALTHOBA RAGETOTEM
Weapon Merchant, Felwood (44), E-5, Bloodvenom Post (102), Tent

ALYISSIA
Warrior Trainer, Teldrassil (80), H-4, Shadowglen (127), In northeast room inside main building

ALYSSA BLAYE
Undercity (88), F-3, The War Quarter, Platform in front of Skull Building

ALYSSA EVA
Reagent Vendor, Duskwood (36), K-4, Darkshire (108), First floor of house

ALYSSA GRIFFITH
Bag Vendor, Stormwind (72), J-5, Old Town, The Protective Hide

ALZZIN THE WILDSHAPER
Feralas (46), G-4, Dire Maul

ALZZIN'S MINION
Feralas (46), G-4, Dire Maul

AMAN
Wetlands (96), A-6, Deepwater Tavern, (Summon) Spawns second floor of inn

AMBASSADOR ARDALAN
Blasted Lands (20), J-2, Nethergarde Keep (120), Top floor of tower facing entrance of keep

AMBASSADOR BERRYBUCK
Council of Darkshire, Duskwood (36), J-5, Darkshire (108), Darkshire Town Hall

AMBASSADOR BLOODRAGE
Rare Spawn, Barrens (18), F-9, Razorfen Downs, Lvl 36 Semi-Rare; Spawns in/ near huts

AMBASSADOR FLAMELASH
Burning Steppes (22), Searing Gorge (64), C-4/D-8, Blackrock Depths

AMBASSADOR INFERNUS
Badlands (16), F-3, Angor Fortress, Basement of fortress

AMBASSADOR MALCIN
Barrens (18), F-9, Razorfen Downs, Huts in hills

AMBASSADOR RAULETH
Hinterlands (50), B-5, Aerie Peak (100)

AMBEREYE BASILISK
Desolace (30), D-5, Mauradon

AMBEREYE REAVER
Desolace (30), D-5, Mauradon

AMBERSHARD CRUSHER
Desolace (30), D-5, Mauradon

AMBERSHARD DESTROYER
Desolace (30), D-5, Mauradon

A-ME 01
Un'Goro Crater (90), I-2, Fungal Rock, Southern section of the cave

AMIE PIERCE
Dustwallow Marsh (38), I-5, Theramore Isle (135), 2nd floor of inn

AMNENNAR THE COLDBRINGER
Barrens (18), F-9, Razorfen Downs

AMY DAVENPORT
Tradeswoman, Redridge Mountains (62), C-5, Lakeshire (117), Roams around of caravan in front of Lakeshire Town Hall

ANA'THEK THE CRUEL
Skullsplitter Chief, Stranglethorn Vale (74), E-5, Ruins of Zul'Mamwe, Patrol with a Skullsplitter Berserker and Skullsplitter Spiritchaser between cave and ruins

ANADYIA
Robe Vendor, Darnassus (26), G-9, Tradesmen's Terrace, Robe shop

ANASTASIA HARTWELL
Mage Trainer, Undercity (88), L-1, The Magic Quarter, Northwest corner of Skull Building

ANATHEMUS
Rare Spawn, Badlands (16), C-7, Lvl 44 Uncommon; Patrols large radius around entire region

ANAYA DAWNRUNNER
Darkshore (24), F-6, G-6, Ameth'Aran, Roams southern part of Ameth'Aran

ANCESTRAL SPIRIT
Mulgore (58), H-2, Red Rocks, On hill within burial ground

ANCHORITE DETAN
Duskwood (36), J-5, Darkshire (108)

ANCIENT CORE HOUND
Burning Steppes (22), Searing Gorge (64), C-4/D-8, The Molten Core

ANCIENT EQUINE SPIRIT
Feralas (46), G-4, Dire Maul

ANCIENT KODO
Desolace (30), F:(5, 6), G-6, Ghost Walker Post (113), Kodo Graveyard

ANCIENT OF LORE
Darnassus (26), F-1, G-1, Craftsmen's Terrace, Northwest of First Aid

ANCIENT OF WAR
Darnassus (26), L:(3, 4), I-4, Warrior's Terrace, South of path

ANCIENT STONE KEEPER
Badlands (16), G-1, Uldaman

ANDER GERMAINE
Warrior Trainer, Stormwind (72), L-5, Old Town, Command Center

ANDI
Stormwind (72), Roams city with Miss Danna

ANDI LYNN
Tanaris (78), H-3, Gadgetzan (113), Northeast corner of town near fire

ANDISS
Armorer & Shieldcrafter, Teldrassil (80), G-4, H-4, Shadowglen (127), Inside main building

ANDORHAL TOWER FOUR
Western Plaguelands (92), F-7, Ruins of Andorhal, Southeastern tower ruins

ANDORHAL TOWER ONE
Western Plaguelands (92), E-7, Ruins of Andorhal, Southwestern tower ruins

ANDORHAL TOWER THREE
Western Plaguelands (92), F-6, Ruins of Andorhal, Central northern tower ruin

ANDORHAL TOWER TWO
Western Plaguelands (92), E-6, Ruins of Andorhal, Northwestern tower ruins

ANDRE FIREBEARD
Tanaris (78), K-5, Lost Rigger Cove, Center of fort

ANDREA BOYNTON
Clothier, Silverpine Forest (68), G-4, The Sepulcher (127), House on right side of sepulcher

ANDREA HALLORAN
Wetlands (96), A-5, Menethil Harbor (119), Roams in and out of house west of keep

ANDREW BROWNELL
Undercity (88), J-3, The Magic Quarter, Stall next to Tailors

ANDREW HARTWELL
Undercity (88), G-2, The War Quarter, Watches fights in War Quarter

ANDREW HILBERT
Trade Goods, Silverpine Forest (68), G-4, The Sepulcher (127), Basement of inn

ANDREW KRIGHTON
Armorer & Shieldcrafter, Elwynn Forest (42), E-7,Goldshire (114), Smithy

ANDRISSA HEARTSPEAR
Eye of the Storm Battlemaster, Orgrimmar (61), J-3

ANDROD FADRAN
Leatherworking Supplies, Arathi Highlands (10), F-5, Refuge Point (124), Roams camp south of Gryphon Master

ANDROD FADREN
Leatherworking Supplies, Arathi Highlands (11), F-5, Refuge Point (124) (124)

ANDROL OAKHAND
Fisherman, Teldrassil (80), G-9, Rut'theran Village (125), By dock

ANDRON GANT
Undercity (88), H:(7, 8), The Apothecarium

ANDRUK
Wind Rider Master, Ashenvale (12), B-4, Zoram'gar Outpost (137)

ANDRUS
Staff Merchant, Darnassus (26), G-9, Tradesmen's Terrace, Staff shop

ANDUIN WRYNN
King of Stormwind, Stormwind (72), L-2, Stormwind Keep, Center of east wing

ANGELA CURTHAS
Warrior Trainer, Undercity (88), F-1, The War Quarter, In Skull Building

ANGELAS MOONBREEZE
Feralas (46), C-4, Feathermoon Stronghold (111), Southeast building

ANGER'REL
Burning Steppes (22), Searing Gorge (64), C-4/D-8, Blackrock Depths

ANGERCLAW BEAR
Felwood (44), E:(7, 8), F:(7, 8), G:(7-9), H:(8, 9)

ANGERCLAW GRIZZLY
Felwood (44), G:(2, 3), H:(1-3), I-2, Irontree Woods, Talonbranch Glade (133)

ANGERCLAW MAULER
Felwood (44), E:(3-6), F:(2, 3, 6, 7), G:(2, 4)

ANGERED INFERNAL
Azshara (14), G-3, Thalassian Base Camp, Near Magus Rimtori

ANGRUN
Superior Herbalist, Stranglethorn Vale (74), C-3, Grom'gol Base Camp (114), Next to cauldron on the northern side of camp

ANGUISHED DEAD
Tirisfal Glades (86), K-3, L-3, Scarlet Monastery

ANGUISHED HIGHBORNE
Winterspring (98), H:(4, 5), Lake Kel'Theril

ANGUS STERN
Head Chef, Stormwind (72), F-9, Mage Quarter, The Blue Recluse

ANILIA
Ashenvale (12), J-4, Xavian, Dryad lying on ground in middle of camp

ANISHAR
Rogue Trainer, Darnassus (26), E-2, Cenarion Enclave, Den, bottom of ramp

ANNORA
Master Enchanter, Badlands (16), G-1, Uldaman

ANSEKHWA
Weapon Master, Thunder Bluff (84), D-6, Lower rise, Trains: 1H Mace, 2H Mace, Staves, & Guns

ANTARIUS
Stable Master, Feralas (46), C-4, Feathermoon Stronghold (111), East side of inn

ANTILOS
Rare Spawn, Azshara (14), A-5, I-2, Legashi Encampment, Lvl 50 Very Rare; Roams south from first spawnpoint and around second

ANTILUS THE SOARER
Feralas (46), C-4, Feathermoon Stronghold (111), Southwest building

ANTLERED COURSER
Stonetalon Mountains (70), D:(1, 2), E:(1, 2), F:(2-4), G:(3, 4), Mirkfallon Lake, Stonetalon Peak

ANTONIO PERELLI
Traveling Salesman, Westfall (94), G-6, Spawns at the intersection south of Sentinel Hill and travels along the road to Darkshire and on to Lakeshire

ANTUR FALLOW
Mulgore (58), D-8, Red Cloud Mesa, Along road leading from Camp Narache

ANTU'SUL
Tanaris (78), E-1, Zul'Farrak

ANUB'SHIAH
Burning Steppes (22), Searing Gorge (64), C-4/D-8, Blackrock Depths

ANUBISATH
Silithus (66), D-5, E-5

ANVILRAGE CAPTAIN
Burning Steppes (22), Searing Gorge (64), C-4/D-8, Blackrock Depths

ANVILRAGE FOOTMAN
Burning Steppes (22), Searing Gorge (64), C-4/D-8, Blackrock Depths

ANVILRAGE GUARDSMAN
Burning Steppes (22), Searing Gorge (64), C-4/D-8, Blackrock Depths

ANVILRAGE MARSHAL
Burning Steppes (22), Searing Gorge (64), C-4/D-8, Blackrock Depths

ANVILRAGE MEDIC
Burning Steppes (22), Searing Gorge (64), C-4/D-8, Blackrock Depths

ANVILRAGE OFFICER
Burning Steppes (22), Searing Gorge (64), C-4/D-8, Blackrock Depths

ANVILRAGE OVERSEER
Burning Steppes (22), Searing Gorge (64), C-4/D-8, Blackrock Depths

ANVILRAGE RESERVIST
Burning Steppes (22), Searing Gorge (64), C-4/D-8, Blackrock Depths

ANVILRAGE SOLDIER
Burning Steppes (22), Searing Gorge (64), C-4/D-8, Blackrock Depths

ANVILRAGE WARDEN
Burning Steppes (22), Searing Gorge (64), C-4/D-8, Blackrock Depths

ANYA MAULRAY
Stable Master, Undercity (88), I-4, The Trade Quarter, Upper Ring of Trade Quarter

APOTHECARY BERARD
Silverpine Forest (68), F-7, Pyrewood Village, Second floor of inn

APOTHECARY DITHERS
Tirisfal Glades (86), K-7, The Bulwark (105), Camp on left side of road

APOTHECARY DITHERS
Western Plaguelands (92), C-6, The Bulwark (105)

APOTHECARY FALTHIS
Rare Spawn, Ashenvale (12), D-3, Bathran's Haunt, Lvl 22 Uncommon; Within haunt to the east

APOTHECARY FAUSTIN
Duskwood (36), L-3, Beggar's Haunt, Left side of tower by entrance

APOTHECARY HELBRIM
Barrens (18), F-3, The Crossroads (107), West of inn

APOTHECARY JOHAAN
Royal Apothecary Society, Tirisfal Glades (86), H-5, Brill (104), House on the right side of road

APOTHECARY JORELL
Arathi Highlands (10), H-6, Go'Shek Farm, First house on left side of farm

APOTHECARY KATRINA
Undercity (88), G-6, The Apothecarium, Roams Apothecarium and Canals

APOTHECARY KEEVER
Royal Apothecary Society, Undercity (88), G-7, The Apothecarium, In laboratory

APOTHECARY LYCANUS
Royal Apothecary Society, Undercity (88), G-6, The Apothecarium, Roams Apothecarium

APOTHECARY LYDON
Royal Apothecary Society, Hillsbrad Foothills (48), G-2, Tarren Mill (133), House on the left

APOTHECARY RENFERREL
Royal Apothecary Society, Silverpine Forest (68), F-4, The Sepulcher (127), Right side of inn under scaffolding

APOTHECARY VALLIA
Undercity (88), G-6, The Apothecarium, Roams Apothecarium, Trade Quarter

APOTHECARY ZAMAH
Thunder Bluff (84), C-3, Spirit Rise, The Pools of Vision

APOTHECARY ZINGE
Royal Apothecary Society, Undercity (88), G-7, The Apothecarium, In laboratory

APPRENTICE HONEYWELL
Hillsbrad Foothills (48), F:(5, 6), Southshore (129)

APPRENTICE KRYTEN
Arathi Highlands (10), F-5, Refuge Point (124), Camp

AQUEMENTAS
Tanaris (78), J-5, Lost Rigger Cove, (Summon) Near circle of stones southwest of fort

ARADOS THE DAMNED
Hillsbrad Foothills (48), A-8, Purgation Isle, In front of tower

ARAGA
Rare Spawn, Alterac Mountains (8), D:(7, 8), E-9, Dalaran, Sofera's Naze, The Headland, Lvl 35 Average Rare; Roams small area around spawn point

ARAJ THE SUMMONER
Western Plaguelands (92), F-7, Ruins of Andorhal, Idle with multiple mobs in the center of city

ARANAE VENOMBLOOD
Herbalist, Hillsbrad Foothills (48), G-2, Tarren Mill (133), Outside of the house on the left

ARANTIR
The Hand of Chaos, Redridge Mountains (62), C-5, Lakeshire (117), L shaped dock west of the bridge

ARASH-ETHIS
Rare Spawn, Feralas (46), D-2, E-2, The Twin Colossals, Lvl 49 Uncommon; Patrols area west of road near mountains

ARATHANDRIS SILVERSKY
Emerald Circle, Felwood (44), G-8, Morlos'Aran, North of road

ARCANE ABERRATION
Feralas (46), G-4, Dire Maul

ARCANE CHIMAEROK
Feralas (46), B:(7, 8), C:(7-9), Isle of Dread

ARCANE FEEDBACK
Feralas (46), G-4, Dire Maul

ARCANE NULLIFIER X-21
Dun Morogh (32), C-4, Gnomeregan

ARCANE TORRENT
Feralas (46), G-4, Dire Maul

ARCANIST DOAN
Tirisfal Glades (86), K-3, L-3, Scarlet Monastery

ARCH DRUID FANDRAL STAGHELM
Boss, Darnassus (26), D-1, Cenarion Enclave, Northwest structure, upper level

ARCH DRUID HAMUUL RUNETOTEM
Thunder Bluff (84), J-3, Elder Rise, Inside Hall of Elders

ARCHAEDAS
Badlands (16), G-1, Uldaman

ARCHAEOLOGIST FLAGONGUT
Explorers' League, Wetlands (96), A-6, Deepwater Tavern, Northeast, upstairs room

ARCHAEOLOGIST HOLLEE
Explorer's League, Darkshore (24), F-4, Auberdine (101), In front of northern building

ARCHBISHOP BENEDICTUS
Boss, Stormwind (72), F-3, Cathedral Square, Cathedral of Light

ARCHIBALD
Weapon Master, Undercity (88), H-3, The War Quarter, Trains: Crossbows, Daggers, 1H Sword, 2H Sword, & Polearms

ARCHIBALD KAVA
Cloth and Leather Armor Merchant, Tirisfal Glades (86), D-6, Deathknell (109), First floor of second house on right side of road

ARCHIVIST GALFORD
Eastern Plaguelands (40), D-2, Stratholme

ARCHMAGE ALLISTARJ
Blasted Lands (20), J-3, Serpent's Coil, Cave interior

ARCHMAGE ANGELA DOSANTOS
Brotherhood of the Light, Eastern Plaguelands (40), K-6, Light's Hope Chapel (118)

ARCHMAGE ANSIREM RUNEWEAVER
Alterac Mountains (8), B-8, Dalaran, Road just north of Lordamere Internment Camp

ARCHMAGE ARUGAL
Silverpine Forest (68), F-7, Shadowfang Keep

ARCHMAGE ATAERIC
Silverpine Forest (68), I-6, Ambermill, Town hall

ARCHMAGE MALIN
Stormwind (72), F-8, Mage Quarter, Next to Tower

ARCHMAGE SHYMM
Mage Trainer, Thunder Bluff (84), B-2, Spirit Rise, The Pools of Vision

ARCHMAGE TEVROSH
Dustwallow Marsh (38), I-5, Theramore Isle (135), Top of central tower

ARCHMAGE XYLEM
Azshara (14), C-4, Bear's Head, Requires quest from Sanath Lim-yo to reach

ARDO DIRTPAW
Redridge Mountains (62), B-2, Rethban Cavern, Idle with several Redridge gnolls in cave

ARDWYN CAILEN
Wand Merchant, Stormwind (72), F:(6, 7), Mage Quarter, Stormwind Staves

AREI
Felwood (44), G-3, Irontree Woods, (Summon) Spawns in Irontree Woods and walks to Ashenvale

ARENA SPECTATOR
Burning Steppes (22), Searing Gorge (64), C-4/D-8, Blackrock Depths

ARGENT DEFENDER
Western Plaguelands (92), C-5, E-8, F-8, Chillwind Camp (107)

ARGENT GUARD
Eastern Plaguelands (40), K-6, Light's Hope Chapel (118)

ARGENT GUARD MANADOS
The Argent Dawn, Darnassus (26), G-2, Craftsmen's Terrace, Argent Dawn

ARGENT GUARD THAELRID
Ashenvale (12), B-2, Blackfathom Deeps

ARGENT OFFICER GARUSH
The Argent Dawn, Tirisfal Glades (86), K-7, The Bulwark (105), Camp on left side of road

ARGENT OFFICER PUREHEART
The Argent Dawn, Western Plaguelands (92), E-8, Chillwind Camp (107), With two Argent Defenders in front of tent

ARGENT QUARTERMASTER HASANA
Western Plaguelands (92), K-7, The Bulwark (105)

ARGENT QUARTERMASTER LIGHTSPARK
The Argent Dawn, Western Plaguelands (92), E-8, Chillwind Camp (107), By lumber pile

ARGENT RIDER
Eastern Plaguelands (40), K-6, Light's Hope Chapel (118)

ARGOS NIGHTWHISPER
Stormwind (72), C-6, The Park, By pool of water

ARIAS'TA BLADESINGER
Warrior Trainer, Darnassus (26), H-3, Warrior's Terrace, Lower northwest platform

ARIENA STORMFEATHER
Gryphon Master, Redridge Mountains (62), D-6, Left of bridge heading into Lakeshire

ARIKARA
Thousand Needles (82), E-4, Darkcloud Pinnacle, Atop small plateau east of water

ARIN'SOR
Ravasaur Trainers, Un'Goro Crater (90), D-2, Hill in far northwestern section of crater

ARIYELL SKYSHADOW
Weapon Merchant, Darnassus (26), H-4, Warrior's Terrace, Lower southwest platform

ARKKORAN CLACKER
Azshara (14), I-4, J:(3-5), K:(3, 4), Temple of Arkkoran

ARKKORAN MUCKDWELLER
Azshara (14), I-4, J:(3-5), K:(3, 4), Temple of Arkkoran

ARKKORAN ORACLE
Azshara (14), I-4, J:(3-5), K-4, Temple of Arkkoran

ARKKORAN PINCER
Azshara (14), I-4, J:(3-5), K-4, Temple of Arkkoran

ARMAND CROMWELL
Fishing Trainer, Undercity (88), K-3, The Magic Quarter, On Dock

ARMORED SCORPID
Durotar (34), E:(3, 4), F:(3-5), G:(2-5), H:(2-4), I:(2, 3)

ARNAK GRIMTOTEM
Thousand Needles (82), E-3, Darkcloud Pinnacle, On northern cliff, north of Darkcloud Pinnacle

ARNOK
First Aid Trainer, Orgrimmar (60), D-8, Valley of Spirit, Survival of the Fittest (near Spirit Lodge)

ARNOLD LELAND
Fishing Trainer, Stormwind (72), G-6, The Canals, Dock

ARRA'CHEA
Mulgore (58), F-2, The Golden Plains, Roams plains

ARTHUR MOORE
Leatherworker Trainer, Undercity (88), J-6, The Rogues' Quarter

ARTHUR THE FAITHFUL
Paladin Trainer, Stormwind (72), F-3, Cathedral Square, Cathedral of Light

ARTILLERYMAN SHELDONORE
Ironforge (52), B-5, The Commons, The Stonefire Tavern

ARTIST RENFRAY
Western Plaguelands (92), I-7, Caer Darrow, Ghost In house by the docks

ARTORIUS THE AMIABLE
Winterspring (98), I-1, Roams northwest of grove

ARUGAL'S VOIDWALKER
Silverpine Forest (68), F-7, Shadowfang Keep

ASHENVALE BEAR
Ashenvale (12), D:(4, 5), E:(3-7), F:(4, 7), G:(4-6), H:(5, 7, 8), I:(7, 8)

ASHENVALE OUTRUNNER
Ashenvale (12), I-7, J:(6, 7), Nightsong Woods, Dor'Danil Barrow Den

ASHENVALE SENTINEL
Ashenvale (12), H-6, Nightsong Woods, Raynewood Retreat

ASHLAN STONESMIRK
Wetlands (96), G-2, Dun Modr, Next to wagons, west of road

ASKA MISTRUNNER
Cooking Trainer, Thunder Bluff (84), F-5, High rise, inside Aska's Kitchen tent

ASORAN
General Goods Vendor, Orgrimmar (60), E-4, Valley of Wisdom, Asoran's Market

ASPECT OF BANALITY
Western Plaguelands (92), I-7, Scholomance

ASPECT OF CORRUPTION
Western Plaguelands (92), I-7, Scholomance

ASPECT OF MALICE
Western Plaguelands (92), I-7, Scholomance

ASPECT OF SHADOW
Western Plaguelands (92), I-7, Scholomance

ASTAIA
Fishing Trainer, Darnassus (26), F-5, Tradesmen's Terrace, Dock

ASTARII STARSEEKER
Priest Trainer, Darnassus (26), E-8, The Temple Gardens, Balcony, north of fountain

ASTERION
Darkshore (24), G-4, Bashal'Aran, In blue-lined structure

ASTOR HADREN
Silverpine Forest (68), G-4, Patrols between the road just east of The Sepulcher and the Gallows' End Tavern in Brill

ASTRANAAR SENTINEL
Ashenvale (12), D-5, E-5, F-6, Astranaar (101), Silverwind Refuge

ATAL'AI CORPSE EATER
Swamp of Sorrows (76), I-5, The Temple of Atal'Hakkar

ATAL'AI DEATHWALKER
Swamp of Sorrows (76), I-5, The Temple of Atal'Hakkar

ATAL'AI DEATHWALKER'S SPIRIT
Swamp of Sorrows (76), I-5, The Temple of Atal'Hakkar

ATAL'AI EXILE
The Hinterlands (50), E-7, Shadra'Alor, Lower left portion of temple

ATAL'AI HIGH PRIEST
Swamp of Sorrows (76), I-5, The Temple of Atal'Hakkar

ATAL'AI PRIEST
Swamp of Sorrows (76), I-5, The Temple of Atal'Hakkar

ATAL'AI SKELETON
Swamp of Sorrows (76), I-5, The
Temple of Atal'Hakkar

ATAL'AI SLAVE
Swamp of Sorrows (76), I-5, The
Temple of Atal'Hakkar

ATAL'AI WARRIOR
Swamp of Sorrows (76), I-5, The
Temple of Atal'Hakkar

ATAL'AI WITCH DOCTOR
Swamp of Sorrows (76), I-5, The
Temple of Atal'Hakkar

ATAL'ALARION
Swamp of Sorrows (76), I-5, The
Temple of Atal'Hakkar

ATEPA
Banker, Thunder Bluff (85), E-6

ATEPU
Banker, Thunder Bluff (84), E-6, Thunder
Bluff Bank

ATHRIDAS BEARMANTLE
Teldrassil (80), G-6, Dolanaar (109),
Outside building north of road

ATHRIKUS NARASSIN
Darkshore (24), H-3, Tower of
Althalaxx, Top of tower

ATURK THE ANVIL
Orgrimmar (60), J-2, Valley of Honor,
Next to the Burning Anvil

AUBERDINE SENTINEL
Darkshore (24), E:(4, 5), F:(4, 5),
Auberdine (101), Mist's Edge, The Long
Wash

AUCTIONEER BEARDO
Auctioneer, Tanaris (78), H-3,
Gadgetzan (113), Auction House

AUCTIONEER BUCKLER
Auctioneer, Ironforge (52), C-7, The
Commons, Auction House

AUCTIONEER CAIN
Auctioneers, Undercity (88), I-4

AUCTIONEER CAZAREZ
Auctioneer, Darnassus (26), G-5

AUCTIONEER CHILTON
Auctioneer, Stormwind (72), H-6

AUCTIONEER EPITWEE
Auctioneers, Undercity (88), I-5

AUCTIONEER FITCH
Auctioneer, Stormwind (72), H-6

AUCTIONEER GOLOTHAS
Auctioneer, Darnassus (26), H-5

AUCTIONEER GRIMFUL
Auctioneer, Orgrimmar (60), G-6, Valley
of Strength, Auction House

AUCTIONEER GRIZZLIN
Auctioneer, Orgrimmar (60), G-6, Valley
of Strength, Auction House

AUCTIONEER GULLEM
Auctioneer, Thunder Bluff (85), D-5

AUCTIONEER JAXON
Auctioneer, Stormwind (72), H-6

AUCTIONEER KREAKY
Auctioneer (Lower Level), Stranglethorn
Vale (74), B-8, Booty Bay (103)

AUCTIONEER KRESKY
Auctioneer, Orgrimmar (60), G-6, Valley
of Strength, Auction House

AUCTIONEER LEEKA
Auctioneers, Undercity (88), J-5

AUCTIONEER LYMPKIN
Auctioneer, Ironforge (52), C-7, The
Commons, Auction House

AUCTIONEER NAXXREMIS
Auctioneers, Undercity (88), H-4

AUCTIONEER O'RELLY
Auctioneer, Stranglethorn Vale (74),
B-8, Booty Bay (103)

AUCTIONEER REDMUSE
Auctioneer, Ironforge (52), C-7, The
Commons, Auction House

AUCTIONEER RHYKER
Auctioneers, Undercity (88), I-5

AUCTIONEER SILVA'LAS
Auctioneer, Darnassus (26), H-5

AUCTIONEER STAMPI
Auctioneer, Thunder Bluff (85), D-5

AUCTIONEER STOCKTON
Auctioneers, Undercity (88), J-4

AUCTIONEER THATHUNG
Auctioneer, Orgrimmar (60), G-6, Valley
of Strength, Auction House

AUCTIONEER TOLON
Auctioneer, Darnassus (26), H-5

AUCTIONEER TRICKET
Auctioneers, Undercity (88), H-5

AUCTIONEER WABANG
Auctioneer, Orgrimmar (60), G-6, Valley
of Strength, Auction House

AUCTIONEER YARLY
Auctioneers, Undercity (88), I-4

AUGUSTUS THE TOUCHED
Eastern Plaguelands (40), B-3,
Terrorweb Tunnel, Cave along western
border

AULD STONESPIRE
Thunder Bluff (84), C-6, Lower rise,
inside tent near elevators

"AUNTIE" BERNICE STONEFIELD
Elwynn Forest (42), D-8, The Stonefield
Farm, Next to well

AURAL GOLDLEAF
Silithus (67), G-4, Cenarion Hold (106)

AURIUS
Eastern Plaguelands (40), D-2,
Stratholme

AURORA SKYCALLER
Eastern Plaguelands (40), H-3,
Northpass Tower, Tower

AUSTIL DE MON
Warrior Trainer, Tirisfal Glades (86), H-5,
Brill (104), First floor of Gallows' End
Tavern

AVALANCHION
World Boss, Azshara (14), J-2, Bitter
Reaches, Roams northern peninsula

AVATAR OF HAKKAR
Swamp of Sorrows (76), I-5, The
Temple of Atal'Hakkar

AVETTE FELLWOOD
Bowyer, Duskwood (36), J-4, Darkshire
(108), Near carriages outside and left of
the Scarlet Raven Inn

AWBIE
Burning Steppes (22), Searing Gorge
(64), C-4/D-8, Blackrock Spire

AWENASA
Stable Master, Thousand Needles (82),
F-5, Freewind Post (112), Outside Inn

AXIE
Innkeeper, Dustwallow Marsh (38), F-7,
Mudsprocket (120)

AXTROZ
Wetlands (96), K-5, Dragonmaw Gates,
Patrols path

AYANNA EVERSTRIDE
Hunter Trainer, Teldrassil (80), G-4,
Shadowglen (127), First room off of
ramp up tree

AZAR STRONGHAMMER
Paladin Trainer, Dun Morogh (32), F-5,
Kharanos (116), Thunderbrew Distillery

AZJ'TORDIN
Feralas (46), J-4, Lariss Pavilion, In
temple, northeast of Camp Mojache

AZORE ALDAMORT
The Argent Dawn, Desolace (30), E-3,
Ethel Rethor, Temple ruins overlooking
sea

AZSHARA SENTINEL
Azshara (14), A-8, Talrendis Point

AZSHIR THE SLEEPLESS
Tirisfal Glades (86), K-3, L-3, Scarlet
Monastery

AZUREGOS
Azshara (14), H-9, Roams the central
area of the southern landmass

AZUROUS
Rare Spawn, Winterspring (98), J-5,
Ice Thistle Hills, Lvl 59 Average Rare;
Wanders hills east of road

AZZERE THE SKYBLADE
Rare Spawn, Barrens (18), E-6, Southern
Barrens, Lvl 25 Uncommon; Patrols
area south of Camp Taurajo

AZZLEBY
Stable Master, Winterspring (98), I-4,
Everlook (110), Outside of Everlook's
entrance

B

BABAGAYA SHADOWCLEFT
Warlock Trainer, Barrens (18), H-3,
Ratchet (122)

BAEL'GAR
Burning Steppes (22), Searing Gorge
(64), C-4/D-8, Blackrock Depths

BAEL'DUN APPRAISER
Mulgore (58), C-5, Bael'dun Digsite

BAEL'DUN DIGGER
Mulgore (58), C-5, D-5, Bael'dun
Digsite

BAEL'DUN EXCAVATOR
Barrens (18), E-8, F:(8, 9), Bael Modan

BAEL'DUN FOREMAN
Barrens (18), E-8, Bael Modan

BAEL'DUN OFFICER
Barrens (18), F-8, Bael Modan

BAEL'DUN RIFLEMAN
Barrens (18), F-8, Bael Modan

BAEL'DUN SOLDIER
Barrens (18), F-8, Bael Modan

BAELOG
Badlands (16), G-1, Uldaman

BAILEY STONEMANTLE
Banker, Ironforge (52), D-6, The
Commons, Vault of Ironforge

BAILIFF CONACHER
Redridge Mountains (62), C-4,
Lakeshire (117), Lakeshire Town Hall

BAILOR STONEHAND
Loch Modan (54), D-4, Thelsamar (134),
Third house left of the path

BAINE BLOODHOOF
Mulgore (58), E-6, Bloodhoof Village
(102), Center of village

BAKER MASTERSON
Western Plaguelands (92), I-8, Caer
Darrow, House inside city walls just
right of entrance

BALANDAR BRIGHTSTAR
Dustwallow Marsh (38), D-3,
Brackenwall Village (104)

BALAI LOK'WEIN
Potions, Scrolls and Reagents,
Dustwallow Marsh (38), D-3,
Brackenwall Village (104), Northern part
of village

BALDRUC
Gryphon Master, Dustwallow Marsh
(38), I-5, Theramore Isle (135),
Southeast near docks

BALE
General Goods, Felwood (44), E-5,
Bloodvenom Post (102), Tent

BALGARAS THE FOUL
Wetlands (96), F-2, H:(2, 3), I-3, Dun
Modr, Direforge Hill, Spawns in a
building at Dun Modr or in northwest
camp in Direforge Hill

BALIR FROSTHAMMER
Dun Morogh (32), D-7, Coldridge Valley
(107), By fence

BALIZAR THE UMBRAGE
Ashenvale (12), D-2, Spawns on road
near Darkshore border

BALNAZZAR
Eastern Plaguelands (40), D-2,
Stratholme

BALOS JACKEN
Dustwallow Marsh (38), D-5, Lost Point,
Landing in tower

BALTHULE SHADOWSTRIKE
Darkshore (24), H-2, South of road,
near a rock west of tower

BALTHUS STONEFLAYER
Skinning Trainer, Ironforge (52), E-3,
The Great Forge, Finespindle's Leather
Goods

BALTUS FOWLER
Warrior Trainer, Undercity (88), F-2, The
War Quarter, In Skull Building

BANAL SPIRIT
Western Plaguelands (92), I-7,
Scholomance

BANALASH
Trade Goods, Swamp of Sorrows (76),
F-5, Stonard (131), Second floor of inn

BANNOK GRIMAXE
Burning Steppes (22), Searing Gorge
(64), C-4/D-8, Blackrock Spire

BARAK KODOBANE
Barrens (18), E-2, The Forgotten Pools,
Foot of structure on hill

BARBED CRUSTACEAN
Ashenvale (12), B-2, Blackfathom
Deeps

BARBED LASHER
Desolace (30), D-5, Mauradon

BARDU SHARPEYE
Tirisfal Glades (86), K-7, The Bulwark
(105), Camp on right side of road

BARDU SHARPEYE
Western Plaguelands (92), C-6, The
Bulwark (105)

BARG
General Supplies, Barrens (18), F-3, The
Crossroads (107), Outside inn

BARIM JURGENSTAAD
Reagent Vendor, Ironforge (52), B-6,
The Commons, Barim's Reagents

**BARISTOLTH OF THE SHIFTING
SANDS**
Silithus (67), G-5, Cenarion Hold (106)

BARITANAS SKYRIVER
Cenarion Circle, Desolace (30), H-1,
Nijel's Point (121), Up southwestern hill

BARITHRAS MOONSHADE
Darkshore (24), F-4, Auberdine (101),
In front of inn

BARKEEP DANIELS
Redridge Mountains (62), C-4,
Lakeshire (117), First floor of Lakeshire
Inn

BARKEEP DOBBINS
Bartender, Elwynn Forest (42),
F-7, Goldshire (114), First floor of Lion's
Pride Inn

BARKEEP HANN
Bartender, Duskwood (36), J-4,
Darkshire (108), Scarlet Raven Inn

BARKEEP KELLY
Bartender, Hillsbrad Foothills (48), F-6,
Southshore (129), First floor of inn

BARKEEP MORAG
Orgrimmar (60), G-7, Valley of
Strength, Inn

BARNABUS
Rare Spawn, Badlands (16), F-7, G-7,
H:(6, 7), Agmond's End, Badlands,
Mirage Flats, Lvl 38 Average Rare;
Roams small area around spawn point

BARNIL STONEPOT
Stranglethorn Vale (74), C-1,
Nesingwary's Expedition, Camp

BARNUM STONEMANTLE
Banker, Ironforge (52), D-6, The
Commons, Vault of Ironforge

BARON AQUANIS
Ashenvale (12), B-2, Blackfathom
Deeps, (Summon)

BARON CHARR
Un'Goro Crater (90), F:(4-6), G-4, G-6,
H:(4-6), Fire Plume Ridge, Patrols
around ridge

BARON GEDDON
Burning Steppes (22), Searing Gorge
(64), C-4/D-8, The Molten Core

BARON LONGSHORE
Barrens (18), H-5, The Merchant Coast,
Camps on coast

BARON REVILGAZ
Stranglethorn Vale (74), B-8, Booty Bay
(103), Third floor balcony of The Salty
Sailor Tavern

BARON RIVENDARE
Eastern Plaguelands (40), D-2,
Stratholme

BARON SILVERLAINE
Silverpine Forest (68), F-7, Shadowfang
Keep

BARON VARDUS
Alterac Mountains (8), H-4, Strahnbrad,
Basement of inn

BARONESS ANASTARI
Eastern Plaguelands (40), D-2,
Stratholme

BAROS ALEXSTON
City Architect, Stormwind (72), G-3,
Cathedral Square, City Hall

BAROS ALEXSTON
Stormwind (72), F-6, The Stockade

BARRENS GIRAFFE
Barrens (18), D:(2, 3), E:(2-5),
F:(1, 2, 4, 5), G:(1-5), H:(1-3)

BARRENS GUARD
Barrens (18), D-3, E-1, F-1, Gold Road,
Honor's Stand, The Mor'shan Rampart

BARRENS KODO
Barrens (18), E:(5, 6, 8)

BART TIDEWATER
Captain of the Maiden's Virtue,
Wetlands (96), A-6, Menethil Harbor
(119), Roams path next to docks and
along docks

BARTENDER LILLIAN
Barkeeper, Dustwallow Marsh (38), I-5,
Theramore Isle (135), Inn

BARTENDER WENTAL
Food and Drinks, Redridge Mountains
(62), C-4, Lakeshire (117), First floor of
Lakeshire Inn

BARTLEBY
Drunk, Stormwind (72), K-4, Old Town,
Roams Old Town to the Pig and Whistle
Tavern

BARTOLO GINSETTI
Hillsbrad Foothills (48), F-5, Southshore
(129), In front of house

BASHANA RUNETOTEM
Thunder Bluff (84), I-3, Elder Rise,
Inside tent near bridge

BASIL FRYE
Journeyman Blacksmith, Undercity (88),
H-3, The War Quarter

BATH'RAH THE WINDWATCHER
Alterac Mountains (8), K-7, Chillwind
Point, Troll platform

BATTLE BOAR HORROR
Barrens (18), F-9, Razorfen Downs

BATTLEBOAR
Mulgore (58), F:(7, 8), G:(7-9),
Brambleblade Ravine

BAYNE
Rare Spawn, Tirisfal Glades (86),
E:(4, 5), F-5, G-4, Stillwater Pond, Lvl
10 Uncommon; Roams small area
around spawn point

BAZIL THREDD
Stormwind (72), F-6, The Stockade

BAZZALAN
Orgrimmar (60), F-5, Ragefire Chasm

BEATEN CORPSE
Barrens (18), F-5, Southern Barrens, Hu
south of ravine

BEETIX FICKLESPRAGG
Silithus (67), G-4, Cenarion Hold (106)

BEFOULED WATER ELEMENTAL
Ashenvale (12), F:(6, 7), G:(6, 7),
Mystral Lake, Silverwind Refuge

BEKA ZIPWHISTLE
Arena Battlemaster, Stormwind (72),
L-1

BELDIN STEELGRILL
Dun Morogh (32), G-5, Steelgrill's
Depot, Outside of left building

BELDRUK DOOMBROW
Paladin Trainer, Ironforge (52), C-1, The
Mystic Ward, Hall of Mysteries

BELFRY BAT
Tirisfal Glades (86), H-5, Brill (104)

BELGROM ROCKMAUL
Orgrimmar (60), I-3, J-3, Valley of
Honor, Hall of the Brave

BELIA THUNDERGRANITE
Pet Trainer, Ironforge (52), J-8, The
Military Ward, Hall of Arms

BELLYGRUB
Redridge Mountains (62), A-5, Roams
on western side of Lake Everstill

BELNISTRASZ
Barrens (18), F-9, Razorfen Downs

BEN TRIAS
Apprentice of Cheese, Stormwind (72),
I-6, Trade District, Trias' Cheese

BENA WINTERHOOF
Alchemist Trainer, Thunder Bluff (84),
E-3, Middle rise, inside Bena's Alchemy
tent

BENGOR
Swamp of Sorrows (76), F-5, Stonard
(131), First floor of inn

BENGUS DEEPFORGE
Artisan Blacksmith, Ironforge (52), G-4,
The Great Forge, Next to anvils

BENIJAH FENNER
Weapon Merchant, Undercity (88), H-3
The War Quarter

BENJAMIN CAREVIN
Duskwood (36), J-5, Darkshire (108),
Second floor of house

BENNY BLAANCO
Westfall (94), E-2, Furlbrow's Pumpkin
Farm, In the house north of the
pumpkin farm

BERA STONEHAMMER
Gryphon Master, Tanaris (78), H-3,
Gadgetzan (113), South of town

BERAM SKYCHASER
Shaman Trainer, Thunder Bluff (84), B-2
Spirit Rise, Inside Hall of Spirits

BERNARD BRUBAKER
Leather Armor Merchant, Redridge
Mountains (62), L-7, Camp

BERNARD GUMP
Florist, Stormwind (72), J-6, The Canals
Fragrant Flowers

BERNIE HEISTEN
Food & Drink, Blasted Lands (20), I-2,
Nethergarde Keep (120), First floor of
left castle

BERSERK OWLBEAST
Winterspring (98), I:(2, 6), J:(2, 6), The
Hidden Grove, Owl Wing Thicket

BERSERK TROGG
Loch Modan (54), I:(6, 7), J:(6, 7),
Ironband's Excavation Site

BESSANY PLAINSWIND
Moonglade (56), G-3, Nighthaven (121), North central side of town, north of moonwell

BESSELETH
Stonetalon Mountains (70), F-7, G-7, Sishir Canyon, Roams area west of path

BETHAINE FLINTHAMMER
Stable Master, Wetlands (96), A-6, Menethil Harbor (119), Outside tavern

BETHAN BLUEWATER
Feralas (46), C-4, Feathermoon Stronghold (111), Top floor of tree building in northeast

BETHOR ICESHARD
Undercity (88), L-2, The Magic Quarter, On Skull Building

BETINA BIGGLEZINK
The Argent Dawn, Eastern Plaguelands (40), K-6, Light's Hope Chapel (118), Roams camp on right side of chapel

BETTY QUIN
Journeyman Enchanter, Stormwind (72), F-6, The Canals, Shop south of stockade

BHAG'THERA
Stranglethorn Vale (74), E:(2, 3), F-2, Mosh'Ogg Ogre Mound, Roams small area around spawn point

BHALDARAN RAVENHADE
Bowyer, Ashenvale (12), F-7, Silverwind Refuge, Center of building

BIBBLY F'UTZBUCKLE
Desolace (30), H-4, Kormek's Hut, Fenced area left of hut

BIBILFAZ FEATHERWHISTLE
Gryphon Master, Western Plaguelands (92), E-8, Chillwind Camp (107), Just south of camp

BIG SAMRAS
Rare Spawn, Hillsbrad Foothills (48), I-3, K:(4, 5), Durnholde Keep, Lvl 27 Semi-Rare; Roams small area around spawn point

BIG WILL
Barrens (18), H-5, Fray Island, (Summon) Fighting pit

BIJOU
Burning Steppes (22), Searing Gorge (64), C-4/D-8, Blackrock Spire

BILBAN TOSSLESPANNER
Warrior Trainer, Ironforge (52), I-9, The Military Ward, Hall of Arms

BILE SLIME
Eastern Plaguelands (40), D-2, Stratholme

BILE SPEWER
Eastern Plaguelands (40), D-2, Stratholme

BILLIBUB COGSPINNER
Engineering Supplier, Stormwind (72), H-1, Dwarven District, North end of district, next to wagon

BILLY
Stormwind (72), Roams city

BILLY MACLURE
Elwynn Forest (42), F-8, The Maclure Vineyards, In front of barn

BIMBLE LONGBERRY
Fruit Vendor, Ironforge (52), E-1, C-3, The Mystic Ward, Roams the ward

BINGLES BLASTENHEIMER
Loch Modan (54), H-5, The Loch, Along the banks of the loch half way down the right side

BINGUS
Weapon Merchant, Ironforge (52), C-2, The Mystic Ward, The Fighting Wizard

BINJY FEATHERWHISTLE
Mechanostrider Pilot, Dun Morogh (32), G-5, Steelgrill's Depot, By mechanostrider's outside of depot

BINK
Mage Trainer, Ironforge (52), C-1, The Mystic Ward, Hall of Mysteries

BINNY SPRINGBLADE
Gnomeregan Exiles, Ironforge (52), F-1, The Forlorn Cavern, Stoneblade's

BIP NIGSTROM
Arena Organizer, Tanaris (78), G-3, Gadgetzan (113)

BIRGITTE CRANSTON
Portal Trainer, Thunder Bluff (85), A-2

BISHOP DELAVEY
Stormwind (72), K-2, L-2, Stormwind Keep, East wing, in south room

BISHOP FARTHING
Stormwind (72), F-2, Cathedral Square, Cathedral of Light

BIXI WOBBLEBONK
Weapon Master, Ironforge (52), H-9, The Military Ward, Timberline Arms, Trains: Crossbows, Daggers, & Throwing Weapons

BJARN
Rare Spawn, Dun Morogh (32), G-6, H-6, I-6, The Tundrid Hills, Lvl 12 Uncommon; Roams small area around spawn point

BLACK BEAR PATRIARCH
Loch Modan (54), E-6, H-3, I:(3, 4), J-4, K-4, The Farstrider Lodge (111), Below Lodge

BLACK BROODLING
Burning Steppes (22), J:(3, 6), K:(2, 3, 5, 6), L:(3-6), Terror Wing Path

BLACK DRAGON WHELP
Redridge Mountains (62), B-7, C:(3, 6-8), D:(6, 7), E:(3, 7), F:(3, 4, 7, 8), G:(4, 7), H:(7, 8), I-7

BLACK DRAGONSPAWN
Burning Steppes (22), G-6, J-6, K:(3, 4), L:(4-6), The Pillar of Ash

BLACK DRAKE
Burning Steppes (22), K:(3, 6), L-4, Terror Wing Path

BLACK GUARD SENTRY
Eastern Plaguelands (40), D-2, Stratholme

BLACK GUARD SWORDSMITH
Eastern Plaguelands (40), D-2, Stratholme

BLACK OOZE
Wetlands (96), C:(5, 6), D-5, F:(2, 3), G-3, H:(3, 4), I:(4, 5)

BLACK RAVAGER
Duskwood (36), G:(5, 6), H-6, I-3, J-4, Brightwood Grove

BLACK RAVAGER MASTIFF
Duskwood (36), G:(5, 6), H-6, I:(3-4), Brightwood Grove

BLACK SLAYER
Blasted Lands (20), G-2, H-4, I:(3, 4), Dreadmaul Hold, Rise of the Defiler, Serpent's Coil

BLACK SLIME
Wetlands (96), G:(5-8), H:(6-8), I-6

BLACK WIDOW HATCHLING
Duskwood (36), C:(4, 5), D:(3-6), E:(3, 5, 6), K:(5, 6), L:(5, 6)

BLACK WYRMKIN
Burning Steppes (22), G-6, J-6, K:(3, 4), L:(4-6), Terror Wing Path

BLACKBREATH CRONY
Burning Steppes (22), Searing Gorge (64), C-4/D-8, Blackrock Depths

BLACKENED BASILISK
Stonetalon Mountains (70), D:(5, 6), E-5, F-4, The Charred Vale, Mirkfallon Lake

BLACKFATHOM MYRMIDON
Ashenvale (12), B-2, Blackfathom Deeps

BLACKFATHOM ORACLE
Ashenvale (12), B-2, Blackfathom Deeps

BLACKFATHOM SEA WITCH
Ashenvale (12), B-2, Blackfathom Deeps

BLACKFATHOM TIDE PRIESTESS
Ashenvale (12), B-2, Blackfathom Deeps

BLACKHAND ASSASSIN
Burning Steppes (22), Searing Gorge (64), C-4/D-8, Blackrock Spire

BLACKHAND DRAGON HANDLER
Burning Steppes (22), Searing Gorge (64), C-4/D-8, Blackrock Spire

BLACKHAND DREADWEAVER
Burning Steppes (22), Searing Gorge (64), C-4/D-8, Blackrock Spire

BLACKHAND ELITE
Burning Steppes (22), Searing Gorge (64), C-4/D-8, Blackrock Spire

BLACKHAND INCARCERATOR
Burning Steppes (22), Searing Gorge (64), C-4/D-8, Blackrock Spire

BLACKHAND IRON GUARD
Burning Steppes (22), Searing Gorge (64), C-4/D-8, Blackrock Spire

BLACKHAND SUMMONER
Burning Steppes (22), Searing Gorge (64), C-4/D-8, Blackrock Spire

BLACKHAND THUG
Burning Steppes (22), Searing Gorge (64), C-4/D-8, Blackrock Spire

BLACKHAND VETERAN
Burning Steppes (22), Searing Gorge (64), C-4/D-8, Blackrock Spire

BLACKLASH
Badlands (16), L-5, Lethlor Ravine, (Summon) Altar protected by Scorched Guardians

BLACKMOSS THE FETID
Rare Spawn, Teldrassil (80), E:(3-4), Wellspring River, Lvl 13 Uncommon; Patrols up and down river

BLACKROCK AMBUSHER
Burning Steppes (22), B:(2, 3), C-5, E-4, Blackrock Stronghold

BLACKROCK ASSASSIN
Redridge Mountains (62), F-4, G-4, Ilgalar

BLACKROCK BATTLEMASTER
Burning Steppes (22), D:(3, 4), E:(3, 4), Blackrock Stronghold

BLACKROCK CHAMPION
Redridge Mountains (62), D-1, Render's Rock, Cave

BLACKROCK CHAMPION
Burning Steppes (22), H:(8, 9), I:(8, 9), Blackrock Pass

BLACKROCK GLADIATOR
Redridge Mountains (62), I:(5, 6), Stonewatch Keep

BLACKROCK GRUNT
Redridge Mountains (62), E-4, F-4, H-4, I:(7, 8), J:(7, 8), Stonewatch Keep

BLACKROCK HUNTER
Redridge Mountains (62), I:(5, 6), Stonewatch Keep

BLACKROCK OUTRUNNER
Redridge Mountains (62), E:(1, 2, 4), F:(2, 4), H:(4, 7), I:(6-8), J:(6-8), K:(6, 7), Render's Rock

BLACKROCK OUTRUNNER
Burning Steppes (22), J-9

BLACKROCK RAIDER
Burning Steppes (22), B-3, E-4, Blackrock Stronghold

BLACKROCK RENEGADE
Redridge Mountains (62), E:(1, 2), F:(1, 2), H:(4, 7), I-6, J:(6, 7), K-7, Render's Camp

BLACKROCK RENEGADE
Burning Steppes (22), I-9, J-9

BLACKROCK SCOUT
Redridge Mountains (62), H:(5, 6), I:(5, 6), Stonewatch Keep

BLACKROCK SENTRY
Redridge Mountains (62), H:(5, 6), I:(5, 6), Stonewatch Keep

BLACKROCK SHADOWCASTER
Redridge Mountains (62), H-5, I:(5, 6), Stonewatch Keep

BLACKROCK SLAYER
Burning Steppes (22), B-3, D:(3-5), E:(3-6), F:(5, 6), G-5, The Pillar of Ash

BLACKROCK SOLDIER
Burning Steppes (22), B-3, D-5, E:(5, 6), F:(5, 6), G-5, The Pillar of Ash

BLACKROCK SORCERER
Burning Steppes (22), D:(3-5), E:(3-6), F:(5, 6), G-5, The Pillar of Ash

BLACKROCK SUMMONER
Redridge Mountains (62), D-1, E-1, F-1, H-4, J-8, Render's Rock, Cave

BLACKROCK SUMMONER
Burning Steppes (22), H:(8, 9), I:(8, 9), J-9, Blackrock Pass

BLACKROCK TRACKER
Redridge Mountains (62), D-1, E-1, Render's Rock, Cave

BLACKROCK TRACKER
Burning Steppes (22), H:(8, 9), I:(8, 9), J-9, Blackrock Pass

BLACKROCK WARLOCK
Burning Steppes (22), A-3, D:(3, 4), E:(3, 4), F:(5, 6), G-5, The Pillar of Ash

BLACKROCK WORG
Burning Steppes (22), B-3, D-5, E-6, F:(5, 6), G-5, The Pillar of Ash

BLACKSMITH RAND
Apprentice Armorer, Tirisfal Glades (86), D-7, Deathknell (109), First house on right side of road

BLACKSMITH VERRINGTON
Hillsbrad Foothills (48), C-5, Hillsbrad Fields (115), Stands idle in or around smithy

BLACKWATER DECKHAND
Arathi Highlands (10), D-8, Faldir's Cove

BLACKWOOD PATHFINDER
Darkshore (24), F:(5, 6), The Long Wash, Twilight Shore, Twilight Vale

BLACKWOOD SHAMAN
Darkshore (24), F:(8, 9), G:(8, 9), Blackwood Den, The Master's Glaive, Twilight Vale

BLACKWOOD TOTEMIC
Darkshore (24), F:(8, 9), G-9, H-3

BLACKWOOD URSA
Darkshore (24), F:(8, 9), G:(8, 9), Blackwood Den, Grove of the Ancients, Twilight Vale

BLACKWOOD WARRIOR
Darkshore (24), F:(8, 9), G-3, H:(3, 4)

BLACKWOOD WINDTALKER
Darkshore (24), F:(5, 6), The Long Wash, Twilight Vale

BLAISE MONTGOMERY
Feralas (46), I-4, Camp Mojache (105), Northeast of inn

BLASTMASTER EMI SHORTFUSE
Dun Morogh (32), C-4, Gnomeregan

BLAZERUNNER
Un'Goro Crater (90), G-5, Fire Plume Ridge, West den on ridge

BLAZING ELEMENTAL
Searing Gorge (64), E:(3-5), F-5, G:(4, 5, 8), The Cauldron

BLAZING FIREGUARD
Burning Steppes (22), Searing Gorge (64), C-4/D-8, Blackrock Depths

BLAZING INVADER
Un'Goro Crater (90), F:(4-6), G:(4-6), Fire Plume Ridge

BLEAK WORG
Silverpine Forest (68), F-7, Shadowfang Keep

BLEAKHEART HELLCALLER
Ashenvale (12), J-5, K-5, Forest Song, Nightsong Woods, Satyrnaar

BLEAKHEART SATYR
Ashenvale (12), J-5, K-5, Forest Song, Nightsong Woods, Satyrnaar

BLEAKHEART SHADOWSTALKER
Ashenvale (12), J-5, Nightsong Woods, Satyrnaar, Xavian

BLEAKHEART TRICKSTER
Ashenvale (12), J-5, Nightsong Woods, Satyrnaar, Xavian

BLEEDING HORROR
Tirisfal Glades (86), J-6, K-6, Balnir Farmstead

BLIGHTED HORROR
Eastern Plaguelands (40), G-5, I:(3, 4), J-4, Blackwood Lake

BLIGHTED SURGE
Eastern Plaguelands (40), H:(7, 8), I:(7, 8), Lake Mereldar

BLIGHTED ZOMBIE
Western Plaguelands (92), F:(5, 6), Dalson's Tears

BLIGHTHOUND
Eastern Plaguelands (40), D-7, The Marris Stead

BLIMO GADGETSPRING
Trade Supplier, Azshara (14), E-9, The Ruined Reaches, Gnome tower

BLIND HUNTER
Rare Spawn, Barrens (18), E-9, Razorfen Kraul, Lvl 32 Rare

BLIND MARY
Duskwood (36), K-6, Inside house

BLINDLIGHT MUCKDWELLER
Ashenvale (12), B-2, Blackfathom Deeps

BLINDLIGHT MURLOC
Ashenvale (12), B-2, Blackfathom Deeps

BLINDLIGHT ORACLE
Ashenvale (12), B-2, Blackfathom Deeps

BLINK DRAGON
Ashenvale (12), G-5, H:(5, 7), Moonwell, Nightsong Woods, Raynewood Retreat

BLISTERPAW HYENA
Tanaris (78), E:(4, 5), F:(3-6), G:(3-6), H:(4-6), I:(4-6)

BLIXREZ GOODSTITCH
Leatherworking Supplies, Stranglethorn Vale (74), B-8, Booty Bay (103), Tan-Your-Hide Leatherworks (shop)

BLIXXRAK
Light Armor Merchant, Winterspring (98), I-4, Everlook (110), Inside northeast building

BLIZRIK BUCKSHOT
Gunsmith, Tanaris (78), G-3, Gadgetzan (113), Western structure

BLIZTIK
Alchemy Supplies Vendor, Duskwood (36), B-5, Raven Hill (123), Second floor of house

BLOOD ELF DEFENDER
Azshara (14), H-3, Thalassian Base Camp

BLOOD ELF RECLAIMER
Azshara (14), G-3, Thalassian Base Camp

BLOOD ELF SURVEYOR
Azshara (14), G-3, Thalassian Base Camp

BLOOD OF AGAMAGGAN
Barrens (18), E-9, Razorfen Kraul

BLOOD SEEKER
Silverpine Forest (68), F-7, Shadowfang Keep

BLOODAXE EVOKER
Burning Steppes (22), Searing Gorge (64), C-4/D-8, Blackrock Spire

BLOODAXE RAIDER
Burning Steppes (22), Searing Gorge (64), C-4/D-8, Blackrock Spire

BLOODAXE SUMMONER
Burning Steppes (22), Searing Gorge (64), C-4/D-8, Blackrock Spire

BLOODAXE VETERAN
Burning Steppes (22), Searing Gorge (64), C-4/D-8, Blackrock Spire

BLOODAXE WARMONGER
Burning Steppes (22), Searing Gorge (64), C-4/D-8, Blackrock Spire

BLOODAXE WORG
Burning Steppes (22), Searing Gorge (64), C-4/D-8, Blackrock Spire

BLOODAXE WORG PUP
Burning Steppes (22), Searing Gorge (64), C-4/D-8, Blackrock Spire

BLOODFEATHER FURY
Teldrassil (80), C-3, D-3, The Oracle Glade

BLOODFEATHER HARPY
Teldrassil (80), D:(3, 4), E-4, The Oracle Glade

BLOODFEATHER MATRIARCH
Teldrassil (80), C-3, D-3, The Oracle Glade

BLOODFEATHER ROGUE
Teldrassil (80), D:(3, 4), E-4, The Oracle Glade

BLOODFEATHER SORCERESS
Teldrassil (80), D:(3, 4), E-4, The Oracle Glade

BLOODFEATHER WIND WITCH
Teldrassil (80), C-3, D-3, The Oracle Glade

BLOODFEN LASHTAIL
Dustwallow Marsh (38), D:(6, 7), E-7, Bloodfen Burrow

BLOODFEN RAPTOR
Dustwallow Marsh (38), D:(1, 3), E:(1-3), F:(1-3), G:(1-4), H:(2-4)

BLOODFEN RAZORMAW
Dustwallow Marsh (38), D:(6, 7), E-7, Bloodfen Burrow

BLOODFEN SCREECHER
Dustwallow Marsh (38), F:(1, 2), Bluefen

BLOODFEN SCYTHECLAW
Dustwallow Marsh (38), D:(4-6), E:(3-6), F:(3-6), The Dragonmurk, Lost Point, The Quagmire

BLOODFURY AMBUSHER
Stonetalon Mountains (70), D-6, The Charred Vale

BLOODFURY HARPY
Stonetalon Mountains (70), D-6, E-5, The Charred Vale

BLOODFURY RIPPER
Stonetalon Mountains (70), C-6, The Charred Vale, Roams northwest area of Charred Vale

BLOODFURY ROGUEFEATHER
Stonetalon Mountains (70), C:(6, 7), D:(6, 7), E:(6, 7), The Charred Vale

BLOODFURY SLAYER
Stonetalon Mountains (70), C:(6, 7), D:(6, 7), E:(6, 7), The Charred Vale

BLOODFURY STORM WITCH
Stonetalon Mountains (70), C:(6, 7), D:(6, 7), E:(6, 7), The Charred Vale

BLOODFURY WINDCALLER
Stonetalon Mountains (70), D-6, The Charred Vale

BLOODHOUND
Burning Steppes (22), Searing Gorge (64), C-4/D-8, Blackrock Depths

B
MAIN INDEX

BLOODHOUND MASTIFF
Burning Steppes (22), Searing Gorge (64), C-4/D-8, Blackrock Depths

BLOODLETTER
Eastern Plaguelands (40), E-8, Carrowshire

BLOODMAGE DRAZIAL
Blasted Lands (20), G-1, Dreadmaul Hold, Next to bonfire

BLOODMAGE LYNNORE
Blasted Lands (20), G-1, Dreadmaul Hold, Next to bonfire

BLOODMAGE THALNOS
Tirisfal Glades (86), K-3, L-3, Scarlet Monastery

BLOODPETAL FLAYER
Un'Goro Crater (90), F:(3, 4, 6, 7), G:(2-4, 6, 7), G:(2-4, 6-8), H:(2-8), I-4

BLOODPETAL LASHER
Un'Goro Crater (90), G-4, H:(3, 4), I:(2-4), J:(3-5, 7), Lakkari Tar Pits, The Marshlands

BLOODPETAL PEST
Un'Goro Crater (90), F-1, Marshal's Refuge (118)

BLOODPETAL THRESHER
Un'Goro Crater (90), G-4, H:(3, 4), I:(2-4), J:(3-5, 7), Lakkari Tar Pits, The Marshlands

BLOODPETAL TRAPPER
Un'Goro Crater (90), C:(4-7), D:(2-8), E:(2-8)

BLOODROAR THE STALKER
Feralas (46), F-6, Feral Scar Vale, In second set of caves

BLOODSAIL DECKHAND
Stranglethorn Vale (74), C-9, Wild Shore

BLOODSAIL ELDER MAGUS
Stranglethorn Vale (74), C-6, The Cape of Stranglethorn, Wild Shore

BLOODSAIL MAGE
Stranglethorn Vale (74), B-7, C:(7, 8)

BLOODSAIL RAIDER
Stranglethorn Vale (74), B-7, C:(7, 8)

BLOODSAIL SEA DOG
Stranglethorn Vale (74), C-6, The Cape of Stranglethorn, Wild Shore

BLOODSAIL SWABBY
Stranglethorn Vale (74), C-9, Wild Shore

BLOODSAIL SWASHBUCKLER
Stranglethorn Vale (74), B:(6, 8, 9), C:(8, 9)

BLOODSAIL WARLOCK
Stranglethorn Vale (74), B:(6, 8, 9), C:(8, 9)

BLOODSCALP AXE THROWER
Stranglethorn Vale (74), B-2, C-2, Bal'lal Ruins, The Savage Coast, Tkashi Ruins

BLOODSCALP BEASTMASTER
Stranglethorn Vale (74), B:(1, 2), Ruins of Zul'Kunda

BLOODSCALP BERSERKER
Stranglethorn Vale (74), A:(1, 2), B-1

BLOODSCALP HEADHUNTER
Stranglethorn Vale (74), A:(1, 2), B-1

BLOODSCALP HUNTER
Stranglethorn Vale (74), A-2, B:(1, 2), Ruins of Zul'Kunda

BLOODSCALP MYSTIC
Stranglethorn Vale (74), A-2, B:(1, 2), Ruins of Zul'Kunda

BLOODSCALP SCAVENGER
Stranglethorn Vale (74), C-2, Tkashi Ruins

BLOODSCALP SCOUT
Stranglethorn Vale (74), A-2, B:(1, 2), Ruins of Zul'Kunda

BLOODSCALP SHAMAN
Stranglethorn Vale (74), B-2, C-2, Bal'lal Ruins, The Savage Coast, Tkashi Ruins

BLOODSCALP WARRIOR
Stranglethorn Vale (74), B-2, C-2

BLOODSCALP WITCH DOCTOR
Stranglethorn Vale (74), A:(1, 2), B-1, Ruins of Zul'Kunda, Zuuldaia Ruins

BLOODSNOUT WORG
Silverpine Forest (68), G:(7, 8), H:(7, 8), The Greymane Wall

BLOODTALON SCYTHEMAW
Durotar (34), E:(2-5), F:(2-5), H:(1, 2)

BLOODTALON TAILLASHER
Durotar (34), F:(3-5), G:(2-5), H:(2-4), I:(2, 3, 7-9), J:(7-9)

BLOODTOOTH GUARD
Ashenvale (12), G-7, Bloodtooth Camp, Mystral Lake

Bloodvenom Post (102) BRAVE
Felwood (44), E-5, Bloodvenom Post (102)

BLUE DRAGONSPAWN
Azshara (14), D:(7, 8), E-8, Forlorn Ridge, Lake Mennar

BLUE SCALEBANE
Azshara (14), E:(7, 8), Lake Mennar

BLUEGILL FORAGER
Wetlands (96), B:(3, 4), C-4, Bluegill Marsh

BLUEGILL MUCKDWELLER
Wetlands (96), A-3, B:(3, 4), C:(3, 4), Bluegill Marsh

BLUEGILL MURLOC
Wetlands (96), A-4, B-4, C-4, Bluegill Marsh

BLUEGILL ORACLE
Wetlands (96), B:(3, 4), Bluegill Marsh

BLUEGILL PUDDLEJUMPER
Wetlands (96), A-4, B:(3, 4), Bluegill Marsh

BLUEGILL RAIDER
Wetlands (96), A:(6, 7), B:(2, 6), C-2, D:(1, 2), Bluegill Marsh

BLUEGILL WARRIOR
Wetlands (96), A:(2, 3), B:(2-4), C-4, Bluegill Marsh

BLUFF RUNNER WINDSTRIDER
Thunder Bluff (84), D-6, Roams all around the rises

BLUFF WATCHERS
Thunder Bluff (84)

BOAHN
Barrens (18), E-4, Wailing Caverns

BOAR SPIRIT
Barrens (18), E-9, Razorfen Kraul

BOGLING
Teldrassil (80), H-7, Lake Al'Ameth, Spawns east of lake next to camp

BOILING ELEMENTAL
Thousand Needles (82), D:(3, 4), E-4, Darkcloud Pinnacle

BOLYUN
Pet Trainer, Ashenvale (12), C-6, Shrine of Aessina, Hidden in a camp near mountains in far southwest of region

BOM'BAY
Witch Doctor in Training, Durotar (34), H-8, Sen'jin Village (126), South side of pond

BOMBUS FINESPINDLE
Leatherworking Supplies, Ironforge (52), E-3, The Great Forge, Finespindle's Leather Goods

BONE CHEWER
Duskwood (36), B-3, C:(3, 4), Raven Hill Cemetery (123)

BONEFLAYER GHOUL
Barrens (18), F-9, Razorfen Downs

BONEPAW HYENA
Desolace (30), E-7, F-7, G-3, H-4, Ethel Rethor, Sar'theris Strand

BOOKIE HEROD
Stranglethorn Vale (74), E:(1, 2), Kurzen's Compound, Roams a small area around spawn point

BOR WILDMANE
Silithus (67), G-5, Cenarion Hold (106)

BORAN IRONCLINK
Armorer, Dun Morogh (32), F-5, Kharanos (116), Smithy

BORAND
Bowyer, Stonetalon Mountains (70), E-6, Sun Rock Retreat (132), South of western structure

BORELGORE
Eastern Plaguelands (40), G-3, Patrols ravines by spawn point

BORER BEETLE
Burning Steppes (22), Searing Gorge (64), C-4/D-8, Blackrock Depths

BORGOSH COREBENDER
Weaponsmith, Orgrimmar (60), J-2, Valley of Honor, Across from Arms of Legend

BORGUS STEELHAND
Weapon Crafter, Stormwind (72), H-1, Dwarven District, Northwest building

BORGUS STOUTARM
Gryphon Master, Burning Steppes (22), K-7, Morgan's Vigil (120), Camp

BORSTAN
Meat Vendor, Orgrimmar (60), G-5, The Drag, Borstan's Firepit

BORYA
Tailoring Supplies, Orgrimmar (60), H-5, The Drag, Magar's Cloth Goods

BOR'ZEHN
Thousand Needles (82), I-6, Ironstone Camp, Camp just west of Shimmering Flats

BOSS COPPERPLUG
Barrens (18), G-1, H-1, Boulder Lode Mine, Southern cave in mine

BOSS GALGOSH
Rare Spawn, Loch Modan (54), I-6, Ironband's Excavation Site, Lvl 22 Uncommon; On excavation platform with a Stonesplitter Geomancer and Berserk Trogg

BOSS THO'GRUN
Badlands (16), I-7, Camp Boff, Patrols with entourage to Camp Wurg (D-6) and Camp Cagg (B-7)

BOULDERFIST BRUTE
Arathi Highlands (10), G:(7, 8), H-7, Boulderfist Hall

BOULDERFIST ENFORCER
Arathi Highlands (10), D:(4, 5), E-4, Boulderfist Outpost

BOULDERFIST LORD
Arathi Highlands (10), B:(6, 7), Boulderfist Hall

BOULDERFIST MAGUS
Arathi Highlands (10), G:(7, 8), Boulderfist Hall

BOULDERFIST MAULER
Arathi Highlands (10), B-7, C:(6, 7), Boulderfist Hall

BOULDERFIST OGRE
Arathi Highlands (10), D:(4, 5), E:(4, 5), Boulderfist Hall

BOULDERFIST SHAMAN
Arathi Highlands (10), B:(6, 7), C:(6, 7), Boulderfist Hall

BOULDERHEART
Rare Spawn, Redridge Mountains (62), L-6, Lvl 25 Semi-Rare; Roams small area around spawn point

BOUNTY HUNTER KOLARK
Orgrimmar (60), I-2, J-2, Valley of Honor, Roamer

BOWEN BRISBOISE
Journeyman Tailor, Tirisfal Glades (86), G-5, Cold Hearth Manor, House on northwestern edge of manor

BOYLE
Undercity (88), G-6, The Apothecarium, On dock near Royal Quarter

BRACK
Rare Spawn, Westfall (94), C-8, Longshore, Lvl 19 Uncommon; Runs entire Longshore coast

BRACKENWALL ENFORCER
Dustwallow Marsh (38), D-3, E-3, Brackenwall Village (104)

BRAELYN FIREHAND
Stonetalon Mountains (70), E-6, Sun Rock Retreat (132), Southeast of western structure, next to water

BRAENNA FLINTCRAG
Priest Trainer, Ironforge (52), C-1, The Mystic Ward, Hall of Mysteries

BRAGOK
Flight Master, Barrens (18), H-4, Ratchet (122)

BRAHNMAR
Armorer, Wetlands (96), A-6, Menethil Harbor (119), Building northeast of tavern

BRAIN EATER
Duskwood (36), B-3, C:(3, 4), Raven Hill Cemetery (123)

BRAINWASHED NOBLE
Westfall (94), D-7, E-7, The Deadmines

BRAK DURNAD
Weaponsmith, Wetlands (96), A-6, Menethil Harbor (119), Building northeast of tavern

BRAKGUL DEATHBRINGER
Warsong Gulch Battlemaster, Orgrimmar (60), J-3, Valley of Honor

BRAKKAR
Wind Rider Master, Felwood (44), E-5, Bloodvenom Post (102), Up hill

BRANCH SNAPPER
Ashenvale (12), F:(4-5), Iris Lake, Circles Iris Lake

BRANDON
Stormwind (72), H-3, The Canals, Dock

BRANDUR IRONHAMMER
Paladin Trainer, Ironforge (52), C-1, The Mystic Ward, Hall of Mysteries

BRANNOCK
Fisherman, Feralas (46), C-4, Feathermoon Stronghold (111), Next to water, northeast of the inn

BRANNOL EAGLEMOON
Clothier, Teldrassil (80), G-6, Dolanaar (109), Inn

BRANSTOCK KHALDER
Priest Trainer, Dun Morogh (32), D-7, Coldridge Valley (107), Anvilmar

BRANT JASPERBLOOM
Herbalist, Dustwallow Marsh (38), H-5, Theramore Isle (135), Hut in west corner

BRAUG DIMSPIRIT
Stonetalon Mountains (70), E-7, Talondeep Path, Just south of the Talondeep Path entrance.

BRAVE CLOUDMANE
Mulgore (58), E-6, Bloodhoof Village (102), Patrols village

BRAVE DARKSKY
Mulgore (58), E-5, Patrols road north of village

BRAVE DAWNEAGLE
Mulgore (58), F-6, Patrols road east of village

BRAVE GREATHOOF
Mulgore (58), E-8, Camp Narache (105), Patrols camp

BRAVE IRONHORN
Mulgore (58), E-6, Bloodhoof Village (102), Patrols village

BRAVE LEAPING DEER
Mulgore (58), F-6, Patrols road east of village

BRAVE LIGHTNINGHORN
Mulgore (58), E-8, Red Cloud Mesa, Patrols east of camp

BRAVE MOONHORN
Thousand Needles (82), D-2, The Great Lift, Next to lift

BRAVE PROUDSNOUT
Mulgore (58), E-8, Camp Narache (105), Patrols camp

BRAVE RAINCHASER
Mulgore (58), E-6, Bloodhoof Village (102), Patrols village

BRAVE ROCKHORN
Mulgore (58), F-6, Patrols road east of village

BRAVE RUNNING WOLF
Mulgore (58), E-8, Camp Narache (105), Patrols camp

BRAVE STONEHIDE
Officer Accessories QM, Orgrimmar (61), E-7

BRAVE STRONGBASH
Mulgore (58), E-6, Bloodhoof Village (102), Patrols village

BRAVE SWIFTWIND
Mulgore (58), F-6, Bloodhoof Village (102), Patrols village

BRAVE WILDRUNNER
Mulgore (58), E-6, Bloodhoof Village (102), Patrols village

BRAVE WINDFEATHER
Mulgore (58), E-8, Camp Narache (105), Patrols camp

BRAWLER
Loch Modan (54), D-9, Stonesplinter Valley, Stand with Grawmug and Gnasher in center of cave

BRAWN
Leatherworking Trainer, Stranglethorn Vale (74), C-3, Grom'gol Base Camp (114), Next orcish carriage directly across from the eastern entrance into camp

BREK STONEHOOF
Mining Trainer, Thunder Bluff (84), C-6, Lower rise, inside Stonehoof Geology tent

BRENWYN WINTERSTEEL
Blade Merchant, Ironforge (52), H-9, The Military Ward, Timberline Arms

BRETTA GOLDFURY
Gun Merchant, Ironforge (52), J-6, The Military Ward, Goldfury's Hunting Supplies

BREWMASTER BILGER
Hillsbrad Foothills (48), F-6, Southshore (129), Basement of inn

BREWMASTER DROHN
Barrens (18), H-4, Ratchet (122), Outside Plate-n-Chain

BREYK
Wind Rider Master, Swamp of Sorrows (76), F-5, Stonard (131), Left of the inn

BRIARTHORN
Warlock Trainer, Ironforge (52), G-1, The Forlorn Cavern, Building to the right of Traveling Fisherman

BRIENNA STARGLOW
Tailoring Supplies, Feralas (46), K-5, Thalanaar, Hill northwest of well in stone structure

BRIGITTE CRANSTON
Portal Trainer, Thunder Bluff (84), C-3, Spirit Rise, The Pools of Vision

BRIKK KEENCRAFT
Master Blacksmith, Stranglethorn Vale (74), C-8, Booty Bay (103), Booty Bay Blacksmith (shop)

BRIMGORE
Dustwallow Marsh (38), F-8, Wyrmbog, Roams along the foothills northwest

BRINE
Barrens (18), E-8, Blackthorn Ridge, Hut on hill

BRINNA VALANAAR
Bowyer, Azshara (14), A-8, Talrendis Point

BRISTLEBACK BATTLEBOAR
Mulgore (58), G:(7-9), H-8, Brambleblade Ravine

BRISTLEBACK GEOMANCER
Barrens (18), D:(4, 5), E:(4, 5), F:(5, 6), Agama'gor, Bramblescar

BRISTLEBACK HUNTER
Barrens (18), D:(4, 5), E:(5, 6), F:(5, 6), Agama'gor, Bramblescar

BRISTLEBACK INTERLOPER
Mulgore (58), G-2, H-2, Red Rocks

BRISTLEBACK QUILBOAR
Mulgore (58), G:(7, 8), H-8, Brambleblade Ravine

BRISTLEBACK SHAMAN
Mulgore (58), G:(7, 8), H:(7, 8), Brambleblade Ravine

BRISTLEBACK THORNWEAVER
Barrens (18), E-5, F:(5, 6), Agama'gor, Bramblescar

BRISTLEBACK WATER SEEKER
Barrens (18), E-5, F:(5, 6), Agama'gor, Bramblescar

BRIVELTHWERP
Ice Cream Vendor, Thousand Needles (82), J-8, Mirage Raceway (119), Next to building west of racetrack

BROCK STONESEEKER
Mining Trainer, Loch Modan (54), E-5, Thelsamar (134), In second house on right of path

BROG HAMFIST
General Supplies, Elwynn Forest (42), F-7, Goldshire (114), First floor of Lion's Pride Inn

BROGG
Stonemaul Survivor, Dustwallow Marsh (38), F-7, Mudsprocket (120)

BROGUN STONESHIELD
Alterac Valley Battlemaster, Darnassus (26), H-4, Warrior's Terrace, Lower southwest platform

BROHANN CASKBELLY
Explorers' League, Stormwind (72), I-2, J-2, Dwarven District, Tavern

BROKEN CADAVER
Eastern Plaguelands (40), D-2, Stratholme

BROKEN TOOTH
Rare Spawn, Badlands (16), G-4, H-2, I-3, Angor Fortress, Dustwind Gulch, Lvl 37 Uncommon; Roams small area around spawn point

BROKESPEAR
Rare Spawn, Barrens (18), F:(4-5), G-4, The Stagnant Oasis, Lvl 17 Uncommon; Stays near spawn points

BRO'KIN
Alchemy Supplies, Alterac Mountains (8), E-4, Ruins of Alterac, Wall along northern side of ruins

BROM KILLIAN
Mining Trainer, Undercity (88), H-4, The War Quarter

BROMBAR HIGGLEBY
The Keymaster, Ironforge (52), G-4, The Great Forge, North of The Great Anvil

BROMIIR ORMSEN
Heavy Armor Merchant, Ironforge (52), D-6, The Commons, Ironforge Armory

BROMOS GRUMMNER
Paladin Trainer, Dun Morogh (32), D-7, Coldridge Valley (107), Anvilmar

BRONK
Alchemy Supplies, Feralas (46), I-4, Camp Mojache (105), East of bridge

BRONK GUZZLEGEAR
Journeyman Engineer, Dun Morogh (32), G-5, Steelgrill's Depot, Basement of right building

RONK STEELRAGE
Armorer & Shieldcrafter, Mulgore (58), E-8, Camp Narache (105), Southwest tent

RONT COLDCLEAVE
Butcher, Hillsbrad Foothills (48), F-6, Southshore (129), Small house right of path

RONTUS
Rare Spawn, Barrens (18), E-8, Blackthorn Ridge, Lvl 27 Average Rare; Spawns near center hut and roams ridge

ROOKE STONEBRAID
Mining Supplier, Stormwind (72), H-2, Dwarven District, Building north of west entrance

ROTHER ANTON
Scarlet Crusade Emissary, Desolace (30), I-1, Nijel's Point (121), Second floor of inn

ROTHER BENJAMIN
Priest Trainer, Stormwind (72), F-3, Cathedral Square, Cathedral of Light

ROTHER CASSIUS
Reagent Vendor, Stormwind (72), F-3, Cathedral Square, Cathedral of Light

ROTHER CROWLEY
Scarlet Crusade Emissary, Stormwind (72), F-3, Cathedral Square, Cathedral of Light

ROTHER DANIL
General Supplies, Elwynn Forest (42), F-4, Northshire Valley (122), Caravan facing abbey

ROTHER JOSHUA
Priest Trainer, Stormwind (72), F-3, Cathedral Square, Cathedral of Light

ROTHER KARMAN
Paladin Trainer, Dustwallow Marsh (38), I-5, Theramore Isle (135), Outside Foothold Citadel

ROTHER KRISTOFF
Stormwind (72), G-4, Cathedral Square, By Fountain

ROTHER MALACH
Undercity (88), G-2, The War Quarter, Watches fights in War Quarter

ROTHER NEALS
Elwynn Forest (42), G-4, Northshire Valley (122), Top floor of abbey

ROTHER NIMETZ
Stranglethorn Vale (74), D-1, Rebel Camp (124), Camp

ROTHER PAXTON
Elwynn Forest (42), G-4, Northshire Valley (122), Library Wing of abbey

ROTHER SAMMUEL
Paladin Trainer, Elwynn Forest (42), G-4, Northshire Valley (122), Hall of Arms of abbey

ROTHER SARNO
Stormwind (72), F-3, Cathedral Square, Cathedral of Light

ROTHER WILHELM
Paladin Trainer, Elwynn Forest (42), E-7, Goldshire (114), Rear entrance of smith

BRUEGAL IRONKNUCKLE
Rare Spawn, Stormwind (72), F-6, The Stockade, Lvl 26 Rare

BRUMERAN
Winterspring (98), I-6, Dun Mandarr, Roams north to The Ruins of Kel'Theril

BRUMN WINTERHOOF
Arathi Highlands (10), D-4, Small camp on hill

BRUTUS
Stranglethorn Vale (74), C-9, Wild Shore

BRUUK BARLEYBEARD
Bartender, Ironforge (52), J-7, The Military Ward, Bruuk's Corner

BRYAN CROSS
Shield Merchant, Stormwind (72), I-4, Old Town, The Silver Sheild

BRYLLIA IRONBRAND
General Good Vendor, Ironforge (52), E-7, The Commons, Fizzlespinner's General Goods

BUBULO ACERBUS
Alliance Cloth Quartermaster, Ironforge (52), J-5, Tinker Town, North of the tram entrance

BULIWYF STONEHAND
Weapon Master, Ironforge (52), H-9, The Military Ward, Timberline Arms, Trains: 1H Axe, 2H Axe, Fist, Guns, 1H Mace, & 2H Mace

BULKREK RAGEFIST
Wind Rider Master, Tanaris (78), H-3, Gadgetzan (113), North of town

BULRUG
Stable Master, Thunder Bluff (84), E-6, On Thunder Bluff's lower rise; In Front of Thunder Bluff Bank & Next to Mail box

BUNTHEN PLAINSWIND
Thunder Bluff Flight Master, Moonglade (56), F-5, Nighthaven (121), Southwest side of town

BURBIK GEARSPANNER
Trade Supplier, Ironforge (52), F-3, The Great Forge, Burbik's Supplies

BURDRAK HARGLHELM
Leather Armor Merchant, Dun Morogh (32), D-4, Brewnall Village, In tent along northwest side of village

BURGLE EYE
Rare Spawn, Dustwallow Marsh (38), H:(1-3), Dreadmurk Shore, Lvl 38 Uncommon; Spawns on the five isles

BURKRUM
Heavy Armor Merchant, Ashenvale (12), I-6, Splintertree Post (129), Near some crates next to inn

BURLY ROCKJAW TROGG
Dun Morogh (32), B:(7, 8), C:(7, 8), D:(7, 8), Coldridge Pass, Coldridge Valley (107)

BURNING BLADE ACOLYTE
Barrens (18), E-2, F-2, Dreadmist Peak

BURNING BLADE ADEPT
Desolace (30), G:(2, 3), H-3, Thunder Axe Fortress

BURNING BLADE APPRENTICE
Durotar (34), F-3, H-1, Skull Rock, Thunder Ridge

BURNING BLADE AUGUR
Desolace (30), G:(2, 3), H-3, Thunder Axe Fortress

BURNING BLADE BRUISER
Barrens (18), E-2, F-2, Dreadmist Peak

BURNING BLADE CRUSHER
Barrens (18), E-2, F-2, Dreadmist Peak

BURNING BLADE CULTIST
Durotar (34), H:(2, 3), Dustwind Cave

BURNING BLADE FANATIC
Durotar (34), F-3, H-1, Skull Rock, Thunder Ridge

BURNING BLADE FELSWORN
Desolace (30), G:(2, 3), H-3, Thunder Axe Fortress

BURNING BLADE INVOKER
Desolace (30), K-8, Shadowbreak Ravine

BURNING BLADE NEOPHYTE
Durotar (34), H-3, Dustwind Cave

BURNING BLADE NIGHTMARE
Desolace (30), K-8, Shadowbreak Ravine

BURNING BLADE REAVER
Desolace (30), G:(2, 3), H-3, Thunder Axe Fortress

BURNING BLADE SEER
Desolace (30), G-3, Thunder Axe Fortress

BURNING BLADE SHADOWMAGE
Desolace (30), G-3, Thunder Axe Fortress

BURNING BLADE SUMMONER
Desolace (30), F:(7, 8), G:(7, 8), K-8, Mannoroc Coven, Shadowbreak Ravine

BURNING BLADE THUG
Durotar (34), H-3, Drygulch Ravine, Dustwind Cave

BURNING BLADE TOXICOLOGIST
Barrens (18), E-2, F-2, Dreadmist Peak

BURNING DESTROYER
Stonetalon Mountains (70), D-7, E-7, The Charred Vale

BURNING EXILE
Arathi Highlands (10), C-3, Circle of West Binding

BURNING FELGUARD
Burning Steppes (22), Searing Gorge (64), C-4/D-8, Blackrock Spire

BURNING FELHOUND
Burning Steppes (22), Searing Gorge (64), C-4/D-8, Blackrock Spire

BURNING IMP
Burning Steppes (22), Searing Gorge (64), C-4/D-8, Blackrock Spire

BURNING RAVAGER
Stonetalon Mountains (70), C-6, D-6, E-6, The Charred Vale

BURROWING THUNDERSNOUT
Burning Steppes (22), Searing Gorge (64), C-4/D-8, Blackrock Depths

BUZZARD
Badlands (16), G:(6, 8), H-6, I:(5-7), Agmond's End

BUZZEK BRACKETSWING
Master Engineer, Tanaris (78), H-3, Gadgetzan (113), Outside inn

BYANCIE
First Aid Trainer, Teldrassil (80), G-6, Dolanaar (109), Bottom floor inside building north of road

C

CADAVEROUS WORM
Feralas (46), G-4, Dire Maul, (Summon)

CAEDAKAR THE VICIOUS
Ashenvale (12), D-2, Spawns on road near Darkshore border

CAELYB
Pet Trainer, Ashenvale (12), F-6, Silverwind Refuge, Right wing of building

CAER DARROW CANNONEER
Western Plaguelands (92), I:(7, 8), Caer Darrow, Located throughout the city

CAER DARROW CITIZEN
Western Plaguelands (92), I-8, J:(7, 8), Caer Darrow, Located throughout the city

CAER DARROW GUARDSMAN
Western Plaguelands (92), I-8, J:(7, 8), Caer Darrow, Located throughout the city

CAER DARROW HORSEMAN
Western Plaguelands (92), I:(7, 8), J:(7, 8), Caer Darrow, Located throughout the city

CAIN FIRESONG
Mage Trainer, Tirisfal Glades (86), H-5, Brill (104), Second floor of Gallows' End Tavern

CAIRNE BLOODHOOF
High Chieftan, Thunder Bluff (84), G-5, High rise, next to bridge to Elder Rise

CAITLIN GRASSMAN
Wetlands (96), A-6, Menethil Harbor (119), Small house east of keep

CALANDRATH
Innkeeper, Silithus (67), G-4, Cenarion Hold (106)

CALEDRA DAWNBREEZE
Stormwind (72), K-3, Stormwind Keep, Petitioner's Chamber

CALIPH SCORPIDSTING
Tanaris (78), I-4, Waterspring Field, Near two tents between hills

CALOR
Duskwood (36), J-5, Darkshire (108), Outside of house

CALVIN MONTAGUE
Tirisfal Glades (86), E-6, Deathknell (109), Roaming just inside wall northeast of town

CAMERICK JONGLEUR
Wandering Minstrel, Wetlands (96), A-6, Menethil Harbor (119), Next to wagon, south of keep

CAMP MOJACHE BRAVE
Feralas (46), I:(4, 5), J-4, Lariss Pavilion, Lower Wilds, Wildwind Lake

CANAGA EARTHCALLER
Durotar (34), F-7, Valley of Trials (136)

CANNIBAL GHOUL
Eastern Plaguelands (40), B:(3, 4), C:(2-4), D:(3, 4), E:(2-4), F:(2-4), Plaguewood

CANNIBAL GHOUL
Eastern Plaguelands (40), D-2, Stratholme

CANNON MASTER WILLEY
Eastern Plaguelands (40), D-2, Stratholme

CANNONEER SMYTHE
Barrens (18), H-6, Northwatch Hold, Top of eastern tower

CANNONEER WHESSAN
Barrens (18), G-5, Northwatch Hold, Top of western tower

CAPTAIN ANDREWS
Red Team Captain, Dustwallow Marsh (38), I-5, Theramore Isle (135), Sparring grounds to northeast

CAPTAIN BELD
Rare Spawn, Dun Morogh (32), K-6, Ironband's Compound, Lvl 11 Common; Basement of compound

CAPTAIN DANUVIN
The People's Militia, Westfall (94), F-5, Sentinel Hill (126), Sentinel Tower

CAPTAIN DARGOL
Tirisfal Glades (86), G-3, Agamand Mills (100), Bottom floor of Agamand Family Crypt

CAPTAIN DIRGEHAMMER
Armor QM, Stormwind (72), K-6

CAPTAIN EVENCANE
Warrior Trainer, Dustwallow Marsh (38), I-5, Theramore Isle (135), 2nd floor of Foothold Citadel

CAPTAIN FAIRMOUNT
Barrens (18), H-5, Northwatch Hold, Top of main tower

CAPTAIN FLAT TUSK
Rare Spawn; Captain of the Battleguard, Durotar (34), F:(4, 5), G-5, Durotar, Razormane Grounds, Lvl 11 Uncommon; Near huts

CAPTAIN GARRAN VIMES
Dustwallow Marsh (38), I-5, Theramore Isle (135), 2nd floor of Foothold Citadel

CAPTAIN GEROGG HAMMERTOE
Rare Spawn, Bael'dun Captain of the Guard, Barrens (18), F-8, Bael'dun Keep, Lvl 27 Average Rare; Second floor of keep

CAPTAIN GRAYSON
Westfall (94), C-8, Westfall Lighthouse, Island near lighthouse

CAPTAIN GREENSKIN
Westfall (94), D-7, E-7, The Deadmines

CAPTAIN HALYNDON
Wetlands (96), B-2, The Lost Fleet, Top of northern ship

CAPTAIN HECKLEBURY SMOTTS
Stranglethorn Vale (74), B-8, Booty Bay (103), On dock near ship launch on the northern side of bay

CAPTAIN IRONHILL
Hillsbrad Foothills (48), I-8, Dun Garok, Stands idle at spawn point

CAPTAIN KEELHAUL
Stranglethorn Vale (74), C-9, Wild Shore, Below deck to the stern of beached ship

CAPTAIN KROMCRUSH
Feralas (46), G-4, Dire Maul

CAPTAIN MELRACHE
Tirisfal Glades (86), K-3, Scarlet Watch Post, Idle with two Scarlet Bodyguards in tower ruins

CAPTAIN NIALS
Arathi Highlands (10), F-5, Refuge Point (124), Camp

CAPTAIN O'NEAL
Weapons QM, Stormwind (72), K-6

CAPTAIN PENTIGAST
Desolace (30), I-1, Nijel's Point (121), Clearing near entrance

CAPTAIN PERRINE
Tirisfal Glades (86), F-7, Idle with a single Scarlet Zealot in tower ruins

CAPTAIN REDPATH
Eastern Plaguelands (40), E-8, Darrowshire, (Summon) Well in the center of town

CAPTAIN RUGELFUSS
Loch Modan (54), C-7, Valley of Kings, Third floor of tower

CAPTAIN SHATTERSKULL
Barrens (18), E-1, Mor'shan Base Camp, Outside entrance to Warsong Gulch

CAPTAIN STEELGUT
Arathi Highlands (10), D-8, Faldir's Cove, Seated by bonfire on hill

CAPTAIN STOUTFIST
Wetlands (96), A-6, Menethil Harbor (119), Second floor of keep

CAPTAIN THALO'THAS BRIGHTSUN
Barrens (18), H-4, Ratchet (122), Outside inn

CAPTAIN THOMAS
Blue Team Captain, Dustwallow Marsh (38), I-5, Theramore Isle (135), Sparring grounds to northeast

CAPTAIN VACHON
Tirisfal Glades (86), K-5, Crusader's Outpost, Idle with a single Scarlet Friar in tower ruins

CAPTAIN VANESSA BELTIS
Azshara (14), H-9, The Ruined Reaches, Inlet

CAPTURED ARKO'NARIN
Felwood (44), E-6, Shadow Hold, Cage at first landing

CAPTURED HAKKARI ZEALOT
Stranglethorn Vale (74), A-2, Yojamba Isle

CAPTURED LEPER GNOME
Dun Morogh (32), F-5, Kharanos (116), Cage in gnomish workshop

CAPTURED MOUNTAINEER
Tirisfal Glades (86), H-5, Brill (104), Basement of Gallows' End Tavern

CAPTURED SCARLET ZEALOT
Tirisfal Glades (86), H-5, Brill (104), Basement of Gallows' End Tavern

CAPTURED SERVANT OF AZORA
Specialist Tailoring Supplies, Redridge Mountains (62), J-8, Render's Valley, By cages in camp

CAPTURED SPRITE DARTER
Feralas (46), H-5, Lower Wilds

CARAVAN MASTER TSET
Azshara (14), E-6, Southridge Beach, Near cliff face and ruins

CARAVANEER RUZZGOT
Stranglethorn Vale (74), B-8, Booty Bay (103), On dock near ship launch on the northern side of bay

CARENDIN HALGAR
Undercity (88), L-2, The Magic Quarter, Geen circle east of Skull Building

CARETAKER ALARIC
Arathi Highlands (10), D-6, Crypt, Roams crypt

CARETAKER ALEN
The Argent Dawn, Eastern Plaguelands (40), K-6, Light's Hope Chapel (118), Next to caravan south of chapel

CARETAKER CAICE
Tirisfal Glades (86), C-7, D-7, Deathknell (109)

CARETAKER FOLSOM
Stormwind (72), D-6, The Canals, Far west end of canals

CARETAKER NEVLIN
Arathi Highlands (10), D-6, Crypt, Roams crypt

CARETAKER SMITHERS
Hillsbrad Foothills (48), F-5, Southshore (129), Graveyard

CARETAKER WESTON
Arathi Highlands (10), D-6, Crypt, Roams crypt

CARLA GRANGER
Cloth Armor Merchant, Stormwind (72), H-6, Trade District, Lionheart Armory

CARLIN REDPATH
The Argent Dawn, Eastern Plaguelands (40), K-6, Light's Hope Chapel (118), Camp on right side of chapel

CARLO AURELIUS
Assassin, Hillsbrad Foothills (48), J-2, K-2, In mountains

CARNIVOUS THE BREAKER
Rare Spawn, Darkshore (24), F-5, F-8, Twilight Vale, Lvl 16 Uncommon; Roams close to spawn point

CAROLAI ANISE
Alchemist Trainer, Tirisfal Glades (86), H-5, Brill (104), House on the right side of road

CAROLYN WARD
Rogue Trainer, Undercity (88), L-7, The Rogues' Quarter, Inside Skull Building

CARRION DEVOURER
Eastern Plaguelands (40), B-3, C:(2-4), D-4, E-4, F:(3, 4), G:(3, 4), H:(2-5), I:(3-5), J:(3, 4), East Wall Tower

CARRION GRUB
Eastern Plaguelands (40), A:(4, 5), B:(5-7), C:(6-9), D:(6-8), E:(6-8), F:(6-8), G:(5-7), H:(5-8), I:(5-8), J:(5-7), K-6

CARRION HORROR
Desolace (30), F-6, G-6, Ghost Walker Post (113), Kodo Graveyard

CARRION LURKER
Western Plaguelands (92), E-5, F:(3-6), G:(3-7)

CARRION RECLUSE
Duskwood (36), B-4, C-4, Raven Hill Cemetery (123)

CARRION SWARMER
Feralas (46), G-4, Dire Maul

CARRION VULTURE
Western Plaguelands (92), D:(5, 6), The Bulwark (105)

CARROSH
Teldrassil (80), F-4, Hills east of Wellspring Lake

CARYSSIA MOONHUNTER
Tribal Leatherworking Trainer, Feralas (46), K-5, Thalanaar, Next to well

CATELYN THE BLADE
Blackwater Raiders, Stranglethorn Vale (74), B-8, Booty Bay (103), Second floor of The Salty Sailor Tavern

CATHERINE LELAND
Fishing Supplier, Stormwind (72), G-6, The Canals, Dock

CAULDRON LORD BILEMAW
Western Plaguelands (92), E-6, Felstone Field, (Summon) Spawns at the base of the cauldron

CAULDRON LORD MALVINIOUS
Western Plaguelands (92), F-5, Dalson's Tears, (Summon) Spawns at the base of the cauldron

CAULDRON LORD RAZARCH
Western Plaguelands (92), G-6, The Writhing Haunt, (Summon) Spawns at the base of the cauldron

CAULDRON LORD SOULWRAITH
Western Plaguelands (92), H-6, Gahrron's Withering, (Summon) Spawns at the base of the cauldron

CAVALIER DURGEN
Western Plaguelands (92), G-2, Patrols up and down tower south of Hearthglen

CAVE CREEPER
Burning Steppes (22), Searing Gorge (64), C-4/D-8, Blackrock Depths

CAVE STALKER
Wetlands (96), F-6, G-6, Thelgen Rock

CAVE YETI
Hillsbrad Foothills (48), E-3, Darrow Hill, In and near cave

CAVERN LURKER
Desolace (30), D-5, Mauradon

CAVERN SHAMBLER
Desolace (30), D-5, Mauradon

CAVERNDEEP AMBUSHER
Dun Morogh (32), C-4, Gnomeregan

CAVERNDEEP BURROWER
Dun Morogh (32), C-4, Gnomeregan

CAVERNDEEP INVADER
Dun Morogh (32), C-4, Gnomeregan

CAVERNDEEP LOOTER
Dun Morogh (32), C-4, Gnomeregan

CAVERNDEEP PILLAGER
Dun Morogh (32), C-4, Gnomeregan

CAVERNDEEP REAVER
Dun Morogh (32), C-4, Gnomeregan

CAWIND TRUEAIM
Gunsmith & Bowyer, Feralas (46), I-4, Camp Mojache (105), Second floor balcony of inn

CAYLAIS MOONFEATHER
Hippogryph Master, Darkshore (24), F-4, Auberdine (101), Hippogryph platform

CAYNRUS
Shield Merchant, Darnassus (26), H-7, Tradesmen's Terrace, Shields shop

CAZ TWOSPROCKET
Gnomeregan Exiles, Dustwallow Marsh (38), I-5, Theramore Isle (135), Blacksmithing hut to west

CAZUL
Orgrimmar (60), F-5, The Cleft of Shadow, Next to Shadowdeep Reagents

CEDRIC STUMPEL
Undercity (88), K-6, The Rogues' Quarter, Roames Rogue Quarter

CEDRIK PROSE
Gryphon Master, Arathi Highlands (11), F-5, Refuge Point (124) (124), Camp

CELEBRAS THE CURSED
Desolace (30), D-5, Mauradon

CELEBRAS THE REDEEMED
Desolace (30), D-5, Mauradon

CELEBRIAN DRYAD
Desolace (30), D-5, Mauradon

CELES EARTHBORNE
Moonglade (56), H-4, Nighthaven (121), On wood platform, north of lake, east of town

CENARION BOTANIST
Stonetalon Mountains (70), D:(1, 2), E:(1, 2), Stonetalon Peak

CENARION PROTECTOR
Ashenvale (12), H-5, Raynewood Retreat

CENARION VINDICATOR
Ashenvale (12), H-5, Raynewood Retreat

CENTAUR PARIAH
Desolace (30), F-9, Mannoroc Coven, Wanders hills and pauses at overlooks

CENTIPAAR SANDREAVER
Tanaris (78), E:(4, 5), The Noxious Lair

CENTIPAAR STINGER
Tanaris (78), E:(4, 5), The Noxious Lair

CENTIPAAR SWARMER
Tanaris (78), E:(4, 5), The Noxious Lair

CENTIPAAR TUNNELER
Tanaris (78), E:(4, 5), F-5, The Noxious Lair, Sandsorrow Watch

CENTIPAAR WASP
Tanaris (78), E:(4, 5), The Noxious Lair

CENTIPAAR WORKER
Tanaris (78), E:(4, 5), The Noxious Lair

CERELLEAN WHITECLAW
Darkshore (24), E-4, Auberdine (101), Dock

CERSEI DUSKSINGER
Swamp of Sorrows (76), F-5, Stonard (131)

CHAL FAIRWIND
Wintersaber Trainers, Winterspring (98), J-3, Outside small shack in hills

CHAMBERMAID PILLACLENCHER
Searing Gorge (64), E-3, The Slag Pit, (Summon) Sleeping quarters

CHAMPION CYSSA DAWNROSE
Paladin Trainer, Undercity (88), H-9

CHARDRYN
Herbalism Supplier, Darnassus (26), F-7, The Temple Gardens, Small building, northeast of temple

CHARITY MIPSY
General Goods, Dustwallow Marsh (38), I-5, Theramore Isle (135), Southeast near docks

CHARLES SEATON
Blade Merchant, Undercity (88), K-5, The Rogues' Quarter, Near Magic Quarter entry

CHARLGA RAZORFLANK
Barrens (18), E-9, Razorfen Kraul

CHARRED ANCIENT
Stonetalon Mountains (70), D:(6, 7), E:(6, 7), The Charred Vale

CHARYS YSERIAN
Arcane Trinkets Vendor, Stormwind (72), E-8, Mage Quarter, Ancient Curios

CHATTER
Rare Spawn, Redridge Mountains (62), G-4, H-5, Alther's Mill, Lvl 23 Uncommon; Roams small area around spawn point

CHAW STRONGHIDE
Journeyman Leatherworker, Mulgore (58), E-6, Bloodhoof Village (102), Northeast tent

CHEF BREANNA
Redridge Mountains (62), B-4, Lakeshire (117), First floor of large house on southwestern side of town

CHEF GRUAL
Duskwood (36), J-4, Darkshire (108), Scarlet Raven Inn

CHEF JESSEN
Hillsbrad Foothills (48), F-6, Southshore (129), First floor of inn

CHEMIST CUELY
Undercity (88), F-7, The Apothecarium, In laboratory

CHEMIST FUELY
Undercity (88), F-7, The Apothecarium, In laboratory

CHEPI
Reagent Vendor, Thunder Bluff (84), D-6, Roams around lower rise

CHESMU
Banker, Thunder Bluff (84), E-6, Thunder Bluff Bank

CHIEF ARCHAEOLOGIST GREYWHISKER
Explorers' League, Darnassus (26), D-8, The Temple of the Moon, Steps west of the temple

CHIEF ENGINEER BILGEWHIZZLE
Gadgetzan Water Co., Tanaris (78), H-3, Gadgetzan (113), Between bank and inn

CHIEF ENGINEER HINDERWEIR VII
Loch Modan (54), F-1, Stonewrought Dam, Under scaffolding on dam wall

CHIEF HAWKWIND
Mulgore (58), E-8, Camp Narache (105), Main tent (north)

CHIEF MURGUT
Ashenvale (12), G-6, Greenpaw Village

CHIEF SHARPTUSK THORNMANTLE
Mulgore (58), H-8, Brambleblade Ravine, Tent in north of ravine

CHIEF UKORZ SANDSCALP
Tanaris (78), E-1, Zul'Farrak

CHIEFTAIN BLOODMAW
Felwood (44), I-1, Felpaw Village, Camp at north side of pond

CHIEFTAIN NEK'ROSH
Wetlands (96), G-5, Angerfang Encampment, Southeast side of camp

CHILLWIND CHIMAERA
Winterspring (98), H:(4, 5), I:(4, 5), J:(2-5)

CHILLWIND RAVAGER
Winterspring (98), H:(2, 3), I:(1-3, 5, 6)

CHIMAERA MATRIARCH
Stonetalon Mountains (70), D-7, The Charred Vale, Roams southeastern section of Charred Vale

CHIMAEROK
Feralas (46), B:(7, 8), C:(7-9), Isle of Dread

CHIMAEROK DEVOURER
Feralas (46), B:(7, 8), C:(7-9), Isle of Dread

CHLOE CURTHAS
Undercity (88), G-2, The War Quarter, Watches fights in War Quarter

CHOK'SUL
Loch Modan (54), K-2, Mo'grosh Stronghold, Cave

CHOMPER
Dun Morogh (32), C-4, Gnomeregan

CHO'RUSH THE OBSERVER
Feralas (46), G-4, Dire Maul

CHRISTI GALVANIS
General Goods, Desolace (30), I-1, Nijel's Point (121), Inn

CHRISTOPH FARAL
Stormwind (72), K-4, Old Town, Roamer - Stops at Pig and Whistle Tavern

CHRISTOPH JEFFCOAT
Tradesman, Hillsbrad Foothills (48), H-2, Tarren Mill (133), First floor of inn

CHRISTOPH WALKER
Warrior Trainer, Undercity (88), F-2, The War Quarter, In Skull Building

CHRISTOPHER DRAKUL
Guild Master, Undercity (88), I-4, The Trade Quarter, East spoke from bank

CHRISTOPHER HEWEN
General Trade Goods Vendor, Westfall (94), F-5, Sentinel Hill (126), Inn

CHROMATIC DRAGONSPAWN
Burning Steppes (22), Searing Gorge (64), C-4/D-8, Blackrock Spire

CHROMATIC ELITE GUARD
Burning Steppes (22), Searing Gorge (64), C-4/D-8, Blackrock Spire

CHROMATIC WHELP
Burning Steppes (22), Searing Gorge (64), C-4/D-8, Blackrock Spire

CHROMIE
Western Plaguelands (92), E-7, Ruins of Andorhal, Second floor of inn

CHRONALIS
Tanaris (78), I-5, Caverns of Time, Near entrance to cavern

CHUCKY "TEN THUMBS"
Stranglethorn Vale (74), D-6, Ruins of Aboraz, Roaming around ruins

CHYLINA
General Supplies, Stonetalon Mountains (70), E-2, Stonetalon Peak, Building north of hippogryphs

CITIZEN WILKES
Hillsbrad Foothills (48), C-4, Hillsbrad Fields (115), Patrols between the town hall, smithy and two houses in the eastern and northern parts of town

CIVILIAN GUARD PARKER
Redridge Mountains (62), A-7, Three Corners

CLACK THE REAVER
Rare Spawn, Blasted Lands (20), G-4, Dreadmaul Post, Lvl 53 Semi-Rare; Patrols to tower ruins at the edge of Serpent's Coil (I-3)

CLAIRA KINDFEATHER
The Hinterlands (50), C-5, Aerie Peak (100), Third floor of tower

CLAIRE WILLOWER
Tirisfal Glades (86), D-7, Deathknell (109), Outside of the first house on right side of road

CLARICE FOSTER
Thunder Bluff (84), C-3, Spirit Rise, The Pools of Vision

CLARISE GNARLTREE
Expert Blacksmith, Duskwood (36), J-5, Darkshire (108), Smithy

CHIEFTAIN BLOODMAW

CLATTERING CRAWLER
Ashenvale (12), A:(2-4), B:(2-4), The Zoram Strand (137), Zoram'gar Outpost (137)

CLATTERING SCORPID
Durotar (34), G:(5, 7), H:(4-8), I:(4, 5, 7)

CLAUDE ERKSINE
Pet Trainer, Loch Modan (54), K-6, The Farstrider Lodge (111), In right hall of lodge

CLAVICUS KNAVINGHAM
Alliance Cloth Quartermaster, Stormwind (72), G-7, Mage Quarter, Duncan's Textiles

CLEFT SCORPID
Badlands (16), G-1, Uldaman

CLERK DALTRY
Duskwood (36), J-5, Darkshire (108), Darkshire Town Hall

CLERK HORACE WHITESTEED
Hillsbrad Foothills (48), C-4, Hillsbrad, Town hall

CLERK LENDRY
Dustwallow Marsh (38), I-5, Theramore Isle (135), 2nd floor of Foothold Citadel

CLIFF BREAKER
Azshara (14), E:(7-9), F:(7-9), G:(7-9), H:(1, 8, 9), I:(1, 2), J:(1-3), K-2, Bitter Reaches, Lake Mennar, Southridge Beach

CLIFF GIANT
Feralas (46), D:(2, 3), Ruins of Ravenwind, The Twin Colossals

CLIFF HADIN
Bowyer, Loch Modan (54), K-6, The Farstrider Lodge (111), On right side of lodge entrance

CLIFF LURKER
Loch Modan (54), F-7, G:(6-8), H:(5-8), I-5

CLIFF STORMER
Barrens (18), B:(2, 3), C:(2, 3) Stonetalon Mountains (70), G-7, H:(7, 9), J:(8, 9), K:(8, 9)

CLIFF THUNDERER
Azshara (14), E:(7-9), F:(7-9), G:(7-9), H:(1, 8, 9), I:(1, 2), J:(1-3), K-2, Bitter Reaches, Legash Encampment, Southridge Beach

CLIFF WALKER
Azshara (14), A-5, C-5, E:(7-9), F:(7-9), G:(7-9), H:(1, 8, 9), I:(1, 2), J:(1-3), K-2

CLIFFWATCHER LONGHORN
Thousand Needles (82), F-5, Freewind Post (112), Outside Inn, next to fire

CLOUD SERPENT
Thousand Needles (82), D:(3, 5), E:(4-6), F-6, G:(5, 6)

CLOUD SKYDANCER
Hippogryph Master, Silithus (67), G-5, Cenarion Hold (106)

CLUNK
The Undermarket, Searing Gorge (64), D-5, The Cauldron, Next to Trade Master Kovic in cave

CLUTCHMOTHER ZAVAS
Rare Spawn, Un'Goro Crater (90), G-8, The Slithering Scar, Lvl 54 Semi-Rare; Inside The Slighering Scar

CLYDE KELLEN
Fisherman, Tirisfal Glades (86), I-5, Brightwater Lake, On the southwest bank of the lake

CLYDE RANTHAL
Leatherworking Supplies, Redridge Mountains (62), L-7, Camp

COAST CRAWL DEEPSEER
Feralas (46), A:(5, 6), B:(5, 6), C:(5, 6), D:(5, 6), Sardor Isle

COAST CRAWL SNAPCLAW
Feralas (46), A:(5, 6), B:(5, 6), C:(5, 6), D:(5, 6), Sardor Isle

COAST STRIDER
Tanaris (78), I:(6, 7), J-6, Southbreak Shore

COASTAL FRENZY
Darkshore (24), D-7, E:(6-8), F:(2, 3), G-2, Mist's Edge

COBALT BROODLING
Winterspring (98), H:(5-6), I-5, Mazthoril

COBALT MAGEWEAVER
Winterspring (98), H:(5, 6), I-5, Mazthoril

COBALT SCALEBANE
Winterspring (98), H:(5, 6), I-5, Mazthoril

COBALT WHELP
Winterspring (98), H:(5, 6), I-5, Mazthoril

COBALT WYRMKIN
Winterspring (98), H:(5, 6), I-5, Mazthoril

COG GLITZSPINNER
Duskwood (36), K-5, Darkshire (108), Second house on left side of road heading into Darkshire from the east

COLD EYE BASILISK
Stranglethorn Vale (74), B-4, C:(4, 5), D:(4, 5), Southern Savage Coast, The Cape of Stranglethorn, The Vile Reef

COLDRIDGE MOUNTAINEER
Dun Morogh (32), D-7, J-4, Coldridge Pass, Coldridge Valley (107)

COLEMAN FARTHING
Tirisfal Glades (86), H-5, Brill (104), First floor of Gallows' End Tavern

COLLIN MAUREN
Stormwind (72), F-8, Mage Quarter, East path leading into Mage Quarter

COLONEL KURZEN
Stranglethorn Vale (74), F-1, The Stockpile, By table to the rear of cave

COMAR VILLARD
Wetlands (96), G-1, Thandol Span, South of collapsed section of bridge

COMBAT MASTER CRITON
Dustwallow Marsh (38), I-5, Theramore Isle (135), Sparring grounds to northeast

COMBAT MASTER SZIGETI
Dustwallow Marsh (38), I-5, Theramore Isle (135), Sparring grounds to northeast

COMMANDER AGGRO'GOSH
Stranglethorn Vale (74), C-3, Grom'gol Base Camp (114), Roams near bonfire center of camp

COMMANDER ALTHEA EBONLOCKE
Leader of the Night Watch, Duskwood (36), J-5, Darkshire (108), In front of the Darkshire Town Hall

COMMANDER AMAREN
Arathi Highlands (10), F-5, Refuge Point (124), Roams camp

COMMANDER ASHLAM VALORFIST
Western Plaguelands (92), E-8, Chillwind Camp (107), In front of tent

COMMANDER ELIGOR DAWNBRINGER
Brotherhood of the Light, Eastern Plaguelands (40), K-6, Light's Hope Chapel (118)

COMMANDER FELSTROM
Rare Spawn, Duskwood (36), A-3, B-4, Dawning Wood Catacombs, Lvl 32 Uncommon; Stands at spawn point

COMMANDER GOR'SHAK
Burning Steppes (22), Searing Gorge (64), C-4/D-8, Blackrock Depths

COMMANDER MAR'ALITH
Silithus (67), G-5, Cenarion Hold (106)

COMMANDER SAMAUL
Dustwallow Marsh (38), I-5, Theramore Isle (135), 2nd floor of Foothold Citadel

COMMANDER SPRINGVALE
Silverpine Forest (68), F-7, Shadowfang Keep

CONDEMNED ACOLYTE
Hillsbrad Foothills (48), A:(7, 8), Purgation Isle, Island

CONDEMNED CLERIC
Hillsbrad Foothills (48), A-8, Purgation Isle, Near top of island

CONDEMNED MONK
Hillsbrad Foothills (48), A-8, Purgation Isle, Island

CONNOR RIVERS
Apprentice Chef, Stormwind (72), F-9, Mage Quarter, The Blue Recluse

CONSERVATOR ILTHALAINE
Teldrassil (80), G-4, H-4, Shadowglen (127), Benches southwest of Aldrassil

CONSTANCE BRISBOISE
Apprentice Clothier, Tirisfal Glades (86), G-6, Cold Hearth Manor, House on northwestern edge of manor

CONSTRICTOR VINE
Desolace (30), D-5, Mauradon

COOK GHILM
Cooking Trainer, Dun Morogh (32), I-5, Gol'Bolar Quarry, Patrols kitchen area of camp

COOK TORKA
Durotar (34), H-4, Razor Hill (124), Western entrance on hill

COOKIE
Westfall (94), D-7, E-7, The Deadmines

OR GRIMTOTEM
Thunder Bluff (84), I-3, Elder Rise, In front of Magatha Grimtotem's tent

ORAL MOONGALE
Azshara (14), C-4, Bear's Head, Up hill to the right of tower

ORALSHELL LURKER
Azshara (14), E-9, F:(4, 7, 9), G:(4, 7, 9), H:(3, 4, 7-9), I:(3, 4, 7-9), J:(7-9), K:(3, 4, 8, 9), L:(2-4)

ORALSHELL TORTOISE
Azshara (14), E:(1, 2), F:(1, 2), G-1, H-1, I-1, J-1, K:(1, 2), L:(1, 2), Jagged Reef

ORAND
Darnassus (26), E-1, Cenarion EnclaBabe, Tree stump, west of the northeast structure

ORBETT SCHNEIDER
Stormwind (72), Roams city

ORE HOUND
Burning Steppes (22), Searing Gorge (64), C-4/D-8, The Molten Core

ORE RAGER
Burning Steppes (22), Searing Gorge (64), C-4/D-8, The Molten Core

ORINA STEELE
Weaponsmith, Elwynn Forest (42), E-7,Goldshire (114), Smithy

ORITHRAS MOONRAGE
Teldrassil (80), G-6, Dolanaar (109), Moonwell south side of Dolanaar

ORK GIZELTON
Desolace (30), H-4, Spawns on road near Kormek's Hut, runs a loop along the roads, and pauses at the hut upon return

ORPORAL BLUTH
Camp Trader, Stranglethorn Vale (74), D-1, Rebel Camp (124), Camp

ORPORAL KALEB
Stranglethorn Vale (74), D-1, Rebel Camp (124), Camp

ORPORAL KEESHAN
Redridge Mountains (62), C-1, Render's Rock, Center of cave

ORPORAL MELKINS
Desolace (30), I-1, Nijel's Point (121), Clearing near entrance

ORPORAL SETHMAN
Stranglethorn Vale (74), D-1, Rebel Camp (124), Camp

ORPORAL TEEKA BLOODSNARL
Frostwolf Clan, Alterac Mountains (8), I-5, Alterac Valley, Cave

ORRIAM
Emerald Circle Flight Master, Felwood (44), G-8, Emerald Sanctuary (110) (110)

ORROSIVE LURKER
Dun Morogh (32), C-4, Gnomeregan

ORROSIVE SAP BEAST
Stonetalon Mountains (70), D:(1, 2), E:(1, 2), Stonetalon Peak, The Talon Den

ORROSIVE SWAMP OOZE
Dustwallow Marsh (38), F:(4-6), G:(5, 6), Beezil's Wreck, The Quagmire

ORRUPT FORCE OF NATURE
Desolace (30), D-5, Mauradon

ORRUPT MINOR MANIFESTATION OF WATER
Silverpine Forest (68), F-4, The Tides Run

ORRUPTED BLOODTALON SCYTHEMAW
Durotar (34), E-6, F:(2, 3), Rocktusk Farm, Thunder Ridge, Tor'kren Farm

ORRUPTED MOTTLED BOAR
Durotar (34), E-4, F-2, Thunder Ridge

ORRUPTED SCORPID
Durotar (34), E-3, F-5, H-1, Jaggedswine Farm, Thunder Ridge

ORRUPTED SPIRIT
Western Plaguelands (92), I-7, Scholomance

ORRUPTED SURF CRAWLER
Durotar (34), H-1, I-2, Bladefist Bay, Deadeye Shore, Skull Rock

ORRUPTOR
Desolace (30), D-5, Mauradon

OUNCILMAN BRUNSWICK
Pyrewood Council, Silverpine Forest (68), G-7, Pyrewood Village, (Summon) Spawns with Lord Mayor Morrison and Councilman Cooper in town hall

OUNCILMAN COOPER
Pyrewood Council, Silverpine Forest (68), G-7, Pyrewood Village, (Summon) Spawns with Lord Mayor Morrison and Councilman Brunswick in town hall

COUNCILMAN HARTIN
Pyrewood Council, Silverpine Forest (68), G-7, Pyrewood Village, (Summon) Spawns with Councilman Higarth and Councilman Wilhelm in town hall

COUNCILMAN HENDRICKS
Pyrewood Council, Silverpine Forest (68), G-7, Pyrewood Village, (Summon) Spawns with Councilman Thatcher in town hall

COUNCILMAN HIGARTH
Pyrewood Council, Silverpine Forest (68), G-7, Pyrewood Village, (Summon) Spawns with Councilman Hartin and Councilman Wilhelm in town hall

COUNCILMAN MILLSTIPE
Council of Darkshire, Duskwood (36), J-5, Darkshire (108), Darkshire Town Hall

COUNCILMAN SMITHERS
Pyrewood Council, Silverpine Forest (68), G-7, Pyrewood Village, (Summon) Spawns in town hall

COUNCILMAN THATCHER
Pyrewood Council, Silverpine Forest (68), G-7, Pyrewood Village, (Summon) Spawns with Councilman Hendricks in town hall

COUNCILMAN WILHELM
Pyrewood Council, Silverpine Forest (68), G-7, Pyrewood Village, (Summon) Spawns with Councilman Hartin and Councilman Higarth in town hall

COUNT REMINGTON RIDGEWELL
House of Nobles, Stormwind (72), K-3, Stormwind Keep, Petitioner's Chamber

COURIER HAMMERFALL
Ironforge (52), Roams entire city

COWARDLY CROSBY
Tailoring Supplies, Stranglethorn Vale (74), B-9, Wild Shore, Small camp on the southernmost tip of Stanglethorn Vale

COYOTE
Westfall (94), C:(3, 4), D:(2-4), E:(2, 3), F:(2-5), G:(1-4), Hills

COYOTE PACKLEADER
Westfall (94), C:(3, 4), D:(2-4), E:(2, 3), F:(3-5), G:(2-4), Gold Coast Quarry

CRACKED GOLEM
Darkshore (24), E:(8, 9), Remtravel's Excavation

CRACKED SKULL SOLDIER
Tirisfal Glades (86), E-3, F-3, Agamand Mills (100)

CRAFTSMAN WILHELM
Brotherhood of the Light, Eastern Plaguelands (40), K-6, Light's Hope Chapel (118)

CRAG BOAR
Dun Morogh (32), D:(5, 6), E:(6, 7), F:(5-7), G:(5, 6)

CRAG COYOTE
Badlands (16), G:(3-5), H:(1-5), I-5, Hammertoe's Digsite, Digsite

CRAG STALKER
Thousand Needles (82), D:(2-4), E:(3, 5, 6), F:(5, 6), G-5, Darkcloud Pinnacle, Freewind Post (112), The Great Lift

CRAIG HEWITT
Hillsbrad Foothills (48), G-3, Tarren Mill (133)

CRAIG NOLLWARD
Cook, Dustwallow Marsh (38), I-5, Theramore Isle (135), Back of inn

CRANE OPERATOR BIGGLEFUZZ
Barrens (18), H-4, Ratchet (122), Tower near dock

CRANK FIZZLEBUB
Stranglethorn Vale (74), B-8, Booty Bay (103), First floor of The Salty Sailor Tavern

CRANKY BENJ
Rare Spawn, Alterac Mountains (8), A-5, Lordamere Lake, Lvl 32 Very Rare; Patrols eastern coast of lake

CRAVEN DROK
Orgrimmar (60), E-5, The Drag, Roams The Cleft of Shadow and The Drag

CRAZED ANCIENT
Ashenvale (12), G:(3, 4), H:(4, 5), Nightsong Woods, Raynewood Retreat

CRAZED OWLBEAST
Winterspring (98), I:(2, 6), J:(2, 6), The Hidden Grove, Owl Wing Thicket

CRAZK SPARKS
Fireworks Merchant, Stranglethorn Vale (74), B-8, Booty Bay (103), Shop on the back side of building near the overturned boat and hanging shark on the eastern side of bay

CREEPING SLUDGE
Desolace (30), D-5, Mauradon

CREEPTHESS
Rare Spawn, Hillsbrad Foothills (48), B-5, C-6, D:(5, 6), Azurelode Mine, Lvl 24 Semi-Rare; Roams small area around spawn point

CREST KILLER
Burning Steppes (22), Searing Gorge (64), C-4/D-8, Blackrock Depths

CRESTING EXILE
Arathi Highlands (10), I-3, Circle of East Binding

CRIER GOODMAN
Stormwind (72), Roams city

CRILDOR
Darnassus (26), C:(2, 3), F-5, The Temple Gardens, Strolls along path, pausing at dock and lake in Cenarion Enclave

CRIMSON BATTLE MAGE
Eastern Plaguelands (40), D-2, Stratholme

CRIMSON BODYGUARD
Eastern Plaguelands (40), D-2, Roams between Stratholme and Tyr's Hand

CRIMSON CONJUROR
Eastern Plaguelands (40), D-2, Stratholme

CRIMSON COURIER
Eastern Plaguelands (40), D-2, Stratholme, Patrols with four Crimson Bodyguards to Tyr's Hand (L-8)

CRIMSON DEFENDER
Eastern Plaguelands (40), D-2, Stratholme

CRIMSON ELITE
Western Plaguelands (92), G-2, (Summon) Both inside the tower and along the road west of the tower

CRIMSON GALLANT
Eastern Plaguelands (40), D-2, Stratholme

CRIMSON GUARDSMAN
Eastern Plaguelands (40), D-2, Stratholme

CRIMSON HAMMERSMITH
Eastern Plaguelands (40), D-2, Stratholme

CRIMSON INITIATE
Eastern Plaguelands (40), D-2, Stratholme

CRIMSON INQUISITOR
Eastern Plaguelands (40), D-2, Stratholme

CRIMSON MONK
Eastern Plaguelands (40), D-2, Stratholme

CRIMSON OOZE
Wetlands (96), F:(2, 3), Ironbeard's Tomb

CRIMSON PRIEST
Eastern Plaguelands (40), D-2, Stratholme

CRIMSON RIFLEMAN
Eastern Plaguelands (40), D-2, Stratholme

CRIMSON SORCERER
Eastern Plaguelands (40), D-2, Stratholme

CRIMSON WHELP
Wetlands (96), H:(3, 4), I:(3-5), J-5, The Green Belt

CROWD PUMMELLER 9-60
Dun Morogh (32), C-4, Gnomeregan

CRUSADER LORD VALDELMAR
Eastern Plaguelands (40), L-8, Tyr's Hand, Patrols in and out of The Scarlet Basilica

CRUSHRIDGE BRUTE
Alterac Mountains (8), F:(3, 4, 6), G:(4-6), Crushridge Hold, Slaughter Hollow

CRUSHRIDGE ENFORCER
Alterac Mountains (8), E:(5, 6), Ruins of Alterac, Ruins

CRUSHRIDGE MAGE
Alterac Mountains (8), E:(4, 5), F-5, Ruins of Alterac, Ruins

CRUSHRIDGE MAULER
Alterac Mountains (8), E:(4, 5), F-5, Ruins of Alterac, Ruins

CRUSHRIDGE OGRE
Alterac Mountains (8), E-3, F:(3-6), G:(3-6), Crushridge Hold, Slaughter Hollow

CRUSHRIDGE PLUNDERER
Alterac Mountains (8), E-5, Ruins of Alterac, Ruins

CRUSHRIDGE WARMONGER
Alterac Mountains (8), D-5, E:(5, 6), Ruins of Alterac, Ruins

CRYPT BEAST
Eastern Plaguelands (40), D-2, Stratholme

CRYPT CRAWLER
Eastern Plaguelands (40), D-2, Stratholme

CRYPT FIEND
Eastern Plaguelands (40), B-3, C:(2, 3), D:(3, 4), E:(3, 4), F-3, I-4, Terrordale

CRYPT HORROR
Eastern Plaguelands (40), I-4, Terrordale

CRYPT ROBBER
Eastern Plaguelands (40), D-8, Terrordale

CRYPT SLAYER
Eastern Plaguelands (40), E-5, F-5, K:(4, 5), The Noxious Glade

CRYPT WALKER
Eastern Plaguelands (40), B-3, C:(2, 3), D:(2-4), E:(3, 4), F-3, Terrordale

CRYSTAL BOUGHMAN
Cooking Trainer, Redridge Mountains (62), B-4, Lakeshire (117), First floor of large house on southwestern side of town

CRYSTAL FANG
Rare Spawn, Burning Steppes (22), Searing Gorge (64), C-4/D-8, Blackrock Spire, Lvl 60 Rare

CRYSTAL SPINE BASILISK
Stranglethorn Vale (74), B-2, E-1, Kurzen's Compound, The Savage Coast

CURATOR THORIUS
Ironforge (52), E-3, F-1, Hall of Explorers, Roams library

CURGLE CRANKLEHOP
Tanaris (78), H-3, Gadgetzan (113), Near Super Egg-O-Matic on north side of town

CURSED ATAL'AI
Swamp of Sorrows (76), I-5, The Temple of Atal'Hakkar

CURSED CENTAUR
Desolace (30), D-5, Mauradon

CURSED DARKHOUND
Tirisfal Glades (86), E:(4-7), F:(4-7), G:(6, 7), G:(3, 6), I:(3-6), J:(3-7), K:(6, 7)

CURSED HIGHBORNE
Darkshore (24), F-6, G-6, Ameth'Aran

CURSED JUSTICAR
Hillsbrad Foothills (48), A-8, Purgation Isle, Island

CURSED MAGE
Eastern Plaguelands (40), B:(3, 4), C:(2-4), D:(3, 4), E:(2-4), F:(2-4), Terrordale

CURSED MARINE
Wetlands (96), B:(2, 3), The Lost Fleet

CURSED OOZE
Felwood (44), E:(6, 7), F:(6, 7), Ruins of Constellas

CURSED PALADIN
Hillsbrad Foothills (48), A:(7, 8), Purgation Isle, Island

CURSED SAILOR
Wetlands (96), B:(2, 3), The Lost Fleet

CURSED SYCAMORE
Feralas (46), F-7, Ruins of Isildien, Roams as far north as the High Wilderness

CUTAC
Cloth & Leather Armor Merchant, Durotar (34), H-4, Razor Hill (124), Northern entrance

CYCLOK THE MAD
Rare Spawn, Tanaris (78), F:(5-7), G:(6, 7), Dunemaul Compound, Eastmoon Ruins, Southmoon Ruins, Lvl 48 Very Rare; Spawns in ruins or compound and sticks close to spawn point

CYCLONE WARRIOR
Silithus (90), D:(4, 5), E:(2, 3), F:(4, 5), G-3, Southwind Village

CYCLONIAN
Alterac Mountains (8), K-6, Chillwind Point, (Summon) Tiki Altar in front of ruins

CYLANIA
Night Elf Armorer, Darnassus (26), H-5, Warrior's Terrace, Lower southwest platform

CYLANIA ROOTSTALKER
Herbalist, Ashenvale (12), F-7, Silverwind Refuge, Left wing of building

CYLINA DARKHEART
Demon Trainer, Elwynn Forest (42), F-7,Goldshire (114), Basement of Lion's Pride Inn

CYNDRA KINDWHISPER
Alchemist Trainer, Teldrassil (80), G-6, Dolanaar (109), Inside house east of inn

CYRIDAN
Leather Armor Merchant, Darnassus (26), G-8, Tradesmen's Terrace, Leather Armor shop

CYROEN
Reagent Vendor, Darnassus (26), E-1, Cenarion Enclave, Northwest structure

CYRUS THEREPENTOUS
Burning Steppes (22), L-3, Slither Rock, Cave

D

DABYRIE LABORER
Arathi Highlands (10), G-4, H-4, Dabyrie's Farmstead,

DABYRIE MILITIA
Arathi Highlands (10), G-4, H:(3, 4), Dabyrie's Farmstead

DADANGA
Un'Goro Crater (90), F-1, Marshal's Refuge (118), Entrance to cave

DAELYSHIA
Hippogryph Master, Ashenvale (12), E-5, Astranaar (101)

DAEOLYN SUMMERLEAF
General Goods, Moonglade (56), F-3, Nighthaven (121), Northwest building

DAERA BRIGHTSPEAR
Hunter Trainer, Ironforge (52), J-9, The Military Ward, Hall of Arms

DAGGERSPINE MARAUDER
Arathi Highlands (10), C:(8, 9), D-9, The Drowned Reef

DAGGERSPINE RAIDER
Arathi Highlands (10), B:(8, 9), C:(8, 9), The Drowned Reef

DAGGERSPINE SCREAMER
Hillsbrad Foothills (48), G:(7, 8), H:(8, 9), Eastern Strand

DAGGERSPINE SHOREHUNTER
Hillsbrad Foothills (48), F:(6, 7), G:(7, 8), Eastern Strand

DAGGERSPINE SHORESTALKER
Hillsbrad Foothills (48), G:(7, 8), H:(8, 9), Eastern Strand

DAGGERSPINE SIREN
Hillsbrad Foothills (48), F-6, G:(6-8), H-8, Eastern Strand

DAGGERSPINE SORCERESS
Arathi Highlands (10), B:(8, 9), C:(8, 9), The Drowned Reef

DAGRI
Raene's Pet, Ashenvale (12), E-5, Astranaar (101), First floor of inn near Raene

DAGUN THE RAVENOUS
Dustwallow Marsh (38), H-1, Dreadmurk Shore, (Summon) Spawns near largest of five isles after an herb is placed on the Seaworn Altar

DAHNE PIERCE
Dustwallow Marsh (38), I-5, Theramore Isle (135), 2nd floor of inn

DAIO THE DECREPIT
Blasted Lands (20), E-5, The Tainted Scar, Altar

DAISY
Race Starter Girl, Thousand Needles (82), K-8, Mirage Raceway (119), Inside racetrack

DAL BLOODCLAW
Ashenvale (12), E-4, Thistlefur Village, Roams between camps

DALAR DAWNWEAVER
Silverpine Forest (68), G-4, The Sepulcher (127), Roams on right side of sepulcher by crates

DALARAN APPRENTICE
Silverpine Forest (68), G:(6, 7), H:(6, 7)

DALARAN BREWMASTER
Silverpine Forest (68), I-6, Ambermill, Caravan right of entrance inside city walls

DALARAN CONJUROR
Silverpine Forest (68), I-6, Ambermill

DALARAN MAGE
Silverpine Forest (68), I:(6, 7), Ambermill

145

DALARAN MINER
Silverpine Forest (68), I-6, Ambermill, Shed left of entrance inside city walls

DALARAN PROTECTOR
Silverpine Forest (68), H:(5-7), I:(6, 7), Ambermill

DALARAN SHIELD GUARD
Alterac Mountains (8), B:(8, 9), Lordamere Internment Camp

DALARAN SPELLSCRIBE
Silverpine Forest (68), I-6, Ambermill

DALARAN SUMMONER
Alterac Mountains (8), A:(7, 8), B:(5-8), C-6, Dalaran

DALARAN THEURGIST
Alterac Mountains (8), B:(8, 9), Lordamere Internment Camp

DALARAN WARDER
Silverpine Forest (68), I-6, J-6, Ambermill, Keep

DALARAN WATCHER
Silverpine Forest (68), H-8, I:(6-8), J:(6, 8)

DALARAN WIZARD
Silverpine Forest (68), I:(6-8), J:(5-8)

DALARAN WORKER
Alterac Mountains (8), A:(7, 8), B:(6, 7), Dalaran

DALIN FORGEWRIGHT
Silverpine Forest (68), G-8, The Greymane Wall, Mounted on horse roaming along wall

DALINDA MALEM
Desolace (30), G-3, Thunder Axe Fortress, Kneeling near chest in center of fortress

DALMOND
General Goods, Darkshore (24), F-4, Auberdine (101), Back terrace of northern building

DALRIA
Trade Goods, Ashenvale (12), E-5, Astranaar (101), Back of building to the southwest

DAMNED SOUL
Deadwind Pass (28), C:(6-8), D:(7, 8), E:(7-9), F-8, Karazhan, Morgan's Plot

DAN GOLTHAS
Journeyman Leatherworker, Undercity (88), J-6, The Rogues' Quarter

DANE LINDGREN
Journeyman Blacksmith, Stormwind (72), I-2, J-2, Dwarven District, At the Forge

DANE WINSLOW
Demon Trainer, Elwynn Forest (42), G-4, Northshire Valley (122), Graveyard on right side of abbey

DANIEL BARTLETT
General Trade Supplier, Undercity (88), I-4, The Trade Quarter, Upper Ring of Trade Quarter

DANIEL ULFMAN
Tirisfal Glades (86), D-6, Deathknell (109)

DANIELLE ZIPSTITCH
Tailoring Supplies, Duskwood (36), K-5, Darkshire (108), Second floor of house

DANK DRIZZLECUT
Mining Trainer, Dun Morogh (32), J-6, Gol'Bolar Quarry, Far end of camp by machinery

DANLAAR NIGHTSHADE
Hunter Trainer, Ashenvale (12), F-6, Silverwind Refuge, Back of building

DANLYIA
Food & Drink Vendor, Teldrassil (80), G-6, Dolanaar (109), Bottom floor inside building north of road

DANNAL STERN
Warrior Trainer, Tirisfal Glades (86), D-6, Deathknell (109), First floor of second house on right side of road

DANNELOR
First Aid Trainer, Darnassus (26), G-1, Craftsmen's Terrace, First Aid shop

DANNIE FIZZWIZZLE
Demon Trainer, Dun Morogh (32), F-5, Kharanos (116), Gnomish camp on right of distillery

DAPHNE STILWELL
Westfall (94), D-9, The Dagger Hills, Roams the nearby orchard

DAR
Swamp of Sorrows (76), F-5, Stonard (131), First floor of inn

DARBEL MONTROSE
Rare Spawn, Arathi Highlands (10), C-7, D-6, Stromgarde Keep (132), Lvl 39 Semi-Rare; Roams with minion near spawn point

DARCY
Waitress, Redridge Mountains (62), C-4, Lakeshire (117), First floor of Lakeshire Inn

DARGH TRUEAIM
Hunter Trainer, Loch Modan (54), K-6, The Farstrider Lodge (111), In right hall of lodge

DARGON
Food & Drink Merchant, Moonglade (56), G-4, Nighthaven (121), At counter of central building

DARIAN SINGH
Fireworks Vendor, Stormwind (72), D-7, Mage Quarter, Pyrotechnics

DARIANNA
Journeyman Leatherworker, Darnassus (26), I-2 , Craftsmen's Terrace, Leatherworking shop

DARK ADEPT
Eastern Plaguelands (40), E-5, F-5, I-4, K:(4, 5), The Fungal Vale

DARK CASTER
Eastern Plaguelands (40), H:(6, 7), Corin's Crossing

DARK CLERIC BERYL
Priest Trainer, Tirisfal Glades (86), H-5, Brill (104), Second floor of Gallows' End Tavern

DARK CLERIC DUESTEN
Priest Trainer, Tirisfal Glades (86), C-7, Deathknell (109), Church

DARK GUARD
Burning Steppes (22), Searing Gorge (64), C-4/D-8, Blackrock Depths

DARK IRON AGENT
Dun Morogh (32), C-4, Gnomeregan

DARK IRON AMBASSADOR
Dun Morogh (32), C-4, Gnomeregan

DARK IRON AMBUSHER
Loch Modan (54), G-7, Spawns at Caravan

DARK IRON BOMBARDIER
Wetlands (96), G-1, Dun Modr

DARK IRON DEMOLITIONIST
Wetlands (96), F-2, H-3, I-3, Dun Modr

DARK IRON DWARF
Wetlands (96), F-2, G-2, H:(2, 3), I-3, Dun Modr

DARK IRON ENTREPRENEUR
Specialty Goods, Wetlands (96), F-2, Dun Modr, Behind bar in southern building

DARK IRON GEOLOGIST
Searing Gorge (64), H-6, I-3, Dustfire Valley

DARK IRON INSURGENT
Loch Modan (54), H:(1, 2), Stonewrought Dam, Eastern side of dam

DARK IRON LOOKOUT
Searing Gorge (64), C-5, D:(5, 6), E-6, F-6

DARK IRON MARKSMAN
Searing Gorge (64), J-2, Dustfire Valley

DARK IRON RAIDER
Loch Modan (54), H:(6, 7), Spawns at Caravan

DARK IRON RIFLEMAN
Wetlands (96), G-2, Dun Modr

DARK IRON SABOTEUR
Wetlands (96), F-2, G:(1, 2), H:(2, 3), I-3, Dun Modr

DARK IRON SAPPER
Loch Modan (54), G-1, Stonewrought Dam

DARK IRON SENTRY
Searing Gorge (64), D:(5, 6), E:(4, 6), F-6, The Slag Pit, Throughout pit

DARK IRON SLAVER
Searing Gorge (64), D:(3-6), E:(2-6), F-4, G-4, The Cauldron

DARK IRON SPY
Dun Morogh (32), K-6, Ironband's Compound

DARK IRON STEAMSMITH
Searing Gorge (64), D-5, E-5, The Cauldron

DARK IRON TASKMASTER
Searing Gorge (64), D:(3-5), E:(2-5), F-4, G-4, The Cauldron

DARK IRON TUNNELER
Wetlands (96), F-2, G-2, H:(2, 3), I-3, Dun Modr

DARK IRON WATCHMAN
Searing Gorge (64), H-6, I-3, Dustfire Valley

DARK KEEPER BETHEK
Burning Steppes (22), Searing Gorge (64), C-4/D-8, Blackrock Depths

DARK KEEPER OFGUT
Burning Steppes (22), Searing Gorge (64), C-4/D-8, Blackrock Depths

DARK KEEPER PELVER
Burning Steppes (22), Searing Gorge (64), C-4/D-8, Blackrock Depths

DARK KEEPER UGGEL
Burning Steppes (22), Searing Gorge (64), C-4/D-8, Blackrock Depths

DARK KEEPER VORFALK
Burning Steppes (22), Searing Gorge (64), C-4/D-8, Blackrock Depths

DARK KEEPER ZIMREL
Burning Steppes (22), Searing Gorge (64), C-4/D-8, Blackrock Depths

DARK SCREECHER
Burning Steppes (22), Searing Gorge (64), C-4/D-8, Blackrock Depths

DARK SHADE
Western Plaguelands (92), I-7, Scholomance

DARK SPRITE
Teldrassil (80), F-5, G-5, Fel Rock

DARK STRAND ADEPT
Ashenvale (12), C-3, D-3, Ruins of Ordil'Aran

DARK STRAND ASSASSIN
Ashenvale (12), C-3, Ruins of Ordil'Aran

DARK STRAND CULTIST
Ashenvale (12), C-3, D-3, Ruins of Ordil'Aran

DARK STRAND ENFORCER
Ashenvale (12), C-3, D-3, Ruins of Ordil'Aran

DARK STRAND EXCAVATOR
Ashenvale (12), C-3, D-3, Ruins of Ordil'Aran

DARK STRAND FANATIC
Darkshore (24), H-3, I-3, Ruins of Mathystra, Tower of Althalaxx

DARK STRAND VOIDCALLER
Darkshore (24), H-3, Tower of Althalaxx

DARK SUMMONER
Cult of the Damned, Eastern Plaguelands (40), D:(2, 3), H:(6, 7), Corin's Crossing

DARKEYE BONECASTER
Tirisfal Glades (86), E:(3, 4), F:(3, 4), Agamand Mills (100)

DARKFANG CREEPER
Dustwallow Marsh (38), D:(5, 6), E:(5, 6), F:(5, 6), Stonemaul Ruins

DARKFANG LURKER
Dustwallow Marsh (38), D:(1, 3-5), E:(1-4), F:(1-4), G:(1-4), H:(2-4)

DARKFANG SPIDER
Dustwallow Marsh (38), D:(1, 3), E:(1-3), F:(1-3), G:(1-4), H:(2-4)

DARKFANG VENOMSPITTER
Dustwallow Marsh (38), D:(4-6), E:(3-6), F:(3-6)

DARKMASTER GANDLING
Western Plaguelands (92), I-7, Scholomance

DARKMIST LURKER
Dustwallow Marsh (38), C-2, D-2, Darkmist Cavern

DARKMIST RECLUSE
Dustwallow Marsh (38), D:(2, 3), Darkmist Cavern

DARKMIST SILKSPINNER
Dustwallow Marsh (38), C-2, D-2, Darkmist Cavern

DARKMIST SPIDER
Dustwallow Marsh (38), D:(2, 3), Darkmist Cavern

DARKMIST WIDOW
Rare Spawn, Dustwallow Marsh (38), D-2, Darkmist Cavern, Lvl 40 Uncommon; Back of cavern

DARKREAVER'S FALLEN CHARGER
Western Plaguelands (92), I-7, Scholomance

DARKSHORE THRESHER
Darkshore (24), D-5, E:(2-6), F-3, Mist's Edge, The Long Wash, Twilight Shore

DARKSLAYER MORDENTHAL
Ashenvale (12), J-7, Dor'Danil Barrow Den, Northwest of barrow den

DARLA HARRIS
Gryphon Master, Hillsbrad Foothills (48), F-5, Southshore (129), Northwest of town near tower

DARN TALONGRIP
Stonetalon Mountains (70), I-9, Malaka'jin, Next to shack

DARNALL
Tailoring Supplies, Moonglade (56), G-3, Nighthaven (121), First floor of northeast building

DARNASSIAN PROTECTOR
Teldrassil (80), B-5, C-5, Rut'theran Village (125)

DARNASSUS SENTINEL
Teldrassil (80), B:(5, 6), C:(5, 6), D-5, G-9, Rut'theran Village (125)

DARNATH BLADESINGER
Warrior Trainer, Darnassus (26), H-3, Warrior's Terrace, Lower northwest platform

DARREN MALVEW
Stablehand, Hillsbrad Foothills (48), F-6, Southshore (129), Right of stable

DARROWSHIRE BETRAYER
Eastern Plaguelands (40), E-8, Darrowshire

DARROWSHIRE DEFENDER
Eastern Plaguelands (40), E-8, Darrowshire

DARSOK SWIFTDAGGER
Barrens (18), F-3, The Crossroads (107), Top of tower south of inn

DART
Rare Spawn, Dustwallow Marsh (38), F-2, Lvl 38 Uncommon; Runs in a circle near spawn point

DARYL RIKNUSSUN
Cooking Trainer, Ironforge (52), H-4, The Great Forge, The Bronze Kettle

DARYL STACK
Master Tailor, Hillsbrad Foothills (48), H-2, Tarren Mill (133), Church

DARYL THE YOUNGLING
Loch Modan (54), K-6, The Farstrider Lodge (111), In left hall of lodge

DARYN LIGHTWIND
Cenarion Lore Keeper, Teldrassil (80), G-9, Rut'theran Village (125), Second floor of building

DASHEL STONEFIST
Stormwind (72), J-4, Old Town, By The Five Deadly Venoms

DAUGHTER OF CENARIUS
Stonetalon Mountains (70), D:(1, 2), E:(1, 2), Stonetalon Peak

DAVID LANGSTON
Stormwind (72), J-5, Old Town, Pig and Whistle Tavern

DAVID TRIAS
Rogue Trainer, Tirisfal Glades (86), D-6, Deathknell (109), First floor of second house on right side of road

DAVIL CROKFORD
Eastern Plaguelands (40), E-8, Darrowshire, (Summon) Town entrance along path

DAVIL LIGHTFIRE
Eastern Plaguelands (40), E-8, Darrowshire, (Summon) Town entrance along path

DAVITT HICKSON
Undercity (88), The Magic Quarter, Wanders Magic Quarter

DAWN BRIGHTSTAR
Arcane Goods, Elwynn Forest (42), I-7, Tower of Azora, Top floor of tower

DAWNWATCHER SELGORM
The Argent Dawn, Darnassus (26), G-2, Craftsmen's Terrace, Argent Dawn

DAWNWATCHER SHAEDLASS
The Argent Dawn, Darnassus (26), G-2, Craftsmen's Terrace, Argent Dawn

DAZALAR
Hunter Trainer, Teldrassil (80), G-6, Dolanaar (109), East of inn

DEADLY CLEFT SCORPID
Badlands (16), G-1, Uldaman

DEADMIRE
Dustwallow Marsh (38), F-5, The Quagmire, Follows the stream southwest and turns around

DEAD-TOOTH JACK
Elwynn Forest (42), L-8, Camp west of bridge heading into Duskwood

DEADWIND BRUTE
Deadwind Pass (28), E-6, F:(6-8), The Vice

DEADWIND MAULER
Deadwind Pass (28), E-6, F:(6-8), G:(7, 8), The Vice

DEADWIND OGRE MAGE
Deadwind Pass (28), E-6, F:(6-8), The Vice

DEADWIND WARLOCK
Deadwind Pass (28), E-6, F:(6-8), G:(7, 8), The Vice

DEADWOOD AVENGER
Felwood (44), H:(1, 2), I:(1, 2), Felpav Village

DEADWOOD DEN WATCHER
Felwood (44), H:(1, 2), I:(1, 2), Felpav Village

DEADWOOD GARDENER
Felwood (44), F:(8, 9), G:(8, 9), Deadwood Village

DEADWOOD PATHFINDER
Felwood (44), F-9, G-9, Deadwood Village

DEADWOOD SHAMAN
Felwood (44), H:(1, 2), I:(1, 2), Felpav Village

DEADWOOD WARRIOR
Felwood (44), F:(8, 9), G:(8, 9), Deadwood Village

DEATH CULTIST
Eastern Plaguelands (40), C-2, D:(3, 4 E:(3, 4), F-3, Plaguewood

DEATH FLAYER
Rare Spawn, Durotar (34), E-5, F-5, Lv 11 Uncommon; Roams clearing south of road

DEATH HOWL
Rare Spawn, Felwood (44), G:(7-8), H-9, Felwood, Morlos'Aran, Lvl 49 Average Rare; Roams near spawn points

DEATH KNIGHT DARKREAVER
Western Plaguelands (92), I-7, Scholomance

DEATH LASH
Feralas (46), G-4, Dire Maul

DEATH SINGER
Eastern Plaguelands (40), D-6, E:(5, 6 F-5, I-3, J:(3-5), K-4, Browman Mill

DEATH SPEAKER JARGBA
Barrens (18), E-9, Razorfen Kraul

DEATHEYE
Rare Spawn, Blasted Lands (20), G:(2, 3), Dreadmaul Hold, Lvl 49 Average Rare; Roams small area arou spawn point

DEATHGUARD ABRAHAM
Tirisfal Glades (86), G-5, Bridge

DEATHGUARD BARTHOLOMEW
Tirisfal Glades (86), H-5, Brill (104)

DEATHGUARD BARTRAND
Tirisfal Glades (86), D-6, Deathknell (109)

DEATHGUARD BURGESS
Tirisfal Glades (86), H-5, Brill (104), Outside of the Brill Town Hall

DEATHGUARD CYRUS
Tirisfal Glades (86), H-5, Brill (104)

DEATHGUARD DILLINGER
Tirisfal Glades (86), H-5, Brill (104), Along road near graveyard

DEATHGUARD ELITE
Tirisfal Glades (86), E-5, H-6, Brill (104

DEATHGUARD GARVIN
Tirisfal Glades (86), H-5, Brill (104)

DEATHGUARD HUMBERT
Hillsbrad Foothills (48), H-2, Tarren Mi (133), Left of church

DEATHGUARD KEL
Tirisfal Glades (86), H-5, Kneeling in front of northeastern entrance to graveyard

DEATHGUARD LAWRENCE
Tirisfal Glades (86), G-5, Brill (104)

DEATHGUARD LINNEA
Tirisfal Glades (86), I-6, In camp outsic of Undercity

DEATHGUARD LUNDMARK
Tirisfal Glades (86), E-5, H-6, Roams Road

DEATHGUARD MORRIS
Tirisfal Glades (86), H-5, Brill (104)

DEATHGUARD MORT
Tirisfal Glades (86), H-5, Brill (104)

DEATHGUARD OLIVAR
Tirisfal Glades (86), D-6, Deathknell (109)

DEATHGUARD PHILLIP
Tirisfal Glades (86), D-6, Deathknell (109)

DEATHGUARD PODRIG
Silverpine Forest (68), F-4, The Sepulcher (127), Outside of inn entrance on left

DEATHGUARD RANDOLPH
Tirisfal Glades (86), D-6, Deathknell (109)

DEATHGUARD ROYANN
Tirisfal Glades (86), D-5, Deathknell (109)

DEATHGUARD SALTAIN
Tirisfal Glades (86), D-7, Deathknell (109), Roaming near the church

DEATHGUARD SAMSA
Hillsbrad Foothills (48), H-2, Tarren Mill (133), Roaming outside of inn

DEATHGUARD SIMMER
Tirisfal Glades (86), E-5, At the fork in the road outside of Deathknell

DEATHGUARD TERRENCE
Tirisfal Glades (86), D-5, Deathknell (109)

DEATHLASH SCORPID
Burning Steppes (22), D:(5, 6), E-3, F:(3, 7), G:(2, 3, 6), H:(5, 6), I:(3-6), J-3

DEATHLY USHER
Blasted Lands (20), G-2, Rise of the Defiler, Summoned on activation of quest

DEATHMAW
Rare Spawn, Burning Steppes (22), I-3, J-6, K:(3, 5), Dreadmaul Rock, Terror Wing Path, Lvl 53 Uncommon; Roams small area around spawn point

DEATH'S HEAD ACOLYTE
Barrens (18), E-9, Razorfen Kraul

DEATH'S HEAD ADEPT
Barrens (18), E-9, Razorfen Kraul

DEATH'S HEAD CULTIST
Barrens (18), F-9, Razorfen Downs

DEATH'S HEAD GEOMANCER
Barrens (18), F-9, Razorfen Downs

DEATH'S HEAD NECROMANCER
Barrens (18), F-9, Razorfen Downs

DEATH'S HEAD PRIEST
Barrens (18), E-9, Razorfen Kraul

DEATH'S HEAD SAGE
Barrens (18), F-9, Razorfen Downs

DEATH'S HEAD SEER
Barrens (18), E-9, Razorfen Kraul

DEATH'S HEAD WARD KEEPER
Barrens (18), E-9, Razorfen Kraul

DEATHSPEAKER SELENDRE
Rare Spawn, Cult of the Damned, Eastern Plaguelands (40), E-5, K:(4, 5), The Fungal Vale, The Noxious Glade, Lvl 56 Uncommon; In camp

DEATHSTALKER ADAMANT
Silverpine Forest (68), F-7, Shadowfang Keep

DEATHSTALKER ERLAND
Silverpine Forest (68), H-1, Malden's Orchard, House northeast of orchard

DEATHSTALKER FAERLEIA
Silverpine Forest (68), G-7, Pyrewood Village, Town hall

DEATHSTALKER LESH
Hillsbrad Foothills (48), A-5, Southpoint Tower, At base of tower

DEATHSTALKER VINCENT
Silverpine Forest (68), F-7, Shadowfang Keep

DEATHSTALKER ZRAEDUS
Duskwood (36), L-3, Beggar's Haunt, Tower entrance

DEATHSTRIKE TARANTULA
Swamp of Sorrows (76), G-6, H:(6, 7), I:(6-8), J:(7, 8)

DEATHSWORN CAPTAIN
Rare Spawn, Silverpine Forest (68), F-7, Shadowfang Keep, Lvl 25 Rare

DECAYING HORROR
Western Plaguelands (92), H:(3, 4), I:(3, 4), The Weeping Cave

DECEDRA WILLHAM
Dustwallow Marsh (38), J-6, Theramore Isle (135), Docks

DECKHAND MOISHE
Arathi Highlands (10), D-8, Faldir's Cove, Bow of ship

DECREPIT DARKHOUND
Tirisfal Glades (86), D-5, E:(4-6), F:(5, 6), G-5, H:(4-6), I:(4-6)

DEEB
Rare Spawn, Tirisfal Glades (86), G-3, H-3, The North Coast, Lvl 12 Uncommon; Stands idle at spawn point

DEEG
Blackwater Raiders, Stranglethorn Vale (74), B-8, Booty Bay (103), Third floor of The Salty Sailor Tavern

DEEK FIZZLEBIZZ
Journeyman Engineer, Loch Modan (54), F-1, Stonewrought Dam, Under scaffolding on dam wall

DEEP BORER
Desolace (30), D-5, Mauradon

DEEP DWELLER
Tanaris (78), I:(6, 7), J:(6, 7), K-6, Southbreak Shore

DEEP LURKER
Swamp of Sorrows (76), I-5, The Temple of Atal'Hakkar

DEEP POOL THRESHFIN
Ashenvale (12), B-2, Blackfathom Deeps

DEEP SEA THRESHADON
Darkshore (24), H-1, I-1, Mist's Edge

DEEP S Burning Steppes (22), Searing Gorge (64), C-4/D-8, Blackrock Depths

DEEP STRIDER
Feralas (46), C-3, D:(3-5), E:(5-7), The Forgotten Coast

DEEPMOSS CREEPER
Stonetalon Mountains (70), G-7, H:(7, 9), I:(8, 9)

DEEPMOSS VENOMSPITTER
Stonetalon Mountains (70), F:(4, 5), G:(4-7), H-6

DEEPMOSS WEBSPINNER
Stonetalon Mountains (70), G-7, H-5, I-4, J:(4, 5)

DEEPROT STOMPER
Desolace (30), D-5, Mauradon

DEEPROT TANGLER
Desolace (30), D-5, Mauradon

DEEPSTRIDER GIANT
Desolace (30), B-9, C-6, F-1, Ethel Rethor, Sar'theris Strand

DEEPSTRIDER SEARCHER
Desolace (30), B-9, C-6, F-1, Mannoroc Coven, Sar'theris Strand

DEFIAS AMBUSHER
Elwynn Forest (42), D-6

DEFIAS BANDIT
Elwynn Forest (42), C-6, D-6, F:(7, 8), G:(6, 8), I-8, J-8, L-8

DEFIAS BLACKGUARD
Westfall (94), D-7, E-7, The Deadmines

DEFIAS BODYGUARD
Elwynn Forest (42), F-9, Jerod's Landing

DEFIAS CAPTIVE
Stormwind (72), F-6, The Stockade

DEFIAS COMPANION
Westfall (94), D-7, E-7, The Deadmines

DEFIAS CONJURER
Westfall (94), D-7, E-7, The Deadmines

DEFIAS CONVICT
Stormwind (72), F-6, The Stockade

DEFIAS CUTPURSE
Elwynn Forest (42), D:(6, 7), E:(5-7), F:(5, 6), Mirror Lake, Mirror Lake Orchard

DEFIAS DIGGER
Westfall (94), D-7, E-7, The Deadmines

DEFIAS DOCKMASTER
Elwynn Forest (42), F-9, Jerod's Landing, House on riverbank

DEFIAS DRONE
Westfall (94), H-7, Tower

DEFIAS ENCHANTER
Duskwood (36), B-7, C-7, G-8, The Yorgen Farmstead

DEFIAS EVOKER
Westfall (94), D-7, E-7, The Deadmines

DEFIAS FOOTPAD
Westfall (94), F-2, G-2, The Jansen Stead

DEFIAS HENCHMAN
Westfall (94), D-7, E-7, The Deadmines

DEFIAS HIGHWAYMAN
Westfall (94), D-8, E-8, F:(7, 8), The Dagger Hills

DEFIAS INMATE
Stormwind (72), F-6, The Stockade

DEFIAS INSURGENT
Stormwind (72), F-6, The Stockade

DEFIAS KNUCKLEDUSTER
Westfall (94), C:(7, 8), D:(7-8), E-8, F:(7, 8), G-6, The Dagger Hills

DEFIAS LOOTER
Westfall (94), B-5, C:(3-6), D:(5-7), E:(2, 6, 7), Gold Coast Quarry

DEFIAS MAGICIAN
Westfall (94), D-7, E-7, The Deadmines

DEFIAS MESSENGER
Westfall (94), E-7, Moonbrook, Roams along the road from Moonbrook to the back of the Jangolode Mine

DEFIAS MINER
Westfall (94), D-7, E-7, The Deadmines

DEFIAS NIGHT BLADE
Duskwood (36), B-7, C-7, F:(7, 8), G-8, The Yorgen Farmstead

DEFIAS NIGHT RUNNER
Duskwood (36), B:(6, 7), C:(6, 7), F-7, G:(7, 8), H-7, The Yorgen Farmstead

DEFIAS OVERSEER
Westfall (94), D-7, E-7, The Deadmines

DEFIAS PATHSTALKER
Westfall (94), C:(7, 8), D:(6, 7), E-8, F:(7, 8), The Dagger Hills

DEFIAS PILLAGER
Westfall (94), B-5, C:(4-6), D:(5-7), E:(6, 7), Gold Coast Quarry

DEFIAS PIRATE
Westfall (94), D-7, E-7, The Deadmines

DEFIAS PRISONER
Stormwind (72), F-6, The Stockade

DEFIAS PROFITEER
Freewheeling Merchant, Westfall (94), E-7, Moonbrook, Top floor of Moonbrook inn

DEFIAS RAIDER
Westfall (94), D-8, Moonbrook

DEFIAS RENEGADE MAGE
Westfall (94), D-8, F-8, The Dagger Hills

DEFIAS ROGUE WIZARD
Elwynn Forest (42), C-6, D-6, G:(6, 8), J:(5, 6), K-5

DEFIAS SMUGGLER
Westfall (94), D-4, E:(2-5), F:(2, 4, 5), Jangolode Mine

DEFIAS SQUALLSHAPER
Westfall (94), D-7, E-7, The Deadmines

DEFIAS STRIP MINER
Westfall (94), D-7, E-7, The Deadmines

DEFIAS TASKMASTER
Westfall (94), D-7, E-7, The Deadmines

DEFIAS THUG
Elwynn Forest (42), G:(4, 5), H:(4, 5), Northshire Valley (122)

DEFIAS TOWER PATROLLER
Westfall (94), I-7, Tower

DEFIAS TOWER SENTRY
Westfall (94), I-7, Tower

DEFIAS TRAITOR
Westfall (94), F-5, Sentinel Hill (126), Sentinel Tower

DEFIAS TRAPPER
Westfall (94), C-3, D-4, E:(2-5), F:(2, 4, 5)

DEFIAS WATCHMAN
Westfall (94), D-7, E-7, The Deadmines

DEFIAS WIZARD
Westfall (94), D-7, E-7, The Deadmines

DEFIAS WORKER
Westfall (94), D-7, E-7, The Deadmines

DEILIA VERANA
Hillsbrad Foothills (48), H-2, Tarren Mill (133)

DEINO
Mage Trainer, Orgrimmar (60), D-8, Valley of Spirit, Darkbriar Lodge

DELFRUM FLINTBEARD
Journeyman Blacksmith, Darkshore (24), F-4, Auberdine (101), In front of northern building

DELGO RAGETOTEM
Axe Merchant, Thunder Bluff (84), F-6, High rise, inside Ragetotem Arms tent

DELGREN THE PURIFIER
Ashenvale (12), D-4, Maestra's Post, Near Stones south of outpost

DELLA
Jessir's Pet, Felwood (44), G-8, Emerald Sanctuary (110), Near Pool

DELLYLAH
Food & Drink Vendor, Teldrassil (80), H-4, Shadowglen (127), Open room in front of main building

DELMANIS THE HATED
Darkshore (24), H-3, Tower of Althalaxx, Roams hills east of tower to bonfire

DEMETRIA
The Scarlet Oracle, Eastern Plaguelands (40), K-8, Tyr's Hand, (Summon) Patrols with nine Scarlet troopers to Stratholme (D-2)

DEMISETTE CLOYCE
Warlock Trainer, Stormwind (72), D-8, Mage Quarter, The Slaughtered Lamb

DEMNUL FARMOUNTAIN
Ironforge (52), J-9, The Military Ward, Hall of Arms

DEMON PORTAL GUARDIAN
Desolace (30), F:(7, 8), G:(7, 8), Mannoroc Coven

DEMON SPIRIT
Desolace (30), G-3, Thunder Axe Fortress

DEN GRUNT
Durotar (34), F-7, G-7, Valley of Trials (136)

DEN MOTHER
Darkshore (24), H-4, Mist's Edge

DENALAN
Teldrassil (80), H-7, Lake Al'Ameth, Camp east of lake

DENATHARION
Druid Trainer, Darnassus (26), D-1, Cenarion Enclave, Northwest structure

DENDRITE STARBLAZE
Moonglade (56), H-3, Nighthaven (121), Second floor of far northeast building on hill

DENDRYTHIS
Food & Drink Vendor, Darnassus (26), F-2, Cenarion Enclave

DENEB WALKER
Scrolls and Potions, Arathi Highlands (10), C-6, Stromgarde Keep (132), Well near church

DENNI'KA
Butcher, Stonetalon Mountains (70), I-9, Malaka'jin, Next to wagon, north of den

DEPUTY FELDON
Redridge Mountains (62), D-6, Next to Gryphon Master outside of Lakeshire

DEPUTY RAINER
Elwynn Forest (42), C-7, Westbrook Garrison, Right of garrison entrance

DEPUTY WILLEM
Elwynn Forest (42), F-4, Northshire Valley (122), Outside to the right of abbey

DERAK NIGHTFALL
Cook, Hillsbrad Foothills (48), H-2, Tarren Mill (133), Between the inn and graveyard

DEREK THE UNDYING
Mage Trainer, Undercity (88), G-2

DERINA RUMDNUL
Wetlands (96), A-6, Menethil Harbor (119), In and out of small house east of keep

DERMOT
Alterac Mountains (8), B-8, Lordamere Internment Camp, Building within camp walls

DERMOT JOHNS
Cloth & Leather Armor Merchant, Elwynn Forest (42), F-4, Northshire Valley (122), Caravan facing abbey

DEROTAIN MUDSIPPER
The Thorium Brotherhood, Tanaris (78), H-3, Gadgetzan (113), Near southern entrance

DESERT RAGER
Silithus (66), D:(4, 5), F:(4, 5)

DESERT RUMBLER
Silithus (66), D-1, E:(1-3), F:(3, 4), G-3, Ravaged Twilight Camp

DESSECUS
Rare Spawn, Felwood (44), H-2, Irontree Cavern, Lvl 56 Semi-Rare; Bottom cave

DETH'RYLL SATYR
Darkshore (24), G-4, Bashal'Aran

DEVIATE ADDER
Barrens (18), E-4, Wailing Caverns

DEVIATE COILER
Barrens (18), E-4, Wailing Caverns

DEVIATE CREEPER
Barrens (18), E-4, Wailing Caverns

DEVIATE CROCOLISK
Barrens (18), E-4, Wailing Caverns

DEVIATE DREADFANG
Barrens (18), E-4, Wailing Caverns

DEVIATE GUARDIAN
Barrens (18), E-4, Wailing Caverns

DEVIATE LASHER
Barrens (18), E-4, Wailing Caverns

DEVIATE MOCASSIN
Barrens (18), E-4, Wailing Caverns

DEVIATE PYTHON
Barrens (18), E-4, Wailing Caverns

DEVIATE RAVAGER
Barrens (18), E-4, Wailing Caverns

DEVIATE SHAMBLER
Barrens (18), E-4, Wailing Caverns

DEVIATE SLAYER
Barrens (18), E-4, Wailing Caverns

DEVIATE STALKER
Barrens (18), E-4, Wailing Caverns

DEVIATE STINGLASH
Barrens (18), E-4, Wailing Caverns

DEVIATE VENOMWING
Barrens (18), E-4, Wailing Caverns

DEVIATE VIPER
Barrens (18), E-4, Wailing Caverns

DEVILSAUR
Un'Goro Crater (90), D:(3, 4), F-8, H:(3, 8), J-4

DEVLIN AGAMAND
Tirisfal Glades (86), F-4, Agamand Mills (100), Roams small area around spawn point

DEVOURING ECTOPLASM
Barrens (18), E-4, Wailing Caverns

DEVOURING OOZE
Western Plaguelands (92), H:(3, 4), I:(3, 4), The Weeping Cave

DEVRAK
Wind Rider Master, Barrens (18), F-3, The Crossroads (107), West of inn

DEWIN SHIMMERDAWN
Alchemy Supplies, Wetlands (96), A-6, Menethil Harbor (119), Building west of keep

DEXTREN WARD
Stormwind (72), F-6, The Stockade

DEZE SNOWBANE
Arathi Basin Battlemaster, Orgrimmar (61), J-3

DHUGRU GORELUST
Warlock Trainer, Durotar (34), H-4, Razor Hill (124), Behind barracks

DIAMOND HEAD
Rare Spawn, Feralas (46), A:(5-6), C:(5-6), Sardor Isle, Lvl 45 Semi-Rare; Seabed off coast of isle

DIATHORUS THE SEEKER
Ashenvale (12), J-7, Demon Fall Ridge, Overlooking central intersection at bottom of dungeon

DIEMETRADON
Un'Goro Crater (90), E-2, F:(3, 6, 7), G:(2-4, 6, 7), H:(2, 5-8)

DIGGER FLAMEFORGE
Rare Spawn, Excavation Specialist, Barrens (18), E-8, Bael Modan, Lvl 24 Uncommon; In excavation site tent

DIGGERSPINE SHORESTALKER
Hillsbrad Foothills (48), H-8, Eastern Strand

DIGMASTER SHOVELPHLANGE
Rare Spawn, Badlands (16), G-1, Uldaman, Lvl 38 Semi-Rare

DINITA STONEMANTLE
Vault Administrator, Ironforge (52), D-6, The Commons, Vault of Ironforge

DINK
Mage Trainer, Ironforge (52), C-1, The Mystic Ward, Hall of Mysteries

DIRANIA SILVERSHINE
Teldrassil (80), H-4, Shadowglen (127), Cauldron southeast of Aldrassil

DIRE CONDOR
Redridge Mountains (62), C-3, D-7, F:(3, 4, 7, 8), G:(4, 5, 7), H:(5, 7, 8), I-7

DIRE MOTTLED BOAR
Durotar (34), F:(3-5), G:(3-5, 7), H:(3-8), H-8, I:(4, 5)

DIRGE QUIKCLEAVE
Trainer/Butcher (Cooking), Tanaris (78), H-3, Gadgetzan (113), Inn

DIRK THUNDERWOOD
Silithus (67), G-4, Cenarion Hold (106)

DISCIPLE OF NARALEX
Barrens (18), E-4, Wailing Caverns

DISEASED BLACK BEAR
Western Plaguelands (92), C-6, D:(5-7), E:(6, 7), The Bulwark (105)

DISEASED FLAYER
Eastern Plaguelands (40), D-6, E:(5, 6), F-5, I-4, J:(4, 5), K-4, The Noxious Glade

DISEASED GHOUL
Western Plaguelands (92), I-7, Scholomance

DISEASED GRIZZLY
Western Plaguelands (92), G:(5, 6), H:(4-6), I:(4-6)

DISEASED WOLF
Western Plaguelands (92), E-5, F:(3-6), G:(3-7)

DISHU
Rare Spawn, Barrens (18), F:(2-3), Lvl 13 Uncommon; Patrols close to spawn points

DISPATCH COMMANDER METZ
The Argent Dawn, Eastern Plaguelands (40), K-6, Light's Hope Chapel (118)

DISPATCH COMMANDER RUAG
Swamp of Sorrows (76), F-5, Stonard (131), Third floor of main hall

DIZZY ONE-EYE
Blackwater Raiders, Stranglethorn Vale (74), B-8, Booty Bay (103), Outside near waterfall on the third level along the eastern side of bay

DOAN KARHAN
Barrens (18), F-6, Southern Barrens, Northeast of Camp Taurajo

DOC MIXILPIXIL
Gnomeregan Exiles, Stormwind (72), L-6, Old Town, SI:7

DOCKMASTER BAREN
Redridge Mountains (62), C-5, Lakeshire (117), In front of shed near docks west of the bridge

DOCTOR DRAXLEGAUGE
Arathi Highlands (10), D-8, Faldir's Cove, Bonfire on hill

DOCTOR GREGORY VICTOR
Trauma Surgeon (First Aid), Arathi Highlands (10), J-4, Hammerfall (115), Inside west building

DOCTOR GUSTAF VANHOWZEN
Trauma Surgeon (First Aid), Dustwallow Marsh (38), I-5, Theramore Isle (135), First floor of Foothold Citadel

DOCTOR HERBERT HALSEY
Alchemist Trainer, Undercity (88), F-7, The Apothecarium, In laboratory

DOCTOR MARSH
Alchemist Trainer, Undercity (88), G-7, The Apothecarium, Near Royal Quarter entry

DOCTOR MARTIN FELBEN
Alchemist Trainer, Undercity (88), F-7, The Apothecarium, In laboratory

DOCTOR THEOLEN KRASTINOV
Western Plaguelands (92), I-7, Scholomance

DOG
Sire, Thousand Needles (82), F-5, Freewind Post (112), Roaming near hut, west of inn

DO'GOL
Dustwallow Marsh (38), D-3, Brackenwall Village (104), Northern part of village

DOLKIN CRAGHELM
Mail Armor Merchant, Ironforge (52), G-9, The Military Ward, Craghelm's Plate and Chain

DOLMAN STEELFURY
Weapon Merchant, Ironforge (52), E:(6, 7), The Commons, Steelfury's Weapon Emporium

DOLORAN SHIELD GUARD
Alterac Mountains (8), B-8, Lordamere Internment Camp

DON GAROK PRIEST
Hillsbrad Foothills (48), I-8, Dun Garok

DON POMPA
Wetlands (96), A-6, Baradin Bay, Northern dock

DONAL OSGOOD
Arathi Basin Battlemaster, Ironforge (52), J-9

DONALD RABONNE
Fisherman, Hillsbrad Foothills (48), F-6, Southshore (129), On docks in front of shed

DONNI ANTHANIA
Crazy Cat Lady, Elwynn Forest (42), F-5, House southwest of Northshire Valley

DONOVA SNOWDEN
Winterspring (98), E-5, Frostfire Hot Springs, Tent in valley

DONYAL TOVALD
Librarian, Stormwind (72), K-1, Stormwind Keep, Royal Library

DOOM'REL
Burning Steppes (22), Searing Gorge (64), C-4/D-8, Blackrock Depths

DOOMFORGE ARCANASMITH
Burning Steppes (22), Searing Gorge (64), C-4/D-8, Blackrock Depths

DOOMFORGE CRAFTSMAN
Burning Steppes (22), Searing Gorge (64), C-4/D-8, Blackrock Depths

DOOMFORGE DRAGOON
Burning Steppes (22), Searing Gorge (64), C-4/D-8, Blackrock Depths

DOOMGUARD COMMANDER
Blasted Lands (20), E-6, F:(6-8), G-7, H-6, I-6, Dark Portal, The Tainted Scar

DOOMGUARD MINION
Feralas (46), G-4, Dire Maul

DOOMWARDER
Desolace (30), F:(7, 8), G:(7, 8), Mannoroc Coven

DOOMWARDER CAPTAIN
Desolace (30), G-8, Mannoroc Coven

DOPE'REL
Burning Steppes (22), Searing Gorge (64), C-4/D-8, Blackrock Depths

DORAN STEELWING
The Hinterlands (50), B-4, Aerie Peak (100), Wildhammer Keep

DORAS
Wind Rider Master, Orgrimmar (60), E-6 , Valley of Strength, The Skytower, top floor

DOREEN BELTIS
Tirisfal Glades (86), H-5, Brill (104)

DORIN SONGBLADE
Armorer, Redridge Mountains (62), D-5, Lakeshire (117), Stable

DORION
Hunter Trainer, Darnassus (26), E-1, Cenarion Enclave, Northeast structure, upper level

DORIS VOLANTHIUS
Armor Quartermaster, Orgrimmar (61), E-7

DORIUS STONETENDER
Searing Gorge (64), H-6, Grimesilt Dig Site, Lying injured in dig site

DORN PLAINSTALKER
Thousand Needles (82), G-4, The Weathered Nook, Den

DOYO'DA
Orgrimmar (60), F-7 , Valley of Strength, Inn

DRAC ROUGHCUT
Tradesman, Loch Modan (54), D-5, Thelsamar (134), Stoutlager Inn

DRACONIC MAGELORD
Azshara (14), E:(7, 8), Lake Mennar

DRACONIC MAGEWEAVER
Azshara (14), D:(7, 8), E:(7, 8), Lake Mennar

DRAENEI EXILE
Swamp of Sorrows (76), C-3, The Harborage

DRAENEI REFUGEE
Blasted Lands (20), G-3, H-3, Rise of the Defiler

DRAG MASTER MIGLEN
Thousand Needles (82), K-8, Mirage Raceway (119), Grandstands at drag strip

DRAGONMAW BATTLEMASTER
Wetlands (96), G-5, Angerfang Encampment

DRAGONMAW BONEWARDER
Wetlands (96), F:(4, 5), G:(4, 5), Angerfang Encampment

DRAGONMAW CENTURION
Wetlands (96), G-5, Angerfang Encampment

DRAGONMAW GRUNT
Wetlands (96), F:(7, 8), G:(6-8), Dun Algaz, Thelgen Rock

DRAGONMAW RAIDER
Wetlands (96), E:(4, 5), F:(4, 5), G:(4, 5), Angerfang Encampment, The Green Belt

DRAGONMAW SCOUT
Wetlands (96), F:(7, 8), G:(7, 8), Dun Algaz

DRAGONMAW SHADOWWARDER
Wetlands (96), G-5, Angerfang Encampment

DRAGONMAW SWAMPRUNNER
Wetlands (96), E-5, F:(4, 5), G:(4, 5), Angerfang Encampment, Whelgar's Excavation Site

DRAKE LINDGREN
General & Trade Supplies, Elwynn Forest (42), K-7, Eastvale Logging Camp, House

DRAKK STONEHAND
Master Leatherworking Trainer, The Hinterlands (50), B-4, Aerie Peak (100), Wildhammer Keep

DRAN DROFFERS
Droffers and Son Salvage, Orgrimmar (60), G-4, The Drag, Droffer and Sons Salvage

DRANH
Skinner, Barrens (18), F-6, Camp Taurajo (106), Near hides

DRAYL
Thunder Bluff (84), G-8, Hunter Rise, On Hunter's Rise in Thunder Bluff

DRAZ'ZILB
Dustwallow Marsh (38), D-3, Brackenwall Village (104), In cave to southeast

DRAZZIT DRIPVALVE
Dustwallow Marsh (38), F-7, Mudsprocket (120)

DREAD FLYER
Desolace (30), D-4, E:(4-6), F:(4-6), G:(4, 5), H:(4-6), J:(1, 4, 5), K:(2, 4, 5)

DREAD GUARD
Feralas (46), G-4, Dire Maul

DREAD RIPPER
Desolace (30), C-8, D-8, G-8, H:(7, 8), Mannoroc Coven, Sar'theris Strand

DREAD SWOOP
Desolace (30), D-7, E:(2-4, 6-8), F:(1-4), G:(1-4, 6, 7), H:(1-4), I:(2-7), J:(3-6), K-4

DREAD WEAVER
Eastern Plaguelands (40), J:(4, 5), K-4, The Noxious Glade

DREADLORD
Blasted Lands (20), E:(6, 7), F:(7, 8), G-7, The Tainted Scar

DREADMAUL BRUTE
Blasted Lands (20), F:(1, 2), G-1, Dreadmaul Hold

DREADMAUL MAULER
Blasted Lands (20), G:(4, 5), Dreadmaul Post

DREADMAUL OGRE
Blasted Lands (20), F:(1, 2), G-1, Dreadmaul Hold

DREADMAUL OGRE MAGE
Blasted Lands (20), F:(1, 2), G-1, Dreadmaul Hold

DREADMAUL WARLOCK
Blasted Lands (20), G:(4, 5), Dreadmaul Post

DREADSCORN
Rare Spawn, Blasted Lands (20), F-3, Altar of Storms, Lvl 57 Uncommon; Patrols to foot of hill in Blasted Lands (F-4)

DREADSTEED SPIRIT
Feralas (46), G-4, Dire Maul

DREADWHISPER
Rare Spawn, Western Plaguelands (92), H-6, Gahrron's Withering, Lvl 58 Semi-Rare; Roams small area around spawn point

DREAMING WHELP
Swamp of Sorrows (76), A:(5, 6), B:(5, 6), Itharius's Cave

DREAMROARER
Feralas (46), F-1, Dream Bough, Roams small land mass

DREAMSCYTHE
Swamp of Sorrows (76), I-5, The Temple of Atal'Hakkar

DREAMSTALKER
Ashenvale (12), L-4, Bough Shadow, Hovers on dais in front of portal

DREAMTRACKER
The Hinterlands (50), I-2, Seradane, Idles at spawn point

DREDGE CRUSHER
Silithus (66), D:(2, 3), E:(2-4), F:(3, 4), G:(3, 4)

DREDGE STRIKER
Silithus (66), E:(1, 2), F:(1, 2), G:(1-3), H:(1-3), Hive'Ashi, Southwind Village

DREDGE WORM
Burning Steppes (22), Searing Gorge (64), C-4/D-8, Blackrock Depths

DREKA'SUR
Felwood (44), E-5, Bloodvenom Post (102), Campfire

DRIZZLIK
Stranglethorn Vale (74), B-8, Booty Bay (103), Tan-Your-Hide Leatherworks (shop)

DROGOTH THE ROAMER
Rare Spawn, Dustwallow Marsh (38), D-1, Bluefen, Lvl 37 Uncommon; Roams throughout Bluefen

DROVNAR STRONGBREW
Alchemy Supplies, Arathi Highlands (10), F-5, Refuge Point (124), Roams camp

DRUID OF THE FANG
Barrens (18), E-4, Wailing Caverns

DRULL
Hillsbrad Foothills (48), J-4, Durnholde Keep, Building in lower level of keep

DRULZEGAR SKRAGHOOK
Desolace (30), B-7, Shadowprey Village (128), Down by dock

DRUM FEL
Arathi Highlands (10), J-3, Hammerfall (115), Platform of north building

DRUNKEN FOOTPAD
Alterac Mountains (8), H:(6, 7), Sofera's Naze

DRUSILLA LA SALLE
Warlock Trainer, Elwynn Forest (42), G-4, Northshire Valley (122), Graveyard on right side of abbey

DRYSNAP CRAWLER
Desolace (30), B:(5-9), C:(3-5, 8), D:(3, 4), Ethel Rethor, Sar'theris Strand

DRYWALLOW CROCOLISK
Dustwallow Marsh (38), D:(2, 3), E:(1-3, F:(2, 3), G:(2-4), H-3, Bluefen, Brackenwall Village (104)

DRYWALLOW DAGGERMAW
Dustwallow Marsh (38), E:(6-8), F:(7, 8), F:(7, 8), The Dragonmurk

DRYWALLOW SNAPPER
Dustwallow Marsh (38), D:(3-6), E:(3-6), F:(4-6), G:(5, 6), The Dragonmurk, The Quagmire

DRYWALLOW VICEJAW
Dustwallow Marsh (38), D:(2-4), E:(1-4), F:(2-4), G:(2-4), H-3, Bluefen, The Quagmire

DRYWHISKER DIGGER
Arathi Highlands (10), L:(3, 4), Drywhisker Gorge

DRYWHISKER KOBOLD
Arathi Highlands (10), K:(3, 4), L-4, Drywhisker Gorge

DRYWHISKER SURVEYOR
Arathi Highlands (10), L-3, Drywhisker Gorge

DUGGAN WILDHAMMER
Rare Spawn, Eastern Plaguelands (40), B-7, C-6, D-8, E-7, The Undercroft, Lvl 55 Semi-Rare; Roams small area around spawn point

DUGHAL STORMWING
Burning Steppes (22), Searing Gorge (64), C-4/D-8, Blackrock Depths

DUHNG
Cook, Barrens (18), G-3, Inside hut east of Crossroads

DUKE HYDRAXIS
Azshara (14), J-7, Bay of Storms, Island off the coast

DUKE NICHOLAS ZVERENHOFF
The Argent Dawn, Eastern Plaguelands (40), K-6, Light's Hope Chapel (118), Camp on right side of chapel

DULCIEA FROSTMOON
Cloth Armor Merchant, Feralas (46), C-4, Feathermoon Stronghold (111), Inn

DUN GAROK MOUNTAINEER
Hillsbrad Foothills (48), I-8, Dun Garok

DUN GAROK RIFLEMAN
Hillsbrad Foothills (48), I-8, Dun Garok

DUN MOROGH MOUNTAINEER
Dun Morogh (32), D:(4, 5), I:(5, 6), L:(3-5)

DUNCAN CULLEN
Light Armor Merchant, Stormwind (72), G-7, Mage Quarter, Duncan's Textiles

DUNE SMASHER
Tanaris (78), E-8, F-8, Uldum, Valley of the Watchers

DUNEMAUL BRUTE
Tanaris (78), F:(5-7), G:(6, 7), Dunemaul Compound, Eastmoon Ruins, Southmoon Ruins

DUNEMAUL ENFORCER
Tanaris (78), F:(5-7), G:(6, 7), Dunemaul Compound, Eastmoon Ruins, Southmoon Ruins

DUNEMAUL OGRE
Tanaris (78), F:(5-7), G:(6, 7), Dunemaul Compound, Eastmoon Ruins, Southmoon Ruins

DUNEMAUL OGRE MAGE
Tanaris (78), F:(5-7), G:(6, 7), Dunemaul Compound, Eastmoon Ruins, Southmoon Ruins

DUNEMAUL WARLOCK
Tanaris (78), F:(5-7), G:(6, 7), Dunemaul Compound, Eastmoon Ruins, Southmoon Ruins

DUNGAR LONGDRINK
Gryphon Master, Stormwind (72), J-6, Trade District, Next to gryphons

DUOKNA
General Goods, Durotar (34), F-7, Valley of Trials (136), Northwest structure

DURIEL MOONFIRE
Ashenvale (12), H-7, Silverwing Outpost

DURIK
Stable Master, Stranglethorn Vale (74), C-3, Grom'gol Base Camp (114)

DURNAN FURCUTTER
Cloth & Leather Armor Merchant, Dun Morogh (32), D-7, Coldridge Valley (107), Anvilmar

DUROTAR TIGER
Durotar (34), I:(8, 9), J:(7-9), Echo Isle

DURTHAM GRELDON
Ironforge (52), G-1, The Forlorn Cavern, South building, inside east entrance

DUSKBAT
Tirisfal Glades (86), C:(6, 7), D:(6, 7), Deathknell (109)

DUSKSTALKER
Rare Spawn, Teldrassil (80), F-8, G-8, Lvl 9 Uncommon; Patrols south of Lake Al'Ameth

DUSKWING
Eastern Plaguelands (40), D-6, Patrols large portion of Eastern Plaguelands

DUST DEVIL
Westfall (94), C:(3, 5, 7), D:(2, 4, 6), E-5, F-4, G:(3, 5), H-7, Gold Coast Quarry, Throughout Westfall

DUST STORMER
Silithus (66), D:(1, 2), E:(1, 2), F-2, G:(1, 2), H:(1, 2), Hive'Ashi, The Crystal Vale

DUSTBELCHER BRUTE
Badlands (16), D-6, I-7, Camp Wurg, Rock and Fire

DUSTBELCHER LORD
Badlands (16), A-9, B-9, Dustbelcher Grotto

DUSTBELCHER MAULER
Badlands (16), A:(7, 8), B:(7, 8), I-7, Dustbelcher Grotto

DUSTBELCHER MYSTIC
Badlands (16), I-7, J:(2, 3), Camp Kosh

DUSTBELCHER OGRE
Badlands (16), D-6, I-7, Dustbelcher Grotto

DUSTBELCHER OGRE MAGE
Badlands (16), A-9, B-9, Dustbelcher Grotto

DUSTBELCHER SHAMAN
Badlands (16), A:(8, 9), B:(7, 8), I-7, Dustbelcher Grotto

DUSTBELCHER WARRIOR
Badlands (16), J-2, Camp Kosh

DUSTBELCHER WYRMHUNTER
Badlands (16), A:(7, 8), B:(7, 8), I-7, Dustbelcher Grotto

DUSTWIND HARPY
Durotar (34), G:(2, 3), H-3, Drygulch Ravine, Razorwind Canyon, Tor'kren Farm

DUSTWIND PILLAGER
Durotar (34), G:(2, 3), H-3, Drygulch Ravine, Jaggedswine Farm, Razorwind Canyon

DUSTWIND SAVAGE
Durotar (34), H:(2, 3), Drygulch Ravine

DUSTWIND STORM WITCH
Durotar (34), H-2, Drygulch Ravine

DUTHORIAN RALL
Stormwind (72), F-2, Cathedral Square, Cathedral of Light

DWANE WERTLE
Chef, Dustwallow Marsh (38), I-5, Theramore Isle (135), First floor of Foothold Citadel

DWUKK
Journeyman Blacksmith, Durotar (34), H-4, Razor Hill (124), Northeast of inn

DYING ARCHAEOLOGIST
Searing Gorge (64), E-3, The Slag Pit, Lying next to the Altar of Suntara

DYING KODO
Desolace (30), F:(1, 2, 5, 6), G:(1, 6, 9), H-9, J-6, Ghost Walker Post (113), Kodo Graveyard

DYSLIX SILVERGRUB
Flight Master, Dustwallow Marsh (38), F-7, Mudsprocket (120)

E

EAGAN PELTSKINNER
Elwynn Forest (42), F-4, Northshire Valley (122), Camp on left side of abbey

EALYSHIA DEWWHISPER
Two Handed Weapon Merchant, Darnassus (26), H-7, Tradesmen's Terrace, Two Handed Weapons shop

EARTHBORER
Orgrimmar (60), F-5, Ragefire Chasm

EARTHCALLER HALMGAR
Barrens (18), E-9, Razorfen Kraul

RTHEN CUSTODIAN
adlands (16), G-1, Uldaman

RTHEN GUARDIAN
adlands (16), G-1, Uldaman

RTHEN HALLSHAPER
adlands (16), G-1, Uldaman

RTHEN ROCKSMASHER
adlands (16), G-1, Uldaman

RTHEN SCULPTOR
adlands (16), G-1, Uldaman

RTHEN STONEBREAKER
adlands (16), G-1, Uldaman

RTHEN STONECARVER
adlands (16), G-1, Uldaman

STVALE LUMBERJACK
lwynn Forest (42), K-6, Eastvale Logging Camp

STVALE PEASANT
lwynn Forest (42), K-7, Eastvale Logging Camp

RU
Disciple of Naralex, Barrens (18), E-4, The Wailing Caverns, Right eye of cave above entrance

HEYAKEE
Barrens (18), G-2, (Summon) Bones northeast of Grol'dom Farm

K'ALOM
Rare Spawn, Ashenvale (12), F-7, G-7, Mystral Lake, Lvl 27 Average Rare; spawns in areas around lake

AN THE HOWLER
Rare Spawn, Dun Morogh (32), E-5, F-5, The Grizzled Den, Lvl 9 Uncommon; n cave

ANA HATETALON
Feralas (46), D-1, Ruins of Ravenwind, (Summon) Use the horn to call her

NA MULLBY
Trade Supplier, Stormwind (72), I-6, Trade District, Everyday Merchandise

RICK KILLIAN
Undercity (88), The War Quarter, Wanders Canals and War Quarter

RIS BARLEYBEARD
Barmaid, Ironforge (52), J-7, The Military Ward, Bruuk's Corner

WARD
Undercity (88), G-2, The War Quarter, Fights Captives in War Quarter

WARD REMINGTON
Guild Tabard Designer, Undercity (88), -4, The Trade Quarter, East spoke from bank

WIN HARLY
General Supplies, Silverpine Forest (68), G-4, The Sepulcher (127), In front of crates on right side of sepulcher

WIN VANCLEEF
Westfall (94), D-7, E-7, The Deadmines

WINA MONZOR
Fletcher, Wetlands (96), A-6, Menethil Harbor (119), Next to wagon, east of keep

FSEE
Pet, Redridge Mountains (62), C-5, Lakeshire (117), L-shaped dock west of the bridge

GAN
Eastern Plaguelands (40), B-3, Terrordale, House

INAR STONEGRIP
Wetlands (96), G-4, Intersection of road to Menethil Harbor and road to Dun Modr

NRIS BRIGHTSPEAR
Hunter Trainer, Stormwind (72), I-2, Dwarven District, Building south of tram entrance

TRIGG
Orgrimmar (60), C-4, Valley of Wisdom, Grommash Hold

LADRIEL
Skinning Trainer, Darnassus (26), I-2, Craftsmen's Terrace, Leatherworking shop

LAINE CAREVIN
Duskwood (36), J-5, Darkshire (108), First floor of house

LAINE TRIAS
Mistress of Cheese, Stormwind (72), I-6, Trade District, Trias' Cheese

LANARIA
Darnassus (26), H-3, Warrior's Terrace, Lower northwest platform

LDER ASHENVALE BEAR
Ashenvale (12), H:(5, 6), I:(5, 6)

ELDER BLACK BEAR
Loch Modan (54), B:(7, 8), C:(1-6), D:(2-4, 6, 7), E:(3, 5-7), Dun Algaz

ELDER CLOUD SERPENT
Thousand Needles (82), A-3, B:(3, 4), G:(4, 5), H-5, Highperch, Whitereach Post, Windbreak Canyon

ELDER CRAG BOAR
Dun Morogh (32), C:(4, 5), D:(3-5), E:(3-5), F:(3, 4), G:(5, 6), H:(5, 6), I:(5, 6), J:(5, 6), K:(4-6)

ELDER CRAG COYOTE
Badlands (16), A-6, B:(6-8), C:(5, 6, 8), D:(5-7), E:(6, 7), F:(6, 7), Apocryphan's Rest

ELDER DARKSHORE THRESHER
Darkshore (24), D:(6, 7, 9), E:(7-9), G:(1, 2), H:(1. 2), I-1, Twilight Shore

ELDER DIEMETRADON
Un'Goro Crater (90), C:(3-7), D:(3-8), E:(2-8), F:(5, 6)

ELDER DRAGONKIN
Swamp of Sorrows (76), J:(4, 5), K:(4, 5), Sorrowmurk

ELDER GRAY BEAR
Hillsbrad Foothills (48), B:(1-6), C:(1-3, 5-7), D:(3, 5, 6), E:(5, 6), G-5, H:(4-6), I:(2, 3, 5-7), J:(3-7), K:(3-5), L-4, Throughout Hillsbrad

ELDER LAKE CREEPER
Silverpine Forest (68), K:(2-4), The Dawning Isles

ELDER LAKE SKULKER
Silverpine Forest (68), K-4, Fenris Isle

ELDER MESA BUZZARD
Arathi Highlands (10), B:(6, 7), C-7, D-7, G-8

ELDER MISTVALE GORILLA
Stranglethorn Vale (74), C:(6, 7)

ELDER MOSS CREEPER
Hillsbrad Foothills (48), G:(5-7), H:(7, 8), I:(6, 7), J-7

ELDER MOTTLED BOAR
Durotar (34), E:(2-5), F:(1-6), G:(1-3), H:(1-3), I:(2, 3)

ELDER MOUNTAIN BOAR
Loch Modan (54), H:(3, 4), I:(3, 4), J:(4, 5), K-5, The Farstrider Lodge (111)

ELDER MYSTIC RAZORSNOUT
Rare Spawn, Barrens (18), G:(2, 3), Thorn Hill, Lvl 15 Uncommon; Eastern Razormane camp

ELDER NIGHTSABER
Teldrassil (80), D-3, E:(3, 4), F:(3, 4), The Oracle Glade, Wellspring Lake

ELDER PLAINSTRIDER
Mulgore (58), C:(2, 3), D:(1-5), E:(1-5), F:(1-5), G:(2-7), H:(3, 5, 6)

ELDER RAGE SCAR
Feralas (46), F-3, Rage Scar Hold

ELDER RAZORMAW
Wetlands (96), D:(1, 2), E-2, I-3, J-3, Raptor Ridge

ELDER SALTWATER CROCOLISK
Stranglethorn Vale (74), A-2, B-2, C:(3, 4)

ELDER SHADOWHORN STAG
Ashenvale (12), G:(3, 4), H:(3-7), I:(5-7), J:(5, 6)

ELDER SHADOWMAW PANTHER
Stranglethorn Vale (74), C-6, D-6

ELDER SHARDTOOTH
Winterspring (98), H-2, I:(1-3, 5, 6)

ELDER STRANGLETHORN TIGER
Stranglethorn Vale (74), C-2, D-2

ELDER THUNDER LIZARD
Desolace (30), C:(7, 8), D:(7, 8), E:(4-6, 8), F:(5, 6, 9), G:(5, 8, 9), H:(5-9), J:(1, 4, 5), K-2

ELDER TIMBERLING
Teldrassil (80), E-3, The Oracle Glade, Wellspring River

ELDER TORNTUSK
The Hinterlands (50), I-8, Jintha'Alor, Chained to altar

ELDIN PARTRIDGE
Undercity (88), F-3, The War Quarter, Platform in front of Skull Building

ELDRAEITH
Herbalism Supplier, Stormwind (72), G-8, Mage Quarter, Alchemy Need

ELDRETH APPARITION
Feralas (46), G-4, Dire Maul

ELDRETH DARTER
Feralas (46), G-4, Dire Maul

ELDRETH PHANTASM
Feralas (46), G-4, Dire Maul

ELDRETH SEETHER
Feralas (46), G-4, Dire Maul

ELDRETH SORCERER
Feralas (46), G-4, Dire Maul

ELDRETH SPECTRE
Feralas (46), G-4, Dire Maul

ELDRETH SPIRIT
Feralas (46), G-4, Dire Maul

ELDRIN
Journeyman Tailor, Elwynn Forest (42), K-7, Eastvale Logging Camp, House

ELEANOR RUSK
General Goods Vendor, Undercity (88), I-5, The Trade Quarter, Upper Ring of Trade Quarter

ELECTROCUTIONER 6000
Dun Morogh (32), C-4, Gnomeregan

ELEMENTAL SLAVE
Alterac Mountains (8), A:(7, 8), B:(5-8), C-6, Dalaran

ELFARRAN
Warsong Gulch Battlemaster, Stormwind (72), L-2, Stormwind Keep, East Wing

ELISA STEELHAND
Blacksmithing Supplies, Darkshore (24), F-4, Auberdine (101), In front of northern building

ELISSA DUMAS
Portal Trainer, Darnassus (26), E-8, The Temple of the Moon, Northeast of fountain

ELIZA
Bride of the Embalmer, Duskwood (36), D-3, Raven Hill Cemetery (123), (Summon) Fresh grave

ELIZA CALLEN
Leather Armor Merchant, Tirisfal Glades (86), H-5, Brill (104), Outside of smithy

ELIZABETH VAN TALEN
Engineer Supplier, Undercity (88), J-7, The Rogues' Quarter

ELKI
Mail Armor Merchant, Thunder Bluff (84), I-6, Lower rise, in Hewa's Armory

ELLANDRIETH
General Goods Vendor, Darnassus (26), I-5, Tradesmen's Terrace, General Goods shop

ELLING TRIAS
Master of Cheese, Stormwind (72), I-6, Trade District, Trias' Cheese

ELLY LANGSTON
Barmaid, Stormwind (72), K-4, Old Town, Pig and Whistle Tavern

ELSHARIN
Mage Trainer, Stormwind (72), F-8, Mage Quarter, Wizard's Sanctum

ELU
Wind Rider Apprentice, Thousand Needles (82), F-5, Freewind Post (112), North side of plateau, opposite inn

ELYNNA
Tailoring Supplies, Darnassus (26), I-2, Craftsmen's Terrace, Tailoring shop

ELYSA
Alterac Mountains (8), E-2, Dandred's Fold, Second floor of house

EMBER WORG
Burning Steppes (22), J-3, K:(2, 3, 5, 6), L:(3-6), Terror Wing Path

EMBERSTRIFE
Dustwallow Marsh (38), G-8, Emberstrife's Den, Southern part of cave on landing

EMERALD OOZE
The Hinterlands (50), J:(6, 7), Jintha'Alor

EMERALDON BOUGHGUARD
Ashenvale (12), K-4, L-4

EMERALDON ORACLE
Ashenvale (12), K-4, L-4, Bough Shadow, Forest Song

EMERALDON TREE WARDER
Ashenvale (12), K-4, L-4, Bough Shadow, Forest Song

EMISSARY GORMOK
Eastern Plaguelands (40), K-6, Light's Hope Chapel (118)

EMOGG THE CRUSHER
Loch Modan (54), J-2, Mo'grosh Stronghold, Patrols a path in front of the three caves

EMPEROR DAGRAN THAURISSAN
Burning Steppes (22), Searing Gorge (64), C-4/D-8, Blackrock Depths

EMRUL RIKNUSSUN
Cooking Supplier, Ironforge (52), H-4, The Great Forge, The Bronze Kettle

ENCRUSTED SURF CRAWLER
Durotar (34), H-1, I:(1, 2), Bladefist Bay, Skull Rock

ENCRUSTED TIDE CRAWLER
Darkshore (24), E-8, H-2, Cliffspring River, Mist's Edge, Twilight Shore

ENFORCER EMILGUND
Rare Spawn, Mulgore (58), D-2, Lvl 11 Uncommon; Venture Co. camp

ENGINEER WHIRLEYGIG
Rare Spawn, Barrens (18), G-1, The Sludge Fen, Lvl 19 Uncommon; Control room

ENLAE
Eye of the Storm Battlemaster, Darnassus (26), H-4

ENOHAR THUNDERBREW
Blasted Lands (20), I-2, Nethergarde Keep (120), Just right of entrance inside keep

ENRAGED FERAL SCAR
Feralas (46), F:(5, 6), Feral Scar Vale

ENRAGED FOULWEALD
Ashenvale (12), G-6, Greenpaw Village

ENRAGED PANTHER
Thousand Needles (82), B-2, Locked in cage, next to destroyed wagons

ENRAGED REEF CRAWLER
Desolace (30), C:(3-5), D:(2-4), Ethel Rethor, Sar'theris Strand

ENRAGED ROCK ELEMENTAL
Badlands (16), H:(8, 9), In hills behind Theldurin the Lost

ENRAGED SILVERBACK GORILLA
Stranglethorn Vale (74), C-7, Mistvale Valley, Spirit Den

ENRAGED STONE SPIRIT
Stonetalon Mountains (70), D-6, E-6, The Charred Vale

ENSLAVED ARCHAEOLOGIST
Searing Gorge (64), D-2, E:(2, 3), The Slag Pit

ENSLAVED DRUID OF THE TALON
Teldrassil (80), E-8, Gnarlpine Hold, Southwest camp

ENTHRALLED ATAL'AI
Swamp of Sorrows (76), I-5, The Temple of Atal'Hakkar

ENTROPIC BEAST
Felwood (44), E-4, F-4, Shatter Scar Vale

ENTROPIC HORROR
Felwood (44), E-4, F-4, Shatter Scar Vale

ENYO
Mage Trainer, Orgrimmar (60), D:(8, 9), Valley of Spirit, Darkbriar Lodge

ERELAS AMBERSKY
Teldrassil (80), G-9, Rut'theran Village (125), First floor of building

ERIC "THE SWIFT"
Badlands (16), G-1, Uldaman

ERICH LOHAN
Stormwind (72), F-8, G-7, Mage Quarter, Roams around district

ERIDAN BLUEWIND
Emerald Circle, Felwood (44), G-8, Emerald Sanctuary (110), Building

ERIK FELIXE
Feralas (46), B-4, Feathermoon Stronghold (111), Next to log west of inn

ERIKA TATE
Cooking Supplier, Stormwind (72), K-4, Old Town, Pig and Whistle Tavern

ERIN
Redridge Mountains (62), C-4, Lakeshire (117)

ERION SHADEWHISPER
Rogue Trainer, Darnassus (26), D-2, Cenarion Enclave, Den, small room on lower level

ERIS HAVENFIRE
Eastern Plaguelands (40), B-2, Plaguewood, On hill (note that the NPC is only visible to Lvl 60 priests that have the Eye of Divinity equipped)

ERMA
Stable Master, Elwynn Forest (42), F-7, Goldshire (114), Outside the Lion's Pride Inn

ERTOG RAGETUSK
Ashenvale (12), I-6, Splintertree Post (129), Up hill to left as you enter main outpost (near watch tower)

ESTELLE GENDRY
Undercity (88), K-7, The Rogues' Quarter, Southwest of Skull Building

ETU RAGETOTEM
Mace & Staff Merchant, Thunder Bluff (84), F-6, High rise, inside Ragetotem Arms tent

EUNICE BURCH
Cooking Trainer, Undercity (88), H-4, The Trade Quarter, West spoke from bank

EVA SARKHOFF
Western Plaguelands (92), J-7, Caer Darrow, Just outside of entrance to Scholomance

EVAN LARSON
Hatter, Stormwind (72), F-8, Mage Quarter, Larson Clothiers

EVERLOOK BRUISER
Winterspring (98), I-4, Everlook (110)

EVIE WHIRLBREW
Alchemy Supplies, Winterspring (98), I-4, Everlook (110), Hut north of entrance

EVISCERATOR
Burning Steppes (22), Searing Gorge (64), C-4/D-8, Blackrock Depths

EVOLVING ECTOPLASM
Barrens (18), E-4, Wailing Caverns

EVONICE SOOTSMOKER
The Thorium Brotherhood, Searing Gorge (64), D-3, Thorium Point (136), Right of tower ramp

EXECUTOR ARREN
Tirisfal Glades (86), D-7, Deathknell (109), Between both houses on right side of road

EXECUTOR ZYGAND
Tirisfal Glades (86), H-5, Brill (104), Mounted outside of the Brill Town Hall

EXPEDITIONARY MOUNTAINEER
Burning Steppes (22), A-6

EXPEDITIONARY PRIEST
Burning Steppes (22), A-6

EXZHAL
Stranglethorn Vale (74), A-2, Yojamba Isle

EYAHN EAGLETALON
Thunder Bluff (84), D-6, Lower rise, near elevator

EYE OF IMMOL'THAR
Feralas (46), G-4, Dire Maul

EYE OF NAXXRAMAS
Eastern Plaguelands (40), D-2, Stratholme

EYELESS WATCHER
Eastern Plaguelands (40), E-5, I-3, J-3, K-5, The Noxious Glade

EZEKIEL GRAVES
Poison Vendor, Undercity (88), J-5, The Rogues' Quarter

F

FAELYSSA
Darnassus (26), D-2, Cenarion Enclave, Southwest structure

FAHRAD
Grand Master Rogue, Hillsbrad Foothills (48), K-2, Balcony of Chateau Ravenholdt

FAHRAK
Ashenvale (12), I-6, Splintertree Post (129), Right of flightpoint

FAHRAN SILENTBLADE
Tools & Supplies, Ashenvale (12), E-5, Astranaar (101), Left as you enter inn from west

FALDREAS GOETH'SHAEL
Ashenvale (12), E-5, Astranaar (101), Outside inn to west

FALDRON
Leatherworking Trainer, Darnassus (26), I-2, Craftsmen's Terrace, Leatherworking shop

FALFINDEL WAYWARDER
Feralas (46), K-5, Thalanaar, Next to well

FALGRAN HASTIL
Dustwallow Marsh (38), I-5, Theramore Isle (135), East side of town

FALKAN ARMONIS
Reagent Vendor, Wetlands (96), A-6, Menethil Harbor (119), Outside building, west of keep

FALKHAAN ISENSTRIDER
Elwynn Forest (42), F-5, Northshire Valley (122), In front of fountain at Northshire Valley entrance

FALLA SAGEWIND
Barrens (18), E-3, F-3, Atop mountain

FALLEN CHAMPION
Tirisfal Glades (86), K-3, L-3, Scarlet Monastery

FALLENROOT HELLCALLER
Ashenvale (12), B-2, Blackfathom Deeps

FALLENROOT ROGUE
Ashenvale (12), B-2, Blackfathom Deeps

FALLENROOT SATYR
Ashenvale (12), B-2, Blackfathom Deeps

FALLENROOT SHADOWSTALKER
Ashenvale (12), B-2, Blackfathom Deeps

FALSTAD WILDHAMMER
The Hinterlands (50), B-5, Aerie Peak (100), Base of Peak fortification

FALTHIR THE SIGHTLESS
Stranglethorn Vale (74), A-2, Yojamba Isle

FAM'RETOR GUARDIAN
Badlands (16), D-5, The Dustbowl, (Summon) Circular seal on ground

FAR SEER MOK'THARDIN
Stranglethorn Vale (74), C-3, Grom'gol Base Camp (114), Scaffolding just left of zepplin tower

FARALORN
General Supplies, Feralas (46), C-4, Feathermoon Stronghold (111), Inn

FARDEL DABYRIE
Arathi Highlands (10), H-4, Dabyrie's Farmstead, Roams in front of shed right of barn

FARGON MORTALAK
Superior Armorer, Stranglethorn Vale (74), B-8, Booty Bay (103), Plate-n-Chain (shop)

FARMER DALSON
Western Plaguelands (92), F-5, Dalson's Tears, (Summon) Spawns at the outhouse

FARMER FURLBROW
Westfall (94), G-2, The Jansen Stead, Cart near Old Blanchy

FARMER GETZ
Hillsbrad Foothills (48), D-4, Hillsbrad Fields (115), Barn on the eastern side of town

FARMER KALABA
Hillsbrad Foothills (48), D-5, Hillsbrad Fields (115), Roams in southernmost farm

FARMER KENT
Hillsbrad Foothills (48), F-6, Southshore (129), Patrols between crop field and docks

FARMER RAY
Hillsbrad Foothills (48), C-3, Hillsbrad Fields (115), First floor of house at northern end of town

FARMER SALDEAN
Westfall (94), F-3, Saldean's Farm, Farmhouse

FARMER SOLLIDEN
Rare Spawn, Tirisfal Glades (86), D-5, E-5, Solliden Farmstead, Lvl 8 Uncommon; Stands idle at spawn point

FARRIN DARIS
Duskwood (36), J-4, Darkshire (108), Inn

FARSEER JAVAD
Shaman Trainer, Ironforge (52), G-3

FARUZA
Apprentice Herbalist, Tirisfal Glades (86), H-5, Brill (104), Between the stable and house on right side of road

FATHER COBB
Priest Trainer, Thunder Bluff (84), B-2, Spirit Rise, The Pools of Vision

FATHER GAVIN
Dun Morogh (32), H-4, Misty Pine Refuge, Altar outside of house

FATHER INIGO MONTOY
Brotherhood of the Light, Eastern Plaguelands (40), K-6, Light's Hope Chapel (118)

FATHER LANKESTER
Priest Trainer, Undercity (88), F-2, The War Quarter, Outside Skull Building

FATHER LAZARUS
Priest Trainer, Undercity (88), F-2, The War Quarter, Outside Skull Building

FAULTY WAR GOLEM
Rare Spawn, Searing Gorge (64), C-6, D-5, E-4, F-7, G-6, The Sea of Cinders, Lvl 46 Semi-Rare; Roams small area around spawn point

FAUSTRON
Wind Rider Master, Moonglade (56), D-7, At end of beaten path, west of road

FEATHERMOON SENTINEL
Feralas (46), C:(4, 5), Feathermoon Stronghold (111), Sardor Isle

FEDFENNEL
Rare Spawn, Elwynn Forest (42), I-4, Stone Cairn Lake, Lvl 12 Uncommon; Stands idle at spawn point

FEEBOZ
Arathi Highlands (10), I-3, Circle of East Binding, Patrols with Fozruck to each of the four Circles of Binding

FEEGLY THE EXILED
Barrens (18), F-9, Bael Modan, Camp overlooking excavation

FEERO IRONHAND
Ashenvale (12), D-4, Maestra's Post, Near Stones south of outpost

FEL LASH
Feralas (46), G-4, Dire Maul

FEL STEED
Silverpine Forest (68), F-7, Shadowfang Keep

FEL'ZERUL
Swamp of Sorrows (76), F-5, Stonard (131), Third floor of main hall

FELA
Heavy Armor Merchant, Thunder Bluff (84), D-4, Middle rise, inside Thunder Bluff Armorers tent

FELBEAST
Blasted Lands (20), G:(3, 5), H:(4-6), I:(3, 4)

FELCULAR
Blasted Lands (20), G-3, Rise of the Defiler, (Summon) Summoned by Razelikh the Defiler at 25% health

FELDER STOVER
Weaponsmith, Burning Steppes (22), K-7, Morgan's Vigil (120), Caravan, left side of camp

FELGUARD
Ashenvale (12), J:(6-8), K:(6, 7), Demon Fall Canyon, Felfire Hill, Nightsong Woods

FELGUARD ELITE
Blasted Lands (20), E:(5, 6), F:(5-7), G:(6, 7), H:(5, 6), I:(5, 6), Dark Portal, The Tainted Scar

FELGUARD SENTRY
Blasted Lands (20), H:(5, 6), I:(5, 6), Dark Portal

FELGUR TWOCUTS
Desolace (30), G-6, Ghost Walker Post (113), Southern hut

FELHOUND
Blasted Lands (20), H:(5, 6), I:(5, 6), Dark Portal

FELICIA DOAN
General Trade Goods Vendor, Undercity (88), I-5, The Trade Quarter, Upper Ring of Trade Quarter

FELICIA GUMP
Herbalism Supplier, Stormwind (72), J-6, The Canals, Fragrant Flowers

FELICIA MALINE
Gryphon Master, Duskwood (36), K-4, Darkshire (108), Right side of road heading into Darkshire from the east

FELIKA
General Trade Good Merchant, Orgrimmar (60), G-5, The Drag, Roams The Drag

FELIX WHINDLEBOLT
Dun Morogh (32), D-7, Coldridge Valley (107), Anvilmar

FELLICENT'S SHADE
Rare Spawn, Tirisfal Glades (86), J-6, Balnir Farmstead, Lvl 12 Uncommon; Patrols a circular path around crop field

FELMUSK FELSWORN
Ashenvale (12), H-5, I-5, Night Run

FELMUSK ROGUE
Ashenvale (12), H:(5, 6), I:(5, 6), Night Run

FELMUSK SATYR
Ashenvale (12), H-5, I-5, Night Run

FELMUSK SHADOWSTALKER
Ashenvale (12), H:(5, 6), I:(5, 6), Night Run

FELNOK STEELSPRING
Winterspring (98), I-4, Everlook (110), East of inn

FELPAW RAVAGER
Felwood (44), G:(2, 3), H:(1-3), I-2, Irontree Woods, Talonbranch Glade (133)

FELPAW SCAVENGER
Felwood (44), E:(3-6), F:(2-4, 6, 7), G:(2-4)

FELPAW WOLF
Felwood (44), E:(7, 8), F:(7, 8), G:(7-9), H-9, Deadwood Village, Emerald Sanctuary (110), Morlos'Aran

FELSLAYER
Ashenvale (12), C-6, D-6, Fire Scar Shrine

FELSTALKER
Durotar (34), F-5, G-5, Burning Blade Coven, Valley of Trials (136)

FELWEAVER SCORNN
Durotar (34), H-1, Skull Rock, Cave (north side or deep in cave)

FEN CREEPER
Wetlands (96), B:(2, 3), C:(2-4), D:(2-4), E-3, F:(3, 4), G:(3-5), H-5

FEN DWELLER
Wetlands (96), B:(4, 5), C:(4, 5), H:(5-7), I:(6, 7)

FENROS
Rare Spawn, Duskwood (36), H-4, Brightwood Grove, Lvl 32 Uncommon; Patrols to two additional worgen camps (I-6, H-3)

FENRUS THE DEVOURER
Silverpine Forest (68), F-7, Shadowfang Keep

FENTHWICK
Rogue Trainer, Ironforge (52), G-1, The Forlorn Cavern, South building, inside east entrance

FENWICK THATROS
Silverpine Forest (68), I-3, Lordamere Lake, Roams at the edge of dock

FERAL CRAG COYOTE
Badlands (16), G:(7, 8), H:(5-7), I:(5-7), Agmond's End

FERAL MOUNTAIN LION
Hillsbrad Foothills (48), G:(5-7), H:(6-8), I-7

FERAL NIGHTSABER
Teldrassil (80), D:(2, 3), E:(2, 3), F:(2, 3), The Oracle Glade

FERAL SCAR YETI
Feralas (46), F:(5, 6), G-6, Feral Scar Vale, High Wilderness

FERAN STRONGWIND
Ashenvale (12), I-7, Nightsong Woods, Camp southwest of Splintertree Post (129)

FEROCIOUS GRIZZLED BEAR
Silverpine Forest (68), G:(2-5), H:(2, 4, 5), Throughout Silverpine

FEROCIOUS RAGE SCAR
Feralas (46), F-3, Rage Scar Hold, The Twin Colossals

FEROCIOUS YETI
Hillsbrad Foothills (48), E-3, Darrow Hill, In and near cave

FEROCITAS THE DREAM EATER
Teldrassil (80), I-5, Gnarlpine camp northeast of Starbreeze Village

FERRA
Feralas (46), G-4, Dire Maul

FETID CORPSE
Duskwood (36), J-4, K:(3, 4), Manor Mistmantle

FETID ZOMBIE
Western Plaguelands (92), G:(6, 7), The Writhing Haunt

FIELD MARSHAL AFRASIABI
Stormwind (72), J-7, Stormwind City, Northeast of statue at entrance

FILLIUS FIZZLESPINNER
Trade Supplier, Ironforge (52), E-7, The Commons, Fizzlespinner's General Goods

FIMBLE FINESPINDLE
Leatherworking Trainer, Ironforge (52), E-3, The Great Forge, Finespindle's Leather Goods

FIN FIZRACKET
Blackwater Raiders, Stranglethorn Vale (74), B-8, Booty Bay (103), Lying under overturned boat on the eastern side of bay

FINBUS GEARGRIND
Expert Engineer, Duskwood (36), K-5, Darkshire (108), Second house on left side of road heading into Darkshire from the east

FINEOUS DARKVIRE
Burning Steppes (22), Searing Gorge (64), C-4/D-8, Blackrock Depths

FINGAT
Rare Spawn, Swamp of Sorrows (76), H-8, Stagalbog Cave, Lvl 43 Semi-Rare; Patrols cave

FINKLE EINHORN
Burning Steppes (22), Searing Gorge (64), C-4/D-8, Blackrock Spire

FIORA LONGEARS
Dustwallow Marsh (38), I-5, Theramore Isle (135), Inn

FIRE BEETLE
Burning Steppes (22), A:(5, 6), B:(6, 7), C-6, D-5, E:(4-6), F-5, G-6, H:(4-6), I-5, J:(3, 4), K:(3, 5, 6), L:(4, 5), Searing Gorge (64), B:(4, 7), C:(5-7), D:(3, 4, 6, 7), E:(4, 5, 7), F:(4, 6, 7), G:(3, 4, 6-8), H-7, I:(3-5), J-2

FIRE ROC
Tanaris (78), E:(4, 5), F-4, G:(4, 5), H:(4, 5), I-4

FIRE SPIRIT
Durotar (34), F-5, Shrine of the Dormant Flame, (Summon) Atop hill near altar

FIREBRAND DARKWEAVER
Burning Steppes (22), Searing Gorge (64), C-4/D-8, Blackrock Spire

FIREBRAND DREADWEAVER
Burning Steppes (22), Searing Gorge (64), C-4/D-8, Blackrock Spire

FIREBRAND GRUNT
Burning Steppes (22), Searing Gorge (64), C-4/D-8, Blackrock Spire

FIREBRAND INVOKER
Burning Steppes (22), Searing Gorge (64), C-4/D-8, Blackrock Spire

FIREBRAND LEGIONNAIRE
Burning Steppes (22), Searing Gorge (64), C-4/D-8, Blackrock Spire

FIREBRAND PYROMANCER
Burning Steppes (22), Searing Gorge (64), C-4/D-8, Blackrock Spire

FIRECALLER RADISON
Rare Spawn, Darkshore (24), F-9, The Master's Glaive, Lvl 19 Semi-Rare; Wanders center isle

FIREGUARD
Burning Steppes (22), Searing Gorge (64), C-4/D-8, Blackrock Depths

FIREGUARD DESTROYER
Burning Steppes (22), Searing Gorge (64), C-4/D-8, Blackrock Depths

FIREGUT BRUTE
Burning Steppes (22), J:(4, 5), K:(4, 5), Dreadmaul Rock

FIREGUT CAPTAIN
Burning Steppes (22), B-3, Dreadmaul Rock

FIREGUT OGRE
Burning Steppes (22), I:(4, 5), J:(3-6), K:(3-5), Dreadmaul Rock

FIREGUT OGRE MAGE
Burning Steppes (22), I:(4, 5), J:(3-5), K:(3-5), Dreadmaul Rock

FIRELORD
Burning Steppes (22), Searing Gorge (64), C-4/D-8, The Molten Core

FIREMANE ASH TAIL
Dustwallow Marsh (38), D-7, E:(6-8), F:(6, 7), The Dragonmurk

FIREMANE FLAMECALLER
Dustwallow Marsh (38), F:(7, 8), G:(7, 8), H-8, The Dragonmurk

FIREMANE SCALEBANE
Dustwallow Marsh (38), D-7, E-7, F:(7, 8), G:(7, 8), H-8, The Dragonmurk

FIREMANE SCOUT
Dustwallow Marsh (38), D-7, E:(6-8), F:(6, 7), The Dragonmurk

FIRESWORN
Burning Steppes (22), Searing Gorge (64), C-4/D-8, The Molten Core

FIRETAIL SCORPID
Burning Steppes (22), A-5, B:(4-7), C:(5, 6), Dreadmaul Rock

FIREWALKER
Burning Steppes (22), Searing Gorge (64), C-4/D-8, The Molten Core

FIRODREN MOONCALLER
Herbalism Trainer, Darnassus (26), F-7, The Temple Gardens, Small building, northeast of temple

FIRST MATE CRAZZ
Blackwater Raiders, Stranglethorn Vale (74), B-8, Booty Bay (103), On the dock just past The Old Port Authority on the eastern side of bay

FIRST MATE FITZSIMMONS
Wetlands (96), A-6, Menethil Harbor (119), Outside tavern

FIRST MATE NILZLIX
Arathi Highlands (10), D-8, Faldir's Cove, Roams around dock

FIRST MATE SNELLIG
Wetlands (96), B-3, The Lost Fleet, Bottom of southern ship

FIRST SERGEANT HOLA'MAHI
Armor Quartermaster, Orgrimmar (61) E-7

FIZIM BLASTWRENCH
Arena BM, Thunder Bluff (85), G-8

FIZZLE BRASSBOLTS
Thousand Needles (82), K-8, Mirage Raceway (119), West of racetrack

FIZZLE DARKSTORM
Durotar (34), F-3, Thunder Ridge, Eastern part of ridge in clearing

FIZZLEBANG BOOMS
Fireworks Vendor, Ironforge (52), J-5, Tinker Town, Things That Go Boom

FLAGGLEMURK THE CRUEL
Rare Spawn, Darkshore (24), E:(6-7), G-2, Mist's Edge, Twilight Shore, Lvl Uncommon; Roams the shore close to spawn point

FLAKK
Trade Supplies, Durotar (34), H-4, Raz Hill (124), Outside barracks

FLAME IMP
Burning Steppes (22), Searing Gorge (64), C-4/D-8, The Molten Core

FLAMEGUARD
Burning Steppes (22), Searing Gorge (64), C-4/D-8, The Molten Core

FLAMEKIN RAGER
Burning Steppes (22), C-6, D-6, E-4, F:(3, 6), G:(5, 6), H-3, I-3, Ruins of Thourissan

FLAMEKIN SPITTER
Burning Steppes (22), G-6, I-6, J:(3-5, 7), Dreadmaul Rock

FLAMEKIN SPRITE
Burning Steppes (22), G-6, I-6, J:(3-5, 7), Dreadmaul Rock

FLAMEKIN TORCHER
Burning Steppes (22), C-6, D-6, E-4, F:(3, 6), G:(5, 6), H-3, I-3, Ruins of Thourissan

FLAMESCALE BROODLING
Burning Steppes (22), A-5, B:(4-7), C:(5, 6), Draco'dar

FLAMESCALE DRAGONSPAWN
Burning Steppes (22), A:(4, 5), B:(4, 5 C:(5-7), D:(5, 7), Blackrock Mountain

FLAMESCALE WYRMKIN
Burning Steppes (22), A:(4, 5), B:(4, 5 C:(6, 7), D:(5, 7), Blackrock Mountain, Road

FLAMESNORTING WHELP
Wetlands (96), I:(3, 4), J:(4, 5), The Green Belt

FLAMEWAKER
Burning Steppes (22), Searing Gorge (64), C-4/D-8, The Molten Core

FLAMEWAKER ELITE
Burning Steppes (22), Searing Gorge (64), C-4/D-8, The Molten Core

FLAMEWAKER HEALER
Burning Steppes (22), Searing Gorge (64), C-4/D-8, The Molten Core

FLAMEWAKER PRIEST
Burning Steppes (22), Searing Gorge (64), C-4/D-8, The Molten Core

FLAMEWAKER PROTECTOR
Burning Steppes (22), Searing Gorge (64), C-4/D-8, The Molten Core

FLATLAND COUGAR
Mulgore (58), C:(3, 4), D:(2-5), E:(3-5 F:(3-5), G:(3-7), H:(5-7)

FLATLAND PROWLER
Mulgore (58), C-2, D:(1, 2), E:(1-3), F:(1-3), G:(2, 3), H:(2, 3, 6, 7)

FLAWLESS DRAENETHYST FRAGMENT
Blasted Lands (20), H-4

FLAWLESS DRAENETHYST SPHERE
Blasted Lands (20), H-4

FLEDGLING CHILLWIND
Winterspring (98), D-5, E:(4, 5), F-4, G:(3-5), H-4

FLEDGLING CHIMAERA
Stonetalon Mountains (70), D-7, E-7, The Charred Vale

FLEDGLING PTERRORDAX
Un'Goro Crater (90), H-4, I:(2, 4), J:(4, 6), K:(4, 6), Ironstone Plateau, Lakkari Tar Pits, The Marshlands

FLEET MASTER FIRALLON
Stranglethorn Vale (74), C-9, Wild Sho

FLEET MASTER SEAHORN
Blackwater Raiders, Stranglethorn Vale (74), B-8, Booty Bay (103), Third floor balcony of The Salty Sailor Tavern

LEETING PLAINSTRIDER
Barrens (18), E:(2-4), F:(1-4), G:(2-4), H:(2-4)

LESH EATER
Duskwood (36), C:(3, 4), Raven Hill Cemetery (123)

LESH GOLEM
Western Plaguelands (92), E-7, F-7, Ruins of Andorhal

LESHFLAYER GHOUL
Eastern Plaguelands (40), D-2, Stratholme

LESHRIPPER
Westfall (94), C:(4, 6), D:(2-7), E:(2, 4-6), F:(2, 6), G:(4, 5), Alexston Farmstead

LINT SHADOWMORE
SI:7, Western Plaguelands (92), E-8, Chillwind Camp (107), In front of ruined building

LORA SILVERWIND
Superior Herbalist, Stranglethorn Vale (74), B-8, Booty Bay (103), All Things Flora (shop)

OBEED
Race Announcer, Thousand Needles (82), K-8, Mirage Raceway (119), Atop Starters tower inside track

DE REAPER 4000
Rare Spawn, Westfall (94), D-5, E-4, F-2, F-7, G-6, Alexston Farmstead, The Dead Acre, Fulbrow's Pumpkin Farm, The Molsen Farm, Moonbrook, Lvl 20 Semi-Rare; Roams around spawn points

OGGY MACKREEL
Arathi Highlands (10), F-9, Thandol Span, Ruins near bridge connecting Arathi Highlands and Wetlands

DREMAN BONDS
Hillsbrad Foothills (48), C-6, Azurelode Mine, Raised wooden platform in mine

DREMAN COZZLE
Stranglethorn Vale (74), E-2, Venture Co. Operations Center, Second floor control room of structure

DREMAN GRILLS
Rare Spawn, Barrens (18), G-1, The Sludge Fen, Lvl 19 Semi-Rare; Patrols derrick

DREMAN JERRIS
Rare Spawn, Western Plaguelands (92), F:(1, 2), Hearthglen, Lvl 62 Uncommon; Roams small area around spawn point

DREMAN MARCRID
Rare Spawn, Western Plaguelands (92), F-3, Northridge Lumber Camp, Lvl 58 Average Rare; Roams small area around spawn point

DREMAN OSLOW
Redridge Mountains (62), D-5, Lakeshire (117), In Lakeshire just left of bridge

DREMAN RIGGER
Rare Spawn, Stonetalon Mountains (70), H-5, I-5, Blackwolf River, Windshear Crag, Lvl 24 Uncommon; West end of the crag

DREMAN SILIXIZ
Barrens (18), F-1, Outside tower northwest of Sludge Fen

DREMAN STONEBROW
Miners' League, Dun Morogh (32), I-6, Gol'Bolar Quarry, Hill overlooking quarry

DREMAN THAZZ'RIL
Durotar (34), G-7, Valley of Trials (136), Road heading east

DREMAN THISTLENETTLE
Westfall (94), D-7, E-7, The Deadmines

DREST LURKER
Loch Modan (54), B:(7, 8), C:(2-6), D:(2-7), E:(3, 7), Silver Stream Mine

DREST MOSS CREEPER
Hillsbrad Foothills (48), A:(4, 5), B:(4, 5), C:(4, 5), F-1, G:(1-4), H:(1-4), I:(1, 3, 4), J-5, Thoughout Hillsbrad

DREST OOZE
Azshara (14), D-7, E-7, H:(2, 3), I:(2, 3), J:(1-3), K:(2, 3)

DREST SPIDER
Elwynn Forest (42), C-7, D:(6, 7), E:(6-8), F:(6-8),Goldshire (114), Mirror Lake, Mirror Lake Orchard

DRESTSTRIDER
Darkshore (24), F:(7, 8), G:(3, 4, 7), H-3, Bashal'Aran, Cliffspring River, Twilight Shore

DRESTSTRIDER FLEDGLING
Darkshore (24), E-9, F:(2-7, 9), G:(2-7)

FORLORN SPIRIT
Westfall (94), D-7, Moonbrook, (Summon) Town hall dais

FORSAKEN ASSASSIN
Ashenvale (12), J-7, Dor'Danil Barrow Den

FORSAKEN BODYGUARD
Arathi Highlands (10), H-6, Patrols the road from Thoradin's Wall to the Go'Shek Farm

FORSAKEN COURIER
, Arathi Highlands (10), H-6, Go'Shek Farm, Patrols with guards along road to Tarren Mill (see Hillsbrad Foothills)

FORSAKEN DARK STALKER
Ashenvale (12), J-7, Dor'Danil Barrow Den

FORSAKEN HERBALIST
Ashenvale (12), D-3, Bathran's Haunt, Ruins of Ordil'Aran

FORSAKEN INFILTRATOR
Ashenvale (12), J-7, Dor'Danil Barrow Den

FORSAKEN INTRUDER
Ashenvale (12), J-7, Dor'Danil Barrow Den

FORSAKEN SCOUT
Ashenvale (12), C-3

FORSAKEN SEEKER
Ashenvale (12), D-3, Bathran's Haunt, Ruins of Ordil'Aran

FORSAKEN THUG
Ashenvale (12), D-3, Bathran's Haunt, Ruins of Ordil'Aran

FOULBELLY
Rare Spawn, Arathi Highlands (10), B-6, Stromgarde Keep (132), Lvl 42 Very Rare; Stands to the right of tower in ogre quarter of keep

FOULMANE
Rare Spawn, Western Plaguelands (92), F-5, Dalson's Tears, Lvl 52 Semi-Rare; Patrols around cauldron

FOULWEALD DEN WATCHER
Ashenvale (12), F-6, G-6, Greenpaw Village

FOULWEALD PATHFINDER
Ashenvale (12), G-6, Greenpaw Village

FOULWEALD SHAMAN
Ashenvale (12), F-6, G-6, Greenpaw Village

FOULWEALD TOTEMIC
Ashenvale (12), F-6, G-6, Greenpaw Village

FOULWEALD URSA
Ashenvale (12), F-6, G-6, Greenpaw Village

FOULWEALD WARRIOR
Ashenvale (12), F-6, G-6, Greenpaw Village, Silverwind Refuge

FOZRUK
Arathi Highlands (10), I-3, Circle of East Binding, Patrols to each of the four Circles of Binding

FRADD SWIFTGEAR
Engineering Supplies, Wetlands (96), C-3, Sundown Marsh, Outside building next to windmill

FRAGGAR THUNDERMANTLE
The Hinterlands (50), B-4, Aerie Peak (100), Wildhammer Keep

FRAHUN SHADEWHISPER
Rogue Trainer, Teldrassil (80), H-4, Shadowglen (127), In northeast room inside main building

FRAMNALI
Ashenvale (12), I-6, Splintertree Post (129), Atop western watch tower

FRANCIS ELIOT
Weapon Merchant, Undercity (88), H-3, The War Quarter

FRANG
Warrior Trainer, Durotar (34), F-7, Valley of Trials (136), Structure to south

FRANKLIN HAMAR
Tailoring Supplies, Redridge Mountains (62), C-4, Lakeshire (117), Second floor of Lakeshire Inn

FRANKLIN LLOYD
Engineer Trainer, Undercity (88), J-7, The Rogues' Quarter

FRANKLIN THE FRIENDLY
Burning Steppes (22), B-7, Draco'dar, Patrols circular path through southwestern portion of Burning Steppes

FRAS SIABI
Eastern Plaguelands (40), D-2, Stratholme

FRAST DOKNER
Apprentice Weaponsmith, Dun Morogh (32), I-6, Gol'Bolar Quarry, Patrols in and out of camp tent

FRAYFEATHER HIPPOGRYPH
Feralas (46), F-6, G-6

FRAYFEATHER PATRIARCH
Feralas (46), F-7, G-7, Frayfeather Highlands, Ruins of Isildien

FRAYFEATHER SKYSTORMER
Feralas (46), F:(6, 7), G-7, Frayfeather Highlands, High Wilderness, Ruins of Isildien

FRAYFEATHER STAGWING
Feralas (46), F:(6, 7), G-6, Frayfeather Highlands, Ruins of Isildien

FREDERICK STOVER
Bow & Arrow Merchant, Stormwind (72), H-6, Trade District, The Empty Quiver

FREEWIND BRAVE
Thousand Needles (82), E-5, F-5, Freewind Post (112)

FREEZING GHOUL
Western Plaguelands (92), G:(6, 7), The Writhing Haunt

FREEZING SPIRIT
Barrens (18), F-9, Razorfen Downs

FREJA NIGHTWING
Leather Armor Merchant, Teldrassil (80), H-4, Shadowglen (127), Inside main building

FREMAL DOOHICKEY
First Aid Trainer, Wetlands (96), A-6, Deepwater Tavern, Southeast, upstairs room

FRENZIED BLACK DRAKE
Burning Steppes (22), L-3, Slither Rock, (Summon) Summoned by Cyrus Therepentous

FRENZIED BLACK DRAKE
Burning Steppes (22), L-3 , Slither Rock

FRENZIED PLAGUEHOUND
Eastern Plaguelands (40), B-3, C:(2-4), D-4, E-4, F:(3, 4), G:(2-4), H:(2-5), I:(3-5), J:(3, 4), East Wall Tower

FRENZIED PTERRORDAX
Un'Goro Crater (90), B:(4, 6), C:(2-7), D:(3-5, 7, 8), E:(2-8)

FREZZA
Zeppelin Master, Durotar (34), H-1, Atop tower

FROST SPECTRE
Barrens (18), F-9, Razorfen Downs

FROSTMANE HEADHUNTER
Dun Morogh (32), B-5, C-5, E-4, G-2, I-4, J-4, Frostmane Hold, Shimmer Ridge

FROSTMANE HIDESKINNER
Dun Morogh (32), B-5, C-5, I-4, J-4, Frostmane Hold

FROSTMANE NOVICE
Dun Morogh (32), D-8, I-4, J-4, Coldridge Valley (107)

FROSTMANE SEER
Dun Morogh (32), E:(3-5), F:(3-5), I-4, J-4, Shimmer Ridge

FROSTMANE SHADOWCASTER
Dun Morogh (32), B-5, C-5, G-2, I-4, J-4, Frostmane Hold

FROSTMANE SNOWSTRIDER
Dun Morogh (32), C-5, E:(3, 4), F-4, G-2, I-4, J-4, Frostmane Hold, Iceflow Lake, Shimmer Ridge

FROSTMANE TROLL
Dun Morogh (32), C-5, E-4, I-4, J-4, Frostmane Hold, Shimmer Ridge

FROSTMANE TROLL WHELP
Dun Morogh (32), B:(7, 8), C- 8, D-8, Coldridge Valley (107)

FROSTMAUL GIANT
Winterspring (98), I:(6, 7), J-7, Frostwhisper Gorge

FROSTMAUL PRESERVER
Winterspring (98), I:(6, 7), J-7, Frostwhisper Gorge

FROSTMAW
Alterac Mountains (8), E-7, Growless Cave, (Summon) Cave south of Ruins of Alterac

FROSTSABER
Winterspring (98), G-2, H:(1, 2), Frostsaber Rock

FROSTSABER COMPANION
Teldrassil (80), B:(5, 6), C:(4, 5), Cenarion Enclave

FROSTSABER CUB
Winterspring (98), G:(1, 2), H:(1, 2), Frostsaber Rock

FROSTSABER HUNTRESS
Winterspring (98), G:(1, 2), H:(1, 2), Frostsaber Rock

FROSTSABER PRIDE WATCHER
Winterspring (98), G-1, H-1, Frostsaber Rock

FROSTSABER STALKER
Winterspring (98), G:(1, 2), H:(1, 2), Frostsaber Rock

FROSTWOLF AMBASSADOR ROKHSTROM
Orgrimmar (60), F-7, Valley of Strength, Alterac Valley Battlemaster

FROSTWOLF BATTLEGUARD
Alterac Mountains (8), I:(5, 6), Alterac Valley

FROZEN SOUL
Barrens (18), F-9, Razorfen Downs

FUNGAL OOZE
Swamp of Sorrows (76), I-5, The Temple of Atal'Hakkar

FUREN LONGBEARD
Stormwind (72), I-2, J-2, Dwarven District, At the forge

FURIOUS STONE SPIRIT
Stonetalon Mountains (70), D-7, E-7, The Charred Vale

FURL SCORNBROW
Durotar (34), G-4, Atop watchtower

FURY SHELDA
Rare Spawn, Teldrassil (80), D:(3-4), The Oracle Glade, Lvl 8 Uncommon; Patrols near harpy camps west of road

FUZRUCKLE
Banker, Barrens (18), H-4, Ratchet (122), Bank

FYLDAN
Cooking Supplier, Darnassus (26), F-2, Craftsmen's Terrace, Cooking shop

FYLDREN MOONFEATHER
Hippogryph Master, Feralas (46), C-4, Feathermoon Stronghold (111), West of inn

FYLERIAN NIGHTWING
Druid Trainer, Darnassus (26), D-1, Cenarion Enclave, Northwest structure

FYR MISTRUNNER
Bread, Thunder Bluff (84), D-5, Lower rise, inside Breads and Grains tent

FYRENNA
Food & Drink, Darnassus (26), I-5, Craftsmen's Terrace, South of path just after entrance to city

---

G

GABRIELLE CHASE
Food & Drink, Burning Steppes (22), K-7, Morgan's Vigil (120), Scaffolding, right side of camp

GADGETZAN BRUISER
Tanaris (78), G-3, H-3, Gadgetzan (113)

GAERIYAN
Tanaris (78), H-2, Gadgetzan (113), Only visible when dead; Northeast of town in hills

GAEROLAS TALVETHREN
Teldrassil (80), I-6, Starbreeze Village, Second floor of southwest building

GAGSPROCKET
Engineering Goods, Barrens (18), H-4, Ratchet (122), Building northeast of town

GAHROOT
Butcher, Barrens (18), F-6, Camp Taurajo (106), Southern building

GAHZ'RILLA
Tanaris (78), E-1, Zul'Farrak

GAKIN THE DARKBINDER
Stormwind (72), D-8, Mage Quarter, The Slaughtered Lamb

GALAK ASSASSIN
Thousand Needles (82), B-3, Whitereach Post

GALAK CENTAUR
Mulgore (58), H-6, I-6, The Rolling Plains

GALAK MARAUDER
Thousand Needles (82), B:(2, 3), E-3, F-3, Camp E'thok, Splithoof Crag, Splithoof Hold

GALAK MAULER
Thousand Needles (82), B:(2, 3), E-3, F-3, Camp E'thok, Splithoof Crag, Splithoof Hold

---

GALAK MESSENGER
Thousand Needles (82), E-3, Splithoof Crag, Runs between Camp E'thok and Splithoof Crag

GALAK OUTRUNNER
Mulgore (58), H-6, I-6, The Rolling Plains

GALAK PACKHOUND
Thousand Needles (82), B-4, Whitereach Post

GALAK SCOUT
Thousand Needles (82), E:(3, 4), F-4

GALAK STORMER
Thousand Needles (82), B:(2, 3), E-3, F-3, Camp E'thok, Splithoof Hold

GALAK WINDCHASER
Thousand Needles (82), E:(3, 4), F-4

GALAK WRANGLER
Thousand Needles (82), E:(3, 4), F-4

GALAMAV THE MARKSMAN
Badlands (16), A-5, Kargath (116), Tower platform

GALEN GOODWARD
Swamp of Sorrows (76), H-2, Caged next to hut

GALGANN FIREHAMMER
Badlands (16), G-1, Uldaman

GALGAR
Durotar (34), F-7, Valley of Trials (136), Northwest structure

GALTHUK
Two-Handed Weapons Merchant, Orgrimmar (60), J-2, Valley of Honor, Arms of Legend

GALVAN THE ANCIENT
Artisan Blacksmith of the Mithril Order, Stranglethorn Vale (74), F-2, By anvil in camp

GAMILI FROSTHIDE
Cloth & Leather Armor Merchant, Dun Morogh (32), F-5, Kharanos (116), Smithy

GAMMERITA
The Hinterlands (50), L-5, The Overlook Cliffs, Patrols the coastline

GAMON
Orgrimmar (60), G-7, Valley of Strength, Inn

GAN'RUL BLOODEYE
Orgrimmar (60), F-4, The Cleft of Shadow, Darkfire Enclave

GANGLED GOLEM
Eastern Plaguelands (40), K-4, The Noxious Glade

GANN STONESPIRE
Barrens (18), E-7, Southern Gold Road, Spawns on Southern Gold Road and pauses at road to Dustwallow Marsh

GANOOSH
Undercity (88), F-6, The Apothecarium, On wooden pathway leading to back of Apothecarium

GAN'ZULAH
Bloodscalp Chief, Stranglethorn Vale (74), B-1, Ruins of Zul'Kunda, Idle with several trolls in the northwestern corner of ruins

GAREK
Badlands (16), I-5, Left of bone pile

GARNEG CHARSKULL
Rare Spawn, Wetlands (96), E-5, F:(4, 5), Angerfang Encampment, Lvl 29 Uncommon; Spawns in a few different camps

GARON HUTCHINS
Silithus (67), G-4, Cenarion Hold (106)

GARR
Burning Steppes (22), Searing Gorge (64), C-4/D-8, The Molten Core

GARR SALTHOOF
Stranglethorn Vale (74), C-9, Wild Shore, Roams below deck of beached ship

GARRICK PADFOOT
Elwynn Forest (42), H-5, Northshire Vineyards, In front of shed

GARRYETH
Banker, Darnassus (26), E-4, Bank

GART MISTRUNNER
Druid Trainer, Mulgore (58), E-8, Camp Narache (105), North tent

GAR'THOK
Durotar (34), H-4, Razor Hill (124), Bunker

GARYL
Tabard Vendor, Orgrimmar (60), E-7, Valley of Strength, Horde Embassy

GASHER
Swamp of Sorrows (76), I-5, The Temple of Atal'Hakkar

GATEKEEPER RAGEROAR
Rare Spawn, Azshara (14), D-3, Timbermaw Hold, Lvl 49 Semi-Rare; Guards gate

GATH'ILZOGG
Warlord of the Blackrock Clan, Redridge Mountains (62), I-5, Stonewatch, Second floor of Stonewatch Keep

GAVIN GNARLTREE
Weaponsmith, Duskwood (36), J-5, Darkshire (108), Roams in and out of smithy

GAXIM RUSTFIZZLE
Stonetalon Mountains (70), G-7, Webwinder Path, Camp east of road

GAZBAN
Stranglethorn Vale (74), A-3, The Savage Coast, Roams around island

GAZIN TENORM
Stormwind (72), F-3, Cathedral Square, Cathedral of Light

GAZLOWE
Barrens (18), H-4, Ratchet (122), Building northeast of town

GAZROG
Barrens (18), F-3, The Crossroads (107), Front of inn

GAZZ'UZ
Durotar (34), H-1, Skull Rock, Deep in cave

GEARCUTTER COGSPINNER
Engineering Supplies, Ironforge (52), I-4, Tinker Town, Springspindle's Gadgets

GEENIA SUNSHADOW
Speciality Dress Maker, Moonglade (56), G-3, Nighthaven (121), First floor of northeast building

GEHENNAS
Burning Steppes (22), Searing Gorge (64), C-4/D-8, The Molten Core

GELIHAST
Ashenvale (12), B-2, Blackfathom Deeps

GELKAK GYROMAST
Darkshore (24), H-2, Mist's Edge, Rocky outcropping off shore

GELKIS EARTHCALLER
Desolace (30), D:(8, 9), E:(8, 9), Bolgan's Hole, Gelkis Village

GELKIS MARAUDER
Desolace (30), D-9, E-9, Bolgan's Hole, Gelkis Village

GELKIS MAULER
Desolace (30), D-9, E-9, Bolgan's Hole, Gelkis Village

GELKIS OUTRUNNER
Desolace (30), D:(8, 9), E:(8, 9), Bolgan's Hole, Gelkis Village

GELKIS SCOUT
Desolace (30), D:(8, 9), E:(8, 9), Bolgan's Hole, Gelkis Village

GELKIS STAMPER
Desolace (30), D:(8, 9), E:(8, 9), Bolgan's Hole, Gelkis Village

GELKIS WINDCHASER
Desolace (30), D:(8, 9), E:(8, 9), Bolgan's Hole, Gelkis Village

GELMAN STONEHAND
Mining Trainer, Stormwind (72), H-2, Dwarven District, Building north of west entrance

GELTHARIS
Ashenvale (12), J-4, Xavian, Far north within Xavian in a small gully

GENAVIE GALLOW
Undercity (88), I-5, The Trade Quarter, Upper Ring of Trade Quarter

GENERAL ANGERFORGE
Burning Steppes (22), Searing Gorge (64), C-4/D-8, Blackrock Depths

GENERAL COLBATANN
Rare Spawn, Winterspring (98), H-5, Mazthoril, Lvl 57 Semi-Rare; Central cavern

GENERAL DRAKKISATH
Burning Steppes (22), Searing Gorge (64), C-4/D-8, Blackrock Spire

GENERAL FANGFERROR
Rare Spawn, Azshara (14), E-5, Temple of Zin-Malor, Lvl 50 Semi-Rare; Top of main temple

GENERAL MARCUS JONATHEN
High Commander of Stormwind Defense, Stormwind (72), I-7, Stormwind City, Next to statue at entrance

GENNIA RUNETOTEM
Druid Trainer, Mulgore (58), F-6, Bloodhoof Village (102), East tent

GEOFF
Stormwind (72), Roams city with Miss Danna

GEOFFREY HARTWELL
Weapon Merchant, Undercity (88), H-3, The War Quarter

GEOFRAM BOULDERTOE
Mining Trainer, Ironforge (52), G-3, The Great Forge, Deep Mountain Mining Guild

GEOLOGIST LARKSBANE
Silithus (67), G-4, Cenarion Hold (106)

GEOLORD MOTTLE
Rare Spawn, Durotar (34), F-4, G-5, Razormane Grounds, Lvl 9 Uncommon; Found near huts

GEOPRIEST GUKK'ROK
Rare Spawn, Barrens (18), E:(4-5), Agama'gor, Lvl 19 Uncommon; Guards Bristleback den

GEORGE CANDARTE
Leatherworking Supplies, Hillsbrad Foothills (48), L-4, Thoradin's Wall, Behind two trees at the far left corner of the wall

GEORGIA
Bat Handler, Eastern Plaguelands (40), K-5, Light's Hope Chapel (118), Camp on left side of chapel

GEORGIO BOLERO
Artisan Tailor, Stormwind (72), G-7, Mage Quarter, Duncan's Textiles

GERALD CRAWLEY
Poison Supplier, Redridge Mountains (62), C-4, Lakeshire (117), Small house on a hill on northwestern side of town

GERARD ABERNATHY
Undercity (88), G-3, The War Quarter, By Mining Trainer, Close to Canal

GERARD TILLER
Elwynn Forest (42), F-8, The Maclure Vineyards, In front of barn

GERECK
Stable Master, Stonetalon Mountains (70), F-6, Sun Rock Retreat (132), Front of inn

GERENZO WRENCHWHISTLE
Stonetalon Mountains (70), H-4, Cragpool Lake, Wood platform above lake

GERIK KOEN
Two Handed Weapon Merchant, Stormwind (72), J-4, Old Town, Heavy Handed Weapons

GERRIG BONEGRIP
Ironforge (52), G-1, The Forlorn Cavern, Building to the right of Traveling Fisherman

GERSHALA NIGHTWHISPER
Darkshore (24), F-4, Auberdine (101), Pavillion east of inn across bridge

GESHARAHAN
Rare Spawn, Barrens (18), E-4, Lushwater Oasis, Lvl 20 Average Rare; Swims in the oasis

GEST
Rogue Trainer, Orgrimmar (60), E-5, The Cleft of Shadow, Shadowswift Brotherhood

GHAK HEALTOUCH
Alchemist Trainer, Loch Modan (54), E-5, Thelsamar (134), In first house on right of path

GHAMOO-RA
Ashenvale (12), B-2, Blackfathom Deeps

GHARASH
Blacksmithing Supplies, Swamp of Sorrows (76), F-5, Stonard (131), Smithy

GHEDE
Thunder Bluff (84), J-2, Elder Rise, Behind Hall of Elders

GHOK BASHGUUD
Rare Spawn, Burning Steppes (22), Searing Gorge (64), C-4/D-8, Blackrock Spire, Lvl 59 Uncommon

GHOK'KAH
Tailoring Supplies, Dustwallow Marsh (38), D-3, Brackenwall Village (104), West entrance

GHOST HOWL
Rare Spawn, Mulgore (58), C-2, D:(1, 4), F-1, Lvl 12 Uncommon; Roams plains in multiple areas

GHOST OF THE PROTECTOR
Eastern Plaguelands (40), E-8, Darrowshire

GHOST WALKER BRAVE
Desolace (30), G:(5, 6), Ghost Walker Post (113), Kodo Graveyard

GHOSTLY CITIZEN
Eastern Plaguelands (40), D-2, Stratholme

GHOSTLY MARAUDER
Desolace (30), D-5, Mauradon

GHOSTLY RAIDER
Desolace (30), D-5, Mauradon

GHOSTPAW ALPHA
Ashenvale (12), G:(3, 4), H:(3-7), I:(5-7), J:(5, 6), Falfarren River, Nightsong Woods, Splintertree Post (129)

GHOSTPAW HOWLER
Ashenvale (12), G:(6, 7), H:(6, 7)

GHOSTPAW RUNNER
Ashenvale (12), B:(2-5), C:(2-6), D:(2-6), E:(5, 6), H:(7, 8), I:(7, 8), J:(6, 7)

GHOUL
Westfall (94), D:(3, 7), G-8

GHOUL RAVENER
Eastern Plaguelands (40), D-2, Stratholme

GHRAWT
Bowyer, Durotar (34), H-4, Razor Hill (124), Northern entrance

GIANT ASHENVALE BEAR
Ashenvale (12), J:(5, 6), K:(4-6), L:(5, 6)

GIANT BUZZARD
Badlands (16), A-7, B:(5, 6), C:(6-8), D:(6-8), E-8, Apocryphan's Rest

GIANT DARKFANG SPIDER
Dustwallow Marsh (38), F:(4, 5), G:(5-7)

GIANT EMBER WORG
Burning Steppes (22), A-5, B:(4-7), C:(5, 6), Blackrock Mountain

GIANT FORESTSTRIDER
Darkshore (24), E:(8, 9), F:(8, 9), G-9, I:(1, 2)

GIANT GRIZZLED BEAR
Silverpine Forest (68), E-2, F:(1, 2), G:(2, 7), H:(5-7)

GIANT MOSS CREEPER
Hillsbrad Foothills (48), B:(2-7), C:(1-3, 5-7), D:(3, 5, 6), E:(5, 6), G-5, H:(4-6), I:(2, 3, 5, 6), J:(3, 5, 6), K:(3-5), L-4

GIANT PLAINS CREEPER
Arathi Highlands (10), E-3, F:(3, 4, 7, 8), G:(5, 6), H:(5-7), Northfold Manor

GIANT SURF GLIDER
Tanaris (78), G:(8, 9), H-9, I:(8, 9), Land's End Beach

GIANT WEBWOOD SPIDER
Teldrassil (80), D:(2, 3), E:(2, 3), F:(2, 3), The Oracle Glade

GIANT WETLANDS CROCOLISK
Wetlands (96), B:(2, 3, 6), C-2, D-2

GIANT YETI
Alterac Mountains (8), D:(4-7), E:(3, 4, 6, 7), F:(6, 7), Growless Cave

GIBBERING GHOUL
Eastern Plaguelands (40), H:(6, 7), Corin's Crossing

GIBBERT
Weapon Merchant, Un'Goro Crater (90), F-1, Marshal's Refuge (118), Near entrance to cave

GIBBLESNIK
Rare Spawn, Thousand Needles (82), G:(4-5), H:(5-6), Windbreak Canyon, Lvl 28 Semi-Rare; Several spawn points around Windbreak Canyons

GIBBLEWILT
Rare Spawn, Dun Morogh (32), C-4, Gnomeregan, Lvl 11 Uncommon; Roams small area around spawn point

GIGGET ZIPCOIL
Trade Supplies, The Hinterlands (50), E-4, The Hinterlands, Gnomish camp on recessed hill east of Quel'Danil Lodge

GIGGLER
Rare Spawn, Desolace (30), F-1, G-1, H:(2-3), I:(2-3), Tethris Aran, Lvl 34 Semi-Rare; Roams near spawn points

GIKKIX
Fisherman, Tanaris (78), J-2, Steamwheedle Port, Small northern hut

GIL
Stormwind (72), Roams city with Karlee

GILLIAN MOORE
Leather Armor Merchant, Undercity (88), J-6, The Rogues' Quarter

GILMORIAN
Rare Spawn, Swamp of Sorrows (76), J-9, The Forbidding Sea, Lvl 43 Average Rare; Patrols up and down the eastern coastline

GILNID
Westfall (94), D-7, E-7, The Deadmines

GILSHALAN WINDWALKER
Teldrassil (80), G-4, Shadowglen (127), By ramp leading up tree

GILTHARES FIREBOUGH
Barrens (18), H-5, Northwatch Hold, First floor of main tower

GILVERADIN SUNCHASER
The Hinterlands (50), D-5, Shindigger's Camp, Camp

GIMBLE THISTLEFUZZ
Expert Enchanter, Ironforge (52), H-4, The Great Forge, Thistlefuzz Arcanery

GIMBLETHORN
Banker, Tanaris (78), H-3, Gadgetzan (113), Bank

GIMLOK RUMDNUL
Wetlands (96), A-6, Menethil Harbor (119), Roaming eastern side of town

GIMRIZZ SHADOWCOG
Warlock Trainer, Dun Morogh (32), F-5, Kharanos (116), Gnomish camp on right of distillery

GINA LANG
Demon Trainer, Tirisfal Glades (86), H-5, Brill (104), Second floor of Gallows' End Tavern

GINA MACGREGOR
Trade Supplies, Westfall (94), G-5, Sentinel Hill (126), At intersection east of the Sentinel Tower

GINNY LONGBERRY
Reagent Vendor, Ironforge (52), D-3, The Mystic Ward, Longberry's Reagents

GINRO HEARTHKINDLE
Feralas (46), C-4, Feathermoon Stronghold (111), Second floor of southeastern building

GISH THE UNMOVING
Rare Spawn, Eastern Plaguelands (40), F-4, J-6, Pestilent Scar, Lvl 56 Average Rare; Patrols between its two spawn points

GITHYISS THE VILE
Teldrassil (80), G-3, Shadowthread Cave, On ledge in back of cave

GIZELTON CARAVAN KODO
Desolace (30), H:(4, 6), Kormek's Hut, Scrabblescrew's Camp

GIZRUL THE SLAVENER
Burning Steppes (22), Searing Gorge (64), C-4/D-8, Blackrock Spire

GIZZIX GRIMEGURGLE
Dustwallow Marsh (38), F-7, Mudsprocket (120)

GLACIER
Rivern's Guardian, Winterspring (98), G-1, Frostsaber Rock, Atop Frostsaber Rock

GLASSHIDE BASILISK
Tanaris (78), E:(2, 3), F:(2-4), G:(2-4), H:(2-4), I:(2, 3), J-3

GLASSHIDE GAZER
Tanaris (78), E:(4-7), F:(4-7), G:(4-7), H:(4-6), I:(4-6)

GLASSHIDE PETRIFIER
Tanaris (78), D:(5-8), E:(5-8), F:(7, 8), G:(7, 8)

GLASSWEB SPIDER
Searing Gorge (64), G:(5, 7), H:(3-5, 7), I:(2, 5), J-2, Tanner Camp

GLOMMUS
Alterac Mountains (8), E-4, Ruins of Alterac, Small house

GLOOM'REL
Burning Steppes (22), Searing Gorge (64), C-4/D-8, Blackrock Depths

GLORANDIIR
Axe Merchant, Darnassus (26), I-6, Tradesmen's Terrace, Weapons shop

GLORDRUM STEELBEARD
Alterac Valley Battlemaster, Ironforge (52), J-9, The Military Ward, Hall of Arms

GLORIA FEMMEL
Cooking Supplies, Redridge Mountains (62), C-4, Lakeshire (117), First floor of Lakeshire Inn

GLORIN STEELBROW
Wetlands (96), A-6, Deepwater Tavern, First floor

GLUGGLE
Rare Spawn, Stranglethorn Vale (74), C-3, Kal'ai Ruins, Lvl 37 Semi-Rare; Patrols between ruins and path heading north

GLUTINOUS OOZE
Un'Goro Crater (90), C:(3-7), D:(3-8), E:(2-8), F:(5, 6), Fire Plume Ridge, Golakka Hot Springs, Terror Run

GLUTTON
Barrens (18), F-9, Razorfen Downs

GILSHALAN WINDWALKER

GLYX BREWRIGHT
Alchemy Supplies, Stranglethorn Vale (74), B-8, Booty Bay (103), Boucher's Cauldron (shop)

GNARL LEAFBROTHER
Rare Spawn, Feralas (46), I-6, The Writhing Deep, Lvl 44 Very Rare; Roam west to the Woodpaw Hills

GNARLED THISTLESHRUB
Tanaris (78), D:(6, 7), E:(6, 7), Thistleshrub Valley

GNARLPINE AMBUSHER
Teldrassil (80), E-5, F-5, Ban'ethil Hollow

GNARLPINE AUGUR
Teldrassil (80), E:(6, 7), F:(6, 8), G-7, Ban'ethil Barrow Den

GNARLPINE AVENGER
Teldrassil (80), D-8, E-8, Gnarlpine Hold

GNARLPINE DEFENDER
Teldrassil (80), D:(6, 7), E:(6, 7), F:(6-8), G:(7, 8), Ban'ethil Barrow Den, Ban'ethil Hollow, Gnarlpine Hold

GNARLPINE GARDENER
Teldrassil (80), H-6, I:(5, 6), Starbreeze Village

GNARLPINE INSTIGATOR
Teldrassil (80), F-6

GNARLPINE MYSTIC
Teldrassil (80), I-5, Ban'ethil Barrow Den

GNARLPINE PATHFINDER
Teldrassil (80), D-8, E-8, Gnarlpine Hold

GNARLPINE SHAMAN
Teldrassil (80), D:(6, 7), E:(6, 7), F:(6-8), G:(7, 8), Ban'ethil Barrow Den, Ban'ethil Hollow, Gnarlpine Hold

GNARLPINE TOTEMIC
Teldrassil (80), D-8, E-8, Gnarlpine Hold

GNARLPINE URSA
Teldrassil (80), H-6, I:(5, 6), Starbreeze Village

GNARLPINE WARRIOR
Teldrassil (80), F:(6, 7), H-6, I:(5, 6), Lake Al'Ameth, Starbreeze Village

GNASHER
Loch Modan (54), D-9, Stonesplinter Valley, With Grawmug and Brawler in center of cave

GNAWBONE
Rare Spawn, Wetlands (96), D-3, E-3, Sundown Marsh, Lvl 24 Average Rare; Patrols mosshide camps north of road across from excavation site

GNAZ BLUNDERFLAME
Engineering Supplies, Stranglethorn Vale (74), F-4, Outside of gnomish workshop

GNOARN
Ironforge (52), I-5, Tinker Town, Outside tram entrance

GNOME ENGINEER
Dun Morogh (32), J-3

GNOMEREGAN EVACUEE
Dun Morogh (32), C-4, Gnomeregan

GOBBLER
Wetlands (96), B-4, Bluegill Marsh, South central section of marsh

GOBLIN CRAFTSMAN
Westfall (94), D-7, E-7, The Deadmines

GOBLIN ENGINEER
Westfall (94), D-7, E-7, The Deadmines

GOBLIN SHIPBUILDER
Westfall (94), D-7, E-7, The Deadmines

GOBLIN WOODCARVER
Westfall (94), D-7, E-7, The Deadmines

GODAN
Enchanter Trainer, Orgrimmar (60), G-, The Drag, Godan's Runeworks

GODRIC ROTHGAR
Armorer & Shieldcrafter, Elwynn Forest (42), F-4, Northshire Valley (122), Caravan facing abbey

GODRICK FARSAN
Undercity (88), L-1, The Magic Quarter, Inside Skull Building

GOGGEROC
Stonetalon Mountains (70), H-9, Boulderslide Cavern, South of water deep in cave

GOGO
Winterspring (98), I-4, Everlook (110), Outside inn

GOL'DIR
Alterac Mountains (8), H-4, Strahnbra, Second floor of inn

GOLDTOOTH
Elwynn Forest (42), E-8, Fargodeep Mine, Rear of mine

GOLEM LORD ARGELMACH
Burning Steppes (22), Searing Gorge (64), C-4/D-8, Blackrock Depths

GOLEMAGG THE INCINERATOR
Burning Steppes (22), Searing Gorge (64), C-4/D-8, The Molten Core

GOLHINE THE HOODED
Druid Trainer, Felwood (44), H-3, Talonbranch Glade (133), Front of building

GOLNIR BOULDERTOE
Mining Supplier, Ironforge (52), G-3, The Great Forge, Deep Mountain Mining Guild

GOLORN FROSTBEARD
Tradesman, Dun Morogh (32), F-5, Kharanos (116), By caravan

GOMA
Orgrimmar (60), G-7, Valley of Strength, Inn

GOR'TESH
Burning Steppes (22), D-5, Entrance of orc burrow

GORALUK ANVILCRACK
Burning Steppes (22), Searing Gorge (64), C-4/D-8, Blackrock Spire

GORBOLD STEELHAND
General Trade Supplier, Darkshore (24), F-4, Auberdine (101), In front of northern building

GORDO
Tirisfal Glades (86), E-5, Patrols along road between the fork near Deathknell and the bridge near Cold Hearth Manor

GORDOK BRUTE
Feralas (46), G-4, Dire Maul

GORDOK BUSHWACKER
Feralas (46), G-4, Dire Maul

GORDOK CAPTAIN
Feralas (46), G-4, Dire Maul

GORDOK ENFORCER
Feralas (46), F:(4, 5), G:(4, 5), H:(3, 5), Dire Maul, High Wilderness

GORDOK HYENA
Feralas (46), F:(4, 5), G:(3, 4), H-4, Dire Maul, High Wilderness

GORDOK MAGE-LORD
Feralas (46), G-4, Dire Maul

GORDOK MASTIFF
Feralas (46), G-4, Dire Maul

GORDOK MAULER
Feralas (46), G:(3, 4), H:(3, 4), Dire Maul

GORDOK OGRE-MAGE
Feralas (46), F-4, G:(3-5), H:(3-5), Dire Maul, High Wilderness

GORDOK REAVER
Feralas (46), G-4, Dire Maul

GORDOK SPIRIT
Feralas (46), G-4, Dire Maul

GORDOK WARLOCK
Feralas (46), G-4, Dire Maul

GORDON WENDHAM
Weapons Merchant, Undercity (88), H-4, The Trade Quarter, Upper Ring of Trade Quarter

GORDUNNI BATTLEMASTER
Feralas (46), G-7, H-7, High Wilderness, Ruins of Isildien

GORDUNNI BRUTE
Feralas (46), G:(5, 6), I:(2, 3), J:(3, 4)

GORDUNNI MAGE-LORD
Feralas (46), G-7, H-7, High Wilderness, Ruins of Isildien

GORDUNNI MAULER
Feralas (46), G:(5-7), High Wilderness, Ruins of Isildien

GORDUNNI OGRE
Feralas (46), I:(2, 3), J:(3, 4), Gordunni Outpost, Lariss Pavilion

GORDUNNI OGRE MAGE
Feralas (46), I:(2, 3), J:(3, 4), Gordunni Outpost, Lariss Pavilion

GORDUNNI SHAMAN
Feralas (46), G:(6, 7), H-7, High Wilderness, Ruins of Isildien

GORDUNNI WARLOCK
Feralas (46), G:(5-7), High Wilderness, Ruins of Isildien

GORDUNNI WARLORD
Feralas (46), G:(6, 7), H-7, High Wilderness, Ruins of Isildien

GOREFANG
Rare Spawn, Silverpine Forest (68), G:(2, 3), H-2, I-1, Malden's Orchard, Silverpine Forest, Lvl 13 Uncommon; Roams small area around spawn point

GOREHOOF THE BLACK
Stonetalon Mountains (70), J-8, Grimtotem Post, Inside eastern hut

GORETUSK
Westfall (94), C:(3, 4, 6-8), D:(2-7), E:(4-6), F-6, G:(4, 5)

GORGON'OCH
Rare Spawn, Burning Steppes (22), J-4, Dreadmaul Rock, Lvl 54 Average Rare

GORINA
Mining Supplier, Orgrimmar (60), I-3, Valley of Honor, Red Canyon Mining

GORISHI HIVE GUARD
Un'Goro Crater (90), F-8, The Slithering Scar

GORISHI HIVE QUEEN
Un'Goro Crater (90), G-8, The Slithering Scar, Northwest chamber

GORISHI REAVER
Un'Goro Crater (90), F:(7-9), G:(7-9), The Slithering Scar

GORISHI STINGER
Un'Goro Crater (90), F:(8, 9), G-8, The Slithering Scar

GORISHI TUNNELER
Un'Goro Crater (90), F:(8, 9), G-8, The Slithering Scar

GORISHI WASP
Un'Goro Crater (90), F:(7-9), G:(7-9), The Slithering Scar

GORISHI WORKER
Un'Goro Crater (90), F:(7-9), G:(7-9), The Slithering Scar

GORKAS
Wind Rider Master, The Hinterlands (50), L-8, Revantusk Village (125), End of dock

GORLASH
Stranglethorn Vale (74), D-7, The Crystal Shore, Roams small area around spawn point

GORM GRIMTOTEM
Thunder Bluff (84), I-3, Elder Rise, In front of Magatha Grimtotem's tent

GOR'MAROK THE RAVAGER
Tanaris (78), F-6, Dunemaul Compound, Cave

GOR'MUL
Arathi Highlands (10), J-3, Hammerfall (115), Gallows

GORN
Badlands (16), A-5, Kargath (116), First floor orc burrow

GORNEK
Durotar (34), F-7, Valley of Trials (136), Entrance of cave

GOROSH THE DERVISH
Burning Steppes (22), Searing Gorge (64), C-4/D-8, Blackrock Depths

GORRIK
Wind Rider Master, Badlands (16), A-5, Kargath (116), Camp

GORZEEKI WILDEYES
Burning Steppes (22), A-3, Altar of Storms, In graveyard above and left of the Altar of Storms

GOTHARD WINSLOW
Undercity (88), L-6, The Rogues' Quarter

GOTHOR BRUMN
Armorer, Loch Modan (54), C-2, Dun Algaz, Algaz Station

GOTRI
Bag Vendor, Orgrimmar (60), G-5, The Drag, Gotri's Traveling Gear

GRACINA SPIRITMIGHT
Darnassus (26), E-8, The Temple of the Moon, Balcony, east of fountain

GRADOK
Loch Modan (54), H-7, Patrols large circular paths with Haren Swifthoof and Thragomm along the eastern side of the loch

GRAHAM VAN TALEN
Apprentice Engineer, Undercity (88), J-7, The Rogues' Quarter

GRAMMA STONEFIELD
Elwynn Forest (42), D-8, The Stonefield Farm, House

GRAND ADMIRAL JES-TERETH
Stormwind (72), L-1, Stormwind Keep, War Room

GRAND CRUSADER DATHROHAN
Eastern Plaguelands (40), D-2, Stratholme

GRAND FOREMAN PUZIK GALLYWIX
Barrens (18), F-1, Top of tower northwest of Sludge Fen

GRAND INQUISITOR ISILLIEN
Western Plaguelands (92), G-2 (Summon) Spawns in the tower south of Hearthglen

GRAND MASON MARBLESTEN
Royal Stonecutters Union, Ironforge (52), C-7, F-5, The Commons, Building next to visitor's center

GRANDPA VISHAS
Rare Spawn, Alterac Mountains (8), D-3, The Uplands, Lvl 34 Common; Inside house

GRANIS SWIFTAXE
Warrior Trainer, Dun Morogh (32), F-5, Kharanos (116), Thunderbrew Distillery

GRANISTAD
Hillsbrad Foothills (48), K-3, Durnholde Keep, Roams a small area northeast of keep

GRARK LORKRUB
Burning Steppes (22), D-3, Blackrock Stronghold, Center of stronghold

GRARNIK GOODSTITCH
Expert Tailor, Stranglethorn Vale (74), B-8, Booty Bay (103), A Tailor to Cities (shop)

GRAUD
General Goods, Arathi Highlands (10), J-3, Hammerfall (115), First floor north building

GRAVE ROBBER
Duskwood (36), B:(4, 5), Raven Hill Cemetery (123)

GRAVELFLINT BONESNAPPER
Darkshore (24), E-9, Remtravel's Excavation

GRAVELFLINT GEOMANCER
Darkshore (24), E-8, Remtravel's Excavation

GRAVELFLINT SCOUT
Darkshore (24), E-8, Remtravel's Excavation

GRAVELSNOUT DIGGER
Thousand Needles (82), A:(1, 2), G:(4, 5), H:(5, 6), I-5, Windbreak Canyon

GRAVELSNOUT FORAGER
Thousand Needles (82), B:(2, 4), C:(3-5), D-5, E-5, G:(4, 5), H-6, The Screeching Canyon, Windbreak Canyon

GRAVELSNOUT KOBOLD
Thousand Needles (82), B:(2, 4), C:(3-5), D:(3, 5), E:(3, 5), F-6, Darkcloud Pinnacle, The Screeching Canyon

GRAVELSNOUT SURVEYOR
Thousand Needles (82), A:(1, 2), H:(5, 6), I-5, Ironstone Camp

GRAVELSNOUT VERMIN
Thousand Needles (82), D-3, E:(3, 5), F-6, Darkcloud Pinnacle

GRAVIS SLIPKNOT
Rare Spawn, Alterac Mountains (8), H-4, Strahnbrad, Lvl 36 Uncommon; Windmill on western side of town

GRAW CORNERSTONE
Mail Armor Merchant, Searing Gorge (64), E-7, Left side of camp

GRAWL
General Goods, Badlands (16), A-5, Kargath (116), First floor orc burrow

GRAWMUG
Loch Modan (54), D-9, Stonesplinter Valley, With Brawler and Gnasher in center of cave

GRAWN THROMWYN
Weaponsmith, Dun Morogh (32), F-5, Kharanos (116), Smithy

GRAWNAL
General Goods, Stonetalon Mountains (70), E-6, Sun Rock Retreat (132), Western building

GRAY BEAR
Hillsbrad Foothills (48), A:(4, 5), B:(4, 5), C-5, F:(1, 2), G:(1-4), H:(1-4), I-1, Tarren Mill (133), Throughout Hillsbrad

GRAY FOREST WOLF
Elwynn Forest (42), H:(6, 7), I:(6, 7), J:(6, 7)

GRAZLE
Felwood (44), I-1, Timbermaw Hold, Near entrance to the hold

GRAZLIX
Armorer & Shieldcrafter, Barrens (18), H-4, Ratchet (122), Plate-n-Chain

GREAT BEAR SPIRIT
Moonglade (56), F-3, Uphill of northwest corner of town

GREAT CAT SPIRIT
Moonglade (56), H-7, South of east side of lake

GREAT COURSER
Stonetalon Mountains (70), D:(1, 2), E:(1, 2), Stonetalon Peak

GREAT FATHER ARCTIKUS
Rare Spawn, Dun Morogh (32), B-5, C-5, Frostmane Hold, Lvl 11 Uncommon; Cave at Frostmane Hold

GREAT GORETUSK
Redridge Mountains (62), A:(5, 7, 8), B:(4, 5, 7), C:(6-8), D:(6-8), E:(1, 2, 7), F:(1-3), G-4
Westfall (94), E-7, F-7, G:(5-7), H:(5, 7)

GREAT WAVETHRASHER
Azshara (14), E-9, F:(7, 9), G:(7, 9), H:(7-9), I:(7-9), J:(7-9), K:(8, 9)

GREATER BARRENS KODO
Barrens (18), E:(6, 8)

GREATER DUSKBAT
Tirisfal Glades (86), D:(4, 5), E:(4-6), F:(4-6), G:(5, 6), H:(4-6), I:(4-6)

GREATER FIREBIRD
Rare Spawn, Tanaris (78), F-4, Abyssal Sands, Lvl 46 Average Rare; Flies throughout northern sands

GREATER FLESHRIPPER
Westfall (94), B-4, G:(5, 6), H-6, The Dead Acre

GREATER KRAUL BAT
Barrens (18), E-9, Razorfen Kraul

GREATER LAVA SPIDER
Searing Gorge (64), B:(7, 8), C:(4-8), D-3, E-7

GREATER OBSIDIAN ELEMENTAL
Burning Steppes (22), C-6, D-6, E-4, F:(3, 6), G:(5, 6), H-3, I-3

GREATER PLAINSTRIDER
Barrens (18), E:(1-4), F:(1-3), G:(2, 3), Grol'dom Farm, The Mor'shan Rampart, Thorn Hill

GREATER ROCK ELEMENTAL
Badlands (16), A:(7, 8), B:(8, 9), C-8, Camp Cagg

GREATER TARANTULA
Redridge Mountains (62), F-4, G-4, I-7, Alther's Mill

GREATER THUNDERHAWK
Barrens (18), E:(7, 8), F:(7, 8), Blackthorn Ridge, Southern Barrens

GREATMOTHER HAWKWIND
Mulgore (58), F-8, Red Cloud Mesa, Water mill southeast of camp

GREEN RECLUSE
Duskwood (36), A:(4-6), B-7, G-2, H-2, I-2, J:(2, 3), Brightwood Grove

GREEN SCALEBANE
Swamp of Sorrows (76), H-4, I-4, J:(4, 6, 7)

GREEN SLUDGE
The Hinterlands (50), G:(4, 5), H-4, I:(4, 5), Skull Rock, Cave

GREEN WYRMKIN
Swamp of Sorrows (76), H:(5, 6), I:(6, 7), K:(5-7), L:(5, 6)

GREENPAW
Teldrassil (80), E-6, Ban'ethil Barrow Den, Lower level of den

GREGAN BREWSPEWER
Feralas (46), E-3, The Twin Colossals, Camp on hill

GREGOR AGAMAND
Tirisfal Glades (86), F-3, Agamand Mills (100), Roams around the windmills to the rear of mill

GREGOR GREYSTONE
The Argent Dawn, Winterspring (98), I-4, Everlook (110), Inside inn

GREGOR MACVINCE
Horse Breeder, Dustwallow Marsh (38), I-5, Theramore Isle (135), Stables to southwest

GREGORY ARDUS
Staff & Mace Merchant, Stormwind (72), F-4, Cathedral Square, Just Maces

GREGORY CHARLES
Rogue Trainer, Undercity (88), L-7, The Rogues' Quarter, Inside Skull Building

GREISHAN IRONSTOVE
Traveling Merchant, Loch Modan (54), C-1, Dun Algaz, Patrols between Dun Algaz, Thelsamar, and the Valley of Kings

GREL'BORG THE MISER
Alterac Mountains (8), E-5, Ruins of Alterac, Patrols between castle basement and Ruins of Alterac (E-4)

GRELIN WHITEBEARD
Dun Morogh (32), C-7, Coldridge Valley (107), Camp

GRELL
Teldrassil (80), G:(4, 5), H-4, Shadowglen (127)

GREAT FATHER ARCTIKUS — *(see GREAT FATHER ARCTIKUS above)*

GRELLKIN
Teldrassil (80), G:(3, 4), H:(3, 4), Shadowglen (127)

GREMLOCK PILSNOR
Cooking Trainer, Dun Morogh (32), F-5, Kharanos (116), Thunderbrew Distillery

GRENIL STEELFURY
Weapon Merchant, Ironforge (52), E-6, The Commons, Steelfury's Weapon Emporium

GRENKA BLOODSCREECH
Thousand Needles (82), C-5, Roguefeather Den, Deep inside den

GRENTHAR
Barrens (18), F-3, The Crossroads (107), Outside inn

GRESHKA
Demon Master, Swamp of Sorrows (76), F-5, Stonard (131), Second floor of main hall

GRETA MOSSHOOF
Emerald Circle, Felwood (44), G-8, Emerald Sanctuary (110), Roams entry path

GRETCHEN DEDMAR
Tirisfal Glades (86), H-5, Brill (104), Second floor of Gallows' End Tavern

GRETCHEN VOGEL
Waitress, Redridge Mountains (62), B-4, Lakeshire (117), Second floor of large house on southwestern side of town

GRETH
Stable Master, Badlands (16), A-5, Kargath (116), Outside orc burrow

GRETHEER
Rare Spawn, Silithus (66), E-2, F-3, G-4, Hive'Regal, Lvl 57 Very Rare; Roams close to spawn points

GRETTA FINESPINDLE
Journeyman Leatherworker, Ironforge (52), E-3, The Great Forge, Finespindle's Leather Goods

GRETTA GANTER
Fisherman Supplies, Dun Morogh (32), D-4, Iceflow Lake, Dock at southwest corner of lake

GREYMIST COASTRUNNER
Darkshore (24), E:(5, 6, 8), F:(2, 3, 6), Mist's Edge, The Long Wash, Twilight Shore

GREYMIST HUNTER
Darkshore (24), E-8, Twilight Shore

GREYMIST NETTER
Darkshore (24), E-7, G-2, Mist's Edge, Twilight Shore

GREYMIST ORACLE
Darkshore (24), E:(8, 9), H-1, Twilight Shore

GREYMIST RAIDER
Darkshore (24), E-5, The Long Wash

GREYMIST SEER
Darkshore (24), E:(6, 7), F:(2, 3, 6), Mist's Edge, The Long Wash, Twilight Shore

GREYMIST TIDEHUNTER
Darkshore (24), E:(8, 9), H-1, Mist's Edge, Twilight Shore

GREYMIST WARRIOR
Darkshore (24), E-8, G-2, Mist's Edge, Twilight Shore

GREZZ RAZORFIST
Warrior Trainer, Orgrimmar (60), J-3, Valley of Honor, Hall of the Brave

GRIF WILDHEART
Hunter Trainer, Dun Morogh (32), F-5, Kharanos (116), On hill at southwest end of town

GRIK'NIR THE COLD
Dun Morogh (32), D-8, Coldridge Valley (107), Cave

GRIM PATRON
Burning Steppes (22), Searing Gorge (64), C-4/D-8, Blackrock Depths

GRIMAND ELMORE
Stormwind (72), H-1, Dwarven District, Northwest Building

GRIMBLE
Shipmaster, Barrens (18), H-4, Ratchet (122), Dock

GRIMBOOZE THUNDERBREW
Westfall (94), E-8, The Dagger Hills, Camp in the Dagger Hills south of Moonbrook

GRIMCLAW
Darkshore (24), F-8, Twilight Vale, Just off road to the east

GRIMESTACK
Stable Master, Stranglethorn Vale (74), B-8, Booty Bay (103), Outside of The Salty Sailor Tavern

GRIMLOK
Badlands (16), G-1, Uldaman

GRIMMAW
Rare Spawn, Teldrassil (80), E-8, Gnarlpine Hold, Lvl 11 Uncommon; Patrols Gnarlpine camps

GRIMNAL
Mail and Plate Merchant, Swamp of Sorrows (76), F-5, Stonard (131), Smithy

GRIMNUR STONEBRAND
Fishing Trainer, Ironforge (52), F-1, The Forlorn Cavern, Traveling Fisherman

GRIMSON THE PALE
Silverpine Forest (68), I-4, Deep Elem Mine, Back on mine

GRIMTAK
Butcher, Durotar (34), H-4, Razor Hill (124), Western entrance on hill

GRIMTOTEM BANDIT
Thousand Needles (82), D:(3, 4), E:(3-4), Darkcloud Pinnacle, The Great Lift

GRIMTOTEM BRUTE
Stonetalon Mountains (70), I-8, J:(8, 9), K:(8, 9), Camp Aparaje, Greatwood Vale, Grimtotem Post

GRIMTOTEM GEOMANCER
Thousand Needles (82), D:(3, 4), E:(3-4), Darkcloud Pinnacle, The Great Lift

GRIMTOTEM MERCENARY
Stonetalon Mountains (70), J:(8, 9), K:(8, 9), Camp Aparaje, Greatwood Vale, Grimtotem Post

GRIMTOTEM NATURALIST
Feralas (46), H:(4, 5), Grimtotem Compound, Lower Wilds

GRIMTOTEM RAIDER
Feralas (46), H:(4, 5), Grimtotem Compound, Lower Wilds

GRIMTOTEM REAVER
Thousand Needles (82), D-4, E:(3, 4), Darkcloud Pinnacle

GRIMTOTEM RUFFIAN
Stonetalon Mountains (70), J:(8, 9), K:(8, 9), Camp Aparaje, Greatwood Vale, Grimtotem Post

GRIMTOTEM SHAMAN
Feralas (46), H:(4, 5), Grimtotem Compound, Lower Wilds

GRIMTOTEM SORCERER
Stonetalon Mountains (70), I-8, J:(8, 9), K-8, Camp Aparaje, Greatwood Vale, Grimtotem Post

GRIMTOTEM STOMPER
Thousand Needles (82), D:(3, 4), E:(3-4), Darkcloud Pinnacle

GRIMUNGOUS
Rare Spawn, The Hinterlands (50), K-5, The Overlook Cliffs, Lvl 50 Very Rare; Patrols the southeastern ridgeline

GRINGER
Wind Rider Master, Stranglethorn Vale (74), B-8, Booty Bay (103), Kalimdor Airlines

GRINIBLIX THE SPECTATOR
Feralas (46), G-4, Dire Maul, On ledge of The Maul

GRINIBLIX THE SPECTATOR
Feralas (46), G-4, Dire Maul

GRINNING DOG
Orgrimmar (60), K-2, Valley of Honor, Arms of Legend

GRISH LONGRUNNER
Thousand Needles (82), D-2, The Great Lift, Next to lift

GRISHA
Wind Rider Master, Searing Gorge (64), D-3, Thorium Point (136), Ridgeline outcropping southwest of camp

GRITJAW BASILISK
Desolace (30), E-3, F:(1-4), G:(1, 2, 4, 6, 7), H:(1-4, 6), I:(2-4), J:(2-4), K:(3, 4)

GRIZLAK
Rare Spawn, Loch Modan (54), D-3, Silver Stream Mine, Lvl 15 Uncommon; Roams small area around spawn point

GRIZLOWE
Shipmaster, Stranglethorn Vale (74), B-8, Booty Bay (103)

GRIZZLE
Burning Steppes (22), Searing Gorge (64), C-4/D-8, Blackrock Depths

GRIZZLE HALFMANE
Alterac Valley Battlemaster, Undercity (88), H-8, Royal Quarter, In Throne room

GRIZZLE SNOWPAW
Rare Spawn, Winterspring (98), J-4, Winterfall Village, Lvl 59 Uncommon; Patrols village

GRIZZLED BLACK BEAR
Loch Modan (54), E:(5-7), F-6, H:(4, 7, 8), I:(4, 5, 7), J:(5, 6), K-7

GRIZZLED IRONFUR BEAR
Feralas (46), F-5, G-5, H-6, I-6

GRIZZLED THISTLE BEAR
Darkshore (24), F:(7-9), G-8

GROD
Leather Armor Merchant, Thunder Bluff (84), D-4, Middle rise, inside Thunder Bluff Armorers tent

GRODDOC APE
Feralas (46), E-5, F-5, G:(5, 6), H-5, I-5

GRODDOC THUNDERER
Feralas (46), D:(1, 2), E:(1-4), F-3, Ruins of Ravenwind, The Twin Colossals

GROKOR
Pet Trainer, Swamp of Sorrows (76), F-5, Stonard (131), Behind orcish carriage left of entrance to main hall

GROL THE DESTROYER
Blasted Lands (20), F-1, Dreadmaul Hold, In center of hold

GROL'DAR
Warlock Trainer, Orgrimmar (60), F-5, The Cleft of Shadow, Darkfire Enclave

GROM'GOL GRUNT
Stranglethorn Vale (74), C-3

GRONDAL MOONBREEZE
Journeyman Tailor, Darkshore (24), F-4, Auberdine (101), Right wing of northern building

GROUM STONEBEARD
Journeyman Blacksmith, Ironforge (52), G-4, The Great Forge, Next to anvils

GROUND POUNDER
Tanaris (78), E-3, F-3, G:(3, 4), H:(3, 4), Noonshade Ruins, Sandsorrow Watch, Waterspring Field

GRUB
Barrens (18), G-3, Inside hut east of Crossroads

GRUBBIS
Dun Morogh (32), C-4, Gnomeregan

GRUBTHOR
Rare Spawn, Silithus (66), E-4, Lvl 58 Semi-Rare; Roams close to spawn points

GRUFF
Un'Goro Crater (90), D:(7-8), E:(7-8), Terror Run, Roams around Terror Run

GRUFF SWIFTBITE
Rare Spawn, Elwynn Forest (42), C-9, Forest's Edge, Lvl 12 Uncommon; Patrols small area around spawn point

GRUHAM RUMDNUL
General Supplies, Wetlands (96), A-6, Menethil Harbor (119), Small house east of keep

GRUK
Barrens (18), G-3, Inside hut east of Crossroads

GRUKLASH
Rare Spawn, Burning Steppes (22), A-3, D-3, E-5, Altar of Storms, Blackrock Stronghold, Lvl 59 Uncommon

GRULL HAWKWIND
Mulgore (58), E-8, Camp Narache (105), Center of camp

GRUM REDBEARD
Winterspring (98), G-3, Starfall Village (130), Caverns in hills behind village

GRUMNUS STEELSHAPER
Armor Crafter, Ironforge (52), G-4, The Great Forge, The Great Anvil

GRUNA
Food & Drink, Burning Steppes (22), H-2, Flame Crest (112), Next to Wind Rider Master

GRUNDEL HARKIN
Armorer, Dun Morogh (32), D-7, Coldridge Valley (107), Anvilmar

GRUNDIG DARKCLOUD
Stonetalon Mountains (70), J-8, Grimtotem Post, Western hut

GRUNT DOGRAN
Barrens (18), E-5, Agama'gor, Eastern hut

GRUNT GARGAL
Badlands (16), A-5, Kargath (116), Group left of orc burrow

GRUNT KOMACK
Orgrimmar (60), Valley of Strength

GRUNT KOR'JA
Durotar (34), H-5, Along southern road leading out from Razor Hill

GRUNT LOGMAR
Barrens (18), F-6, Camp Taurajo (106), Western entrance

GRUNT THARLAK
Swamp of Sorrows (76), F-5, Stonard (131), Guarding holding pen in northwest corner of camp

GRUNT ZUUL
Swamp of Sorrows (76), F-5, Stonard (131), Guarding holding pen in northwest corner of camp

GRUNTER
Rare Spawn, Blasted Lands (20), H-3, I-3, Serpent's Coil, Lvl 50 Very Rare; Roams small area around spawn point

GRUUL DARKBLADE
Weaponsmith, Azshara (14), B-5, Valormok

GRYAN STOUTMANTLE
The People's Militia, Westfall (94), G-5, Sentinel Hill (126), Sentinel Tower

GRYFE
Flight Master, Un'goro Crater (90), F-1, Marshal's Refuge (118)

GRYPHON MASTER TALONAXE
The Hinterlands (50), B-4, Aerie Peak (100), Inside of Peak fortification

GRYTH THURDEN
Gryphon Master, Ironforge (52), G-5, The Great Forge, Next to Gryphons

GUARD ADAMS
Redridge Mountains (62), C-5, Lakeshire (117), Patrols around Lakeshire

GUARD ASHLOCK
Redridge Mountains (62), D-6, Patrols back and forth over the bridge heading into Lakeshire

GUARD BERTON
Redridge Mountains (62), C-5, Lakeshire (117), Next to mailbox outside of Lakeshire Inn

GUARD BYRON
Dustwallow Marsh (38), I-5, Theramore Isle (135), Outside inn to north

GUARD CLARKE
Redridge Mountains (62), C-5, Lakeshire (117), Patrols around Lakeshire

GUARD EDWARD
Dustwallow Marsh (38), I-5, Theramore Isle (135), Sparring grounds to northeast

GUARD FENGUS
Feralas (46), G-4, Dire Maul

GUARD HIETT
Redridge Mountains (62), D-6, Roams right of bridge heading into Lakeshire

GUARD HOWE
Redridge Mountains (62), D-6, Left of bridge heading into Lakeshire

GUARD JARAD
Dustwallow Marsh (38), I-5, Theramore Isle (135), Sparring grounds to northeast

GUARD KAHIL
Dustwallow Marsh (38), I-5, Theramore Isle (135), Sparring grounds to northeast

GUARD LANA
Dustwallow Marsh (38), I-5, Theramore Isle (135), Sparring grounds to northeast

GUARD LASITER
Dustwallow Marsh (38), I-5, Theramore Isle (135), East archery range

GUARD MOL'DAR
Feralas (46), G-4, Dire Maul

GUARD NARRISHA
Dustwallow Marsh (38), I-5, Theramore Isle (135), Sparring grounds to northeast

GUARD PARKER
Redridge Mountains (62), A-7, Three Corners, Patrols a circular path around the area

GUARD PEARCE
Redridge Mountains (62), D-6, Right of bridge heading into Lakeshire

GUARD ROBERTS
Elwynn Forest (42), F-7, Crystal Lake, Kneeling by a tree at the edge of the lake

GUARD SLIP'KIK
Feralas (46), G-4, Dire Maul

GUARD TARK
Dustwallow Marsh (38), I-5, Theramore Isle (135), Sparring grounds to northeast

GUARD TARUC
Barrens (18), G-3, Inside hut east of Crossroads

GUARD THOMAS
Elwynn Forest (42), J-7, Left of bridge

GUARD WACHABE
Thousand Needles (82), F-5, Freewind Post (112), Northwest of inn, next to pole

GUARDIAN OF ELUNE
Winterspring (98), J-6, Owl Wing Thicket, (Summon) Behind altar

GUBBER BLUMP
Darkshore (24), E-4, Auberdine (101), On beach near hippogryph platform

GUILLAUME SOROUY
Journeyman Blacksmith, Silverpine Forest (68), F-4, The Sepulcher (127), Basement of inn

GUNDER THORNBUSH
Tradesman, Duskwood (36), J-4, Darkshire (108), Scarlet Raven Inn

GUNTHER ARCANUS
Tirisfal Glades (86), I-4, Gunther's Retreat, Large island in the center of Brightwater Lake

GUNTHER WELLER
Weapons Merchant, Stormwind (72), H-6, Trade District, Weller's Arsenal

GURDA RAGESCAR
Ashenvale (12), I-7, Nightsong Woods, Camp to southwest of Splintertree Post (129)

GURDA WILDMANE
Desolace (30), G-6, Ghost Walker Post (113), Southern hut

GURUBASHI WARRIOR
Stranglethorn Vale (74), E-2, F-2, Zul'Gurub

GUSTING VORTEX
Tanaris (78), E:(4-6), F:(4-7), G:(4, 5), H:(4, 5), I:(4-6)

GUTHRUM THUNDERFIST
Gryphon Master, The Hinterlands (50), B-5, Aerie Peak (100), Left of Peak fortification entrance

GUTSPILL
Duskwood (36), J-8, Roland's Doom, Patrols the length of the mine

GUZZLING PATRON
Burning Steppes (22), Searing Gorge (64), C-4/D-8, Blackrock Depths

GWENNA FIREBREW
Barmaid, Ironforge (52), B-5, The Commons, The Stonefire Tavern

GWENNYTH BLY'LEGGONDE
Darkshore (24), F-4, Auberdine (101), Hippogryph platform

GWINA STONEBRANCH
Herbalism Supplier, Ironforge (52), G-6, The Great Forge, Ironforge Physician

GWYN FARROW
Mushroom Merchant, Silverpine Forest (68), G-4, The Sepulcher (127), In front of crates on right side of sepulcher

GYLL
Gryphon Master, Stranglethorn Vale (74), B-8, Booty Bay (103), Southern Skies Platform

GYTH
Burning Steppes (22), Searing Gorge (64), C-4/D-8, Blackrock Spire

H

HAARKA THE RAVENOUS
Rare Spawn, Tanaris (78), H-7, The Gaping Chasm, Lvl 50 Average Rare; Spawns in one of the chambers and sticks close to spawn point

HADOKEN SWIFTSTRIDER
Feralas (46), I-4, Camp Mojache (105), Between tents, near waterfall

HAE'WILANI
Weapons Vendor, Desolace (30), C-7, Shadowprey Village (128), Small eastern structure

HAGAR LIGHTNINGHOOF
Thousand Needles (82), F-5, Freewind Post (112), Next to western bridge

HAGG TAURENBANE
Rare Spawn, Razormane Champion, Barrens (18), D-8, E-8, Blackthorn Ridge, Lvl 26 Uncommon

HAGGARD REFUGEE
Silverpine Forest (68), G:(8, 9), The Greymane Wall

HAGGLE
Ironforge (52), L-5, The Deeprun Tram Roams around Deeprun Tram

HAGGRUM BLOODFIST
Azshara (14), B-5, Valormok

HAGRUS
Reagents Vendor, Orgrimmar (60), E-5, The Cleft of Shadow, Shadowdeep Reagents

HAHK'ZOR
Rare Spawn, Burning Steppes (22), J:(4, 5), K-4, Dreadmaul Rock, Lvl 54 Semi-Rare; Roams small area around spawn point

HAHRANA IRONHIDE
Master Leatherworker, Feralas (46), I-4, Camp Mojache (105), Big western tent

HAI'ZAN
Butcher, Durotar (34), H-7, Sen'jin Village (126), Northern part of village

HAKKAR'I BLOODKEEPER
Swamp of Sorrows (76), I-5, Temple of Atal'Hakkar

HAKKAR'I FROST WING
Swamp of Sorrows (76), I-5, Temple of Atal'Hakkar

HAKKARI PRIEST
Stranglethorn Vale (74), E-2, F-2, Zul'Gurub

HAKKAR'I SAPPER
Swamp of Sorrows (76), I-5, The Temple of Atal'Hakkar

HAL MCALLISTER
Fish Merchant, Hillsbrad Foothills (48), F-6, Southshore (129), Edge of docks

HALDARR FELSWORN
Azshara (14), B-6, Haldarr Encampment

HALDARR SATYR
Azshara (14), B-6, Haldarr Encampment

HALDARR TRICKSTER
Azshara (14), B-6, Haldarr Encampment

HALEH
Winterspring (98), H-5, Mazthoril, Atop mountain, reachable by portal deep in Mazthoril

HALIJA WHITESTRIDER
Clothier, Barrens (18), F-3, The Crossroads (107), Southern entrance

HALJAN OAKHEART
General Goods, Ashenvale (12), E-5, Astranaar (101), Right as you enter building to the southwest

HALYCON
Burning Steppes (22), Searing Gorge (64), C-4/D-8, Blackrock Spire

HAMHOCK
Stormwind (72), F-6, The Stockade

HAMLIN ATKINS
Mushroom Farmer, Tirisfal Glades (86), H-5, Brill (104), Patrols along road between the mausoleum and the graveyard and the eastern and western city limits of Brill

HAMMERED PATRON
Burning Steppes (22), Searing Gorge (64), C-4/D-8, Blackrock Depths

HAMMERFALL GRUNT
Arathi Highlands (10), H:(5, 6), I:(5, 6), Hammerfall (115)

HAMMERFALL GUARDIAN
Arathi Highlands (10), J:(3, 4), K-4, Hammerfall (115)

HAMMERFALL PEON
Arathi Highlands (10), H:(5, 6), I:(5, 6), Hammerfall (115)

HAMMERSPINE
Rare Spawn, Dun Morogh (32), J-5, Gol'Bolar Quarry, Lvl 12 Uncommon; Roams small area around spawn point

HAMMERTOE GREZ
Badlands (16), G-1, Uldaman

HAMMON KARWN
Superior Tradesman, Arathi Highlands (10), F-5, Refuge Point (124), Camp

HANASHI
Weapon Master, Orgrimmar (60), K-2, Valley of Honor, Arms of Legend, Trains: Bows, 1H Axe, 2H Axe, Staves & Thrown

HANA'ZUA
Durotar (34), F-6, Valley of Trials (136), Laying in the shade of a tree to the west

HAND OF RAVENCLAW
Silverpine Forest (68), H-3, I:(3, 4), The Decrepit Ferry, East of road near lake

HANDOR
Cloth & Leather Armor Merchant, Orgrimmar (60), H-4, The Drag, Kodohide Leatherworkers

HANDS SPRINGSPROCKET
Dun Morogh (32), D-7, Coldridge Pass, Outside of pass entrance

HANK THE HAMMER
The Mithril Order, Stormwind (72), H-2, Dwarven District, By Forge

HANNAH
Redridge Mountains (62), B-4, Lakeshire (117), Western point of Lake Everstill

HANNAH AKELEY
Reagent Supplier, Undercity (88), K-2, The Magic Quarter, Outside Skull Building

HANNAH BLADELEAF
Alliance Outrunner, Barrens (18), F-8, Southern Barrens, Spawns at border to Dustwallow Marsh and travels north to Lushwater Oasis

HANS WESTON
Armorer & Shieldsmith, Dustwallow Marsh (38), I-5, Theramore Isle (135), Blacksmithing hut to west

HANS ZANDIN
Hillsbrad Foothills (48), G-2 , Tarren Mill (133), Orchard

HANSEL HEAVYHANDS
The Thorium Brotherhood, Searing Gorge (64), D-3, Thorium Point (136), Right side of tower

HAR'ALEN
Ashenvale (12), I-6, Splintertree Post (129), Building just north of flightpoint

HARANT IRONBRACE
Armorer & Shieldcrafter, Mulgore (58), E-6, Bloodhoof Village (102), Northeast tent

HARB CLAWHOOF
Kodo Mounts, Mulgore (58), E-6, Bloodhoof Village (102), Northern clearing

HARB FOULMOUNTAIN
Rare Spawn, Thousand Needles (82), D-3, E-3, Darkcloud Pinnacle, Lvl 27 Uncommon; Patrols across three small plateaus, north of pinnacle

HARBINGER BALTHAZAD
Undercity (88), Canals, Roams inner circle

HAREN KANMAE
Superior Bowyer, Stranglethorn Vale (74), B-8, Booty Bay (103), Swift Flights (shop) on the northern side of The Old Port Authority

HAREN SWIFTHOOF
Loch Modan (54), H-7, Patrols large circular paths with Gradok and Thragomm along the eastern side of the loch

HARGGAN
Blacksmithing Supplies, The Hinterlands (50), B-4, Aerie Peak (100), Wildhammer Keep

HARGIN MUNDAR
Wetlands (96), A-6, Menethil Harbor (119), Deepwater Tavern, Roams in and out of tavern

HARICK BOULDERDRUM
Wands Merchant, Ironforge (52), C-2, The Mystic Ward, The Fighting Wizard

HARKEN WINDTOTEM
Mulgore (58), F-6, Bloodhoof Village (102), East tent

HARKLAN MOONGROVE
Alchemy Supplies, Ashenvale (12), F-7, Silverwind Refuge, Left wing of building

HARKLANE
Fish Vendor, Feralas (46), C-5, Feathermoon Stronghold (111), Southwest building

HARLAN BAGLEY
Stormwind (72), H:(5, 6), Trade District, Lionheart Armory

HARLO BARNABY
Wetlands (96), A-5, Menethil Harbor (119), Front of keep

HARLO WIGGLESWORTH
Winterspring (98), I-4, Everlook (110), Outside inn

HARLON THORNGUARD
Armorer & Shieldsmith, Darkshore (24), F-4, Auberdine (101), Left wing of northern building

HARLOWN DARKWEAVE
Leatherworking Supplies, Ashenvale (12), C-6, Shrine of Aessina, Hidden in a camp near mountains in far southwest of region

HARN LONGCAST
Fishing Supplies, Mulgore (58), E-6, Bloodhoof Village (102), North tents

HARNOR
Food & Drink, Desolace (30), G-5, Ghost Walker Post (113), Western hut

HAROLD RAIMS
Apprentice Weaponsmith, Tirisfal Glades (86), D-7, Deathknell (109), First house on right side of road

HAROLD RIGGS
Fishing Trainer, Wetlands (96), A-6, Menethil Harbor (119), Dock

HAROMM
Shaman Trainer, Swamp of Sorrows (76), F-6, Stonard (131), Scaffolding just inside camp walls left of southern entrance

HARROC
Durotar (34), H-3, Garden next to house

HARRUK
Pet Trainer, Durotar (34), H-4, Razor Hill (124), Bunker

HARRY BURLGUARD
Stormwind (72), J-5, Old Town, Pig and Whistle Tavern

HARTASH
Weapon Merchant, Swamp of Sorrows (76), F-5, Stonard (131), Smithy

HARUTT THUNDERHORN
Warrior Trainer, Mulgore (58), E-8, Camp Narache (105), Main tent (north)

HARVEST GOLEM
Westfall (94), C:(4, 5), D-5, E:(3, 6, 7), F:(3, 4), G:(3, 4), Saldean's Farm

HARVEST REAPER
Westfall (94), G-6, H-6, The Dead Acre

HARVEST WATCHER
Westfall (94), D-5, E:(3, 4), F:(2, 3), Saldean's Farm

HASTAT THE ANCIENT
Felwood (44), G-3, Irontree Woods, (Summon) Talk to the ancients on the island

HATE SHRIEKER
Eastern Plaguelands (40), C-3, D-3, E:(2, 3), H:(6, 7), Corin's Crossing

HATE'REL
Burning Steppes (22), Searing Gorge (64), C-4/D-8, Blackrock Depths

HATECREST MYRMIDON
Feralas (46), B:(6, 7), Isle of Dread

HATECREST SCREAMER
Feralas (46), B:(5, 6), C:(5, 6), Ruins of Solarsal, Sardor Isle

HATECREST SERPENT GUARD
Feralas (46), B:(6, 7), Isle of Dread, Shalzaru's Lair

HATECREST SIREN
Feralas (46), B:(5, 6), C:(5, 6), Ruins of Solarsal, Sardor Isle

HATECREST SORCERESS
Feralas (46), B:(6, 7), Isle of Dread, Shalzaru's Lair

HATECREST WARRIOR
Feralas (46), B:(5, 6), C:(5, 6), Ruins of Solarsal, Sardor Isle

HATECREST WAVE RIDER
Feralas (46), B:(5, 6), C:(5, 6), Ruins of Solarsal, Sardor Isle

HATEFURY BETRAYER
Desolace (30), I:(1, 2), J:(1-3), K:(1-3), Sargeron

HATEFURY FELSWORN
Desolace (30), I:(1, 2), J:(1-3), K:(1-3), Sargeron

HATEFURY HELLCALLER
Desolace (30), I:(1, 2), J:(1-3), K:(1-3), Sargeron

HATEFURY ROGUE
Desolace (30), I:(1, 2), J:(1-3), K:(1-3), Sargeron

HATEFURY SHADOWSTALKER
Desolace (30), I:(1, 2), J:(1-3), K:(1-3), Sargeron

HATEFURY TRICKSTER
Desolace (30), I:(1, 2), J:(1-3), K:(1-3), Sargeron

HAUGHTY MODISTE
Fashion Designer, Tanaris (78), J-2, Steamwheedle Point (130)

HAUNTED SERVITOR
Silverpine Forest (68), F-7, Shadowfang Keep

HAUNTING PHANTASM
Tirisfal Glades (86), K-3, L-3, Scarlet Monastery

HAUNTING SPIRIT
Curse spell effect, Silverpine Forest (68), F-7, Shadowfang Keep

HAUNTING VISION
Western Plaguelands (92), H:(5, 6), I:(5, 6), Gahrron's Withering

HAYOC
Dustwallow Marsh (38), D-3, Brackenwall Village (104), West entrance

HAZZALI SANDREAVER
Tanaris (78), G-7, H:(6-8), The Gaping Chasm

HAZZALI STINGER
Tanaris (78), G:(7, 8), H:(6-8), I:(6, 7), The Gaping Chasm

HAZZALI SWARMER
Tanaris (78), G:(7, 8), H:(6-8), I:(6, 7), The Gaping Chasm

HAZZALI TUNNELER
Tanaris (78), G-7, H:(6-8), The Gaping Chasm

HAZZALI WASP
Tanaris (78), G:(7, 8), H:(6-8), I:(6, 7), The Gaping Chasm

HAZZALI WORKER
Tanaris (78), G-7, H:(6-8), The Gaping Chasm

HAZZAS
Swamp of Sorrows (76), I-5, The Temple of Atal'Hakkar

HEARTHSINGER FORRESTEN
Rare Spawn, Eastern Plaguelands (40), D-2, Stratholme, Lvl 57 Rare

HEARTRAZOR
Thousand Needles (82), A-4, B-4, Highperch, Patrols entrance to Highperch

HEAVY WAR GOLEM
Searing Gorge (64), C-5, D:(5, 6), E:(4-6), F:(4, 6), The Cauldron

HECHT COPPERPINCH
Smokywood Pastures, Barrens (18), E-1, Mor'shan Base Camp, Outside entrance to Warsong Gulch

HECKLEFANG HYENA
Barrens (18), D:(2, 3), E:(2-4), F:(1, 2, 4, 5), G:(1-5), H:(1-4)

HECKLEFANG HYENA
Durotar (34), D:(2, 5), E:(1, 2, 5, 6)

HECKLEFANG SNARLER
Barrens (18), E:(4-6), F:(5, 6), Agama'gor, Bramblescar, Southern Barrens

HECKLEFANG STALKER
Barrens (18), E:(7, 8), F:(7, 8), Blackthorn Ridge, Southern Barrens

HEDERINE INITIATE
Winterspring (98), H:(8, 9), I:(7-9), J-8, Darkwhisper Gorge

HEDERINE MANASTALKER
Winterspring (98), H:(8, 9), I:(8, 9), J-8, Darkwhisper Gorge

HEDERINE SLAYER
Winterspring (98), H:(8, 9), I:(8, 9), J-8, Darkwhisper Gorge

HED'MUSH THE ROTTING
Rare Spawn, Eastern Plaguelands (40), E-7, G-3, H-5, Crown Guard Tower, Eastwall Tower, Northpass Tower, Lvl 57 Very Rare; Roams small area around spawn point

HEDRUM THE CREEPER
Burning Steppes (22), Searing Gorge (64), C-4/D-8, Blackrock Depths

HEGGIN STONEWHISKER
Rare Spawn, Bael'dun Chief Engineer, Barrens (18), E-8, Bael Modan, Lvl 24 Uncommon; Crane

HEGNAR RUMBLESHOT
Gunsmith, Dun Morogh (32), E-6, Camp

HEGNAR SWIFTAXE
Axe Merchant, Ironforge (52), H-9, The Military Ward, Timberline Arms

HEINRICH STONE
Blade Merchant, Stormwind (72), K-4, Old Town, Honest Blades

HEKKRU
Stable Master, Swamp of Sorrows (76), F-5, Stonard (131), Next to mailbox out side of inn

HELCULAR'S REMAINS
Hillsbrad Foothills (48), F-5, Southshore (129), Graveyard

HELDAN GALESONG
Fisherman, Darkshore (24), E-6, Twilight Shore, Grassy outcropping near shore

HELENA ATWOOD
Undercity (88), H-2, The War Quarter, Shooting at target

HELENDIS RIVERHORN
Burning Steppes (22), K-7, Morgan's Vigil (120), House ruins, left side of camp

HELENE PELTSKINNER
Skinner, Elwynn Forest (42), F-6, Goldshire (114), House facing Crystal Lake

HELENIA OLDEN
Trade Supplies, Dustwallow Marsh (38), I-5, Theramore Isle (135), Southern house

HELGRUM THE SWIFT
Swamp of Sorrows (76), F-5, Stonard (131), Third floor of main hall

HEMATOS
Rare Spawn, Burning Steppes (22), D-3, Blackrock Mountain, Lvl 60 Very Rare; Patrols circular path around Draco'dar

HEMATUS
Badlands (16), L-5, Lethlor Ravine, (Summon) Altar protected by Scorched Guardians

HEMET NESINGWARY
Stranglethorn Vale (74), C-1, Nesingwary's Expedition, Camp

HEMMIT ARMSTRONG
Hillsbrad Foothills (48), E-6, Southshore (129), Inn

HENCHMAN VALIK
Alterac Mountains (8), H-7, Sofera's Naze, Right of camp on hill

HENEN RAGETOTEM
Thunder Bluff (84), G-8, Hunter Rise, In front of Hunter's Hall on Hunter Rise in Thunder Bluff

HENRY CHAPAL
Gunsmith, Redridge Mountains (62), C-4, Lakeshire (117), Small house on a hill on northwestern side of town

HENRY STERN
Recipe Trainer (Cooking), Barrens (18), F-9, Razorfen Downs

HENZE FAULK
Elwynn Forest (42), J-5, Heroes' Vigil, Lying on hill facing megalith formation

HEPZIBAH SEDGEWICK
Undercity (88), K-6, The Rogues' Quarter, Wanders Rogues' Quarter and Canals

HERALATH FALLOWBROOK
Barrens (18), E-9, Razorfen Kraul

HERALD MOONSTALKER
Darnassus (26), D-4, The Temple Gardens, Roams path throughout city

HERBALIST POMEROY
Herbalism Trainer, Elwynn Forest (42), E-5, Secluded house on hill

HERBLE BAUBBLETUMP
Engineering and Mining Supplies, Duskwood (36), K-5, Darkshire (108), Outside the second house on left side of road heading into Darkshire from the east

HEROD
Tirisfal Glades (86), K-3, L-3, Scarlet Monastery

HESUWA THUNDERHORN
Pet Trainer, Thunder Bluff (84), F-8, Hunter Rise, In building west of Hunter's Hall

HETAERA
Azshara (14), H-5, Hetaera's Clutch, Roams underwater and among the outer islands

HEWA
Cloth Armor Merchant, Thunder Bluff (84), E-6 , Lower rise, in Hewa's Armory

HEXED TROLL
Durotar (34), J:(8, 9), Echo Isles

HEZRUL BLOODMARK
Barrens (18), E-4, Lushwater Oasis, Circles the oasis, pausing at camps

HGARTH
Artisan Enchanter, Stonetalon Mountains (70), F-6, Sun Rock Retreat (132), Alone on a cliff northeast of inn

HIEROPHANT THEODORA MULVADANIA
Badlands (16), A-5, Kargath (116), Bonfire left of orc burrow

HIGH CHIEF WINTERFALL
Winterspring (98), J-4, Winterfall Village, Spawns in upper cave

HIGH EXECUTOR DARTHALIA
Hillsbrad Foothills (48), H-2, Tarren Mill (133), Roams in front of church

HIGH EXECUTOR DERRINGTON
Tirisfal Glades (86), K-7, The Bulwark (105), Camp on left side of road

HIGH EXECUTOR DERRINGTON
Western Plaguelands (92), C-5, The Bulwark (105)

HIGH EXECUTOR HADREC
Silverpine Forest (68), F-4, The Sepulcher (127), Basement of inn

HIGH EXPLORER MAGELLAS
Explorers' League, Ironforge (52), I-2, Hall of Explorers, Out front of library

HIGH GENERAL ABBENDIS
Rare Spawn, Eastern Plaguelands (40), K-8, L-8, Tyr's Hand, Lvl 59 Uncommon; Second floor of castle or in The Scarlet Basilica

HIGH INQUISITOR FAIRBANKS
Tirisfal Glades (86), K-3, L-3, Scarlet Monastery

HIGH INQUISITOR WHITEMANE
Tirisfal Glades (86), K-3, L-3, Scarlet Monastery

HIGH INTERROGATOR GERSTAHN
Burning Steppes (22), Searing Gorge (64), C-4/D-8, Blackrock Depths

HIGH JUSTICE GRIMSTONE
Burning Steppes (22), Searing Gorge (64), C-4/D-8, Blackrock Depths

HIGH OVERLORD SAURFANG
Orgrimmar (60), F:(7, 8), Valley of Strength, Near main entrance

HIGH PRIEST ROHAN
Priest Trainer, Ironforge (52), C-1, The Mystic Ward, Hall of Mysteries

HIGH PRIEST THEL'DANIS
Western Plaguelands (92), G-8, Uther's Tomb, Patrols in and out of tomb

HIGH PRIESTESS HAI'WATNA
Rare Spawn, Stranglethorn Vale (74), F-2, Zul'Gurub, Lvl 57 Semi-Rare; Ruins just before the entrance to Zul'Gurub

HIGH PRIESTESS LAURENA
Priest Trainer, Stormwind (72), F-3, Cathedral Square, Cathedral of Light

HIGH PRIESTESS MACDONNELL
Anchorite Truuen, Western Plaguelands (93), E-8, Chillwind Camp (107) (107)

HIGH PRIESTESS OF THAURISSAN
Burning Steppes (22), Searing Gorge (64), C-4/D-8, Blackrock Depths

HIGH PROTECTOR LORIK
Western Plaguelands (92), F-2, Hearthglen, Patrols path around city

HIGH PROTECTOR TARSEN
Western Plaguelands (92), F-3, Northridge Lumber Camp, Patrols around lumber mill

HIGH SORCERER ANDROMATH
Stormwind (72), F-8, Mage Quarter, Wizard's Sanctum

HIGH TINKER MEKKATORQUE
King of Gnomes, Ironforge (52), I-5, Tinker Town, Out front of tram entrance

HIGHBORNE APPARITION
Azshara (14), A-7, Shadowsong Shrine

HIGHBORNE LICHLING
Azshara (14), A-7, Haldarr Encampment, Shadowsong Shrine

HIGHBORNE SUMMONER
Feralas (46), G-4, Dire Maul

HIGHLAND FLESHSTALKER
Arathi Highlands (10), F:(7, 8), G:(6-8), H-6, River

HIGHLAND LASHTAIL
Wetlands (96), D-2, E-2, H:(2-4), Direforge Hill

HIGHLAND RAPTOR
Wetlands (96), E-2, F-2, G:(2, 3), H:(2-4), Direforge Hill, Ironbeard's Tomb

HIGHLAND RAZORMAW
Wetlands (96), D-2, E-2, I:(3, 4), J:(3, 4), Direforge Hill, Raptor Ridge

HIGHLAND SCYTHECLAW
Wetlands (96), D-2, E-2, H:(2-4), Direforge Hill, The Green Belt

HIGHLAND STRIDER
Arathi Highlands (10), B:(3, 4), C:(2-4), D:(2-4), E:(4-7), F:(3-6, 8), G:(3-5), H:(4, 5), I:(3-5), J:(3-5), K-3

HIGHLAND THRASHER
Arathi Highlands (10), B:(4-6), C-5, D:(5, 6), E:(3, 4, 6, 7), F:(3, 4, 6), G-6, H-7, I-6, Northfold Manor

HIGHLORD BOLVAR FORDRAGON
Boss, Stormwind (72), L-2, Stormwind Keep, Center of east wing

HIGHLORD DEMITRIAN
Silithus (66), D-1, Ravaged Twilight Camp, Far northwest of camp on hill

HIGHLORD MASTROGONDE
Rare Spawn, Searing Gorge (64), A-4, C-3, Firewatch Ridge, Lvl 51 Uncommon; Roams small area around spawn point

HIGHLORD OMOKK
Burning Steppes (22), Searing Gorge (64), C-4/D-8, Blackrock Spire

HIGHLORD TAELAN FORDRING
Highlord of the Scarlet Crusade, Western Plaguelands (92), E-1, Mardenholde Keep, Second floor of keep

HIGHPERCH CONSORT
Thousand Needles (82), A:(3, 4), G-4, Highperch

HIGHPERCH SOARER
Thousand Needles (82), A-4, B-4, Highperch, Flies around Highperch

HIGHPERCH WYVERN
Thousand Needles (82), A:(3, 4), G-4, Highperch

HIGHVALE MARKSMAN
The Hinterlands (50), D-5, E:(4, 5), Quel'Danil Lodge

HIGHVALE OUTRUNNER
The Hinterlands (50), D-5, E:(4, 5), Quel'Danil Lodge

HIGHVALE RANGER
The Hinterlands (50), D:(4, 5), E:(4, 5), Quel'Danil Lodge

HIGHVALE SCOUT
The Hinterlands (50), D-5, E:(4, 5), Quel'Danil Lodge

HILARY
Redridge Mountains (62), C-5, Lakeshire (117), L-shaped dock west of the bridge

HILLSBRAD APPRENTICE BLACKSMITH
Hillsbrad Foothills (48), C:(4, 5), Hillsbrad Fields (115), Forge

HILLSBRAD COUNCILMAN
Hillsbrad Foothills (48), C:(4, 5), Hillsbrad Fields (115)

HILLSBRAD FARMER
Hillsbrad Foothills (48), C:(3-5), D:(4, 5), Hillsbrad Fields (115), Orchard

HILLSBRAD FARMHAND
Hillsbrad Foothills (48), C:(3, 4), D-4, Hillsbrad Fields (115)

HILLSBRAD FOOTMAN
Hillsbrad Foothills (48), C:(4, 5), D-5, Hillsbrad Fields (115)

HILLSBRAD FOREMAN
Hillsbrad Foothills (48), B(5, 6), C:(5, 6), Azurelode Mine, Mine

HILLSBRAD MINER
Hillsbrad Foothills (48), B:(5, 6), C:(5, 6), Azureload Mine, Mine

HILLSBRAD PEASANT
Hillsbrad Foothills (48), C:(4, 5), D:(4, 5), Hillsbrad Fields (115)

HILLSBRAD SENTRY
Hillsbrad Foothills (48), B-6, C-6, Azureload Mine, Mine

HILLSBRAD TAILOR
Hillsbrad Foothills (48), D-4, Hillsbrad Fields (115), House northeast of southernmost crop field

HIMMIK
Food & Drink, Winterspring (98), I-4, Everlook (110), Inside inn

HIN DENBURG
Zeppelin Master, Tirisfal Glades (86), H-6, Zepplin tower just north of Undercity

HISSPERAK
Rare Spawn, Desolace (30), E:(4-6), F-5, G-5, Kodo Graveyard, Lvl 37 Semi-Rare; Roams area northwest of the Kodo Graveyard

HISTORIAN KARNIK
Ironforge (52), K-1, Hall of Explorers, The Library

HITAH'YA THE KEEPER
The Hinterlands (50), I-9, Jintha'Alor, Patrols with two Vilebranch Aman'zasi Guards around glowing rock

HIVE'ASHI AMBUSHER
Silithus (66), G-3, Southwind Village

HIVE'ASHI DEFENDER
Silithus (66), E-1, F:(1, 2), Hive'Ashi

HIVE'ASHI DRONE
Silithus (66), G-3, Southwind Village

HIVE'ASHI SANDSTALKER
Silithus (66), E-1, F:(1, 2), Hive'Ashi

HIVE'ASHI STINGER
Silithus (66), E-1, F:(1-3), G:(2, 3), Hive'Ashi

HIVE'ASHI SWARMER
Silithus (66), E-1, F:(1-3), G:(2, 3), Hive'Ashi

HIVE'ASHI WORKER
Silithus (66), F:(1, 2), Hive'Ashi

HIVE'REGAL AMBUSHER
Silithus (66), F:(4, 5), G:(4, 5), H-4, Hive'Regal

HIVE'REGAL BURROWER
Silithus (66), F-4, G:(4, 5), Hive'Regal

HIVE'REGAL HIVE LORD
Silithus (66), F:(4, 5), G:(4, 5), H-4, Hive'Regal

HIVE'REGAL SLAVEMAKER
Silithus (66), F:(4, 5), G:(4, 5), H-4, Hive'Regal

HIVE'REGAL SPITFIRE
Silithus (66), F:(4, 5), G:(4, 5), H-4, Hive'Regal

HIVE'ZORA HIVE SISTER
Silithus (66), D:(3, 4), E:(3, 4), Hive'Zora

HIVE'ZORA REAVER
Silithus (66), D:(3, 4), E:(3, 4), Hive'Zora

HIVE'ZORA TUNNELER
Silithus (66), D:(3, 4), E:(3, 4), Hive'Zora

HIVE'ZORA WASP
Silithus (66), D:(3, 4), E:(3, 4), Hive'Zora

HIVE'ZORA WAYWATCHER
Silithus (66), D:(3, 4), E:(3, 4), Hive'Zora

HJOLDIR STONEBLADE
Blade Merchant, Ironforge (52), F-1, The Forlorn Cavern, Stoneblade's

HOGAN FERENCE
Duskwood (36), J-5, Darkshire Town Hall

HOGGER
Elwynn Forest (42), C-9, Forest's Edge, Roams small area around spawn point

HOGOR THUNDERHOOF
Guns Merchant, Thunder Bluff (84), F-6, High rise, inside Thunderhoof's Firearms

HOGRAL BAKKAN
Rogue Trainer, Dun Morogh (32), F-5, Kharanos (116), Thunderbrew Distillery

HOL'ANYEE MARSHAL
Un'Goro Crater (90), F-1, Marshal's Refuge (118), Entrance to cave

HOLDOUT MEDIC
Dun Morogh (32), C-4, Gnomeregan

HOLDOUT TECHNICIAN
Dun Morogh (32), C-4, Gnomeregan

HOLDOUT WARRIOR
Dun Morogh (32), J-4

HOLT THUNDERHORN
Hunter Trainer, Thunder Bluff (84), G-9, Hunter Rise, Inside Hunter's Hall

HOMER STONEFIELD
Fruit Seller, Elwynn Forest (42), D-8, The Stonefield Farm, In front of barn

HOMING ROBOT OOX-09/HL
The Hinterlands (50), G-4, The Hinterlands, Lying on rock at the southern end of cove

HOMING ROBOT OOX-17/TN
Tanaris (78), I-6, In hills

HOMING ROBOT OOX-22/FE
Feralas (46), F-6, Feral Scar Vale, Laying in clearing

HONNI GOLDENOAT
Baker, Loch Modan (54), D-5, Thelsamar (134), Stoutlager Inn

HORATIO MONTOGOMERY, M.D. STATUE
Stormwind (72), L-6, Old Town, SI:7

HORDE AXE THROWER
Barrens (18), E-3

HORDE DEFENDER
Barrens (18), E-3, The Forgotten Pools

HORDE DEFORESTER
Ashenvale (12), I:(7, 8), K:(5, 6)

HORDE ELITE
Barrens (18), E-1, Mor'shan Base Camp

HORDE GRUNT
Ashenvale (12), I:(7, 8), K:(5, 6)

HORDE GUARD
Barrens (18), E-6, F-3, G-2, H-2

HORDE LABORER
Barrens (18), E-1, Mor'shan Base Camp

HORDE PEON
Ashenvale (12), I:(7, 8), K:(5, 6)

HORDE SCOUT
Ashenvale (12), I:(7, 8), K:(5, 6)

HORDE SHAMAN
Ashenvale (12), I:(7, 8), K:(5, 6), L-6

HORDE SUPPLY CRATE (5)
The Hinterlands (50), H-5, I:(4, 5), Skulk Rock, Five crates are placed randomly within cave

HORGUS THE RAVAGER
Eastern Plaguelands (40), E-8, Darrowshire, (Summon) Downed tree right side of path heading into town

HORIZON SCOUT COOK
Azshara (14), F-9, The Ruined Reaches, South of camp on border of Great Sea in back cabin of ship beneath debris

HORIZON SCOUT CREWMAN
Azshara (14), F-9, G-9, The Ruined Reaches, At beach and inlet

HORIZON SCOUT ENGINEER
Azshara (14), F-9, The Ruined Reaches, South of camp on border of Great Sea in back cabin of ship beneath debris

HORIZON SCOUT FIRST MATE
Azshara (14), F-9, The Ruined Reaches, South of camp on border of Great Sea in back cabin of ship beneath debris

HORNIZZ BRIMBUZZLE
Desolace (30), F-6, Kodo Graveyard, Camp on hills to east

HORTHUS
Reagents Vendor, Orgrimmar (60), E-6, Valley of Strength, Spitfire Reagents

HOUNDMASTER GREBMAR
Raid Sub-Boss, Burning Steppes (22), Searing Gorge (64), C-4/D-8, Blackrock Depths

HOUNDMASTER LOKSEY
Tirisfal Glades (86), K-3, L-3, Scarlet Monastery

HOWIN KINDFEATHER
The Hinterlands (50), C-5, Aerie Peak (100), Third floor of tower

HRAGRAN
Cloth and Leather Armor Merchant, Stranglethorn Vale (74), C-3, Grom'gol Base Camp (114), Under tent in front of zepplin tower

HRAQ
Blacksmithing Supplier, Barrens (18), F-3, The Crossroads (107), Western entrance

HRAUG
Demon Trainer, Durotar (34), F-7, Valley of Trials (136), Back of cave

HUKKU
Swamp of Sorrows (76), I-5, The Temple of Atal'Hakkar

HUKLAH
Cloth & Leather Armor Merchant, Durotar (34), F-7, Valley of Trials (136)

HULA'MAHI
Reagents and Herbs, Barrens (18), F-3, The Crossroads (107), West of inn

HULDAR
Loch Modan (54), G-7, The Loch, Next to dynamite filled carriage on the southern end of loch

HULFDAN BLACKBEARD
Rogue Trainer, Ironforge (52), G-1, The Forlorn Cavern, South building, inside east entrance

HULFNAR STONETOTEM
Mulgore (58), F-6, Bloodhoof Village (102), Combat ground east of village

HULKING FERAL SCAR
Feralas (46), F-6, Feral Scar Vale

HULKING GRITJAW BASILISK
Desolace (30), D-4, E:(4-6), F:(4-6), G:(4, 5), H:(4-6), J:(1, 4, 5), K:(2, 4, 5), Ghost Walker Post (113), Kodo Graveyard, Sargeron

HULKING MOUNTAIN LION
Alterac Mountains (8), D:(8, 9), E:(3, 8, 9), F:(2, 7-9), H-3, I-5, J:(5, 6), K:(5, 6)

HUMAN SKULL
Eastern Plaguelands (40), D-7, The Marris Stead

HUMAR THE PRIDELORD
Barrens (18), H-3, North of Ratchet

HUNGERING DEAD
Tirisfal Glades (86), I-4, Brightwater Lake

HUNGERING WRAITH
Western Plaguelands (92), H:(5, 6), I:(5, 6), Gahrron's Withering

HUNTRESS NHEMAI
Teldrassil (80), F:(5-6), G-6, Dolanaar (109), Patrols road between Dolanaar and east of Ban'ethil Hollow

HUNTRESS YAELIURA
Teldrassil (80), F:(5-6), G-6, Dolanaar (109), Patrols road between Dolanaar and east of Ban'ethil Hollow

HUNSTMAN LEOPOLD
The Scarlet Crusade, Eastern Plaguelands (40), K-6, Light's Hope Chapel (118)

HUNTSMAN MARKHOR
Stable Master, The Hinterlands (50), L-8, Revantusk Village (125), To the right of hut on southeast side of village

HUNTSMAN RADLEY
Western Plaguelands (92), H-4, Stand idle with wolf in small camp to the right of path heading towards Hearthglen

HURAAN
Hillsbrad Foothills (48), F-6, Southshore (129)

HURICANIAN
Rare Spawn, Silithus (66), D-1, The Crystal Vale, Lvl 58 Uncommon; Roams vale

HURKLOR
Blacksmithing Supplies, Stranglethorn Vale (74), B-8, Booty Bay (103), Plate-n-Chain (shop)

HURLEY BLACKBREATH
Burning Steppes (22), Searing Gorge (64), C-4/D-8, Blackrock Depths

HUUM WILDMANE
Silithus (67), G-4, Cenarion Hold (106)

HYDRAXIAN HONOR GUARD
Azshara (14), J:(7, 8), K-7, Bay of Storms

HYDROLING
Feralas (46), G-4, Dire Maul

HYDROMANCER VELRATHA
Tanaris (78), E-1, Zul'Farrak

HYDROSPAWN
Feralas (46), G-4, Dire Maul

I

IAN STROM
Rogue Trainer, Stranglethorn Vale (74), B-8, Booty Bay (103), Second floor of The Salty Sailor Tavern

ICE CLAW BEAR
Dun Morogh (32), C:(4-6), D:(3-6), E:(3-5), F:(3, 6), G:(4-6), H:(4-6), I:(5, 6), J-5, K-5

ICE THISTLE MATRIARCH
Winterspring (98), J:(4, 5), K-4, Ice Thistle Hills

ICE THISTLE PATRIARCH
Winterspring (98), J:(4, 5), K-4, Ice Thistle Hills

ICE THISTLE YETI
Winterspring (98), H-3, I:(3, 4), J:(4, 5), K-4, Starfall Village (130), Ice Thistle Hills

IDRIANA
Banker, Darnassus (26), E-4, Bank

ILIFAR
Blasted Lands (20), G-3, Rise of the Defiler, (Summon) Summoned by Razelikh the Defiler at 75% health

ILKRUD MAGTHRULL
Ashenvale (12), C-6, Fire Scar Shrine, Near the altar to the north

ILLIYANA
Ashenvale (12), C-5, Shrine of Aessina, Center of Shrine

ILLIYANA MOONBLAZE
Silverwing Supply Officer, Ashenvale (12), H-8, Silverwing Grove, In tent to the right of ramp

ILLUSION OF JANDICE BAROV
Western Plaguelands (92), I-7, Scholomance

ILLUSIONARY PHANTASM
Tirisfal Glades (86), K-3, L-3, Scarlet Monastery

ILLYANIE
Cloth Armor Merchant, Stonetalon Mountains (70), E-2, Stonetalon Peak, House west of hipporgryphs

ILLYANNA RAVENOAK
Feralas (46), G-4, Dire Maul

ILSA CORBIN
Warrior Trainer, Stormwind (72), L-5, Old Town, Command Center

ILYENIA MOONFIRE
Weapon Master, Darnassus (26), H-5, Warrior's Terrace, Lower southwest platform, Trains: Bows, Daggers, Fist, Thrown, & Staves

IMELDA
Stormwind (72), C-5, The Park, Northwest section

IMMOLATUS
Rare Spawn, Felwood (44), F-4, Shatte Scar Vale, Lvl 56 Semi-Rare; Roams eastern craters

IMMOL'THAR
Feralas (46), G-4, Dire Maul

IMPSY
Niby's Minion, Felwood (44), F-5, Bloodvenom Falls, North of pond near dock

INCENDOSAUR
Searing Gorge (64), D-5, E:(2-5), F:(2-4), The Slag Pit, Northern area of the pit

INFERNAL BODYGUARD
Felwood (44), F-4, Shatter Scar Vale

INFERNAL SENTRY
Felwood (44), F-4

INFERNO ELEMENTAL
Searing Gorge (64), B-5, C:(4, 6-8), D:(4, 6, 8), E-6, F-6, Firewatch Ridge, Lava

INFILTRATOR HAMEYA
Eastern Plaguelands (40), I-2, Zul'Mashar, Patrols circular path around graves

INFILTRATOR MARKSEN
Swamp of Sorrows (76), F-5, Stonard (131), Holding pen in northwest corner of camp

INGO WOOLYBUSH
Explorers' League, Dustwallow Marsh (38), I-5, Theramore Isle (135), 2nd floor of inn

INGRYS STONEBROW
Cloth Armor Merchant, Ironforge (52), E-1, The Mystic Ward, Maeva's Mystic Apparel

INITIATE AMAKKAR
Badlands (16), A-5, Kargath (116), Group left of orc burrow

INJURED PEASANT
Eastern Plaguelands (40), C-2

INNKEEPER ABEQWA
Innkeeper, Thousand Needles (82), F-5, Freewind Post (112), Inn

INNKEEPER ADEGWA
Innkeeper, Arathi Highlands (10), J-3, Hammerfall (115), First floor north building

INNKEEPER ALLISON
Innkeeper, Stormwind (72), H-7, Trade District, The Gilded Rose

INNKEEPER ANDERSON
Innkeeper, Hillsbrad Foothills (48), F-6, Southshore (129), First floor of inn

INNKEEPER BATES
Innkeeper, Silverpine Forest (68), F-4, The Sepulcher (127), Right side of entrance to inn

INNKEEPER BELM
Innkeeper, Dun Morogh (32), F-5, Kharanos (116), Thunderbrew Distillery

INNKEEPER BOORAND PLAINSWIND
Innkeeper, Barrens (18), F-3, The Crossroads (107), Inn

INNKEEPER BRIANNA
Innkeeper, Redridge Mountains (62), C-4, Lakeshire (117), First floor of Lakeshire Inn

INNKEEPER BYULA
Innkeeper, Barrens (18), F-6, Camp Taurajo (106), Inn

INNKEEPER FARALIA
innkeeper, Stonetalon Mountains (71), E-2, Stonetalon Peak (131)

INNKEEPER FARLEY
Innkeeper, Elwynn Forest (42), F-7, Goldshire (114), First floor of Lion' Pride Inn

INNKEEPER FIREBREW
Innkeeper, Ironforge (52), B-5, The Commons, The Stonefire Tavern

INNKEEPER FIZZGRIMBLE
Innkeeper, Tanaris (78), H-3, Gadgetzan (113), Inn

INNKEEPER GREUL
Innkeeper, Feralas (46), I-4, Camp Mojache (105), Inn

INNKEEPER GROSK
Innkeeper, Durotar (34), H-4, Razor Hi (124)

INNKEEPER GRYSHKA
Innkeeper, Orgrimmar (60), G-7, Valle of Strength, Inn

INNKEEPER HEARTHSTOVE
Innkeeper, Loch Modan (54), D-5, Thelsamar (134), Stoutlager Inn

INNKEEPER HEATHER
Innkeeper, Westfall (94), F-5, Sentinel Hill (126), Inn

INNKEEPER HELBREK
Innkeeper, Wetlands (96), A-6, Deepwater Tavern, By bar

INNKEEPER JANENE
Innkeeper, Dustwallow Marsh (38), I-5, Theramore Isle (135), Inn

INNKEEPER JAYKA
Innkeeper, Stonetalon Mountains (70), F-6, Sun Rock Retreat (132), Inn

INNKEEPER KARAKUL
Innkeeper, Swamp of Sorrows (76), F-5, Stonard (131), First floor of inn

INNKEEPER KAUTH
Innkeeper, Mulgore (58), E-6, Bloodhoof Village (102), Inn

INNKEEPER KAYLISK
Innkeeper, Ashenvale (12), I-6, Splintertree Post (129), Center of inn

INNKEEPER KELDAMYR
Innkeeper, Teldrassil (80), G-6, Dolanaar (109), Inn

INNKEEPER KIMLYA
Innkeeper, Ashenvale (12), E-5, Astranaar (101), Second floor of inn

INNKEEPER LYSHAERYA
Innkeeper, Desolace (30), I-1, Nijel's Point (121), Inn

INNKEEPER NORMAN
Innkeeper, Undercity (88), I-4, The Trade Quarter, Upper Ring of Trade Quarter

INNKEEPER PALA
Innkeeper, Thunder Bluff (84), E-6, Building near bridges to Hunter's Rise

INNKEEPER RENEE
Innkeeper, Tirisfal Glades (86), H-5, Brill (104), First floor of Gallows' End Tavern

INNKEEPER SAELIENNE
Innkeeper, Darnassus (26), I:(1, 2), Craftsmen's Terrace, Inn

INNKEEPER SHAUSSIY
Innkeeper, Darkshore (24), F-4, Auberdine (101), First floor of inn

INNKEEPER SHAY
Innkeeper, Hillsbrad Foothills (48), H-2, Tarren Mill (133), First floor of inn

INNKEEPER SHUL'KAR
Innkeeper, Badlands (16), A-5, Kargath (116), First floor orc burrow

INNKEEPER SHYRIA
Innkeeper, Feralas (46), C-4, Feathermoon Stronghold (111), Inn

INNKEEPER SIKEWA
Innkeeper, Desolace (30), C-7, Shadowprey Village (128), Inn

INNKEEPER SKINDLE
Innkeeper, Stranglethorn Vale (74), B-8, Booty Bay (103), First floor of The Salty Sailor Tavern

INNKEEPER THULBEK
Innkeeper, Stranglethorn Vale (74), C-3, Grom'gol Base Camp (114)

INNKEEPER THULFRAM
Innkeeper, The Hinterlands (50), B-4, Aerie Peak (100), Wildhammer Keep

INNKEEPER TRELAYNE
Innkeeper, Duskwood (36), J-4, Darkshire (108), Scarlet Raven Inn

INNKEEPER VIZZIE
Innkeeper, Winterspring (98), I-4, Everlook (110), Inside inn

INNKEEPER WILEY
Innkeeper, Barrens (18), H-4, Ratchet (122), Inn

INSANE GHOUL
Duskwood (36), K-7, Tranquil Gardens Cemetery, Roams in church

INSTRUCTOR MALICIA
Western Plaguelands (92), I-7, Scholomance

INTERROGATOR VISHAS
Tirisfal Glades (86), K-3, L-3, Scarlet Monastery

IRENE SURESHOT
Gunsmith, Loch Modan (54), K-6, The Farstrider Lodge (111), On left side of lodge entrance

IRONAYA
Badlands (16), G-1, Uldaman

IRONBACK
Rare Spawn, The Hinterlands (50), L:(5, 6), The Overlook Cliffs, Lvl 51 Semi-Rare; Roams small area around spawn point

IRONBARK PROTECTOR
Feralas (46), G-4, Dire Maul

IRONBEAK HUNTER
Felwood (44), E-4:(4-6), F:(2, 4-7), G:(2-4)

IRONBEAK OWL
Felwood (44), E-7, F:(7, 8), G:(7, 8), H:(8, 9), Deadwood Village, Emerald Sanctuary (110), Morlos'Aran

IRONBEAK SCREECHER
Felwood (44), G:(2, 3), H:(1-3), I-2, Felpaw Village, Irontree Woods, Talonbranch Glade (133)

IRONEYE THE INVINCIBLE
Thousand Needles (82), L:(7-8), Mirage Raceway (119), The Shimmering Flats, Far east near cliffs

IRONFORGE GUARD
Dun Morogh (32), F-4, G:(2-4), H:(2, 3), I:(2, 3), J:(2-4), Gates of Ironforge, Kharanos (116), Steelgrill's Depot

IRONFORGE MOUNTAINEER
Dun Morogh (32), E-6, F:(4-6), G-5, H-5, I:(2, 5), J:(2-4)

IRONFUR BEAR
Feralas (46), F-5, G:(5, 6), H:(4, 5), I:(3-5), J:(4, 5), K:(4, 5)

IRONFUR PATRIARCH
Feralas (46), D:(1, 2), E:(1-4), F-3, Rage Scar Hold, Ruins of Ravenwind, The Twin Colossals

IRONHIDE DEVILSAUR
Un'Goro Crater (90), D:(3, 4), F-8, H:(3, 8), J-4

IRONJAW BASILISK
Stranglethorn Vale (74), D-5, Crystalvein Mine

IRONPATCH
Stranglethorn Vale (74), C-9, Wild Shore, On Boat

IRONSPINE
Tirisfal Glades (86), K-3, L-3, Scarlet Monastery

IRONTREE STOMPER
Felwood (44), F-3, G:(2, 3), Irontree Woods

IRONTREE WANDERER
Felwood (44), F-3, G:(2, 3), Irontree Woods

IRONUS COLDSTEEL
Special Weapon Crafter, Ironforge (52), G-4, The Great Forge, The Great Anvil

IRONZAR
Weaponsmith, Barrens (18), H-4, Ratchet (122), Ironzar's Imported Weaponry

IRRADIATED HORROR
Dun Morogh (32), C-4, Gnomeregan

IRRADIATED INVADER
Dun Morogh (32), C-4, Gnomeregan

IRRADIATED PILLAGER
Dun Morogh (32), C-4, Gnomeregan

IRRADIATED SLIME
Dun Morogh (32), C-4, Gnomeregan

ISABELLA
Mage Trainer, Tirisfal Glades (86), C-7, Deathknell (109), Church

ISHA AWAK
Barrens (18), H-5, The Merchant Coast, Northwatch Hold, Swims off the shore

ISHAMUHALE
Barrens (18), G-3, Thorn Hill, (Summon) Spawns on southeast side of Thorn Hill

ISLEN WATERSEER
Barrens (18), H-4, The Tidus Stair, Outside hut

ITHARIUS
Swamp of Sorrows (76), B-7, Itharius's Cave, Cave

IVAR THE FOUL
Silverpine Forest (68), H-1, The Ivar Patch, Barn

IVERRON
Teldrassil (80), G-3, Shadowglen (127), Up hill west of entrance to Shadowthread Cave

IVY LEAFRUNNER
Emerald Circle, Felwood (44), G-8, Emerald Sanctuary (110), Tent

IZZY COPPERGRAB
Banker, Winterspring (98), I-4, Everlook (110), Inside building directly north of inn

J

J.D. COLLIE
Un'Goro Crater (90), F-1, Marshal's Refuge (118), Northwest chamber of cave

J.D. SHADESONG
Silithus (67), G-4, Cenarion Hold (106)

JABBERING GHOUL
Western Plaguelands (92), E-6, Felstone Field, Roams near cauldron

JABBEY
General Goods, Tanaris (78), J-2, Steamwheedle Port, Big northern building

JACK STERLING
Winterspring (98), I-4, Everlook (110), Outside northeast building

JACOB
Angelas' Pet, Feralas (46), C-4, Feathermoon Stronghold (111), Southeastern building

JADE
Rare Spawn, Swamp of Sorrows (76), I-5, Temple of Atal'Hakkar, Lvl 47 Very Rare; Entrance to the Temple of Atal'Hakkar

JADE OOZE
The Hinterlands (50), G:(4, 5), H:(4, 5), I:(4, 5), Skull Rock, Cave

JADE SLUDGE
The Hinterlands (50), I:(7, 8), Jintha'Alor

JADEFIRE BETRAYER
Felwood (44), E-2, F:(2, 6, 7), Jadefire Run

JADEFIRE FELSWORN
Felwood (44), D:(6, 7), E:(6-8), F:(8, 9), Jadefire Run, Ruins of Constellas

JADEFIRE HELLCALLER
Felwood (44), E:(2, 6), F:(2, 6, 7), Jadefire Run, Shadow Hold

JADEFIRE ROGUE
Felwood (44), D:(6, 7), E:(6, 7), Ruins of Constellas

JADEFIRE SATYR
Felwood (44), E-8, F:(8, 9), Jadefire Run

JADEFIRE SHADOWSTALKER
Felwood (44), D:(6, 7), E:(6, 7), Ruins of Constellas

JADEFIRE TRICKSTER
Felwood (44), E:(2, 6), F:(2, 6, 7), Jadefire Run, Shadow Hold

JADEMIR BOUGHGUARD
Feralas (46), E:(1, 2), F:(1, 2), Jademir Lake, Oneiros, Ruins of Ravenwind

JADEMIR ORACLE
Feralas (46), E:(1, 2), F:(1, 2), Jademir Lake, Oneiros, Ruins of Ravenwind

JADEMIR TREE WARDER
Feralas (46), E:(1, 2), F:(1, 2), Jademir Lake, Oneiros, Ruins of Ravenwind

JADENVIS SEAWATCHER
Reagent Vendor, Feralas (46), C-4, Feathermoon Stronghold (111), North of inn on dock

JADESPINE BASILISK
Badlands (16), G-1, Uldaman

JAEANA
Meat Vendor, Darnassus (26), H-5, Tradesmen's Terrace, Roams around Fletcher & Weapons shops

JAEDENAR ADEPT
Felwood (44), E-6, Barrow Dens, Jaedenar, Shrine of the Deceiver

JAEDENAR CULTIST
Felwood (44), E-6, Barrow Dens, Jaedenar, Shrine of the Deceiver

JAEDENAR DARKWEAVER
Felwood (44), E:(5, 6), F-5, Jadefire Run, Shadow Hold

JAEDENAR ENFORCER
Felwood (44), E:(5, 6), F-5, Jadefire Run, Shadow Hold

JAEDENAR GUARDIAN
Felwood (44), E-6, Barrow Dens, Jaedenar, Shadow Hold, Shrine of the Deceiver

JAEDENAR HOUND
Felwood (44), E-6, Barrow Dens, Jaedenar, Shrine of the Deceiver

JAEDENAR HUNTER
Felwood (44), E:(5, 6), Jadefire Run, Shadow Hold

JAEDENAR LEGIONNAIRE
Felwood (44), E:(5, 6), Shadow Hold

JAEDENAR WARLOCK
Felwood (44), E:(5, 6), Shadow Hold

JAELYSIA
Stable Master, Darkshore (24), F-4, Auberdine (101), In front of inn

JAGGED ROCK ELEMENTAL
Alterac Mountains (8), B-7, Dalaran

JAGUERO STALKER
Stranglethorn Vale (74), D:(8, 9), Jaguero Isle, Wild Shore

JAHAN HAWKWING
Leather & Mail Armor Merchant, Barrens (18), F-3, The Crossroads (107), Western entrance

JAILOR BORHUIN
Alterac Mountains (8), I-4, Strahnbrad, First floor of house

JAILOR ESTON
Hillsbrad Foothills (48), J-4, Durnholde Keep, Roams small area around spawn point

JAILOR MARLGEN
Hillsbrad Foothills (48), J-4, Durnholde Keep, Roams small area around spawn point

JALANE AYROLE
Master Shadoweave Tailor, Stormwind (72), D-8, Mage Quarter, The Slaughtered Lamb

JALINDA SPRIG
Burning Steppes (22), K-7, Morgan's Vigil (120), Tower ruins, center of camp

JALINDE SUMMERDRAKE
Rare Spawn, The Hinterlands (50), D-5, E:(4, 5), Quel'Danil Lodge, Lvl 49 Uncommon; Roams small area around spawn point

JAMES CLARK
Elwynn Forest (42), K-7, Eastvale Logging Camp, House in front of crop field

JAMES HALLORAN
Wetlands (96), A-5, Menethil Harbor (119), Roaming outside house to the west of keep

JAMES VAN BRUNT
Blacksmith Trainer, Undercity (88), I-3, The War Quarter

JAMIE NOR
Tirisfal Glades (86), H-5, Brill (104)

JAMIN
Redridge Mountains (62), C-5, Lake Everstill, Dock

JAMMAL'AN THE PROPHET
Swamp of Sorrows (76), I-5, The Temple of Atal'Hakkar

JANDI
Herbalism Trainer, Orgrimmar (60), G-4, The Drag, Jandi's Arboretum

JANDIA
Trade Supplies, Thousand Needles (82), F-5, Freewind Post (112), Inn

JANDICE BAROV
Western Plaguelands (92), I-7, Scholomance

JANDRIA
Priest Trainer, Darnassus (26), E-8, Temple of the Moon, Just inside temple, north of fountain

JANET HOMMERS
Food & Drink, Desolace (30), I-1, Nijel's Point (121), Inn

JANEY ANSHIP
Stormwind (72), F-8, Mage Quarter, Roamer - sits by tower

JANGDOR SWIFTSTRIDER
Leatherworking Supplies, Feralas (46), I-4, Camp Mojache (105), Big western tent

JANICE FELSTONE
Western Plaguelands (92), E-5, Felstone Field, Second floor of house

JANNA BRIGHTMOON
Clothier, Teldrassil (80), H-4, Shadowglen (127), Second level of main building

JANNOK BREEZESONG
Rogue Trainer, Teldrassil (80), G-6, Dolanaar (109), Inn

JANNOS IRONWILL
Superior Macecrafter, Arathi Highlands (10), F-5, Refuge Point (124), Camp

JANNOS LIGHTHOOF
Druid Trainer, Feralas (46), I-4, Camp Mojache (105), In tent, east of water

JANOS HAMMERKNUCKLE
Weaponsmith, Elwynn Forest (42), F-4, Northshire Valley (122), Caravan facing abbey

JANSEN UNDERWOOD
Blacksmithing Supplies, Stranglethorn Vale (74), C-8, Booty Bay (103), Booty Bay Blacksmith (shop)

JAQUILINA DRAMET
Superior Axecrafter, Stranglethorn Vale (74), C-1, Nesingwary's Expedition, Camp

JAREL MOOR
Bartender, Stormwind (72), D-7, Mage Quarter, The Slaughtered Lamb

JARETH WILDWOODS
Darnassus (26), I-6, Tradesmen's Terrace, East of General Goods

JARK
General Goods, Durotar (34), H-4, Razor Hill (124), Barracks

JARKAL MOSSMELD
Badlands (16), A-5, Kargath (116), Second floor orc burrow

JARON STONESHAPER
Explorers' League, Winterspring (98), H-3, Starfall Village (130), Terrace of main building

JARQUIA
Swamp of Sorrows (76), L:(5, 6), Misty Reed Strand, Roams small area around spawn point

JARRODENUS
Hippogryph Master, Azshara (14), A-8, Talrendis Point

JARTSAM
Nightsaber Riding Instructor, Darnassus (26), E-1, Cenarion Enclave, Intersection of paths

JARUND STOUTSTRIDER
The Cenarion Circle, Silithus (66), K-2, Valor's Rest (137), Hut south of road

JARVEN THUNDERBREW
Dun Morogh (32), F-5, Kharanos (116), Thunderbrew Distillery

JASE FARLANE
Trade Supplies, Eastern Plaguelands (40), K-6, Light's Hope Chapel (118), Camp on left side of chapel

JASON LEMIEUX
Mushroom Seller, Hillsbrad Foothills (48), G-2, Tarren Mill (133), Patrols "figure eight" path around town

JASON MATHERS
Fishmonger, Elwynn Forest (42), F-6, Crystal Lake, Dock

JASPER FEL
Shady Dealer, Stormwind (72), L-6, Old Town, SI:7

JAWN HIGHMESA
General Goods, Thousand Needles (82), F-5, Freewind Post (112), Inn

JAXIN CHONG
Alchemist Trainer, Stranglethorn Vale (74), B-8, Booty Bay (103), Boucher's Cauldron (shop)

JAYLA
Skinner, Ashenvale (12), F-6, Silverwind Refuge, Center of building

JAYSIN LANYDA
Poisons and Reagents, Hillsbrad Foothills (48), F-6, Southshore (129), Second floor of inn

JAZ
Burning Steppes (22), Searing Gorge (64), C-4/D-8, Blackrock Depths

JAZZIK
General Supplies, Barrens (18), H-4, Ratchet (122), Jazzik's General Goods

JAZZRIK
Blacksmithing Supplies, Badlands (16), F-5, Valley of Fangs, Camp

JED RUNEWATCHER
Rare Spawn, Burning Steppes (22), Searing Gorge (64), C-4/D-8, Blackrock Spire, Lvl 59 Uncommon

JEDIGA
Azshara (14), B-5, Valormok

JEEDA
Apprentice Witch Doctor, Stonetalon Mountains (70), F-6, Sun Rock Retreat (132), Second floor of inn

JEEN'RA NIGHTRUNNER
Hunter Trainer, Darnassus (26), E-1, Cenarion Enclave, Top of structure, connected to the northeast structure

JEENA FEATHERBOW
Bowyer, Teldrassil (80), G-6, Dolanaar (109), Inn

J'EEVEE
Western Plaguelands (92), I-7, Scholomance

JEKYLL FLANDRING
Rewards Vendor, Alterac Mountains (8), I-6, Left camp outside Alterac Valley (Horde)

JEMMA QUIKSWITCH
Journeyman Engineer, Ironforge (52), I-4, Tinker Town, Springspindle's Gadgets

JE'NEU SANCREA
The Earthen Ring, Ashenvale (12), B-4, Zoram'gar Outpost (137), Northern Structure

JENN LANGSTON
Stormwind (72), Old Town, Roams Old Town

JENNA LEMKENILLI
Journeyman Engineer, Darkshore (24), F-4, Auberdine (101), In front of northern building

JENNABINK POWERSEAM
Tailoring Supplies & Specialty Goods, Wetlands (96), A-6, Menethil Harbor (119), Second floor of building west of keep

JENNEA CANNON
Mage Trainer, Stormwind (72), F-8, Mage Quarter, Wizard's Sanctum

JENOVA STONESHIELD
Stable Master, Stormwind (72), I-2, Dwarven District, South of tram entrance

JENSEN FARRAN
Bowyer, Dustwallow Marsh (38), I-5, Theramore Isle (135), East archery range

JEN'SHAN
Hunter Trainer, Durotar (34), F-7, Valley of Trials (136), Structure to south

JEREMIAH PAYSON
Cockroach Vendor, Undercity (88), I-4, The Trade Quarter, Under Bridge in Trade Quarter

JERGOSH THE INVOKER
Orgrimmar (60), F-5, Ragefire Chasm

JER'KAI MOONWEAVER
Feralas (46), H-4, Lower Wilds, In hills overlooking Grimtotem Compound

JERN HORNHELM
Loch Modan (54), E-5, Thelsamar (134), In second house on right of path

JES'RIMON
Orgrimmar (60), G-3, The Drag, Yelmak's Alchemy and Potions, top floor

JESSARA CORDELL
Enchanting Supplies, Stormwind (72), F-6, The Canals, Shop south of stockade

JESSE HALLORAN
Wetlands (96), A-5, Menethil Harbor (119), Roams in and out of house west of keep

JESSICA CHAMBERS
Innkeeper, Eastern Plaguelands (40), K-6, Light's Hope Chapel (118)

JESSICA REDPATH
Winterspring (98), I-4, Everlook (110), Inside inn

JESSIR MOONBOW
Felwood (44), G-8, Emerald Sanctuary (110), Near pool

JEWEL
Troyas' Pet, Feralas (46), C-4, Feathermoon Stronghold (111), Southeastern building

JEZELLE PRUITT
Undercity (88), K-1, The Magic Quarter, Green circle west of Skull Building

JEZIBA
Western Plaguelands (92), E-7, Ruins of Andorhal, Second floor of inn

JHAG
Apprentice Enchanter, Orgrimmar (60), G-4, The Drag, Godan's Runeworks

JHAWNA OATWIND
Baker, Mulgore (58), E-6, Bloodhoof Village (102), Mill

JHORDY LAPFORGE
Engineer, Tanaris (78), H-3, Gadgetzan (113), Transporter northeast of cage

JILLIAN TANNER
Leatherworking Supplies, Stormwind (72), J-5, Old Town, The Protective Hide

JIMMY
Stormwind (72), Roams city with Miss Danna

JIMMY THE BLEEDER
Rare Spawn, Alterac Mountains (8), F-8, H-7, Corrahn's Dagger, Sofera's Naze, Lvl 27 Average Rare; Roams around camp

JIN'SORA
Bow Merchant, Orgrimmar (60), J-4, Valley of Honor, Orgrimmar Bowyer

JINAR'ZILLEN
Desolace (30), B-7, Shadowprey Village (128), Dock

JINKY TWIZZLEFIXXIT
Engineering Supplies, Thousand Needles (82), K-8, Mirage Raceway (119), Tent west of racetrack

JIN'ROKH THE BREAKER
Stranglethorn Vale (74), A-2, Yojamba Isle

JIN'ZALLAH THE SANDBRINGER
Tanaris (78), F-3, Sandsorrow Watch, In hut near east watchtower

JITTERS
Duskwood (36), B-6, Raven Hill (123), Circling well in town

JOACHIM BRENLOW
Bartender, Stormwind (72), F-9, Mage Quarter, The Blue Recluse

JOANNA WHITEHALL
Undercity (88), G-3, The War Quarter, By Mining Trainer, Close to Canal

JOCASTE
Hunter Trainer, Darnassus (26), E-1, Cenarion Enclave, Northeast structure

JOHAN FOCHT
Miner, Silverpine Forest (68), F-4, The Sepulcher (127), Basement of inn

JOHN BURNSIDE
Banker, Stormwind (72), H-7, Trade District, Stormwind Counting House

JOHN TURNER
Ironforge (52), C-5, E-8, The Commons, Roams The Commons

JONATHAN CAREVIN
Duskwood (36), J-5, Darkshire (108), First floor of house

JONATHAN CHAMBERS
Bag Vendor, Undercity (88), I-6, The Rogues' Quarter, Near Apothecarium entry

JONDOR STEELBROW
Guild Master, Ironforge (52), D-8, The Commons, Ironforge Visitor's Center

JON-JON THE CROW
Stranglethorn Vale (74), C-5, Ruins of Jubuwal, Camp

JORAH ANNISTON
Undercity (88), K-4, The Magic Quarter, Near Rogues' Quarter entry

JORB
Lizzarik's Bodyguard, Barrens (18), G-4, Ratchet (122)

JORDAN STILWELL
Dun Morogh (32), G-4, Gates of Ironforge, Next to anvil outside of Ironforge

JORGEN
Stormwind (72), K-8, Valley of Heroes, Northeast of entrance

JORIK KERRIDAN
Rogue Trainer, Elwynn Forest (42), G-4, Northshire Valley (122), Abbey stable

JORMUND STONEBROW
Expert Tailor, Ironforge (52), F-3, The Great Forge, Stonebrow's Clothier

JORN SKYSEER
Barrens (18), F-6, Camp Taurajo (106), Outside southern building

JORY ZAGA
Darkshore (24), J-2, Hut, northeast of lake

JOSEF GREGORIAN
Artisan Tailor, Undercity (88), J-3, The Magic Quarter

JOSEPH DIRTE
Waste Management, Western Plaguelands (92), I-7, Caer Darrow, In front of shed left of entrance to Scholomance

JOSEPH MOORE
Leatherworking Supplies, Undercity (88), J-6, The Rogues' Quarter

JOSEPH REDPATH
Western Plaguelands (92), G-7, Sorrow Hill, (Summon) Spawns at gravestone Eastern Plaguelands (40), E-8, Darrowshire, (Summon) Well in the center of town

JOSEPHINE LISTER
Master Shadowweave Tailor, Undercity (88), L-2, The Magic Quarter, Outside Skull Building

JOSHUA KIEN
General Supplies, Tirisfal Glades (86), D-6, Deathknell (109), First floor of second house on right side of road

JOSHUA MACLURE
Vintner, Elwynn Forest (42), F-9, The Maclure Vineyards, Next to well on the south side of farm

JOVIL
Eye of the Storm Battlemaster, Stormwind (72), L-1

JOY AR'NARETH
Azshara (14), C-4, Bear's Head, Requires quest from Sanath Lim-yo to reach

JUBAHL CORPSESEEKER
Demon Trainer, Ironforge (52), G-1, The Forlorn Cavern, First building on north from east entrance

JUBIE GADGETSPRING
Engineering Supplier, Azshara (14), E-9, The Ruined Reaches, Gnome tower

JUDGE THELGRAM
Hillsbrad Foothills (48), A-8, Purgation Isle, To the right of tower

JUGKAR GRIM'ROD
Desolace (30), G-8, Mannoroc Coven, Northeast of ruins

JULI STORMKETTLE
Mage Trainer, Ironforge (52), C-1, The Mystic Ward, Hall of Mysteries

JULIA GALLINA
Wine Vendor, Stormwind (72), H-7, The Canals, Gallina Winery

JUNGLE STALKER
Stranglethorn Vale (74), B-5, C:(4, 5)

JUNGLE THUNDERER
Stranglethorn Vale (74), D:(3, 4), E:(3, 4)

JUN'HA
Tailoring Supplies, Arathi Highlands (10), J-4, Hammerfall (115), Inside west building

JUNIOR APOTHECARY HOLLAND
Royal Apothecary Society, Tirisfal Glades (86), G-5, Brill (104), Patrols back and forth in graveyard between the gazeebo and northeastern entrance

JUSTIN
Stormwind (72), H-3, The Canals, Dock

JUSTINE DEMALIER
Stormwind Recruiter, Stormwind (72), H-6, Trade District, Next to tree

JUTAK
Blade Trader, Stranglethorn Vale (74), B-8, Booty Bay (103)

JUVENILE SNOW LEOPARD
Dun Morogh (32), E-6, F-6, Coldridge Pass, The Grizzled Den

JYN STONEHOOF
Weapon's Merchant, Thunder Bluff (84), D-6, Lower rise, in Thunder Bluff Weapons tent

K

KAAL SOULREAPER
Warlock Trainer, Undercity (88), L-2, The Magic Quarter, Inside Skull Building

KADRAK
Barrens (18), F-1, The Mor'shan Rampart, Top of eastern tower

KAELA SHADOWSPEAR
Stonetalon Mountains (70), G-7, Webwinder Path, Hill between road and Windshear Crag

KAELYSTIA HATEBRINGER
Mage Trainer, Undercity (88), L-1, The Magic Quarter, Inside Skull Building

KAERBRUS
Hunter Trainer, Felwood (44), H-3, Talonbranch Glade (133), Near pond

KAGA MISTRUNNER
Meat Vendor, Thunder Bluff (84), F-5, High rise, in Kodo Steak and Ribs tent

KAGORO
Dustwallow Marsh (38), D-3, Brackenwall Village (104)

KAH MISTRUNNER
Fishing Trainer, Thunder Bluff (84), F-5, High rise, in Mountaintop Bait & Tackle tent

KAITA DEEPFORGE
Blacksmithing Supplies, Stormwind (72), H-2, Dwarven District, At the Forge

KAJA
Guns and Ammo Merchant, Orgrimmar (60), , Valley of Strength, Boomstick Imports

KAL
Druid Trainer, Teldrassil (80), G-6, Dolanaar (109), Moonwell south side of Dolanaar

KALARAN WINDBLADE
Searing Gorge (64), D-4, Amongst Mutilated Dark Iron Remains

KALDAN FELMOON
Specialist Leatherworking Supplies, Barrens (18), E-4, Wailing Caverns

KALI HEALTOUCH
Herbalist, Loch Modan (54), D-5, Thelsamar (134), On porch of first house on right of path

KALI REMIK
Durotar (34), H-7, Sen'jin Village (126), Atop northern structure

KALIN WINDFLIGHT
Feralas (46), E-2, The Twin Colossals, Atop eastern colossal

KALLDAN FELMOON
Specialist Leatherworking Supplies, Barrens (18), E-4, The Wailing Caverns, Right eye of cave above entrance

KALTUNK
Durotar (34), F-7, Valley of Trials (136), Center fire

KALYIMAH STORMCLOUD
Bags & Sacks, Barrens (18), F-3, The Crossroads (107), Southern entrance

KAM DEEPFURY
Stormwind (72), F-6, The Stockade

KAMARI
Journeyman Leatherworker, Orgrimmar (60), H-4, The Drag, Kodohide Leatherworkers

KANATI GREYCLOUD
Thousand Needles (82), B-3, Whitereach Post, Front of hut

KANDAAR
Eye of the Storm Battlemaster, Ironforge (52), J-9

KANDRIS DREAMSEEKER
Shaman Trainer, Orgrimmar (60), D-4, Valley of Wisdom, Grommash Hold

KANIA
Enchanting Supplier, Silithus (67), G-4, Cenarion Hold (106)

KAPLAK
Rogue Trainer, Durotar (34), H-4, Razor Hill (124), Bunker

KAR STORMSINGER
Kodo Riding Instructor, Mulgore (58), E-6, Bloodhoof Village (102), Northern clearing

KARA ADAMS
Shield Crafter, Redridge Mountains (62), D-5, Lakeshire (117), Stable

KARANG AMAKKAR
Ashenvale (12), B-4, Zoram'gar Outpost (137), Center of outpost

KARD RAGETOTEM
Sword and Dagger Merchant, Thunder Bluff (84), F-6, High rise, inside Ragetotem Arms tent

KAREN TAYLOR
Mining and Smithing Supplies, Redridge Mountains (62), D-5, Lakeshire (117), By carriage in front of Lakeshire Town Hall

KARETH
Blade Merchant, Orgrimmar (60), E-5, The Cleft of Shadow, The Slow Blade

KARGAL BATTLESCAR
Barrens (18), H-2, Far Watch Post, Southside of road

KARL BORAN
Wetlands (96), A-6, Menethil Harbor (119), Dock

KARLEE CHADDIS
Stormwind (72), Roams city

KARM IRONQUILL
Mining Supplies, Loch Modan (54), E-5, Thelsamar (134), In second house on right of path

KARN STONEHOOF
Expert Blacksmith, Thunder Bluff (84), D-6, Lower rise, next to pond

KARNA REMTRAVEL
Un'Goro Crater (90), F-1, G-1, Lakkari Tar Pits, Next to northeast tar pit

KAROLEK
Leatherworking Trainer, Orgrimmar (60), H-4, The Drag, Kodohide Leatherworkers

KAROS RAZOK
Bat Handler, Silverpine Forest (68), G-4, The Sepulcher (127), Left of road heading into sepulcher

KARREL GRAYVES
Tirisfal Glades (86), D-6, Deathknell (109)

KARRINA MEKENDA
Pet Trainer, Stormwind (72), I-2, Dwarven District, Building south of tram entrance

KARTOSH
Warlock Trainer, Swamp of Sorrows (76), F-5, Stonard (131), Second floor of main hall

KALI HEALTOUCH

KARTRA BLOODSNARL
Alterac Valley Battlemaster, Orgrimmar (60), J-3, Valley of Honor

KARUS
Banker, Orgrimmar (60), F-7, Valley of Strength

KARY THUNDERHORN
Hunter Trainer, Thunder Bluff (84), G-9 Hunter Rise, Inside Hunter's Hall

KASHOCH THE REAVER
Rare Spawn, Winterspring (98), I-7, Frostwhisper Gorge, Lvl 60 Average Rare; Guards tower in gorge

KASKK
Rare Spawn, Desolace (30), F-7, G:(7-8) Mannoroc Coven, Lvl 40 Very Rare; Patrols spawn points

KAT SAMPSON
Leather Armor Merchant, Loch Modan (54), K-6, The Farstrider Lodge (111), left center of lodge

KATAR
Swamp of Sorrows (76), K-7, Misty Reed Strand, Just above banks near Misty Reed Post

KATHERINE THE PURE
Paladin Trainer, Stormwind (72), F-3, Cathedral Square, Cathedral of Light

KATHRUM AXEHAND
Axe Merchant, Stormwind (72), H-1, Dwarven District, Northwest Building

KATIE HUNTER
Horse Breeder, Elwynn Forest (42), L-6, Eastvale Logging Camp, Corale

KATIS
Wand Merchant, Orgrimmar (60), E-5, The Cleft of Shadow, Ironwood Staves and Wands

KATOOM THE ANGLER
Trainer/Fishing Trainer and Supplies, The Hinterlands (50), L-8, Revantusk Village (125), On crate on docka

KATRINA ALLIESTAR
Herbalism Supplier, Undercity (88), G-5, The Apothecarium, Near War Quarter entry

KATRINA TURNER
Tanaris (78), G-3, Gadgetzan (113)

KAWNIE SOFTBREEZE
General Goods, Mulgore (58), E-8, Camp Narache (105), North tent

KAYA FLATHOOF
Stonetalon Mountains (70), J-8, Grimtotem Post, Western hut

KAYLA SMITHE
Demon Trainer, Tirisfal Glades (86), C-7, Deathknell (109), Church

KAYNETH STILLWIND
Ashenvale (12), K-4, Forest Song, Northwest of Forest Song

KAYREN SOOTHALLOW
General Goods, Hillsbrad Foothills (48), H-2, Tarren Mill (133), Outside of inn

KAZAN MOGOSH
Food & Drink Merchant, Dun Morogh (32), I-5, Gol'Bolar Quarry, Patrols kitchen area of camp

KAZKAZ THE UNHOLY
Swamp of Sorrows (76), I-5, The Temple of Atal'Hakkar

KAZON
Rare Spawn, Redridge Mountains (62), D-1, Render's Camp, Lvl 27 Uncommon; Idle by hut

KEBOK
Stranglethorn Vale (74), B-8, Booty Bay (103), Third floor of The Salty Sailor Tavern

KEEG GIBN
Ale & Wine, Dun Morogh (32), D-5, Brewnall Village, By caravan

KEENA
Trade Goods, Arathi Highlands (10), J-3, Hammerfall (115), First floor north building

KEEPER ALBAGORM
Stonetalon Mountains (71), E-2, Stonetalon Peak (131), Next to moonwell

KEEPER BEL'DUGUR
Undercity (88), G-5, The Apothecarium In front of bridge

KEEPER BEL'VARIL
Hillsbrad Foothills (48), G-2, Tarren Mill (133), House on the right side

KEEPER MARANDIS
Hippogryph Master, Desolace (30), H-1, Nijel's Point (121), Building on southwestern hill

EEPER ORDANUS
Ashenvale (12), H-5, Raynewood Retreat, Top floor of building

EEPER REMULOS
Moonglade (56), E-4, Shrine of Remulos, Next to tree

EGAN DARKMAR
Alterac Mountains (8), B-8, Lordamere Internment Camp, Third floor of building west of camp

EINA
Bowyer, Teldrassil (80), H-4, Shadowglen (127), Open room in front of main building

ELDAS
Pet Trainer, Teldrassil (80), G-6, Dolanaar (109), East of inn

ELDRAN
Orgrimmar (60), D-6, Talon Gate, Near South Fury River entrance

ELDRIC BOUCHER
Arcane Goods Vendor, Stormwind (72), H-6, Trade District, Pestle's Apothecary

ELEK SKYKEEPER
Emerald Circle, Felwood (44), G-8, Emerald Sanctuary (110), Between tent and building

ELGRUK BLOODAXE
Weapon Crafter, Orgrimmar (60), J-2, Valley of Honor, Arms of Legend

ELLY GRANT
Stormwind (72), C-5, The Park, Roams park

ELM HARGUNTH
Warsong Supply Officer, Barrens (18), E-1, Mor'shan Base Camp, Outside entrance to Warsong Gulch

ELOMIR IRONHAND
Maces & Staves, Ironforge (52), H-9, The Military Ward, Timberline Arms

ELSEY YANCE
Cook, Stranglethorn Vale (74), B-8, Booty Bay (103), Good Food (shop) on the northern side of The Old Port Authority

ELSTRUM STONEBREAKER
Warrior Trainer, Ironforge (52), I-9, The Military Ward, Hall of Arms

ELSUWA
Stable Master, Barrens (18), F-6, Camp Taurajo (106), Outside inn

ELT THOMASIN
Loch Modan (54), K-6, The Farstrider Lodge (111), In left rear of lodge

ELV STERNHAMMER
Warrior Trainer, Ironforge (52), J-9, The Military Ward, Hall of Arms

ENATA DABYRIE
Arathi Highlands (10), H-4, Dabyrie's Farmstead, House on hill

ENDOR KABONKA
Master of Cooking Recipes, Stormwind (72), K-4, Old Town, Pig and Whistle Tavern

EN'JAI
Priest Trainer, Durotar (34), F-7, Valley of Trials (136)

ENNAH HAWKSEYE
Gunsmith, Mulgore (58), E-6, Bloodhoof Village (102), Northeast tent

EN'ZIGLA
Stonetalon Mountains (70), I-9, Malaka'jin, Next to shack

ER RAGETOTEM
Warrior Trainer, Thunder Bluff (84), G-9, Hunter Rise, Inside Hunter's Hall

ERAS WOLFHEART
Arathi Basin Battlemaster, Darnassus (26), H-4

ERGUL BLOODAXE
Warsong Gulch Battlemaster, Thunder Bluff (84), G-9, Hunter Rise, Between bridges in a tent

ERLONIAN EVERSHADE
Druid of the Claw, Darkshore (24), G-8, Grove of the Ancients, Sleeping in clearing near the water

ERNOBEE
Dun Morogh (32), C-4, Gnomeregan

ERR IRONSIGHT
The Hinterlands (50), C-5, Aerie Peak (100), First floor of tower

ERSOK PROND
Tradesman, Wetlands (96), A-6, Deepwater Tavern, Next to stairs

ERYN SYLVIUS
Rogue Trainer, Elwynn Forest (42), F-7, Goldshire (114), Second floor of Lion's Pride Inn

---

KEYL SWIFTCLAW
Silithus (67), G-4, Cenarion Hold (106)

KHAELYN STEELWING
Gryphon Master, Eastern Plaguelands (40), K-6, Light's Hope Chapel (118), Camp on right side of chapel

KHAN DEZ'HEPAH
Desolace (30), J:(4-5), Kolkar Village, Big hut or landing

KHAN HRATHA
Desolace (30), C-5, Valley of Spears, (Summon) Under stone bridge

KHAN JEHN
Desolace (30), I-8, Magram Village, Big hut

KHAN SHAKA
Desolace (30), E-9, Bolgan's Hole, Deep in caverns

KHARA DEEPWATER
Fishing Supplies, Loch Modan (54), E-4, The Loch, On porch of house on the western shore of loch

KHARAN MIGHTHAMMER
Burning Steppes (22), Searing Gorge (64), C-4/D-8, Blackrock Depths

KHARDAN PROUDBLADE
Weaponsmith, Teldrassil (80), G-4, H-4, Shadowglen (127), Inside main building

KHAREDON
Light Armor Merchant, Moonglade (56), H-3, Nighthaven (121), First floor of far northeast building on hill

KHELDEN BREMEN
Mage Trainer, Elwynn Forest (42), G-4, Northshire Valley (122), Second floor of abbey

KHUR HORNSTRIKER
Reagent Vendor, Silithus (67), G-5, Cenarion Hold (106)

KIBLER
Burning Steppes (22), H-2, Flame Crest (112), Cave

KIERAN
Weapon Merchant, Darnassus (26), I-6, Tradesmen's Terrace, Weapons shop, second floor

KIKNIKLE
Stylish Clothier, Barrens (18), E-4, Near mountains west of oasis

KILDAR
Wolf Riding Instructor, Orgrimmar (60), I-1, Valley of Honor, Outside of Hunter's Hall

KIL'HALA
Journeyman Tailor, Barrens (18), F-3, The Crossroads (107), Southern entrance

KIL'HIWANA
Fisherman, Ashenvale (12), B-4, Zoram'gar Outpost (137), Near coast

KILLANNOC MACLEOD
Barrens (18), H-5, Fray Island, Outside southern building

KILLIAN HAGEY
Skinning Trainer, Undercity (88), J-6, The Rogues' Quarter

KILLIAN SANATHA
Fisherman, Silverpine Forest (68), E-2, North Tide's Run, Camp along shoreline

KILLIUM BOULDERTOE
Stable Master, The Hinterlands (50), B-5, Aerie Peak (100), Wildhammer Keep

KILRAM
Winterspring (98), I-4, Everlook (110), North building

KILXX
Fisherman, Barrens (18), H-4, Ratchet (122), Near dock

KIMBERLY GRANT
Stormwind (72), C-5, The Park, Roams park

KIMBERLY HIETT
Fletcher, Redridge Mountains (62), C-4, Lakeshire (117), First floor of Lakeshire Inn

KIM'JAEL
Azshara (14), G-2, Legash Encampment, Camp atop tor

KINDAL MOONWEAVER
Feralas (46), H-4, Lower Wilds, In hills overlooking Grimtotem Compound

KINELORY
Arathi Highlands (10), H-5, Go'Shek Farm, Hill northwest of farm

KING BANGALASH
Stranglethorn Vale (74), D-4, Roams small area around spawn point

KING GORDOK
Feralas (46), G-4, Dire Maul

KING MAGNI BRONZEBEARD
Lord of Ironforge, Ironforge (52), E-5, The Great Forge, The High Seat

---

KING MOSH
Un'Goro Crater (90), D:(3-5), E:(3-4), Golakka Hot Springs, Spawns in different spots north of springs

KING MUKLA
Stranglethorn Vale (74), D-9, Jaguero Isle, Roams small area around spawn point

KING TERENAS MENETHRILL II
King's Tomb, Undercity (88), I-4, Ruins of Lordaeron

KIN'WEELAY
Stranglethorn Vale (74), C-3, Grom'gol Base Camp (114), To the left of forge

KIRA SONGSHINE
Traveling Baker, Elwynn Forest (42), F-7, Goldshire (114), Patrols between the Gates of Stormwind and the two roads in southern Goldshire

KIREENA
Trade Goods, Desolace (30), G-5, Ghost Walker Post (113), Western hut

KIRGE STERNHORN
Barrens (18), E-6, Camp Taurajo (106), North of road

KIRITH THE DAMNED
Blasted Lands (20), J-3, Serpent's Coil, Cave interior

KIRK MAXWELL
Stable Master, Westfall (94), F-5, Sentinel Hill (126), Outside Inn

KIRO
War Harness Maker, Orgrimmar (60), I-4, Valley of Honor, Kiro's Harnesses

KIRSTA DEEPSHADOW
Western Plaguelands (92), G-3, Northridge Lumber Camp, Kneeling by carriage along path to the northeast of camp

KIRTONOS THE HERALD
Western Plaguelands (92), I-7, Scholomance

KITHA
Demon Trainer, Durotar (34), H-4, Razor Hill (124), Behind barracks

KITHAS
Enchanting Supplier, Orgrimmar (60), G-4, The Drag, Godan's Runeworks

KITTA FIREWIND
Artisan Enchanter, Elwynn Forest (42), I-7, Tower of Azora, Top floor of tower

KIXXLE
Potions & Herbs, Wetlands (96), G-4, Next to road to Dun Modr, by bridge

KIZZ BLUNTSTRIKE
Macecrafter, Stranglethorn Vale (74), B-8, Booty Bay (103), Cuts-n-Bruises Incorporated (shop) on the southern side of The Old Port Authority

KLANNOC MACLEOD
Barrens (18), H-5, Fray Island, Outside southern building

KLAVEN MORTWAKE
Westfall (94), I-7, The Dust Plains, Top of tower

KLOCKMORT SPANNERSPAN
Ironforge (52), I-5, Tinker Town, Outside Springspindle's Gadgets

KNAZ BLUNDERFLAME
Engineering Supplies, Stranglethorn Vale (74), F-4, Outside of gnomish workshop

KNOT THIMBLEJACK
Feralas (46), G-4, Dire Maul

KOBOLD DIGGER
Westfall (94), E-2, Gold Coast Quarry

KOBOLD GEOMANCER
Elwynn Forest (42), H-6, I-6, Jasperlode Mine

KOBOLD MINER
Elwynn Forest (42), H:(5, 6), I:(5, 6), Fargodeep Mine, Jasperlode Mine

KOBOLD TUNNELER
Elwynn Forest (42), E:(8, 9), Fargodeep Mine, The Maclure Vineyards, The Stonefield Farm

KOBOLD VERMIN
Elwynn Forest (42), F:(3, 4), G-4, Echo Ridge Mine, Northshire Valley (122)

KOBOLD WORKER
Elwynn Forest (42), F:(3, 4), G:(3, 4), Echo Ridge Mine, Northshire Valley (122)

KODO BULL
Mulgore (58), C:(2, 3), D:(4, 7), E-2, G-2

KODO CALF
Mulgore (58), C:(2, 3), D:(4, 7), E-2, G-2

KODO MATRIARCH
Mulgore (58), C:(2, 3), D:(4, 7), E-2, G-2

KODO SPIRIT
Desolace (30), F-6, G-6, Kodo Graveyard, Southwest in graveyard

KOITER
Fallen Hero, Twincruiser, Barrens (18), E-3, Shrine of the Fallen Warrior, North of Wailing Caverns, south of road

KOLKAR AMBUSHER
Desolace (30), I:(4, 5), Kolkar Village

KOLKAR BATTLE LORD
Desolace (30), I:(4, 5), J:(4, 5), Kolkar Village

KOLKAR BLOODCHARGER
Barrens (18), E-4, F-4, G:(4, 5), Lushwater Oasis, The Stagnant Oasis, The Wailing Caverns

KOLKAR CENTAUR
Desolace (30), I:(4, 5), J:(4, 5), Kolkar Village

KOLKAR DESTROYER
Desolace (30), I:(4, 5), J:(4, 5), Kolkar Village

KOLKAR DRUDGE
Durotar (34), G-8, H-8, Darkspear Strand, Kolkar Crag

KOLKAR INVADER
Barrens (18), E-3, The Crossroads (107), The Forgotten Pools

KOLKAR MARAUDER
Barrens (18), F:(4, 5), G:(4, 5), Lushwater Oasis, The Stagnant Oasis

KOLKAR MAULER
Desolace (30), I:(4, 5), J:(4, 5), Kolkar Village

KOLKAR OUTRUNNER
Durotar (34), G-8, Kolkar Crag

KOLKAR PACK RUNNER
Barrens (18), E-4, F-4, G:(4, 5), Lushwater Oasis, The Stagnant Oasis

KOLKAR PACKHOUND
Barrens (18), E-4, F-4, G:(4, 5), Lushwater Oasis, The Stagnant Oasis

KOLKAR SCOUT
Desolace (30), I:(4, 5), J:(4, 5), Kolkar Village

KOLKAR STORMER
Barrens (18), E:(2-4), F-4, G-4, The Forgotten Pools, Lushwater Oasis, The Stagnant Oasis

KOLKAR STORMSEER
Barrens (18), E-3, The Forgotten Pools

KOLKAR WAYLAYER
Desolace (30), I:(4, 5), Kolkar Village

KOLKAR WINDCHASER
Desolace (30), I:(4, 5), J:(4, 5), Kolkar Village

KOLKAR WRANGLER
Barrens (18), E:(2-4), F-4, The Forgotten Pools, Lushwater Oasis

KOMA
Banker, Orgrimmar (60), F-7, Valley of Strength

KOMIN WINTERHOOF
Herbalism Trainer, Thunder Bluff (84), F-4, Middle rise, in Holistic Herbalism tent

KON YELLOWEYES
Thunder Bluff (84), G-8, Hunter Rise, In front of Hunter's Hall

KONDA
Stranglethorn Vale (74), C-7, Mistvale Valley, (Summon) Spawns in with several gorillas

KOR'GELD
Alchemy Supplier, Orgrimmar (60), G-3, The Drag, Yelmak's Alchemy and Potions

KOR'GHAN
Orgrimmar (60), F-5, The Drag, In building above Dark Earth Fungus and Mushrooms

KOR'GRESH COLDRAGE
Arathi Highlands (10), G-8, Boulderfist Hall, Inside lower of two caves at Boulderfist Hall

KOR'JUS
Mushroom Vendor, Orgrimmar (60), F-5, The Cleft of Shadow, Darkearth Fungus and Mushrooms

KORFAX
Champion of the Light, Eastern Plaguelands (40), K-6, Light's Hope Chapel (118)

KORIN FEL
Arathi Highlands (10), J-3, Hammerfall (115), Platform of north building

---

KORRA
Ashenvale (12), E-5, Astranaar (101), First floor of inn near Raene

KORRAN
Barrens (18), F-3, The Crossroads (107), Western entrance

KORU
Mace and Staff Vendor, Orgrimmar (60), K-2, Valley of Honor, Arms of Legend, second floor

KOVORK
Rare Spawn, Arathi Highlands (10), D-5, Boulderfist Outpost, Lvl 36 Uncommon; Inside cave at Boulder'gor

KOZISH
Orgrimmar (60), G-7, Valley of Strength, Inn

KRAGG
Hunter Trainer, Stranglethorn Vale (74), C-3, Grom'gol Base Camp (114), Just inside camp walls to the left of western entrance

KRAH'RANIK
Darkshore (24), J-2, Hut, northeast of lake

KRAK
Armorer, Dustwallow Marsh (38), D-3, Brackenwall Village (104), Northern part of village

KRAKK
Superior Armorer, Stranglethorn Vale (74), C-3, Grom'gol Base Camp (114), Next to anvil by forge

KRAKLE
Un'Goro Crater (90), D-5, Golakka Hot Springs, West of big spring, next to big rock

KRAKLE'S THERMOMETER
Un'Goro Crater (90), F-5, G:(4-5), H-5, Fire Plume Ridge, Found in a few spots on ridge

KRANAL FISS
Barrens (18), G-2, Grol'dom Farm, Roams outside tower east of farm

KRANG STONEHOOF
Warrior Trainer, Mulgore (58), F-6, Bloodhoof Village (102), Combat ground east of village

KRATHOK MOLTENFIST
Orgrimmar (60), J-2, Valley of Honor, Across from Arms of Legend

KRAUL BAT
Barrens (18), E-9, Razorfen Kraul

KRAVEL KOALBEARD
Thousand Needles (82), K-8, Mirage Raceway (119), West of racetrack

KRAY
Alchemist Trainer, Thunder Bluff (84), E-3, Middle rise, inside Bena's Alchemy tent

KRAZEK
Stranglethorn Vale (74), B-8, Booty Bay (103), Third floor of The Salty Sailor Tavern

KREENIG SNARLSNOUT
Barrens (18), G-3, Thorn Hill, Roams northeast side of hill

KREG BILMN
General Supplies, Dun Morogh (32), F-5, Kharanos (116), Thunderbrew Distillery

KREGG KEELHAUL
Rare Spawn, Tanaris (78), J-5, K-5, Lost Rigger Cove, Lvl 47 Uncommon; In west building, ship being built, or far ship at dock

KRELDIG UNGOR
Reclaimers Inc., Desolace (30), I-1, Nijel's Point (121), Between paths leading to flight point and inn

KRELLACK
Rare Spawn, Silithus (66), G-2, Southwind Village, Lvl 56 Semi-Rare; Roams close to spawn points

KRESH
Barrens (18), E-4, Wailing Caverns

KRETHIS SHADOWSPINNER
Rare Spawn, Silverpine Forest (68), E-1, The Skittering Dark, Lvl 15 Uncommon; Roaming in or around cave

KRIGGON TALSONE
Fisherman, Westfall (94), D-9, Longshore, Dock on southern tip of jutty

KRINKLE GOODSTEEL
Blacksmithing Supplies, Tanaris (78), H-3, Gadgetzan (113), Near southern entrance

KRIS LEGACE
Freewheeling Tradeswoman, Hillsbrad Foothills (48), J-4, Durnholde Keep, Just below rear of ruins in the upper level of keep

KRISS GOLDENLIGHT
Eastern Plaguelands (40), G-3, Northpass Tower, Tower

KRISTY GRANT
Feralas (46), K-5, Thalanaar, Roaming northwest of well

KRIXIL SLOGSWITCH
Food & Drink, Dustwallow Marsh (38), F-7, Mudsprocket (120)

KROG
Dustwallow Marsh (38), D-3, Brackenwall Village (104), Center of village

KROLG
Ashenvale (12), G-7, Mystral Lake, South near mountain inlet

KROM STOUTARM
Ironforge (52), J-1, Hall of Explorers, The Library

KROM'GRUL
Rare Spawn, Burning Steppes (22), J:(4, 5), K:(4, 5), Dreadmaul Rock, Lvl 54 Common; Roams small area around spawn point

KROND
Butcher, Stonetalon Mountains (70), E-6, Sun Rock Retreat (132), Western building

KROSHIUS
Felwood (44), F-4, Shatter Scar Vale, North of the eastern crater

KROUM
Wind Rider Master, Azshara (14), B-5, Valormok, North of camp

KRUEG SKULLSPLITTER
Feralas (46), I-4, Camp Mojache (105), Next to tent, east of water

KRULMOO FULLMOON
Leatherworking Trainer, Barrens (18), F-6, Camp Taurajo (106), Southern building

KRUMN
Guild Master, Thunder Bluff (84), D-6, Lower rise, in Thunder Bluff Civic Information tent

KRUNN
Miner, Durotar (34), H-4, Razor Hill (124), Northeast of inn

KRUSK
Hillsbrad Foothills (48), H-2, Tarren Mill (133), Church

KUL TIRAS MARINE
Durotar (34), H:(5, 6), I:(5, 6), Scuttle Coast, Tiragarde Keep

KUL TIRAS SAILOR
Durotar (34), H:(5, 6), I:(5, 6), Scuttle Coast, Tiragarde Keep

KULLEG STONEHORN
Skinning Trainer, Feralas (46), I-4, Camp Mojache (105), Big western tent

KULWIA
Trade Supplies, Stonetalon Mountains (70), E-6, Sun Rock Retreat (132), South of western structure

KUM'ISHA THE COLLECTOR
Blasted Lands (20), H-4, Rise of the Defiler, Behind ruins wall

KUNA THUNDERHORN
Bowyer & Fletching Goods, Thunder Bluff (84), E-4, Middle rise, inside Thunderhorn's Archery tent

KUNDRIC ZANDEN
Hillsbrad Foothills (48), E-5, Southshore (129), Church

KURAY'BIN
Ashenvale (12), I-6, Splintertree Post (129), Foot of outlying watch tower near road

KURDEN BLOODCLAW
Warsong Gulch Battlemaster, Undercity (88), G-9, Royal Quarter

KURDRAM STONEHAMMER
Mining Trainer, Darkshore (24), F-4, Auberdine (101), In front of northern building

KURDROS
Hillsbrad Foothills (48), K-3, Durnholde Keep, Roams a small area northeast of keep

KURGUL
Demon Trainer, Orgrimmar (60), F-5, The Cleft of Shadow, Darkfire Enclave

KURLL
Food & Drink, Azshara (14), B-5, Valormok, Bivouac

KURM STONEHOOF
Mining Supplier, Thunder Bluff (84), C-6, Lower rise, inside Stonehoof Geology tent

KURMOKK
Rare Spawn, Stranglethorn Vale (74), D-6, Ruins of Aboraz, Lvl 42 Very Rare; Patrols through Mistvale Valley toward the road heading into Booty Bay

KURRAN STEELE
Cloth & Leather Armor Merchant, Elwynn Forest (42), E-6, Goldshire (114), Smithy

KURUK
General Goods, Thunder Bluff (84), D-6, Lower rise, inside Kuruk's Goods tent

KURZEN COMMANDO
Stranglethorn Vale (74), E-1, Kurzen's Compound

KURZEN HEADSHRINKER
Stranglethorn Vale (74), E-1, Kurzen's Compound

KURZEN JUNGLE FIGHTER
Stranglethorn Vale (74), E:(1, 2), Kurzen's Compound

KURZEN MEDICINE MAN
Stranglethorn Vale (74), E:(1, 2), Kurzen's Compound

KURZEN MINDSLAVE
Mogh the Undying's Minion, Stranglethorn Vale (74), E-5, Ruins of Zul'Mamwe, (Summon) By campfire

KURZEN WAR PANTHER
Stranglethorn Vale (74), E-1, The Stockpile

KURZEN WAR TIGER
Stranglethorn Vale (74), E-1, The Stockpile

KURZEN WITCH DOCTOR
Stranglethorn Vale (74), E-1, The Stockpile

KURZEN WRANGLER
Stranglethorn Vale (74), E-1, The Stockpile

KURZEN'S AGENT
Stranglethorn Vale (74), D-1, (Summon) Two agents spawn in near the path leading to the Rebel Camp (124)

KUZ
Barrens (18), E-8, Blackthorn Ridge, Roams the ridge

K'WAII
General Goods, Durotar (34), H-7, Sen'jin Village (126), Main floor of big hut

KYLANNA
Alchemist Trainer, Ashenvale (12), F-7, Silverwind Refuge, Left wing of building

KYLANNA WINDWHISPER
Master Alchemist, Feralas (46), C-4, Feathermoon Stronghold (111), Bottom floor of tree building in northeast

KYM WILDMANE
Druid Trainer, Thunder Bluff (84), I-3, Elder Rise, Inside Hall of Elders

KYNDRI
Baker, Darkshore (24), F-4, Auberdine (101), First floor of inn

KYRA BOUCHER
Reagent Vendor, Stormwind (72), H-6, Trade District, Pestle's Apothecary

KYRA WINDBLADE
Warrior Trainer, Teldrassil (80), G-6, Dolanaar (109), Inn

KYRAI
Poison Vendor, Darnassus (26), D-2, Cenarion Enclave, Southwest structure

KZAN THORNSLASH
Weaponsmith, Durotar (34), F-7, Valley of Trials (136)

KZIXX
Rare Goods, Duskwood (36), K-2, By carriage

L

LADY ANACONDRA
Barrens (18), E-4, Wailing Caverns

LADY HEDERINE
Rare Spawn, Winterspring (98), H-8, Darkwhisper Gorge, Lvl 61 Very Rare; Deep within the gorge

LADY HOTESHEM
Arathi Basin Battlemaster, Stormwind (72), L-1

LADY ILLUCIA BAROV
Western Plaguelands (92), I-7, Scholomance

LADY JAINA PROUDMOORE
Ruler of Theramore, Dustwallow Marsh (38), I-5, Theramore Isle (135), Top of central tower

LADY KATRANA PRESTOR
Stormwind (72), L-2, Stormwind Keep, Center of east wing

LADY MOONGAZER
Darkshore (24), F-6, G-6, Ameth'Aran, Roams southern part of Ameth'Aran

LADY PALANSEER
Armor Quartermaster, Orgrimmar (61), E-7

LADY SAREVESS
Ashenvale (12), B-2, Blackfathom Deeps

LADY SATHRAH
Teldrassil (80), E-3, F-3, The Oracle Glade, Patrols north of The Oracle Glade east towards the hills

LADY SESSPIRA
Rare Spawn, Azshara (14), D-5, Ruins of Eldarath, Lvl 51 Uncommon; Patrols the ruins

LADY SEVINE
Blasted Lands (20), F-3, Altar of Storms, Rear of altar on right side

LADY SYLVANUS WINDRUNNER
Boss, Banshee Queen, Undercity (88), H-9, Royal Quarter, In Throne room

LADY SZALLAH
Rare Spawn, Feralas (46), B-7, Isle of Dread, Lvl 46 Uncommon; Roams various areas outside of Shalzaru's Lair

LADY VESPIA
Rare Spawn, Ashenvale (12), B:(2-3), The Zoram Strand (137), Lvl 22 Uncommon; Roams coastline

LADY VESPIRA
Rare Spawn, Darkshore (24), I-2, Ruins of Mathystra, Lvl 22 Semi-Rare; Roams throughout ruins

LADY ZEPHRIS
Rare Spawn, Hillsbrad Foothills (48), H-9, Eastern Strand, Lvl 33 Uncommon; Patrols southeastern coastline

LAER STEPPERUNNER
Food & Drink, Thousand Needles (82), B-3, Whitereach Post, Next to hut

LAGO BLACKWRENCH
Ironforge (52), F-1, The Forlorn Cavern, Outside Traveling Fisherman

LAH'MAWHANI
Trade Supplies, Desolace (30), B-7, Shadowprey Village (128), Down by dock

LAIRD
Fish Vendor, Darkshore (24), F-4, Auberdine (101), First floor of inn

LAIRN
Banker, Darnassus (26), E-4, Bank

LAKE CREEPER
Silverpine Forest (68), K-3, L:(2, 3), The Dawning Isles

LAKE FRENZY
Silverpine Forest (68), I:(2-4), J:(2, 4), K:(1, 4), L:(1-3), Lordamere Lake

LAKE SKULKER
Silverpine Forest (68), J:(3, 4), K:(3, 4), Fenris Isle

LAKOTA WINDSONG
Thousand Needles (82), E-3, Darkcloud Pinnacle, On northern cliff, north of Darkcloud Pinnacle

LAKOTA'MANI
Barrens (18), E-5, F-5, Agama'gor, Bramblescar, Patrols across Southern Gold Road

LALINA SUMMERMOON
Journeyman Enchanter, Darnassus (26), H-1, Craftsmen's Terrace, Enchanting shop

LAMAR VEISILLI
Fruit Seller, Redridge Mountains (62), B-5, Lakeshire (117), Behind small house on southwestern side of town

LAND RAGER
Tanaris (78), E:(5, 6), F:(5-7), G:(4, 5), I:(5, 6)

LAND WALKER
Feralas (46), D:(2, 3), Ruins of Ravenwind, The Twin Colossals

LANDRIA
Bow Merchant, Darnassus (26), H-6, Tradesmen's Terrace, Fletcher

LANDSLIDE
Desolace (30), D-5, Mauradon

LANIE REED
Gryphon Master, Searing Gorge (64), D-3, Thorium Point (136), Ridgeline outcropping southeast of camp

LANKA FARSHOT
Hunter Trainer, Mulgore (58), E-8, Camp Narache (105), Main tent (north)

LANTI'GAH
Barrens (18), E-3, Roams road west of Crossroads

LAPRESS
Rare Spawn, Silithus (66), G-5, Hive'Regal, Lvl 60 Very Rare; Spawns in far southeast of hive and roams hive

LAR PROWLTUSK
Durotar (34), H-7, Sen'jin Village (126), Between two rocks west of the village

LARA MOORE
Leather Armor Merchant, Stormwind (72), H-6, Trade District, Lionheart Armory

LARD
Innkeeper, The Hinterlands (50), L-8, Revantusk Village (125), First floor of inn on eastern side of village

LARDAN
Leatherworking Supplies, Ashenvale (12), E-5, Astranaar (101), Second floor library of northwest building (south of road)

LARGE CRAG BOAR
Dun Morogh (32), D-5, E:(3, 5), F:(3-6), G:(4-6), H-5, I-5

LARGE VILE SLIME
Western Plaguelands (92), H:(3, 4), I:(3, 4), The Weeping Cave

LARHKA
Beverage Merchant, Barrens (18), F-3, The Crossroads (107), Inn

LARIIA
Priest Trainer, Darnassus (26), E-9, The Temple of the Moon, South of fountain

LARIMAINE PURDUE
Portal Trainer, Stormwind (72), F-8, Mage Quarter, Wizard's Sanctum

LARION
Un'Goro Crater (90), F-1, Marshal's Refuge (118), South of cave

LARIS GEARDAWDLE
Ironforge (52), K-2, Hall of Explorers, The Library

LAR'KORWI
Un'Goro Crater (90), K-5, The Marshlands, (Summon) Attacks uphill into clearing

LAR'KORWI MATE
Un'Goro Crater (90), H:(5-8), I:(5-8), J:(5, 6), The Marshlands

LARS
Duskwood (36), A-3, The Hushed Bank, Camp

LASHTAIL RAPTOR
Stranglethorn Vale (74), C:(2, 3), D:(2, 3)

LATHERION
Barrens (18), F-6, Southern Barrens

LATHORIC THE BLACK
Searing Gorge (64), E-3, The Slag Pit, (Summon) Spawns next to Obsidion

LATRONICUS MOONSPEAR
Feralas (46), C-5, Feathermoon Stronghold (111), Southwest building

LAUGHING SISTER
Ashenvale (12), G:(5, 6), H:(5, 6), Nightsong Woods, Raynewood Retreat

LAUREN NEWCOMB
Light Armor Merchant, Undercity (88), I-4, The Trade Quarter, Upper Ring of Trade Quarter

LAURNA MORNINGLIGHT
Priest Trainer, Teldrassil (80), G-6, Dolanaar (109), Bottom floor inside building north of road

LAU'TIKI
Fisherman, Durotar (34), H-8, Darkspear Strand, Structure on coast

LAVA ANNIHILATOR
Burning Steppes (22), Searing Gorge (64), C-4/D-8, The Molten Core

LAVA CRAB
Burning Steppes (22), A-3, B-4, C:(5, 6), D:(3, 5-7), E:(4, 5), F:(5, 6), G:(5, 6), H:(3, 4), I:(3, 6), J:(3-5, 7), Found near lava pools and streams Searing Gorge (64), C:(3, 4, 6, 7), D:(4, 7, 8), E:(3-6), F:(5, 6), G:(4, 5, 7, 8), Near lava pools

LAVA ELEMENTAL
Burning Steppes (22), Searing Gorge (64), C-4/D-8, The Molten Core

LAVA REAVER
Burning Steppes (22), Searing Gorge (64), C-4/D-8, The Molten Core

LAVA SPAWN
Burning Steppes (22), Searing Gorge (64), C-4/D-8, The Molten Core

LAVA SURGER
Burning Steppes (22), Searing Gorge (64), C-4/D-8, The Molten Core

LAVINIA CROWE
Enchanter Trainer, Undercity (88), H-6, The Apothecarium, Near Rogues Quarter entry

LAWRENCE SCHNEIDER
Journeyman Tailor, Stormwind (72), G-7, Mage Quarter, Duncan's Textiles

LAYO STARSTRIKE
The Cenarion Circle, Silithus (66), K-2, Valor's Rest (137), Hut south of road

LAZIPHUS
Stable Master, Tanaris (78), H-3, Gadgetzan (113), Outside inn

LAZY PEON
Durotar (34), F-6, G:(6, 7), Valley of Trials (136), Sleeping or working around trees

LEE BROWN
Fisherman, Elwynn Forest (42), F-6, Crystal Lake, Dock

LEECH STALKER
Wetlands (96), F-6, G:(6, 7), H:(6, 7), Dun Algaz, Mosshide Fen

LEECH WIDOW
Rare Spawn, Wetlands (96), G-6, Thelgen Rock, Lvl 24 Uncommon; Patrols southwest area of cave

LEGACKI
Winterspring (98), I-4, Everlook (110), East of inn

LEGASHI HELLCALLER
Azshara (14), F-2, G-2, H:(2, 3), I-2, Bitter Reaches, Legash Encampment, Thalassian Base Camp

LEGASHI ROGUE
Azshara (14), F-2, G-2, H:(2, 3), I-2, Legash Encampment, Thalassian Base Camp, The Shattered Strand

LEGASHI SATYR
Azshara (14), F-2, G-2, H:(2, 3), I-2, Legash Encampment, Thalassian Base

LEGION HOUND
Ashenvale (12), J:(7, 8), K-7, Demon Fall Canyon

LELANAI
Saber Handler, Darnassus (26), E-1, Cenarion Enclave, Intersection of paths

LENNY "FINGERS" MCCOY
Stormwind (72), J-4, Old Town, Across from The Five Deadly Venoms

LEO SARN
Enchanting Supplies, Silverpine Forest (68), H-8, Camp

LEONA THARPE
Undercity (88), G-3, The War Quarter, By Mining Trainer, Close to Canal

LEONARD PORTER
Leatherworking Supplies, Western Plaguelands (92), E-8, Chillwind Camp (107), Behind ruined house

LEONID BARTHALOMEW THE REVERED
The Argent Dawn, Eastern Plaguelands (40), K-6, Light's Hope Chapel (118), Patrols in and out of chapel

LEPER GNOME
Dun Morogh (32), C-4, Frostmane Hold, Gnomeregan

LEPRITHUS
Rare Spawn, Westfall (94), D-3, G-8, The Dust Plains, Lvl 19 Uncommon; Appears near coffin/tombstones under tree

LEPROUS ASSISTANT
Dun Morogh (32), C-4, Gnomeregan

LEPROUS DEFENDER
Dun Morogh (32), C-4, Gnomeregan

LEPROUS MACHINESMITH
Dun Morogh (32), C-4, Gnomeregan

LEPROUS TECHNICIAN
Dun Morogh (32), C-4, Gnomeregan

LESSER FELGUARD
Ashenvale (12), C-6, D-6, Fire Scar Shrine

LESSER INFERNAL
Desolace (30), F:(7, 8), G:(7, 8), Mannoroc Coven

LESSER ROCK ELEMENTAL
Badlands (16), B-4, C:(4, 5), D-5, The Dustbowl, Hill Side

LESSER WATER ELEMENTAL
Stranglethorn Vale (74), A:(2, 3), B-4, The Savage Coast, The Vile Reef

...HLAS
eralas (46), F-1, Dream Bough, Roams
mall land mass

...HTENDRIS
eralas (46), G-4, Dire Maul

...INGTON MORTAIM
ortal Trainer, Undercity (88), L-2, The
agic Quarter, On Skull Building

...LORT
adlands (16), A-5, Kargath (116),
ower platform

...HUNTER
esolace (30), F-8, G-8, J-7, K-8,
annoroc Coven, Shadowbreak Ravine

...SPRITE
eadwind Pass (28), D:(6-8), E:(6, 8),
arazhan, Sleeping Gorge

...RARIAN MAE PALEDUST
xplorers' League, Ironforge (52), J-1,
all of Explorers, The Library

...ILLIN
are Spawn, Darkshore (24), G-4,
ashal'Aran, Lvl 14 Uncommon;
Wanders through ruins

...UTENANT BENEDICT
urotar (34), I-6, Tiragarde Keep,
eceiving room of castle

...UTENANT DOREN
tranglethorn Vale (74), D-1, Rebel
amp (124), Camp

...UTENANT FANGORE
edridge Mountains (62), K-4, Galardell
alley, Roams small area around spawn
oint

...UTENANT FARREN ORINELLE
illsbrad Foothills (48), F-6, Southshore
(29), First floor of inn

...UTENANT HAGGERDIN
lterac Mountains (8), E-8, The
eadland, Left camp outside Alterac
alley

...UTENANT JACKSPRING
Weapons QM, Stormwind (72), K-6

...UTENANT KARTER
Mount Vendor, Stormwind (72), K-6

...UTENANT ROTIMER
tormpike Guard Recruitment Officer,
ronforge (52), E-6, The Commons,
utside Bank

...UTENANT SANDERS
irisfal Glades (86), L-4, Venomweb
ale, Patrols an arc around camp

...EUTENANT TRISTIA
Armor QM, Stormwind (72), K-6

...EUTENANT VALORCALL
rathi Highlands (10), G-4, Dabyrie's
armstead, Patrols along road to
tromgarde Keep

...GHTNING HIDE
urotar (34), F:(2, 3), Thunder Ridge

...L TIMMY
oy with kittens, Stormwind (72),
athedral Square, The Canals, Roams
athedral Square and The Canals

...LADRIS MOONRIVER
shenvale (12), D-4, Maestra's Post,
Back porch of outpost

...LITH THE LITHE
Winterspring (98), I-4, Everlook (110),
Inside building directly north of inn

...LLIAM SPARKSPINDLE
xpert Engineer, Stormwind (72), H-1,
warven District, North end of district,
by tent

...LLITH NEFARA
Tirisfal Glades (86), I-4, Brightwater
Lake, (Summon) Spawns on small island
in the center of Brightwater Lake

...LLY
Enchanting Supplies, Silverpine Forest
(68), F-5, Camp

...LYN DARKRIVER
Ashenvale (12), C-5, Shrine of Aessina,
Roams north side of Shrine

...LYSSIA NIGHTBREEZE
Alchemist Trainer, Stormwind (72), G-8,
Mage Quarter, Alchemy Needs

...NA HEARTHSTOVE
Stable Master, Loch Modan (54), D-5,
Thelsamar (134), Outside of inn to the
left of entrance

...NA STOVER
Bow & Gun Merchant, Stormwind (72),
H-6, Trade District, The Empty Quiver

...INDEA RABONNE
Tackle and Bait, Hillsbrad Foothills (48),
F-6, Southshore (129), On docks in
front of shed

LINDROS
Azshara (14), H-9, The Ruined Reaches,
Inlet

LINDSAY ASHLOCK
General Supplies, Redridge Mountains
(62), C-5, Lakeshire (117), Next to
caravan in front of Lakeshire Town Hall

LINGERING HIGHBORNE
Azshara (14), D:(4-6), E-5, Ruins of
Eldarath, Temple of Zin-Malor

LINKEN
Un'Goro Crater (90), F-1, Marshal's
Refuge (118), South of cave, next to
hollowed out stump

LISAN PIERCE
Stormwind (72), F-8, Mage Quarter,
Roams and sits by tower

LISBETH SCHNEIDER
Clothier, Stormwind (72), G-5, The
Canals, Canal Tailor and Fit Shop

LISSYPHUS FINESPINDLE
Light Armor Merchant, Ironforge (52),
G-9, The Military Ward, Craghelm's
Plate and Chain

LIV RIZZLEFIX
Workshop Assistant, Barrens (18), H-4,
Ratchet (122), Building near dock

LIVING BLAZE
Un'Goro Crater (90), F:(5, 6), G:(4-6),
Fire Plume Ridge

LIVING DECAY
Eastern Plaguelands (40), G:(6, 7), H-6,
I-6, J-6, Pestilent Scar

LIVING STORM
Tanaris (78), E:(6, 8), F-7

LIZBETH CROMWELL
Fishing Supplier, Undercity (88), K-3,
The Magic Quarter, On Dock

LIZZARIK
Weapon Dealer, Barrens (18), G-4,
Ratchet (122), South of road

LLANA
Reagent Supplies, Ashenvale (12), E-5,
Astranaar (101), Northwest building
(north of road)

LLANE BESHERE
Warrior Trainer, Elwynn Forest (42), G-4,
Northshire Valley (122), Hall of Arms
of abbey

LO'GROSH
Rare Spawn, Alterac Mountains (8),
F-3, G-5, Crushridge Hold, Slaughter
Hollow, Lvl 39 Average Rare; Roams
small area around spawn point

LOCH CROCOLISK
Loch Modan (54), G:(2-6), H:(2-6), The
Loch

LOCH FRENZY
Loch Modan (54), E:(2, 3), F:(1-3),
G:(1-3), The Loch, In lake

LOCHEED
Searing Gorge (64), H-6, Grimesilt Dig
Site, Wooden outhouse

LOCKE OKARR
Ashenvale (12), I-6, Splintertree Post
(129), North of outlying watch tower
near road

LOGANAAR
Druid Trainer, Moonglade (56), G-4,
Nighthaven (121), Next to moonwell,
by northern section of lake

LOGANNAS
Alchemy Supplies, Feralas (46), C-4,
Feathermoon Stronghold (111), Bottom
floor of tree building in northeast

LOH'ATU
Azshara (14), A-8, Talrendis Point, Tent

LOHGAN EVA
Tailoring Supplies, Duskwood (36), K-4,
Darkshire (108), First floor of house

LOK ORCBANE
Barrens (18), D-8, Blackthorn Ridge,
Westernmost hut on ridges

LOKHTOS DARKBARGAINER
Burning Steppes (22), Searing Gorge
(64), C-4/D-8, Blackrock Depths

LOLO THE LOOKOUT
Arathi Highlands (10), D-8, Faldir's
Cove, Roams on hill opposite dock

LOMAC GEARSTRIP
Ironforge (52), J-5, Tinker Town,
Outside tram entrance

LONGBRAID THE GRIM
Wetlands (96), G-2, Dun Modr, Next to
wagons, west of road

LONGTOOTH HOWLER
Feralas (46), F-5, G-5, H:(5, 6), I:(5, 6)

LONGTOOTH RUNNER
Feralas (46), B:(4, 5), C-5, H:(4, 5),
I:(3-5), J:(4, 5), K:(4, 5)

**LOOKOUT CAPTAIN LOLO
LONGSTRIKER**
The Thorium Brotherhood, Searing
Gorge (64), D-3, Thorium Point (136),
Left of tower ramp

LOORANA
Food & Drink, Feralas (46), I-4, Camp
Mojache (105), East of inn

LORAMUS THALIPEDES
Azshara (14), H-7, Bay of Storms,
Southern end of island, near cave

LORAX
Winterspring (98), I-7, Frostwhisper
Gorge, Southeast of gorge

LORD ALEXEI BAROV
Western Plaguelands (92), I-7,
Scholomance

LORD ALIDEN PERENOLDE
Alterac Mountains (8), E-2, Dandred's
Fold, Second floor of house

LORD ANGLER
Rare Spawn, Dustwallow Marsh (38),
G-6, Tidefury Cove, Lvl 44 Average
Rare; Roams the cove

LORD ARKKOROC
Azshara (14), J-4, Temple of Arkkoran,
Top floor of temple above entrance

LORD AZRETHOC
Desolace (30), G-8, Mannoroc Coven,
Roams eastern clearing

LORD BANEHOLLOW
Felwood (44), E-6, Shadow Hold, Top
floor of the final area

LORD BAURLES K. WISHOCK
House of Nobles, Stormwind (72), K-3,
Stormwind Keep, Petitioner's Chamber

LORD CAPTAIN WYRMAK
Rare Spawn, Swamp of Sorrows (76),
H-4, Lvl 45 Uncommon; Patrols the
upper right portion of swampland
surrounding the Temple of Atal'Hakkar

LORD COBRAHN
Barrens (18), E-4, Wailing Caverns

LORD CONDAR
Rare Spawn, Loch Modan (54), H-8,
J-7, K-7, Ironband's Excavation Site,
The Farstrider Lodge (111), Lvl 15
Semi-Rare; Roams small area around
spawn point

LORD CYRIK BLACKFORGE
Barrens (18), E-8, Bael Modan, Landing
pad

LORD DARKSCYTHE
Rare Spawn, Eastern Plaguelands (40),
D-3, E:(3, 4), F-3, Plaguewood, Lvl 57
Average Rare; Roams small area around
spawn point

LORD ELLO EBONLOCKE
Mayor of Darkshire, Duskwood (36),
J-5, Darkshire (108), Darkshire Town
Hall

LORD FALCONCREST
Arathi Highlands (10), C-6, Stromgarde
Keep (132), Third floor castle

LORD GRAYSON SHADOWBREAKER
Paladin Trainer, Stormwind (72), F-3,
Cathedral Square, Cathedral of Light

LORD GREGOR LESCOVAR
Stormwind (72), K-1, Stormwind Keep,
Royal Library

LORD HEL'NURATH
Feralas (46), G-4, Dire Maul

LORD INCENDIUS
Burning Steppes (22), Searing Gorge
(64), C-4/D-8, Blackrock Depths

LORD JORACH RAVENHOLDT
Hillsbrad Foothills (48), K-2, Second
floor of Chateau Ravenholdt

LORD KAZZAK
Raid Boss, Blasted Lands (20), E-8,
The Tainted Scar, Roams medium area
around spawn point

LORD KRAGARU
Desolace (30), C-1, Ranzajar Isle,
Serpent Statue

LORD LAKMAERAN
Feralas (46), C-7, Isle of Dread, Roams
hill near Chimaeroks

LORD MALATHROM
Rare Spawn, Duskwood (36), C:(2, 3),
Dawning Wood Catacombs, Lvl 31
Uncommon; Roams small area around
spawn point

LORD MALDAZZAR
Rare Spawn, Western Plaguelands
(92), F-8, G:(7, 8), Sorrow Hill, Lvl 56
Uncommon; Roams small area around
spawn point

LORD MAXWELL TYROSUS
The Argent Dawn, Eastern Plaguelands
(40), K-6, Light's Hope Chapel (118),
Chapel

LORD MAYOR MORRISON
Pyrewood Council, Silverpine Forest
(68), G-7, Pyrewood Village, (Summon)
Spawns with Councilman Brunswick and
Councilman Cooper in town hall

LORD MELENAS
Teldrassil (80), G-5, Fel Rock, Ledge in
middle of cave

LORD PYTHAS
Barrens (18), E-4, Wailing Caverns

LORD ROCCOR
Rare Spawn, Burning Steppes (22),
Searing Gorge (64), C-4/D-8, Blackrock
Depths, Lvl 51 Rare

LORD SAKRASIS
Rare Spawn, Stranglethorn Vale (74),
B-6, Nek'Mani Wellspring, Lvl 45
Uncommon; Far end of bridge in front
of altar

LORD SERPENTIS
Barrens (18), E-4, Wailing Caverns

LORD SINSLAYER
Rare Spawn, Darkshore (24), H-3,
Cliffspring Falls, Lvl 15 Uncommon; In
caves

LORD TIRION FORDRING
Order of the Silver Hand, Western
Plaguelands (92), G-3, (Summon) Rides
in along path and fights elites

LORD TONY ROMANO
Rogue Trainer, Stormwind (72), L-6, Old
Town, SI:7

LORD VICTOR NEFARIUS
Burning Steppes (22), Searing Gorge
(64), C-4/D-8, Blackrock Spire

LORD VYLETONGUE
Desolace (30), D-5, Mauradon

LOREKEEPER JAVON
Feralas (46), G-4, Dire Maul

LOREKEEPER KILDRATH
Feralas (46), G-4, Dire Maul

LOREKEEPER LYDROS
Feralas (46), G-4, Dire Maul

LOREKEEPER MYKOS
Feralas (46), G-4, Dire Maul

LOREKEEPER POLKELT
Western Plaguelands (92), I-7,
Scholomance

LOREKEEPER RAINTOTEM
Mulgore (58), G-3, Red Rocks, Small
camp near tree

LORELAE WINTERSONG
Trade Supplies, Moonglade (56), G-4,
Nighthaven (121), Central building

LOREMASTER DIBBS
Hillsbrad Foothills (48), F-6, Southshore
(129), In front of small house

LORGUS JETT
Ashenvale (12), B-2, Blackfathom
Deeps

LORO
Swamp of Sorrows (76), I-5, The
Temple of Atal'Hakkar

LORUK FORESTSTRIDER
Ashenvale (12), I-6, Splintertree Post
(129), In entrance of northern caves

LOSLOR RUDGE
Engineering Supplies, Dun Morogh
(32), G-5, Steelgrill's Depot, In front of
barrels outside of right building

LOST BARRENS KODO
Barrens (18), D-2, E:(2-4), F:(1, 4, 5),
G:(2, 4)

LOST ONE CHIEFTAIN
Rare Spawn, Swamp of Sorrows
(76), H-2, Fallow Sanctuary, Lvl 39
Semi-Rare; Idle near huts in the
northwest corner of camp

LOST ONE COOK
Rare Spawn, Swamp of Sorrows
(76), H-2, Fallow Sanctuary, Lvl 37
Uncommon; Idle by one of the two
cauldrons in camp

LOST ONE FISHERMAN
Swamp of Sorrows (76), F:(3, 4), G-3,
H-3, Fallow Sanctuary

LOST ONE HUNTER
Swamp of Sorrows (76), G-3, H:(2, 3),
Fallow Sanctuary

LOST ONE MUCKDWELLER
Swamp of Sorrows (76), G-3, H:(2, 3),
I-2, Fallow Sanctuary

LOST ONE MUDLURKER
Swamp of Sorrows (76), F:(3, 4), G-3,
The Shifting Mire

LOST ONE RIFTSEEKER
Swamp of Sorrows (76), H:(2, 3), Fallow
Sanctuary

LOST ONE SEER
Swamp of Sorrows (76), H:(2, 3), Fallow
Sanctuary

LOST SOUL
Rare Spawn, Tirisfal Glades (86), F-4,
G-5, Agamand Mills (100), Lvl 6
Uncommon; Roams small area around
spawn point

LOST WHELP
Wetlands (96), H:(3-5), I:(4, 5),
Mosshide Fen, The Green Belt

LOTHERIAS
Darnassus (26), I-2 , Craftsmen's
Terrace, Leatherworking shop

LOTHOS RIFTWAKER
Burning Steppes (22), Searing Gorge
(64), C-4/D-8, The Molten Core

LOTWIL VERIATUS
Badlands (16), H-4, The Dustbowl,
Camp

LOUIS WARREN
Weapons Merchant, Undercity (88),
H-4, The Trade Quarter, Upper Ring of
Trade Quarter

LUCAN CORDELL
Expert Enchanter, Stormwind (72), F-6,
The Canals, Shop south of stockade

LUCIAN FENNER
Undercity (88), K-7, The Rogues'
Quarter, Near anvil and forge

LUCIEN SARKHOFF
Western Plaguelands (92), J-7, Caer
Darrow, Just outside of entrance to
Scholomance

LUCIEN TOSSELWRENCH
Badlands (16), H-4, The Dustbowl,
Camp

LUCIFRON
Burning Steppes (22), Searing Gorge
(64), C-4/D-8, The Molten Core

LUCILLE CASTLETON
Robe Vendor, Undercity (88), J-3, The
Magic Quarter

LUCIUS
Redridge Mountains (62), C-5,
Lakeshire (117), L-shaped dock west of
the bridge

LUI'MALA
Fisherman, Desolace (30), B-7,
Shadowprey Village (128), Dock

LUMAK
Fishing Trainer, Orgrimmar (60), I-3 ,
Valley of Honor, Lumak's Fishing

LUMBERJACK
Westfall (94), F-5, Sentinel Hill (126)

LUNACLAW
Darkshore (24), F-4

LUNNIX SPROCKETSLIP
Mining Supplies, Winterspring (98),
I-4, Everlook (110), Inside building east
of inn

LUPINE DELUSION
Silverpine Forest (68), F-7, Shadowfang
Keep

LUPINE HORROR
Silverpine Forest (68), F-7, Shadowfang
Keep

LUPOS
Rare Spawn, Duskwood (36), C-3, D-3,
E-3, H-3, I-3, J-3, Brightwood Grove,
The Darkened Bank, Lvl 23 Uncommon;
Roams small area around spawn point

LURKING FERAL SCAR
Feralas (46), F-5, (Summon) Appears in
ambush

LUTHER PICKMAN
Warlock Trainer, Undercity (88), L-2,
The Magic Quarter, Inside Skull Building

LYESA STEELBROW
Guild Tabard Vendor, Ironforge (52),
D-8, The Commons, Ironforge Visitor's
Center

LYLANDRIS
Warsong Gulch Battlemaster, Ironforge
(52), J-9, The Military Ward, Hall of
Arms

LYON MOUNTAINHEART
Ironforge (52), I-1, Hall of Explorers,
The Library

LYRAI
General Supplies, Teldrassil (80), H-4,
Shadowglen (127), Second level of
main building

LYRANNE FEATHERSONG
Food & Drink, Winterspring (98), H-3,
Starfall Village (130), North end of main
building

LYRIA DU LAC
Warrior Trainer, Elwynn Forest (42), E-7,Goldshire (114), Rear entrance of smith

LYRLIA BLACKSHIELD
Eye of the Storm BM, Undercity (88), H-9

LYSHEANA
Guild Master, Darnassus (26), I-2 , Craftsmen's Terrace, Southeast building, second floor

LYSTA BANCROFT
Undercity (88), G-2, The War Quarter, Watches fights in War Quarter

M

MA STONEFIELD
Elwynn Forest (42), D-8, The Stonefield Farm, In front of house

MABEL SOLAJ
General Goods Vendor, Duskwood (36), J-4, Darkshire (108), Scarlet Raven Tavern

MAD MAGGLISH
Barrens (18), E-4, The Wailing Caverns

MADAME EVA
Duskwood (36), K-4, Darkshire (108), First floor of house

MADISON
Redridge Mountains (62), C-5, Lake Everstill, Dock

MAETHRYA
Hippogryph Master, Wintersprinq (98), I-4, Everlook (110), Northeast of town

MAEVA SNOWBRAID
Robe Merchant, Ironforge (52), E-1, The Mystic Ward, Maeva's Mystical Apparel

MAGAR
Expert Tailor, Orgrimmar (60), H-5, The Drag, Magar's Cloth Goods

MAGATHA GRIMTOTEM
Thunder Bluff (84), I-3, Elder Rise, Inside tent on Elder Rise, guarded by Cor and Gorm Grimtotem

MAGE HUNTER
Desolace (30), G:(7, 8), H-7, Mannoroc Coven

MAGENIUS
Reagents Vendor, Orgrimmar (60), E-4, Valley of Wisdom, Asoran's Market

MAGGA
Durotar (34), F-7, Valley of Trials (136), Structure to south

MAGGOT EYE
Tirisfal Glades (86), H-3, Garren's Haunt, Shed at northern end of crop field

MAGGRAN EARTHBINDER
Stonetalon Mountains (70), F-6, Sun Rock Retreat (132), Outside inn

MAGINOR DUMAS
Master Mage, Stormwind (72), F-8, Mage Quarter, Wizard's Sanctum

MAGIS SPARKMANTLE
Mage Trainer, Dun Morogh (32), F-5, Kharanos (116), Thunderbrew Distillery

MAGISTER HAWKHELM
Rare Spawn, Azshara (14), G-3, Thalassian Base Camp, Lvl 52 Average Rare; Roams close to spawn points

MAGISTER KALENDRIS
Feralas (46), G-4, Dire Maul

MAGISTRATE BARTHILAS
Eastern Plaguelands (40), D-2, Stratholme

MAGISTRATE BLUNTNOSE
Loch Modan (54), D-4, Thelsamar (134), Outside of second house on left of path

MAGISTRATE BURNSIDE
Hillsbrad Foothills (48), C-4, Hillsbrad, Town hall

MAGISTRATE HENRY MALEB
Hillsbrad Foothills (48), E-6, Southshore (129), Southshore Town Hall

MAGISTRATE MARDUKE
Western Plaguelands (92), I-7, Scholomance, Ghost in throne room of pre-instance portion of Scholomance

MAGISTRATE SEVREN
Tirisfal Glades (86), H-5, Brill (104), Brill Town Hall

MAGISTRATE SOLOMON
Redridge Mountains (62), C-4, Lakeshire (117), Lakeshire Town Hall

MAGISTRIX ELOSAI
Thousand Needles (82), F-5, Freewind Post (112) (112)

MAGMA ELEMENTAL
Searing Gorge (64), B-5, C:(6, 7), D:(4, 6-8), E:(3-6), F:(5, 6), G:(4, 5, 7, 8), The Cauldron

MAGMADAR
Burning Steppes (22), Searing Gorge (64), C-4/D-8, The Molten Core

MAGMAKIN
Burning Steppes (22), Searing Gorge (64), C-4/D-8, The Molten Core

MAGMAR FELLHEW
Loch Modan (54), I-7, Ironband's Excavation Site, Camp outside of excavation site

MAGMUS
Burning Steppes (22), Searing Gorge (64), C-4/D-8, Blackrock Depths

MAGNUS FROSTWAKE
Western Plaguelands (92), I-8, Caer Darrow, Ghost in smithy

MAGOSH
Rare Spawn, Loch Modan (54), I-7, Ironband's Excavation Site, Lvl 21 Uncommon; With two Stonesplitter Diggers on hilltop in center excavation site

MAGRAM BONEPAW
Desolace (30), I:(7, 8), J-8, Magram Village

MAGRAM MARAUDER
Desolace (30), I:(7, 8), J:(7, 8), Magram Village

MAGRAM OUTRUNNER
Desolace (30), I:(7, 8), J:(6, 7), Magram Village

MAGRAM PACK RUNNER
Desolace (30), I:(7, 8), J-8, Magram Village

MAGRAM SCOUT
Desolace (30), I:(7, 8), J:(6, 7), Magram Village

MAGRAM STORMER
Desolace (30), I:(7, 8), J:(7, 8), Magram Village

MAGRAM WINDCHASER
Desolace (30), I:(7, 8), J:(6-8), Magram Village

MAGRAM WRANGLER
Desolace (30), I:(7, 8), J:(6-8), Magram Village

MAGRAMI SPECTRE
Desolace (30), H-9, I-9, Valley of Bones

MAGREGAN DEEPSHADOW
Badlands (16), G-1, Uldaman

MAGRIN RIVERMANE
Mulgore (58), E-6, Bloodhoof Village (102), Inn

MAGRONOS THE UNYIELDING
Rare Spawn, Blasted Lands (20), G-4, Dreadmaul Post, Lvl 56 Average Rare; Roams small area around spawn point

MAGTOOR
Swamp of Sorrows (76), C-3, The Harborage, Idle in draenei camp

MAGUS RIMTORI
Azshara (14), G-3, Thalassian Base Camp, East of the base camp

MAGUS TIRTH
Thousand Needles (82), K-8, Mirage Raceway (119), West grandstands

MAGUS WORDEEN VOIDGLARE
Hillsbrad Foothills (48), G-2, Tarren Mill (133), House on the right

MAHANI
Expert Tailor, Barrens (18), F-6, Camp Taurajo (106), Southern building

MAHNOTT ROUGHWOUND
Weaponsmith, Mulgore (58), E-6, Bloodhoof Village (102), Northeast tent

MAHREN SKYSEER
Barrens (18), H-4, The Tidus Stair, Outside hut

MAHU
Leatherworking & Tailoring Supplies, Thunder Bluff (84), E-4, Middle rise, inside Thunder Bluff Armorers tent

MAI'AH
Mage Trainer, Durotar (34), F-7, Valley of Trials (136), Structure to south

MAIDEN'S VIRTUE CREWMAN
Wetlands (96), A-6, Baradin Bay, Menethil Harbor (119)

MAI'LAHII
Fishing Supplies, Desolace (30), B-7, Shadowprey Village (128), Down by dock

MAI'ZOTH
Stranglethorn Vale (74), F-3, Mosh'Ogg Ogre Mound, Idle with several ogres in the rear of cave

MAJOR MATTINGLY
Stormwind (72), I-8, Stormwind City, Southwest of statue at entrance

MAJOR SAMUELSON
Stormwind City Guard, Stormwind (72), K-2, Stormwind Keep, East wing, north room

MAJORDOMO EXECUTUS
Burning Steppes (22), Searing Gorge (64), C-4/D-8, The Molten Core

MAK
Journeyman Leatherworker, Thunder Bluff (84), D-4, Middle rise, inside Thunder Bluff Armorers tent

MAKABA FLATHOOF
Barrens (18), D-3, Camp at Stonetalon border

MAKARU
Mining Trainer, Orgrimmar (60), I-3, Valley of Honor, Red Canyon Mining

MAKASGAR
Durotar (34), I-7, Darkspear Strand, Coast of northernmost edge of strand

MAKRINNI RAZORCLAW
Azshara (14), E-9, F:(7, 9), G:(7, 9), H:(7-9), I:(7-9), K:(8, 9)

MAKRINNI SCRABBLER
Azshara (14), G-4, H:(3, 4), I-4, J-5, K:(3, 4), L:(2-4)

MAKRINNI SNAPCLAW
Azshara (14), E:(1, 2), F:(1, 2), G-1, H-1, I-1, J-1, K:(1, 2), L:(1, 2), Jagged Reef

MAKRURA CLACKER
Durotar (34), H-8, I:(4-9), J:(5-9), K-7, Darkspear Strand, Echo Isles, Scuttle Coast

MAKRURA ELDER
Durotar (34), I:(1-4), Bladefist Bay

MAKRURA SHELLHIDE
Durotar (34), H-8, I:(4-9), J:(5-9), K-7, Darkspear Strand, Echo Isles, Scuttle Coast

MAKRURA SNAPCLAW
Durotar (34), I:(1-4), Bladefist Bay, Deadeye Shore, Scuttle Coast

MALAKAI CROSS
Priest Trainer, Thunder Bluff (84), B-2, Spirit Rise, The Pools of Vision

MALCOMB WYNN
Apprentice Enchanter, Undercity (88), H-6, The Apothecarium, Near Rogues' Quarter entry

MALDRYN
Druid Trainer, Stormwind (72), C-5, The Park, By pool of water

MALEKI THE PALLID
Eastern Plaguelands (40), D-2, Stratholme

MALFORMED DEFIAS DRONE
Westfall (94), H-7, Circles tower

MALFUNCTIONING REAVER
Rare Spawn, Burning Steppes (22), J-3, K:(3, 6), L-5, Dreadmaul Rock, Terror Wing Path, Lvl 56 Semi-Rare; Roams small area around spawn point

MALGIN BARLEYBREW
Bael'dun Morale Officer, Barrens (18), F-8, Bael'dun Keep, Back of right wing

MALICIOUS SPIRIT
Western Plaguelands (92), I-7, Scholomance

MALISSA
Poison Supplier, Duskwood (36), K-4, Darkshire (108), Outside the first house on right side of road heading into Darkshire from the east

MALIYNN
Food & Drink Vendor, Ashenvale (12), E-5, Astranaar (101), First floor of inn

MALLEN SWAIN
Tailoring Supplies, Hillsbrad Foothills (48), G-2, Tarren Mill (133), Roams near well

MALOR THE ZEALOUS
Eastern Plaguelands (40), D-2, Stratholme

MALORNE BLADELEAF
Herbalist, Teldrassil (80), G-6, Dolanaar (109), Inside house east of inn

MALOSH
Warrior Trainer, Swamp of Sorrows (76), F-5, Stonard (131), First floor of inn

MALTON DROFFERS
Droffer and Sons Salvage, Orgrimmar (60), G-4, The Drag, Droffer and Sons Salvage

MALURESSIAN
Stable Master, Ashenvale (12), E-5, Astranaar (101), Entrance of inn across from mailbox

MALUX
Skinning Trainer, Desolace (30), B-7, Shadowprey Village (128), Landing of western structure

MALVOR
Herbalist, Moonglade (56), F-5, Nighthaven (121), Small house next to a moonwell, north of western section of lake

MALYFOUS DARKHAMMER
The Thorium Brotherhood, Wintersprinq (98), I-4, Everlook (110), West of inn, near south wall

MALYGEN
General Goods, Felwood (44), I-3, Talonbranch Glade (133), Behind building near gazebo

MANA BURST
Feralas (46), G-4, Dire Maul

MANA EATER
Desolace (30), G-7, Mannoroc Coven

MANA REMNANT
Feralas (46), G-4, Dire Maul

MANA SPRITE
Deadwind Pass (28), D:(6-8), E:(6, 8), Karazhan, Sleeping Gorge

MANA SURGE
Dustwallow Marsh (38), F-6, The Quagmire

MANACLAW
Wintersprinq (98), H-5, Mazthoril, Deep in caverns

MANAHOUND
Blasted Lands (20), E:(5, 6), F:(6-8), G-7, H-6, I-6, Dark Portal, The Tainted Scar

MANGECLAW
Dun Morogh (32), K-4, North Gate Outpost, Top of a deadend hill on the left side of the outpost

MANGLED CADAVER
Eastern Plaguelands (40), D-2, Stratholme

MANGLETOOTH
Barrens (18), F-6, Camp Taurajo (106), Cage near west entrance

MANGORN FLINTHAMMER
Heavy Armor Merchant, Ironforge (52), D-6, The Commons, Ironforge Armory

MANGY DUSKBAT
Tirisfal Glades (86), D:(6, 7), Deathknell (109)

MANGY MOUNTAIN BOAR
Loch Modan (54), D-6, E:(5, 6), F:(6, 7), G:(6, 7), H:(5, 6), I:(5-7), J:(5, 7), K-7, Ironband's Excavation Site

MANGY NIGHTSABER
Teldrassil (80), H:(3, 4), Shadowglen (127)

MANGY SILVERMANE
The Hinterlands (50), B-5, C:(5, 6), D-5, The Hinterlands

MANGY WOLF
Elwynn Forest (42), B:(7, 8), C:(7, 8), D:(6-8), E:(6, 7), F:(5-7), G:(6, 7), H:(6, 7)

MANI WINTERHOOF
Alchemy Supplies, Thunder Bluff (84), E-3, Middle rise, inside Bena's Alchemy tent

MANIFESTATION OF WATER
Barrens (18), H-4, The Tidus Stair, (Summon)

MANKRIK
Barrens (18), F-3, The Crossroads (107), Southern entrance

MANNOROC LASHER
Ashenvale (12), J:(6-8), K:(6, 7), Demon Fall Canyon, Felfire Hill, Nightsong Woods

MAQUELL EBONWOOD
Tirisfal Glades (86), D-6, Deathknell (109), Roams from Church to Inn

MARANDIS' SISTER
Desolace (30), C-8, H-1, Nijel's Point (121), Sar'theris Strand

MARAUDINE BONEPAW
Desolace (30), E-6, Valley of Spears

MARAUDINE KHAN ADVISOR
Desolace (30), C-5, Valley of Spears

MARAUDINE MARAUDER
Desolace (30), C:(5, 6), D:(5, 6), Maraudon, Valley of Spears

MARAUDINE MAULER
Desolace (30), C:(5, 6), D:(5, 6), Maraudon, Valley of Spears

MARAUDINE PRIEST
Desolace (30), D-5, Mauradon

MARAUDINE SCOUT
Desolace (30), C:(6, 7), D:(5-7), E-6, Maraudon, Valley of Spears

MARAUDINE STORMER
Desolace (30), C:(5, 6), D-5, Maraudon, Valley of Spears

MARAUDINE WINDCHASER
Desolace (30), C:(5, 6), D:(5, 6), Maraudon, Valley of Spears

MARAUDINE WRANGLER
Desolace (30), C:(6, 7), D:(5-7), E-6, Maraudon, Valley of Spears

MARAUDING CORPSE
Eastern Plaguelands (40), E-8, Darrowshire

MARAUDING OWLBEAST
The Hinterlands (50), I-5, The Hinterlands

MARAUDING SKELETON
Eastern Plaguelands (40), E-8, Darrowshire

MARCEL DABYRIE
Arathi Highlands (10), G-4, Dabyrie's Farmstead, Roams in stable

MARCUS BEL
Alliance Outrunner, Barrens (18), F-8, Southern Barrens, Spawns at border to Dustwallow Marsh and travels north to Lushwater Oasis

MARDA WELLER
Weapons Merchant, Stormwind (72), H-6, Trade District, Weller's Arsenal

MARDANT STRONGOAK
Druid Trainer, Teldrassil (80), G-4, Shadowglen (127), First room off of ramp up tree

MARDRACK GREENWELL
Food & Drink, Feralas (46), C-4, Feathermoon Stronghold (111), Inn

MARDUK BLACKPOOL
Western Plaguelands (92), I-7, Scholomance

MAREK IRONHEART
Loch Modan (54), K-6, The Farstrider Lodge (111), In right hall of lodge

MAREZ COWL
Arathi Highlands (10), D:(5, 6), Stromgarde Keep (132), Roams in Stromgarde Keep

MARGOL THE RAGER
Searing Gorge (64), I-8, Patrols the canyons around cave

MARGOZ
Durotar (34), H-2, Tent

MARIA LUMERE
Alchemy Supplies, Stormwind (72), G-8, Mage Quarter, Alchemy Need

MARIE HOLDSTON
Weaponsmith, Dustwallow Marsh (38), I-5, Theramore Isle (135), Blacksmithing hut to west

MARIN NOGGENFOGGER
Tanaris (78), H-3, Gadgetzan (113), Outside entrance to Auction House

MARION CALL
Rogue Trainer, Tirisfal Glades (86), H-5, Brill (104), Second floor of Gallows' End Tavern

MARIS GRANGER
Skinning Trainer, Stormwind (72), J-5, Old Town, The Protective Hide

MARISA DU'PAIGE
Westfall (94), D-7, E-7, The Deadmines

MARJAK KEENBLADE
Weaponsmith, Mulgore (58), E-8, Camp Narache (105), Southwest tent

MARK OF DETONATION
Eastern Plaguelands (40), C-2, D:(3, 4), E:(2, 4), F-3, Plaguewood

MARKEL SMYTHE
Stranglethorn Vale (74), B-8, Booty Bay (103)

MARLA FOWLER
Undercity (88), G-2, The War Quarter, Watches fights in War Quarter

MARLENE REDPATH
Western Plaguelands (92), F-8, Sorrow Hill, Roams inside house on western side of graveyard

MARLETH BARLEYBREW
Dun Morogh (32), D-4, Brewnall Village, Under scaffolding

MARLI WISHRUNNER
Feralas (46), C-2, The Twin Colossals, Off road near western colossal

MARRYK NURRIBIT
Mage Trainer, Dun Morogh (32), D-7, Coldridge Valley (107), Back room of Anvilmar (first floor)

MARSH FLESHEATER
Swamp of Sorrows (76), H:(7, 8), I:(7-9), K:(7, 8), L:(2, 3, 5-7), Misty Reed Strand

MARSH INKSPEWER
Swamp of Sorrows (76), H:(7, 8), I:(7-9), K:(7-9), L:(5-7), Misty Reed Strand

MARSH MURLOC
Swamp of Sorrows (76), K:(8, 9), Misty Reed Strand

MARSH ORACLE
Swamp of Sorrows (76), H-8, L:(2, 3, 5-7), Misty Reed Strand

MARSHAL DUGHAN
Elwynn Forest (42), E-7,Goldshire (114), In front of smithy

MARSHAL HAGGARD
Elwynn Forest (42), L-7, Eastvale Logging Camp, Under lantern post in front of house

MARSHAL MARRIS
Redridge Mountains (62), D-5, Lakeshire (117), In Lakeshire just right of bridge

MARSHAL MAXWELL
Burning Steppes (22), K-7, Morgan's Vigil (120), Adjacent to camp entrance

MARSHAL MCBRIDE
Elwynn Forest (42), F-4, Northshire Valley (122), In hallway just inside abbey

MARSHAL REDPATH
Hillsbrad Foothills (48), F-6, Southshore (129), Right of Southshore Town Hall

MARSHAL REGINALD WINDSOR
Burning Steppes (22), Searing Gorge (64), C-4/D-8, Blackrock Depths

MARTEK THE EXILED
Badlands (16), F-5, Valley of Fangs, Camp

MARTHA ALLIESTAR
Herbalism Trainer, Undercity (88), G-5, The Apothecarium, Near War Quarter entry

MARTHA STRAIN
Demon Trainer, Undercity (88), L-2, The Magic Quarter, Inside Skull Building

MARTHA STRAIN
Tirisfal Glades (86), D-6, Deathknell (109)

MARTIE JAINROSE
Redridge Mountains (62), B-4, Lakeshire (117), Outside small house on southwestern side of town

MARTIN LINDSEY
Arathi Basin Battlemaster, Thunder Bluff (85), G-8

MARTINE TRAMBLAY
Fishing Supplies, Tirisfal Glades (86), I-6, By wagon at fork in road

MA'RUK WYRMSCALE
Rare Spawn, Wetlands (96), G-7, Dun Algaz, Lvl 25 Uncommon; Patrols water south of windmill

MARUKAI
Ashenvale (12), B-4, Zoram'gar Outpost (137), Southern structure

MARVON RIVETSEEKER
Tanaris (78), H-5, Broken Pillar, In west corner

MARY EDRAS
First Aid Trainer, Undercity (88), J-5, The Rogues' Quarter, Directly across from Skull Building

MASAT T'ANDR
Superior Leatherworker, Swamp of Sorrows (76), C-3, The Harborage, Idle in draenei camp

MASTER APOTHECARY FARANELL
Undercity (88), G-7, The Apothecarium, In laboratory

MASTER DIGGER
Rare Spawn, Westfall (94), E-2, Jangolode Mine, Lvl 15 Uncommon; In back of mine

MASTER FEARDRED
Rare Spawn, Azshara (14), H:(2-3), Legash Encampment, Lvl 51 Average Rare

MASTER GADRIN
Durotar (34), H-7, Sen'jin Village (126), Center pond

MASTER KANG
Hillsbrad Foothills (48), J-2, Next to sparing ring right of Chateau Ravenholdt

MASTER MATHIAS SHAW
Leader of SI:7, Stormwind (72), K-6, Old Town, SI:7

MASTER MECHANIC CASTPIPE
Ironforge (52), J-5, Tinker Town, Outside tram entrance

MASTER PYREANOR
Paladin trainer, Orgrimmar (61), D-4

MASTER SERGEANT BIGGINS
Officeer Accessories QM, Stormwind (72), K-6

MASTER SMITH BURNINATE
The Thorium Brotherhood, Searing Gorge (64), D-3, Thorium Point (136), Right side of camp next to the forge

MASTER VORNAL
Durotar (34), H-7, Sen'jin Village (126), Center pond

MASTER WOOD
Stormwind (72), I-5, Old Town, Command Center

MASTOK WRILEHISS
Ashenvale (12), I-6, Splintertree Post (129), Between cave entrance and inn

MATERO ZESHUWAL
Demon Trainer, Barrens (18), H-3, Ratchet (122)

MATHIEL
Darnassus (26), H-4, Warrior's Terrace, Lower southwest platform

MATHREDIS FIRESTAR
Burning Steppes (22), H-2, Flame Crest (112), Right of scaffolding

MATHRENGYL BEARWALKER
Druid Trainer, Darnassus (26), D-1, Cenarion Enclave, Northwest structure, on balcony

MATT JOHNSON
Mining Trainer, Duskwood (36), J-5, Darkshire (108), Outside to the rear of smithy

MATTHEW HOOPER
Fishing Trainer, Redridge Mountains (62), C-5, Lakeshire (117), Straight dock west of the bridge

MATTIE ALRED
Undercity (88), G-3, The War Quarter, Wanders Canals and War Quarter

MAUR GRIMTOTEM
Orgrimmar (60), F-5, Ragefire Chasm

MAUR RAINCALLER
Mulgore (58), E-6, Bloodhoof Village (102), North part of camp

MAURIN BONESPLITTER
Desolace (30), G-5, Ghost Walker Post (113), Northern plateau

MAURY "CLUB FOOT" WILKINS
Stranglethorn Vale (74), C-5, Ruins of Jubuwal, Ruins near camp

MAVORIS CLOUDSBREAK
Ashenvale (12), J-7, Dor'Danil Barrow Den, Deep within den in a side passage

MAVRALYN
Leather Armor & Leatherworking Supplies, Darkshore (24), F-4, Auberdine (101), Left wing of northern building

MAX LUNA
Arena Battlemaster, Tanaris (78), H-3, Gadgetzan (113)

MAXAN ANVOL
Priest Trainer, Dun Morogh (32), F-5, Kharanos (116), Thunderbrew Distillery

MAXIMILLIAN CROWE
Warlock Trainer, Elwynn Forest (42), F-7,Goldshire (114), Basement of Lion's Pride Inn

MAXIMILLION
Warlock Trainer, Tirisfal Glades (86), D-6, Deathknell (109), Church

MAXTON STRANG
Mail Armor Merchant, Desolace (30), I-1, Nijel's Point (121), Northwestern ruins

MAXWORT UBERGLINT
Burning Steppes (22), H-2, Flame Crest (112), Under scaffolding

MAYARA BRIGHTWING
Burning Steppes (22), K-7, Morgan's Vigil (120), Adjacent to camp entrance

MAYBELL MACLURE
Elwynn Forest (42), F-9, The Maclure Vineyards, House

MAYBESS RIVERBREEZE
Emerald Circle, Felwood (44), F-8, Near a pool west of the road

MAYDA THANE
Cobbler, Stormwind (72), J-4, Old Town, Thane's Boots

MAYWIKI OF ZULDAZAR
Stranglethorn Vale (74), A-2, Yojamba Isle

MAZEN MAC'NADIR
Academy of Arcane Arts and Sciences, Stormwind (72), F-6, The Canals, Building South of Stockade

MAZK SNIPESHOT
Engineering Supplies, Stranglethorn Vale (74), B-8, Booty Bay (103), Boomstick Imports East (shop) on the southern side of The Old Port Authority

MAZZRANACHE
Mulgore (58), C-4, Roams across Mulgore to the eastern hills and back

MCGAVAN
The Mithril Order, Stranglethorn Vale (74), C-8, Booty Bay (103), In front of forge outside of Booty Bay Blacksmith

ME'LYNN
Expert Tailor, Darnassus (26), H-2, Craftsmen's Terrace, Tailoring shop

MEBOK MIZZYRIX
Barrens (18), H-4, Ratchet (122), Outside Ironzar's Imported Weaponry

MECHANICAL GUARDIAN
Dun Morogh (32), C-4, Gnomeregan

MECHANICAL SENTRY
Dun Morogh (32), C-4, Gnomeregan

MECHANO-FLAMEWALKER
Dun Morogh (32), C-4, Gnomeregan

MECHANO-FROSTWALKER
Dun Morogh (32), C-4, Gnomeregan

MECHANO-TANK
Dun Morogh (32), C-4, Gnomeregan

MEDIC HELAINA
Dustwallow Marsh (38), I-5, Theramore Isle (135), Sparring grounds to northeast

MEDIC TAMBERLYN
Dustwallow Marsh (38), I-5, Theramore Isle (135), Sparring grounds to northeast

MEELA DAWNSTRIDER
Shaman Trainer, Mulgore (58), E-8, Camp Narache (105), North tent

MEGGI PEPPINROCKER
Winterspring (98), I-4, Everlook (110), Roams town

MEILOSH
Felwood (44), I-1, Timbermaw Hold, Central intersection

MEKGINEER THERMAPLUGG
Dun Morogh (32), C-4, Gnomeregan

MEHLAR DAWNBLADE
Tirisfal Glades (86), K-7, The Bulwark (105) (105)

MELARITH
Teldrassil (80), G-6, Dolanaar (109), Inn

MELEA
Mail Armor Merchant, Darnassus (26), H-7, Tradesmen's Terrace, Mail Armor shop

MELIA
Western Plaguelands (92), I-8, Caer Darrow, Ghost By fountain

MELIKA ISENSTRIDER
Assistant Innkeeper, Elwynn Forest (42), F-7,Goldshire (114), First floor of Lion's Pride Inn

MELIRI
Weaponsmith, Moonglade (56), G-4, Nighthaven (121), Just inside southeast building

MELISARA
Hillsbrad Foothills (48), H-2, Tarren Mill (133), Right of church

MELITHAR STAGHELM
Teldrassil (80), H-4, Shadowglen (127), On steps leading to main building

MELIZZA BRIMBUZZLE
Desolace (30), D-5, Valley of Spears, Caged outside of large hut

MELOR STONEHOOF
Thunder Bluff (84), G-8, Hunter Rise, In front of Hunter's Hall

MELRIS MALAGAN
Captain of the Guard, Stormwind (72), H-6, Trade District, Next to tree

MENARA VOIDRENDER
Barrens (18), H-3, Ratchet (122), Tower in eastern hills

MENETHIL SENTRY
Wetlands (96), A:(5, 6), Baradin Bay, Menethil Bay, Menethil Harbor (119)

MENNET CARKAD
Undercity (88), L-7, The Rogues' Quarter, In front of Skull Building

MERCUTIO FILTHGORGER
Eastern Plaguelands (40), D-8, The Undercroft, (Summon) Behind crypt by carriage

MERELYSSA
Blade Merchant, Darnassus (26), I-6, Tradesmen's Terrace, Weapons shop

MERI IRONWEAVE
Armorer & Shieldcrafter, Teldrassil (80), G-6, Dolanaar (109), Inn

MERIDETH CARLSON
Horse Breeder, Hillsbrad Foothills (48), F-6, Southshore (129), Stable

MERILL PLEASANCE
Tabard Vendor, Undercity (88), I-4, The Trade Quarter, East spoke from bank

MERISSA STILWELL
Elwynn Forest (42), F-4, Northshire Valley (122), Caravan facing abbey

MERRIN ROCKWEAVER
Wetlands (96), E-5, Whelgar's Excavation Site, Den across the bridge in east section of site

MESA BUZZARD
Arathi Highlands (10), B-5, D:(5, 6), E:(2-4, 6, 7), F-3, G-7, H:(6, 7)

MESA EARTH SPIRIT
Mulgore (58), F-8, Kodo Rock, (Summon) Earth side of rock

MESHLOK THE HARVESTER
Rare Spawn, Desolace (30), D-5, Mauradon, Lvl 48 Rare

MEVEN KORGAL
Tirisfal Glades (86), D-7, Deathknell (109), In front of tent

MEZZIR THE HOWLER
Rare Spawn, Winterspring (98), E-4, Frostfire Hot Springs, Lvl 55 Uncommon; Roams to the west

MIAO'ZAN
Alchemist Trainer, Durotar (34), H-7, Sen'jin Village (126), Northwest structure

MIBLON SNARLTOOTH
Feralas (46), E-1, Ruins of Ravenwind, Steps of ruins

MICHA YANCE
Trade Goods, Hillsbrad Foothills (48), F-5, Southshore (129), First floor of house

MICHAEL
Stable Master, Dustwallow Marsh (38), I-5, Theramore Isle (135), Outside inn to north

MICHAEL GARRETT
Bat Handler, Undercity (88), I-5, The Trade Quarter, Upper Ring of Trade Quarter

MICHELLE BELLE
Physician, Elwynn Forest (42), F-7,Goldshire (114), Second floor of Lion's Pride Inn

MICKEY LEVINE
Tirisfal Glades (86), K-7, The Bulwark (105), Camp on right side of road

MICKEY LEVINE
Western Plaguelands (92), C-6, The Bulwark (105)

MIJAN
Swamp of Sorrows (76), I-5, The Temple of Atal'Hakkar

MIKAL PIERCE
Dustwallow Marsh (38), I-5, Theramore Isle (135), 2nd floor of inn

MIKE MILLER
Bread Merchant, Westfall (94), G-5, Sentinel Hill (126), At intersection east of the Sentinel Tower

MIKEY
Stormwind (72), Roams city with Miss Danna

MIKHAIL
Bartender, Wetlands (96), A-6, Deepwater Tavern, Near bar

MILES DEXTER
Rogue Trainer, Undercity (88), L-7, The Rogues' Quarter, Inside Skull Building

MILES WELSH
Priest Trainer, Thunder Bluff (84), B-2, Spirit Rise, The Pools of Vision

MILLA FAIRANCORA
Alchemist Trainer, Darnassus (26), G-2, Craftsmen's Terrace, Alchemy shop

MILLI FEATHERWHISTLE
Mechanostrider Merchant, Dun Morogh (32), G-5, Steelgrill's Depot, By mechanostrider's outside of depot

MILLIE GREGORIAN
Tailoring Supplies, Undercity (88), J-3, The Magic Quarter

MILLY OSWORTH
Elwynn Forest (42), G-4, Northshire Valley (122), Next to carriage near the abbey stable

MILSTAFF STORMEYE
Portal Trainer, Ironforge (52), C-1, The Mystic Ward, Hall of Mysteries

MILTON BEATS
Giver of the Beatings, Hillsbrad Foothills (48), J-2, Cave leading to Chateau Ravenholdt

MILTON SHEAF
Librarian, Stormwind (72), K-1, Stormwind Keep, Royal Library

MINDLESS SKELETON
Eastern Plaguelands (40), D-2, Stratholme

MINDLESS UNDEAD
Eastern Plaguelands (40), D-2, Stratholme

MINDLESS ZOMBIE
Tirisfal Glades (86), C-6, D-6, Deathknell (109)

MINER HACKETT
Hillsbrad Foothills (48), C:(5, 6), Azurelode Mine, (Random spawn)

MINER JOHNSON
Westfall (94), D-7, E-7, The Deadmines

MINION OF MORGANTH
Morganth's Guardian, Redridge Mountains (62), K-5, Tower of Ilgalar, (Summon) Summoned by Morganth during boss encounter

MINION OF SETHIR
Teldrassil (80), D-2, The Oracle Glade, North of the glade on tree branches

MINOR MANIFESTATION OF AIR
Thousand Needles (82), H-5, Within rock pattern atop plateau

MINOR MANIFESTATION OF EARTH
Durotar (34), G-7, Spirit Rock

MINOR MANIFESTATION OF FIRE
Durotar (34), F-6, Shrine of the Dormant Flame

MINOR MANIFESTATION OF WATER
Silverpine Forest (68), F-4, The Tides Run, Coast of pond

MIRADOR
Eastern Plaguelands (40), A-4, Thondroril River, Roams by house on banks of Thondroril River

MIRAN
Loch Modan (54), G-7, The Loch, Next to dynamite filled carriage at the southern end of loch

MIRE LORD
Swamp of Sorrows (76), A-3, Misty Valley, Cave

MIREFIN COASTRUNNER
Dustwallow Marsh (38), G:(1, 2), H:(1-3), I-3, Dreadmurk Shore

MIREFIN MUCKDWELLER
Dustwallow Marsh (38), G:(1, 2), H:(1-3), I-3, Dreadmurk Shore

MIREFIN MURLOC
Dustwallow Marsh (38), G-2, H-2, Dreadmurk Shore

MIREFIN ORACLE
Dustwallow Marsh (38), G-1, H:(1-3), I-3, Dreadmurk Shore

MIREFIN PUDDLEJUMPER
Dustwallow Marsh (38), G-2, H-2, Dreadmurk Shore

MIREFIN WARRIOR
Dustwallow Marsh (38), G-1, H:(1-3), I-3, Dreadmurk Shore

MIRELLE TREMAYNE
Heavy Armor Merchant, Undercity (88), H-3, The War Quarter

MIRELOW
Rare Spawn, Wetlands (96), B:(3, 4), C:(2-4), Bluegill Marsh, Sundown Marsh, Lvl 25 Semi-Rare; Patrols water west and south of windmill and around bluegill camps

MIRKET
Warlock Trainer, Orgrimmar (60), F-5, The Cleft of Shadow, Darkfire Enclave

MISHA
Desolace (30), G-1, Spawns on road near Stonetalon border and patrols roads with Rexxar

MISHA TOR'KREN
Durotar (34), G-3, Tor'kren Farm, Farmhouse

MISHELLENA
Hippogryph Master, Felwood (44), H-3, Talonbranch Glade (133), North of building

MISHIKI
Herbalist, Durotar (34), H-7, Sen'jin Village (126), West structure

MISHTA General Trade Goods Vendor, Silithus (67), G-5, Cenarion Hold (106)

MISS DANNA School Mistress, Stormwind (72), Roams city

MIST Teldrassil (80), C-3, The Oracle Glade, West of glade

MIST CREEPER Silverpine Forest (68), E-1, The Skittering Dark, Cave

MIST HOWLER Rare Spawn, Ashenvale (12), C:(2-3), D-1, Lvl 22 Semi-Rare; Roams forest near spawn points

MISTINA STEELSHIELD Alliance Cloth Quartermaster, Ironforge (52), F-3, The Great Forge, Outside Stonebrow's Clothier

MISTRESS NAGMARA Burning Steppes (22), Searing Gorge (64), C-4/D-8, Blackrock Depths

MISTVALE GORILLA Stranglethorn Vale (74), D-2, Lake Nazferiti

MISTWING RAVAGER Azshara (14), H:(2, 3), I:(2, 3), J:(1-3), K:(2, 3), Bitter Reaches, Thalassian Base Camp, The Shattered Strand

MISTWING ROGUE Azshara (14), A-8, B-8, C-8, D:(7, 8), E-7, Forlorn Ridge, Lake Mennar, Ruins of Eldarath

MITHRAS IRONHILL Stormwind (72), K-1, Stormwind Keep, War Room

MITH'RETHIS THE ENCHANTER Rare Spawn, The Hinterlands (50), I-8, J-8, Jintha'Alor, Lvl 52 Average Rare; Roams from camp to camp

MITSUWA Ashenvale (12), B-4, Zoram'gar Outpost (137), Southern structure

MIZZLE THE CRAFTY Feralas (46), G-4, Dire Maul

MOBILE ALERT SYSTEM Dun Morogh (32), C-4, Gnomeregan

MOGG Barrens (18), E-1, Roams in and out of building west of road

MOGH THE UNDYING Skullsplitter Clan Witchdoctor, Stranglethorn Vale (74), E-5, Ruins of Zul'Mamwe, By campfire

MO'GROSH BRUTE Loch Modan (54), I-2, J:(1-3), K:(1, 2), Mo'grosh Stronghold

MO'GROSH ENFORCER Loch Modan (54), H:(2, 3), I:(2, 3), J:(2, 3), Mo'grosh Stronghold

MO'GROSH MYSTIC Loch Modan (54), I-2, J:(1-3), K-2, Mo'grosh Stronghold

MO'GROSH OGRE Loch Modan (54), H:(2, 3), I:(2, 3), J:(2, 3), Mo'grosh Stronghold

MO'GROSH SHAMAN Loch Modan (54), H:(2, 3), I:(2, 3), J:(2, 3), Mo'grosh Stronghold

MOJO THE TWISTED Rare Spawn, Blasted Lands (20), F-1, G-2, Dreadmaul Hold, Lvl 48 Uncommon; Roams small area around spawn point

MOKK THE SAVAGE Stranglethorn Vale (74), C-7, Mistvale Valley, (Summon) Spawns in with several gorillas

MOK'RASH Stranglethorn Vale (74), B-7, Janeiro's Point, Southern end of island

MOKTAR KRIN Thousand Needles (82), I-6, Ironstone Camp, Camp just west of Shimmering Flats

MOLOK THE CRUSHER Rare Spawn, Arathi Highlands (10), G-8, Boulderfist Hall, Lvl 39 Semi-Rare; Westernmost point in cave

MOLT THORN Rare Spawn, Swamp of Sorrows (76), C-5, D-4, The Shifting Mire, Lvl 42 Average Rare; Patrols back and forth between connecting bridges along the western waterways

MOLTEN DESTROYER Burning Steppes (22), Searing Gorge (64), C-4/D-8, The Molten Core

MOLTEN ELEMENTAL Orgrimmar (60), F-5, Ragefire Chasm

MOLTEN GIANT Burning Steppes (22), Searing Gorge (64), C-4/D-8, The Molten Core

MOLTEN WAR GOLEM Burning Steppes (22), Searing Gorge (64), C-4/D-8, Blackrock Depths

MONGRESS Rare Spawn, Felwood (44), F:(7-8), Lvl 50 Very Rare; Roams near spawn points

MONIKA SENGUTZ Hillsbrad Foothills (48), H-2, Tarren Mill (133), First floor of inn

MONNOS THE ELDER Rare Spawn, Azshara (14), H-9, K-2, Bitter Reaches, Lvl 54 Uber-Rare; Roams across northern and southern peninsulas

MONSTROUS CRAWLER Swamp of Sorrows (76), I-9, J:(1, 9), K:(1, 9), L:(1-9), Misty Reed Strand

MONSTROUS OOZE Wetlands (96), F:(2, 3), I:(4, 5), J:(4, 5), Direforge Hill, Ironbeard's Tomb

MONSTROUS PLAGUEBAT Eastern Plaguelands (40), B-3, C:(2-4), D-4, E-4, F:(3-4), G:(2-4), H:(2-5), I:(3-5), J:(3, 4), Plaguewood

MONTARR Lorekeeper, Thousand Needles (82), F-5, Freewind Post (112), Next to hut, west of inn

MONTY Rat Extermination Specialist, Ironforge (52), L-5, The Deeprun Tram, Deeprun Tram

MOODAN SUNGRAIN Baker, Mulgore (58), E-8, Camp Narache (105), Mill

MOON PRIESTESS AMARA Teldrassil (80), F:(5-6), G-6, Dolanaar (109), Patrols road between Dolanaar and east of Ban'ethil Hollow

MOONGLADE WARDEN Moonglade (56), E-4, F:(3-5), G:(3, 4), H-3, I-6, J:(5, 6), Nighthaven (121)

MOONKIN Darkshore (24), F:(4, 5), G:(4, 5)

MOONKIN ORACLE Darkshore (24), G-5

MOONRAGE ARMORER Silverpine Forest (68), G-7, Preywood Village

MOONRAGE BLOODHOWLER Silverpine Forest (68), G:(7, 8), H:(7, 8), I-4, In hills

MOONRAGE DARKRUNNER Silverpine Forest (68), G:(2, 3), H:(2, 3), Valagan's Field, Farm

MOONRAGE DARKSOUL Silverpine Forest (68), F:(2, 3), G-3, I-4, North Tide's Hollow

MOONRAGE ELDER Silverpine Forest (68), F-7, G-7, Preywood Village

MOONRAGE GLUTTON Silverpine Forest (68), F:(2, 3), G:(2, 3), H:(1, 2), North Tide's Hollow

MOONRAGE LEATHERWORKER Silverpine Forest (68), G-7, Preywood Village

MOONRAGE SENTRY Silverpine Forest (68), F-7, G-7, Preywood Village

MOONRAGE TAILOR Silverpine Forest (68), G-7, Preywood Village

MOONRAGE WATCHER Silverpine Forest (68), F-7, G-7, Preywood Village

MOONRAGE WHITESCALP Silverpine Forest (68), G:(3, 4), H:(2-5), The Shining Strand

MOONSTALKER Darkshore (24), F:(2, 5-8), G:(2-4, 6, 7), H:(2-4)

MOONSTALKER MATRIARCH Darkshore (24), E:(8, 9), F-9, G-9, I-1, Mist's Edge, The Master's Glaive, Twilight Vale

MOONSTALKER RUNT Darkshore (24), F:(2-6), G:(2-6), Ameth'Aran, Bashal'Aran, Mist's Edge

MOONSTALKER SIRE Darkshore (24), E:(8, 9), F:(7-9), G:(8, 9), I-1

MOONTOUCHED OWLBEAST Winterspring (98), I:(2, 6), J:(2, 6), The Hidden Grove, Owl Wing Thicket

MOORA Felwood (44), E-6, Shadow Hold, Anteroom after spiral tunnel

MOORANE HEARTHGRAIN Baker, Barrens (18), F-3, The Crossroads (107), Eastern entrance

MOORANTA Skinning Trainer, Thunder Bluff (84), E-4, Middle rise, next to Thunder Bluff Armorers

MOORAT LONGSTRIDE General Goods, Mulgore (58), E-6, Bloodhoof Village (102), Northeast tent

MORBENT FEL Duskwood (36), B-3, Forlorn Rowe, Second floor of house

MORDRESH FIRE EYE Barrens (18), F-9, Razorfen Downs

MOREN RIVERBEND Moonglade (56), G-4, Nighthaven (121), West wing of southeast building

MORG GNARLTREE Armorer, Duskwood (36), J-5, Darkshire (108), Smithy

MORGAINE THE SLY Rare Spawn, Elwynn Forest (42), D-6, Mirror Lake Orchard, Lvl 10 Uncommon; House next to lake

MORGAN LADIMORE Duskwood (36), B-3, Forlorn Rowe, (Summon) Fresh grave

MORGAN PESTLE Stormwind (72), H-6, Trade District, Pestle's Apothecary

MORGAN STERN Dustwallow Marsh (38), I-5, Theramore Isle (135), Inn

MORGAN THE COLLECTOR Elwynn Forest (42), J-8, Brackwell Pumpkin Patch, In house with Erlan Drudgemoor and Surena Caledon

MORGANTH Redridge Mountains (62), K-5, Tower of Ilgalar, Idle on top floor of tower

MORGANUS Stable Master, Tirisfal Glades (86), H-5, Brill (104), In front of stable

MORGG STORMSHOT Stormwind (72), I-2 , Dwarven District, West of tavern

MORGUM Leather Armor Merchant, Orgrimmar (60), G-7, Valley of Strength, Soran's Leather and Steel

MORHAN COPPERTONGUE Metalsmith, Loch Modan (54), D-5, Thelsamar (134), On porch of first house on left of path

MORI HILDELVE Dun Morogh (32), K-4, North Gate Outpost, Corpse at foot of a deadend hill on left side of the outpost

MORIN CLOUDSTALKER Mulgore (58), F-6, Travels road east of village

MOR'LADIM Duskwood (36), B-4, Forlorn Rowe, Patrols a circular path around Raven Hill Cemetery, Forlorn Rowe, and the entrance to the Dawning Wood Catacombs

MORLEY BATES Fungus Vendor, Undercity (88), K-2, The Magic Quarter, Roams Magic Quarter

MORLEY EBERLEIN Clothier, Elwynn Forest (42), I-7, Tower of Azora, Second floor of tower

MORPHAZ Swamp of Sorrows (76), I-5, The Temple of Atal'Hakkar

MORRIDUNE Ashenvale (12), B-2, Blackfathom Deeps

MORRIS LAWRY Stormwind (72), F-5, G-5, The Canals, Just east of The Finest Thread

MOR'ROGAL Stonetalon Mountains (70), F-6, Sun Rock Retreat (132), Hut on cliff south of inn

MORTA'GYA THE KEEPER The Hinterlands (50), G-7, The Altar of Zul, Top of altar

MORTIMER MONTAGUE Banker, Undercity (88), I-4, The Trade Quarter

MOR'VEK Ravasaur Trainers, Un'Goro Crater (90), J-7, The Marshlands, East of far south tip of river

MOR'ZUL BLOODBRINGER Burning Steppes (22), A-3, Altar of Storms, Graveyard above and left of the Altar of Storms

MOSARN Thunder Bluff (84), F-8, Hunter Rise, In building west of Hunter's Hall

MOSH'OGG BRUTE Stranglethorn Vale (74), C-3, D-3, Mizjah Ruins, The Savage Coast

MOSH'OGG BUTCHER Stranglethorn Vale (74), F-3, Mosh'Ogg Ogre Mound

MOSH'OGG LORD Stranglethorn Vale (74), F-3, Mosh'Ogg Ogre Mound

MOSH'OGG MAULER Stranglethorn Vale (74), F-3, Mosh'Ogg Ogre Mound

MOSH'OGG SHAMAN Stranglethorn Vale (74), F-3, Mosh'Ogg Ogre Mound

MOSH'OGG SPELLCRAFTER Stranglethorn Vale (74), F-3, Mosh'Ogg Ogre Mound

MOSH'OGG WARMONGER Stranglethorn Vale (74), E-3. F-3, Mosh'Ogg Ogre Mound

MOSH'OGG WITCH DOCTOR Stranglethorn Vale (74), C-3, D-3, Mizjah Ruins, The Savage Coast

MOSS STALKER Silverpine Forest (68), E:(1, 2), F-2, The Skittering Dark, Cave

MOSSFLAYER CANNIBAL Eastern Plaguelands (40), H:(2, 3), I:(2, 3), J-2, Zul'Masha

MOSSFLAYER SCOUT Eastern Plaguelands (40), H:(2, 3), I:(2, 3), J-2, Zul'Masha

MOSSFLAYER SHADOWHUNTER Eastern Plaguelands (40), H:(2, 3), I:(2, 3), J-2, Zul'Masha

MOSSFLAYER ZOMBIE Eastern Plaguelands (40), D-8, The Undercroft

MOSSHIDE ALPHA Wetlands (96), D-3, E-3, Saltspray Glen, Sundown Marsh

MOSSHIDE BRUTE Wetlands (96), D-3, E-3, F-3, Saltspray Glen, Sundown Marsh

MOSSHIDE FENRUNNER Wetlands (96), C-4, D:(3, 4), E-3, F:(3, 4), G-3, H:(5, 6), I:(5, 6), Mosshide Fen, Sundown Marsh

MOSSHIDE GNOLL Wetlands (96), G-7, H:(6-8), I:(6, 7), Dun Algaz, Mosshide Fen

MOSSHIDE MISTWEAVER Wetlands (96), E-3, F-3, G-3, H-6, I-7, Ironbeard's Tomb, Mosshide Fen

MOSSHIDE MONGREL Wetlands (96), H:(5-7), I:(5-7), Mosshide Fen

MOSSHIDE MYSTIC Wetlands (96), D-3, E-3, Saltspray Glen, Sundown Marsh

MOSSHIDE TRAPPER Wetlands (96), C-4, D:(3, 4), E-3, F-3, G-3, Bluegill Marsh, Saltspray Glen, Sundown Marsh

MOSSHOOF COURSER Azshara (14), D-7, E:(7, 8), F:(1-4, 7, 8), G:(2-4, 8, 9), H:(1, 2, 8), I:(2, 3), J:(2, 3), K:(2, 3)

MOSSHOOF RUNNER Azshara (14), A:(5-7), B:(5-7), Haldarr Encampment, Shadowsong Shrine, Valormok

MOSSHOOF STAG Azshara (14), A-8, B:(7, 8), C-8, D-8, Lake Mennar

MOT DAWNSTRIDER Journeyman Enchanter, Thunder Bluff (84), E-4, Middle rise, next to Dawnstrider Enchantments

MOTEGA FIREMANE Thousand Needles (82), B-3, Whitereach Post, Next to hut

MOTHER FANG Rare Spawn, Elwynn Forest (42), H-5, Jasperlode Mine, Lvl 10 Uncommon; Roams in mine

MOTHER SMOLDERWEB Burning Steppes (22), Searing Gorge (64), C-4/D-8, Blackrock Spire

MOTLEY GARMASON Wetlands (96), G-2, Dun Modr, Next to wagons, west of road

MOTTLED BOAR Durotar (34), F:(6, 7), G:(6, 7), Hidden Path, Valley of Trials (136)

MOTTLED DRYWALLOW CROCOLISK Dustwallow Marsh (38), D:(5, 6), E:(5, 6), F:(5, 6), G:(5, 6), Beezil's Wreck, The Dragonmurk, The Quagmir

MOTTLED RAPTOR Wetlands (96), B-5, C:(4-6), D:(4, 5), E-4, Black Channel Marsh, Menethil Bay, Whelgar's Excavation Site

MOTTLED RAZORMAW Wetlands (96), D-5, E-5, Whelgar's Excavation Site

MOTTLED SCREECHER Wetlands (96), C:(5, 6), D:(4, 5), Black Channel Marsh, Menethil Bay

MOTTLED SCYTHECLAW Wetlands (96), D:(4, 5), E:(4, 5), Whelgar's Excavation Site

MOTTLED WORG Silverpine Forest (68), G:(1-3), H:(1, 2), I:(1, 2), Thoughout Silverpine

MOUNTAIN BOAR Loch Modan (54), C:(1-5), D:(2-4), E:(3, 4)

MOUNTAIN BUZZARD Loch Modan (54), I:(5, 7), J:(5-7), K:(6-8), The Farstrider Lodge (111)

MOUNTAIN COUGAR Mulgore (58), D:(8, 9), E:(8, 9), F-9, G-9, Red Cloud Mesa

MOUNTAIN LION Alterac Mountains (8), D:(7-9), E:(8, 9), F:(7-9), G-8, I-5, J:(5, 6), K:(5, 6)

MOUNTAIN YETI Alterac Mountains (8), D:(6, 7), E-7, Growless Cave

MOUNTAINEER ANGST Loch Modan (54), F-1, Stonewrought Dam, Roams dam

MOUNTAINEER BARLEYBREW Dun Morogh (32), L-5, South Gate Outpost, Next to tower

MOUNTAINEER BARN Loch Modan (54), F-1, Stonewrought Dam, Roams dam

MOUNTAINEER BROKK Loch Modan (54), C:(1, 2), Dun Algaz

MOUNTAINEER COBBLEFLINT Loch Modan (54), B-7, Valley of Kings, In front of tower

MOUNTAINEER CRAGG Loch Modan (54), D-4, Thelsamar (134

MOUNTAINEER DALK Loch Modan (54), D-4, E-4, Thelsamar (134)

MOUNTAINEER DOKKIN Wetlands (96), G-8, H-8, Dun Algaz, Patrols tunnel

MOUNTAINEER DOLF Dun Morogh (32), F-5, Kharanos (116), Kneeling on cliff edge left of the path leading to Kharanos

MOUNTAINEER DROKEN Loch Modan (54), D-5, Thelsamar (134

MOUNTAINEER FLINT Loch Modan (54), C-2, D-4, Algaz Station, Roams road

MOUNTAINEER GANN Loch Modan (54), B-2, North Gate Pass

MOUNTAINEER GRAVELGAW Loch Modan (54), C-8, Valley of Kings, By tower entrance

MOUNTAINEER GRUGELM Wetlands (96), G-8, H-8, Dun Algaz, Patrols tunnel

MOUNTAINEER GWARTH Loch Modan (54), D-4, Thelsamar (134

MOUNTAINEER HAGGIS Loch Modan (54), E-1, Stonewrought Dam

MOUNTAINEER HAGIL Loch Modan (54), G-1 , Stonewrought Dam

MOUNTAINEER HAMMERFALL Loch Modan (54), C-2, Algaz Station

MOUNTAINEER HARN Loch Modan (54), D-5, Thelsamar (134

MOUNTAINEER KADRELL Loch Modan (54), D-5, Thelsamar (134 Patrols along path running through Thelsamar

MOUNTAINEER KALMIR Loch Modan (54), Valley of Kings, Roams road

MOUNTAINEER KAMDAR Loch Modan (54), D-4, Thelsamar (134

OUNTAINEER LANGARR
Loch Modan (54), D-5, Thelsamar (134)

OUNTAINEER LUXST
Loch Modan (54), C-2, Algaz Station, ower

OUNTAINEER MODAX
Loch Modan (54), E-4, Thelsamar (134)

OUNTAINEER MORLIC
Loch Modan (54), F-1, Stonewrought Jam, By engineer tent

OUNTAINEER MORRAN
Loch Modan (54), C-2, Algaz Station, Roams from Algaz Station to road

OUNTAINEER NAARTH
Loch Modan (54), B-7, Valley of Kings, Roams road

OUNTAINEER OSMOK
Loch Modan (54), D-5, Thelsamar (134)

OUNTAINEER PEBBLEBITTY
Loch Modan (54), B-8, Valley of Kings, Mounted by mountain pass heading into Searing Gorge

OUNTAINEER RHAREN
Wetlands (96), H-8, Dun Algaz, Stands guard of tunnel

OUNTAINEER ROCKGAR
Loch Modan (54), C-1, Dun Algaz, By mountain pass heading into Wetlands

OUNTAINEER ROGHAN
Loch Modan (54), D-5, Thelsamar (134)

OUNTAINEER STORMPIKE
Loch Modan (54), C-2, Dun Algaz, Algaz Station

OUNTAINEER THALOS
Dun Morogh (32), C-7, Coldridge Pass, On road heading to pass entrance

OUNTAINEER THAR
Wetlands (96), H-8, Dun Algaz, Stands guard of tunnel

OUNTAINEER TYRAW
Loch Modan (54), B-7, Valley of Kings

OUNTAINEER VEEK
Loch Modan (54), B-8, B-7, Valley of Kings

OUNTAINEER WALLBANG
Loch Modan (54), C-7, Valley of Kings, First floor of tower

OUNTAINEER WUAR
Loch Modan (54), D-4, Thelsamar (134)

OUNTAINEER YUTTHA
Loch Modan (54), C-2, Algaz Station

OUNTAINEER ZAREN
Loch Modan (54), B-7, C-6, Valley of Kings, Roams road

OUNTAINEER ZWARN
Loch Modan (54), B-7, C-6, Algaz Station, Tent

OUNTED IRONFORGE MOUNTAINEER
Dun Morogh (32), J:(2, 3)

R. SMITE
Westfall (94), D-7, E-7, The Deadmines

RS. WINTERS
General Supplies, Tirisfal Glades (86), H-5, Brill (104), Standing by carriage left of Gallows' End Tavern

UAD
Rare Spawn, Tirisfal Glades (86), D-4, Whispering Shore, Lvl 10 Uncommon; Patrols in and along shoreline

UCK FRENZY
Barrens (18), H-5, Fray Island

UCK SPLASH
Searing Gorge (64), A:(3, 4), Firewatch Ridge, In the pools

UCKRAKE
Alterac Mountains (8), E-5, Ruins of Alterac, Town Hall

UCKSHELL CLACKER
Dustwallow Marsh (38), F:(3, 4), G:(4, 5), H:(4, 5), Dustwallow Bay

UCKSHELL PINCER
Dustwallow Marsh (38), H:(6, 7), Tidefury Cove

UCKSHELL RAZORCLAW
Dustwallow Marsh (38), G-6, Tidefury Cove

UCKSHELL SCRABBLER
Dustwallow Marsh (38), G-6, H-7, Tidefury Cove

UCKSHELL SNAPCLAW
Dustwallow Marsh (38), F:(3, 4), G:(4, 5), H:(4, 5), Dustwallow Bay

UCULENT OOZE
Un'Goro Crater (90), H:(3, 4), I:(3, 4), J:(2-4, 6, 7), Lakkari Tar Pits, The Marshlands

MUDCRUSH DURTFEET
Dustwallow Marsh (38), D-4, Small camp south of Brackenwall Village

MUDDUK
Superior Cook, Stranglethorn Vale (74), C-3, Grom'gol Base Camp (114), Under scaffolding just inside camp walls to the right of western entrance

MUDROCK BORER
Dustwallow Marsh (38), G-6, H:(5, 6), Dustwallow Bay, Tidefury Cove

MUDROCK BURROWER
Dustwallow Marsh (38), F:(3, 4), G:(4, 5), H:(4, 5), Dustwallow Bay

MUDROCK SNAPJAW
Dustwallow Marsh (38), G-6, H:(5, 6), Dustwallow Bay, Tidefury Cove

MUDROCK SPIKESHELL
Dustwallow Marsh (38), G:(1, 2), H:(1-4), I:(1-4), Dreadmurk Shore, Theramore Isle, Witch Hill

MUDROCK TORTOISE
Dustwallow Marsh (38), G:(1, 2), H:(1-4), I:(1-4), Dreadmurk Shore, Theramore Isle

MUDSNOUT GNOLL
Hillsbrad Foothills (48), G-6, H-6, Nethander Stead

MUDSNOUT SHAMAN
Hillsbrad Foothills (48), H-6, Nethander Stead

MUG'THOL
Alterac Mountains (8), E-5, Ruins of Alterac, Second floor of castle

MUGGLEFIN
Rare Spawn, Ashenvale (12), C-4, Lake Falathim, Lvl 23 Semi-Rare; Roams near spawn points

MUGLASH
Ashenvale (12), B-4, Zoram'gar Outpost (137), Southeast structure

MUIGIN
Un'Goro Crater (90), F-1, Marshal's Refuge (118), Southeast of cave

MUIREDON BATTLEFORGE
Ironforge (52), C-1, The Mystic Ward, Hall of Mysteries

MUKDRAK
Journeyman Engineer, Durotar (34), H-4, Razor Hill (124), Northeast of inn

MULGORE PROTECTOR
Mulgore (58), D-8, Red Cloud Mesa

MULGRIS DEEPRIVER
Western Plaguelands (92), G-6, The Writhing Haunt, Lying in house on the nothern side of farm

MULL THUNDERHORN
Mulgore (58), E-6, Bloodhoof Village (102), Outside east tent

MUMMIFIED ATAL'AI
Swamp of Sorrows (76), I-5, The Temple of Atal'Hakkar

MURA RUNTETOTEM
Silverpine Forest (68), F-4, The Sepulcher (127), Left side of inn by fireplace

MURAGUS
Staff Merchant, Orgrimmar (60), E-5, The Cleft of Shadow, Ironwood Staves and Wands

MURDALOC
Badlands (16), G-7, Agmond's End, Roams camp

MURDEROUS BLISTERPAW
Rare Spawn, Tanaris (78), H-4, Lvl 43 Very Rare; Roams from one set of hills to the other

MUREN STORMPIKE
Ironforge (52), J-9, The Military Ward, Hall of Arms

MURK SLITHERER
Swamp of Sorrows (76), I-5, The Temple of Atal'Hakkar

MURK SPITTER
Swamp of Sorrows (76), I-5, The Temple of Atal'Hakkar

MURK THRESHER
Dustwallow Marsh (38), G-6, H:(5, 6), Dustwallow Bay, Tidefury Cove

MURK WORM
Swamp of Sorrows (76), I-5, The Temple of Atal'Hakkar

MURKDEEP
Darkshore (24), E-8, Twilight Shore, Spawns off shore

MURKGILL FORAGER
Stranglethorn Vale (74), C:(2, 3), Kal'ai Ruins

MURKGILL HUNTER
Stranglethorn Vale (74), C:(2, 3), Kal'ai Ruins

MURKGILL LORD
Stranglethorn Vale (74), C-3, Kal'ai Ruins

MURKGILL ORACLE
Stranglethorn Vale (74), C-3, Kal'ai Ruins

MURKGILL WARRIOR
Stranglethorn Vale (74), C:(2, 3), Kal'ai Ruins

MURKSHALLOW SNAPCLAW
Ashenvale (12), B-2, Blackfathom Deeps

MURLOC
Elwynn Forest (42), G:(6, 7), H:(6, 7), Crystal Lake

MURLOC COASTRUNNER
Westfall (94), D-1, E-1, F-1, Longshore

MURLOC FLESHEATER
Redridge Mountains (62), E:(4, 5), F:(5-7), G:(6, 7), H-6, Lake Everstill

MURLOC FORAGER
Elwynn Forest (42), G-9, H-8, I-8, J:(8, 9), K:(4-6, 8, 9)

MURLOC HUNTER
Westfall (94), B:(3-6), C-3, Longshore

MURLOC LURKER
Elwynn Forest (42), J-8, K:(4-6, 8, 9), L:(8, 9), Stone Cairn Lake

MURLOC MINOR ORACLE
Westfall (94), C-2, D:(1, 2), E-1, Longshore

MURLOC MINOR TIDECALLER
Redridge Mountains (62), F:(6, 7), G:(6, 7), H-6, Lake Everstill

MURLOC NETTER
Westfall (94), C:(2, 3), D:(1, 2), Longshore

MURLOC NIGHTCRAWLER
Redridge Mountains (62), K-6, Stonewatch Falls

MURLOC ORACLE
Westfall (94), B:(5-7), C-8, Longshore

MURLOC RAIDER
Westfall (94), E-1, F-1, Longshore

MURLOC SCOUT
Redridge Mountains (62), E:(4, 5), F-5, G-5, H-5, Lake Everstill

MURLOC SHORESTRIKER
Redridge Mountains (62), F:(6, 7), G-7, Lake Everstill

MURLOC STREAMRUNNER
Elwynn Forest (42), G:(6, 7), H:(6, 7), Crystal Lake

MURLOC TIDECALLER
Redridge Mountains (62), G-5, H-5, K-6, Lake Everstill

MURLOC TIDEHUNTER
Westfall (94), B-7, C-8, Longshore

MURLOC WARRIOR
Westfall (94), B:(3-5), C:(2, 3), Longshore

MURNDAN DERTH
Gunsmith, Wetlands (96), A-6, Menethil Harbor (119), Building northeast of tavern

MURPHY WEST
Wetlands (96), A-6, Menethil Harbor (119), First floor of keep, next to stairs

MUSHGOG
Rare Spawn, Feralas (46), G-4, Dire Maul, Lvl 60 Rare

MUSHGOG
Feralas (46), G-4, The Maul, In arena

MUTANUS THE DEVOURER
Barrens (18), E-4, Wailing Caverns

MUTATED VENTURE CO. DRONE
Barrens (18), F-1, First floor of tower northeast of Sludge Fen

MUURAN
Superior Macecrafter, Desolace (30), G-6, Ghost Walker Post (113), Outside center hut

MU'UTA
Bowyer, Arathi Highlands (10), J-3, Hammerfall (115), Next to forge

MUX MANASCRAMBLER
Tanaris (78), H-3, Gadgetzan (113)

MYDRANNUL
General Goods Vendor, Darnassus (26), I-5, Warrior's Terrace, South of path just after entrance to city

MYIZZ LUCKYCATCH
Superior Fisherman, Stranglethorn Vale (74), B-8, Booty Bay (103), On the eastern side of the bay directly beneath hanging shark

MY'LANNA
Food & Drink Merchant, Moonglade (56), F-3, Nighthaven (121), Northwest building

MYLENTHA RIVERBEND
Moonglade (56), G-3, Nighthaven (121), Second floor of northeast building

MYLINI FROSTMOON
Weapon Merchant, Felwood (44), I-3, Talonbranch Glade (133) (133)

MYLOR SUNDERFURY
Ironforge (52), G-4, The Great Forge, North of The Great Anvil

MYRA TYRNGAARDE
Bread Vendor, Ironforge (52), C-6, D-8, The Commons, Roams in a circle

MYRANDA THE HAG
Western Plaguelands (92), G-8, Sorrow Hill, On tree stump where path forks

MYRIAM MOONSINGER
Barrens (18), F-9, Razorfen Downs, Atop large bramble in dark area

MYROKOS SILENTFORM
Hillsbrad Foothills (48), K-2, First floor of Chateau Ravenholdt

MYSTIC YAYO'JIN
Reagent Vendor, The Hinterlands (50), L-8, Revantusk Village (125), Roams hut on eastern side of village

MYSTLASH FLAYER
Ashenvale (12), A:(2-4), The Zoram Strand (137)

MYSTLASH HYDRA
Ashenvale (12), A:(2-4), B:(2, 3), The Zoram Strand (137), Zoram'gar Outpost (137)

MYTHIDAN
Mace & Staff Merchant, Darnassus (26), I-6, Tradesmen's Terrace, Weapons shop

MYTHRIN'DIR
General Trade Supplier, Darnassus (26), H-2, Craftsmen's Terrace, General Trade shop

MYZRAEL
Arathi Highlands (10), I-3, (Summon) Shard of Myzrael

N

NAAL MISTRUNNER
Cooking Supplier, Thunder Bluff (84), F-5, High rise, outside Aska's Kitchen tent

NADIA VERNON
Bowyer, Silverpine Forest (68), G-4, The Sepulcher (127), Next to house on the right side of sepulcher

NADYIA MANEWEAVER
Journeyman Leatherworker, Teldrassil (80), E-5, House at end of road

NAELA TRANCE
Bowyer, Wetlands (96), A-6, Menethil Harbor (119), Next to wagon, east of keep

NAGA EXPLORER
Stranglethorn Vale (74), B:(6, 7)

NAGAZ
Alterac Mountains (8), E-2, Dandred's Fold, First floor of house

NAG'ZEHN
Thousand Needles (82), I-6, Ironstone Camp, Camp just west of Shimmering Flats

NAGULON
Barrens (18), H-3, Ratchet (122)

NAK
Barrens (18), E-8, Blackthorn Ridge, Roams the ridge

NALESETTE WILDBRINGER
Pet Trainer, Felwood (44), H-3, Talonbranch Glade (133), Front of building

NALPAK
Disciple of Naralex, Barrens (18), E-4, The Wailing Caverns, Right eye of cave above entrance

NALPAK
Barrens (18), E-4, Wailing Caverns

NAMDO BIZZZLE
Engineering Supplies, Dun Morogh (32), C-4, Gnomeregan

NAN MISTRUNNER
Fruit Vendor, Thunder Bluff (84), E-4, Middle rise, in Fruits and Vegetables tent

NANCY VISHAS
Alterac Mountains (8), D-3, The Uplands, Patrols between house and dock

NANDAR BRANSON
Alchemy Supplies, Hillsbrad Foothills (48), F-6, Southshore (129), Small house on left of path

NANTAR
Baker, Ashenvale (12), E-5, Astranaar (101), First floor of inn

NARA MEIDEROS
Priest Trainer, Stormwind (72), C-5, The Park, By pool of water

NARA WILDMANE
Thunder Bluff (84), I-3, Elder Rise, Inside Hall of Elders

NARAIN SOOTHFANCY
Tanaris (78), J-2, Steamwheedle Port, Engineer tower to the north of the port

NARAM LONGCLAW
Weaponsmith, Darkshore (24), F-4, Auberdine (101), Back terrace of northern building

NARAXIS
Rare Spawn, Duskwood (36), L-5, Lvl 27 Uncommon; Cave

NARG THE TASKMASTER
Rare Spawn, Elwynn Forest (42), E-8, Fargodeep Mine, Lvl 10 Uncommon; Roams in mine

NARGAL DEATHEYE
Weaponsmith, Barrens (18), F-3, The Crossroads (107), Western entrance

NARGATT
Food & Drink, Stranglethorn Vale (74), C-3, Grom'gol Base Camp (114), Scaffolding just left of zepplin tower

NARIANNA
Bowyer, Moonglade (56), G-4, Nighthaven (121), East wing of southeast building

NARILLASANZ
Rare Spawn, Alterac Mountains (8), J:(5, 6), K:(4-6), Chillwind Point, Lvl 44 Semi-Rare; Patrols area between lake and road

NARJ DEEPSLICE
Butcher, Arathi Highlands (10), F-5, Refuge Point (124), Roams in camp

NARKK
Pirate Supplies, Stranglethorn Vale (74), B-8, Booty Bay (103), Nautical Needs (shop) on the northern side of The Old Port Authority

NARM FAULK
Dun Morogh (32), K-6, Ironband's Compound, Dead on hill at the southern end of Helm's Bed Lake

NARM SKYCHASER
Shaman Trainer, Mulgore (58), F-6, Bloodhoof Village (102), East tent

NARNIE
Pet, Redridge Mountains (62), C-4, Lakeshire (117), First floor of Lakeshire Inn

NARRET SHADOWGROVE
Trades Supplies, Teldrassil (80), G-6, Dolanaar (109), Middle floor inside building north of road

NARTOK
Warlock Trainer, Durotar (34), F-7, Valley of Trials (136), Back of cave

NARV HIDECRAFTER
Expert Leathercrafter, Desolace (30), G-6, Ghost Walker Post (113), Center hut

NAT PAGLE
Artisan Fisherman, Dustwallow Marsh (38), H-6, Tidefury Cove, On isle in the cove

NATA DAWNSTRIDER
Enchanting Supplies, Thunder Bluff (84), E-4, Middle rise, next to Dawnstrider Enchantments

NATAKA LONGHORN
Desolace (30), G-6, Ghost Walker Post (113), Center hut

NATHANIEL DUMAH
Western Plaguelands (92), E-8, Chillwind Camp (107), In front of shed by ruined building

NATHANIEL STEENWICK
Thrown Weapons Merchant, Undercity (88), K-5, The Rogues' Quarter, Near Magic Quarter entry

NATHANOS BLIGHTCALLER
Champion of the Banshee Queen, Eastern Plaguelands (40), D-7, The Marris Stead, In front of house with two Blighthounds

NATHERIL RAINCALLER
General Goods, Winterspring (98), H-3, Starfall Village (130), South end of main building

NAZEER BLOODPIKE
Dustwallow Marsh (38), D-3, Brackenwall Village (104), West entrance

NAZGREL
Advisor to Thrall, Orgrimmar (60), C:(3, 4), Valley of Wisdom, Grommash Hold

NEAL ALLEN
Engineering & General Goods Supplier, Wetlands (96), A-6, Menethil Harbor (119), Northeast room on first floor of keep

NECROFIEND
Western Plaguelands (92), I-7, Scholomance

NECROMANCER
Cult of the Damned, Eastern Plaguelands (40), C-2, D:(2-4), E:(3, 4), F-3, Plaguewood, In structures

NEEDLES COUGAR
Thousand Needles (82), A:(1-3), B:(2-4), C:(2-5), D:(4, 5), E-5, F:(5, 6), G:(4, 5), H:(5, 6), I:(5, 6)

NEEKA BLOODSCAR
Badlands (16), A-5, Kargath (116), Tower platform

NEEMA
Waitress, Hillsbrad Foothills (48), F-6, Southshore (129), First floor of inn

NEERU FIREBLADE
Orgrimmar (60), E-5, The Cleft of Shadow, Building ouside Ragefire Chasm entry

NEFARU
Rare Spawn, Duskwood (36), I-8, J-8, Roland's Doom, Lvl 34 Uncommon; Roams small area around spawn point

NEGOLASH
Stranglethorn Vale (74), C-8, Wild Shore, (Summon) Patrols to the ruined lifeboat on shore

NEKRUM GUTCHEWER
Tanaris (78), E-1, Zul'Farrak

NELSON THE NICE
Silithus (66), I-4, Hive'Zora, Roams south to the Twilight Outpost, down to the wall and back

NEMETH HAWKEYE
Farstriders, Stranglethorn Vale (74), C-3, Grom'gol Base Camp (114)

NERGAL
General Goods Vendor, Un'Goro Crater (90), F-1, Marshal's Refuge (118), Near entrance to cave

NERRIST
Trade Goods, Stranglethorn Vale (74), C-3, Grom'gol Base Camp (114), Just inside camp walls to the right of eastern entrance

NERUB'ENKAN
Eastern Plaguelands (40), D-2, Stratholme

NESSA SHADOWSONG
Fishing Supplies, Teldrassil (80), G-9, Rut'theran Village (125), At intersection

NETHER MAIDEN
Desolace (30), F:(7, 8), G-7, Mannoroc Coven

NETHER SISTER
Desolace (30), G-8, Mannoroc Coven

NETHER SORCERESS
Desolace (30), F:(7, 8), G:(7, 8), Mannoroc Coven

NETHERGARDE ANALYST
Blasted Lands (20), I-2, J:(1, 2), Nethergarde Keep (120)

NETHERGARDE CLERIC
Blasted Lands (20), I:(1, 2), Nethergarde Keep (120)

NETHERGARDE ELITE
Blasted Lands (20), I-2, J-2, Nethergarde Keep (120)

NETHERGARDE ENGINEER
Blasted Lands (20), H-1, I-1, J-1, K-1, Garrison Armory, Nethergarde Keep (120)

NETHERGARDE FOREMAN
Blasted Lands (20), H-1, I-1, J-1, K-1, Garrison Armory, Nethergarde Keep (120)

NETHERGARDE MINER
Blasted Lands (20), H-1, I-1, J-1, K-1, Garrison Armory, Nethergarde Keep (120)

NETHERGARDE OFFICER
Blasted Lands (20), I-2, J-2, Nethergarde Keep (120)

NETHERGARDE RIFTWATCHER
Blasted Lands (20), I-2, J-2, Nethergarde Keep (120)

NETHERGARDE SOLDIER
Blasted Lands (20), I:(1-3), J:(1-3), Garrison Armory, Nethergarde Keep (120), Serpent's Coil

NETHERWALKER
Feralas (46), G-4, Dire Maul

NEWTON BURNSIDE
Banker, Stormwind (72), H-7, Trade District, Stormwind Counting House

NEZ'RAZ
Zeppelin Master, Stranglethorn Vale (74), C-3, Grom'gol Base Camp (114), Atop tower

NEZZLIOK THE DIRE
Bloodscalp Clan Witchdoctor, Stranglethorn Vale (74), B-1, Ruins of Zul'Kunda, Idle with several trolls in the northwestern corner of ruins

NIBY THE ALMIGHTY
Felwood (44), F-5, Shatter Scar Vale, North of pond near dock

NICHOLAS ATWOOD
Gun Merchant, Undercity (88), I-3, The War Quarter

NIDA WINTERHOOF
Herbalism Supplier, Thunder Bluff (84), F-4, Middle rise, in front of Holistic Herbalism

NIGHT WEB MATRIARCH
Tirisfal Glades (86), C-6, Night Web's Hollow

NIGHT WEB SPIDER
Tirisfal Glades (86), C-6, Night Web's Hollow

NIGHTBANE DARK RUNNER
Duskwood (36), H:(4, 5, 7), I:(4-8), Brightwood Grove

NIGHTBANE SHADOW WEAVER
Duskwood (36), H:(3-5, 7), I:(4-8), Brightwood Grove

NIGHTBANE TAINTED ONE
Duskwood (36), H-8, I-8, J:(7, 8)

NIGHTBANE VILE FANG
Duskwood (36), H-8, I-8, J-7

NIGHTBANE WORGEN
Duskwood (36), H:(3-5, 7), I:(3, 4, 6, 7), Brightwood Grove

NIGHTLASH
Silverpine Forest (68), G-2, The Dead Field, Spawns (on timer) in the center of crop field

NIGHTMARE ECTOPLASM
Barrens (18), E-4, Wailing Caverns

NIGHTMARE SCALEBANE
Swamp of Sorrows (76), I-5, The Temple of Atal'Hakkar

NIGHTMARE SUPPRESSOR
Swamp of Sorrows (76), I-5, The Temple of Atal'Hakkar

NIGHTMARE WANDERER
Swamp of Sorrows (76), I-5, The Temple of Atal'Hakkar

NIGHTMARE WHELP
Swamp of Sorrows (76), I-5, The Temple of Atal'Hakkar

NIGHTMARE WYRMKIN
Swamp of Sorrows (76), I-5, The Temple of Atal'Hakkar

NIGHTSABER
Teldrassil (80), F:(5, 6), G:(5, 6), H:(5, 6), I-5

NIGHTSABER STALKER
Teldrassil (80), D-6, E:(5-7), F:(7, 8), G-7, H-7, Dolanaar (109), Lake Al'Ameth, Pools of Arlithrien

NIGHTSHADE
Jeen'ra's Pet, Darnassus (26), E-1, Cenarion Enclave, Top of structure, connected to the northeast structure

NIJEL'S POINT GUARD
Desolace (30), H-1, I:(1, 2), Nijel's Point (121)

NIKOVA RASKOL
Stormwind (72), J-4, Old Town, Hanging out in Old Town street

NILITH LOKRAV
Searing Gorge (64), E-7, Kneeling on right side of camp

NILLEN ANDEMAR
Macecrafter, Loch Modan (54), E-1, Stonewrought Dam, By keg on cart on dam wall

NIMAR THE SLAYER
Rare Spawn, Arathi Highlands (10), I:(6, 7), J-6, Witherbark Village, Lvl 37 Uncommon; Roams in village

NIMBOYA
Stranglethorn Vale (74), C-3, Grom'gol Base Camp (114), Just inside camp walls near cauldron by the northern entrance

NINA LIGHTBREW
Alchemy Supplies, Blasted Lands (20), J-2, Nethergarde Keep (120), Top floor of tower facing entrance of keep

NIOMA
Leatherworking Supplies, The Hinterlands (50), B-4, Aerie Peak (100), Wildhammer Keep

NIPSY
Stormwind (72), I-1, Dwarven District, Deeprun Tram

NISSA AGAMAND
Tirisfal Glades (86), F-4, Agamand Mills (100), Patrols two story house on right side of mill

NISSA FIRESTONE
First Aid Trainer, Ironforge (52), G-6, The Great Forge, Ironforge Physician

NITTLEBUR SPARKFIZZLE
Mage Trainer, Ironforge (52), C-1, The Mystic Ward, Hall of Mysteries

NIXX SPROCKETSPRING
Master Goblin Engineer, Tanaris (78), H-3, Gadgetzan (113), Northeast hut

NIXXRAK
Heavy Armor Merchant, Winterspring (98), I-4, Everlook (110), Inside northeast building

NIXXRAX FILLAMUG
Food & Drink, Stranglethorn Vale (74), B-8, Booty Bay (103), Behind the bar on the first floor of The Salty Sailor Tavern

NIZZIK
Venture Armor Salesman, Stonetalon Mountains (70), H-4, Cragpool Lake, Wood platform above lake, next to wheel

NOBORU THE CUDGEL
Swamp of Sorrows (76), G-3, Patrols with two Lost One Muckdwellers between spawn point and an area near the Harborage with two Lost One Muckdwellers

NOGG
Expert Engineer, Orgrimmar (60), I-3, J-3, Valley of Honor, Nogg's Machine Shop

NOGGLE FICKLESPRAGG
Silithus (67), G-4, Cenarion Hold (106)

NORI PRIDEDRIFT
Dun Morogh (32), C-7, Coldridge Valley (107), Camp

NORTHSHIRE GUARD
Elwynn Forest (42), F-5, Northshire Valley (122)

NORTHSPRING HARPY
Feralas (46), D:(1, 2), Ruins of Ravenwind

NORTHSPRING ROGUEFEATHER
Feralas (46), D:(1, 2), Ruins of Ravenwind

NORTHSPRING SLAYER
Feralas (46), D:(1, 2), Ruins of Ravenwind

NORTHSPRING WINDCALLER
Feralas (46), D:(1, 2), Ruins of Ravenwind

NOVICE ELRETH
Tirisfal Glades (86), C-7, Deathknell (109), Church

NOVICE THAIVAND
Hillsbrad Foothills (48), H-2, Tarren Mill (133), Graveyard

NOXIOUS PLAGUEBAT
Eastern Plaguelands (40), F-6, G:(5, 6), H:(5, 6), I:(6, 7), J:(6, 7), K-7

NOXIOUS SLIME
Desolace (30), D-5, Maraudon

NOXXION
Desolace (30), D-5, Maraudon

NOXXIOUS ESSENCE
Desolace (30), D-5, Maraudon

NOXXIOUS SCION
Desolace (30), D-5, Maraudon

NURSE LILLIAN
Stormwind (72), F-6, The Canals, Top of steps to stockade

NURSE NEELA
First Aid Trainer, Tirisfal Glades (86), H-5, Brill (104), First floor of Gallows' End Tavern

NYOMA
Cooking Supplies, Teldrassil (80), G-6, Dolanaar (109), Next to cauldron southeast of inn

NYRILL
Xylem's Apprentice, Azshara (14), C-5, Requires quest from Sanath Lim-yo to reach

NYSE
Wind Rider Master, Thousand Needles (82), F-5, Freewind Post (112), North side of plateau, opposite inn

O

OAKENSCOWL
Teldrassil (80), G-7, Lake Al'Ameth, In den south of lake

OAKPAW
Rare Spawn, Ashenvale (12), F-6, G-6, Greenpaw Village, Lvl 27 Semi-Rare; Roams throughout village

OASIS SNAPJAW
Barrens (18), E-4, F-4, G-4, Lushwater Oasis, The Stagnant Oasis

OBEN RAGECLAW
Teldrassil (80), E-6, Ban'ethil Barrow Den, Room in south section of den

OBI
Un'Goro Crater (90), D-2, Hill in far northwestern section of crater

OBSIDIAN ELEMENTAL
Burning Steppes (22), G-6, I-6, J:(3-5, 7), Blackrock Pass

OBSIDIAN GOLEM
Badlands (16), G-1, Uldaman

OBSIDIAN SENTINEL
Badlands (16), G-1, Uldaman

OBSIDIAN SHARD
Badlands (16), G-1, Uldaman

OBSIDION
Searing Gorge (64), E-2, The Slag Pit, (Summon) Animates when Lathoric the Black encounter is triggered

OCCULUS
Tanaris (78), I-5, Caverns of Time, Land bridge leading to cavern

ODO THE BLINDWATCHER
Silverpine Forest (68), F-7, Shadowfang Keep

OFFICER AREYN
Accessories Quartermaster, Stormwind (72), K-5, Old Town, Outside SI:7

OFFICER BRADY
Stormwind (72), Roams city

OFFICER GOTHINA
Undercity Commendations, Undercity (88), H-4

OFFICER IRONBEARD
Ironforge Commendations, Ironforge (52), F-5

OFFICER JAXON
Stormwind (72), Roams city

OFFICER LUNALIGHT
Darnassus Commendations, Darnassus (26), E-4

OFFICER MALOOF
Stormwind Commendations, Stormwind (72), H-6

OFFICER POMEROY
Stormwind (72), Roams city

OFFICER PORTERHOUSE
Gnomeregan Commendations, Ironforge (52), F-5

OFFICER REDBLADE
Orgrimmaar Commendations, Orgrimmar (61), E-4

OFFICER THUNDERSTRIDER
Thunderbluff Commendations, Thunder Bluff (85), D-6

OFFICER VU'SHALAY
Darkspear Commendations, Orgrimmar (61), E-4

OGG'MARR
Butcher, Dustwallow Marsh (38), D-3, Brackenwall Village (104), Northern part of village

OGGLEFLINT
Orgrimmar (60), F-5, Ragefire Chasm

OGLETHORPE OBNOTICUS
Master Gnome Engineer, Stranglethorn Vale (74), B-8, Booty Bay (103), Small house on third level along the eastern side of bay

OGOM THE WRETCHED
Swamp of Sorrows (76), I-5, The Temple of Atal'Hakkar

OGRABISI
Burning Steppes (22), Searing Gorge (64), C-4/D-8, Blackrock Depths

OGROMM
Hunter Trainer, Swamp of Sorrows (76), F-5 Stonard (131), Behind orcish carriage left of entrance to main hall

OGRON
Dustwallow Marsh (38), E-4, Just off road

OGTINC
Azshara (14), E-4, The Shattered Strand, Overlooking ruins atop cliff

OGUNARO WOLFRUNNER
Riding Wolf (Kennel Master), Orgrimmar (60), I-1, Valley of Honor, Outside of Hunter's Hall

OHANAKO
Two Handed Weapon Merchant, Thunder Bluff (84), F-6, High rise, inside Ragetotem Arms tent

OK'THOR THE BREAKER
Raid Sub-Boss, Burning Steppes (22), Searing Gorge (64), C-4/D-8, Blackrock Depths

OKLA
Barrens (18), G-2, Grol'dom Farm, Roams tower east of farm

OKOTHOS IRONRAGER
Armorsmith, Orgrimmar (60), J-2, Valley of Honor

OL' BEASLEY
Stormwind (72), J-4, Old Town, Across from The Five Deadly Venoms

OL' EMMA
Stormwind (72), H-4, The Canals, Roams around Cathedral Square and Canals

OL' SOOTY
Loch Modan (54), D-6, Grizzlepaw Ridge, Roams area along the southwestern end of the loch

OLAF
Badlands (16), G-1, Uldaman

OLD BLANCHY
Westfall (94), G-2, The Jansen Stead, Near Furlbrows

OLD CLIFF JUMPER
Rare Spawn, The Hinterlands (50), C:(5, 6), The Hinterlands, Lvl 42 Semi-Rare; Patrols small area around spawn point

OLD GRIZZLEGUT
Rare Spawn, Feralas (46), G-6, H-4, Lower Wilds, Ruins of Isildien, Lvl 43 Very Rare; Roams in a wide area

OLD ICEBEARD
Dun Morogh (32), E-5, Chill Breeze Valley, Roams small area around spawn point

OLD IRONBARK
Feralas (46), G-4, Dire Maul

OLD MAN HEMING
Fisherman, Stranglethorn Vale (74), B-8, Booty Bay (103), The Happy Bobber (shop)

OLD MURK-EYE
Westfall (94), C-8, Longshore, Roams southern part of Longshore

OLD SERRA'KIS
Ashenvale (12), B-2, Blackfathom Deeps

OLD VICEJAW
Rare Spawn, Silverpine Forest (68), H:(5, 6), Lvl 14 Uncommon; Roams small area around spawn point

OLIVER DWOR
Apprentice Weaponsmith, Tirisfal Glades (86), H-5, Brill (104), Smithy

OLIVIA BURNSIDE
Banker, Stormwind (72), H-7, Trade District, Stormwind Counting House

OLLANUS
Light Armor Merchant, Orgrimmar (60), G-7, Valley of Strength, Soran's Leather and Steel

OLM THE WISE
Rare Spawn, Cenarion Circle, Felwood (44), G:(2-3), H:(1-3), Irontree Woods, Lvl 52 Average Rare; Roams near spawn points

OLMIN BURNINGBEARD
Hunter Trainer, Ironforge (52), J-8, The Military Ward, Hall of Arms

OLTHRAN CRAGHELM
Heavy Armor Merchant, Ironforge (52), G-9, The Military Ward, Craghelm's Plate and Chain

OLVIA
Meat Vendor, Orgrimmar (60), E-7, Valley of Strength, Chop House

OMGORN THE LOST
Rare Spawn, Tanaris (78), F:(6, 7), G:(6, 7), Dunemaul Compound, Eastmoon Ruins, Southmoon Ruins, Lvl 50 Semi-Rare; Roams a wide path around spawn point

OMUSA THUNDERHORN
Wind Rider Master, Barrens (18), E-6, Camp Taurajo (106), Western entrance

ONGEKU
Swamp of Sorrows (76), H-2, Fallow Sanctuary, Roams small area around spawn point

ONIN MACHAMMAR
Dun Morogh (32), C-4, Gnomeregan, Stealthed on top of helipad

ONU
Darkshore (24), G-8, Grove of the Ancients, Center of temple

ONYXIA
Raid Boss, Dustwallow Marsh (38), G-8, Onyxia's Lair

ONYXIAN WARDER
Dustwallow Marsh (38), G-8, Onyxia's Lair

ONYXIAN WHELP
Dustwallow Marsh (38), G-8, Onyxia's Lair

OOZEWORM
Rare Spawn, Dustwallow Marsh (38), D:(6-7), E-6, The Den of Flame, The Dragonmurk, Lvl 42 Very Rare; Roams spawn points

OOZLINGS
Swamp of Sorrows (76), I-5, The Temple of Atal'Hakkar

OPHEK
Durotar (34), H-4, Razor Hill (124), Behind barracks

OPHELIA MONTAGUE
Banker, Undercity (88), I-4, The Trade Quarter

OPUS
Burning Steppes (22), I:(2, 3)

OR'KALAR
Arathi Highlands (10), B:(6, 7), C-6, Stromgarde Keep (132), Ogre quarter of Stromgarde Keep

ORALIUS
Burning Steppes (22), K-7, Morgan's Vigil (120), Next to Gryphon Master

ORAN SNAKEWRITHE
Undercity (88), J-3, The Magic Quarter, Stall next to Tailors

ORENDIL BROADLEAF
Ashenvale (12), D-4, Maestra's Post, Near Stones to the south of main outpost

ORENTHIL WHISPERWIND
Teldrassil (80), G-4, H-4, Shadowglen (127), Benches southwest of Aldrassil

ORGRIMMAR GRUNT
Durotar (34), E-1, F-1, G-1, H-1, Valley of Trials (136)

ORIK'ANDO
Feralas (46), I-4, Camp Mojache (105), Next to tent, east of water

ORM STONEHOOF
Thunder Bluff (84), D-6, Lower rise, next to pond

ORMAK GRIMSHOT
Hunter Trainer, Orgrimmar (60), H-2, Valley of Honor, Hunter's Hall

ORMER IRONBRAID
Wetlands (96), E-5, Whelgar's Excavation Site, Just across bridge in east section of site

ORMOK
Rogue Trainer, Orgrimmar (60), E-5, The Cleft of Shadow, Next to Shadowswift Brotherhood building

ORMYR FLINTEYE
Rogue Trainer, Ironforge (52), G-1, The Forlorn Cavern, South building, inside east entrance

ORNERY PLAINSTRIDER
Barrens (18), D:(2, 3), E:(1, 2, 4, 5), F:5, G:(1, 3-5), H-3

OROKK OMOSH
Orgrimmar (60), J-2, Valley of Honor, Across from Arms of Legend

ORPHAN MATRON BATTELWALL
Orgrimmar (60), J-2, Valley of Honor, Building near Lumak's Fishing

ORPHAN MATRON NIGHTINGALER
Stormwind (72), G-4, Cathedral Square, Outside Orphanage

ORWIN GIZZNICK
Feralas (46), I-4, Camp Mojache (105), East of inn, next to water

OSBORNE THE NIGHT MAN
Rogue Trainer, Stormwind (72), K-5, Old Town, Outside SI:7

OSRIC STRANG
Heavy Armor Merchant, Stormwind (72), K-5, Old Town, Limited Immunity

OTHO MOJI'KO
Cooking Supplier, The Hinterlands (50), L-8, Revantusk Village (125), Dancing in hut on southeast side of village

OTT
Weaponsmith, Hillsbrad Foothills (48), G-3, Tarren Mill (133), Caravan at southern end of town

OTTO
Arathi Highlands (10), C-6, Stromgarde Keep (132), Third floor of castle

OUTCAST NECROMANCER
Desolace (30), H-9, I-9, Valley of Bones

OUTFITTER ERIC
Speciality Tailoring Supplies, Ironforge (52), F-3, The Great Forge, Stonebrow's Clothier

OUTHOUSE
Western Plaguelands (92), F-5, Dalson's Tears, Located on the north end of the farm behind the house and barn

OVERLORD MOK'MOROKK
Dustwallow Marsh (38), D-3, Brackenwall Village (104), Center of village

OVERLORD RAMTUSK
Barrens (18), E-9, Razorfen Kraul

OVERLORD ROR
Felwood (44), G-9, Deadwood Village, Southern camp

OVERLORD RUNTHAK
Orgrimmar (60), F:(7, 8), Valley of Strength, Near main entrance

OVERLORD WYRMTHALAK
Burning Steppes (22), Searing Gorge (64), C-4/D-8, Blackrock Spire

OVERMASTER PYRON
Burning Steppes (22), Searing Gorge (64), C-4/D-8, Blackrock Depths

OVERSEER GLIBBY
Barrens (18), G-1, The Sludge Fen

OVERSEER MALTORIUS
Searing Gorge (64), E-4, The Slag Pit, Roams with two Dark Iron Sentry's around upper level platform

OVERSEER OILFIST
The Thorium Brotherhood, Searing Gorge (64), D-3, Thorium Point (136), Second floor of tower

OWATANKA
Barrens (18), E-6, F-6, Southern Barrens, Roams areas south and east of Camp Taurajo

OWEN VAUGHN
Reagent Vendor, Stormwind (72), E-7, Mage Quarter, Essential Components

OX
The Mithril Order, Orgrimmar (60), J-2, Valley of Honor, Across from Arms of Legend

OZZIE TOGGLEVOLT
Dun Morogh (32), F-5, Kharanos (116), In gnomish building

P

PA MACLURE
Elwynn Forest (42), F-9, The Maclure Vineyards, In front of house

PACK KODO
Thousand Needles (82), B-3, Whitereach Post, Next to hut

PACKMASTER STONEBRUISER
Brotherhood of the Light, Eastern Plaguelands (40), K-6, Light's Hope Chapel (117)

PAIGE CHADDIS
Stormwind (72), Roams city with Karlee

PAIGE FELIXE
Feralas (46), B-4, Feathermoon Stronghold (111), Next to log west of inn

PAINED
Dustwallow Marsh (38), I-5, Theramore Isle (135), Top of central tower

PAKWA
Bag Vendor, Thunder Bluff (84), D-6, Lower rise, in front of Kuruk's Goods tent

PALEMANE POACHER
Mulgore (58), C-6, F-7, G-7, Palemane Rock, Winterhoof Water Well

PALEMANE SKINNER
Mulgore (58), C-6, D-6, E-7, F-7, G-7, Palemane Rock, Red Cloud Mesa, Winterhoof Water Well

PALEMANE TANNER
Mulgore (58), C-6, D-6, E-7, F-7, G-7, Palemane Rock, Red Cloud Mesa

PAMELA REDPATH
Eastern Plaguelands (40), E-8, Darrowshire, Roams house ruins in northwestern part of town

PAND STONEBINDER
First Aid Trainer, Thunder Bluff (84), C-2, Spirit Rise, Inside Spiritual Healing tent

PANTHER
Stranglethorn Vale (74), B:(1, 2), C:(1, 2), E-1

PANZOR THE INVINCIBLE
Rare Spawn, Burning Steppes (22), Searing Gorge (64), C-4/D-8, Blackrock Depths, Lvl 57 Rare

PAO'KA SWIFTMOUNTAIN
Thousand Needles (82), B-4, Highperch, Entrance to Highperch

PARQUAL FINTALLAS
Undercity (88), F-7, The Apothecarium, On the bridge

PAT
Stormwind (72), Roams city with Miss Danna

PATCHWORK HORROR
Eastern Plaguelands (40), D-2, Stratholme

PATHSTRIDER
Eastern Plaguelands (40), G-2, Quel'Lithien Lodge

PATRICE DWYER
Poison Supplies, Silverpine Forest (68), F-4, The Sepulcher (127), Left side of inn by fireplace

PATRICK GARRETT
Undercity (88), I-5, The Trade Quarter, Upper Ring of Trade Quarter

PATRICK MILLS
Azshara (14), H-9, The Ruined Reaches, Inlet

PAVAL REETHE
Dustwallow Marsh (38), E-4, Camp on small island

PAWE MISTRUNNER
Thunder Bluff (84), B-3, Spirit Rise, Ouside of tents

PAXTON GANTER
Fisherman, Dun Morogh (32), E-4, Iceflow Lake, Fishing at a break in the ice on lake

PEACEKEEPER SECURITY SUIT
Dun Morogh (32), C-4, Gnomeregan

PELTURAS WHITEMOON
Ashenvale (12), E-5, Astranaar (101), Southeast building

PENNY
Stable Master, Redridge Mountains (62), C-5, Lakeshire (117), Next to stack of kegs outside of Lakeshire Inn

PEPHREDO
Mage Trainer, Orgrimmar (60), D:(8, 9), Valley of Spirit, Darkbriar Lodge

PERIA LAMENUR
Pet Trainer, Dun Morogh (32), F-5, Kharanos (116), In caravan

PESTERHIDE HYENA
Thousand Needles (82), B:(2, 4), C:(2-5), D:(2-5), E:(3, 5, 6), F:(5, 6), G-5

PESTERHIDE SNARLER
Thousand Needles (82), A:(1-3), B:(2-4), G:(4, 5), H:(5, 6), I:(5, 6)

PETER GALEN
Master Dragonscale Leatherworker, Azshara (14), D-6, Ruins of Eldarath, Camp in hills south of ruins

PETRA GROSSEN
Un'Goro Crater (90), F-1, Marshal's Refuge (118), Entrance to cave

PETRIFIED GUARDIAN
Feralas (46), G-4, Dire Maul

PETRIFIED TREANT
Feralas (46), G-4, Dire Maul

PHALANX
Burning Steppes (22), Searing Gorge (64), C-4/D-8, Blackrock Depths

PHANTIM
Ashenvale (12), L-4, Bough Shadow, Patrols area near portal

PHASE LASHER
Feralas (46), G-4, Dire Maul

PHIN ODELIC
Hillsbrad Foothills (48), F-6, Southshore (129), Right of inn by carriage

PIERCE SHACKLETON
Mage Trainer, Undercity (88), L-1, The Magic Quarter, Inside Skull Building

PIKKLE
Miner, Tanaris (78), G-3, Gadgetzan (113), Southwestern hut

PILLAR OF AMETHYST
Badlands (16), L-6, Lethlor Ravine, Pillar on hill

PILLAR OF DIAMOND
Badlands (16), L-3, Lethlor Ravine, Pillar on hill

PILLAR OF OPAL
Badlands (16), K-7, Lethlor Ravine, Pillar on hill

PILOT BELLOWFIZ
Dun Morogh (32), G-5, Steelgrill's Depot, By siege tank outside of depot

PILOT HAMMERFOOT
Dun Morogh (32), L-4, North Gate Outpost, By siege tank next to tower

PILOT LONGBEARD
Ironforge Siege Brigade, Ironforge (52), J-9, The Military Ward, Hall of Arms

PILOT STONEGEAR
Dun Morogh (32), G-5, Steelgrill's Depot, By siege tank outside of depot

PILOT WIZZLECRANK
Barrens (18), G-1, Hut

PILOT XIGGS FUSELIGHTER
Azshara (14), J-9, The Ruined Reaches, Landing pad on island

PIMGIB
Feralas (46), G-4, Dire Maul

PITER VERANCE
Weaponsmith & Armorer, Dustwallow Marsh (38), I-5, Theramore Isle (135), First floor of Foothold Citadel

PITHWICK
Bag Vendor, Ironforge (52), E-7, The Commons, Fizzlespinner's General Goods

PIXEL
Ashenvale (12), I-6, Splintertree Post (129), On crates to right of flightpoint

PIZNIK
Stonetalon Mountains (70), J-6, Windshear Mine, West deadend of mine

PIZZNUKLE
Leather Armor Merchant, Barrens (18), E-4, Near mountains west of oasis

PLAGUE GHOUL
Eastern Plaguelands (40), D-2, Stratholme

PLAGUE LURKER
Western Plaguelands (92), G:(5, 6), H:(4-6), I:(4-6)

PLAGUE MONSTROSITY
Eastern Plaguelands (40), G-5, I:(3, 4), J-4, Blackwood Lake

PLAGUE RAVAGER
Eastern Plaguelands (40), H:(7, 8), I:(7, 8), Lake Mereldar

PLAGUE SPREADER
Duskwood (36), B-3, C:(3, 4), Raven Hill Cemetery (123)

PLAGUEBAT
Eastern Plaguelands (40), A:(4, 5), B:(5-7), C:(6-8), D:(6-9), E:(6-8), F:(6-8), G:(7, 8), H:(7, 8), I:(7, 8), J-8

PLAGUED HATCHLING
Western Plaguelands (92), I-7, Scholomance

PLAGUED PEASANT
Eastern Plaguelands (40), C-2, Plaguewood

PLAGUED RAT
Eastern Plaguelands (40), D-2, Stratholme

PLAGUEHOUND
Eastern Plaguelands (40), F-6, G:(5, 6), H:(5, 6), I:(5-7), J:(6, 7), K-7

PLAGUEHOUND RUNT
Eastern Plaguelands (40), A:(4, 5), B:(5-7), C:(6-8), D:(6-9), E:(6-8), G:(7, 8), H:(7, 8), I:(7, 8), J-8

PLAGUELAND TERMITE
Western Plaguelands (92), F-3

PLAGUEMAW THE ROTTING
Barrens (18), F-9, Razorfen Downs

PLAINS CREEPER
Arathi Highlands (10), B:(4, 5), C:(3-5), D:(2, 3, 5, 6), E:(3-7), F:(4, 6, 7), G:(3-6), H:(3-5), I:(3-6), J:(3-6), K-3, Refuge Point (124), Outside Refuge Point (124) and throughout highlands

PLAINSTRIDER
Mulgore (58), E:(7-9), F:(7-9), Camp Narache (105), Kodo Rock

PLATED STEGODON
Un'Goro Crater (90), C:(5-7), D:(6-8), E:(6-8), Golakka Hot Springs, Terror Run

"PLUCKY" JOHNSON
Thousand Needles (82), K-8, Mirage Raceway (119)

PLUGGER SPAZZRING
Burning Steppes (22), Searing Gorge (64), C-4/D-8, Blackrock Depths

POISON SPRITE
Desolace (30), D-5, Mauradon

POOKA
Barrens (18), E-1, Roams in and out of building west of road

PORANNA SNOWBRAID
Tailoring Supplies, Ironforge (52), F-3, The Great Forge, Stonebrow's Clothier

PORTHANNIUS
Teldrassil (80), H-5, Shadowglen (127), Side of road leading out of Shadowglen

POSTMASTER MALOWN
Eastern Plaguelands (40), D-2, Stratholme

POZZIK
Thousand Needles (82), K-8, Mirage Raceway (119), Inside racetrack

PRAIRIE STALKER
Mulgore (58), C:(3, 4), D:(2-5), E:(3-5), F:(3-5), G:(3-7), H:(5-7)

PRAIRIE WOLF
Mulgore (58), C-8, D:(5-8), E:(5-7), F:(6, 7), G:(6, 7)

PRAIRIE WOLF ALPHA
Mulgore (58), C-2, D:(1, 2), E:(1-3), F:(1-3), G:(2, 3), H:(2, 3, 6, 7)

PRATE CLOUDSEER
Thousand Needles (82), G-4, The Weathered Nook, Front of den

PRATT MCGRUBBEN
Leatherworking Supplies, Feralas (46), C-4, Feathermoon Stronghold (111), Behind Inn, next to water

PRECIOUS
Un'Goro Crater (90), E:(4-8), F-6, F-8, G:(6-8), Golakka Hot Springs, The Slithering Scar, Terror Run, Walks big area from The Slithering Scar to north of the springs

"PRETTY BOY" DUNCAN
Stranglethorn Vale (74), B-7, Southern Savage Coast, Roams around shoreline camp

PRIDEWING CONSORT
Stonetalon Mountains (70), E-4, F:(4, 5), G-4, Mirkfallon Lake

PRIDEWING PATRIARCH
Rare Spawn, Stonetalon Mountains (70), F:(4-5), G-4, Mirkfallon Lake, Lvl 25 Uncommon; Spawns in mountains east or south of Mirkfallon Lake

PRIDEWING SKYHUNTER
Stonetalon Mountains (70), F-5, G-4, Mirkfallon Lake

PRIDEWING SOARER
Stonetalon Mountains (70), E-4, F-4, Mirkfallon Lake, Soars between high ledges northwest of lake and in middle of lake

PRIDEWING WYVERN
Stonetalon Mountains (70), F:(4, 5), G-4, Mirkfallon Lake

PRIESTESS ALATHEA
Priest Trainer, Darnassus (26), E-8, Temple of the Moon, Balcony, north of fountain

PRIESTESS A'MOORA
Darnassus (26), D-9, Temple of the Moon, Balcony, west of fountain

PRIESTESS ANETTA
Priest Trainer, Elwynn Forest (42), G-4, Northshire Valley (122), Room behind the Library Wing of abbey

PRIESTESS JOSETTA
Priest Trainer, Elwynn Forest (42), F-7, Goldshire (114), Second floor of Lion's Pride Inn

PRIESTESS OF ELUNE
Winterspring (98), J-6, Owl Wing Thicket, (Summon) Near altar

PRIMAL OOZE
Un'Goro Crater (90), E-2, F:(3, 6, 7), G:(2-4, 6, 7), H:(2, 5-8), J-3

PRIMAL TORNTUSK
The Hinterlands (50), L-8, Revantusk Village (125), Second floor of inn on eastern side of village

PRIMITIVE OWLBEAST
The Hinterlands (50), E-6, F:(4-7), G:(4-6), H:(4-6), The Hinterlands

PRIMORDIAL BEHEMOTH
Desolace (30), D-5, Mauradon

PRINCE GALEN TROLLBANE
Arathi Highlands (10), D-6, Stromgarde Keep (132), Roams church near crypt

PRINCE KELLEN
Rare Spawn, Desolace (30), J-2, Sargeron, Lvl 33 Average Rare; Top of hill or east by hill

PRINCE NAZJAK
Rare Spawn, Arathi Highlands (10), C:(8, 9), The Drowned Reef, Lvl 41 Very Rare; Roams in the reef

PRINCE RAZE
Rare Spawn, Ashenvale (12), J:(4-5), Xavian, Lvl 32 Uncommon; Can be found near delta, next to a totem in middle of camp, or next to Geltharis

PRINCE THUNDERAAN
Silithus (66), D-1, Ravaged Twilight Camp, (Summon)

PRINCE TORTHELDRIN
Feralas (46), G-4, Dire Maul

PRINCE XAVALIS
Felwood (44), E-6, Shadow Hold, Small incline in first room

PRINCESS
Elwynn Forest (42), J-8, Brackwell Pumpkin Patch, Roams with two Porcine Entourage around pumpkin patch

PRINCESS MOIRA BRONZEBEARD
Burning Steppes (22), Searing Gorge (64), C-4/D-8, Blackrock Depths

PRINCESS POOBAH
Stranglethorn Vale (74), D-8, Jaguero Isle, Small camp on the northern side of island

PRINCESS TEMPESTRIA
Winterspring (98), H-4, Lake Kel'Theril, Spawns on the lake

PRINCESS THERADRAS
Desolace (30), D-5, Mauradon

PRISONER OF JIN'ZIL
Stonetalon Mountains (70), J-9, Malaka'jin, Den, inside one of three cages

PRIVATE HENDEL
Dustwallow Marsh (38), F-2, Dock near small camp

PRIVATE MERLE
Stranglethorn Vale (74), D-1, Rebel Camp (124), Camp

PRIVATE THORSEN
Stranglethorn Vale (74), D-1, Rebel Camp (124), Patrols between camp and an area down the hill

PRIVATEER BLOADS
Stranglethorn Vale (74), B-8, Booty Bay (103), Idle in front of Stranglethorn Trust Bank

PRIVATEER GROY
Dustwallow Marsh (38), I-5, Theramore Isle (135), Southeast near docks

PROFESSOR PHIZZLETHORPE
Arathi Highlands (10), D-8, Faldir's Cove, By bonfire on hill

PROSPECTOR GEHN
Explorers' League, Dun Morogh (32), I-5, Gol'Bolar Quarry, By caravan along back wall of camp

PROSPECTOR GUNSTAN
Explorers' League, Tanaris (78), E-8, Valley of the Watchers, Camp near entrance to Uldum

PROSPECTOR IRONBAND
Loch Modan (54), I-7, Ironband's Excavation Site, Camp outside of excavation site

PROSPECTOR IRONBOOT
Tanaris (78), J-3, Steamwheedle Port, Outside southern building

PROSPECTOR KHAZGORM
Explorer's League, Barrens (18), F-9, Bael Modan, Roams southeast area in excavation

PROSPECTOR REMTRAVEL
Explorer's League, Darkshore (24), E-8, Remtravel's Excavation, Behind rock

PROSPECTOR RYEDOL
Badlands (16), H-4, Camp

PROSPECTOR STONEHEWER
Alterac Mountains (8), E-8, The Headland, Right camp outside Alterac Valley (Alliance)

PROSPECTOR STORMPIKE
Ironforge (52), J-1, Hall of Explorers, Library

PROSPECTOR WHELGAR
Wetlands (96), E-5, Whelgar's Excavation Site, Den across the bridge in east section of site

PROTECTOR BIALON
Westfall (94), F-5, Sentinel Hill (126), Outside Sentinel Tower

PROTECTOR DENI
Westfall (94), F-5, Sentinel Hill (126), Outside Saw Mill

PROTECTOR DORANA
Westfall (94), G-5, Sentinel Hill (126), Spawns near the merchants outside Sentinel Hill and roams south along the road

PROTECTOR DUTFIELD
Westfall (94), G-5, Sentinel Hill (126), Roams Sentinel Tower

PROTECTOR GARIEL
Westfall (94), F-5, Sentinel Hill (126), Outside Sentinel Tower

PROTECTOR KORELOR
Westfall (94), F-5, Sentinel Hill (126), Spawns near the Saw Mill and roams to the bridge leading to Duskwood

PROTECTOR LEICK
Westfall (94), F-5, Sentinel Hill (126), Outside Saw Mill

PROTECTOR WEAVER
Westfall (94), G-5, Sentinel Hill (126), Circles top of Sentinel Tower

PROWLER
Elwynn Forest (42), I-4, J:(4, 6-8), K:(4, 6-8), L:(6-8), Eastvale Logging Camp, Ridgepoint Tower, Stone Cairn Lake

PRYNNE
Gnomeregan Exiles, Ironforge (52), F-1, The Forlorn Cavern, Stoneblade's

PTERRORDAX
Un'Goro Crater (90), F:(7, 9), G:(1, 2, 7, 9), H:(1, 2, 5, 7, 9), J-5

PUSILLIN
Feralas (46), G-4, Dire Maul

PUTRID GARGOYLE
Eastern Plaguelands (40), B:(6, 7), C:(2, 7, 9), D:(3, 6, 7), E:(2, 4, 6-8), F:(3, 6-8), G:(5, 8), H:(5-8), I:(5, 7), J:(5, 7), Plaguewood

PUTRID SHRIEKER
Eastern Plaguelands (40), C-4, D-4, F-4, G:(3, 4), H:(3-5), I:(4, 5), J-3, Quel'Lithien Lodge

PUTRIDIUS
Rare Spawn, Western Plaguelands (92), F-7, Ruins of Andorhal, Lvl 58 Uber-Rare; Roamd around city

PUTRIDUS SATYR
Desolace (30), D-5, Mauradon

PUTRIDUS SHADOWSTALKER
Desolace (30), D-5, Mauradon

PUTRIDUS TRICKSTER
Desolace (30), D-5, Mauradon

PYALL SILENTSTRIDE
Cook, Mulgore (58), E-6, Bloodhoof Village (102), Northeast tent

PYGMY SURF CRAWLER
Durotar (34), H-8, I:(4-8), J:(5, 6)

PYGMY TIDE CRAWLER
Darkshore (24), E:(4, 5), F-4, Auberdine, The Long Wash, Mist's Edge

PYGMY VENOM WEB SPIDER
Duskwood (36), A:(3-7), B:(3, 7), C-3, D-3, E-2, F-2, G:(1, 2), H-2, I-2, J-2, K-2, L-2, The Darkened Bank

PYREWOOD ARMORER
Silverpine Forest (68), G-7, Pyrewood Village, Smithy

PYREWOOD ELDER
Silverpine Forest (68), F-7, G-7, Preywood Village

PYREWOOD LEATHERWORKER
Silverpine Forest (68), G-7, Pyrewood Village, House next to inn

PYREWOOD SENTRY
Silverpine Forest (68), F-7, G-7, Preywood Village

PYREWOOD TAILOR
Silverpine Forest (68), G-7, Pyrewood Village, Patrols between house and smithy

PYREWOOD WATCHER
Silverpine Forest (68), F-7, G-7, Preywood Village

PYROGUARD EMBERSEER
Burning Steppes (22), Searing Gorge (64), C-4/D-8, Blackrock Spire

PYROMANCER LOREGRAIN
Burning Steppes (22), Searing Gorge (64), C-4/D-8, Blackrock Depths

Q

QEEJU
Stable Master, Ashenvale (12), I-6, Splintertree Post (129)

QIA
Trade Goods Supplies, Winterspring (98), I-4, Everlook (110), Inside building directly north of inn

QIAGA THE KEEPER
The Hinterlands (50), G-7, The Altar of Zul, Top of altar

QIROT
Rare Spawn, Feralas (46), I-6, The Writhing Deep, Lvl 47 Uncommon; In hive

QIXDI GOODSTITCH
Cloth Armor and Accessories, Stranglethorn Vale (74), B-8, Booty Bay (103), Tan-Your-Hide Leatherworks (shop)

QIZZIK
Banker, Tanaris (78), H-3, Gadgetzan (113), Bank

QUAE
Arathi Highlands (10), H-5, Go'Shek Farm, Hill northwest of farm

QUARRY SLAVE
Burning Steppes (22), Searing Gorge (64), C-4/D-8, Blackrock Depths

QUARRYMASTER THESTEN
Miners' League, Dun Morogh (32), J-5, Gol'Bolar Quarry, Under tent along back wall of camp

QUARTERMASTER HICKS
Master Weaponsmith, Elwynn Forest (42), C-7, Westbrook Garrison, First floor armory in garrison

QUARTERMASTER HUDSON
Armorer & Shieldcrafter, Elwynn Forest (42), C-7, Westbrook Garrison, First floor armory in garrison

QUARTERMASTER LEWIS
Quartermaster, Westfall (94), G-5, Sentinel Tower, Sentinel Tower

QUARTERMASTER LUNGERTZ
Blasted Lands (20), J-2, Nethergarde Keep (120), Stable

QUARTERMASTER MIRANDA BREECHLOCK
The Argent Dawn, Eastern Plaguelands (40), K-6, Light's Hope Chapel (118), Camp on right side of chapel

QUARTERMASTER ZIGRIS
Rare Spawn, Burning Steppes (22), Searing Gorge (64), C-4/D-8, Blackrock Spire, Lvl 59 Uncommon

QUEL'LITHIEN PROTECTOR
Eastern Plaguelands (40), G-2, Quel'Lithien Lodge

QUENTIN
Thousand Needles (82), K-8, Mirage Raceway (119), West grandstands

QUILGUARD CHAMPION
Barrens (18), E-9, Razorfen Kraul

QUINN
Tanaris (78), G-3, Gadgetzan (113), Outside southwestern hut

QUINN YORICK
Silverpine Forest (68), H-1, The Ivar Patch, Second floor of house

QUINTIS JONESPYRE
Feralas (46), C-4, Feathermoon Stronghold (111), Top floor of tree building in northeast

QUIXXIL
Un'Goro Crater (90), F-1, Marshal's Refuge (118), South of cave

R

RABID BLISTERPAW
Tanaris (78), D:(5-8), E:(5-8), F:(4-8), G:(4, 5, 7, 8)

RABID BONEPAW
Desolace (30), E-4, G-4, Scrabblescrew's Camp

RABID CRAG COYOTE
Badlands (16), J:(3, 4), K:(3, 4), Dustwind Gulch

RABID DIRE WOLF
Duskwood (36), A:(3-7), B-3, C-3, D:(2, 3), E:(2, 3), F-2, G-2, H-2, I-2, J:(2, 3), K-2, Brightwood Grove

RABID LONGTOOTH
Feralas (46), D:(1, 2), E:(1-4), F-3, Ruins of Ravenwind, The Twin Colossals

RABID SHADOWHIDE GNOLL
Redridge Mountains (62), J:(4-6), Galardell Valley

RABID SHARDTOOTH
Winterspring (98), H-7, I-7, J-7, Frostwhisper Gorge

RABID THISTLE BEAR
Darkshore (24), F:(2, 5-8), G:(2-4, 6, 7), H:(2-4)

RABINE SATURNA
Moonglade (56), G-4, Nighthaven (121), South wing of southeast building

RACE MASTER KRONKRIDER
Thousand Needles (82), K-8, Mirage Raceway (119), Atop Starters tower inside track

RACHEL
Redridge Mountains (62), C-4, Lakeshire (117)

RADNAAL MANEWEAVER
Skinner, Teldrassil (80), E-5, Outside house

RAEDON DUSKSTRIKER
Alliance Cloth Quartermaster, Darnassus (26), I-2, Craftsmen's Terrace, Tailoring shop

RAENA FLINTHAMMER
Light Armor Merchant, Ironforge (52), D-6, The Commons, Ironforge Armory

RAENE WOLFRUNNER
Ashenvale (12), E-5, Astranaar (101), First floor of inn near Korra and Dagri

RAGE SCAR YETI
Feralas (46), F-3, Rage Scar Hold

RAGE TALON CAPTAIN
Burning Steppes (22), Searing Gorge (64), C-4/D-8, Blackrock Spire

RAGE TALON DRAGON GUARD
Burning Steppes (22), Searing Gorge (64), C-4/D-8, Blackrock Spire

RAGE TALON DRAGONSPAWN
Burning Steppes (22), Searing Gorge (64), C-4/D-8, Blackrock Spire

RAGE TALON FIRE TONGUE
Burning Steppes (22), Searing Gorge (64), C-4/D-8, Blackrock Spire

RAGE TALON FLAMESCALE
Burning Steppes (22), Searing Gorge (64), C-4/D-8, Blackrock Spire

RAGECLAW
Teldrassil (80), E-6, Ban'ethil Barrow Den, Roams circular path in northern section of den

RAGEFIRE SHAMAN
Orgrimmar (60), F-5, Ragefire Chasm

RAGEFIRE TROGG
Orgrimmar (60), F-5, Ragefire Chasm

RAGEPAW
Rare Spawn, Felwood (44), G-9, Deadwood Village, Lvl 51 Uncommon; Roams southern area of camp

RAGEREAVER GOLEM
Burning Steppes (22), Searing Gorge (64), C-4/D-8, Blackrock Depths

RAGGED GHOUL
Western Plaguelands (92), I-7, Scholomance

RAGGED JOHN
Burning Steppes (22), H-2, Flame Crest (112), Right of scaffolding

RAGGED OWLBEAST
Winterspring (98), D:(4, 5), E:(4, 5), F-4, G:(3-5), H-4, Frostfire Hot Springs, Timbermaw Post

RAGGED SCAVENGER
Tirisfal Glades (86), D-6, E-6, Deathknell (109)

RAGGED TIMBER WOLF
Dun Morogh (32), C:(7, 8), D:(7, 8), Coldridge Valley (107)

RAGGED YOUNG WOLF
Dun Morogh (32), C:(7, 8), D:(7, 8), Coldridge Valley (107)

RAGGLESNOUT
Boss, Barrens (18), F-9, Razorfen Downs

RAGING AGAM'AR
Barrens (18), E-9, Razorfen Kraul

RAGING CLIFF STORMER
Stonetalon Mountains (70), F:(3, 4), G:(3, 4), H:(4-7), I:(4, 6), J:(4, 5)

RAGING DUNE SMASHER
Tanaris (78), E-8, F-8, Uldum, Valley of the Watchers

RAGING MOONKIN
Darkshore (24), G:(4, 5)

RAGING OWLBEAST
Winterspring (98), H-3, I:(3, 4), Moon Horror Den, Everlook

RAGING REEF CRAWLER
Darkshore (24), D-9, E-9, H:(1, 2), I-Mist's Edge, Twilight Shore

RAGING ROT HIDE
Silverpine Forest (68), J:(2, 3), Fenris

RAGING THUNDER LIZARD
Desolace (30), D-7, E:(2-4, 6-8), F:(1-4, 7), G:(2-4), H:(3, 4), I:(5-7), J:(5, 6)

RAGNAR THUNDERBREW
Dun Morogh (32), F-5, Kharanos (11 Outside of distillery

RAGNAROS
Burning Steppes (22), Searing Gorge (64), C-4/D-8, The Molten Core

RAHAURO
Thunder Bluff (84), I-3, Elder Rise, Outside of Magatha Grimtotem's ter

RAIDER BORK
Mount QM, Orgrimmar (61), E-7

RAIDER JHASH
Durotar (34), H-4, Razor Hill (124), Spawns at trough in Razor Hill and patrols to the Den and back

RAIDER KERR
Durotar (34), H-4, Razor Hill (124), Spawns at trough in Razor Hill and patrols to the Den and back

RAKAIAH
Felwood (44), E-6, Shadow Hold, Alt room

RAK'SHIRI
Rare Spawn, Winterspring (98), G:(1, H-1, Frostsaber Rock, Lvl 57 Semi-Ra Roams base of rock

RALEIGH ANDREAN
Ex-Chef, Undercity (88), I-4, The Trad Quarter, West spoke from bank

RALEIGH THE DEVOUT
Hillsbrad Foothills (48), F-6, Southsho (129), Second floor of inn

RALLIC FINN
Bowyer, Elwynn Forest (42), L-7, Eastvale Logging Camp, Next to targ

RALSTON FARNSLEY
Horde Cloth Quartermaster, Undercit (88), J-3, The Magic Quarter, Quest Giver

RAMSTEIN THE GORGER
Eastern Plaguelands (40), D-2, Stratholme

RAN BLOODTOOTH
Ashenvale (12), G-7, Bloodtooth Cam Far south deep in camp

RAND RHOBART
Skinner, Tirisfal Glades (86), I-6, In ca outside of Undercity

RANDAL HUNTER
Horse Riding Instructor, Elwynn Fores (42), L-6, Eastvale Logging Camp, Corale

RANDAL WORTH
Journeyman Leatherworker, Stormwir (72), J-5, Old Town, The Protective H

RANDOLPH MONTAGUE
Banker, Undercity (88), I-4, The Trade Quarter

RANE YORICK
Deathstalker, Silverpine Forest (68), H-1, The Ivar Patch, In front of house

RANGER
Eastern Plaguelands (40), G-2, Quel'Lithien Lodge

RANGER LORD HAWKSPEAR
Rare Spawn, Eastern Plaguelands (40), G-2, Quel'Lithien Lodge, Lvl 60 Uncommon; Patrols lodge

RANIK
Trade Supplies, Barrens (18), H-4, Ratchet (122), Jazzik's General Goods

RANN FLAMESPINNER
Tailoring Supplies, Loch Modan (54), D-5, Thelsamar (134), Porch of third house north of path

RANSHALLA
Winterspring (98), I-6, Owl Wing Thicket, Off road to east by pillar

RARC
Armorer & Shieldcrafter, Durotar (34) F-7, Valley of Trials (136)

RARTAR
Alchemy Supplies, Swamp of Sorrows (76), F-5, Stonard (131), Second floor of inn

RAS FROSTWHISPER
Western Plaguelands (92), I-7, Scholomance

RASCAL SPRITE
Teldrassil (80), G-5, Fel Rock

ASCHAL THE COURIER
Feralas (46), I-6, The Writhing Deep, Cocoon in hive

RAGLASH
Horde Cloth Quartermaster, Orgrimmar (60), H-5, The Drag, Magar's Cloth Goods

ATCHET BRUISER
Barrens (18), G-4, H-4, Ratchet (122)

ATHORIAN
Rare Spawn, Barrens (18), E-2, F-2, Dreadmist Den, Lvl 15 Uncommon; In cave atop Dreadmist Peak

ATSLIN MAIME
Tirisfal Glades (86), H-5, Brill (104), First floor of Gallows' End Tavern

ATTLECAGE SKELETON
Tirisfal Glades (86), D-6, Agamand Mills (100)

ATTLECAGE SOLDIER
Tirisfal Glades (86), E-4, F:(3, 4), Agamand Mills (100)

ATTLEGORE
Western Plaguelands (92), I-7, Scholomance

AU CLIFFRUNNER
Thousand Needles (82), F-5, Freewind Post (112), Inn

AVAGE
Rare Spawn, Blasted Lands (20), G-4, I-4, Lvl 51 Semi-Rare; Roams small area around spawn point

AVAGED CADAVER
Eastern Plaguelands (40), D-2, Stratholme

AVAGED CORPSE
Tirisfal Glades (86), F-5, G:(4-6)

AVASAUR
Un'Goro Crater (90), H:(6-8), I:(6-8), The Marshlands, The Slithering Scar

AVASAUR HUNTER
Un'Goro Crater (90), H:(5, 6), I:(5, 6), J:(5, 6), The Marshlands

AVASAUR MATRIARCH
Un'Goro Crater (90), H-7, I:(6, 7), The Marshlands

AVASAUR RUNNER
Un'Goro Crater (90), H:(6-8), I:(6-8), The Marshlands

AVENCLAW APPARITION
Silverpine Forest (68), G-2, The Dead Field

AVENCLAW CHAMPION
Silverpine Forest (68), H:(3, 4), The Decrepit Ferry, East of road near lake

AVENCLAW DRUDGER
Silverpine Forest (68), I-7, Beren's Peril, Cave

AVENCLAW GUARDIAN
Silverpine Forest (68), I-7, Beren's Peril, Cave

AVENCLAW RAIDER
Silverpine Forest (68), G:(5, 6), Olsen's Farthing, Farm

AVENCLAW REGENT
Rare Spawn, Desolace (30), J-2, Sargeron, Lvl 22 Uncommon; Southwest of Nijel's Point

AVENCLAW SERVANT
Silverpine Forest (68), H:(3, 4), The Decrepit Ferry, East of road near lake

AVENCLAW SLAVE
Silverpine Forest (68), G-5, H:(1, 2), The Ivar Patch, Farm

AVENHOLDT ASSASSIN
Assassin's League, Hillsbrad Foothills (48), K-2, Ravenholdt Manor, In and around the Ravenholdt Manor

AVENHOLDT GUARD
Hillsbrad Foothills (48), J:(1, 2), K-2

AVENOUS DARKHOUND
Tirisfal Glades (86), K:(4, 5), L:(4, 5), Venomweb Vale

AWRK
First Aid Trainer, Durotar (34), H-4, Razor Hill (124), Barracks

AYAN DAWNRISEN
Azshara (14), C-4, Bear's Head, Requires quest from Sanath Lim-yo to reach

AYNE
Cenarion Circle, Eastern Plaguelands (40), K-6, Light's Hope Chapel (118)

AYTAF
Loramus's Guardian, Azshara (14), H-7, Bay of Storms, Patrols near Loramus

AZAL'BLADE
Badlands (16), A-5, Kargath (116), Group left of orc burrow

RAZBO RUSTGEAR
Weapon and Armor Merchant, Dustwallow Marsh (38), F-7, Mudsprocket (120)

RAZE
Nilith's Guardian, Searing Gorge (64), E-7, Behind Nilith Lokrav on right side of camp

RAZELIKH THE DEFILER
Blasted Lands (20), G-3, Rise of the Defiler, (Summon) Summoned by player via Altar of the Defiler

RAZOR HILL GRUNT
Durotar (34), G-4, H-4, Razor Hill (124)

RAZORBEAK GRYPHON
The Hinterlands (50), D-7, E:(4, 5), F:(4, 6), G-5, H-6

RAZORBEAK SKYLORD
The Hinterlands (50), H-6, I:(4, 6)

RAZORCLAW THE BUTCHER
Silverpine Forest (68), F-7, Shadowfang Keep

RAZORFEN BATTLEGUARD
Barrens (18), E-9, F-9, Razorfen Downs, Southern Gold Road

RAZORFEN BEAST TRAINER
Barrens (18), E-9, Razorfen Kraul

RAZORFEN BEASTMASTER
Barrens (18), E-9, Razorfen Kraul

RAZORFEN DEFENDER
Barrens (18), E-9, Razorfen Kraul

RAZORFEN DUSTWEAVER
Barrens (18), E-9, Razorfen Kraul

RAZORFEN EARTHBREAKER
Barrens (18), E-9, Razorfen Kraul

RAZORFEN GEOMANCER
Barrens (18), E-9, Razorfen Kraul

RAZORFEN GROUNDSHAKER
Barrens (18), E-9, Razorfen Kraul

RAZORFEN HANDLER
Barrens (18), E-9, Razorfen Kraul

RAZORFEN QUILGUARD
Barrens (18), E-9, Razorfen Kraul

RAZORFEN SERVITOR
Barrens (18), E-9, F-9, Razorfen Downs, Razorfen Kraul, Southern Gold Road

RAZORFEN SPEARHIDE
Barrens (18), E-9, Razorfen Kraul

RAZORFEN STALKER
Barrens (18), E-9, Razorfen Kraul

RAZORFEN THORNWEAVER
Barrens (18), F-9, Razorfen Downs

RAZORFEN TOTEMIC
Barrens (18), E-9, Razorfen Kraul

RAZORFEN WARDEN
Barrens (18), E-9, Razorfen Kraul

RAZORFEN WARRIOR
Barrens (18), E-9, Razorfen Kraul

RAZORLASH
Desolace (30), D-5, Mauradon

RAZORMANE BATTLEGUARD
Durotar (34), F:(4, 5), G-4, Razormane Grounds

RAZORMANE DEFENDER
Barrens (18), G:(2, 3), Thorn Hill

RAZORMANE DUSTRUNNER
Durotar (34), F:(4, 5), G-4, Razormane Grounds

RAZORMANE GEOMANCER
Barrens (18), G:(2, 3), Thorn Hill

RAZORMANE HUNTER
Barrens (18), F:(2, 3), G:(2, 3), Thorn Hill

RAZORMANE MYSTIC
Barrens (18), G-3, Thorn Hill

RAZORMANE PATHFINDER
Barrens (18), E-8, Blackthorn Ridge, Southern Barrens

RAZORMANE QUILBOAR
Durotar (34), F-5, G-5, H-5, Razormane Grounds

RAZORMANE SCOUT
Durotar (34), F-5, G-5, H-5, Razormane Grounds

RAZORMANE SEER
Barrens (18), D-8, E-8, Blackthorn Ridge, Southern Gold Road

RAZORMANE STALKER
Barrens (18), E-8, Blackthorn Ridge, Southern Gold Road

RAZORMANE THORNWEAVER
Barrens (18), F:(2, 3), G-3, Gold Road, Thorn Hill

RAZORMANE WARFRENZY
Barrens (18), D-8, E-8, Blackthorn Ridge

RAZORMANE WATER SEEKER
Barrens (18), F:(2, 3), G-3, Gold Road, Thorn Hill

RAZORMAW MATRIARCH
Rare Spawn, Wetlands (96), I-3, J-3, Raptor Ridge, Lvl 31 Uncommon; Spawns in western or northeastern chamber of cave

RAZORTALON
Rare Spawn, The Hinterlands (50), D:(5, 7), E-5, F-5, Bogen's Ledge, Lvl 44 Average Rare; Roams small area around spawn point

RAZZERIC
Thousand Needles (82), K-8, Mirage Raceway (119), Inside racetrack

RAZZLE SPRYSPROCKET
Dun Morogh (32), F-5, Kharanos (116), In gnomish building

REANIMATED CORPSE
Western Plaguelands (92), I-7, Scholomance

REBAN FREERUNNER
Pet Trainer, Mulgore (58), E-6, Bloodhoof Village (102), North tents

REBECCA LAUGHLIN
Tabard Vendor, Stormwind (72), I-7, Trade District, Stormwind Visitor's Center

REBEL WATCHMAN
Stranglethorn Vale (74), D-1, Rebel Camp (124), Patrols back and forth in camp

RED DRAGONSPAWN
Wetlands (96), K:(4, 5), Dragonmaw Gates, Raptor Ridge

RED JACK FLINT
Wetlands (96), A-6, Menethil Harbor (119), First floor of keep, next to stairs

RED SCALEBANE
Wetlands (96), K-5, L-5, Dragonmaw Gates

RED WHELP
Wetlands (96), H:(4, 5), I-5, Mosshide Fen, The Green Belt

RED WYRMKIN
Wetlands (96), K:(4, 5), L-5, Dragonmaw Gates, Raptor Ridge

REDPATH MILITIA
Eastern Plaguelands (40), E-8, Darrowshire, (Summon) Path heading into town

REDPATH THE CORRUPTED
Eastern Plaguelands (40), E-8, Darrowshire, (Summon) Path heading into town

REDRIDGE ALPHA
Redridge Mountains (62), C-2, Redridge Canyons

REDRIDGE BASHER
Redridge Mountains (62), B-3, C:(2, 3), D:(2, 3), Redridge Canyons

REDRIDGE BRUTE
Redridge Mountains (62), B:(3, 4), C:(3, 4), D-2, E:(3, 4), Redridge Canyons

REDRIDGE DRUDGER
Redridge Mountains (62), B-3, Rethban Caverns

REDRIDGE MONGREL
Redridge Mountains (62), A-6, B-6, C-8, D-8, E-7, Lakeridge Highway

REDRIDGE MYSTIC
Redridge Mountains (62), B:(3, 4), C:(2-4), D:(2, 3), E:(3, 4), Redridge Canyons

REDRIDGE POACHER
Redridge Mountains (62), C-8, D-8, E-7, Lakeridge Highway

REDRIDGE THRASHER
Redridge Mountains (62), A-6, B-6, C-8, D-8, Three Corners

REDROCK EARTH SPIRIT
Durotar (34), G:(7, 8)

REDSTONE BASILISK
Blasted Lands (20), H-3, I-3, Serpent's Coil

REDSTONE CRYSTALHIDE
Blasted Lands (20), G:(3-5), H:(4-6), Dark Portal, Dreadmaul Post, Rise of the Defiler

REEF CRAWLER
Darkshore (24), E:(7, 8), G-2, H-2, Cliffspring River, Mist's Edge, Twilight Shore

REESE LANGSTON
Tavernkeeper, Stormwind (72), J-5, Old Town, Pig and Whistle Tavern

Refuge Point (124)E DEFENDER
Arathi Highlands (10), F:(4, 5), G:(4, 5), Refuge Point (124)

REGGIFUZ
Stable Master, Barrens (18), H-4, Ratchet (122), Front of inn

---

REGINA HALLORAN
Wetlands (96), A-5, Menethil Harbor (119), House, west of keep

REGINALD GRIMSFORD
Undercity (88), The Magic Quarter, Wanders Magic Quarter

REGNUS THUNDERGRANITE
Hunter Trainer, Ironforge (52), I-8, The Military Ward, Hall of Arms

REGTHAR DEATHGATE
Barrens (18), E-3, Bunker along road west of Crossroads

REJOLD BARLEYBREW
Dun Morogh (32), D-4, Brewnall Village, Under scaffolding

REKK'TILAC
Rare Spawn, Searing Gorge (64), C-7, D-3, F-7, G-3, H-7, I-7, Tanner Camp, The Sea of Cinders, Thorium Point (136), Lvl 48 Average Rare; Stands idle at spawn point

REKKUL
Poison Vendor, Orgrimmar (60), E-5, The Cleft of Shadow, Rekkul's Poisons

RELARA WHITEMOON
Ashenvale (12), E-5, Astranaar (101), On bed in southeast building

RELLIAN GREENSPYRE
Darnassus (26), E-2, Cenarion Enclave, Next to bridge

REMA SCHNEIDER
Stormwind (72), G:(5, 6), The Canals, Canal Tailor and Fit Shop

REMAINS OF TREY LIGHTFORGE
Felwood (44), E-6, Shadow Hold, On altar in altar room

REMEN MARCOT
Elwynn Forest (42), F-7, Goldshire (114), Basement of Lion's Pride Inn

REMORSEFUL HIGHBORNE
Winterspring (98), H-4, The Ruins of Kel'Theril, In ruins

REMY "TWO TIMES"
Elwynn Forest (42), F-7, Goldshire (114), Standing by the road at the far end of town

RENATO GALLINA
Stormwind (72), H-6, Trade District, Outside Pestle's Apothecary

RENDOW
Feralas (46), K-5, Thalanaar, Northwest of well

RENN'AZ
Ammunition Vendor, The Hinterlands (50), L-8, Revantusk Village (125) (125)

RENZIK "THE SHIV"
SI:7 Operative, Stormwind (72), K-6, Old Town, SI:7

RESIDUAL MONSTROSITY
Feralas (46), G-4, Dire Maul

RESSAN THE NEEDLER
Rare Spawn, Tirisfal Glades (86), E-7, F:(6, 7), G-6, Nightmare Vale, Lvl 11 Uncommon; Roams a small area around spawn point

RESTLESS SHADE
Deadwind Pass (28), C:(6-8), D:(7, 8), E:(7-9), F-8, Karazhan, Morgan's Plot

RETHEROKK THE BERSERKER
Rare Spawn, The Hinterlands (50), G:(6, 7), H-6, The Altar of Zul, Lvl 48 Uncommon; Roams around base of altar

RETHIEL THE GREENWARDEN
Wetlands (96), H-4, The Green Belt, In bare spot, east of road to Dun Modr

RETHILGORE
Silverpine Forest (68), F-7, Shadowfang Keep

REVANTUSK DRUMMER
The Hinterlands (50), L-8, Revantusk Village (125)

REVANTUSK WATCHER
The Hinterlands (50), K-8, L-8, Revantusk Village (125)

REVELOSH
Badlands (16), G-1, Uldaman

REX ASHIL
Rare Spawn, Silithus (66), F-2, Hive'Ashi, Lvl 57 Average Rare; Patrols above and within hive

REX PIXEM
Arena BM, Undercity (88), H-9

REXXAR
Champion of the Horde, Desolace (30), G-1, Spawns on road near Stonetalon Mts. border and patrols roads with Misha

REYNA STONEBRANCH
Herbalism Trainer, Ironforge (52), G-6, The Great Forge, Ironforge Physician

---

REZLAK
Tinkers' Union, Durotar (34), G-2, Along road south of Orgrimmar entrance

RHAG GARMASON
Wetlands (96), G-2, Dun Modr, Next to wagons, west of road

RHAHK'ZOR
Westfall (94), D-7, E-7, The Deadmines

RHAPSODY SHINDIGGER
The Hinterlands (50), D-5, Shindigger's Camp, Camp

RHIANNON DAVIS
Expert Tailor, Undercity (88), J-3, The Magic Quarter

RHINAG
Durotar (34), F-2, Among boulders south of Rocktusk Farm

RIBBLY SCREWSPIGOT
Burning Steppes (22), Searing Gorge (64), C-4/D-8, Blackrock Depths

RIBBLY'S CRONY
Burning Steppes (22), Searing Gorge (64), C-4/D-8, Blackrock Depths

RIBCHASER
Rare Spawn, Redridge Mountains (62), A-6, D-8, Lakeridge Highway, Three Corners, Lvl 17 Uncommon; Patrols around gnoll camp

RICHARD KERWIN
Warlock Trainer, Undercity (88), L:(1, 2), The Magic Quarter, Northeast corner of Skull Building

RICHARD VAN BRUNT
Undercity (88), G-2, The War Quarter, Watches fights in War Quarter

RICKLE GOLDGRUBBER
Banker, Stranglethorn Vale (74), B-8, Booty Bay (103), Stranglethorn Trust Bank

RICTER
Alterac Mountains (8), B-8, Lordamere Internment Camp, Roams inside camp walls

RIDGE HUNTRESS
Badlands (16), D-5, E-5, F:(5-7), G:(5-8), H:(4-8), I:(5-7), J-7, The Dustbowl, Plains

RIDGE STALKER
Badlands (16), E-4, F:(4, 5), G-4, H:(1-3), I:(3-5), J:(3, 4), The Dustbowl

RIDGE STALKER PATRIARCH
Badlands (16), A:(6, 7), B:(5-8), C:(6-8), D:(6-8), Apocryphan's Rest

RIELD MARSHAL OSLIGHT
Arathi Highlands (11), F-5, Refuge Point (124) (124)

RIFLEMAN TORRIG
Silithus (67), G-5, Cenarion Hold (106)

RIGGER GIZELTON
Desolace (30), H-4, Spawns on road near Kormek's Hut, runs a loop along the roads, and pauses at the hut upon return

RIGGLEFUZZ
Badlands (16), F-5, Valley of Fangs, Camp

RIKQIZ
Leatherworking Supplies, Stranglethorn Vale (74), B-8, Booty Bay (103), Two story house on third level along the eastern side of bay

RILAN HOWARD
Winterspring (98), I-1, Small camp near hills

RILEY WALKER
Undercity (88), G-2, The War Quarter, Watches fights in War Quarter

RILLI GREASYGOB
Orgrimmar (60), I-3, J-3, Valley of Honor, Nogg's Machine Shop

RIMBLAT EARTHSHATTERER
The Earthen Ring, Eastern Plaguelands (40), K-6, Light's Hope Chapel (118)

RINGO
Un'Goro Crater (90), G-5, Fire Plume Ridge, East den on ridge

RIN'JI
Witherbark Troll, The Hinterlands (50), E-5, Quel'Danil Lodge, Cage towards the rear of main lodge

RIPPA
Rare Spawn, Stranglethorn Vale (74), B-6, Southern Savage Coast, Lvl 44 Very Rare; Patrols the cove on the northern side of The Cape of Stranglethorn

RIPSCALE
Rare Spawn, Dustwallow Marsh (38), E-5, F:(5-6), The Quagmire, Lvl 39 Semi-Rare; Roams swamp

RISEN ABERRATION
Western Plaguelands (92), I-7, Scholomance

RISEN BONEWARDER
Western Plaguelands (92), I-7, Scholomance

RISEN CONSTRUCT
Western Plaguelands (92), I-7, Scholomance

RISEN GUARD
Western Plaguelands (92), I-7, Scholomance

RISEN GUARDIAN
Western Plaguelands (92), I-7, Scholomance

RISEN LACKEY
Western Plaguelands (92), I-7, Scholomance

RISEN PROTECTOR
Western Plaguelands (92), I-7, Scholomance

RISEN WARRIOR
Western Plaguelands (92), I-7, Scholomance

RIVER CROCOLISK
Stranglethorn Vale (74), C-1, D:(1, 2), Lake Nazferiti

RIVERN FROSTWIND
Wintersaber Trainers, Winterspring (98), G-1, Frostsaber Rock, Atop Frostsaber Rock

RIVERPAW BANDIT
Westfall (94), E-6, F:(6, 7), G-7, H-7, Stendel's Pond

RIVERPAW BRUTE
Westfall (94), B-5, C-7, E-6, F:(6, 7), G-7, H-1, The Dust Plains

RIVERPAW GNOLL
Westfall (94), D-2, E:(1, 2), F:(1, 2), G-1, The Jansen Stead

RIVERPAW HERBALIST
Westfall (94), B-6, C:(5-7), Alexston Farmstead

RIVERPAW MINER
Westfall (94), B-5, C:(4, 5), Gold Coast Quarry

RIVERPAW MONGREL
Westfall (94), B:(6, 7), C:(3, 5-7), D-3

RIVERPAW MYSTIC
Westfall (94), G:(7, 8), H:(7, 8), The Dust Plains

RIVERPAW OUTRUNNER
Elwynn Forest (42), C:(8, 9), I:(4, 5), J-4, K-4, Forest's Edge

RIVERPAW OVERSEER
Westfall (94), G-8, H-8, The Dust Plains

RIVERPAW RUNT
Elwynn Forest (42), C:(8, 9), D:(8, 9), I:(4, 5), J-4, Forest's Edge

RIVERPAW SCOUT
Westfall (94), C:(3, 5), D:(2, 3), E:(1, 2), F:(1, 2), G-1, The Jansen Stead

RIVERPAW SHAMAN
Westfall (94), D-2, Jangolode Mine

RIVERPAW TASKMASTER
Westfall (94), F-7, G:(7, 8), H:(7, 8), The Dust Plains

RIZNEK
Drink Vendor, Thousand Needles (82), K:(7-8), Mirage Raceway (119), Roams infield of racetrack from drag strip grandstands to starting tower

RIZZ LOOSEBOLT
Engineering Supplies, Alterac Mountains (8), F-4, Slaughter Hollow, Captive in cage on left of cave

RIZZLE BRASSBOLTS
Thousand Needles (82), J-8, Mirage Raceway (119), Building west of racetrack

RO'BARK
Rare Spawn, Hillsbrad Foothills (48), H-6, Nethander Stead, Lvl 28 Uncommon; Patrols crop field

ROBERT AEBISCHER
Superior Armorsmith, Hillsbrad Foothills (48), F-5, Southshore (129), Behind small house left of path

ROBERT GOSSOM
Undercity (88), G-2, The War Quarter, Watches fights in War Quarter

ROBERTO PUPELLYVERBOS
Merlot Connoisseur, Stormwind (72), H-7, The Canals, Gallina Winery

ROC
Tanaris (78), E-3, F-3, G:(3, 4), H:(3, 4)

ROCK BORER
Desolace (30), D-5, Mauradon

ROCK ELEMENTAL
Badlands (16), B:(3, 4), C-4, E:(7, 8), F:(7-9), G:(8, 9), Kargath

ROCK STALKER
Silithus (66), D:(4, 5), E:(4, 5), F:(4, 5), G:(4, 5), H-4, The Scarab Dais

ROCK WORM
Desolace (30), D-5, Mauradon

ROCKBITER
Feralas (46), D-2, The Twin Colossals, Camp southwest of western colossal

ROCKHIDE BOAR
Elwynn Forest (42), F:(7-9), G:(7, 8), H:(7, 8), I:(7, 8), J:(7, 8), Brackwell Pumpkin Patch, Jerod's Landing

ROCKJAW AMBUSHER
Dun Morogh (32), J:(5, 6), K-6, Gol'Bolar Quarry, Helm's Bed Lake, Ironband's Compound

ROCKJAW BACKBREAKER
Dun Morogh (32), J-6, K:(5, 6), Gol'Bolar Quarry, Helm's Bed Lake, Ironband's Compound

ROCKJAW BONESNAPPER
Dun Morogh (32), J:(5, 6), K:(5, 6), Gol'Bolar Quarry, Helm's Bed Lake, Ironband's Compound

ROCKJAW RAIDER
Dun Morogh (32), D-7, E:(6, 7), Coldridge Pass

ROCKJAW SKULLTHUMPER
Dun Morogh (32), I-6, J:(5, 6), Gol'Bolar Quarry

ROCKJAW TROGG
Dun Morogh (32), B:(7, 8), C:(7, 8), D:(7, 8), Coldridge Pass, Coldridge Valley (107)

ROCKLANCE
Barrens (18), G-4, The Stagnant Oasis, Patrols the oasis

ROCKWING GARGOYLE
Eastern Plaguelands (40), D-2, Stratholme

ROCKWING SCREECHER
Eastern Plaguelands (40), D-2, Stratholme

ROETTEN STONEHAMMER
Reclaimers Inc., Ironforge (52), I-2, Hall of Explorers, Out front of library

ROGER
Redridge Mountains (62), C-5, Lake Everstill

ROGGO HARLBARROW
Wetlands (96), G-2, Dun Modr, Next to wagons, west of road

ROGUE BLACK DRAKE
Burning Steppes (22), A-6

ROGUE FLAME SPIRIT
Stonetalon Mountains (70), D:(5, 6), E:(5, 6), F-4, The Charred Vale, Mirkfallon Lake

ROGUE ICE THISTLE
Winterspring (98), D-5, E:(4, 5), F:(3, 4), G:(3-5), H-4, Frostfire Hot Springs, Timbermaw Post

ROGUE VALE SCREECHER
Feralas (46), D-4, E:(4-6), F-5, G-5

ROGVAR
Master Alchemist, Swamp of Sorrows (76), F-5, Stonard (131), Second floor of main hall

ROHAN THE ASSASSIN
The Scarlet Crusade, Eastern Plaguelands (40), K-6, Light's Hope Chapel (118)

ROHH THE SILENT
Rare Spawn, Redridge Mountains (62), J:(3, 4), K:(5, 6), Galardell Valley, Stonewatch Falls, Tower of Ilgalar, Lvl 26 Semi-Rare; Stands idle at spawn point

ROK ORHAN
Feralas (46), I-4, Camp Mojache (105), Spawns near western mill and walks to the eastern mill

ROK'ALIM THE POUNDER
Thousand Needles (82), A:(2-3), B-4, C-4, Spawns in a few different spots along southeastern plateaus

ROKAR BLADESHADOW
Durotar (34), H-3, Farmhouse

ROKARO
Champion of the Horde, Desolace (30), C-7, Shadowprey Village (128)

ROLAND GEARDABBLER
Azshara (14), F-9, The Ruined Reaches, South of camp on border of Great Sea in back cabin of ship beneath debris

ROLE DREUGER
Duskwood (36), J-5, Darkshire Town Hall

ROLOCH
Rare Spawn, Stranglethorn Vale (74), D-3, Mizjah Ruins, Lvl 38 Average Rare; Patrols between ruins and the path to the north

ROMAN
Stormwind (72), H-3, The Canals, Dock

RONALD BURCH
Cooking Supplier, Undercity (88), H-4, The Trade Quarter, West spoke from bank

ROOGUG
Barrens (18), E-9, Razorfen Kraul

ROOKERY GUARDIAN
Burning Steppes (22), Searing Gorge (64), C-4/D-8, Blackrock Spire

ROOKERY HATCHER
Burning Steppes (22), Searing Gorge (64), C-4/D-8, Blackrock Spire

ROOKERY WHELP
Burning Steppes (22), Searing Gorge (64), C-4/D-8, Blackrock Spire

ROON WILDMANE
Desolace (30), C-7, Shadowprey Village (128), Near entrance

RORGISH JOWL
Rare Spawn, Ashenvale (12), E-4, Thistlefur Village, Lvl 25 Uncommon; Roams camp near spawn locations

RORY
Western Plaguelands (92), I-7, Caer Darrow, Roams around the dock on the western side of city

ROT HIDE BRUISER
Silverpine Forest (68), J:(2, 3), Fenris Isle

ROT HIDE BRUTE
Silverpine Forest (68), J:(2-4), Fenris Isle

ROT HIDE GLADERUNNER
Silverpine Forest (68), G-2, The Dead Field

ROT HIDE GNOLL
Tirisfal Glades (86), G:(3, 4), H:(3, 4), Garren's Haunt

ROT HIDE GRAVEROBBER
Tirisfal Glades (86), G:(4, 5)

ROT HIDE MONGREL
Tirisfal Glades (86), G-3, H:(3, 4), Garren's Haunt

ROT HIDE MYSTIC
Silverpine Forest (68), G-2, The Dead Field

ROT HIDE PLAGUE WEAVER
Silverpine Forest (68), J:(2-4), Fenris Isle

ROT HIDE SAVAGE
Silverpine Forest (68), J:(2, 3), Fenris Isle

ROTGATH STONEBEARD
Expert Blacksmith, Ironforge (52), G-4, The Great Forge, Next to anvils

ROTGRIP
Desolace (30), D-5, Mauradon

ROTHOS
The Hinterlands (50), I-3, Seradane, Patrols around portal

ROTTED ONE
Duskwood (36), C:(3, 4), Raven Hill Cemetery (123)

ROTTING AGAM'AR
Barrens (18), E-9, Razorfen Kraul

ROTTING ANCESTOR
Tirisfal Glades (86), F-3, G-3, Agamand Mills (100)

ROTTING BEHEMOTH
Western Plaguelands (92), H:(3, 4), I:(3, 4), The Weeping Cave

ROTTING CADAVER
Western Plaguelands (92), F:(5, 6), Dalson's Tears

ROTTING DEAD
Tirisfal Glades (86), F:(5, 6), G:(5, 6)

ROTTING GHOUL
Western Plaguelands (92), G:(6, 7), The Writhing Haunt

ROTTING HIGHBORNE
Feralas (46), G-4, Dire Maul

ROTTING SLIME
Ashenvale (12), I:(7, 8), J:(6, 7), Felfire Hill, Nightsong Woods, Dor'Danil Barrow Den, Warsong Labor Camp

ROTTING SLIME
Barrens (18), E-OUT

ROTTING SLUDGE
Eastern Plaguelands (40), G:(6, 7), H-6, I-6, J:(5, 6), Pestilent Scar

ROXXIK
Engineer Trainer, Orgrimmar (60), J-3, Valley of Honor, Nogg's Machine Shop

ROYAL FACTOR BATHRILOR
Stormwind Census, Stormwind (72), G-3, Cathedral Square, City Hall

ROYAL HISTORIAN ARCHESONUS
Ironforge (52), E-5, The Great Forge, The High Seat

ROYAL OVERSEER BAUHAUS
Undercity Census, Undercity (88), J-4, The Trade Quarter, By Guild Master, East spoke from bank

RUDRA AMBERSTILL
Dun Morogh (32), I-5, Amberstill Ranch, By building

RUGA RAGETOTEM
Barrens (18), F-6, Camp Taurajo (106), Southern building

RUKLAR THE TRAPPER
Elwynn Forest (42), I-6, Jasperlode Mine, Small camp to the right of mine entrance

RUMBLER
Rare Spawn, Badlands (16), A-8, B-9, Camp Cagg, Lvl 45 Uncommon; Roams small area around spawn point

RUMBLING EXILE
Arathi Highlands (10), E:(5, 6), Circle of Inner Binding

RUMSER FIZZLEBRACK
Tanaris (78), G-3, Gadgetzan (113)

RUMSTAG PROUDSTRIDER
Horde Cloth Quartermaster, Thunder Bluff (84), F-4, Middle rise, inside Thunder Bluff Armorers tent

RUNK WINDTAMER
Wind Rider Master, Silithus (67), G-5, Cenarion Hold (106)

RUPERT BOCH
Warlock Trainer, Tirisfal Glades (86), H-5, Brill (104), Second floor of Gallows' End Tavern

RUPPO ZIPCOIL
Engineering Supplies, The Hinterlands (50), E-4, The Hinterlands, Gnomish camp on recessed hill east of Quel'Danil Lodge

RUSTY HARVEST GOLEM
Westfall (94), F:(2, 3), G-2, Furlbrow's Pumpkin Patch

RUUL EAGLETALON
Mulgore (58), E-6, Bloodhoof Village (102), South tent

RUUL ONESTONE
Rare Spawn, Arathi Highlands (10), B-7, The Tower of Arathor, Lvl 39 Average Rare; Roams the top floor of tower

RUUL SNOWHOOF
Ashenvale (12), E-3, Thistlefur Hold, Cage in water in back of hold

RUUZEL
Ashenvale (12), A-2, The Zoram Strand (137), Patrols entire island

RUUZLU
Tanaris (78), E-1, Zul'Farrak

RUW
Herbalism Trainer, Feralas (46), I-4, Camp Mojache (105), East of bridge

RUZAN
Durotar (34), F-7, Valley of Trials (136)

RWAG
Rogue Trainer, Durotar (34), F-7, Valley of Trials (136)

RYBRAD CLODBANK
Weaponsmith, Dun Morogh (32), D-7, Coldridge Valley (107), Anvilmar

RYNTHARIEL THE KEYMASTER
Stonetalon Mountains (70), C-2, The Talon Den, Southern room of den

S

SAEAN
Loch Modan (54), G-7, The Loch, (Summon) Attacks player and NPC's during escort

SAENORION
Leatherworking Supplies, Darnassus (26), I-2 , Craftsmen's Terrace, Leatherworking shop

SAERN PRIDERUNNER
Thunder Bluff (84), G-8, Hunter Rise, Inside Tent next to Hunter's Hall

SAGE KOROLUSK
Feralas (46), I-4, Camp Mojache (105), Patrols road north of inn

SAGE PALERUNNER
Feralas (46), I-4, Camp Mojache (105), Small tent near waterfall

SAGE TRUTHSEEKER
Thunder Bluff (84), C-5, Inside bridge Spirit Rise

SAGORNE CRESTRIDER
Shaman Trainer, Orgrimmar (60), D-4, Valley of Wisdom, Grommash Hold

SAHOC
Weapon Master, Orgrimmar (61), K-2

SAHRAN BLOODSHADOW
Tirisfal Glades (86), G-6 , H-5, Brill (10

SAH'RHEE
Barrens (18), F-9, Razorfen Downs

SALAZAR BLOCH
Book Dealer, Undercity (88), K-4, The Magic Quarter, Near Rogues' Quarter entry

SALFA
Winterspring (98), D4, Frostfire Hot Springs, West edge of Felwood

SALIA
Felwood (44), E-6, Shadow Hold, Anteroom after spiral tunnel

SALMA SALDEAN
Westfall (94), F-3, Saldean's Farm, Farmhouse

SALT FLATS SCAVENGER
Thousand Needles (82), I:(5-7), J:(5-7), K:(6, 7), L-6, Ironstone Camp, The Shimmering Flats, Weazel's Crater

SALT FLATS VULTURE
Thousand Needles (82), I:(8, 9), J-9, K:(7, 8), L-8, Tahonda Ruins, The Rustmaul Dig Site, The Shimmering Fl...

SALTSCALE FORAGER
Stranglethorn Vale (74), B-3, Bal'lal Ruins, The Savage Coast, The Vile Ree...

SALTSCALE HUNTER
Stranglethorn Vale (74), B-3, The Savage Coast, The Vile Reef

SALTSCALE ORACLE
Stranglethorn Vale (74), B-3, The Vile Reef

SALTSCALE TIDE LORD
Stranglethorn Vale (74), B-3, The Vile Reef

SALTSCALE WARRIOR
Stranglethorn Vale (74), B-3, The Savage Coast, The Vile Reef

SALTSPITTLE MUCKDWELLER
Ashenvale (12), C-4, Lake Falathim

SALTSPITTLE ORACLE
Ashenvale (12), C-4, Lake Falathim

SALTSPITTLE PUDDLEJUMPER
Ashenvale (12), C:(4, 5), Lake Falathim

SALTSPITTLE WARRIOR
Ashenvale (12), C:(4, 5), Lake Falathim

SALTSTONE BASILISK
Thousand Needles (82), I:(5-6), J:(5-7) K-6, Ironstone Camp, The Shimmering Flats, Weazel's Crater

SALTSTONE CRYSTALHIDE
Thousand Needles (82), I-8, J:(,6-9), K:(5-9), L:(6-8), Tahonda Ruins, The Shimmering Flats, Weazel's Crater

SALTSTONE GAZER
Thousand Needles (82), J:(8, 9), K:(8, Tahonda Ruins, The Shimmering Flats, Mirage Raceway

SALTWATER CROCOLISK
Stranglethorn Vale (74), A-2, B-2, C:(3, 4)

SALTWATER SNAPJAW
The Hinterlands (50), K:(6-9), L:(4-9), Overlook Cliffs, Coast

SAMANTHA SHACKELTON
Undercity (88), J-3, The Magic Quarter, Stall next to Tailors

SAMANTHA SWIFTHOOF
Stranglethorn Vale (74), D-1, Patrols between the bridge into Duskwood an... the entrance to Booty Bay

SAMMY
Western Plaguelands (92), I-8, Caer Darrow, Ghost By fountain

SAMOR FESTIVUS
Shady Dealer, Wetlands (96), A-6, Deepwater Tavern, Northwest, upstairs room

SAMUEL FIPPS
Tirisfal Glades (86), D-6, Deathknell (109), Ruined camp on right side of road heading out of town

SAMUEL HAWKE
League of Arathor Supply Officer, Arat... Highlands (11), F-5, Refuge Point (124, (124)

SAMUEL VAN BRUNT
Blacksmith Supplier, Undercity (88), H-3, The War Quarter

...ANA
Mail Armor Merchant, Orgrimmar (60), G-7, Valley of Strength, Soran's Leather and Steel

...ANATH LIM-YO
Azshara (14), C-5, Camp in foothills

...AND CRAWLER
Westfall (94), D-1, E-1, F-1, Longshore

...AND SKITTERER
Silithus (66), E:(1, 2), F:(1, 2), G:(1-3), H:(1-3), Southwind Village

...ANDAHL
Warlock Trainer, Stormwind (72), D-8, Mage Quarter, The Slaughtered Lamb

...ANDFURY AXE THROWER
Tanaris (78), E-3, F:(2, 3), Sandsorrow Watch, Zul'Farrak

...ANDFURY BLOOD DRINKER
Tanaris (78), E-1, Zul'Farrak

...ANDFURY CRETIN
Tanaris (78), E-1, Zul'Farrak

...ANDFURY EXECUTIONER
Tanaris (78), E-1, Zul'Farrak

...ANDFURY FIRECALLER
Tanaris (78), E-3, F:(2, 3), Sandsorrow Watch, Zul'Farrak

...ANDFURY GUARDIAN
Tanaris (78), E-1, Zul'Farrak

...ANDFURY HIDESKINNER
Tanaris (78), E-3, F:(2, 3), Sandsorrow Watch, Zul'Farrak

...ANDFURY SHADOWCASTER
Tanaris (78), E-1, Zul'Farrak

...ANDFURY SHADOWHUNTER
Tanaris (78), E-1, Zul'Farrak

...ANDFURY SOUL EATER
Tanaris (78), E-1, Zul'Farrak

...ANDFURY WITCH DOCTOR
Tanaris (78), E-1, Zul'Farrak

...ANUYE RUNETOTEM
Leather Armor Merchant, Barrens (18), F-6, Camp Taurajo (106), Near hides

...AP BEAST
Stonetalon Mountains (70), D:(1, 2), E:(1, 2), F:(2-4), G:(3, 4), Mirkfallon Lake, Stonetalon Peak, The Talon Den

...AR BROWNEYE
Winterspring (98), I-1, Small camp near hills

...ARA BALLOO
Ironforge (52), I-7, The Military Ward, North patio

...ARA PIERCE
Dustwallow Marsh (38), I-5, Theramore Isle (135), 2nd floor of inn

...ARA TIMBERLAIN
Elwynn Forest (42), K-7, Eastvale Logging Camp, Front steps of house

...ARAH GOODE
Stable Master, Silverpine Forest (68), F-4, The Sepulcher (127), Outside of inn entrance on right

...ARAH KILLIAN
Mining Supplier, Undercity (88), H-4, The War Quarter

...ARAH RAYCROFT
General Goods, Hillsbrad Foothills (48), F-5, Southshore (129), Second floor of house

...ARAH TANNER
Master Elemental Leatherworker, Searing Gorge (64), H-7, Tanner Camp, In front of tent

...ARGATH
Ashenvale (12), D-4, Maestra's Post, Near Stones south of main outpost

...ARILUS FOULBORNE
Barrens (18), E-2, Dreadmist Peak, Atop Dreadmist Peak

...ARIN STARLIGHT
Darnassus (26), C-5, The Temple Gardens, South of teleporter

...ARK RAGETOTEM
Warrior Trainer, Thunder Bluff (84), G-9, Hunter Rise, Inside Hunter's Hall

...ARKOTH
Durotar (34), F-7, Valley of Trials (136), Roams western hills

...ARLEK
Orgrimmar (60), G-5, The Drag, Building south of Jandi's Arboretum

...ARLTOOTH
Wetlands (96), D-5, Whelgar's Excavation Site, On upper ledge, in southwestern section of site

...AROK
Orgrimmar (60), G-7, Valley of Strength, Inn

SARU STEELFURY
Blacksmith Trainer, Orgrimmar (60), K-2, Valley of Honor, The Bruning Anvil

SATURATED OOZE
Swamp of Sorrows (76), I-5, The Temple of Atal'Hakkar

SAVAGE OWLBEAST
The Hinterlands (50), H:(4-6), I:(4-6), J:(5, 6), The Hinterlands

SAVANNAH HIGHMANE
Barrens (18), F:(2, 3), G-3, Gold Road

SAVANNAH HUNTRESS
Barrens (18), F:(1-3), G:(2, 3), Gold Road, Thorn Hill

SAVANNAH MATRIARCH
Barrens (18), H-3, Thorn Hill

SAVANNAH PATRIARCH
Barrens (18), E:(1, 2), G-3, H-3, The Dry Hills

SAVANNAH PROWLER
Barrens (18), D:(2, 3), E:(2-4), F:(1, 2), G:(1-4), H:(1-3), Boulder Lode Mine, The Dry Hills

SAVANNE
Fishing Supplies, Feralas (46), C-5, Feathermoon Stronghold (111), Southwest building

SAWFIN FRENZY
Swamp of Sorrows (76), H-6, I:(4-6), J-5, Pool of Tears

SAWTOOTH CROCOLISK
Swamp of Sorrows (76), F-4, G:(3-5), H-3, I-2, The Shifting Mire

SAWTOOTH SNAPPER
Swamp of Sorrows (76), I-9, J:(1-3, 6, 9), K:(1-7, 9), L:(2, 3, 8, 9), Sorrowmurk

SAYOC
Weapon Master, Orgrimmar (60), J-2, Valley of Strength, Arms of Legend, Trains: Bows, Daggers, Fist Weapons, 1H Axe, 2H Axe, Thrown

SCALD
Rare Spawn, Searing Gorge (64), D-5, G-4, The Cauldron, Lvl 49 Average Rare; Patrols path near spawn point

SCALDING BROODLING
Burning Steppes (22), D:(5, 6), E-3, F:(3, 7), G:(2, 3, 6), H:(5, 6), I:(3-6), J-3

SCALDING DRAKE
Burning Steppes (22), D-6, F-7, I-6

SCALDING ELEMENTAL
Thousand Needles (82), D:(3, 4), E-4, Darkcloud Pinnacle, Splithoof Crag

SCALDING WHELP
Badlands (16), J-5, K:(3, 5-7), L:(3, 4, 6), Lethor Ravine

SCALE BELLY
Rare Spawn, Stranglethorn Vale (74), F-5, Crystalvein Mine, Lvl 45 Uncommon; Mine

SCALEBANE CAPTAIN
Swamp of Sorrows (76), H-4, I-4, J:(4-7), K:(4, 5)

SCALEBANE LIEUTENANT
Wetlands (96), L:(5, 6), Grim Batol

SCALEBANE ROYAL GUARD
Wetlands (96), K-7, L:(6, 7), Grim Batol

SCALEBEARD
Rare Spawn, Azshara (14), G-5, Bay of Storms, Lvl 52 Uncommon; Spawns in Scalebeard's Cave and roams

SCARAB
Tanaris (78), E-1, Zul'Farrak

SCARGIL
Rare Spawn, Hillsbrad Foothills (48), B-7, C-7, Western Strand, Lvl 30 Uncommon

SCARLET ABBOT
Tirisfal Glades (86), K-3, L-3, Scarlet Monastery

SCARLET ADEPT
Tirisfal Glades (86), K-3, L-3, Scarlet Monastery

SCARLET ARCHMAGE
Eastern Plaguelands (40), J-8, K:(7, 8), L:(7, 8), Tyr's Hand

SCARLET ASSASSIN
Western Plaguelands (92), I:(2, 3), Northridge Lumber Camp

SCARLET AUGUR
Tirisfal Glades (86), K-3, The Grand Vestibule, Scarlet Monastery

SCARLET AUGUR
Tirisfal Glades (86), K-3, L-3, Scarlet Monastery

SCARLET AVENGER
Western Plaguelands (92), G:(2, 4), H-4, Northridge Lumber Camp

SCARLET BEASTMASTER
Tirisfal Glades (86), K-3, L-3, Scarlet Monastery

SCARLET BODYGUARD
Tirisfal Glades (86), K:(2, 3), Scarlet Watch Post

SCARLET CAVALIER
Western Plaguelands (92), E-1, Mardenholde Keep

SCARLET CENTURIAN
Tirisfal Glades (86), K-3, L-3, Scarlet Monastery

SCARLET CHAMPION
Tirisfal Glades (86), K-3, L-3, Scarlet Monastery

SCARLET CHAPLAIN
Tirisfal Glades (86), K-3, L-3, Scarlet Monastery

SCARLET CLERIC
Eastern Plaguelands (40), I-8, J:(7, 8), K:(7, 8), Scarlet Base Camp

SCARLET COMMANDER MARJHAN
The Scarlet Crusade, Eastern Plaguelands (40), K-6, Light's Hope Chapel (118)

SCARLET COMMANDER MOGRAINE
Tirisfal Glades (86), K-3, L-3, Scarlet Monastery

SCARLET CONJURER
Tirisfal Glades (86), K-3, L-3, Scarlet Monastery

SCARLET CONVERT
Tirisfal Glades (86), D:(6, 7), E:(6, 7), Deathknell (109)

SCARLET CURATE
Eastern Plaguelands (40), K:(7, 8), L:(7, 8), Tyr's Hand

SCARLET DEFENDER
Tirisfal Glades (86), K-3, L-3, Scarlet Monastery

SCARLET DISCIPLE
Tirisfal Glades (86), K-3, The Grand Vestibule, Scarlet Monastery, Scarlet Monastery

SCARLET DIVINER
Tirisfal Glades (86), K-3, L-3, Scarlet Monastery

SCARLET ENCHANTER
Eastern Plaguelands (40), I-8, J:(7, 8), K:(7, 8), Scarlet Base Camp

SCARLET EVOKER
Tirisfal Glades (86), K-3, L-3, Scarlet Monastery

SCARLET EXECUTIONER
Rare Spawn, Western Plaguelands (92), F-2, Hearthglen, Lvl 60 Very Rare; Roams in tower on the southern end of city

SCARLET FRIAR
Tirisfal Glades (86), J:(5, 6), K:(2-6), L-4, Scarlet Watch Post

SCARLET GALLANT
Tirisfal Glades (86), K-3, L-3, Scarlet Monastery

SCARLET GUARDSMAN
Tirisfal Glades (86), K-3, L-3, Scarlet Monastery

SCARLET HIGH CLERIST
Rare Spawn, Western Plaguelands (92), G-2, Lvl 63 Average Rare; Spawns inside or on top of tower south of Hearthglen

SCARLET HUNTER
Western Plaguelands (92), E-5, G-4

SCARLET INITIATE
Tirisfal Glades (86), D-7, E:(6, 7), Deathknell (109)

SCARLET INTERROGATOR
Rare Spawn, Western Plaguelands (92), F-1, Hearthglen, Lvl 61 Uncommon; Spawns on the first or second floor of tower in the northeast corner of city

SCARLET INVOKER
Western Plaguelands (92), E-5, G-4

SCARLET JUDGE
Rare Spawn, Western Plaguelands (92), E-2, Hearthglen, Lvl 60 Semi-Rare; Roams in town hall

SCARLET KNIGHT
Western Plaguelands (92), F-3, G-4, H-4, Dalson's Tears, Northridge Lumber Camp

SCARLET LUMBERJACK
Western Plaguelands (92), F:(3, 4), Northridge Lumber Camp

SCARLET MAGE
Western Plaguelands (92), G-4, H-4, Northridge Lumber Camp

SCARLET MAGICIAN
Tirisfal Glades (86), K:(3, 4), Scarlet Monastery, Whispering Gardens

SCARLET MAGUS
Western Plaguelands (92), F:(1, 2), Hearthglen

SCARLET MEDIC
Western Plaguelands (92), E-5, G-4, Dalson's Tears, Felstone Field, Ruins of Andorhal

SCARLET MISSIONARY
Western Plaguelands (92), E-6, F:(6, 7), G-7, Tower

SCARLET MONK
Tirisfal Glades (86), K-3, L-3, Scarlet Monastery

SCARLET MYRMIDON
Tirisfal Glades (86), K-3, L-3, Scarlet Monastery

SCARLET NEOPHYTE
Tirisfal Glades (86), J-3, K:(2, 3), Scarlet Watch Post

SCARLET PALADIN
Western Plaguelands (92), E:(1, 2), F:(1, 2), Hearthglen

SCARLET PRAETORIAN
Eastern Plaguelands (40), J-8, K:(7, 8), L:(7, 8), Tyr's Hand

SCARLET PRESERVER
Tirisfal Glades (86), K:(3, 4), Whispering Gardens

SCARLET PRIEST
Western Plaguelands (92), E-2, F:(1, 2), Hearthglen

SCARLET PROTECTOR
Tirisfal Glades (86), K-3, L-3, Scarlet Monastery

SCARLET SCOUT
Tirisfal Glades (86), K:(3, 4), L-3, Scarlet Monastery, Whispering Gardens

SCARLET SCRYER
Tirisfal Glades (86), K-3, L-3, Scarlet Monastery

SCARLET SENTINEL
Western Plaguelands (92), E:(1, 2), F:(1, 2), Hearthglen, Northridge Lumber Camp

SCARLET SENTRY
Tirisfal Glades (86), K-3, The Grand Vestibule, Scarlet Monastery, Scarlet Monastery

SCARLET SMITH
Rare Spawn, Western Plaguelands (92), F-1, Hearthglen, Lvl 58 Uncommon; Spawns in around to the right of smithy

SCARLET SOLDIER
Tirisfal Glades (86), K-3, L-3, Scarlet Monastery

SCARLET SORCERER
Tirisfal Glades (86), K-3, L-3, Scarlet Monastery

SCARLET SPELLBINDER
Western Plaguelands (92), G:(2, 4), H-4, Mardenholde Keep

SCARLET TORTURER
Tirisfal Glades (86), K-3, L-3, Scarlet Monastery

SCARLET TRACKING HOUND
Tirisfal Glades (86), K-3, L-3, Scarlet Monastery

SCARLET TRAINEE
Tirisfal Glades (86), K-3, L-3, Scarlet Monastery

SCARLET TROOPER
Eastern Plaguelands (40), K-8, Roams between Stratholme and Tyr's Hand

SCARLET VANGUARD
Tirisfal Glades (86), J:(3, 4), K:(2-4), Scarlet Watch Post

SCARLET WARDER
Eastern Plaguelands (40), I-8, J:(7, 8), K:(7, 8), Scarlet Base Camp

SCARLET WARRIOR
Tirisfal Glades (86), C-5, D:(4, 5), Crusader's Outpost, Tower

SCARLET WIZARD
Tirisfal Glades (86), K-3, L-3, Scarlet Monastery

SCARLET WORKER
Western Plaguelands (92), F:(1, 2), Mardenholde Keep

SCARLET ZEALOT
Tirisfal Glades (86), F:(6, 7), G-7, J:(5, 6), K:(5, 6), L-4, Venomweb Vale, Camp

SCARRED CRAG BOAR
Dun Morogh (32), J:(5, 6), K:(3-6), L:(3-5), Helm's Bed Lake, Ironband's Compound

SCARSHIELD ACOLYTE
Burning Steppes (22), Searing Gorge (64), C-4/D-8, Blackrock Spire

SCARSHIELD GRUNT
Burning Steppes (22), Searing Gorge (64), C-4/D-8, Blackrock Spire

SCARSHIELD LEGIONNAIRE
Burning Steppes (22), Searing Gorge (64), C-4/D-8, Blackrock Spire

SCARSHIELD RAIDER
Burning Steppes (22), Searing Gorge (64), C-4/D-8, Blackrock Spire

SCARSHIELD SENTRY
Burning Steppes (22), Searing Gorge (64), C-4/D-8, Blackrock Spire

SCARSHIELD SPELLBINDER
Burning Steppes (22), Searing Gorge (64), C-4/D-8, Blackrock Spire

SCARSHIELD WARLOCK
Burning Steppes (22), Searing Gorge (64), C-4/D-8, Blackrock Spire

SCARSHIELD WORG
Burning Steppes (22), Searing Gorge (64), C-4/D-8, Blackrock Spire

SCHOLAR RUNETHORN
Feralas (46), C-4, Feathermoon Stronghold (111), Circles path in front of inn

SCHOLOMANCE ACOLYTE
Western Plaguelands (92), I-7, Scholomance

SCHOLOMANCE ADEPT
Western Plaguelands (92), I-7, Scholomance

SCHOLOMANCE DARK SUMMONER
Western Plaguelands (92), I-7, Scholomance

SCHOLOMANCE HANDLER
Western Plaguelands (92), I-7, Scholomance

SCHOLOMANCE NECROLYTE
Western Plaguelands (92), I-7, Scholomance

SCHOLOMANCE NECROMANCER
Western Plaguelands (92), I-7, Scholomance

SCHOLOMANCE NEOPHYTE
Western Plaguelands (92), I-7, Scholomance

SCHOLOMANCE OCCULTIST
Western Plaguelands (92), I-7, Scholomance

SCHOLOMANCE STUDENT
Western Plaguelands (92), I-7, Scholomance

SCOOTY
Chief Engineer, Stranglethorn Vale (74), B-8, Booty Bay (103), By the Gnomeregan Polytransporter underneath the Southern Skies Platform

SCORCHED BASILISK
Stonetalon Mountains (70), D-7, E-7, The Charred Vale

SCORCHED GUARDIAN
Badlands (16), L:(5, 6), Lethor Ravine

SCORCHING ELEMENTAL
Un'Goro Crater (90), F:(5, 6), G:(4-6), Fire Plume Ridge

SCORPASHI LASHER
Desolace (30), D-7, E:(4-7), F:(5-7), G-5, H:(5, 6), I:(6, 7), J:(1, 4-6), K-2

SCORPASHI SNAPPER
Desolace (30), F-1, G:(1, 2, 6, 7), H:(1-4, 6), I:(2-4), J:(2-4), K:(3, 4)

SCORPASHI VENOMLASH
Desolace (30), C:(7, 8), D:(7, 8), E-8, F-9, G:(8, 9), H:(7-9)

SCORPID DUNEBURROWER
Tanaris (78), I-8, Caverns of Time

SCORPID DUNESTALKER
Tanaris (78), D:(5-8), E:(4-8), F:(4-8), G:(4-8), H:(5, 6), I:(5, 6)

SCORPID HUNTER
Tanaris (78), G:(3, 4), H:(2-4), I:(2, 3), J-3

SCORPID REAVER
Thousand Needles (82), I:(5-7), J:(5-7), K:(6, 7), L-6, Ironstone Camp, The Shimmering Flats, Weazel's Crater

SCORPID TAIL LASHER
Tanaris (78), E:(2, 3), F:(2-4), G:(2-4), H:(4, 5), I:(4, 5)

SCORPID TERROR
Thousand Needles (82), I:(7, 8), J:(7-9), K:(7-9), L:(7, 8), Tahonda Ruins, The Rustmaul Dig Site, The Shimmering Flats

SCORPID WORKER
Durotar (34), F:(6, 7), G:(6, 7), Valley of Trials (136)

SCORPOK STINGER
Blasted Lands (20), F-3, G:(2, 3), H-3, I:(3, 4), Dark Portal, Dreadmaul Hold, Rise of the Defiler

SCOTT CAREVIN
Mushroom Seller, Duskwood (36), K-5, Darkshire (108), First floor of house

SCOURGE ARCHER
Eastern Plaguelands (40), C-2

SCOURGE CHAMPION
Eastern Plaguelands (40), D-6, E:(5, 6), F-5, J:(4, 5), K-4, Browman Mill

SCOURGE GUARD
Eastern Plaguelands (40), I-4, Northdale

SCOURGE SOLDIER
Eastern Plaguelands (40), B:(3, 4), C:(2-4), D:(2-4), E:(2-4), F:(2-4), Plaguewood

SCOURGE SUMMONING CRYSTAL
Western Plaguelands (92), E:(6, 7), F:(6, 7), Ruins of Andorhal, The crystals spawn inside each of the four tower ruins within the city

SCOURGE WARDER
Eastern Plaguelands (40), C-3, D-3, E:(2, 3), H:(6, 7), Plaguewood

SCOUT BLOODFIST
Silithus (67), G-5, Cenarion Hold (106)

SCOUT GALIAAN
The People's Militia, Westfall (94), F-5, Sentinel Hill (126), Sawmill

SCOUT RIELL
The People's Militia, Westfall (94), G-5, Sentinel Tower, Top of Sentinel Tower

SCOUT THARR
Orgrimmar (60), Valley of Honor, Roams between Valleys of Strength and Honor

SCREECHING HARPY
Thousand Needles (82), C:(5, 6), Roguefeather Den, The Screeching Canyon

SCREECHING ROGUEFEATHER
Thousand Needles (82), C:(5, 6), Roguefeather Den, The Screeching Canyon

SCREECHING WINDCALLER
Thousand Needles (82), C:(5, 6), Roguefeather Den, The Screeching Canyon

SCRYER
Winterspring (98), H-5, Mazthoril, Deep in caverns

SEA CRAWLER
Westfall (94), C-2, D-2, Longshore

SEA ELEMENTAL
Feralas (46), C:(3, 4), D:(3, 4), E:(4-7), F-5, The Forgotten Coast

SEA SPRAY
Feralas (46), C:(3, 4), D:(3, 4), E:(4-7), F-5, The Forgotten Coast

"SEA WOLF" MACKINLEY
Stranglethorn Vale (74), B-8, Booty Bay (103), Building along the eastern side of bay near the hanging shark

SEARING BLADE CULTIST
Orgrimmar (60), F-5, Ragefire Chasm

SEARING BLADE ENFORCER
Orgrimmar (60), F-5, Ragefire Chasm

SEARING BLADE WARLOCK
Orgrimmar (60), F-5, Ragefire Chasm

SEARING GHOUL
Western Plaguelands (92), E:(6, 7), F:(6, 7), G:(6, 7), Ruins of Andorhal, Idle with Araj the Summoner in the center of city

SEARING HATCHLING
Dustwallow Marsh (38), E:(6-8), F:(6-8), G:(7, 8), The Dragonmurk

SEARING INFERNAL
Ashenvale (12), J:(6-8), K:(6, 7), Felfire Hill, Nightsong Woods, Dor'Danil Barrow Den, Warsong Labor Camp

SEARING LAVA SPIDER
Searing Gorge (64), F:(3, 6, 7), G:(2-4, 6-8), The Sea of Cinders

SEARING ROC
Tanaris (78), E:(6-8), F:(6, 7)

SEARING WHELP
Dustwallow Marsh (38), E:(6-8), F:(6-8), G:(7, 8), The Dragonmurk

SEARN FIREWARDER
Orgrimmar (60), D-5, Valley of Wisdom, Grommash Hold

SEARSCALE DRAKE
Burning Steppes (22), B:(2-4, 7), C:(4, 6), Blackrock Mountain

SEBASTIAN MELOCHE
Armorer, Silverpine Forest (68), F-4, The Sepulcher (127), Basement of inn

SECOND MATE SHANDRIL
Azshara (14), F-9, The Ruined Reaches, Kneeling on isle south of camp

SECURITY CHIEF BILGEWHIZZLE
Tanaris (78), J-3, Steamwheedle Port, Southern building

SEEKER AQUALON
Rare Spawn, Redridge Mountains (62), H-5, I-6, J-6, Lake Everstill, Stonewatch Falls, Lvl 21 Average Rare; Patrols the waterway connecting Lake Everstill with Stonewatch Falls

SEEKER CROMWELL
Undercity (88), I-5, K-7, The Trade Quarter, Roams Trade and Rogue Quarter

SEEKER THOMPSON
Undercity (88), I-5, L-2, The Trade Quarter, Roams Trade and Magic Quarter

SEER GRAYTONGUE
Mulgore (58), E-9, Red Cloud Mesa, Southern hills

SEER RAVENFEATHER
Mulgore (58), E-8, Camp Narache (105), Sitting by totem

SEER WISERUNNER
Mulgore (58), C-4, Cave

SEERETH STONEBREAK
Barrens (18), D-3, Camp at Stonetalon border

SEETH'REL
Burning Steppes (22), Searing Gorge (64), C-4/D-8, Blackrock Depths

SEIKWA
Stable Master, Mulgore (58), E-6, Bloodhoof Village (102), Outside inn

SE'JIB
Master Tribal Leatherworker, Stranglethorn Vale (74), D-4, Hut just south of Mizjah Ruins

SELENDRA
Cenarion Circle, Desolace (30), C-8, Sar'theris Strand, Under tree on beach

SELINA PICKMAN
Undercity (88), The Magic Quarter, Roams Magic Quarter

SELINA WESTON
Alchemy & Herbalism Supplies, Tirisfal Glades (86), H-5, Brill (104), In front of a half buried shed behind the Brill Town Hall

SELLANDUS
Expert Tailor, Stormwind (72), F-8, Mage Quarter, Larson Clothiers

SENANI THUNDERHEART
Ashenvale (12), I-6, Splintertree Post (129), Right of inn

SENATOR BARIN REDSTONE
Ironforge (52), E-5, The Great Forge, The High Seat

SENATOR MEHR STONEHALLOW
Dun Morogh (32), I-6, Gol'Bolar Quarry, Quarry camp by tent

SENIOR SURVEYOR FIZZLEDOWSER
Gadgetzan Water Co., Tanaris (78), G-3, Gadgetzan (113), Atop mound near far west wall

SENIR WHITEBEARD
Dun Morogh (32), F-5, Kharanos (116), In Caravan

SEN'JIN WATCHER
Durotar (34), H-7, Sen'jin Village (126)

SENTINEL AMARASSAN
Stonetalon Mountains (70), C-2, D:(1-2), Stonetalon Peak, Patrols path to Talon Den

SENTINEL ARYNIA CLOUDSBREAK
Teldrassil (80), D-3, The Oracle Glade, East of road next to moonwell

SENTINEL DALIA SUNBLADE
Darnassus (26), E-9, The Temple of the Moon, South of fountain

SENTINEL ELISSA STARBREEZE
Darkshore (24), F-4, Auberdine (101), Second floor of eastern building

SENTINEL FARSONG
Ashenvale (12), H-8, Silverwing Grove, Left of ramp

SENTINEL GLYNDA NAL'SHEA
Darkshore (24), F-4, Auberdine (101), Off path leading east out of town

SENTINEL KELDARA SUNBLADE
Azshara (14), B-6, Haldarr Encampment, Lying in tent atop temple ruins

SENTINEL KYRA STARSONG
Teldrassil (80), G-6, Dolanaar (109), Inn

SENTINEL MELYRIA FROSTSHADOW
Ashenvale (12), C-5, Shrine of Aessina, Center of Shrine

SENTINEL ONAEYA
Ashenvale (12), D-4, Maestra's Post, Left of ramp into main outpost

SENTINEL SELARIN
Darkshore (24), F-4, Auberdine (101), North of Auberdine

SENTINEL SHAYA
Teldrassil (80), G-6, Lake Al'Ameth, South of Dolanaar, near graveyard

SENTINEL SHAYLA NIGHTBREEZE
Teldrassil (80), D-5, E-5, Patrols road outside Darnassus

SENTINEL THENYSIL
Ashenvale (12), E-5, Astranaar (101), Entrance of northwest building

SENTINEL TYSHA MOONBLADE
Darkshore (24), F-6, Twilight Vale, Kneeling beside tree east of road

SENTINEL VALENE STARSTRIKE
Ashenvale (12), F-6, Silverwind Refuge (128), Right wing of building

SENTRY POINT CAPTAIN
Dustwallow Marsh (38), H-4, Sentry Point, Tower

SENTRY POINT GUARD
Dustwallow Marsh (38), H-4, Sentry Point

SEOMAN GRIFFITH
Leather Armor Merchant, Stormwind (72), J-5, Old Town, Protective Hide

SERENA BLOODFEATHER
Barrens (18), D-1, The Dry Hills, Far north

SERGE HINOTT
Alchemist Trainer, Hillsbrad Foothills (48), G-2, Tarren Mill (133), House on the left

SERGEANT BA'SHA
Accessories Quartermaster, Orgrimmar (60), E-7, Valley of Strength, Standing outside Hall of Legends

SERGEANT BRASHCLAW
Rare Spawn, Westfall (94), D-3, Lvl 18 Uncommon; Guards gnoll camp in copse of trees

SERGEANT DE VRIES
Morale Officer, Elwynn Forest (42), C-7, Westbrook Garrison, First floor kitchen in garrison

SERGEANT DURGEN STORMPIKE
Alterac Mountains (8), E-8, Alterac Valley, Cave

SERGEANT HOUSER
Sergeant, Undercity (88), F-3, The War Quarter, Platform in front of Skull Building

SERGEANT MACLEAR
Arathi Highlands (11), F-5, Refuge Point (124) (124)

SERGEANT MAJOR CLATE
Armor QM, Stormwind (72), K-6

SERGEANT MALTHUS
Stranglethorn Vale (74), E-1, The Stockpile, Idle near cauldron in the back of cave

SERGEANT RUTGAR
Sergeant, Undercity (88), F-3, The War Quarter, Platform in front of Skull Building

SERGEANT THUNDERHORN
Weapon Quartermaster, Orgrimmar (61), E-7

SERGEANT YOHWA
Stranglethorn Vale (74), D-1, Rebel Camp (124), Camp

SERGRA DARKTHORN
Barrens (18), F-3, The Crossroads (107), Eastern entrance

SERIADNE
Stable Master, Teldrassil (80), G-6, Dolanaar (109), East of inn

SERIL SCOURGEBANE
Winterspring (98), I-4, Everlook (110), Inside building directly north of inn

SERVANT OF ALLISTARJ
Blasted Lands (20), I:(3-5), Dark Portal, Serpent's Coil, 3 servants (one per location), each roaming a small area around spawn point

SERVANT OF ARKKOROC
Azshara (14), G:(4-7), H:(4-7), I:(4-7), J:(5-7), Bay of Storms, Hetaera's Clutch, Southridge Beach

SERVANT OF AZORA
Elwynn Forest (42), I-7, Tower of Azora

SERVANT OF GROL
Blasted Lands (20), F-1, G-4, Dreadmaul Hold, Dreadmaul Post, 3 servants (two at DH, one at DP)

SERVANT OF HORGUS
Eastern Plaguelands (40), E-8, Darrowshire

SERVANT OF ILGALAR
Redridge Mountains (62), K-5, Tower of Ilgalar

SERVANT OF RAZELIKH
Blasted Lands (20), H:(5, 6), I:(5, 6), Dark Portal, Situated along the outer lip of the Dark Portal

SERVANT OF SEVINE
Blasted Lands (20), F:(3, 4), Altar of Storms, 3 servants (two at BL, one at AoS)

SERVO
Badlands (16), H:(4, 5), The Dustbowl, Patrols around camp

SETHIR THE ANCIENT
Teldrassil (80), D-2, On branches north of The Oracle Glade

SETIS
Rare Spawn, Silithus (66), E-5, The Scarab Wall, Lvl 61 Uber-Rare; Spawns in front of the wall and roams the length of northern Silithus

SEVERED DREAMER
Ashenvale (12), J-7, Dor'Danil Barrow Den

SEVERED DRUID
Ashenvale (12), J-7, Dor'Danil Barrow Den

SEVERED KEEPER
Ashenvale (12), J-7, Dor'Danil Barrow Den

SEVERED SLEEPER
Ashenvale (12), J-7, Dor'Danil Barrow Den

SEWA MISTRUNNER
Fishing Supplier, Thunder Bluff (84), F-5, High rise, outside Mountaintop Bait & Tackle tent

SHADE OF AMBERMOON
Silithus (66), G-3, Southwind Village, Terrace of building

SHADE OF ELURA
Darkshore (24), E-5, The Long Wash, Underwater near shipwreck

SHADE OF ERANIKUS
Swamp of Sorrows (76), I-5, The Temple of Atal'Hakkar

SHADETHICKET BARK RIPPER
Ashenvale (12), H:(6-8), I:(5-8), J:(5-7), K:(6, 7)

SHADETHICKET MOSS EATER
Ashenvale (12), F:(4, 5), Iris Lake

SHADETHICKET ORACLE
Ashenvale (12), I-8, Fallen Sky Lake, Island in center of lake

SHADETHICKET RAINCALLER
Ashenvale (12), D:(6, 7), E-6, Ruins of Stardust

SHADETHICKET STONE MOVER
Ashenvale (12), H:(6-8), I:(5-8), J:(5-7), K:(6, 7)

SHADETHICKET WOOD SHAPER
Ashenvale (12), D:(6, 7), E-6, Ruins of Stardust

SHADI MISTRUNNER
Trade Goods Supplier, Thunder Bluff (84), D-6, Lower rise, in Trade Goods and Supplies tent

SHADOW
Dorion's Pet, Darnassus (26), E-1, Cenarion Enclave, Northeast structure, upper level

SHADOW CHARGER
Silverpine Forest (68), F-7, Shadowfang Keep

SHADOW HUNTER VOSH'GAJIN
Burning Steppes (22), Searing Gorge (64), C-4/D-8, Blackrock Spire

SHADOW LORD FEL'DAN
Felwood (44), E-6, Shadow Hold, Anteroom after spiral tunnel

SHADOW PANTHER
Swamp of Sorrows (76), H-6, I:(3, 7), J:(2, 3, 7, 8), K:(2, 3, 6, 7), L:(4-6), Sorrowmurk

SHADOW PRIEST ALLISTER
Silverpine Forest (68), G-4, The Sepulcher (127), In front of tombstone in graveyard

SHADOW PRIEST SARVIS
Tirisfal Glades (86), C-7, Deathknell (109), Church

SHADOW PRIESTESS VANDIS
Tirisfal Glades (86), K-7, The Bulwark (105), Camp on right side of road

SHADOW SPRITE
Teldrassil (80), G-5, Fel Rock

SHADOWCLAW
Rare Spawn, Darkshore (24), F-4, Lvl Uncommon; Roams near Auberdine

SHADOWED SPIRIT
Western Plaguelands (92), I-7, Scholomance

SHADOWFANG DARKSOUL
Silverpine Forest (68), F-7, Shadowfang Keep

SHADOWFANG GLUTTON
Silverpine Forest (68), F-7, Shadowfang Keep

SHADOWFANG MOONWALKER
Silverpine Forest (68), F-7, Shadowfang Keep

SHADOWFANG RAGETOOTH
Silverpine Forest (68), F-7, Shadowfang Keep

SHADOWFANG WHITESCALP
Silverpine Forest (68), F-7, Shadowfang Keep

SHADOWFANG WOLFGUARD
Silverpine Forest (68), F-7, Shadowfang Keep

SHADOWFORGE AMBUSHER
Badlands (16), G-1, Uldaman

SHADOWFORGE ARCHAEOLOGIST
Badlands (16), G-1, Uldaman

SHADOWFORGE CHANTER
Badlands (16), F-3, G-3, Angor Fortress

SHADOWFORGE CITIZEN
Burning Steppes (22), Searing Gorge (64), C-4/D-8, Blackrock Depths

SHADOWFORGE COMMANDER
Rare Spawn, Badlands (16), F-3, Angor Fortress, Lvl 40 Semi-Rare; Patrols second floor of fortress

SHADOWFORGE DARKCASTER
Badlands (16), G-1, Uldaman

SHADOWFORGE DARKWEAVER
Badlands (16), H-3, Hammertoe's Digsite

SHADOWFORGE DIGGER
Badlands (16), G-1, Marker's Terrace

SHADOWFORGE DIGGER
Badlands (16), G-1, Uldaman

SHADOWFORGE FLAME KEEPER
Burning Steppes (22), Searing Gorge (64), C-4/D-8, Blackrock Depths

SHADOWFORGE GEOLOGIST
Badlands (16), G-1, Uldaman

SHADOWFORGE PEASANT
Burning Steppes (22), Searing Gorge (64), C-4/D-8, Blackrock Depths

SHADOWFORGE RELIC HUNTER
Badlands (16), G-1, Uldaman

SHADOWFORGE RUFFIAN
Badlands (16), G-1, Uldaman

SHADOWFORGE SENATOR
Burning Steppes (22), Searing Gorge (64), C-4/D-8, Blackrock Depths

SHADOWFORGE SHARPSHOOTER
Badlands (16), G-1, Uldaman

SHADOWFORGE SURVEYOR
Badlands (16), G-1, Marker's Terrace, Uldaman

SHADOWFORGE TUNNELER
Badlands (16), H-3, Hammertoe's Digsite

SHADOWFORGE WARRIOR
Badlands (16), F:(3, 4), G-3, Angor Fortress

SHADOWGLEN SENTINEL
Teldrassil (80), G-4, H:(4, 5), Shadowglen (127)

SHADOWHIDE ASSASSIN
Redridge Mountains (62), J:(4, 5), K:(4, 5), Galardell Valley

SHADOWHIDE BRUTE
Redridge Mountains (62), J:(3-5), K:(3, 4), Galardell Valley

SHADOWHIDE DARKWEAVER
Redridge Mountains (62), J:(3-5), K:(4-6), L:(5, 6), Galardell Valley

SHADOWHIDE GNOLL
Redridge Mountains (62), J:(4-6), Galardell Valley

SHADOWHIDE SLAYER
Redridge Mountains (62), J:(3-5), K:(4-6), L:(5, 6), Galardell Valley

SHADOWHIDE WARRIOR
Redridge Mountains (62), J:(3-5), K:(3-6), L:(5, 6), Galardell Valley

HADOWHORN STAG
Ashenvale (12), E:(6, 7), F:(5, 6), G:(5-6)

HADOWMAGE
Eastern Plaguelands (40), E-5, F-5, K:(4, 5), The Fungal Vale

HADOWMAGE VIVIAN LAGRAVE
Badlands (16), A-5, Kargath (116), Bonfire left of orc burrow

HADOWMAW PANTHER
Stranglethorn Vale (74), C-4, D:(3-5), E:(3, 4), F:(2, 3)

HADOWPREY GUARDIAN
Desolace (30), B-7, C-7, Sar'theris Strand, Shadowprey Village (128)

HADOWPRIEST SEZZ-ZIZ
Tanaris (78), E-1, Zul'Farrak

HADOWSHARD RUMBLER
Desolace (30), D-5, Mauradon

HADOWSHARD SMASHER
Desolace (30), D-5, Mauradon

HADOWSILK POACHER
Searing Gorge (64), G-3

HADOWSWORN ADEPT
Blasted Lands (20), I:(3-5), J:(3, 5), Dark Portal, Serpent's Coil

HADOWSWORN CULTIST
Blasted Lands (20), I:(3-5), J:(3, 5), Dark Portal, Serpent's Coil

HADOWSWORN DREADWEAVER
Blasted Lands (20), F:(3, 4), Altar of Storms

HADOWSWORN ENFORCER
Blasted Lands (20), F:(3, 4), Altar of Storms

HADOWSWORN THUG
Blasted Lands (20), I:(3-5), J:(3, 5), Dark Portal, Serpent's Coil

HADOWSWORN WARLOCK
Blasted Lands (20), F:(3, 4), Altar of Storms

HADOWY ASSASSIN
Hillsbrad Foothills (48), E:(5, 6), F:(5, 6), Southshore (129), Spawn behind Magistrate's building after warning to protect the Magistrate

HADRA
The Venom Queen, The Hinterlands (50), E-7, Shadra'Alor, (Summon) Small pond in center of village

HADUMBRA
Ashenvale (12), H-5, Raynewood Retreat, Spawns just north of Raynewood Retreat and roams to a clearing south of Howling Vale and back

HAEL'DRYN
Ashenvale (12), G-5, Moonwell, Near moonwell

HAETHIS DARKOAK
Hippogryph Master, Silithus (66), I-1, Valor's Rest (137), South of road

HAHIAR
Loramus's Guardian, Azshara (14), H-7, Bay of Storms, Patrols near Loramus

HAILIEA
Stormwind (72), C-5, E-5, The Park, Roams The Park

HAINA FULLER
First Aid Trainer, Stormwind (72), F-3, Cathedral Square, Cathedral of Light

HAKES O'BREEN
Arathi Highlands (10), D-8, Faldir's Cove, Dock

HAKY" PHILLIPE
Stranglethorn Vale (74), B-8, Booty Bay (103), On dock near ship launch

HALDYN
Clothier, Darkshore (24), F-4, Auberdine (101), Right wing of northern building

HALOMON
Weaponsmith, Teldrassil (80), G-6, Dolanaar (109), Inn

HALUMON
Tabard Vendor, Darnassus (26), I-2, Craftsmen's Terrace, Southeast building, second floor

HAMBLING HORROR
Tirisfal Glades (86), I-4, Brightwater Lake

HAN'TI
Fruit Vendor, Orgrimmar (60), D-5, Valley of Strength, Stranglethorn Imported Fruits

HANDA
Priest Trainer, Teldrassil (80), H-4, Shadowglen (127), Third level of main building

HANDA THE SPINNER
Rare Spawn, Loch Modan (54), K-5, Lvl 19 Semi-Rare; Roams small area around spawn point

SHANDRINA
Trade Goods, Ashenvale (12), F-6, Silverwind Refuge, Right wing of building

SHANDRIS FEATHERMOON
General of the Sentinel Army, Feralas (46), C-5, Feathermoon Stronghold (111), Southwest building

SHA'NI PROUDTUSK
Burning Steppes (22), J-5, Dreadmaul Rock, (Summon) Altar with remains

SHANKYS
Fishing Supplier, Orgrimmar (60), I-3, Valley of Honor, Lumak's Fishing

SHARA BLAZEN
Hillsbrad Foothills (48), H-2, Tarren Mill (133), Outside of inn

SHARD OF MYZRAEL
Quest Item, Arathi Highlands (10), I-3, West of Circle of East Binding

SHARDI
Wind Rider Master, Dustwallow Marsh (38), D-3, Brackenwall Village (104), Southwest part of village

SHARDTOOTH BEAR
Winterspring (98), E:(4, 5), F:(3, 4), G:(3-5), H-4, Frostfire Hot Springs, Timbermaw Post

SHARDTOOTH MAULER
Winterspring (98), H:(3-5), I:(3-5), J:(3-5), Starfall Village (130), Everlook, Winterfall Village

SHARLINDRA
Undercity (88), H-9, Royal Quarter, In Throne room

SHARPBEAK
The Hinterlands (50), H-7, Jintha'Alor, Cage on mountain northeast of altar

SHARPBEAK'S FATHER
The Hinterlands (50), G-6, The Altar of Zul, (Summon) Flies to Sharpbeak

SHARPBEAK'S MOTHER
The Hinterlands (50), G-6, The Altar of Zul, (Summon) Flies to Sharpbeak

SHARPTALON
Ashenvale (12), J-6, Nightsong Woods, Spawns north of southern bridge and roams southern side of road heading west

SHARPTOOTH FRENZY
Stranglethorn Vale (74), C:(1, 4), D:(1-4), C-7, D:(3, 4), River

SHAWN
Redridge Mountains (62), C-5, Lakeshire (117), L-shaped dock west of the bridge

SHAY LEAFRUNNER
Feralas (46), D-1, Ruins of Ravenwind, In northwestern ruins along hill

SHAYIS STEELFURY
Armor Crafter, Orgrimmar (60), J-2, Valley of Honor

SHAZZRAH
Burning Steppes (22), Searing Gorge (64), C-4/D-8, The Molten Core

SHEAL RUNETOTEM
Druid Trainer, Thunder Bluff (84), J-3, Elder Rise, Inside Hall of Elders

SHEENDRA TALLGRASS
Trade Supplies, Feralas (46), I-4, Camp Mojache (105), Big western tent

SHELBY STONEFLINT
Stable Master, Dun Morogh (32), F-5, Kharanos (116), Outside of distillery

SHELDON VAN CROY
Cloth Armor Merchant, Undercity (88), J-3, The Magic Quarter

SHELDRAS MOONTREE
Druid Trainer, Stormwind (72), C-6, The Park, By pool of water

SHELENE RHOBART
Journeyman Leatherworker, Tirisfal Glades (86), I-6, In camp outside of Undercity

SHELGRAYN
Stable Master, Desolace (30), I-1, Nijel's Point (121), Outside inn

SHELLEI BRONDIR
Gryphon Master, Wetlands (96), A-6, Menethil Harbor (119), South of keep

SHELLENE
Orphanage matron, Stormwind (72), G-4, Cathedral Square, Orphanage

SHEN'DRALAR ANCIENT
Feralas (46), G-4, Dire Maul

SHEN'DRALAR PROVISIONER
Feralas (46), G-4, Dire Maul

SHEN'DRALAR SPIRIT
Feralas (46), G-4, Dire Maul

SHEN'DRALAR ZEALOT
Feralas (46), G-4, Dire Maul

SHENTHUL
Rogue Trainer, Orgrimmar (60), E-5, The Cleft of Shadow, Shadowswift Brotherhood

SHERI ZIPSTITCH
Tailoring Supplies, Duskwood (36), K-4, Darkshire (108), Second floor of house

SHERMAN FEMMEL
Butcher, Redridge Mountains (62), C-4, Lakeshire (117), First floor of Lakeshire Inn

SHEZA WILDMANE
Thunder Bluff (84), H-3, Elder Rise, In front of Elder Rise Drums

SHI'ALUNE
Kaerbrus' Pet, Felwood (44), H-3, Talonbranch Glade (133), Near pond

SHIKRIK
Shaman Trainer, Durotar (34), F-7, Valley of Trials (136)

SHILL DINGER
Burning Steppes (22), Searing Gorge (64), C-4/D-8, Blackrock Depths

SHIM'LA
Orgrimmar (60), H-2, Valley of Honor, Near Hunter's Hall entrance

SHIMRA
General Trade, Orgrimmar (60), F-8, Valley of Strength, Orgrimmar General Store

SHINDRELL SWIFTFIRE
Ashenvale (12), E-5, Astranaar (101), Northern entrance

SHIZZLE
Un'Goro Crater (90), F-1, Marshal's Refuge (118), South of cave

SHLEIPNARR
Rare Spawn, Searing Gorge (64), H-4, Lvl 47 Very Rare; Patrols path near spawn point

SHOJA'MY
Stable Master, Durotar (34), H-4, Razor Hill (124), Outside inn

SHOMA
Weapon Vendor, Orgrimmar (60), K-2, Valley of Honor, Arms of Legend

SHONI THE SHILENT
Stormwind (72), H-1, Dwarven District, Next to well

SHORE CRAWLER
Westfall (94), B:(6-8), C:(8, 9), D-9, Longshore

SHORE STRIDER
Feralas (46), C-3, D:(3-5), E:(5-7), The Forgotten Coast

SHORT JOHN MITHRIL
Stranglethorn Vale (74), C-5, Gurubashi Arena, (Summon) Spawns in the western seats of the arena every 3 hours

SHREEV
Tanaris (78), G-3, Gadgetzan (113), Outside northwestern hut

SHRIEKING BANSHEE
Eastern Plaguelands (40), D-2, Stratholme

SHRIKE BAT
Badlands (16), G-1, Uldaman

SHYLAMIIR
Herbalism Trainer, Stormwind (72), B-5, The Park, Northwest Building

SHYLENAI
Owl Trainer, Darnassus (26), I-5, Warrior's Terrace, South of path just after entrance to city

SHYN
Wind Rider Master, Feralas (46), I-4, Camp Mojache (105), East of inn

SHYRKA WOLFRUNNER
Stable Master, Feralas (46), I-4, Camp Mojache (105), Outside big western tent

SHY-ROTAM
Winterspring (98), G-1, Frostsaber Rock, On the rock (spawns for quest)

SIAN'DUR
Hunter Trainer, Orgrimmar (60), H-2, Valley of Honor, Hunter's Hall

SIAN'TSU
Shaman Trainer, Orgrimmar (60), D-4, Valley of Wisdom, Grommash Hold

SIAN-ROTAM
Winterspring (98), G-1, Frostsaber Rock, On the rock (spawns for quest)

SICKLY REFUGEE
Silverpine Forest (68), G:(8, 9), The Greymane Wall

SIDA
Wetlands (96), A-6, Menethil Harbor (119), Outside house east of keep

SIEGE GOLEM
Rare Spawn, Badlands (16), F-4, Angor Fortress, Lvl 40 Average Rare; Patrols path to an area of Badlands just south of Kargath (A-6)

SIGRUN IRONHEW
Badlands (16), H-4, Camp

SIKWA
Stable Master, Barrens (18), F-3, The Crossroads (107), Behind inn

SILAS ZIMMER
Undercity (88), L-2, The Magic Quarter, Outside of Skull Building

SILDANAIR
Warrior Trainer, Darnassus (26), H-4, Warrior's Terrace, Middle of terrace

SILITHID CREEPER
Barrens (18), E-7, F-7, Field of Giants, Southern Barrens

SILITHID GRUB
Barrens (18), E-7, F-7, Field of Giants, Southern Barrens

SILITHID HARVESTER
Barrens (18), E-7, Field of Giants

SILITHID HIVE DRONE
Thousand Needles (82), H-8, I:(8, 9), J-8, The Rustmaul Dig Site, The Shimmering Flats

SILITHID INVADER
Thousand Needles (82), H-8, I:(8, 9), The Rustmaul Dig Site

SILITHID RAVAGER
Thousand Needles (82), H-8, I:(8, 9), The Rustmaul Dig Site

SILITHID SEARCHER
Thousand Needles (82), I:(8, 9), J-8, The Rustmaul Dig Site, The Shimmering Flats

SILITHID SWARMER
Barrens (18), E-7, F-7, Field of Giants, Southern Barrens

SILT CRAWLER
Swamp of Sorrows (76), J:(1, 9), K:(1, 2, 7, 8), L:(2, 3, 7, 8), Misty Reed Strand

SILVA FIL'NAVETH
Darnassus Flight Master, Moonglade (56), F-4, Nighthaven (121), Southwest side of town

SILVARIA
Pet Trainer, Darnassus (26), E-1, Cenarion Enclave, Northeast structure, upper level

SILVERBACK PATRIARCH
Stranglethorn Vale (74), C-7, D:(6, 7), Mistvale Valley, Ruins of Aboraz, The Crystal Shore

SILVERMANE HOWLER
The Hinterlands (50), E-6, F:(4-7), G:(4-6), H:(4-6), The Hinterlands

SILVERMANE STALKER
The Hinterlands (50), H:(4-6), I:(4-6), J:(4-6), K:(5, 6), L-5, Overlook Cliffs, Along Hills

SILVERMANE WOLF
The Hinterlands (50), D:(5-7), E:(4-6), F:(4, 5), The Hinterlands

SILVERPINE DEATHGUARD
Guard, Silverpine Forest (68), G-4, The Sepulcher (127)

SILVERWING ELITE
Ashenvale (12), H-8, Fallen Sky Lake, Silverwing Grove, Silverwing Outpost

SILVERWING SENTINEL
Ashenvale (12), H-7, Nightsong Woods, Silverwing Outpost

SILVERWING WARRIOR
Ashenvale (12), H-7, Nightsong Woods, Silverwing Outpost

SIMON TANNER
Leatherworking Trainer, Stormwind (72), J-5, Old Town, The Protective Hide

SIMONE CANTRELL
Landscape Architect, Hillsbrad Foothills (48), J-2, Garden to the right of Chateau Ravenholdt

SIMONE THE INCONSPICUOUS
Un'Goro Crater (90), E:(4-8), F-6, F-8, G:(6-8), Golakka Hot Springs, The Slithering Scar, Terror Run, Walks big area from The Slithering Scar to north of the springs

SINDA
Leather Armor Merchant, Teldrassil (80), G-6, Dolanaar (109), Inn

SIN'DALL
Stranglethorn Vale (74), C-2, Tkashi Ruins, Roams small area around spawn point

SINDRAYL
Hippogryph Master, Moonglade (56), G-7, East of small body of water, south of lake

SINGE
Pet, Redridge Mountains (62), I-5, Stonewatch, Second floor of Stonewatch Keep

SINGED BASILISK
Stonetalon Mountains (70), C-6, D:(6, 7), E-6, The Charred Vale

SINGER
Rare Spawn, Arathi Highlands (10), D-3, Northfold Manor, Lvl 34 Uncommon; Roams in farm

SIR MALORY WHEELER
Arathi Basin BM, Undercity (88), H-9

SIR S. J. ERLGADIN
Stranglethorn Vale (74), C-1, Nesingwary's Expedition, Camp

SIRE MAXIMUS ADAM
Arathi Basin BM, Arathi Highlands (11), F-5, Refuge Point (124) (124)

SIRRA VON'INDI
Historian of Darkshire, Duskwood (36), J-5, Darkshire (108), Darkshire Town Hall

SISTER AQUINNE
Novice Priestess, Darnassus (26), C-4, The Temple Gardens, South of teleporter

SISTER HATELASH
Rare Spawn, Mulgore (58), D-1, Lvl 11 Uncommon; Northwest nest

SISTER OF CELEBRIAN
Desolace (30), D-5, Mauradon

SISTER RATHTALON
Barrens (18), D-1, The Dry Hills, Roams the nest

SISTER RIVEN
Stonetalon Mountains (70), C-7, D-7, The Charred Vale, Patrols across Charred Vale

SKARR THE UNBREAKABLE
Rare Spawn, Feralas (46), G-4, Dire Maul, Lvl 58 Rare

SKARR THE UNBREAKABLE
Feralas (46), G-4, The Maul, In arena

SKELETAL ACOLYTE
Western Plaguelands (92), E:(6, 7), F:(6, 7), G:(6, 7), Ruins of Andorhal, Idle with Araj the Summoner in the center of city

SKELETAL BERSERKER
Eastern Plaguelands (40), D-2, Stratholme

SKELETAL EXECUTIONER
Western Plaguelands (92), E:(6, 7), F:(6, 7), G:(6, 7), Ruins of Andorhal, Idle with Araj the Summoner in the center of city

SKELETAL FIEND
Duskwood (36), B:(4, 5), C:(4, 5), Raven Hill Cemetery (123)

SKELETAL FLAYER
Western Plaguelands (92), D:(5, 6), E:(5, 6), F:(7, 8), G:(7, 8), Sorrow Hill

SKELETAL FROSTWEAVER
Barrens (18), F-9, Razorfen Downs

SKELETAL GUARDIAN
Eastern Plaguelands (40), D-2, Stratholme

SKELETAL HEALER
Duskwood (36), A-4, B:(3, 4), Raven Hill Cemetery (123)

SKELETAL HIGHBORNE
Feralas (46), G-4, Dire Maul

SKELETAL HORROR
Duskwood (36), A:(4, 5), B:(4, 5), C:(4, 5), K-6, Raven Hill Cemetery (123)

SKELETAL MAGE
Duskwood (36), K-7, Tranquil Gardens Cemetery

SKELETAL MINER
Westfall (94), D-7, E-7, The Deadmines

SKELETAL RAIDER
Duskwood (36), A:(3, 4), B:(3, 4), Raven Hill Cemetery (123)

SKELETAL SERVANT
Eastern Plaguelands (40), D-3, Stratholme

SKELETAL SHADOWCASTER
Barrens (18), F-9, Razorfen Downs

SKELETAL SORCERER
Western Plaguelands (92), D-6, E:(5, 6), G-8, Sorrow Hill

SKELETAL SUMMONER
Barrens (18), F-9, Razorfen Downs

SKELETAL TERROR
Western Plaguelands (92), F-5, Dalson's Tears

SKELETAL WARDER
Duskwood (36), A:(3, 4), B:(3, 4), Raven Hill Cemetery (123)

SKELETAL WARLORD
Western Plaguelands (92), E:(6, 7), F:(6, 7), Ruins of Andorhal, Idle with Araj the Summoner in the center of city

SKELETAL WARRIOR
Duskwood (36), K-7, Tranquil Gardens Cemetery

SKHOWL
Rare Spawn, Alterac Mountains (8), D:(5, 6), E-4, F-6, Growless Cave, Ruins of Alterac, Lvl 36 Semi-Rare; Roams small area around spawn point

SKITTERING CRUSTACEAN
Ashenvale (12), B-2, Blackfathom Deeps

SKOLMIN GOLDFURY
Bow Merchant, Ironforge (52), J-6, The Military Ward, Goldfury's Hunting Supplies

SKORN WHITECLOUD
Mulgore (58), E-6, Bloodhoof Village (102), Outside inn

SKUERTO
Arathi Highlands (10), F-5, Refuge Point (124), Camp

SKUL
Rare Spawn, Eastern Plaguelands (40), D-2, Stratholme, Lvl 58 Rare

SKULKING CORPSE
Western Plaguelands (92), I-7, Scholomance

SKULLSPLITTER AXE THROWER
Stranglethorn Vale (74), D-4, E:(3, 4), Ruins of Zul'Mamwe

SKULLSPLITTER BEASTMASTER
Stranglethorn Vale (74), E:(4, 5), Ruins of Zul'Mamwe

SKULLSPLITTER BERSERKER
Stranglethorn Vale (74), E-5, Ruins of Zul'Mamwe

SKULLSPLITTER HEADHUNTER
Stranglethorn Vale (74), E-5, Ruins of Zul'Mamwe

SKULLSPLITTER HUNTER
Stranglethorn Vale (74), E:(4, 5), Ruins of Zul'Mamwe

SKULLSPLITTER MYSTIC
Stranglethorn Vale (74), D-4, E:(3, 4), Ruins of Zul'Mamwe

SKULLSPLITTER SCOUT
Stranglethorn Vale (74), E:(4, 5), Ruins of Zul'Mamwe

SKULLSPLITTER SPIRITCHASER
Stranglethorn Vale (74), E-5, Ruins of Zul'Mamwe

SKULLSPLITTER WARRIOR
Stranglethorn Vale (74), D-4, E:(3, 4), Ruins of Zul'Mamwe

SKULLSPLITTER WITCH DOCTOR
Stranglethorn Vale (74), E:(4, 5), Ruins of Zul'Mamwe

SKUM
Barrens (18), E-4, Wailing Caverns

SKY SHADOW
Deadwind Pass (28), B-4, C:(3-6), D:(2, 4-6), E-5, Deadman's Crossing, Deadwind Ravine, Sleeping Gorge

SKYMANE GORILLA
Stranglethorn Vale (74), D:(8, 9), Jaguero Isle

SLAGG
Superior Butcher, Arathi Highlands (10), J-3, Hammerfall (115), Platform of north building

SLARK
Rare Spawn, Westfall (94), F-1, Longshore, Lvl 15 Uncommon; Runs entire Longshore coast

SLAUGHTERHOUSE PROTECTOR
Eastern Plaguelands (40), D-3, E-2, Plaguewood

SLAVE MASTER BLACKHEART
Rare Spawn, Searing Gorge (64), E:(2-4), The Slag Pit, Lvl 50 Uncommon; Roams small area around spawn point

SLAVE WORKER
Searing Gorge (64), D:(2-5), E:(2-5), F-4, The Cauldron, Mines

SLAVERING EMBER WORG
Burning Steppes (22), D:(5, 6), E-3, F:(3, 7), G:(2, 3, 6), H:(5, 6), I:(3-6), J-3

SLAVERING GHOUL
Western Plaguelands (92), D-6, E:(5, 6), F:(7, 8), G:(7, 8), Sorrow Hill

SLAVERING WORG
Silverpine Forest (68), F-7, Shadowfang Keep

SLEEBY
Arathi Highlands (10), I-3, Circle of East Binding, Patrols with Fozruck to each of the four Circles of Binding

SLIME MAGGOT
Swamp of Sorrows (76), I-5, The Temple of Atal'Hakkar

SLIMESHELL MAKRURA
Barrens (18), H:(4, 5), The Merchant Coast, The Tidus Stair

SLIN SKYCHASER
Shaman Trainer, Thunder Bluff (84), B-2, Spirit Rise, Inside Hall of Spirits

SLITHERBLADE MYRMIDON
Desolace (30), C:(1, 2), D:(1, 2), E:(1, 2), Sar'theris Strand

SLITHERBLADE NAGA
Desolace (30), D:(2, 3), E-2, Ethel Rethor, Sar'theris Strand

SLITHERBLADE ORACLE
Desolace (30), C:(1, 2), D:(1, 2), E:(1, 2), Sar'theris Strand

SLITHERBLADE RAZORTAIL
Desolace (30), C:(1, 2), D:(1, 2), Sar'theris Strand

SLITHERBLADE SEA WITCH
Desolace (30), C:(1, 2), D:(1, 2), Sar'theris Strand

SLITHERBLADE SORCERESS
Desolace (30), C-1, D:(1-3), E:(1, 2), Ethel Rethor, Sar'theris Strand

SLITHERBLADE TIDEHUNTER
Desolace (30), C:(1, 2), D-1, E-1, Sar'theris Strand

SLITHERBLADE WARRIOR
Desolace (30), C-1, D:(1-3), E:(1, 2), Ethel Rethor, Sar'theris Strand

SLOAN MCCOY
Poison Supplier, Stormwind (72), K-6, Old Town, SI:7

SLUDGE BEAST
Rare Spawn, Barrens (18), G-1, The Sludge Fen, Lvl 19 Semi-Rare; In sludge

SLUDGINN
Rare Spawn, Wetlands (96), A-7, B-7, Lvl 30 Average Rare; South of Menethil Harbor, in hills across water

SLY GARRETT
Shady Goods, Stranglethorn Vale (74), B-8, Booty Bay (103), Outside of fireworks shop on the eastern side of bay

SMALL CRAG BOAR
Dun Morogh (32), B:(7, 8), C:(7, 8), D-7, Coldridge Pass, Coldridge Valley (107)

SMEED SCRABBLESCREW
Desolace (30), H-6, Scrabblescrew's Camp, In front of hut

SMILING JIM
Dustwallow Marsh (38), I-5, Theramore Isle (135), Sitting outside inn to north

SMITH ARGUS
Journeyman Blacksmith, Elwynn Forest (42), E-6, Goldshire (114), Smithy

SMITH SLAGTREE
Blacksmithing Supplies, The Hinterlands (50), L-8, Revantusk Village (125), Makeshift smithy on right side of village

SMOKEY LARUE
Eastern Plaguelands (40), K-6, Light's Hope Chapel (118), Camp on left side of chapel

SMOLDAR
Rare Spawn, Searing Gorge (64), C-6, Lvl 50 Semi-Rare; Patrols the northwestern portion of the zone

SMOLDERTHORN AXE THROWER
Burning Steppes (22), Searing Gorge (64), C-4/D-8, Blackrock Spire

SMOLDERTHORN BERSERKER
Burning Steppes (22), Searing Gorge (64), C-4/D-8, Blackrock Spire

SMOLDERTHORN HEADHUNTER
Burning Steppes (22), Searing Gorge (64), C-4/D-8, Blackrock Spire

SMOLDERTHORN MYSTIC
Burning Steppes (22), Searing Gorge (64), C-4/D-8, Blackrock Spire

SMOLDERTHORN SEER
Burning Steppes (22), Searing Gorge (64), C-4/D-8, Blackrock Spire

SMOLDERTHORN SHADOW HUNTER
Burning Steppes (22), Searing Gorge (64), C-4/D-8, Blackrock Spire

SMOLDERTHORN SHADOW PRIEST
Burning Steppes (22), Searing Gorge (64), C-4/D-8, Blackrock Spire

SMOLDERTHORN WITCH DOCTOR
Burning Steppes (22), Searing Gorge (64), C-4/D-8, Blackrock Spire

SMUDGE THUNDERWOOD
Poison Vendor, Hillsbrad Foothills (48), K-2, Basement of Chateau Ravenholdt

SNAGGLESPEAR
Rare Spawn, Mulgore (58), F-7, Lvl 9 Uncommon; Camp

SNANG
Journeyman Tailor, Orgrimmar (60), H-5, The Drag, Magar's Cloth Goods

SNAP JAW
Alterac Mountains (8), K-6, Chillwind Point, River

SNAPJAW
Hillsbrad Foothills (48), G-5, River

SNAPJAW CROCOLISK
Stranglethorn Vale (74), D:(2-4)

SNAPPING CRUSTACEAN
Ashenvale (12), B-2, Blackfathom Deeps

SNARL
Expert Blacksmith, Orgrimmar (60), J-2, Valley of Honor, Across from Arms of Legend

SNARLER
Rare Spawn, Feralas (46), I-4, Lariss Pavilion, Lvl 42 Uncommon; Spawns near delta and roams southeast

SNARLFLARE
Rare Spawn, Redridge Mountains (62), D-6, E-3, F-3, Alther's Mill, Lvl 18 Uncommon; Roams small area around spawn point

SNARLMANE
Rare Spawn, Silverpine Forest (68), J:(2, 3), Fenris Keep, Lvl 23 Uncommon; Stands idle at spawn point

SNEED
Westfall (94), D-7, E-7, The Deadmines

SNEED'S SHREDDER
Westfall (94), D-7, E-7, The Deadmines

SNICKERFANG HYENA
Blasted Lands (20), I:(3, 4), Serpent's Coil

SNORT THE HECKLER
Rare Spawn, Barrens (18), D-3, Lvl 17 Uncommon; Roams southwest of Forgotten Pools

SNOW LEOPARD
Dun Morogh (32), C:(4, 5), D:(3-5), E:(3, 4), F:(3, 6), G:(5, 6), H:(5, 6), I-6, K-4

SNOW TRACKER WOLF
Dun Morogh (32), F-5, G:(4, 5), Kharanos (116)

SNURK BUCKSQUICK
Zeppelin Master, Durotar (34), H-1, Atop tower

SOARING RAZORBEAK
The Hinterlands (50), B-5, C-5, The Hinterlands

SOGNAR CLIFFBEARD
Meat Vendor, Ironforge (52), H-8, I-7, The Military Ward, Roams The Military Ward

SOLAKAR FLAMEWREATH
Burning Steppes (22), Searing Gorge (64), C-4/D-8, Blackrock Spire

SOLEIL STONEMANTLE
Banker, Ironforge (52), D-6, The Commons, Vault of Ironforge

SOLM HARGRIN
Rogue Trainer, Dun Morogh (32), D-7, Coldridge Valley (107), Anvilmar

SOMNUS
Swamp of Sorrows (76), J-7, Patrols a circular path around swamp land near the southeastern coast line

SON OF ARKKOROC
Azshara (14), G:(4-7), H:(4-7), I:(4-7), J:(5-7), Bay of Storms, Hetaera's Clutch, Southridge Beach

SON OF ARUGAL
Silverpine Forest (68), F-3, G:(3, 8), Roam

SON OF ARUGAL
Silverpine Forest (68), F-7, Shadowfang Keep

SON OF CENARIUS
Stonetalon Mountains (70), D:(1, 2), E:(1, 2), Stonetalon Peak

SON OF FLAME
Burning Steppes (22), Searing Gorge (64), C-4/D-8, The Molten Core

SOOLIE BERRYFIZZ
Alchemy Supplies, Ironforge (52), I-5, Tinker Town, Berryfizz's Potions and Mixed Drinks

SORAN
Banker, Orgrimmar (60), F-7, Valley of Strength

SORCERER ASHCROMBE
Silverpine Forest (68), F-7, Shadowfang Keep

SOREK
Warrior Trainer, Orgrimmar (60), J-3, Valley of Honor, Hall of the Brave

SORIID THE DEVOURER
Rare Spawn, Tanaris (78), E:(4, 5), The Noxious Lair, Lvl 50 Uncommon; Spawns in multiple chambers

SORROW SPINNER
Swamp of Sorrows (76), A-5, B-5, C:(4-6), D:(3, 5, 6), E:(3, 4), F-3, I-3

SOULLESS GHOUL
Western Plaguelands (92), E:(6, 7), F:(6, 7), G:(6, 7), Ruins of Andorhal, Idle with Araj the Summoner in the center of city

SOUTHERN SAND CRAWLER
Stranglethorn Vale (74), B:(8, 9), C:(7-9), D-7, Jaguero Isle, Wild Shore

SOUTHSEA BRIGAND
Barrens (18), H:(4, 5), The Merchant Coast, Northwatch Hold

SOUTHSEA CANNONEER
Barrens (18), H:(4, 5), The Merchant Coast, The Tidus Stair

SOUTHSEA CUTTHROAT
Barrens (18), G:(4, 5), H:(4, 5), The Merchant Coast

SOUTHSEA DOCK WORKER
Tanaris (78), J-5, K-5, Lost Rigger Cove

SOUTHSEA FREEBOOTER
Tanaris (78), J:(4, 5), K-5, Lost Rigger Cove

SOUTHSEA PIRATE
Tanaris (78), J:(4, 5), K-5, Lost Rigger Cove

SOUTHSEA PRIVATEER
Barrens (18), G:(4, 5), H:(4, 5), The Merchant Coast

SOUTHSEA SWASHBUCKLER
Tanaris (78), J-5, K-5, Lost Rigger Cove

SOUTHSHORE GUARD
Hillsbrad Foothills (48), E:(5, 6), F:(5, 6), Southshore (129)

SOVIK
Engineering Supplies, Orgrimmar (60), J-3, Valley of Honor, Nogg's Machine Shop

SPACKLE THORNBERRY
Demon Trainer, Stormwind (72), D-8, Mage Quarter, The Slaughtered Lamb

SPARK NILMINER
Un'Goro Crater (90), F-1, Marshal's Refuge (118), Entrance to cave

SPARKLESHELL BORER
Thousand Needles (82), J:(8, 9), K:(8, 9), Tahonda Ruins, The Rustmaul Dig Site, The Shimmering Flats

SPARKLESHELL SNAPPER
Thousand Needles (82), I-8, J:(7, 8), K:(5-8), L:(6-8), The Rustmaul Dig Site, The Shimmering Flats, Weazel's Crater

SPARKLESHELL TORTOISE
Thousand Needles (82), I:(6, 7), J:(5-7), K:(5, 6), Ironstone Camp, The Shimmering Flats, Weazel's Crater

SPAWN OF HAKKAR
Swamp of Sorrows (76), I-5, The Temple of Atal'Hakkar

SPECTRAL ATTENDANT
Western Plaguelands (92), F-7, Ruins of Andorhal, Idle with Araj the Summoner in the center of city

SPECTRAL BETRAYER
Eastern Plaguelands (40), G-5, Blackwood Lake

SPECTRAL CITIZEN
Eastern Plaguelands (40), D-2, Stratholme

SPECTRAL CORPSE
Eastern Plaguelands (40), G-6, The Infectis Scar, North near a sword with a glowing aura

SPECTRAL DEFENDER
Eastern Plaguelands (40), G-5, Blackwood Lake

SPECTRAL MARAUDER
Eastern Plaguelands (40), G-6, The Infectis Scar, North near a sword with a glowing aura

SPECTRAL PROJECTION
Western Plaguelands (92), I-7, Scholomance

SPECTRAL RESEARCHER
Western Plaguelands (92), I-7, Scholomance

SPECTRAL TEACHER
Western Plaguelands (92), I-7, Scholomance

SPECTRAL TUTOR
Western Plaguelands (92), I-7, Scholomance

SPELL EATER
Winterspring (98), H:(5, 6), I-5, Mazthoril

SPELLMAW
Winterspring (98), H-5, Mazthoril, Outside near entrance

SPEWED LARVA
Desolace (30), D-5, Maraudon

SPIGOT OPERATOR LUGLUNKET
Gadgetzan Water Co., Tanaris (78), H-Gadgetzan (113), Between bank and in

SPIKED STEGODON
Un'Goro Crater (90), C:(5-7), D:(6-8), E:(6-8), Golakka Hot Springs, Terror R

SPINED CRAWLER
Ashenvale (12), A:(2-4), B:(2-4), The Zoram Strand (137), Zoram'gar Outpo (137)

SPIRE SCARAB
Burning Steppes (22), Searing Gorge (64), C-4/D-8, Blackrock Spire

SPIRE SCORPID
Burning Steppes (22), Searing Gorge (64), C-4/D-8, Blackrock Spire

SPIRE SPIDER
Burning Steppes (22), Searing Gorge (64), C-4/D-8, Blackrock Spire

SPIRE SPIDERLING
Burning Steppes (22), Searing Gorge (64), C-4/D-8, Blackrock Spire

SPIRESTONE BATTLE LORD
Rare Spawn, Burning Steppes (22), Searing Gorge (64), C-4/D-8, Blackroc Spire, Lvl 58 Uncommon

SPIRESTONE BATTLE MAGE
Burning Steppes (22), Searing Gorge (64), C-4/D-8, Blackrock Spire

SPIRESTONE BUTCHER
Burning Steppes (22), Searing Gorge (64), C-4/D-8, Blackrock Spire

SPIRESTONE ENFORCER
Burning Steppes (22), Searing Gorge (64), C-4/D-8, Blackrock Spire

SPIRESTONE LORD MAGUS
Burning Steppes (22), Searing Gorge (64), C-4/D-8, Blackrock Spire

SPIRESTONE MYSTIC
Burning Steppes (22), Searing Gorge (64), C-4/D-8, Blackrock Spire

SPIRESTONE OGRE MAGUS
Burning Steppes (22), Searing Gorge (64), C-4/D-8, Blackrock Spire

SPIRESTONE REAVER
Burning Steppes (22), Searing Gorge (64), C-4/D-8, Blackrock Spire

SPIRESTONE WARLORD
Burning Steppes (22), Searing Gorge (64), C-4/D-8, Blackrock Spire

SPIRIT OF GELK
The Second Kahn, Desolace (30), C-6, Maraudon, Middle tier of purple sectio

SPIRIT OF KIRITH
Blasted Lands (20), J-3, Serpent's Coil, (Summon) Spawns upon killing Kirith the Damned

SPIRIT OF KOLK
The First Kahn, Desolace (30), C-6, Maraudon, Near entrance to purple section

SPIRIT OF MAGRA
The Third Kahn, Desolace (30), C-6, Maraudon, Crystal cave in orange section near giant crystal

SPIRIT OF MARAUDOS
The Fourth Khan, Desolace (30), D-5, Maraudon

SPIRIT OF MINSHINA
Durotar (34), H-7, Sen'jin Village (126), (Summon) Find his skull

SPIRIT OF TREY LIGHTFORGE
Felwood (44), E-6, Jaedenar, (Summon Appears outside of Shadow Hold entrance

SPIRIT OF VENG
The Fifth Khan, Desolace (30), D-5, Maraudon

PITEFLAYER
Rare Spawn, Blasted Lands (20), I-5, Dark Portal, Lvl 52 Semi-Rare; Patrols to tower ruins at the edge of Serpent's Coil (I-3)

PITELASH BATTLEMASTER
Azshara (14), H:(8, 9), I:(8, 9), H:(8, 9), I:(8, 9), Ravencrest Monument

PITELASH MYRMIDON
Azshara (14), E:(4-6), F:(4-7)

PITELASH RAIDER
Azshara (14), F-9, The Ruined Reaches

PITELASH SCREAMER
Azshara (14), B:(5, 6), C:(5, 6), D:(4-6)

PITELASH SERPENT GUARD
Azshara (14), D:(5, 6), E:(5, 6), Ruins of Eldarath, Temple of Zin-Malor

PITELASH SIREN
Azshara (14), D:(5, 6), E:(4-6), F:(4-7), Ruins of Eldarath, The Shattered Strand, Southridge Beach, Temple of Zin-Malor

PITELASH WARRIOR
Azshara (14), B:(5, 6), C:(5, 6), D:(4-6)

PITELASH WITCH
Azshara (14), F-9, The Ruined Reaches

SPLINTER FIST ENSLAVER
Duskwood (36), E-8, Vul'Gol Ogre Mound

SPLINTER FIST FIRE WEAVER
Duskwood (36), E-7, Vul'Gol Ogre Mound

SPLINTER FIST FIREMONGER
Duskwood (36), D-7, E-8, Vul'Gol Ogre Mound

SPLINTER FIST OGRE
Duskwood (36), E-7, Vul'Gol Ogre Mound

SPLINTER FIST TASKMASTER
Duskwood (36), D-7, E-7, Vul'Gol Ogre Mound

SPLINTER FIST WARRIOR
Duskwood (36), D:(7, 8), E-8, Vul'Gol Ogre Mound

SPLINTERBONE CAPTAIN
Barrens (18), F-9, Razorfen Downs

SPLINTERBONE CENTURIAN
Barrens (18), F-9, Razorfen Downs

SPLINTERBONE SKELETON
Barrens (18), F-9, Razorfen Downs

SPLINTERBONE WARRIOR
Barrens (18), F-9, Razorfen Downs

SPLINTERED SKELETON
Western Plaguelands (92), I-7, Scholomance

SPLINTERTREE GUARD
Ashenvale (12), B-4, I:(6, 7)

SPLINTERTREE RAIDER
Ashenvale (12), I-7, Nightsong Woods, Silverwing Outpost

SPOT
Dustwallow Marsh (38), I-5, Theramore Isle (135), Outside Foothold Citadel

SPRAGGLE FROCK
Un'Goro Crater (90), F-1, Marshal's Refuge (118), Near entrance to cave, next to sign

SPRINGSPINDLE FIZZLEGEAR
Engineer Trainer, Ironforge (52), I-5, Tinker Town, Springspindles Gadgets

SPRINKLE
Tanaris (78), G-3, Gadgetzan (113), Outside northwestern hut

SPRITE DARTER
Feralas (46), H:(4, 5), I-5, Camp Mojache (105), Lower Wilds, Woodpaw Hills

SPRITE DRAGON
Feralas (46), D-2, E:(1, 3), F-3, Ruins of Ravenwind, The Twin Colossals

SPRITE JUMPSPROCKET
Journeyman Engineer, Stormwind (72), H-1, Dwarven District, North end of district, by tent

SPROGGER
Stranglethorn Vale (74), B-8, Booty Bay (103), On dock near ship launch on the northern side of bay

SPROK
Dun Morogh (32), C-4, Gnomeregan

SPUTTERVALVE
Tinkers' Union, Barrens (18), H-4, Ratchet (122), Stall near bank

"SQUEALER" THORNMANTLE
Mulgore (58), H-8, Brambleblade Ravine, Cave in center of ravine

SQUIDDIC
Rare Spawn, Redridge Mountains (62), G-7, Lake Everstill, Lvl 19 Uncommon; Patrols back and forth just offshore by the murloc camp

SQUIRE LEOREN MAL'DERATH
Stable Master, Silithus (67), G-5, Cenarion Hold (106)

SQUIRE MALTRAKE
Searing Gorge (64), D-4, Patrols a semicircle around Kalaran Windblade

SRANDA
Light Armor & Weapons Merchant, Badlands (16), A-5, Kargath (116), Forge left of orc burrow

SRAZZ
Pie Vendor, Ironforge (52), E-4, The Great Forge, Circles Great Forge

SRI'SKULK
Rare Spawn, Tirisfal Glades (86), K-5, L:(4, 5), Venomweb Vale, Lvl 13 Uncommon; Roams small area around spawn point

STALVAN MISTMANTLE
Duskwood (36), K-4, Manor Mistmantle, House

STANLEY
Hillsbrad Foothills (48), C-3, Hillsbrad Fields (115), Dog house outside house at northern end of town

STARN
Gunsmith & Bowyer, Thousand Needles (82), F-5, Freewind Post (112), Next to hut, west of inn

STARVING BLISTERPAW
Tanaris (78), E:(2, 3), F:(2, 3), G:(2-4), H:(2-4), I:(2, 3), J-3

STARVING BONEPAW
Desolace (30), G-2, I-4, J:(3, 4), Thunder Axe Fortress

STARVING BUZZARD
Badlands (16), G-3, H-1, I:(2-4), Dustwind Gulch, Uldaman

STARVING DIRE WOLF
Duskwood (36), A:(3-7), B:(2, 3), C-3, D:(2, 3), E-2, F-2, G:(1, 2), H-2, I-2, J-2, K-2, L-2, The Darkened Bank

STARVING MOUNTAIN LION
Hillsbrad Foothills (48), D:(3, 4), E:(3-5), F:(3-5), G-4, Throughout Hillsbrad

STARVING SNICKERFANG
Blasted Lands (20), F-3, G:(2, 3), H-3, Dreadmaul Hold, Rise of the Defiler

STARVING WINTER WOLF
Dun Morogh (32), D-4, Iceflow Lake

STEELJAW SNAPPER
Tanaris (78), I:(2, 3), J:(2-4), K-4

STEELSNAP
Thousand Needles (82), A:(2-3), B:(2-3), Camp E'thok, Spawns at Camp E'thok and roams around plateaus

STEGODON
Un'Goro Crater (90), C:(5-7), D:(6-8), E:(6-8), Golakka Hot Springs, Terror Run

STEN STOUTARM
Dun Morogh (32), D-7, Coldridge Valley (107), By keg on cart

STEPHANIE TURNER
Stormwind (72), I-6, Trade District, Outside Everyday Merchandise

STEPHEN BHARTEC
Tirisfal Glades (86), D-6, Deathknell (109)

STEPHEN RYBACK
Cooking Trainer, Stormwind (72), K-4, Old Town, Pig and Whistle Tavern

STEVEN
Stormwind (72), Roams city with Miss Danna

STEVEN BLACK
Stable Master, Duskwood (36), J-5, Darkshire (108), Outside of Scarlet Raven Inn

STEVEN LOHAN
Stormwind (72), F-9, Mage Quarter, The Blue Recluse

STINGLASHER
Feralas (46), I-6, The Writhing Deep, Spawns in center of west hive and travels to east hive and back

"STINKY" IGNATZ
Dustwallow Marsh (38), F-2, Kneeling near crate and barrels

STITCHED HORROR
Eastern Plaguelands (40), B-4, C:(2, 3), D:(3, 4), E:(2-4), F:(2-4), H:(6, 7), Plaguewood, Stratholme

STITCHES
Gift of the Embalmer, Duskwood (36), D-3, Raven Hill Cemetery (123), (Summon) Behind locked cage

STOLEY
Tanaris (78), J-2, Steamwheedle Port, Southern building

STOLID SNAPJAW
Desolace (30), D-5, Maraudon

STOMA THE ANCIENT
Felwood (44), G-3, Irontree Woods, (Summon) Talk to the ancients on the island

STOMPER KREEG
Feralas (46), G-4, Dire Maul

STONARD CARTOGRAPHER
Swamp of Sorrows (76), F-5, Stonard (131), Scaffolding northeast of camp just past orc borrows

STONARD EXPLORER
Swamp of Sorrows (76), F:(4, 5), J:(1, 7), Stonard (131)

STONARD GRUNT
Swamp of Sorrows (76), E-5, F:(5, 6), Stonard (131)

STONARD HUNTER
Swamp of Sorrows (76), J:(7, 8), K:(7, 8), Stonard (131)

STONARD ORC
Swamp of Sorrows (76), E-5, F-5, Stonard (131)

STONARD SCOUT
Swamp of Sorrows (76), B-5, D-6, E-5, Stonard (131)

STONARD SHAMAN
Swamp of Sorrows (76), K-8, Stonard (131)

STONARD WAYFINDER
Swamp of Sorrows (76), F-5, Stonard (131)

STONE BEHEMOTH
Darkshore (24), E:(8, 9), Remtravel's Excavation

STONE FURY
Alterac Mountains (8), H-4, K-4

STONE GOLEM
Badlands (16), F-3, Angor Fortress

STONE GUARD ZARG
Weapon Quartermaster, Orgrimmar (61), E-7

STONE GUARDIAN
Un'Goro Crater (90), F-3, G-4, J:(4, 6-8), Fire Plume Ridge, Lakkari Tar Pits, The Marshlands

STONE KEEPER
Badlands (16), G-1, Uldaman

STONE MAW BASILISK
Stranglethorn Vale (74), C-1, D-1

STONE RUMBLER
Barrens (18), E-9, Razorfen Kraul

STONE STEWARD
Badlands (16), G-1, Uldaman

STONE WATCHER OF NORGANNON
Tanaris (78), F-8, Uldum, (Summon) Platinum discs from Uldaman are necessary

STONEARM
Rare Spawn, Barrens (18), E:(2-3), Lvl 15 Uncommon; Roams Kolkar villages around the pools

STONELASH FLAYE
Silithus (66), D:(4, 5), E:(4, 5), F:(4, 5), G:(4, 5), H-4, Southwind Village

STONELASH PINCER
Silithus (66), D:(2, 3), E:(2-4), F:(3, 4), G:(3, 4)

STONELASH SCORPID
Silithus (66), E:(1, 2), F:(1, 2), G:(1-3), H:(1-3), Southwind Village

STONESPINE
Rare Spawn, Eastern Plaguelands (40), D-2, Stratholme, Lvl 60 Rare

STONESPLINTER BONESNAPPER
Loch Modan (54), D-9, E:(8, 9), G:(2, 3), Stonesplinter Valley

STONESPLINTER DIGGER
Loch Modan (54), I:(6, 7), J:(6, 7), Ironband's Excavation Site

STONESPLINTER GEOMANCER
Loch Modan (54), I:(6, 7), J:(6, 7), Ironband's Excavation Site

STONESPLINTER SCOUT
Loch Modan (54), C:(5-7), D:(7, 8), Stonesplinter Valley

STONESPLINTER SEER
Loch Modan (54), C:(8, 9), D:(8, 9), E-8, F:(2, 3), G-2, Stonesplinter Valley

STONESPLINTER SHAMAN
Loch Modan (54), D-9, E:(8, 9), G:(2, 3), Stonesplinter Valley

STONESPLINTER SKULLTHUMPER
Loch Modan (54), C:(8, 9), D:(8, 9), E-8, F:(2, 3), G-2, Stonesplinter Valley

STONESPLINTER TROGG
Loch Modan (54), C:(5-7), D:(7, 8), Stonesplinter Valley

STONETALON GRUNT
Stonetalon Mountains (70), E-7, F-6, Sun Rock Retreat (132)

STONETUSK BOAR
Elwynn Forest (42), D:(8, 9), E:(7-9), F:(7-9), Fargodeep Mine, The Maclure Vineyards, The Stonefield Farm

STONEVAULT AMBUSHER
Badlands (16), G-1, Uldaman

STONEVAULT BASHER
Badlands (16), J:(4, 5), Dustwind Gulch

STONEVAULT BASHER
Badlands (16), G-1, Uldaman

STONEVAULT BONESNAPPER
Badlands (16), G:(6, 7), H:(6, 7), Agmond's End

STONEVAULT BRAWLER
Badlands (16), G-1, Uldaman

STONEVAULT CAVE HUNTER
Badlands (16), G-1, Uldaman

STONEVAULT CAVE LURKER
Badlands (16), G-1, Uldaman

STONEVAULT FLAMEWEAVER
Badlands (16), G-1, Uldaman

STONEVAULT GEOMANCER
Badlands (16), G-1, Uldaman

STONEVAULT MAULER
Badlands (16), G-1, Uldaman

STONEVAULT ORACLE
Badlands (16), G-1, Uldaman

STONEVAULT ROCKCHEWER
Badlands (16), G-1, Uldaman

STONEVAULT SEER
Badlands (16), J:(4, 5), Dustwind Gulch, Uldaman

STONEVAULT SHAMAN
Badlands (16), G-7, H-7, Agmond's End

STORM BAY ORACLE
Azshara (14), E:(7, 9), G:(7, 9), H:(7-9), I:(7-9), J:(7-9), K:(8, 9), The Ruined Reaches, Southridge Beach

STORM BAY WARRIOR
Azshara (14), E:(1, 2), F:(1, 2), G:(1, 4), H:(1, 3, 4), I:(1, 3, 4), J-1, K:(1-5), L:(1-4), Jagged Reef, The Shattered Strand, Tower of Eldara

STORM SHADOWHOOF
Felwood (44), I-5, Everlook

STORMHIDE
Barrens (18), E:(7, 8), F:(7, 8)

STORMPIKE BATTLEGUARD
Alterac Mountains (8), D-7, E-8, The Headland, Alliance entrance

STORMSCALE MYRMIDON
Darkshore (24), H-2, I:(1-3), Ruins of Mathystra

STORMSCALE SIREN
Darkshore (24), H:(3, 4), Cliffspring Falls, Cliffspring River

STORMSCALE SORCERESS
Darkshore (24), H-2, I-2, Ruins of Mathystra

STORMSCALE TOXICOLOGIST
Darkshore (24), H-3, Cliffspring Falls

STORMSCALE WARRIOR
Darkshore (24), I-2, Ruins of Mathystra

STORMSCALE WAVE RIDER
Darkshore (24), H:(3, 4), Cliffspring Falls, Cliffspring River

STORMSNOUT
Barrens (18), E:(4-6), F:(5, 6)

STORMWIND CITY GUARD
Elwynn Forest (42), D:(4, 5), Valley of Heroes

STORMWIND GUARD
Elwynn Forest (42), B-8, C:(7, 8), E-6, F:(5, 7), J-7, L-8

STRAHAD FARSAN
Barrens (18), H-3, Ratchet (122), Tower in eastern hills

STRANGLETHORN RAPTOR
Stranglethorn Vale (74), B-2, Ruins of Zul'Kunda, The Savage Coast

STRANGLETHORN TIGER
Stranglethorn Vale (74), B-1, C:(1, 2), D:(1, 2), E:(1, 2)

STRANGLETHORN TIGRESS
Stranglethorn Vale (74), C-4, D:(3-5), E:(2, 3), F:(2, 3)

STRASHAZ HYDRA
Dustwallow Marsh (38), I-2, J-2, Alcaz Island

STRASHAZ MYRMIDON
Dustwallow Marsh (38), J:(1, 2), K-2, Alcaz Island

STRASHAZ SIREN
Dustwallow Marsh (38), J:(1, 2), Alcaz Island

STRASHAZ SORCERESS
Dustwallow Marsh (38), J:(1, 2), K-2, Alcaz Island

STRASHAZ WARRIOR
Dustwallow Marsh (38), J:(1, 2), Alcaz Island

STRATHOLME COURIER
Eastern Plaguelands (40), D-2, Stratholme

STRIDER CLUTCHMOTHER
Darkshore (24), E-9, Remtravel's Excavation, Twilight Vale, Wanders with fledglings

STRIGID HUNTER
Teldrassil (80), D:(3, 4), E:(4, 5), F:(3, 4), The Oracle Glade, Wellspring Lake

STRIGID OWL
Teldrassil (80), F:(5, 6), G:(5-7), H:(5, 6), I:(5, 6), Dolanaar (109), Lake Al'Ameth, Starbreeze Village

STRIGID SCREECHER
Teldrassil (80), D-5, E:(5-8), F:(7, 8), G:(7, 8), H:(7, 8), Gnarlpine Hold, Lake Al'Ameth, Pools of Arlithrien

STROMGARDE CAVALRYMAN
Arathi Highlands (10), G-4, Stromgarde Keep (132)

STROMGARDE DEFENDER
Arathi Highlands (10), C-6, D-6, Stromgarde Keep (132)

STROMGARDE TROLL HUNTER
Arathi Highlands (10), C-6, Stromgarde Keep (132)

STROMGARDE VINDICATOR
Arathi Highlands (10), C-6, D-6, Stromgarde Keep (132)

STRUMNER FLINTHEEL
Armor Crafter, Blasted Lands (20), J-2, Nethergarde Keep (120), Smithy

STUART FLEMING
Fisherman, Wetlands (96), A-6, Menethil Harbor (119), Dock

SUBTERRANEAN DIEMETRADON
Desolace (30), D-5, Maraudon

SUCCUBUS MINION
Morganth's Minion, Redridge Mountains (62), K-5, Tower of Ilgalar, (Summon) Summoned by Morganth

SUFFERING HIGHBORNE
Winterspring (98), H:(4, 5), Lake Kel'Theril, The Ruins of Kel'Theril

SUFFERING VICTIM
Tirisfal Glades (86), K-3, L-3, Scarlet Monastery

SULFURON HARBINGER
Burning Steppes (22), Searing Gorge (64), C-4/D-8, The Molten Core

SULHASA
Wind Rider Master, Silithus (66), I-1, Valor's Rest (137), North of road

SUL'LITHUZ ABOMINATION
Tanaris (78), E-1, Zul'Farrak

SUL'LITHUZ BROODLING
Tanaris (78), E-1, Zul'Farrak

SUL'LITHUZ SANDCRAWLER
Tanaris (78), E-1, Zul'Farrak

SUMI
Blacksmithing Supplier, Orgrimmar (60), J-2, K-2, Valley of Honor, The Burning Anvil

SUMMONED BLACKHAND DREADWEAVER
Burning Steppes (22), Searing Gorge (64), C-4/D-8, Blackrock Spire

SUMMONED BLACKHAND VETERAN
Burning Steppes (22), Searing Gorge (64), C-4/D-8, Blackrock Spire

SUMMONED GUARDIAN
Arathi Highlands (10), B-7, Stromgarde Keep (132), (Summon) Base of tower

SUNN RAGETOTEM
Staff Merchant, Thunder Bluff (84), F-5, High rise, in Rainsticks tent

SUNSCALE LASHTAIL
Barrens (18), E:(1-4), F:(2, 3), G-3, The Crossroads (107), Gold Road, Thorn Hill

SUNSCALE SCREECHER
Barrens (18), D:(2, 3), E:(2-4), F:(1-5), G:(1-5), H:(1-4)

SUNSCALE SCYTHECLAW
Barrens (18), D:(2, 3), E:(1, 2, 4, 5), F-5, G:(1, 3-5), H-3

SUPER-SELLER 680
Desolace (30), E-8, North of road

SUPERVISOR FIZSPROCKET
Mulgore (58), G-3, H-5, The Venture Co. Mine, Deep in southern part of mine

SUPERVISOR LUGWIZZLE
Barrens (18), G-1, The Sludge Fen, Patrols derrick

SUPERVISOR RAELEN
Elwynn Forest (42), K-7, Eastvale Logging Camp, Next to carriage by logging operation

SURA WILDMANE
War Harness Vendor, Thunder Bluff (84), F-5, High rise, between Ragetotem Arms and Aska's Kitchen

SURENA CALEDON
Elwynn Forest (42), J-8, Brackwell Pumpkin Patch, In house with Morgan the Collector and Erlan Drudgemoor

SURF CRAWLER
Durotar (34), I:(2, 3, 7-9), J:(7-9), K-7

SURF GLIDER
Tanaris (78), I-6, J:(5, 6), Lost Rigger Cove, Southbreak Shore

SUSAN TILLINGHAST
Undercity (88), K-6, The Rogues' Quarter, Roams Rouge Quarter

SUZANNE
Stormwind (72), F-8, Mage Quarter, Roamer - sits by tower

SUZETTA GALLINA
Stormwind (72), H-7, The Canals, Gallina Winery

SVEN YORGEN
Duskwood (36), A-3, The Hushed Bank, Camp

"SWAMP EYE" JARL
Dustwallow Marsh (38), G-3, Swamplight Manor, In front of farmhouse

SWAMP JAGUAR
Swamp of Sorrows (76), A-6, B:(4-6), C:(3-6), D:(3-5), E:(3-5), F-4, G-4

SWAMP OOZE
Dustwallow Marsh (38), D:(5, 6), E:(5, 6), F:(5, 6), The Dragonmurk, Lost Point, The Quagmire

SWAMPWALKER
Swamp of Sorrows (76), A:(3, 4), B:(3, 4), F-4, G:(3, 4), Stagalbog Cave, Roams small area around spawn point

SWAMPWALKER ELDER
Swamp of Sorrows (76), A:(3, 4), B-3, Misty Valley

SWART
Shaman Trainer, Durotar (34), H-4, Razor Hill (124), Barracks

SWIFTMANE
Barrens (18), G-3, Runs across plateau northwest of Ratchet

SWINEGART SPEARHIDE
Barrens (18), E:(4-5), Agama'gor, Guards near hills

SWIRLING VORTEX
Thousand Needles (82), I:(5-7), J:(5-7, 9), K:(6-8), L:(6, 8), Tahonda Ruins, The Shimmering Flats

SWOOP
Mulgore (58), D:(4, 5), E:(4, 5), F:(3-5), G:(4-7)

SYDNEY UPTON
Staff Merchant, Undercity (88), J-3, The Magic Quarter

SYLISTA
Stable Master, Stormwind (72), D-5, The Park, By Owl Statue

SYLVANNA FORESTMOON
Alchemist Trainer, Darnassus (26), G-2, Craftsmen's Terrace, First floor

SYNDICATE ASSASSIN
Alterac Mountains (8), E:(1, 2), F-2, Sofera's Naze

SYNDICATE CONJUROR
Arathi Highlands (10), C-6, D-6, Stromgarde Keep (132)

SYNDICATE ENFORCER
Alterac Mountains (8), E:(1, 2), F-2, Sofera's Naze

SYNDICATE FOOTPAD
Alterac Mountains (8), F-8, H:(6, 7), Sofera's Naze

SYNDICATE HIGHWAYMAN
Arathi Highlands (10), D:(2, 3), E-3, Northfold Manor

SYNDICATE MAGUS
Arathi Highlands (10), C-6, D-6, Stromgarde Keep (132)

SYNDICATE MERCENARY
Arathi Highlands (10), D-3, Northfold Manor

SYNDICATE PATHSTALKER
Arathi Highlands (10), D-3, Northfold Manor

SYNDICATE PROWLER
Arathi Highlands (10), C-6, D-6, Stromgarde Keep (132)

SYNDICATE ROGUE
Hillsbrad Foothills (48), H-5, I-4, J:(4, 5), Durnholde Keep

SYNDICATE SABOTEUR
Alterac Mountains (8), F-2, G:(2, 3), H-3, Dalaran

SYNDICATE SENTRY
Alterac Mountains (8), F-2, G:(2, 3), H:(3, 4), Sofera's Naze

SYNDICATE SHADOW MAGE
Hillsbrad Foothills (48), H-5, I-4, J:(4, 5), K-4, Durnholde Keep

SYNDICATE SPY
Alterac Mountains (8), H:(4, 5), I:(4, 5), Sofera's Naze

SYNDICATE THIEF
Alterac Mountains (8), F-8, H:(6, 7), Sofera's Naze

SYNDICATE WATCHMAN
Hillsbrad Foothills (48), H-5, I-4, J:(4, 5), K-4, Durnholde Keep

SYNDICATE WIZARD
Alterac Mountains (8), H:(4, 7), I-4, Sofera's Naze

SYNGE
Gun Merchant, Thousand Needles (82), K-8, Mirage Raceway (119), Inside racetrack, next to building

SYRAL BLADELEAF
Teldrassil (80), G-6, Dolanaar (109), Outside building north of road

SYURANA
Trade Goods, Winterspring (98), H-3, Starfall Village (130), just inside main building

SYURNA
Rogue Trainer, Darnassus (26), D-2, E-2, Cenarion Enclave, Den, west of path

T

TABETHA
Dustwallow Marsh (38), F-6, The Quagmire, Farmhouse

TABLET OF THE SEVEN
Burning Steppes (22), F-4, Ruins of Thaurissan, Doodad at base of dwarven statue

TAGAIN
Cloth Armor Merchant, Thunder Bluff (84), E-4, Middle rise, inside Thunder Bluff Armorers tent

TAH WINTERHOOF
Thunder Bluff (84), F-5, High rise, inside Winterhoof Totems tent

TAI'TASI
Trade Supplies, Durotar (34), H-7, Sen'jin Village (126), Main floor of big hut

TAIGA WISEMANE
Desolace (30), C-7, Shadowprey Village (128), Up hill near gong

TAI'JIN
Priest Trainer, Durotar (34), H-4, Razor Hill (124), Barracks

TAIM RAGETOTEM
Alterac Valley Battlemaster, Thunder Bluff (84), G-8, Hunter Rise, Between bridges in a tent

TAINTED OOZE
Felwood (44), E:(5, 6), F:(5, 6), Felwood

TAJARRI
Moonglade (56), E-4, Shrine of Remulos, Northeast of tree

TAKAR THE SEER
Barrens (18), F-6, Southern Barrens, Northeast of Camp Taurajo

TAKATA STEELBLADE
Desolace (30), G-5, Ghost Walker Post (113), Near western end of bridge

TAKK THE LEAPER
Rare Spawn, Barrens (18), G-1, Lvl 19 Semi-Rare; Roams ridge southeast of Sludge Fen

TAKRIN PATHSEEKER
Durotar (34), H-4, Razor Hill (124), Western entrance

TAL
Wind Rider Master, Thunder Bluff (84), E-5, At the top of large circular staircase

TALADAN
Expert Enchanter, Darnassus (26), H-1, Craftsmen's Terrace, Enchanting shop

TALAELAR
Fish Vendor, Darnassus (26), F-6, Tradesmen's Terrace, Dock

TALDAN
Drink Vendor, Darkshore (24), F-4, Auberdine (101), First floor of inn

TALEN
Ashenvale (12), B-4, Campfire along hills

TALENDRIA
Desolace (30), I-1, Nijel's Point (121), Northwestern ruins

TALIN KEENEYE
Dun Morogh (32), C-7, Coldridge Valley (107), Small camp along road

TALLONKAI SWIFTROOT
Teldrassil (80), G-6, Dolanaar (109), Upper floor inside building north of road

TALLOW
Hillsbrad Foothills (48), G-2, Tarren Mill (133), In between the house and inn on the left

TALLY BERRYFIZZ
Alchemist Trainer, Ironforge (52), I-5, Tinker Town, Berryfizz's Potions and Mixed Drinks

TALO THORNHOOF
Feralas (46), I-4, Camp Mojache (105), In tent, east of bridge

TALONED SWOOP
Mulgore (58), D:(1, 2), E:(1-3), F:(1-3), G:(2, 3), H:(6, 7)

TALVASH DEL KISSEL
Ironforge (52), E-1, The Mystic Ward, North of Maeva's

TAMAR
Leatherworking Supplies, Orgrimmar (60), H-4, The Drag, Kodohide Leatherworkers

TAMARO
Orgrimmar (60), G-5, The Drag, Building south of Jandi's Arboretum

TAMED BATTLE BOAR
Barrens (18), E-9, Razorfen Kraul

TAMED HYENA
Barrens (18), E-9, Razorfen Kraul

TAMMRA WINDFIELD
Stonetalon Mountains (70), F-6, Sun Rock Retreat (132), By bonfire, east of building

TAMRA STORMPIKE
Rare Spawn, Hillsbrad Foothills (48), I-8, Dun Garok, Lvl 28 Uncommon; Roams a small area around spawn point

TAND
Basket Weaver, Thunder Bluff (84), E-3, Middle rise, near elevators

TANDAAN LIGHTMANE
Leather Armor Merchant, Ashenvale (12), E-5, Astranaar (101), Northwest buildling (south of road)

TANEEL DARKWOOD
Ashenvale (12), J-7, Dor'Danil Barrow Den, Across first bridge and in a side room

TANGLED HORROR
Swamp of Sorrows (76), A:(3, 4), G:(4, 5), H:(4, 5), I:(3, 4, 7), J:(3, 7, 8), K:(6, 7), Misty Valley

TANNOK FROSTHAMMER
Innkeeper's Assistant, Dun Morogh (32), F-5, Kharanos (116), Thunderbrew Distillery

TANNYSA
Herbalism Trainer, Stormwind (72), F-8, G-8, Mage Quarter, Across from Alchemy Needs

TANSY PUDDLEFIZZ
Fishing Supplier, Ironforge (52), F-1, The Forlorn Cavern, Traveling Fisherman

TAPOKE "SLIM" JAHN
Wetlands (96), A-6, Deepwater Tavern, Northwest corner of first floor

TAR BEAST
Un'Goro Crater (90), F:(3, 4), H:(3, 4), I-3, Fungal Rock, Lakkari Tar Pits

TAR CREEPER
Un'Goro Crater (90), F:(3, 4), H:(3, 4), I-3, Fungal Rock, Lakkari Tar Pits

TAR LORD
Un'Goro Crater (90), E-2, F:(2, 3), G:(2, 3), Fungal Rock, Lakkari Tar Pits

TAR LURKER
Un'Goro Crater (90), E-2, F:(2, 3), G:(2, 3), Lakkari Tar Pits

TARA COLDGAZE
Hillsbrad Foothills (48), G-3, Tarren Mill (133)

TARAGAMAN THE HUNGERER
Orgrimmar (60), F-5, Ragefire Chasm

TARGOT JINGLEPOCKET
Arathi Highlands (11), F-5, Refuge Point (124) (124)

TARANTULA
Redridge Mountains (62), A:(7-9), B-7, C:(7, 8), D-7, Lakeridge Highway

TARBAN HEARTHGRAIN
Baker, Barrens (18), G-3, Outside hut east of Crossroads

TARG
Alterac Mountains (8), E-5, Ruins of Alterac, Church

TARGORR THE DREAD
Stormwind (72), F-6, The Stockade

TARHUS
Reagent Vendor, Feralas (46), I-4, Camp Mojache (105), Inn

TARHUS
Reagent Vendor, Feralas (46), G-4, Dire Maul

TARI'QA
Trade Supplies, Barrens (18), F-3, The Crossroads (107), Outside inn

TARINDRELLA
Teldrassil (80), G-4, Shadowglen (127), Spawns near big tree, west of Aldrassil and roams west of road

TARKREU SHADOWSTALKER
Thousand Needles (82), I-6, Ironstone Camp, Camp just west of Shimmering Flats

TARN
Leatherworking Trainer, Thunder Bluff (84), E-4, Middle rise, inside Thunder Bluff Armorers tent

TARONN REDFEATHER
Emerald Circle, Felwood (44), G-8, Emerald Sanctuary (110), Tent

TARREL ROCKWEAVER
Wetlands (96), A-5, Menethil Harbor (119), Bridge to town

TARREN MILL DEATHGUARD
Hillsbrad Foothills (48), G:(2, 3), H:(2, 3), Tarren Mill (133)

TARSHAW JAGGEDSCAR
Warrior Trainer, Durotar (34), H-4, Razor Hill (124), Barracks

TASKMASTER FIZZULE
Barrens (18), G-1, Near tower northwest of Sludge Fen

TASKMASTER SCRANGE
The Thorium Brotherhood, Searing Gorge (64), D-3, Thorium Point (136), Right side of camp under scaffolding

TASKMASTER WHIPFANG
Stonetalon Mountains (70), H-5, Blackwolf River, Windshear Crag, Spawns around river, west of Windshear Crag

TATTERNACK STEELFORGE
Barrens (18), F-6, Camp Taurajo (106), North side of camp

TAUR STONEHOOF
Blacksmithing Supplies, Thunder Bluff (84), D-6, Lower rise, next to pond

TAVERNKEEP SMITTS
Duskwood (36), J-4, Darkshire (108), Scarlet Raven Inn

TAWNY GRISETTE
Mushroom Vendor, Undercity (88), I-5, The Trade Quarter, Roams - Upper Ring of Trade Quarter

TAZAN
Barrens (18), H-4, The Merchant Coast, Roams camp at Merchant Coast

TECHBOT
Dun Morogh (32), C-4, Gnomeregan

TEG DAWNSTRIDER
Expert Enchanter, Thunder Bluff (84), E-4, Middle rise, inside Dawnstrider Enchantments tent

TEL'ATHIR
Alchemist Trainer, Stormwind (72), G-8, Mage Quarter, Alchemy Needs

TELDRASSIL SENTINEL
Teldrassil (80), D-3, E-3, F-4, G-6, Shadowglen (127)

TELEPORTER TO RUT'THERAN VILLAGE
Teleporter, Darnassus (26), C-4, D-4, The Temple Gardens, West of bank

TELF JOOLAM
Durotar (34), F-6, Shrine of the Dormant Flame, Atop the hill near the fire shrine

TELONIS
Leatherworking Trainer, Darnassus (26), I-2 , Craftsmen's Terrace, Leatherworking shop

TELOREN
Hippogryph Master, Stonetalon Mountains (70), E-2, Stonetalon Peak, Next to hippogryphs and moonwell

TELURINON MOONSHADOW
Herbalism Trainer, Wetlands (96), A-6 Menethil Harbor (119), Building west of keep

TEMPERED WAR GOLEM
Searing Gorge (64), H-6, I-3, Dustfire Valley

TENARON STORMGRIP
Teldrassil (80), G-4, H-4, Shadowglen (127), Second room at end of ramp up tree

TENDRIS WARPWOOD
Feralas (46), G-4, Dire Maul

TENELL LEAFRUNNER
Emerald Circle, Felwood (44), G-8, Emerald Sanctuary (110), Roams entry path

TEPA
Expert Tailor, Thunder Bluff (84), E-4, Middle rise, inside Thunder Bluff Armorers tent

TEREMUS THE DEVOURER
World Boss, Blasted Lands (20), J-5, Roams Blasted Lands (excluding The Tainted Scar)

TERENTHIS
Darkshore (24), F-4, Auberdine (101), First floor of eastern building

TERL ARAKOR
Wetlands (96), D-4, Next to wagon ju[...] north of main road

TERONIS' CORPSE
Ashenvale (12), C-4, Lake Falathim, North side of center island

TERRORSPARK
Rare Spawn, Burning Steppes (22), E-[...] F-4, G-4, H-4, I-3, Lvl 55 Average Rar[...] Roams small area around spawn point

TERROWULF FLESHRIPPER
Ashenvale (12), F-4, G-4, Nightsong Woods, Howling Vale

TERROWULF PACKLORD
Rare Spawn, Ashenvale (12), G-4, Howling Vale, Lvl 32 Average Rare; In front of structure

TERROWULF SHADOW WEAVER
Ashenvale (12), F-4, G-4, Nightsong Woods, Howling Vale

TERRY PALIN
Lumberjack, Elwynn Forest (42), L-6, Eastvale Logging Camp, In logging operation

TETHIS
Stranglethorn Vale (74), B-5, C:(4, 5), Gurubashi Arena, The Cape of Stranglethorn, Roams small area arou[...] spawn point

THADDEUS WEBB
Enchanting Supplies, Undercity (88), H-6, The Apothecarium, Near Rogues' Quarter entry

THADIUS GRIMSHADE
Blasted Lands (20), J-2, Nethergarde Keep (120), Top floor of tower facing entrance of keep

THALGUS THUNDERFIST
Weapon Merchant, Ironforge (52), H-9 The Military Ward, Timberline Arms

THALIA AMBERHIDE
Thousand Needles (82), F-5, Freewind Post (112), Inn

THALON
Wind Rider Master, Desolace (30), B-7 Shadowprey Village (128), End of dock

THAL'TRAK PROUDTUSK
Badlands (16), A-5, Kargath (116), Group left of orc burrow

THAMARIAN
Darkshore (24), E-4, Auberdine (101), Dock

THAMNER POL
Physician, Dun Morogh (32), F-5, Kharanos (116), Thunderbrew Distillery

THANTHALDIS SNOWGLEAM
Rewards Vendor, Alterac Mountains (8), E-8, The Headland, Camp outside Alterac Valley

THAREK BLACKSTONE
Armorer, Dun Morogh (32), F-5, Kharanos (116), Smithy

THARG
Dustwallow Marsh (38), D-3, Brackenwall Village (104), East entranc[...]

HARIL'ZUN
Redridge Mountains (62), I-6, Stonewatch, With several orcs in camp just inside defensive walls near the southern entrance to the fortification

HARLIDUN
Stable Master, Arathi Highlands (10), J-3, Hammerfall (115), Platform of north building

HARM
Wind Rider Master, Stonetalon Mountains (70), E-6, Sun Rock Retreat (132), South of western structure, next to water

HARNARIUN TREETENDER
Darkshore (24), F-4, Auberdine (101), Outside eastern building

HARYNN BOUDEN
Trade Supplies, Elwynn Forest (42), E-7, Goldshire (114), In caravan by road at the far end of town

HAURIS BALGARR
Rare Spawn, Burning Steppes (22), F-4, G-4, H-4, I-4, Ruins of Thaurissan, Lvl 57 Uncommon; Roams small area around spawn point

HAURISSAN AGENT
Burning Steppes (22), F-4, G-4, H-4, I-4, Ruins of Thaurissan

HAURISSAN FIREWALKER
Burning Steppes (22), F-4, G-4, H-4, I-4, Ruins of Thaurissan

HAURISSAN SPY
Burning Steppes (22), F-4, G-4, H-4, I-4, Ruins of Thaurissan

HE BEAST
Burning Steppes (22), Searing Gorge (64), C-4/D-8, Blackrock Spire

HE CLEANER
Eastern Plaguelands (40), C-2, Plaguewood, (Summon) During Priest epic staff quest to "clean" area

HE EVALCHARR
Rare Spawn, Azshara (14), A-5, B-6, Haldarr Encampment, Lvl 48 Very Rare; Roams area east of Southfury River

HE HUSK
Rare Spawn, Western Plaguelands (92), H-4, I:(3, 4), The Weeping Cave, Lvl 62 Very Rare; Roams small area around spawn point

HE NAMELESS PROPHET
Desolace (30), C-6, Maraudon, Foot of entry stairwell

HE ONGAR
Rare Spawn, Felwood (44), E-5, Bloodvenom River, Lvl 51 Very Rare; Roams river near spawn point

HE PLAINS VISION
Mulgore (58), E-6, Bloodhoof Village (102), (Summon) Spawns and runs to a cave

HE RAKE
Mulgore (58), F-2, The Golden Plains, Prowls plains

HE RAVENIAN
Western Plaguelands (92), I-7, Scholomance

HE RAZZA
Rare Spawn, Feralas (46), G-4, Dire Maul, The Maul, Lvl 60 Rare; In arena

HE REAK
Rare Spawn, The Hinterlands (50), G:(4, 5), I-4, Agol'watha, Skulk Rock, The Creeping Ruin, Lvl 49 Very Rare; Roams small area around spawn point

HE ROT
Rare Spawn, Dustwallow Marsh (38), G-6, Beezil's Wreck, Lvl 43 Average Rare; Roams the area around the wreck

HE SCOURGE CAULDRON
Western Plaguelands (92), E-6, F-5, G-6, H-6, Dalson's Tears, Felstone Field, Gahrron's Withering, The Writhing Haunt, Large stationary cauldron

HE THRESHWACKONATOR 4100
The First Mate, Darkshore (24), H-2, Mist's Edge, On beach near little inlet

HE UNFORGIVEN
Raid Sub-Boss, Eastern Plaguelands (40), D-2, Stratholme

HE WINDREAVER
World Boss, Silithus (66), E-1, Hive'Ashi, Spawns north near hills and roams to Twilight Post

HEKA THE MARTYR
Tanaris (78), E-1, Zul'Farrak

HELDURIN THE LOST
Badlands (16), H-8, Agmond's End, Camp

THELGRUM STONEHAMMER
Mining Supplier, Darkshore (24), F-4, Auberdine (101), In front of northern building

THELMAN SLATEFIST
Alterac Valley Battlemaster, Stormwind (72), L-1, Stormwind Keep, East wing

THENAN
Arathi Highlands (10), E-6, Circle of Inner Binding, (Summon) Crcle of Inner Binding

THEOCRITUS
Mage of Tower Azora, Elwynn Forest (42), I-7, Tower of Azora, Top floor of tower

THEODORE GRIFFS
Undercity (88), F-7, The Apothecarium, In laboratory

THEODORE MONT CLAIRE
Stable Master, Hillsbrad Foothills (48), H-2, Tarren Mill (133), Next to mailbox outside inn

THEODRUS FROSTBEARD
Priest Trainer, Ironforge (52), C-1, The Mystic Ward, Hall of Mysteries

THERADRIM GUARDIAN
Desolace (30), D-5, Maraudon

THERADRIM SHARDLING
Desolace (30), D-5, Maraudon

THERAMORE DESERTER
Dustwallow Marsh (38), D-5, Lost Point, The Quagmire

THERAMORE GUARD
Dustwallow Marsh (38), H:(4, 5), I:(4-6), J:(5, 6), Theramore Isle (135)

THERAMORE INFILTRATOR
Dustwallow Marsh (38), D-4, E:(2-4), F-3, Bluefen

THERAMORE LIEUTENANT
Dustwallow Marsh (38), I-5, Theramore Isle (135)

THERAMORE PRACTICING GUARD
Dustwallow Marsh (38), I-5, Theramore Isle (135)

THERAMORE SENTRY
Dustwallow Marsh (38), E-3, F-2, North Point Tower

THERAMORE SKIRMISHER
Dustwallow Marsh (38), E-4

THERESA
Gerard's Mind Slave, Undercity (88), G-3, G-2, The War Quarter, Roams to Father Lankester

THERESA MOULAINE
Robe Vendor, Stormwind (72), G-4, Cathedral Square, Righteous Plates

THERIDRAN
Druid Trainer, Stormwind (72), C-5, The Park, By pool of water

THERSA WINDSONG
Undercity (88), G-7, The Apothecarium, In laboratory

THERUM DEEPFORGE
Expert Blacksmith, Stormwind (72), H-2, Dwarven District, At the Forge

THERYLUNE
Darkshore (24), F-9, The Master's Glaive, Center isle of lake

THERYSIL
Ashenvale (12), C-5, Shrine of Aessina, North, just outside of shrine

THERZOK
Orgrimmar (60), E-5, The Cleft of Shadow, Shadowswift Brotherhood

THESSALA HYDRA
Desolace (30), D-5, Maraudon

THIEF CATCHER FARMOUNTAIN
Ironforge (52), Roams between Military Ward and the Commons

THIEF CATCHER SHADOWDELVE
Ironforge (52), Roams between Mystic Ward and the Commons

THIEF CATCHER THUNDERBREW
Ironforge (52), Roams between the Commons and the Hall of Explorers via the Great Forge

THISTLE BEAR
Darkshore (24), F:(2-6), G:(2-6)

THISTLE BOAR
Teldrassil (80), G:(3, 4), H:(3, 4), Shadowglen (127)

THISTLE CUB
Darkshore (24), H-4

THISTLEFUR AVENGER
Ashenvale (12), D:(4, 5), E:(3-4), Astranaar (101), Thistlefur Village

THISTLEFUR DEN WATCHER
Ashenvale (12), E:(3, 4), Thistlefur Hold

THISTLEFUR PATHFINDER
Ashenvale (12), D-4, E:(3, 4), Thistlefur Hold, Thistlefur Village

THISTLEFUR SHAMAN
Ashenvale (12), D:(4, 5), E:(3, 4), Astranaar (101), Thistlefur Hold, Thistlefur Village

THISTLEFUR TOTEMIC
Ashenvale (12), E:(3, 4), F-4, Thistlefur Village

THISTLEFUR URSA
Ashenvale (12), E:(3, 4), F-4, Thistlefur Hold, Thistlefur Village

THISTLEHEART
Warlock Trainer, Ironforge (52), G-1, The Forlorn Cavern, Building to the right of Traveling Fisherman

THISTLESHRUB DEW COLLECTOR
Tanaris (78), D:(6, 7), E:(6, 7), Thistleshrub Valley

THISTLESHRUB ROOTSHAPER
Tanaris (78), D:(6, 7), E:(6, 7), Thistleshrub Valley

THOMAS
Altar Boy, Stormwind (72), F-3, Cathedral Square, Cathedral of Light

THOMAS ARLENTO
Tirisfal Glades (86), H-5, Brill (104)

THOMAS BOOKER
Wetlands (96), A-5, Menethil Harbor (119), Training horse outside stables

THOMAS MILLER
Baker, Stormwind (72), I-6, Trade District, Roamer of Trade District

THOMAS MORDAN
Reagent Vendor, Undercity (88), I-4, The Trade Quarter, Upper Ring of Trade Quarter

THONTEK RUMBLEHOOF
Mulgore (58), F-6, Bloodhoof Village (102), Combat ground east of village

THONYS PILLARSTONE
Journeyman Enchanter, Ironforge (52), H-4, The Great Forge, Thistlefuzz Arcanery

THOR
Gryphon Master, Westfall (94), G-5, Sentinel Hill (126)

THORA FEATHERMOON
Alliance Outrunner, Barrens (18), F-8, Southern Barrens, Spawns at border to Dustwallow Marsh and travels north to Lushwater Oasis

THORFIN STONESHIELD
Hunter Trainer, Stormwind (72), I-2, Dwarven District, Building south of tram entrance

THORGAS GRIMSON
Hunter Trainer, Dun Morogh (32), D-7, Coldridge Valley (107), Anvilmar

THORGRUM BORRELSON
Gryphon Master, Loch Modan (54), D-5, Thelsamar (134), Right side of path leading into town

THORIUM BROTHERHOOD LOOKOUT
Lookout, Searing Gorge (64), D-3, Thorium Point (136)

THORK
Barrens (18), F-3, The Crossroads (107), Tower south of inn

THORKAF DRAGONEYE
Master Dragonscale Leatherworker, Badlands (16), I-6, Small camp to right of bone pile

THORN EATER GHOUL
Barrens (18), F-9, Razorfen Downs

THORVALD DEEPFORGE
Loch Modan (54), C-7, Valley of Kings, First floor of tower

THOTAR
Hunter Trainer, Durotar (34), H-4, Razor Hill (124), Bunker

THRAG STONEHOOF
Journeyman Blacksmith, Thunder Bluff (84), D-6, Lower rise, next to pond

THRAGOMM
Loch Modan (54), H-7, Patrols large circular paths with Gradok and Haren Swifthoof along the eastern side of the loch

THRALL
Orgrimmar (60), C:(3, 4), Valley of Wisdom, Grommash Hold

THRALOSH
Cloth & Leather Armor Merchant, Swamp of Sorrows (76), F-5, Stonard (131), Smithy

THRAN KHORMAN
Warrior Trainer, Dun Morogh (32), D-7, Coldridge Valley (107), Anvilmar

THRASHTAIL BASILISK
Stranglethorn Vale (74), D-5, Crystalvein Mine

THRAWN BOLTAR
Blacksmithing Supplies, Dun Morogh (32), F-5, Kharanos (116), Smithy

THREGGIL
Rare Spawn, Teldrassil (80), G-5, Fel Rock, Lvl 6 Uncommon; Runs around water in western section of cave

THRUMN
Tabard Vendor, Thunder Bluff (84), D-6, Lower rise, in front of Thunder Bluff Civic Information tent

THULE RAVENCLAW
Silverpine Forest (68), J-2, Fenris Keep, Second floor of keep

THULMAN FLINTCRAG
Guns Vendor, Stormwind (72), H:(1, 2), Dwarven District, Building west of forge

THULTASH
Food & Drink Vendor, Swamp of Sorrows (76), F-5, Stonard (131), Scaffolding right of entrance to main hall

THULTAZOR
Arcane Goods Vendor, Swamp of Sorrows (76), F-5, Stonard (131), Scaffolding by tree in the center of camp

THUND
Apprentice Engineer, Orgrimmar (60), J-3, Valley of Honor, Nogg's Machine Shop

THUNDER LIZARD
Durotar (34), F:(2, 3), Thunder Ridge

THUNDERHAWK CLOUDSCRAPER
Barrens (18), E:(6, 7), F-6, Camp Taurajo (106), Southern Barrens, Southern Gold Road

THUNDERHAWK HATCHLING
Barrens (18), E:(4-6), F:(5, 6), Agama'gor, Bramblescar, Southern Barrens

THUNDERHEAD
Barrens (18), E:(6, 7), F-6, Camp Taurajo (106), Field of Giants, Southern Barrens

THUNDERHEAD CONSORT
Azshara (14), E:(7, 8), F:(7, 8), G:(7-9), H:(2, 3, 8, 9), I:(1-3), J:(2, 3), K:(2, 3)

THUNDERHEAD HIPPOGRYPH
Azshara (14), A:(5, 6), B:(5-7), Haldarr Encampment, Valormok

THUNDERHEAD PATRIARCH
Azshara (14), E:(7, 8), F:(7, 8), G:(7-9), H:(2, 3, 8, 9), I:(1-3), J:(2, 3), K:(2, 3)

THUNDERHEAD SKYSTORMER
Azshara (14), F:(1-4), G:(2-4), H:(1, 2), Legash Encampment, Thalassian Base Camp, Ursolan

THUNDERHEAD STAGWING
Azshara (14), A-8, B-8, C-8, D:(4, 5, 8), E:(2-4), F:(3, 4)

THUNDERHEART
Badlands (16), A-5, Kargath (116), Group left of orc burrow

THUNDERING BOULDERKIN
Thousand Needles (82), A:(1-3), H:(5, 6), I:(5, 6), Ironstone Camp, Windbreak Canyon

THUNDERING EXILE
Arathi Highlands (10), G-5, Circle of Outer Binding

THUNDERING INVADER
Azshara (14), J:(2, 3), K:(2, 3), Bitter Reaches, The Shattered Strand

THUNDERSTOMP
Rare Spawn, Barrens (18), E-8, Southern Barrens, Lvl 24 Uncommon; Roams clearing near Dustwallow Marsh border

THUNDERSTOMP STEGODON
Un'Goro Crater (90), C:(5-7), D:(6-8), E:(6-8), Golakka Hot Springs, Terror Run

THUNDRIS WINDWEAVER
Darkshore (24), F-4, Auberdine (101), Back terrace of northern building

THUN'GRIM FIREGAZE
Barrens (18), G-3, Atop Thorn Hill

THURGRUM DEEPFORGE
Blacksmithing Supplies, Ironforge (52), G-4, The Great Forge, Next to anvils

THURMAN AGAMAND
Tirisfal Glades (86), E-3, Agamand Mills (100), Roams on the western side of mill near dropoff

THURMAN MULLBY
General Goods Vendor, Stormwind (72), I-6, Trade District, Everyday Merchandise

THURMAN SCHNEDIER
Stormwind (72), F-8, Mage Quarter, Larson Clothiers

THUROS LIGHTFINGERS
Rare Spawn, Elwynn Forest (42), D-6, G:(6, 8), L-8, Crystal Lake, Jerod's Landing, Mirror Lake, Lvl 11 Uncommon; Stands idle at spawn point

THURSTON XANE
Mage Trainer, Thunder Bluff (84), B-2, Spirit Rise, The Pools of Vision

THUUL
Portal Trainer, Orgrimmar (60), D:(8, 9), Valley of Spirit, Darkbriar Lodge, top floor

THUWD
Skinning Trainer, Orgrimmar (60), H-4, The Drag, Kodohide Leatherworkers

THUZADIN ACOLYTE
Eastern Plaguelands (40), D-2, Stratholme

THUZADIN NECROMANCER
Eastern Plaguelands (40), D-2, Stratholme

THUZADIN SHADOWCASTER
Eastern Plaguelands (40), D-2, Stratholme

THYN'TEL BLADEWEAVER
Darnassus (26), H-4, Warrior's Terrace, Middle of terrace

THYSSIANA
Hippogryph Master, Feralas (46), K-5, Thalanaar, North of well

THYSTA
Wind Rider Master, Stranglethorn Vale (74), C-3, Grom'gol Base Camp (114), Inside camp walls to the right of eastern entrance

TICK
Tanaris (78), I-5, Caverns of Time, Land bridge leading to cavern

TIDE CRAWLER
Darkshore (24), E:(6, 7), F:(2, 3, 7), Mist's Edge, Twilight Shore

TIDERESS
Ashenvale (12), F-7, Mystral Lake, Roams underwater and on center island

TIEV MORDUNE
Silverpine Forest (68), F-4, North Tide's Run, Crouched on coastal hill behind megalith

TIGOR SKYCHASER
Shaman Trainer, Thunder Bluff (84), B-2, Spirit Rise, Inside Hall of Spirits

TILLI THISTLEFUZZ
Enchanting Supplies, Ironforge (52), H-4, The Great Forge, Thistlefuzz Arcanery

TIMBER
Rare Spawn, Dun Morogh (32), D-4, Iceflow Lake, Lvl 10 Uncommon; Large island at center of lake

TIMBER WOLF
Elwynn Forest (42), F:(3-5), G:(4, 5), Echo Ridge Mine, Northshire Valley (122)

TIMBERLING
Teldrassil (80), G:(6, 7), H:(6, 7), Dolanaar (109), Lake Al'Ameth

TIMBERLING BARK RIPPER
Teldrassil (80), F-7, G-7, Lake Al'Ameth

TIMBERLING MIRE BEAST
Teldrassil (80), E:(3, 4), The Oracle Glade, Wellspring River

TIMBERLING TRAMPLER
Teldrassil (80), E-4, G-7, Lake Al'Ameth, Wellspring Lake, Wellspring River

TIMBERMAW DEN WATCHER
Azshara (14), D-3, E:(2, 3), F:(2, 3), Timbermaw Hold, Ursolan

TIMBERMAW PATHFINDER
Azshara (14), C:(4, 5), D:(4, 5), Bear's Head, Ruins of Eldarath

TIMBERMAW SHAMAN
Azshara (14), D-3, E:(2, 3), F:(2, 3), Timbermaw Hold, Ursolan

TIMBERMAW TOTEMIC
Azshara (14), C-5, D:(4, 5), Bear's Head, Timbermaw Hold

TIMBERMAW URSA
Azshara (14), E:(2, 3), F:(2, 3), Timbermaw Hold, Ursolan

TIMBERMAW WARRIOR
Azshara (14), C:(4, 5), D:(4, 5), Bear's Head, Ruins of Eldarath, Timbermaw Hold

TIMBERWEB RECLUSE
Azshara (14), B-5, C-5, D:(4, 5), E:(2-4), F-3

TIMMY THE CRUEL
Eastern Plaguelands (40), D-2, Stratholme

TIMOTHY CLARK
Wetlands (96), A-6, Menethil Harbor (119), Second floor of keep

TIMOTHY WELDON
Heavy Armor Merchant, Undercity (88), H-4, The Trade Quarter, Upper Ring of Trade Quarter

TIMOTHY WORTHINGTON
Master Tailor, Dustwallow Marsh (38), I-5, Theramore Isle (135), 2nd floor of building in south corner

TINK SPROCKETWHISTLE
Engineering Supplies, Dun Morogh (32), C-4, Gnomeregan

TINKEE STEAMBOIL
Burning Steppes (22), H-2, Flame Crest (112), Under scaffolding

TINKERER GIZLOCK
Desolace (30), D-5, Mauradon

TINKERER SNIGGLES
Barrens (18), F-1, Building southwest of Sludge Fen

TINKERWIZ
Journeyman Engineer, Barrens (18), H-4, Ratchet (122), Building northeast of town

TINKMASTER OVERSPARK
Master Gnome Engineer, Ironforge (52), J-5, Tinker Town, Outside tram entrance

TIRION FORDRING
Eastern Plaguelands (40), A-4, Thondroril River, In front of house on banks of Thondoril River

TIRISFAL FARMER
Tirisfal Glades (86), D-5, E-5, Solliden Farmstead

TIRISFAL FARMHAND
Tirisfal Glades (86), D-5, E-5, Solliden Farmstead

TISA MARTINE
Ironforge (52), J-7, The Military Ward, Bruuk's Corner

TIYANI
Food & Drink Vendor, Darkshore (24), G-8, Grove of the Ancients, Center of temple

TIZA BATTLEFORGE
Ironforge (52), C-1, The Mystic Ward, Hall of Mysteries

TOBIAS SEECHER
Burning Steppes (22), Searing Gorge (64), C-4/D-8, Blackrock Depths

TODDRICK
Butcher, Elwynn Forest (42), F-7, Goldshire (114), First floor of Lion's Pride Inn

TOG RUSTSPROCKET
Dun Morogh (32), F-5, Kharanos (116), Gnomish camp on right of distillery

TOGNUS FLINTFIRE
Journeyman Blacksmith, Dun Morogh (32), F-5, Kharanos (116), Smithy

TOG'THAR
Hillsbrad Foothills (48), J-4, Durnholde Keep, In ruins in the upper level of keep

TOK'KAR
Swamp of Sorrows (76), K-8, Misty Reed Post, Next to bonfire in camp

TOLDREN DEEPIRON
Priest Trainer, Ironforge (52), C-1, The Mystic Ward, Hall of Mysteries

TOMAS
Cook, Elwynn Forest (42), F-7, Goldshire (114), First floor of Lion's Pride Inn

TOMB FIEND
Barrens (18), F-9, Razorfen Downs

TOMB REAVER
Barrens (18), F-9, Razorfen Downs

TOMMY JOE STONEFIELD
Elwynn Forest (42), D-9, The Stonefield Farm, By river bank west of farm

TONGA RUNETOTEM
Barrens (18), F-3, The Crossroads (107), Southern entrance

TOOGA
Tanaris (78), D-6, E:(6, 7), Thistleshrub Valley, Roams valley and south

TOPPER MCNABB
Stormwind (72), H-6, Trade District, Northwest alley

TOR'PHAN
Cloth & Leather Armor Merchant, Orgrimmar (60), H-5, The Drag, Magar's Cloth Goods

TOREK
Ashenvale (12), I-7, Nightsong Woods, East of road leading to Barrens

TOR'GAN
Arathi Highlands (10), J-4, Hammerfall (115), Outside fence east building

TORM RAGETOTEM
Warrior Trainer, Thunder Bluff (84), G-9, Hunter Rise, Inside Hunter's Hall

TORMENTED OFFICER
Silverpine Forest (68), F-7, Shadowfang Keep

TORMENTED SPIRIT
Rare Spawn, Tirisfal Glades (86), E-3, Agamand Mills (100), Lvl 8 Uncommon; Patrols the northwestern edge of mill

TORMUS DEEPFORGE
Ironforge (52), F-4 , The Great Forge, The Great Anvil

TORN
Banker, Thunder Bluff (84), E-6, Thunder Bluff Bank

TORN FIN COASTRUNNER
Hillsbrad Foothills (48), B:(6, 7), C-7, D-7, Western Strand, Coast

TORN FIN MUCKDWELLER
Hillsbrad Foothills (48), A-6, B:(6, 7), C-7, Western Strand, Coast

TORN FIN ORACLE
Hillsbrad Foothills (48), D-7, E:(6, 7), F-6, Western Strand, Coast

TORN FIN TIDEHUNTER
Hillsbrad Foothills (48), C-7, D-7, E:(6, 7), F:(6, 7), Western Strand, Coast

TORN SCREAMER
Eastern Plaguelands (40), B:(3, 4), C:(2-4), D:(3, 4), E:(2-4), F:(2-4), Plaguewood

TORN SCROLL
Eastern Plaguelands (40), D-8, The Undercroft, Crypt

TORQ IRONBLAST
Gunsmith, Dustwallow Marsh (38), I-5, Theramore Isle (135), First floor of Foothold Citadel

TORREN SQUAREJAW
Explorers' League, Loch Modan (54), E-5, Thelsamar (134), Second house on right of path

TORTA
Tanaris (78), J-3, Steamwheedle Port, Small cove south of the port

TORTURED DRUID
Silithus (66), G-3, H-3, Southwind Village

TORTURED SENTINEL
Silithus (66), G-3, H-3, Southwind Village

TORWA PATHFINDER
Un'Goro Crater (90), J-7, On hill, next to waterfall

TOSAMINA
Orgrimmar (60), I-2 , Valley of Honor, In building with Horde orphans

TOWN CRIER
Duskwood (36), J-5

TOXIC HORROR
Felwood (44), G-3, Irontree Woods

TRACKMASTER ZHERIN
Thousand Needles (82), K-8, Mirage Raceway (119), Grandstands at drag strip

TRADE MASTER KOVIC
The Undermarket, Searing Gorge (64), D-5, The Cauldron, Next to Clunk in cave

TRAINED RAZORBEAK
The Hinterlands (50), B:(5, 6), C:(5, 6), The Hinterlands

TRAK'GEN
General Goods, Orgrimmar (60), F-8, Valley of Strength, Orgimmar General Store

TRAN'REK
Tanaris (78), H-3, Gadgetzan (113), Near crane to north

TRAUGH
Expert Blacksmith, Barrens (18), F-3, The Crossroads (107), Western entrance

TRAVIST BOSK
Undercity (88), F-3, The War Quarter, Platform in front of Skull building

TRAYEXIR
Weapon Merchant, Durotar (34), H-7, Sen'jin Village (126), Main floor of big hut

TREANT SPIRIT
Felwood (44), G-3, Irontree Woods

TRENTON LIGHTHAMMER
The Mithril Order, Tanaris (78), H-3, Gadgetzan (113), Near southern entrance

TRESHALA FALLOWBROOK
Darnassus (26), I-7, Tradesmen's Terrace, Across second story bridge from Weapons shop

TRIANNA
Journeyman Tailor, Darnassus (26), I-2 , Craftsmen's Terrace, Tailoring shop

TRISTANE SHADOWSTONE
Dun Morogh (32), D-4, Brewnall Village, Patrols between scaffolding and half way along road heading south out of village

TRIXIE QUIKSWITCH
Expert Engineer, Ironforge (52), I-4, Tinker Town, Springspindle's Gadgets

TROYAS MOONBREEZE
Feralas (46), C-4, Feathermoon Stronghold (111), Southeastern building

TRUK WILDBEARD
Bartender, The Hinterlands (50), B-4, Aerie Peak (100), Wildhammer Keep

TRULL FAILBANE
Felwood (44), E-5, Bloodvenom Post (102) (102), Campfire

TSUNAMAN
Stonetalon Mountains (70), F-6, Sun Rock Retreat (132), Outside hut on cliff south of inn

TSU'ZEE
Rare Spawn, Feralas (46), G-4, Dire Maul, Lvl 59 Rare

TUKK
General Goods Vendor, Desolace (30), C-7, Shadowprey Village (128), Near entrance

TUMI
Heavy Armor Merchant, Orgrimmar (60), K-2, Valley of Honor, The Burning Anvil

TUNDRA MACGRANN
Dun Morogh (32), D-5, Chill Breeze Valley, Camp in front of cave on hill

TUNKK
Leatherworking Supplies, Arathi Highlands (10), J-3, Hammerfall (115), Inside east building

TUNNEL RAT DIGGER
Loch Modan (54), D:(2, 3), Silver Stream Mine, Mine

TUNNEL RAT FORAGER
Loch Modan (54), C-4, D-2, E:(1, 2), Silver Stream Mine, Front of mine

TUNNEL RAT GEOMANCER
Loch Modan (54), D:(2, 3), Silver Stream Mine, Mine

TUNNEL RAT KOBOLD
Loch Modan (54), C-4, D-2, E:(1, 2), Silver Stream Mine, Mine

TUNNEL RAT SCOUT
Loch Modan (54), B-3, C:(3, 4), D:(2, 3), Silver Stream Mine, Mine

TUNNEL RAT SURVEYOR
Loch Modan (54), D:(2, 3), Silver Stream Mine, Mine

TUNNEL RAT VERMIN
Loch Modan (54), B-3, C:(3, 4), D:(1-3), E:(1-3), Silver Stream Mine, Front of mine

TURAK RUNETOTEM
Druid Trainer, Thunder Bluff (84), J-3, Elder Rise, Inside Hall of Elders

TURHAW
Butcher, Thousand Needles (82), F-5, Freewind Post (112), Next to hut, west of inn

TURIAN
Thrown Weapons Merchant, Darnassus (26), H-6, Tradesmen's Terrace, Thrown Weapons shop

TURUK AMBERSTILL
Dwarven Weaponsmith, Dun Morogh (32), I-5, Amberstill Ranch, On porch of building

TUTEN'KASH
Barrens (18), F-9, Razorfen Downs

TWAIN
Stormwind (72), Roams city with Miss Danna

TWIGGY FLATHEAD
The Announcer, Barrens (18), I-5, Fray Island, Bleechers

TWILIGHT ACOLYTE
Ashenvale (12), B-2, Blackfathom Deeps

TWILIGHT AQUAMANCER
Ashenvale (12), B-2, Blackfathom Deeps

TWILIGHT AVENGER
Silithus (66), D:(2, 4, 5), E:(2, 3), F:(2, 3), Twilight Base Camp, Twilight Outpost, Twilight Post

TWILIGHT BODYGUARD
Burning Steppes (22), Searing Gorge (64), C-4/D-8, Blackrock Depths

TWILIGHT DARK SHAMAN
Searing Gorge (64), A:(3, 4), B:(3, 4), Firewatch Ridge

TWILIGHT DISCIPLE
Darkshore (24), F:(8, 9), The Master's Glaive, Twilight Vale

TWILIGHT ELEMENTALIST
Ashenvale (12), B-2, Blackfathom Deeps

TWILIGHT EMISSARY
Burning Steppes (22), Searing Gorge (64), C-4/D-8, Blackrock Depths

TWILIGHT FIRE GUARD
Searing Gorge (64), A:(3, 4), B:(3, 4), C:(2, 3), Firewatch Ridge

TWILIGHT GEOLORD
Silithus (66), D:(2, 4, 5), E:(2, 3), F:(2, 3), Twilight Base Camp, Twilight Outpost, Twilight Post

TWILIGHT GEOMANCER
Searing Gorge (64), A:(3, 4), B:(3, 4), C:(2, 3), Firewatch Ridge

TWILIGHT IDOLATER
Searing Gorge (64), C-3, Firewatch Ridge

TWILIGHT LORD EVERUN
Rare Spawn, Silithus (66), D-5, E-2, F-3, Twilight Base Camp, Twilight Outpost, Twilight Post, Lvl 60 Uncommon; Roams respective camp

TWILIGHT LORD KELRIS
Ashenvale (12), B-2, Blackfathom Deeps

TWILIGHT LORESEEKER
Ashenvale (12), B-2, Blackfathom Deeps

TWILIGHT MASTER
Silithus (66), D:(4, 5), Twilight Outpost

TWILIGHT REAVER
Ashenvale (12), B-2, Blackfathom Deeps

TWILIGHT RUNNER
Stonetalon Mountains (70), D:(1, 2), E:(1, 2), Stonetalon Peak

TWILIGHT SHADOWMAGE
Ashenvale (12), B-2, Blackfathom Deeps

TWILIGHT STONECALLER
Silithus (66), D:(4, 5), E-2, F:(2, 3), Twilight Base Camp, Twilight Outpost

TWILIGHT THUG
Darkshore (24), F:(8, 9), H:(3, 4), The Master's Glaive, Twilight Vale

TWILIGHT'S HAMMER AMBASSADOR
Burning Steppes (22), Searing Gorge (64), C-4/D-8, Blackrock Depths

TWILIGHT'S HAMMER EXECUTIONER
Burning Steppes (22), Searing Gorge (64), C-4/D-8, Blackrock Depths

TWILIGHT'S HAMMER TORTURER
Burning Steppes (22), Searing Gorge (64), C-4/D-8, Blackrock Depths

TWIZWICK SPROCKETGRIND
Journeyman Engineer, Mulgore (58), H-3, In hills northeast of north entrance to Venture Co. Mine

TYLER
Undercity (88), G-2, The War Quarter, Fights captives in War Quarter

TYMOR
Ironforge (52), D-1, The Mystic Ward, Building to the right of Hall of Mysteries

TYNNUS VENOMSPROUT
Shady Dealer, Ironforge (52), G-1, The Forlorn Cavern, Top of steps, just inside east entrance

TYRANDE WHISPERWIND
High Priestess of Elune, Darnassus (26), E-8, The Temple of the Moon, Balcony, north of fountain

TYRANIS MALEM
Desolace (30), G-3, Thunder Axe Fortress, Center of smaller fortress

TYRANT DEVILSAUR
Un'Goro Crater (90), D:(3, 4), F-8, H:(3, 8), J-4

TYRION
Stormwind (72), K-1, Stormwind Keep, Courtyard

TYRION'S SPYBOT
Stormwind (72), K-1, Stormwind Keep, Courtyard

u

U'CHA
Un'Goro Crater (90), I-2, Fungal Rock, Northern section of cave

UG'THOK
Journeyman Blacksmith, Orgrimmar (60), J-2, Valley of Honor, Across from Arms of Legend

UHGAR
Weaponsmith, Durotar (34), H-4, Razor Hill (124), Northeast of inn

UHK'LOC
Rare Spawn, Un'Goro Crater (90), I-2, Fungal Rock, Lvl 53 Uncommon; Northern section of cave

UKOR
Durotar (34), H-7, Near signpost on road

UKRA'NOR
Staff Merchant, Orgrimmar (60), C-7, Valley of Spirit, Skyfury Staves

ULA'ELEK
Durotar (34), H-7, Sen'jin Village (126), Outside big hut

ULAG THE CLEAVER
Tirisfal Glades (86), H-5, Brill (104), (Summon) Spawns in front of the mausoleum in the graveyard

ULATHEK
Felwood (44), E-6, Shadow Hold, Northwest cave across bridge after spiral tunnel

ULBREK FIREHAND
Stable Master, Ironforge (52), I-8, The Military Ward, Hall of Arms

ULFIR IRONBEARD
Hunter Trainer, Stormwind (72), I-2, Dwarven District, Building south of tra[...] entrance

ULLANNA
Trade Supplies, Darkshore (24), G-8, Grove of the Ancients, Center of temp[...]

ULTHAAN
Butcher, Ashenvale (12), F-6, Silverwi[...] Refuge (128)

ULTHAM IRONHORN
Ram Riding Instructor, Dun Morogh (32), I-5, Amberstill Ranch, By hay bai[...] in corral

ULTHIR
Alchemy Supplies, Darnassus (26), G-[...] Craftsmen's Terrace, Alchemy shop

UMA BARTULM
Herbalism & Alchemy Supplies, Dustwallow Marsh (38), H-5, Theramo[...] Isle (135), Hut in west corner

UMARON STRAGARELM
Winterspring (98), I-4, Everlook (110), Near the machinery along the east wa[...]

UMBER
Moonglade (56), F-4, Nighthaven (12[...] Just outside northwest building on wooden walkway

UMBRANSE THE SPIRITSPEAKER
Winterspring (98), J-3, Inside small shack in hills

UMI RUMPLESNICKER
Winterspring (98), I-4, Everlook (110), Behind building directly north of entrance

UMPI
Hillsbrad Foothills (48), G-2, Tarren Mi[...] (133), House on the left

UNA
Leatherworker Trainer, Thunder Bluff (84), D-4, Middle rise, inside Thunder Bluff Armorers tent

UNA JI'RO
Darkshore (24), J-2, Big structure, nort[...] of lake

UNDEAD DYNAMITER
Westfall (94), D-7, E-7, The Deadmine[...]

UNDEAD EXCAVATOR
Westfall (94), D-7, E-7, The Deadmine[...]

UNDEAD POSTMAN
Eastern Plaguelands (40), D-2, Stratholme

UNDEAD RAVAGER
Desolace (30), H:(8, 9), I:(8, 9), Valley of Bones

UNDEAD SCARAB
Eastern Plaguelands (40), D-2, Stratholme

UNDERTAKER MORDO
Tirisfal Glades (86), C-8, Deathknell (109), Outside of Shadow Grave

NFETTERED SPIRIT
Tirisfal Glades (86), K-3, L-3, Scarlet Monastery

NGER STATFORTH
Horse Breeder, Wetlands (96), A-5, Menethil Harbor (119), Outside stables

N'GORO GORILLA
Un'Goro Crater (90), H-2, I-2, Fungal Rock, Lakkari Tar Pits

N'GORO STOMPER
Un'Goro Crater (90), H-2, I-2, Fungal Rock, Lakkari Tar Pits

N'GORO THUNDERER
Un'Goro Crater (90), I-2, Fungal Rock, Lakkari Tar Pits

NLIVING ATAL'AI
Swamp of Sorrows (76), I-5, The Temple of Atal'Hakkar

NLIVING CARETAKER
Deadwind Pass (28), C:(6-8), D:(7, 8), E:(7-9), F-8, Karazhan, Morgan's Plot

NLIVING MOSSFLAYER
Eastern Plaguelands (40), D-8, The Undercroft

NLIVING RESIDENT
Deadwind Pass (28), C:(6-8), D:(7, 8), E:(7-9), F-8, Karazhan, Morgan's Plot

NSEEN SERVANT
Eastern Plaguelands (40), H:(6, 7), Corin's Crossing

NSTABLE CORPSE
Western Plaguelands (92), I-7, Scholomance

N'THUWA
Mage Trainer, Durotar (34), H-7, Sen'jin Village (126), Small hut to southeast

R'KYO
Priest Trainer, Orgrimmar (60), D-9, Valley of Spirit, Spirit Lodge

RDA
Wind Rider Master, Arathi Highlands (10), J-3, Hammerfall (115), Camp

R'DAN
Felwood (44), E-6, Shadow Hold, Top floor of the final area

REK THUNDERHORN
Hunter Trainer, Thunder Bluff (84), G-9, Hunter Rise, Inside Hunter's Hall

ROK DOOMHOWL
Burning Steppes (22), Searing Gorge (64), C-4/D-8, Blackrock Spire

ROK ENFORCER
Burning Steppes (22), Searing Gorge (64), C-4/D-8, Blackrock Spire

ROK OGRE MAGUS
Burning Steppes (22), Searing Gorge (64), C-4/D-8, Blackrock Spire

RSAL THE MAULER
Teldrassil (80), E-8, Gnarlpine Hold, Patrols southwest camp

RSANGOUS
Ashenvale (12), I-7, Spawns west of Mystral Lake and roams in a loop to the northwest

RSIUS
Winterspring (98), H-3, Roams hills

RSOL'LOK
Rare Spawn, Ashenvale (12), J-5, K-6, Nightsong Woods, Satyrnaar, Warsong Lumber Camp, Lvl 31 Semi-Rare

RSULA DELINE
Warlock Trainer, Stormwind (72), D-8, Mage Quarter, The Slaughtered Lamb

RSYN GHULL
Mage Trainer, Thunder Bluff (84), B-2, Spirit Rise, The Pools of Vision

RTHARO
Weapon Merchant, Orgrimmar (60), F-7, Valley of Strength, The Shattered Axe

RTRAN CLANBRINGER
Guild Master, Orgrimmar (60), E-7, Valley of Strength, Horde Embassy

RUSON
Rare Spawn, Teldrassil (80), I-6, Starbreeze Village, Lvl 7 Uncommon; Patrols road in village

THAN STILLWATER
Fisherman, Mulgore (58), E-6, Stonebull Lake, North end of lake

THEK THE WISE
Desolace (30), D-8, Gelkis Village, Hut on hill

THEL'NAY
Mage Trainer, Orgrimmar (60), D:(8, 9), Valley of Spirit, Darkbriar Lodge

THIL MOONCALL
Ashenvale (12), J-7, Dor'Danil Barrow Den, Northeast cave at bottom of den

UTHOK
General Supplies, Stranglethorn Vale (74), C-3, Grom'gol Base Camp (114), By orcish carriage just inside camp walls to the right of western entrance

UTHRAR THREX
Journeyman Tailor, Ironforge (52), F-3, The Great Forge, Stonebrow's Clothier

UTHROK
Bowyer & Gunsmith, Barrens (18), F-3, The Crossroads (107), Western entrance

UTTNAR
Butcher, Arathi Highlands (10), J-3, Hammerfall (115), Platform of north building

UZZEK
Barrens (18), G-2, Camp near tree

V

VAEAN
Enchanting Supplies, Darnassus (26), H-1, Craftsmen's Terrace, Enchanting shop

VAELAN
Burning Steppes (22), Searing Gorge (64), C-4/D-8, Blackrock Spire

VAELASTRASZ THE RED
Burning Steppes (22), Searing Gorge (64), C-4/D-8, Blackrock Spire

VAGASH
Dun Morogh (32), H-5, I-5, Amberstill Ranch, Patrols in and around cave above ranch

VAHGRUK
Wind Rider Master, Burning Steppes (22), H-2, Flame Crest (112), Right of cave

VAHLARRIEL DEMONSLAYER
Desolace (30), I-1, Nijel's Point (121), Near entrance

VALDARON
Tailoring Supplies, Darkshore (24), F-4, Auberdine (101), Right wing of northern building

VALDRED MORAY
Silverpine Forest (68), G-8, The Greymane Wall, Patrols between the camps along right side of wall

VALE SCREECHER
Feralas (46), F-5, G:(5, 6)

VALGAR HIGHFORGE
Paladin Trainer, Ironforge (52), C-1, The Mystic Ward, Hall of Mysteries

VALSTAG IRONJAW
Wetlands (96), A-6, Menethil Harbor (119), Just inside keep

VALUSHA
Ashenvale (12), I-6, Splintertree Post (129)

VAMPIRIC DUSKBAT
Tirisfal Glades (86), E:(6, 7), F:(6, 7), G-6, H:(3, 4), I:(3-6), J:(3-7), K:(4-7), L-4

VANCE UNDERGLOOM
Journeyman Enchanter, Tirisfal Glades (86), H-5, Brill (104), Second floor of Gallows' End Tavern

VARG WINDWHISPER
Leather Armor Merchant, Mulgore (58), E-6, Bloodhoof Village (102), Northeast tent

VARGUS
Bladesmith, Silithus (67), G-4, Cenarion Hold (106)

VARIA HARDHIDE
Armor Merchant, Mulgore (58), E-8, Camp Narache (105), Southwest tent

VARIAN WRYNN
King of Stormwind, Dustwallow Marsh (38), J-2, Alcaz Island, Underground dungeon in east camp

VARIMATHRAS
Boss, Undercity (88), H-9, Royal Quarter, In Throne room

VAR'JUN
Mulgore (58), E-6, Bloodhoof Village (102), Outside main tent

VARK BATTLESCAR
Skinning Trainer, Desolace (30), B-7, Shadowprey Village (128), Top of western structure

VARO'THEN'S GHOST
Rare Spawn, Azshara (14), A:(7-8), B-7, Lvl 48 Uncommon; Roams area north of road among ruins

VARTRUS THE ANCIENT
Felwood (44), G-3, Irontree Woods, (Summon) Talk to the ancients on the island

VAULT WARDEN
Badlands (16), G-1, Uldaman

VAZARIO LINKGREASE
Master Goblin Engineer, Barrens (18), H-4, Ratchet (122), Building northeast of town

VECTUS
Western Plaguelands (92), I-7, Scholomance

VEENIX
Venture Co. Merchant, Stonetalon Mountains (70), G-5, Windshear Crag, In mountains, west of the river

VEHENA
Horde Cloth Quartermaster, Orgrimmar (60), D-9, Valley of Spirit, Darkbriar Lodge

VEJREK
Dun Morogh (32), C-6, Chill Breeze Valley, Outside troll hut

VELDAN LIGHTFOOT
Leather Armor Merchant, Elwynn Forest (42), C-7, Westbrook Garrison, First floor armory in garrison

VELINDE STARSONG
Duskwood (36), J-8, Roland's Doom, (Summon) Dirt pile

VELMA WARNAM
Undead Horse Riding Instructor, Tirisfal Glades (86), H-5, Brill (104), Stable

VELORA NITELY
Undercity (88), I-4, The Trade Quarter, Upper Ring of Trade Quarter

VEL'RIN FANG
Durotar (34), H-7, Sen'jin Village (126), Structure left of big hut

VENDOR-TRON 1000
Desolace (30), H-4, Spawns when caravan is at Kormek's hut

VENGEFUL ANCIENT
Rare Spawn, Stonetalon Mountains (70), C-7, D-7, The Charred Vale, Lvl 29 Uncommon; Roams the vale

VENGEFUL SURGE
Arathi Highlands (10), E-8

VENOM BELCHER
Eastern Plaguelands (40), D-2, Stratholme

VENOM MIST LURKER
Western Plaguelands (92), C-6, D:(5-7), E:(6, 7), The Bulwark (105)

VENOM WEB SPIDER
Duskwood (36), A:(3-7), B:(3, 7), C-3, D-3, E-2, F-2, G-2, H-2, I-2, J-2, K-2, The Darkened Bank

VENOMHIDE RAVASAUR
Un'Goro Crater (90), H:(5, 6), I:(5, 6), J:(5, 6), The Marshlands

VENOMLASH SCORPID
Badlands (16), G-1, Uldaman

VENOMOUS CLOUD SERPENT
Thousand Needles (82), A:(3, 4), C:(3-5), D-5, E:(5, 6), G:(5, 6), Camp E'thok, Darkcloud Pinnacle, The Screeching Canyon

VENOMTAIL SCORPID
Durotar (34), E:(3, 5, 6), F:(2, 3, 5), G-2, H:(1, 2)

VENOMTIP SCORPID
Burning Steppes (22), J-3, K:(2, 3, 5, 6), L:(3-6), Dreadmaul Rock

VENTURE CO. BUILDER
Stonetalon Mountains (70), H-4, Cragpool Lake

VENTURE CO. DEFORESTER
Stonetalon Mountains (70), H:(4, 5), I:(4-6), J:(5, 6), Blackwolf River, Cragpool Lake, Windshear Crag

VENTURE CO. DRONE
Westfall (94), I-7, Circles tower

VENTURE CO. DRONE
Barrens (18), F-1, Patrols outside tower northeast of Sludge Fen

VENTURE CO. DRUDGER
Barrens (18), F-1, G-1, The Sludge Fen

VENTURE CO. ENFORCER
Barrens (18), G-1, H-1, Boulder Lode Mine

VENTURE CO. ENGINEER
Stonetalon Mountains (70), H-4, Cragpool Lake

VENTURE CO. FOREMAN
Stranglethorn Vale (74), D:(4, 5)

VENTURE CO. GEOLOGIST
Stranglethorn Vale (74), B-1, D:(2, 3), E:(2, 3)

VENTURE CO. HIRELING
Mulgore (58), F:(6, 7), Winterhoof Water Well

VENTURE CO. LABORER
Mulgore (58), E:(4, 5), F:(5, 7), Ravaged Caravan, Thunderhoof Water Well, Winterhoof Water Well

VENTURE CO. LOGGER
Stonetalon Mountains (70), H:(4, 5), I:(4-6), J:(5, 6), Blackwolf River, Cragpool Lake, Windshear Crag

VENTURE CO. LOOKOUT
Barrens (18), F-1

VENTURE CO. LUMBERJACK
Stranglethorn Vale (74), E-2

VENTURE CO. MACHINE SMITH
Stonetalon Mountains (70), H-4, Cragpool Lake

VENTURE CO. MECHANIC
Stranglethorn Vale (74), B-1, D-2, E-2

VENTURE CO. MERCENARY
Barrens (18), G-1, The Sludge Fen

VENTURE CO. MINER
Stranglethorn Vale (74), B-1, C-1

VENTURE CO. OPERATOR
Stonetalon Mountains (70), H-5, I:(4, 5), J:(5, 6), Blackwolf River, Cragpool Lake, Windshear Crag

VENTURE CO. OVERSEER
Barrens (18), G-1, H-1, Boulder Lode Mine

VENTURE CO. PATROLLER
Barrens (18), F-1

VENTURE CO. PEON
Barrens (18), F-1

VENTURE CO. SHREDDER
Stranglethorn Vale (74), E:(2, 3)

VENTURE CO. STRIP MINER
Stranglethorn Vale (74), D:(4, 5)

VENTURE CO. SURVEYOR
Stranglethorn Vale (74), D:(4, 5)

VENTURE CO. TASKMASTER
Mulgore (58), E:(4, 5), F-5, Ravaged Caravan, Stonebull Lake, Thunderhorn Water Well

VENTURE CO. TINKERER
Stranglethorn Vale (74), D:(4, 5)

VENTURE CO. WORKBOSS
Stranglethorn Vale (74), B-1, E-2

VENTURE CO. WORKER
Mulgore (58), D:(1, 2), E-1, G:(4, 5), H:(3-5), The Venture Co. Mine, Wildmane Water Well

VENYA MARTHAND
Tirisfal Glades (86), C-7, Deathknell (109), Church

VERA NIGHTSHADE
Ashenvale (12), I-6, Splintertree Post (129), Sitting in inn

VERDAN THE EVERLIVING
Barrens (18), E-4, Wailing Caverns

VERDANTINE BOUGHGUARD
The Hinterlands (50), I:(2, 3), J:(1-3), Seradane

VERDANTINE ORACLE
The Hinterlands (50), I:(2, 3), J:(1-3), Seradane

VERDANTINE TREE WARDER
The Hinterlands (50), I:(2, 3), J:(1-3), Seradane

VEREK
Burning Steppes (22), Searing Gorge (64), C-4/D-8, Blackrock Depths

VEREN TAILSTRIDER
Thunder Bluff (84), E-4, Middle rise, inside Thunder Bluff Armorers tent

VERIFONIX
Rare Spawn, Stranglethorn Vale (74), D-6, The Cape of Stranglethorn, Lvl 42 Average Rare; Patrols a circular path around ridgeline stopping periodically to mine

VERNA FURLBROW
Westfall (94), G-2, The Jansen Stead, Cart near Old Blanchy

VERNER OSGOOD
Redridge Mountains (62), D-5, Lakeshire (117), Stable

VERNON HALE
Bait and Tackle Supplier, Redridge Mountains (62), C-5, Lakeshire (117), Behind shed near docks on western side of town

VEROG THE DERVISH
Barrens (18), F-4, Spawns on structure west of Stagnant Oasis

VERON AMBERSTILL
Ram Breeder, Dun Morogh (32), I-5, Amberstill Ranch, By carriage in front of corral

VESPRYSTUS
Hippogryph Master, Teldrassil (80), G-9, Rut'theran Village (125), By Hipporgryphs

VEXSPINDLE
Cloth & Leather Armor Merchant, Barrens (18), H-4, Ratchet (122), Plate-n-Chain

VEYZHAK THE CANNIBAL
Rare Spawn, Swamp of Sorrows (76), I-5, The Temple of Atal'Hakkar, Lvl 48 Uncommon

VHAN
Journeyman Tailor, Thunder Bluff (84), E-4, Middle rise, inside Thunder Bluff Armorers tent

VHARR
Superior Weaponsmith, Stranglethorn Vale (74), C-3, Grom'gol Base Camp (114), Next to forge

VICIOUS FALLOUT
Dun Morogh (32), C-4, Gnomeregan

VICIOUS GRAY BEAR
Hillsbrad Foothills (48), D:(3, 4), E:(3-5), F:(3-5), G-4, H-4, I:(3-5), J-5, Thoughout Hillsbrad

VICIOUS GRELL
Teldrassil (80), F-5, G-5, Fel Rock

VICIOUS NIGHT WEB SPIDER
Tirisfal Glades (86), K:(5, 6), L:(5, 6), Venomweb Vale

VICIOUS OWLBEAST
The Hinterlands (50), D:(5-7), E:(4-6), F:(4, 5), The Hinterlands

VICTOR BARTHOLOMEW
Undercity (88), K-1, The Magic Quarter, Green circle west of Skull Building

VICTOR WARD
Journeyman Tailor, Undercity (88), J-3, The Magic Quarter

VIDRA HEARTHSTOVE
Loch Modan (54), D-5, Thelsamar (134), Stoutlager Inn

VIKKI LONSAV
General Goods, Arathi Highlands (10), F-5, Refuge Point (124), Camp

VIKTORI PRISM'ANTRAS
Duskwood (36), K-5, Darkshire (108), First house on left side of road heading into Darkshire from the east

VILE BAT
Silverpine Forest (68), F-7, Shadowfang Keep

VILE FAMILIAR
Durotar (34), F-5, G:(5, 6), Burning Blade Coven, Valley of Trials (136)

VILE FIN LAKESTALKER
Silverpine Forest (68), J:(2, 4, 5), K-2, The Dawning Isles

VILE FIN MINOR ORACLE
Tirisfal Glades (86), B-4, C:(4, 5), D-4, E-3, G-3, H-3, I:(2, 3), J-3, Whispering Shore, Coast

VILE FIN MUCKDWELLER
Tirisfal Glades (86), B-4, C:(4, 5), D-4, E-3, H-3, I:(2, 3), J-3

VILE FIN ORACLE
Silverpine Forest (68), J:(2, 4, 5), K-2, The Dawning Isles

VILE FIN PUDDLEJUMPER
Tirisfal Glades (86), C:(4, 5), D-4, G-3, H-3, Whispering Shore, Coast

VILE FIN SHORECREEPER
Silverpine Forest (68), K-3, L-3, The Dawning Isles

VILE FIN SHREDDER
Silverpine Forest (68), H:(2, 3), I:(1-3), J-1, The Shining Strand

VILE FIN TIDECALLER
Silverpine Forest (68), K-3, L-3, The Dawning Isles

VILE FIN TIDEHUNTER
Silverpine Forest (68), H:(2, 3), I:(1-3), J-1, The Shining Strand

VILE LARVA
Desolace (30), D-5, Mauradon

VILE OOZE
Felwood (44), E-5, Shadow Hold

VILE PRIESTESS HEXX
The Hinterlands (50), I-8, Jintha'Alor, Patrols between altar and cave entrance

VILE SLIME
Western Plaguelands (92), H-4, I:(3, 4), The Wheeping Cave

VILE SPRITE
Darkshore (24), G-4, Bashal'Aran

VILE STING
Thousand Needles (82), I-7, J-7, The Shimmering Flats, Roams west side of Shimmering Flats, near old camp

VILE TUTOR
Cult of the Damned, Eastern Plaguelands (40), H:(6, 7), Corin's Crossing

VILE'REL
Burning Steppes (22), Searing Gorge (64), C-4/D-8, Blackrock Depths

VILEBRANCH AMAN'ZASI GUARD
The Hinterlands (50), H:(7, 8), I-8, J-8, Jintha'Alor

VILEBRANCH AMBUSHER
The Hinterlands (50), J-6, Jintha'Alor

VILEBRANCH AXE THROWER
The Hinterlands (50), F:(6, 7), G:(6, 7), The Altar of Zul

VILEBRANCH BERSERKER
The Hinterlands (50), I:(6, 7), J-7, Jintha'Alor

VILEBRANCH BLOOD DRINKER
The Hinterlands (50), I:(6-8), J-8, Jintha'Alor

VILEBRANCH HEADHUNTER
The Hinterlands (50), J-7, Jintha'Alor

VILEBRANCH HIDESKINNER
The Hinterlands (50), I:(6-8), J:(7, 8), Jintha'Alor

VILEBRANCH KIDNAPPER
The Hinterlands (50), L-4, The Hinterlands, Island off coast

VILEBRANCH RAIDING WOLF
The Hinterlands (50), I:(6-8), Jintha'Alor

VILEBRANCH SCALPER
The Hinterlands (50), G:(6, 7), H:(4, 6), J:(4, 5), K-5, Shaol'Watha

VILEBRANCH SHADOW HUNTER
The Hinterlands (50), I:(6-8), J-7, Jintha'Alor

VILEBRANCH SHADOWCASTER
The Hinterlands (50), I:(6, 7), J:(6, 7), Jintha'Alor

VILEBRANCH SOOTHSAYER
The Hinterlands (50), G:(6, 7), H-4, J-4, K-5, Shaol'Watha

VILEBRANCH SOUL EATER
The Hinterlands (50), I:(6-8), J-8, Jintha'Alor

VILEBRANCH WARRIOR
The Hinterlands (50), I-6, J:(6, 7), Jintha'Alor

VILEBRANCH WITCH DOCTOR
The Hinterlands (50), G-7, I-6, J-7, Jintha'Alor

VILEBRANCH WOLF PUP
The Hinterlands (50), F-7, G:(6, 7), H-6, I:(6, 7), J-7, Jintha'Alor

VINASIA
Cloth Armor Merchant, Darnassus (26), H-7, Tradesmen's Terrace, Cloth Armor shop

VINCENT HYAL
Wetlands (96), A-6, Deepwater Tavern, First floor

VINDICATOR PALANAAR
Ashenvale (12), E-5, Astranaar (101)

VINNA WAYNE
Hillsbrad Foothills (48), H-2, Tarren Mill (133), Graveyard

VIRA YOUNGHOOF
First Aid Trainer, Mulgore (58), E-6, Bloodhoof Village (102), Inn

VISH KOZUS
Captain of the Guard, Silithus (67), G-5, Cenarion Hold (106)

VIVIANNA
Trade Supplies, Feralas (46), C-4, Feathermoon Stronghold (111), Inn

VIZNIK GOLDGRUBBER
Banker, Stranglethorn Vale (74), B-8, Booty Bay (103), Stranglethorn Trust Bank

VIZZKLICK
Tailoring Supplies, Tanaris (78), G-3, Gadgetzan (113), Outside western structure

VOGGAH DEATHGRIP
Alterac Mountains (8), I-6, Camp outside Alterac Valley

VOICE OF ELUNE
Winterspring (98), J-6, Owl Wing Thicket, (Summon) Altar

VOL'JIN
Boss, Orgrimmar (60), C-4, Valley of Wisdom, Grommash Hold

VOLCHAN
Rare Spawn, Burning Steppes (22), K-6, Terror Wing Path, Lvl 60 Uncommon; Patrols a circular path around Dreadmaul Rock to the east

VOLCOR
Darkshore (24), G-8, Blackwood Den, Sitting in cave

VOLOREN
Fishing Supplier, Darnassus (26), F-6, Tradesmen's Terrace, Dock

VOODOO TROLL
Durotar (34), J:(8, 9), Echo Isles

VORIYA
Darkshore (24), J-2, Upper level of hut south of lake

VORLUS VILEHOOF
Teldrassil (80), F-6, Moonwell in hills

VORN SKYSEER
Mulgore (58), E-8, Camp Narache (105), Southwest tent

VORREL SENGUTZ
Tirisfal Glades (86), K-3, L-3, Scarlet Monastery

VORSHA THE LASHER
Ashenvale (12), A-3, The Zoram Strand (137), Off coast northwest of outpost

VOSUR BRAKTHEL
Alchemist Trainer, Ironforge (52), I-5, Tinker Town, Berryfizz's Potions and Mixed Drinks

VRANG WILDGORE
Weaponsmith & Armorcrafter, Barrens (18), E-1, Small inlet among hills

VROK BLUNDERBLAST
Gunsmith, Loch Modan (54), D-4, Thelsamar (134), Porch of house on hill on left of path

VULTROS
Rare Spawn, Westfall (94), C-7, E-4, E-6, F-2, G-7, H-6, The Dead Acre, The Dust Plains, Furlbrow's Pumpkin Farm, Stendel's Pond, Westfall, Lvl 26 Average Rare; Roams around spawn points

VYRIN SWIFTWIND
Loch Modan (54), K-6, The Farstrider Lodge (111), Rear of lodge

W

WAILING ANCESTOR
Tirisfal Glades (86), F-3, G-3, Agamand Mills (100)

WAILING BANSHEE
Eastern Plaguelands (40), D-2, Stratholme

WAILING DEATH
Western Plaguelands (92), H:(5, 6), I:(5, 6), Gahrron's Withering

WAILING GUARDSMAN
Silverpine Forest (68), F-7, Shadowfang Keep

WAILING HIGHBORNE
Darkshore (24), F-6, G-6, Ameth'Aran

WAILING SPECTRE
Deadwind Pass (28), C:(6-8), D:(7, 8), E:(7-9), F-8, Karazhan, Morgan's Plot

WALDOR
Journeyman Leatherworker, Barrens (18), E-4, The Wailing Caverns, Right eye of cave above entrance

WALDOR
Journeyman Leatherworker, Barrens (18), E-4, Wailing Caverns

WALLACE THE BLIND
Weaponsmith, Silverpine Forest (68), G-8, The Greymane Wall, Under scaffolding along left side of wall

WALTER ELLINGSON
Heavy Armor Merchant, Undercity (88), H-4, The Magic Quarter, Upper Ring of Trade Quarter

WANDERING BARRENS GIRAFFE
Barrens (18), E:(4-6), F:(5, 6)

WANDERING EYE OF KILROGG
Feralas (46), G-4, Dire Maul

WANDERING PROTECTOR
Ashenvale (12), H-4

WANDERING SKELETON
Western Plaguelands (92), F-5, Dalson's Tears, Patrols path around outhouse

WANDERING SPIRIT
Tirisfal Glades (86), J-6, Balnir Farmstead

WAR GOLEM
Rare Spawn, Badlands (16), G:(1, 3), H-3, Angor Fortress, Hammertoe's Digsite, The Maker's Terrace, Lvl 36 Semi-Rare; Roams small area around spawn point

WAR MASTER VOONE
Burning Steppes (22), Searing Gorge (64), C-4/D-8, Blackrock Spire

WAR PARTY KODO
Thousand Needles (82), I-6, Ironstone Camp, Camp just west of Shimmering Flats

WAR REAVER
Burning Steppes (22), F-4, G:(3, 4), H:(3, 4), I-4, Ruins of Thourissan

WARBRINGER CONSTRUCT
Burning Steppes (22), Searing Gorge (64), C-4/D-8, Blackrock Depths

WARCALLER GORLACH
Orgrimmar (60), Valley of Wisdom, Roams most of Orgrimmar (except for Valley of Honor)

WARCHIEF REND BLACKHAND
Burning Steppes (22), Searing Gorge (64), C-4/D-8, Blackrock Spire

WARD GUARDIAN
Barrens (18), E-9, Razorfen Kraul

WARDEN BELAMOORE
Alterac Mountains (8), B-8, Lordamere Internment Camp, Third floor of building left of camp

WARDEN HARO
Silithus (67), G-4, Cenarion Hold (106)

WARDEN THELWATER
Stormwind (72), F-6, The Canals, Top of steps to stockade

WARDER STILGISS
Burning Steppes (22), Searing Gorge (64), C-4/D-8, Blackrock Depths

WARG DEEPWATER
Fisherman, Loch Modan (54), E-4, The Loch, In front of house on the western shore of loch

WARLEADER KRAZZILAK
Tanaris (78), F-3, Sandsorrow Watch, Atop watchtower

WARLORD GORETOOTH
Badlands (16), A-5, Kargath (116), Tower platform

WARLORD KOLKANIS
Rare Spawn, Durotar (34), F-8, Kolkar Crag, Lvl 9 Uncommon; Outside hut (left as you enter, middle of chasm to right, or in the back)

WARLORD KRELLIAN
Azshara (14), E-5, Temple of Zin-Malor, Dais in main temple

WARLORD KROM'ZAR
Barrens (18), E-3, Spawns near orc bunkers

WARLORD THRESH'JIN
Rare Spawn, Eastern Plaguelands (40), I-2, J-2, Mazra'Alor, Zul'Mashar, Lvl 58 Uncommon; Stands idle at spawn point

WARMASTER LAGGROND
Frostwolf Clan, Alterac Mountains (8), I-6, Alterac Valley, Cave

WAROSH
Burning Steppes (22), Searing Gorge (64), C-4/D-8, Blackrock Spire

WARPWOOD CRUSHER
Feralas (46), G-4, Dire Maul

WARPWOOD GUARDIAN
Feralas (46), G-4, Dire Maul

WARPWOOD MOSS FLAYER
Felwood (44), G-2, H:(2, 3), Irontree Cavern, Irontree Woods

WARPWOOD SHREDDER
Felwood (44), G-2, H:(2, 3), Irontree Cavern, Irontree Woods

WARPWOOD STOMPER
Feralas (46), G-4, Dire Maul

WARPWOOD TANGLER
Feralas (46), G-4, Dire Maul

WARPWOOD TREANT
Feralas (46), G-4, Dire Maul

WARSONG OUTRIDER
Ashenvale (12), L-5, Nightsong Woods, Southfury River, Warsong Lumber Camp

WARSONG RUNNER
Ashenvale (12), B-4, The Zoram Strand (137), Zoram'gar Outpost (137)

WARSONG SCOUT
Ashenvale (12), I-6, Nightsong Woods, Splintertree Post (129)

WARSONG SHREDDER
Ashenvale (12), I-7, K-5, Nightsong Woods, Warsong Labor Camp, Warsong Lumber Camp

WARUG
Desolace (30), J-7, Magram Village, Northeast of pool

WARUG'S BODYGUARD
Desolace (30), J-7, Magram Village, Northeast of pool

WASHTE PAWNE
Barrens (18), D-8, E:(7-8), Blackthorn Ridge, Southern Barrens, Roams clearing near Blackthorn Ridge

WASTEWANDER ASSASSIN
Tanaris (78), H-4, I:(3, 4), J-4, Waterspring Field, Wavestrider Beach

WASTEWANDER BANDIT
Tanaris (78), I:(2-4), Noonshade Ruins, Waterspring Field, Wavestrider Beach

WASTEWANDER ROGUE
Tanaris (78), H-4, I:(3, 4), Waterspring Field, Wavestrider Beach

WASTEWANDER SCOFFLAW
Tanaris (78), J-4, Wavestrider Beach

WASTEWANDER SHADOW MAGE
Tanaris (78), H-4, I:(2-4), J-4, Noonshade Ruins, Waterspring Field, Wavestrider Beach

WASTEWANDER THIEF
Tanaris (78), I:(2-4), Noonshade Ruins, Waterspring Field, Wavestrider Beach

WATCH COMMANDER ZALAPHIL
Rare Spawn, Durotar (34), I-6, Tiragarde Keep, Lvl 9 Uncommon; Receiving room of castle

WATCHER BACKUS
The Night Watch, Duskwood (36), J-4, Darkshire (108), Patrols between the north edge of Darkshire and the road up to the fork (J-3)

WATCHER BIGGS
Swamp of Sorrows (76), C-6, Idle next to carriage in southwestern swamp land

WATCHER BROWNELL
The Night Watch, Duskwood (36), J-4, Darkshire (108), Outside on the right of the Scarlet Raven Inn

WATCHER BUKOURIS
Duskwood (36), J-5

WATCHER CALLAHAN
The Night Watch, Duskwood (36), K-2, By carriage

WATCHER CORWIN
Duskwood (36), J-5, Darkshire (108)

WATCHER CUTFORD
Duskwood (36), J-5, F-6, Darkshire (108), Roams road

WATCHER DODDS
The Night Watch, Duskwood (36), F-7, By felled log in camp

WATCHER FRAZER
Duskwood (36), J-5, Darkshire (108)

WATCHER GELWIN
Duskwood (36), J-5, Darkshire (108), Patrols road from Darkshire to Rotting Orchard

WATCHER HARTIN
Duskwood (36), J-4, Darkshire (108)

WATCHER HUTCHINS
Duskwood (36), F-7, Darkshire (108)

WATCHER JAN
Duskwood (36), K-5, Darkshire (108)

WATCHER JORDEN
Duskwood (36), J-5, J-6, Darkshire (108), Roams road

WATCHER KEEFER
Duskwood (36), J-5, Darkshire (108)

WATCHER KELLER
Duskwood (36), K-4, Darkshire (108)

WATCHER LADIMORE
The Night Watch, Duskwood (36), J-5, Darkshire (108), Patrols around the center of town

WATCHER MAHAR BA
Blasted Lands (20), J-2, Nethergarde Keep (120), Top floor of tower facing entrance of keep

WATCHER MERANT
Duskwood (36), J-5, Darkshire (108), Patrols road from Darkshire to Rotting Orchard

WATCHER MOCARSKI
Duskwood (36), J-5, Darkshire (108)

WATCHER PAIGE
Duskwood (36), F-7, Darkshire (108), Crossroad south of Twilight Grove

WATCHER PETRAS
Duskwood (36), K-5, Darkshire (108), Roams road

WATCHER ROYCE
Duskwood (36), K-5, Darkshire (108)

WATCHER SARYS
Duskwood (36), J-5, Darkshire (108)

WATCHER SELKIN
Duskwood (36), J-5, Darkshire (108), Patrols road from Darkshire to Rotting Orchard

WATCHER THAYER
Duskwood (36), J-5, Darkshire (108), Patrols road from Darkshire to Rotting Orchard

WATCHER WOLLPERT
Duskwood (36), K-5, Darkshire (108)

WATCHMAN DOOMGRIP
Burning Steppes (22), Searing Gorge (64), C-4/D-8, Blackrock Depths

WATCHMASTER SORIGAL
Duskwood (36), K-5, Darkshire (108), By barrel filled carriage on the right side of road heading into Darkshire from the east

WATER SPIRIT
Silverpine Forest (68), F-4, The Tides Run, Coast of pond

WATERY INVADER
Winterspring (98), H-4, Lake Kel'Theril

WAVE STRIDER
Feralas (46), C-3, D:(3-5), E:(5-7), The Forgotten Coast

WAVETHRASHER
Azshara (14), G-4, H:(3, 4), I:(3, 4), J-4, K:(3, 4), L:(2-4)

WEAPON TECHNICIAN
Burning Steppes (22), Searing Gorge (64), C-4/D-8, Blackrock Depths

WEAVER
Swamp of Sorrows (76), I-5, The Temple of Atal'Hakkar

WEBWOOD LURKER
Teldrassil (80), F:(5, 6), G:(5, 6), H:(5, 6), I-6, Dolanaar (109), Lake Al'Ameth, Starbreeze Village

WEBWOOD SILKSPINNER
Teldrassil (80), D-3, E:(3-5), F:(3, 4), The Oracle Glade, Wellspring Lake, Wellspring River

WEBWOOD SPIDER
Teldrassil (80), G:(2, 3), H-3, Shadowglen (127), Shadowthread Cave

WEBWOOD VENOMFANG
Teldrassil (80), D-5, E:(5-8), F:(7, 8), G:(7, 8), H-7

WELDON BAROV
House of Barov, Western Plaguelands (92), E-8, Chillwind Camp (107), By well

WENDIGO
Dun Morogh (32), E:(4, 5), F-5, The Grizzled Den

WENIKEE BOLTBUCKET
Barrens (18), F-1, Outside tower near Ashenvale border

WENNA SILKBEARD
Special Goods Dealer, Wetlands (96), C-3, Sundown Marsh, Building next to windmill

WERG THICKBLADE
Leatherworking Supplies, Tirisfal Glades (86), K-7, The Bulwark (105), Camp on left side of road

WERG THICKBLADE
Western Plaguelands (92), C-6, The Bulwark (105)

WESLEY
Stable Master, Hillsbrad Foothills (48), F-6, Southshore (129), Right of inn by mailbox

WESTFALL WOODWORKER
Westfall (94), F-5, Sentinel Hill (126)

WETLANDS CROCOLISK
Wetlands (96), B:(3, 5, 6), C:(3, 4, 6), D:(2, 3), E:(3, 4), F:(3, 4), G-4

WHARFMASTER DIZZYWIG
Barrens (18), H-4, Ratchet (122), Dock

WHARFMASTER LOZGIL
Stranglethorn Vale (74), B-8, Booty Bay (103), On dock near ship launch on the northern side of bay

WHIP LASHER
Feralas (46), G-4, Dire Maul

WHIRLING INVADER
Silithus (66), D:(1, 2), E:(1, 2), The Crystal Vale, Ravaged Twilight Base Camp

WHIRLWIND RIPPER
Desolace (30), D-7, E:(2-4, 6-8), F:(1-4, 7), G:(2-4, 6, 7), H:(3, 4, 6), I:(5-7), J:(5, 6)

WHIRLWIND SHREDDER
Desolace (30), C:(7, 8), D:(7, 8), E-8, F-9, G:(8, 9), H:(7-9), Gelkis Village, Mannoroc Coven, Sar'theris Strand

WHIRLWIND STORMWALKER
Desolace (30), D-4, E:(4-6), F:(4-6), G:(4, 5), H:(4-6), J:(1, 4, 5), K:(2, 4, 5)

WHISKEY SLIM
Blackwater Raiders, Stranglethorn Vale (74), B-8, Booty Bay (103), First floor of The Salty Sailor Tavern

WHIT WANTMAL
Duskwood (36), K-4, Darkshire (108), First house on the right side of road heading into Darkshire from the east

WHUUT
Alchemist Trainer, Orgrimmar (60), G-3, The Drag, Yelmak's Alchemy and Potions

WIGCIK
Superior Fisherman, Stranglethorn Vale (74), B-8, Booty Bay (103), In building on first level along the southern side of the bay

WIK'TAR
Fish Merchant & Supplies, Ashenvale (12), B-4, Zoram'gar Outpost (137), Outside western structure

WILD BUCK
Ashenvale (12), B:(2-4), C:(2-4), D:(2-4)

WILD GRELL
Darkshore (24), G-4, Bashal'Aran

WILD GRYPHON
Hillsbrad Foothills (48), J-3, K:(3, 4), Durnholde Keep, Behind keep

WILDER THISTLENETTLE
Stormwind (72), J-2, Dwarven District, Tavern

WILDHAMMER SENTRY
The Hinterlands (50), B-5, Aerie Peak (100)

WILDSPAWN BETRAYER
Feralas (46), G-4, Dire Maul

WILDSPAWN FELSWORN
Feralas (46), G-4, Dire Maul

WILDSPAWN HELLCALLER
Feralas (46), G-4, Dire Maul

WILDSPAWN IMP
Feralas (46), G-4, Dire Maul

WILDSPAWN ROGUE
Feralas (46), G-4, Dire Maul

WILDSPAWN SATYR
Feralas (46), G-4, Dire Maul

WILDSPAWN SHADOWSTALKER
Feralas (46), G-4, Dire Maul

WILDSPAWN TRICKSTER
Feralas (46), G-4, Dire Maul

WILDTHORN LURKER
Ashenvale (12), J:(5, 6), K:(4-6), L:(5, 6)

WILDTHORN STALKER
Ashenvale (12), B-5, C:(4-6), D:(4-6), E:(3-6), F:(4, 5), H:(7, 8), I:(7, 8), J:(6, 7)

WILDTHORN VENOMSPITTER
Ashenvale (12), G:(6, 7), H:(5-7), I:(5, 6)

WILEY THE BLACK
Redridge Mountains (62), C-4, Lakeshire (117), Second floor of Lakeshire Inn

WILHELM STRANG
Mail Armor Merchant, Stormwind (72), K-5, Old Town, Limited Immunity

WILLIAM MACGREGOR
Bowyer, Westfall (94), G-5, Sentinel Hill (126), At intersection east of the Sentinel Tower

WILLIAM MONTAGUE
Banker, Undercity (88), I-4, The Trade Quarter

WILLIAM PESTLE
Elwynn Forest (42), F-7, Goldshire (114), First floor of Lion's Pride Inn

WILLIDEN MARSHAL
Un'Goro Crater (90), F-1, Marshal's Refuge (118), Entrance to cave

WILLIX THE IMPORTER
Barrens (18), E-9, Razorfen Kraul

WILLOW
Twilight's Hammer, Desolace (30), H-4, Kormek's Hut, Inside hut

WILMA RANTHAL
Skinning Trainer, Redridge Mountains (62), L-7, Camp

WIND HOWLER
Barrens (18), E-9, Razorfen Kraul

WINDCALLER KALDON
Silithus (67), G-5, Cenarion Hold (106)

WINDCALLER PROUDHORN
Silithus (67), G-4, Cenarion Hold (106)

WINDCALLER YESSENDRA
Silithus (67), G-4, Cenarion Hold (106)

WINDFURY HARPY
Mulgore (58), C-4, D-4, H-7, The Rolling Plains

WINDFURY MATRIARCH
Mulgore (58), C:(2, 3), D-1, F-1, G:(1, 2), The Golden Plains, Windfury Ridge

WINDFURY SORCERESS
Mulgore (58), C:(2, 3), D-1, F-1, G:(1, 2), The Golden Plains, Windfury Ridge

WINDFURY WIND WITCH
Mulgore (58), C-4, D-4, H-7, The Rolling Plains

WINDSHEAR DIGGER
Stonetalon Mountains (70), I-6, J-6, Blackwolf River, Windshear Crag, Windshear Mine

WINDSHEAR GEOMANCER
Stonetalon Mountains (70), I-6, J-6, Blackwolf River, Windshear Crag, Windshear Mine

WINDSHEAR OVERLORD
Stonetalon Mountains (70), I-6, J-6, Blackwolf River, Windshear Crag, Windshear Mine

WINDSHEAR STONECUTTER
Stonetalon Mountains (70), I-6, Windshear Mine

WINDSHEAR TUNNEL RAT
Stonetalon Mountains (70), I-6, Windshear Mine

WINDSHEAR VERMIN
Stonetalon Mountains (70), I-6, Windshear Mine

WINIFRED KERWIN
Undercity (88), K-1, The Magic Quarter, Green circle west of Skull Building

WINKEY
Tanaris (78), I-6, Southbreak Shore, Small island off coast

WINNA HAZZARD
Felwood (44), E-5, Bloodvenom Post (102), Up hill

WINSTONE WOLFE
, Hillsbrad Foothills (48), K-2, , First floor of Chateau Ravenholdt

WINTER WOLF
Dun Morogh (32), D-4, E-5, F:(4, 5), G:(4, 5), Iceflow Lake, Kharanos (116), Steelgrill's Depot

WINTERFALL AMBUSHER
Winterspring (98), E-4, Timbermaw Post

WINTERFALL DEN WATCHER
Winterspring (98), E-4, F-4, J:(3, 4), Timbermaw Post, Timbermaw Village

WINTERFALL PATHFINDER
Winterspring (98), E:(3, 4), F-4, Timbermaw Post

WINTERFALL RUNNER
Felwood (44), H-1, Felpaw Village, Northwest camp

WINTERFALL RUNNER
Winterspring (98), D-3, Roams between Felwood entrance and Winterfall Village

WINTERFALL SHAMAN
Winterspring (98), J:(3, 4), Winterspring Village

WINTERFALL TOTEMIC
Winterspring (98), D-4, E-4, F-4, Timbermaw Post

WINTERFALL URSA
Winterspring (98), J-4, Winterspring Village

WINTERSPRING OWL
Winterspring (98), H:(3, 5), I:(3-5), J:(3-5)

WINTERSPRING SCREECHER
Winterspring (98), H-2, I:(1-3, 5, 6)

WIRY SWOOP
Mulgore (58), D:(5-8), E-7, F:(6, 7), G:(6, 7), Palemane Rock, Stonebull Lake, Winterhoof Water Well

WITCH DOCTOR JIN'ZIL
Stonetalon Mountains (70), J-9, Malaka'jin, Inside den

WITCH DOCTOR MAU'RI
Orgrimmar (60), D-8, Valley of Spirit, On center stepping stone in pond

WITCH DOCTOR MAV'ARI
Winterspring (98), I-4, Everlook (110)

WITCH DOCTOR UNBAGWA
Stranglethorn Vale (74), C-6, Spirit Den, Cave

WITCH DOCTOR UZER'I
Feralas (46), I-4, Camp Mojache (105), Outside big western tent

WITCH DOCTOR ZUM'RAH
Tanaris (78), E-1, Zul'Farrak

WITCHWING AMBUSHER
Barrens (18), D:(1, 2), The Dry Hills

WITCHWING HARPY
Barrens (18), D:(1, 2), E:(1, 2), The Dry Hills

WITCHWING ROGUEFEATHER
Barrens (18), D:(1, 2), E:(1, 2), The Dry Hills

WITCHWING SLAYER
Barrens (18), D:(1, 2), The Dry Hills

WITCHWING WINDCALLER
Barrens (18), D:(1, 2), The Dry Hills

WITHERBARK AXE THROWER
Arathi Highlands (10), H-7, I:(6, 7), J-6, Witherbark Village

WITHERBARK BERSERKER
Arathi Highlands (10), C:(6, 7)

WITHERBARK BROODGUARD
The Hinterlands (50), D-7, E:(6, 7), F:(6, 7), Shadra'Alor

WITHERBARK CALLER
The Hinterlands (50), E:(7, 8), F:(6, 7), Shadra'Alor

WITHERBARK HEADHUNTER
Arathi Highlands (10), H-7, I:(7, 8), J:(4, 6-8), K-4, Witherbark Village

WITHERBARK HIDESKINNER
The Hinterlands (50), D-6, E-6, Hiri'Watha

WITHERBARK SADIST
The Hinterlands (50), E:(6, 7), F-7, Shadra'Alor

WITHERBARK SCALPER
The Hinterlands (50), C:(5, 6), D:(5, 6), Zan'Watha

WITHERBARK SHADOW HUNTER
Arathi Highlands (10), I-8, J:(7, 8), Witherbark Village

WITHERBARK SHADOWCASTER
Arathi Highlands (10), D:(4-5), E:(4-5), J-4, K-4, Witherbark Village

WITHERBARK TROLL
Arathi Highlands (10), D:(4, 5), E:(4, 5), J-4, K-4, Witherbark Village

WITHERBARK VENOMBLOOD
The Hinterlands (50), D-6, E-6, Hiri'Watha

WITHERBARK WITCH DOCTOR
Arathi Highlands (10), D:(4, 5), H-7, I:(6, 7), J:(6, 7), Witherbark Village

WITHERBARK ZEALOT
The Hinterlands (50), C-6, D:(5, 6), Zan'Watha

WITHERED ANCIENT
Ashenvale (12), G:(3, 4), H:(4, 5), Nightsong Woods, Raynewood Retreat

WITHERED BATTLE BOAR
Barrens (18), F-9, Razorfen Downs

WITHERED PROTECTOR
Felwood (44), G-3, Irontree Woods

WITHERED QUILGUARD
Barrens (18), F-9, Razorfen Downs

WITHERED REAVER
Barrens (18), F-9, Razorfen Downs

WITHERED SPEARHIDE
Barrens (18), F-9, Razorfen Downs

WITHERED WARRIOR
Barrens (18), F-9, Razorfen Downs

WITHERHEART THE STALKER
Rare Spawn, The Hinterlands (50), E-7, Shadra'Alor, Lvl 45 Semi-Rare; Patrols while stealthed around small pond

WITHERVINE BARK RIPPER
Dustwallow Marsh (38), D:(2, 3, 5), E:(2-4), F-2, G:(2, 3), H-2, Bluefen, Brackenwall Village (104), The Quagmire

WITHERVINE CREEPER
Dustwallow Marsh (38), D-2, E-2, F-2, G:(2, 3), H-2, Bluefen

WITHERVINE MIRE BEAST
Dustwallow Marsh (38), D:(3, 5), E:(3-6), F:(5, 6), The Dragonmurk, The Quagmire

WITHERVINE RAGER
Dustwallow Marsh (38), D-5, E:(5, 6), F:(5, 6), The Dragonmurk, The Quagmire

WIXXRAK
Weaponsmith & Gunsmith, Winterspring (98), I-4, Everlook (110), Inside northeast building

WIZBANG CRANKTOGGLE
Darkshore (24), F-4, Auberdine (101), Third floor of inn

WIZLO BEARINGSHINER
Thousand Needles (82), B-3, Whitereach Post, Next to hut

WIZZLE BRASSBOLTS
Thousand Needles (82), K-8, Mirage Raceway (119), West of racetrack

WIZZLECRANK'S SHREDDER
Barrens (18), G-1, The Sludge Fen, North side of Sludge Fen

WOLF MASTER NANDOS
Silverpine Forest (68), F-7, Shadowfang Keep

WOLFGUARD WORG
Silverpine Forest (68), F-7, Shadowfang Keep

WOO PING
Weapon Master, Stormwind (72), H-6, Trade District, Weller's Arsenal, Trains: Crossbows, Daggers, Polearms, Staves, 1H Swords, & 2H Swords

WOOD LURKER
Loch Modan (54), H:(2, 3), J:(3, 4), K-4

WOODPAW ALPHA
Feralas (46), E-4, H:(5, 6), I:(5, 6), J-6

WOODPAW BRUTE
Feralas (46), E-4, H-5, I:(4, 5), J-5

WOODPAW MONGREL
Feralas (46), H-5, I:(4, 5), J-5, Grimtotem Compound, Lower Wilds, Woodpaw Hills

WOODPAW MYSTIC
Feralas (46), E-4, H:(5, 6), I:(5, 6), J-6

WOODPAW REAVER
Feralas (46), E-4, H:(5, 6), I:(5, 6), J-6

WOODPAW TRAPPER
Feralas (46), H-5, I:(4, 5), J-5, Grimtotem Compound, Lower Wilds, Woodpaw Hills

WOODSMAN
Eastern Plaguelands (40), G-2, Quel'Lithien Lodge

WOOLY KODO
Barrens (18), E:(6, 8), Wooly Kodo

WORB STRONGSTITCH
Light Armor Merchant, Feralas (46), I-4, Camp Mojache (105), Big western tent

WORG
Silverpine Forest (68), F-5, G:(4, 5), I-1, J-1, Thoughout Silverpine

WRAHK
Tailoring Supplies, Barrens (18), F-3, The Crossroads (107), Southern entrance

WRATH HAMMER CONSTRUCT
Burning Steppes (22), Searing Gorge (64), C-4/D-8, Blackrock Depths

WRATHTAIL MYRMIDON
Ashenvale (12), A:(2, 3), B-3, The Zoram Strand (137), Zoram'gar Outpost (137)

WRATHTAIL PRIESTESS
Ashenvale (12), A:(2, 3), B-3, The Zoram Strand (137), Zoram'gar Outpost (137)

WRATHTAIL RAZORTAIL
Ashenvale (12), A-3, B:(2, 3), The Zoram Strand (137), Zoram'gar Outpost (137)

WRATHTAIL SEA WITCH
Ashenvale (12), A:(2, 3), B:(2, 3), The Zoram Strand (137), Zoram'gar Outpost (137)

WRATHTAIL SORCERESS
Ashenvale (12), A:(2, 3), B:(2, 3), The Zoram Strand (137)

WRATHTAIL WAVE RIDER
Ashenvale (12), A:(2, 3), B:(2, 3), The Zoram Strand (137), Zoram'gar Outpost (137)

WREN DARKSPRING
Demon Trainer, Dun Morogh (32), D-7, Coldridge Valley (107), Anvilmar

WRENIX THE WRETCHED
Barrens (18), H-4, Ratchet (122), Shack northeast of town

WRENIX'S GIZMOTRONIC APPARATUS
Barrens (18), H-4, Ratchet (122), Shack northeast of town

WRETCHED ZOMBIE
Tirisfal Glades (86), C-6, D-6, Deathknell (109)

WRINKLE GOODSTEEL
Superior Armor Crafter, Tanaris (78), G-3, Gadgetzan (113), Western structure

WRITHING HIGHBORNE
Darkshore (24), F-6, G-6, Ameth'Aran

WRITHING MAGE
Hillsbrad Foothills (48), A-8, Purgation Isle, Island

WU SHEN
Warrior Trainer, Stormwind (72), L:(4, 5), Old Town, Command Center

WUARK
Armorer & Shieldcrafter, Durotar (34), H-4, Razor Hill (124), Northeast of inn

WULAN
Cooking Supplies, Desolace (30), C-7, Shadowprey Village (128), Top of tall eastern structure

WUNNA DARKMANE
Trade Goods, Mulgore (58), E-6, Bloodhoof Village (102), Northeast tent

WYND NIGHTCHASER
Winterspring (98), H-3, Starfall Village (130), Terrace of main building

WYNNE LARSON
Robe Merchant, Stormwind (72), F-8, Mage Quarter, Larson Clothiers

WYRMKIN DREAMWALKER
Swamp of Sorrows (76), H:(5, 6), I:(6, 7), K:(5-7), L:(5, 6)

WYRMKIN FIREBRAND
Wetlands (96), L:(5, 6), Grim Batol

X

XABRAXXIS
Darkshore (24), H-3, Cliffspring Falls, South of river

XAI'ANDER
Weaponsmith, Ashenvale (12), E-5, Astranaar (101), Left as you enter southwest building

XANDAR GOODBEARD
General Supplies, Loch Modan (54), K-6, The Farstrider Lodge (111), Center of lodge

XANIS FLAMEWEAVER
Thunder Bluff (84), B-2, Spirit Rise, Sitting in front of Hall of Spirits

XAN'TIS
Snake Vendor, Orgrimmar (60), A-6, C-8, Valley of Spirit, Roams Valley of Spirits

XAO'TSU
Pet Trainer, Orgrimmar (61), H-2

XAR'TI
Raptor Riding Trainer, Durotar (34), H-7, Sen'jin Village (126), Among raptors south of village

XAVARIC
Felwood (44), E:(2-3), Jadefire Run, Western camp in hills

XAVATHRAS
Felwood (44), E-7, Ruins of Constellas, Western camp near cliff edge

XAVIAN BETRAYER
Ashenvale (12), J:(4, 5), Satyrnaar, Xavian

XAVIAN FELSWORN
Ashenvale (12), J:(4, 5), Satyrnaar, Xavian

XAVIAN ROGUE
Ashenvale (12), J:(4, 5), Satyrnaar, Xavian

XEN'TO
Cooking Supplier, Orgrimmar (60), G-5, The Drag, Borstan's Firepit

XEN'ZILLA
Stonetalon Mountains (70), I-9, Malaka'jin, Small structure

XIGGS FUSELIGHTER
Ironforge (52), J-9, The Military Ward, Hall of Arms

XIGGS FUSELIGHTER'S FLYINGMACHINE
Azshara (14), K-9, The Ruined Reaches, East of landing pad

XIZK GOODSTITCH
Tailoring Supplies, Stranglethorn Vale (74), B-8, Booty Bay (103), A Tailor to Cities (shop)

XIZZER FIZZBOLT
Engineering Supplies, Winterspring (98), I-4, Everlook (110), Inside building directly south of entrance

XOA'TSU
Pet Trainer, Orgrimmar (60), H:(1, 2), Valley of Honor, Behind Hunter's Hall

XON'CHA
Stable Master, Orgrimmar (60), I:(1-2), Valley of Honor, Outside o Hunter's Hall

XOR'JUUL
Hunter Trainer, Orgrimmar (60), H-2, Valley of Honor, Hunter's Hall

XOROTHIAN DREADSTEED
Feralas (46), G-4, Dire Maul

XOROTHIAN IMP
Feralas (46), G-4, Dire Maul

XT:4
Stonetalon Mountains (70), I-5, Windshear Crag, East of logging camp

XT:9
Stonetalon Mountains (70), G-5, H:(5-6), Windshear Crag, West and south of turn in river

X'YERA
Priest Trainer, Orgrimmar (60), D-9, Valley of Spirit, Spirit Lodge, top floor

XYLINNIA STARSHINE
Expert Enchanter, Feralas (46), C-4, Feathermoon Stronghold (111), Southeast of inn

Y

YALDA
Darkshore (24), F-4, Auberdine (101), House on hill

YAMA SNOWHOOF
Ashenvale (12), I-6, Splintertree Post (129), Inn

YANNI STOUTHEART
General Supplies, Loch Modan (54), D-5, Thelsamar (134), Stoutlager Inn

YARLYN AMBERSTILL
Pet Vendor, Dun Morogh (32), I-5, Amberstill Ranch, Patrols circular path around ranch

YARR HAMMERSTONE
Mining Trainer, Dun Morogh (32), G-5, Steelgrill's Depot, Basement of right building

YARROG BANESHADOW
Durotar (34), G-6, Burning Blade Coven, On ledge in back of cave

YAW SHARPMANE
Hunter Trainer, Mulgore (58), E-6, Bloodhoof Village (102), North tents

YEH'KINYA
Tanaris (78), J-2, Steamwheedle Port, Outside northern building

YELMAK
Alchemist Trainer, Orgrimmar (60), G-3, The Drag, Yelmak's Alchemy and Potions

YELNAGI BLACKARM
Durotar (34), H-4, Razor Hill (124), Inn

YENNIKU
Darkspear Hostage, Stranglethorn Vale (74), D-6, Ruins of Aboraz, Northwestern corner of ruins

YLDAN
Bag Merchant, Darnassus (26), I-5, Tradesmen's Terrace, Bags shop

YONADA
Tailoring & Leatherworking Supplies, Barrens (18), F-6, Camp Taurajo (106), Southern building

YONN DEEPCUT
Skinner, Mulgore (58), E-6, Bloodhoof Village (102), Northeast tent

YORBA SCREWSPIGOT
Tanaris (78), J-2, Steamwheedle Port, Southern building

YORI CRACKHELM
Dun Morogh (32), D-7, Coldridge Valley (107), Next to caravan

YORUS BARLEYBREW
Redridge Mountains (62), C-4, Lakeshire (117), First floor of Lakeshire Inn

YOUNG ARIKARA
Thousand Needles (82), F-5, Freewind Post (112), Next to western bridge

YOUNG BLACK BEAR
Dun Morogh (32), D-6, E:(6, 7), F:(4-7), G-5, I-1, Kharanos (116), Steelgrill's Depot, The Grizzled Den

YOUNG BLACK RAVAGER
Duskwood (36), B:(6-8), C:(6-8), D-6, E-6, F:(6-8), G:(6, 7), H-6, I-3, J-3, Brightwood Grove

YOUNG CHIMAERA
Stonetalon Mountains (70), C-6, D-6, E-6, The Charred Vale

YOUNG DIEMETRADON
Un'Goro Crater (90), G-2, H:(3, 4), I:(3, 4), J:(2-4, 6, 7), Lakkari Tar Pits, The Marshlands

YOUNG FLESHRIPPER
Westfall (94), D:(2, 3), E:(2-4), F:(4), G:(1-4)

YOUNG FOREST BEAR
Elwynn Forest (42), C:(7-9), E-9, F:(7-9), G:(7, 8), H:(7, 8), I:(6-8), J:(6-8), K:(6, 8), L:(6-8)

YOUNG GORETUSK
Westfall (94), C:(3, 4), D:(2-4), E:(2-4), F:(2-5), G:(1-4)

YOUNG JUNGLE STALKER
Stranglethorn Vale (74), C-5, Gurubashi Arena, The Cape of Stranglethorn

YOUNG LASHTAIL RAPTOR
Stranglethorn Vale (74), C-3, Grom'gol Base Camp (114), The Savage Coast

YOUNG MESA BUZZARD
Arathi Highlands (10), B:(4, 5), C:(2, 4), D:(2, 3), E:(4, 6), F-6, G:(4, 5), I:(4, 5), J-5, Along hills

YOUNG MOONKIN
Darkshore (24), F:(4, 5), G:(4, 5)

YOUNG MURK THRESHER
Dustwallow Marsh (38), F:(3, 4), G:(4, 5), H:(4, 5), Dustwallow Bay

YOUNG NIGHT WEB SPIDER
Tirisfal Glades (86), C:(5, 6), Deathknell (109)

YOUNG NIGHTSABER
Teldrassil (80), G-4, H:(4, 5), Shadowglen (127)

YOUNG PANTHER
Stranglethorn Vale (74), C-2, D:(1, 2), E:(1, 2), Kurzen's Compound, Tkashi Ruins

YOUNG PRIDEWING
Stonetalon Mountains (70), H-6, J:(4, 5), The Talondeep Path, Windshear Crag

YOUNG REEF CRAWLER
Darkshore (24), E:(5, 6), F:(3, 5), Mist's Edge, The Long Wash, Twilight Shore

YOUNG SAWTOOTH CROCOLISK
Swamp of Sorrows (76), C:(4, 5), D:(3-5), E:(3-5)

YOUNG SCAVENGER
Tirisfal Glades (86), C:(6, 7), D:(6, 7), Deathknell (109)

YOUNG STRANGLETHORN RAPTOR
Stranglethorn Vale (74), B-2, Ruins of Zul'Kunda, The Savage Coast

YOUNG STRANGLETHORN TIGER
Stranglethorn Vale (74), C:(1, 2), D:(1, 2), Nesingwary's Expedition, Rebel Camp (124), Tkashi Ruins

YOUNG THISTLE BOAR
Teldrassil (80), G-4, H:(4, 5), Shadowglen (127)

YOUNG THRESHADON
Loch Modan (54), F:(3-6), H:(4, 5), The Loch

YOUNG WAVETHRASHER
Azshara (14), E:(1, 2), F:(1, 2), G-1, H-1, I-1, J-1, K:(1, 2), L:(1, 2), Jagged Reef

YOUNG WENDIGO
Dun Morogh (32), E-5, F-5, The Grizzled Den

YOUNG WETLANDS CROCOLISK
Wetlands (96), A-5, B:(4-6), C:(3, 4), D:(3, 4), E-4, G:(3, 4), H:(4-7), I:(6, 7)

YOUNG WOLF
Elwynn Forest (42), E-6, F:(4-6), G-4, Echo Ridge Mine, Northshire Valley (122)

YOWLER
Redridge Mountains (62), B-3, Redridge Canyons, With several gnolls in camp

YUGREK
Wind Rider Master, Winterspring (98), I-4, Everlook (110), Northwest of town

YUKA SCREWSPIGOT
Burning Steppes (22), H-2, Flame Crest (112), Cave

YVETTE FARTHING
Tirisfal Glades (86), H-5, Brill (104), First floor of Gallows' End Tavern

Z

ZACHARIAH POST
Undead Horse Merchant, Tirisfal Glades (86), H-5, Brill (104), Stable

ZAELDARR THE OUTCAST
Eastern Plaguelands (40), D-8, The Undercroft, Crypt

ZAETAR'S SPIRIT
Desolace (30), D-5, Mauradon

ZALAS WITHERBARK
Rare Spawn, Arathi Highlands (10), J-8, Witherbark Village, Lvl 40 Uber-Rare; Cave south of village

ZALASHJI
Tanaris (78), J-3, Zalashji's Den, Cave on coast

ZALAZANE
Durotar (34), J-9, Echo Isles, Roams southern part of village

ZALDIMAR WEFHELLT
Mage Trainer, Elwynn Forest (42), F-7, Goldshire (114), Second floor of Lion's Pride Inn

ZAMAEL LUNTHISTLE
Searing Gorge (64), C-3, Firewatch Ridge, Cage next to lava pool

ZAMAN
Loramus's Guardian, Azshara (14), H-7, Bay of Storms, Patrols near Loramus

ZAMEK
Thousand Needles (82), K-8, Mirage Raceway (119), Inside racetrack, next to building

ZAMJA
Cooking Trainer, Orgrimmar (60), G-5, The Drag, Borstan's Firepit

ZAN SHIVSPROKET
Speciality Engineer, Hillsbrad Foothills (48), K-2, Basement of Chateau Ravenholdt

ZANARA
Bowyer, Dustwallow Marsh (38), D-3, Brackenwall Village (104), West entrance

ZANDALAR ENFORCER
Stranglethorn Vale (74), A-2, Yojamba Isle

ZANDALAR HEADSHRINKER
Stranglethorn Vale (74), A-2, Yojamba Isle

ZANDALARIAN EMISSARY
Stranglethorn Vale (74), B-8, Booty Bay (103)

ZANDO'ZAN
Orgrimmar (60), E-5, The Cleft of Shadow, Shadowswift Brotherhood

ZANE BRADFORD
Wand Vendor, Undercity (88), J-3, The Magic Quarter

ZANGEN STONEHOOF
Thunder Bluff (84), F-5, High rise, in the center of the rise

ZANKAJA
Orgrimmar (60), D-6, Valley of Strength, Near highest bridge from Skytower

ZANNOK HIDEPIERCER
Leatherworking Supplies, Silithus (66), K-2, Valor's Rest (137), South of road

ZANSOA
Fishing Supplies, Durotar (34), H-7, Sen'jin Village (126), Main floor of big hut

ZANZIL HUNTER
Stranglethorn Vale (74), C-5, D-6, Ruins of Jubuwal

ZANZIL NAGA
Stranglethorn Vale (74), C-5, D-6, Ruins of Jubuwal

ZANZIL THE OUTCAST
Stranglethorn Vale (74), D-6, Ruins of Aboraz, By bonfire in ruins

ZANZIL WITCH DOCTOR
Stranglethorn Vale (74), C-5, D-6, Ruins of Jubuwal

ZANZIL ZOMBIE
Stranglethorn Vale (74), C-5, D-6, Ruins of Jubuwal

ZAP FARLINGER
Unbalanced Engineer, Winterspring (98), I-4, Everlook (110), Transporter outside of bank

ZAPETTA
Zeppelin Master, Tirisfal Glades (86), H-6, Zepplin tower just north of Undercity

ZARDETH OF THE BLACK CLAW
Stormwind (72), D-8, Mage Quarter, The Slaughtered Lamb

ZARENA CROMWIND
Superior Weaponsmith, Stranglethorn Vale (74), B-8, Booty Bay (103), Cuts-n-Bruises Incorporated (shop) on the southern side of The Old Port Authority

ZARGH
Butcher, Barrens (18), F-3, The Crossroads (107), East of inn

ZARICOTL
Rare Spawn, Badlands (16), E:(5, 6), H-6, The Dustbowl, Mirage Flats, Lvl 55 Uncommon; Roams small area around spawn point

ZARISE
Bat Handler, Hillsbrad Foothills (48), G-2, Tarren Mill (133), To the left just outside town

ZARLMAN TWO-MOONS
Mulgore (58), E-6, Bloodhoof Village (102), Northern clearing

ZARRIN
Cook, Teldrassil (80), G-6, Dolanaar (109), Next to cauldron southeast of inn

ZARUK
Arathi Highlands (10), J-4, Hammerfall (115), Inside fence east building

ZAYUS
High Priest, Orgrimmar (60), D-9, Valley of Spirit, Spirit Lodge, top floor

ZAZO
Orgrimmar (60), G-7, Valley of Strength, Inn

ZEAL'AYA
Herbalism Supplier, Orgrimmar (60), G-4, The Drag, Jandi's Arboretum

ZEGGON BOTSNAP
Arena Battlemaster, Orgrimmar (61), J-3

ZEKKIS
Swamp of Sorrows (76), I-5, The Temple of Atal'Hakkar

ZEL'MAK
Warrior Trainer, Orgrimmar (60), J-3, Valley of Honor, Hall of the Brave

ZEM LEEWARD
Redridge Mountains (62), C-5, Lakeshire (117), Straight dock west of the bridge

ZENDO'JIAN
Weapon Vendor, Orgrimmar (60), K-2, Valley of Honor, Arms of Legend

ZENGU
Arathi Highlands (10), J-3, Hammerfall (115), Platform of north building

ZENN FOULHOOF
Teldrassil (80), H-6, West of main road, south of intersection to Starbreeze Village

ZERILLIS
Rare Spawn, Wetlands (96), E-1, Zul'Farrak, Lvl 45 Rare

ZERILLIS
Tanaris (78), E-1, Zul'Farrak

ZEVRIM THORNHOOF
Feralas (46), G-4, Dire Maul

ZEVROST
Warlock Trainer, Orgrimmar (60), F-5, The Cleft of Shadow, Darkfire Enclave

ZGGI
Zardeth's Minion, Stormwind (72), D-8, Mage Quarter, The Slaughtered Lamb

ZHEVRA CHARGER
Barrens (18), D:(2, 3), E:(1, 2, 4-7), F:(5, 6), G:(1, 3, 5), H:(3, 5)

ZHEVRA RUNNER
Barrens (18), E:(2-5), F:(1-4), G:(2-4), H:(2-4)

ZIGGURAT PROTECTOR
Eastern Plaguelands (40), C-2, D:(3, 4), E-4, F-3, Plaguewood

ZIKKEL
Banker, Barrens (18), H-4, Ratchet (122), Bank

ZILZIBIN DRUMLORE
Orgrimmar (60), G-5, The Drag, Building south of Jandi's Arboretum

ZIXIL
Merchant Supreme, Hillsbrad Foothills (48), G-3, Patrols with Overwatch Mark I between Tarren Mill and Southshore

ZIZ FIZZIKS
Stonetalon Mountains (70), G-6, Windshear Crag, In small house in mountains, just north of Webwinder Path

ZIZZEK
Fisherman, Barrens (18), H-4, Ratchet (122), Front of inn

ZJOLNIR
Raptor Handler, Durotar (34), H-7, Sen'jin Village (126), Among raptors south of village

ZLAGK
Butcher, Durotar (34), F-7, Valley of Trials (136), Northwest structure

ZNORT
Arathi Highlands (10), I-3, Circle of East Binding, Patrols with Fozruck to each of the four Circles of Binding

ZOLO
Swamp of Sorrows (76), I-5, The Temple of Atal'Hakkar

ZOR LONETREE
Elder Far Seer, Orgrimmar (60), D-4, Valley of Wisdom, Grommash Hold

ZORA
Rare Spawn, Silithus (66), D-4, Hive'Zora, Lvl 59 Average Rare; Roams hive

ZORBIN FANDAZZLE
Feralas (46), E-4, The Forgotten Coast, Tent near dock

ZUDD
Pet Trainer, Stranglethorn Vale (74), C-Grom'gol Base Camp (114), By crates inside camp walls to the left of western entrance

ZUKK'ASH STINGER
Feralas (46), I-6, J-6, The Writhing Deep

ZUKK'ASH TUNNELER
Feralas (46), I:(6, 7), J-6, The Writhing Deep

ZUKK'ASH WASP
Feralas (46), I-6, The Writhing Deep

ZUKK'ASH WORKER
Feralas (46), I-6, The Writhing Deep

ZUL'AREK HATEFOWLER
Rare Spawn, The Hinterlands (50), D-6, E-6, Hiri'Watha, Zun'Watha, Lvl 43 Uncommon; Roams small area around spawn point

ZUL'BRIN WARPBRANCH
Rare Spawn, Eastern Plaguelands (40), I-2, J-2, Mazra'Alor, Zul'Mashar, Lvl 59 Semi-Rare; Stands idle at spawn point

ZUL'FARRAK DEAD HERO
Tanaris (78), E-1, Zul'Farrak

ZUL'FARRAK ZOMBIE
Tanaris (78), E-1, Zul'Farrak

ZUL'LOR
Swamp of Sorrows (76), I-5, The Temple of Atal'Hakkar

ZULRG
Weaponsmith, Dustwallow Marsh (38), D-3, Brackenwall Village (104), Center of village

ZUN'DARTHA
Swamp of Sorrows (76), F-5, Stonard (131), Right of entrance to inn

ZUREETHA FARGAZE
Durotar (34), F-7, Valley of Trials (136), Structure to south

ZUZUBEE
Race Announcer, Thousand Needles (82), K-8, Mirage Raceway (119), Grandstands at drag strip

ZZARC' VUL
Duskwood (36), E-8, Vul'Gol Ogre Mound, Roams small area around spawn point

FLIGHT MASTERS

ALLIANCE

REGION	MINI REGION	GRID LOC
Arathi Highlands (10)	Refuge Pointe (124)	F-5
Ashenvale (12)	Astranaar (101)	E-5
Azshara (14)	Talrendis Point	A-8
Blasted Lands (20)	Nethergarde Keep (120)	J-2
Burning Steppes (22)	Morgan's Vigil (120)	K-7
Darkshore (24)	Auberdine (101)	F-4
Desolace (30)	Nijel's Point (121)	H-1
Duskwood (36)	Darkshire (108)	K-4
Dustwallow Marsh (38)	Mudsproccket (120)	F-7
	Theramore Isle (135)	I-5
Eastern Plaguelands (40)	Light's Hope Chapel (116)	K-6
Felwood (44)	Emerald Sanctuary (110)	G-8
	Talonbranch Glade (133)	H-3
Feralas (46)	Feathermoon Stronghold (111)	C-4
	Thalanaar	K-5
Hillsbrad Foothills (48)	Southshore (129)	F-5
Hinterlands (50)	Aerie Peak (100)	B-5
Ironforge (52)	The Great Forge	G-5
Loch Modan (54)	Thelsamar (129)	D-5
Moonglade (56)		G-7
Redridge Mountains (62)	Lakeshire (117)	D-6
Searing Gorge (64)	Thorium Point (136)	D-3
Silithus (66)	Cenarion Hold (106)	G-3
Stonetalon Mountains (70)	Stonetalon Peak (131)	D-1
Stormwind (72)	Trade District	J-6
Stranglethorn Vale (74)	Booty Bay (103)	B-8
	Rebel Camp (124)	C-1
Tanaris (78)	Gadgetzan (113)	H-3
Teldrassil (80)	Rut'theran Village (125)	G-9
Un'Goro Crater (90)	Marshal's Refuge (118)	F-1
Western Plaguelands (92)	Chillwind Camp (107)	F-8
Westfall (94)	Sentinel Hill (126)	G-5
Wetlands (96)	Menethil Harbor (119)	A-6
Winterspring (98)	Everlook (110)	I-4

HORDE

REGION	MINI REGION	GRID LOC
Arathi Highlands (10)	Hammerfall (115)	J-3
Ashenvale (12)	Zoram'gar Outpost (137)	B-4
Azshara (14)	Valormok	B-5
Badlands (16)	Kargath (116)	A-5
Barrens (18)	Camp Taurajo (106)	E-6
	The Crossroads (107)	F-3
Burning Steppes (22)	Flame Crest (112)	H-2
Desolace (30)	Shadowprey Village (128)	B-7
Dustwallow Marsh (38)	Brackenwall Village (104)	E-3
	Mudsprocket (120)	F-7
Eastern Plaguelands (40)	Light's Hope Chapel (118)	K-5
Felwood (44)	Bloodvenom Post (102)	E-5
	Emerald Sanctuary (110)	G-8
Feralas (46)	Camp Mojache (105)	I-4
Hillsbrad Foothills (48)	Tarren Mill (133)	G-2
Hinterlands (50)	Revantusk Village (125)	L-8
Moonglade (56)		D-7
Orgrimmar (60)	Valley of Strength	E-6
Searing Gorge (64)	Thorium Point (136)	D-3
Silithus (66)	Cenarion Hold (106)	G-3
Silverpine Forest (68)	The Sepulcher (127)	G-4
Stonetalon Mountains (70)	Sun Rock Retreat (132)	E-6
Stranglethorn Vale (74)	Booty Bay (103)	B-8
	Grom'gol Base Camp (114)	C-3
Swamp of Sorrows (76)	Stonard (131)	F-5
Tanaris (78)	Gadgetzan (113)	H-3
Thousand Needles (82)	Freewind Post (112)	F-5
Thunder Bluff (84)		E-5
Undercity (88)	The Trade Quarter	I-5
Un'Goro Crater (90)	Marshal's Refuge (118)	F-1
Winterspring (98)	Everlook (110)	I-4

MISCELLANEOUS

INNKEEPERS

REGION	MINI REGION	GRID LOC
Arathi Highlands (10)	Hammerfall (115)	J-3
Ashenvale (12)	Splintertree Post (129)	I-6
	Astranaar (101)	E-5
Badlands (16)	Kargath (116)	A-5
Barrens (18)	The Crossroads (107)	F-3
	Camp Taurajo (106)	E-6
	Ratchet (122)	H-4
Darkshore (24)	Auberdine (101)	F-4
Darnassus (26)	Craftsmen's Terrace	I:(1, 2)
Desolace (30)	Nijel's Point (121)	I-1
	Shadowprey Village (128)	C-7
Dun Morogh (32)	Kharanos (116)	F-5
Durotar (34)	Razor Hill (124)	H-4
Duskwood (36)	Darkshire (108)	J-4
Dustwallow Marsh (38)	Brackenwall Village (104)	E-3
	Mudsprocket (120)	F-7
	Theramore Isle (135)	I-5
Eastern Plaguelands (40)	Light's Hope Chapel (116)	K-6
Elwynn Forest (42)	Goldshire (114)	F-7
Feralas (46)	Camp Mojache (105)	I-4
	Feathermoon Stronghold (111)	C-4
Hillsbrad Foothills (48)	Southshore (129)	F-6
	Tarren Mill (133)	H-2
Hinterlands (50)	Aerie Peak (100)	B-4
	Revantusk Village (125)	L-8
Ironforge (52)	The Commons	B-5
Loch Modan (54)	Thelsamar (134)	D-5
Mulgore (58)	Bloodhoof Village (102)	E-6
Orgrimmar (60)	Valley of Strength	G-7
Redridge Mountains (62)	Lakeshire (117)	C-4
Silithus (66)	Cenarion Hold (106)	G-4
Silverpine Forest (68)	The Sepulcher (127)	F-4
Stonetalon Mountains (70)	Sun Rock Retreat (132)	F-6
Stormwind (72)	Trade District	H:(6, 7)
Stranglethorn Vale (74)	Booty Bay (103)	B-8
Swamp of Sorrows (76)	Stonard (131)	F-5
Tanaris (78)	Gadgetzan (113)	H-3
Teldrassil (80)	Dolanaar (109)	G-6
Thousand Needles (82)	Freewind Post (112)	F-5
Thunder Bluff (84)		E-6
Tirisfal Glades (86)	Brill (104)	H-5
Undercity (88)	The Trade Quarter	I-4, J-4
Westfall (94)	Sentinel Hill (126)	F-5
Wetlands (96)	Menethil Harbor (119)	A-6
Winterspring (98)	Everlook (110)	I-4

MOUNT TRAINERS

REGION	TITLE	NAME	MINI REGION	GRID LOC	NOTES
Elwynn Forest (42)	Horse Riding Instructor	Randal Hunter	Eastvale Logging Camp	L-6	Corral
Mulgore (58)	Kodo Riding Instructor	Kar Stormsinger	Bloodhoof Village (102)	E-6	Northern clearing
Darnassus (26)	Nightsaber Riding Instructor	Jartsam	Cenarion Enclave	E-1	Intersection of paths
Dun Morogh (32)	Mechanostrider Pilot	Binjy Featherwhistle	Steelgrill's Depot	G-5	By mechanostrider's outside of depot
	Ram Riding Instructor	Ultham Ironhorn	Amberstill Ranch	I-5	By hay bails in corral
Durotar (34)	Raptor Riding Trainer	Xar'Ti	Sen'jin Village (126)	H-7	Among raptors south of village
Tirisfal Glades (86)	Undead Horse Riding Instructor	Velma Warnam	Brill (104)	H-5	Stable
Winterspring (98)	Wintersaber Trainers	Chal Fairwind		J-3	Outside small shack in hills
	Wintersaber Trainers	Rivern Frostwind	Frostsaber Rock	G-1	Atop Frostsaber Rock
Orgrimmar (60)	Wolf Riding Instructor	Kildar	Valley of Honor	I-1	Outside of Hunter's Hall

WEAPON MASTERS

REGION	NAME	MINI REGION	GRID LOC	NOTES
Darnassus (26)	Ilyenia Moonfire	Warrior's Terrace	H-5	Lower southwest platform, Trains: Bows, Daggers, Fist, Thrown, & Staves
Ironforge (52)	Bixi Wobblebonk	The Military Ward	H-9	Timberline Arms, Trains: Crossbows, Daggers, & Throwing Weapons
	Buliwyf Stonehand	The Military Ward	H-9	Timberline Arms, Trains: 1H Axe, 2H Axe, Fist, Guns, 1H Mace, & 2H Mace
Orgrimmar (60)	Hanashi	Valley of Honor	J-2	Arms of Legend, Trains: Bows, 1H Axe, 2H Axe, Staves, & Thrown
	Sayoc	Valley of Strength	J-2	Arms of Legend, Trains: Bows, Daggers, Fist Weapons, 1H Axe, 2H Axe, Thrown
Stormwind (72)	Woo Ping	Trade District	H-6	Weller's Arsenal, Trains: Crossbows, Daggers, Polearms, Staves, 1H Swords, & 2H Swords
Thunder Bluff (84)	Ansekhwa		D-6	Lower rise, Trains: 1H Mace, 2H Mace, Staves, & Guns
Undercity (88)	Archibald	The War Quarter	H-3	Trains: Crossbows, Daggers, 1H Sword, 2H Sword, & Polearms

CLASS TRAINERS

DRUID TRAINERS

Region	Name	Mini Region	Grid Loc	Notes
Darnassus (26)	Denatharion	Cenarion Enclave	D-1	Northwest structure
Darnassus (26)	Fylerian Nightwing	Cenarion Enclave	D-1	Northwest structure
Darnassus (26)	Mathrengyl Bearwalker	Cenarion Enclave	D-1	Northwest structure, on balcony
Felwood (44)	Golhine the Hooded	Talonbranch Glade (133)	H-3	Front of building
Feralas (46)	Jannos Lighthoof	Camp Mojache (105)	I-4	In tent, east of water
Moonglade (56)	Loganaar	Nighthaven (121)	G-4	Next to moonwell, by northern section of lake
Mulgore (58)	Gennia Runetotem	Bloodhoof Village (102)	F-6	East tent
Mulgore (58)	Gart Mistrunner	Camp Narache (105)	E-8	North tent
Stormwind (72)	Maldryn	The Park	C-5	By pool of water
Stormwind (72)	Sheldras Moontree	The Park	C-6	By pool of water
Stormwind (72)	Theridran	The Park	C-5	By pool of water
Teldrassil (80)	Kal	Dolanaar (109)	G-6	Moonwell south side of Dolanaar
Teldrassil (80)	Mardant Strongoak	Shadowglen (127)	G-4	First room off of ramp up tree
Thunder Bluff (84)	Kym Wildmane	Elder Rise	I-3	Inside Hall of Elders
Thunder Bluff (84)	Sheal Runetotem	Elder Rise	J-3	Inside Hall of Elders
Thunder Bluff (84)	Turak Runetotem	Elder Rise	J-3	Inside Hall of Elders

HUNTER TRAINERS

Region	Name	Mini Region	Grid Loc	Notes
Ashenvale (12)	Alenndaar Lapidaar	Shrine of Aessina	C-6	Hidden in a camp near mountains in far southwest of region
Ashenvale (12)	Danlaar Nightshade	Silverwind Refuge	F-6, G-6	Back of building
Darnassus (26)	Dorion	Cenarion Enclave	E-1	Northeast structure, upper level
Darnassus (26)	Jeen'ra Nightrunner	Cenarion Enclave	E-1	Top of structure, connected to the northeast structure
Darnassus (26)	Jocaste	Cenarion Enclave	E-1	Northeast structure
Dun Morogh (32)	Thorgas Grimson	Coldridge Valley (107)	D-7	Anvilmar
Dun Morogh (32)	Grif Wildheart	Kharanos (116)	F-5	On hill at southwest end of town
Durotar (34)	Jen'shan	Valley of Trials (136)	F-7	Structure to south
Durotar (34)	Thotar	Razor Hill (124)	H-4	Bunker
Felwood (44)	Kaerbrus	Talonbranch Glade (133)	H-3	Near pond
Ironforge (52)	Daera Brightspear	The Military Ward	J-9	Hall of Arms
Ironforge (52)	Olmin Burningbeard	The Military Ward	J-8	Hall of Arms
Ironforge (52)	Regnus Thundergranite	The Military Ward	I-8	Hall of Arms
Loch Modan (54)	Dargh Trueaim	The Farstrider Lodge	K-6	In right hall of lodge
Mulgore (58)	Lanka Farshot	Camp Narache (105)	E-8	Main tent (north)
Mulgore (58)	Yaw Sharpmane	Bloodhoof Village (102)	E-6	North tents
Orgrimmar (60)	Ormak Grimshot	Valley of Honor	H-2	Hunter's Hall
Orgrimmar (60)	Sian'dur	Valley of Honor	H-2	Hunter's Hall
Orgrimmar (60)	Xor'Juul	Valley of Honor	H-2	Hunter's Hall
Stormwind (72)	Einris Brightspear	Dwarven District	I-2, J-2	Building south of tram entrance
Stormwind (72)	Thorfin Stoneshield	Dwarven District	I-1, I-3	Building south of tram entrance
Stormwind (72)	Ulfir Ironbeard	Dwarven District	I-2	Building south of tram entrance
Stranglethorn Vale (74)	Kragg	Grom'gol Base Camp (114)	C-3	Just inside camp walls to the left of western entrance
Swamp of Sorrows (76)	Ogromm	Stonard (131)	F-5	Behind orcish carriage left of entrance to main hall
Teldrassil (80)	Ayanna Everstride	Shadowglen (127)	G-4	First room off of ramp up tree
Teldrassil (80)	Dazalar	Dolanaar (109)	G-6	East of inn
Thunder Bluff (84)	Holt Thunderhorn	Hunter Rise	G-9	Inside Hunter's Hall
Thunder Bluff (84)	Kary Thunderhorn	Hunter Rise	G-9	Inside Hunter's Hall
Thunder Bluff (84)	Urek Thunderhorn	Hunter Rise	G-9	Inside Hunter's Hall

MAGE TRAINERS

Region	Name	Mini Region	Grid Loc	Notes
Dun Morogh (32)	Magis Sparkmantle	Kharanos (116)	F-5	Thunderbrew Distillery
Dun Morogh (32)	Marryk Nurribit	Coldridge Valley (107)	D-7	Back room of Anvilmar (first floor)
Durotar (34)	Mai'ah	Valley of Trials (136)	F-7	Structure to south
Durotar (34)	Un'Thuwa	Sen'jin Village (126)	H-7	Small hut to southeast
Elwynn Forest (42)	Khelden Bremen	Northshire Valley (122)	G-4	Second floor of abbey
Elwynn Forest (42)	Zaldimar Wefhellt	Goldshire (114)	F-7	Second floor of Lion's Pride Inn
Ironforge (52)	Bink	The Mystic Ward	C-1	Hall of Mysteries
Ironforge (52)	Dink	The Mystic Ward	C-1	Hall of Mysteries
Ironforge (52)	Juli Stormkettle	The Mystic Ward	C-1	Hall of Mysteries
Ironforge (52)	Nittlebur Sparkfizzle	The Mystic Ward	C-1	Hall of Mysteries
Orgrimmar (60)	Deino	Valley of Spirit	D-8	Darkbriar Lodge
Orgrimmar (60)	Enyo	Valley of Spirit	D:(8, 9)	Darkbriar Lodge
Orgrimmar (60)	Pephredo	Valley of Spirit	D:(8, 9)	Darkbriar Lodge
Orgrimmar (60)	Uthel'nay	Valley of Spirit	D:(8, 9)	Darkbriar Lodge
Stormwind (72)	Elsharin	Mage Quarter	F-8	Wizard's Sanctum
Stormwind (72)	Jennea Cannon	Mage Quarter	F-8	Wizard's Sanctum
Stormwind (72)	Maginor Dumas (Master Mage)	Mage Quarter	F-8	Wizard's Sanctum
Thunder Bluff (84)	Archmage Shymm	Spirit Rise	C-3	The Pools of Vision
Thunder Bluff (84)	Thurston Xane	Spirit Rise	C-3	The Pools of Vision
Tirisfal Glades (86)	Cain Firesong	Brill (104)	H-5	Second floor of Gallows' End Tavern
Tirisfal Glades (86)	Isabella	Deathknell (109)	C-7	Church
Undercity (88)	Anastasia Hartwell	The Magic Quarter	L-1	Northwest corner of Skull Building
Undercity (88)	Kaelystia Hatebringer	The Magic Quarter	L-1	Inside Skull Building
Undercity (88)	Pierce Shackleton	The Magic Quarter	L-1	Inside Skull Building

PORTAL TRAINERS

Region	Name	Mini Region	Grid Loc	Notes
Darnassus (26)	Elissa Dumas	The Temple of the Moon	E-8	Northeast of fountain
Ironforge (52)	Milstaff Stormeye	The Mystic Ward	C-1	Hall of Mysteries
Orgrimmar (60)	Thuul	Valley of Spirit	D:(8, 9)	Darkbriar Lodge, top floor
Stormwind (72)	Larimaine Purdue	Mage Quarter	F-8	Wizard's Sanctum
Thunder Bluff (84)	Brigitte Cranston	Spirit Rise	C-3	The Pools of Vision
Undercity (88)	Lexington Mortaim	The Magic Quarter	L-1	On Skull Building

PALADIN TRAINERS

Region	Name	Mini Region	Grid Loc	Notes
Dun Morogh (32)	Azar Stronghammer	Kharanos (116)	F-5	Thunderbrew Distillery
Dun Morogh (32)	Bromos Grummner	Coldridge Valley (107)	D-7	Anvilmar
Dustwallow Marsh (38)	Brother Karman	Theramore Isle (135)	I-5	Outside Foothold Citadel
Elwynn Forest (42)	Brother Sammuel	Northshire Valley (122)	G-4	Hall of Arms of abbey
Elwynn Forest (42)	Brother Wilhelm	Goldshire (114)	E-7	Rear entrance of smith
Ironforge (52)	Beldruk Doombrow	The Mystic Ward	C-1	Hall of Mysteries
Ironforge (52)	Brandur Ironhammer	The Mystic Ward	C-1	Hall of Mysteries
Ironforge (52)	Valgar Highforge	The Mystic Ward	C-1	Hall of Mysteries
Stormwind (72)	Arthur the Faithful	Cathedral Square	F-3	Cathedral of Light
Stormwind (72)	Katherine the Pure	Cathedral Square	F-3	Cathedral of Light
Stormwind (72)	Lord Grayson Shadowbreaker	Cathedral Square	F-3	Cathedral of Light

PRIEST TRAINERS

Region	Name	Mini Region	Grid Loc	Notes
Darnassus (26)	Astarii Starseeker	The Temple Gardens	E-8	Balcony, north of fountain
Darnassus (26)	Priestess Alathea	The Temple of the Moon	E-8	Balcony, north of fountain
Darnassus (26)	Jandria	The Temple of the Moon	E-8	Just inside temple, north of fountain
Darnassus (26)	Lariia	The Temple of the Moon	E-9	South of fountain
Dun Morogh (32)	Branstock Khalder	Coldridge Valley (107)	D-7	Anvilmar
Dun Morogh (32)	Maxan Anvol	Kharanos (116)	F-5	Thunderbrew Distillery
Durotar (34)	Tai'jin	Razor Hill (124)	H-4	Barracks
Durotar (34)	Ken'jai	Valley of Trials (136)	F-7	
Elwynn Forest (42)	Priestess Josetta	Goldshire (114)	F-7	Second floor of Lion's Pride Inn
Elwynn Forest (42)	Priestess Anetta	Northshire Valley (122)	G-4	Room behind the Library Wing of abbey
Ironforge (52)	Braenna Flintcrag	The Mystic Ward	C-1	Hall of Mysteries
Ironforge (52)	High Priest Rohan	The Mystic Ward	C-1	Hall of Mysteries
Ironforge (52)	Theodrus Frostbeard	The Mystic Ward	C-1	Hall of Mysteries
Ironforge (52)	Toldren Deepiron	The Mystic Ward	C-1	Hall of Mysteries
Orgrimmar (60)	Ur'kyo	Valley of Spirit	D-9	Spirit Lodge
Orgrimmar (60)	X'Yera	Valley of Spirit	D-9	Spirit Lodge, top floor
Stormwind (72)	Brother Benjamin	Cathedral Square	F-3	Cathedral of Light
Stormwind (72)	Brother Joshua	Cathedral Square	F-3	Cathedral of Light
Stormwind (72)	High Priestess Laurena	Cathedral Square	F-3	Cathedral of Light
Stormwind (72)	Nara Meideros	The Park	C-5	By pool of water
Teldrassil (80)	Laurna Morninglight	Dolanaar (109)	G-6	Bottom floor inside building north of road
Teldrassil (80)	Shanda	Shadowglen (127)	H-4	Third level of main building
Thunder Bluff (84)	Father Cobb	Spirit Rise	C-3	The Pools of Vision
Thunder Bluff (84)	Malakai Cross	Spirit Rise	C-3	The Pools of Vision
Thunder Bluff (84)	Miles Welsh	Spirit Rise	C-3	The Pools of Vision
Thunder Bluff (84)	Ursyn Ghull	Spirit Rise	C-3	The Pools of Vision
Tirisfal Glades (86)	Dark Cleric Beryl	Brill (104)	H-5	Second floor of Gallows' End Tavern
Tirisfal Glades (86)	Dark Cleric Duesten	Deathknell (109)	C-7	Church
Undercity (88)	Aelthalyste	The War Quarter	G-2	Outside Skull Building
Undercity (88)	Father Lankester	The War Quarter	G-2	Outside Skull Building
Undercity (88)	Father Lazarus	The War Quarter	F-2	Outside Skull Building

PET TRAINERS

Region	Name	Mini Region	Grid Loc	Notes
Ashenvale (12)	Bolyun	Shrine of Aessina	C-6	Hidden in a camp near mountains in far southwest of region
Ashenvale (12)	Caelyb	Silverwind Refuge	F-6	Right wing of building
Darnassus (26)	Silvaria	Cenarion Enclave	E-1	Northeast structure, upper level
Dun Morogh (32)	Peria Lamenur	Kharanos (116)	F-5	In caravan
Durotar (34)	Harruk	Razor Hill (124)	H-4	Bunker
Felwood (44)	Nalesette Wildbringer	Talonbranch Glade (133)	H-3	Front of building
Ironforge (52)	Belia Thundergranite	The Military Ward	J-8	Hall of Arms
Loch Modan (54)	Claude Erksine	The Farstrider Lodge (111)	K-6	In right hall of lodge
Mulgore (58)	Reban Freerunner	Bloodhoof Village (102)	E-6	North tents
Orgrimmar (60)	Xoa'tsu	Valley of Honor	H:(1, 2)	Behind Hunter's Hall
Stormwind (72)	Karrina Mekenda	Dwarven District	I-2	Building south of tram entrance
Stranglethorn Vale (74)	Zudd	Grom'gol Base Camp (114)	C-3	By crates inside camp walls to the left of western entrance
Swamp of Sorrows (76)	Grokor	Stonard (131)	F-5	Behind orcish carriage left of entrance to main hall
Teldrassil (80)	Keldas	Dolanaar (109)	G-6	East of inn
Thunder Bluff (84)	Hesuwa Thunderhorn	Hunter Rise	F-8	In building west of Hunter's Hall

ROGUE TRAINERS

REGION	NAME	MINI REGION	GRID LOC	NOTES
Darnassus (26)	Anishar	Cenarion Enclave	E-2	Den, bottom of ramp
	Erion Shadewhisper	Cenarion Enclave	D-2	Den, small room on lower level
	Syurna	Cenarion Enclave	D-2, E-2	Den, west of path
Dun Morogh (32)	Solm Hargrin	Coldridge Valley (107)	D-7	Anvilmar
	Hogral Bakkan	Kharanos (116)	F-5	Thunderbrew Distillery
Durotar (34)	Kaplak	Razor Hill (124)	H-4	Bunker
	Rwag	Valley of Trials (136)	F-7	
Elwynn Forest (42)	Keryn Sylvius	Goldshire (114)	F-7	Second floor of Lion's Pride Inn
	Jorik Kerridan	Northshire Valley (122)	G-4	Abbey stable
Hillsbrad Foothills (48)	Fahrad (Grand Master Rogue)		K-2	Balcony of Chateau Ravenholdt
Ironforge (52)	Fenthwick	The Forlorn Cavern	G-1	South building, inside east entrance
	Hulfdan Blackbeard	The Forlorn Cavern	G-1	South building, inside east entrance
	Ormyr Flinteye	The Forlorn Cavern	G-1	South building, inside east entrance
Orgrimmar (60)	Gest	The Cleft of Shadow	E-5	Shadowswift Brotherhood
	Ormok	The Cleft of Shadow	E-5	Next to Shadowswift Brotherhood building
	Shenthul	The Cleft of Shadow	E-5	Shadowswift Brotherhood
Stormwind (72)	Lord Tony Romano	Old Town	L-6	SI:7
	Osborne the Night Man	Old Town	K-5	Outside SI:7
Stranglethorn Vale (74)	Ian Strom	Booty Bay (103)	B-8	Second floor of The Salty Sailor Tavern
Teldrassil (80)	Jannok Breezesong	Dolanaar (109)	G-6	Inn
	Frahun Shadewhisper	Shadowglen (127)	H-4	In northeast room inside main building
Tirisfal Glades (86)	Marion Call	Brill (104)	H-5	Second floor of Gallows' End Tavern
	David Trias	Deathknell (109)	D-6	First floor of second house on right side of road
Undercity (88)	Carolyn Ward	The Rogues' Quarter	L-7	Inside Skull Building
	Gregory Charles	The Rogues' Quarter	L-7	Inside Skull Building
	Miles Dexter	The Rogues' Quarter	L-7	Inside Skull Building

SHAMAN TRAINERS

REGION	NAME	MINI REGION	GRID LOC	NOTES
Durotar (34)	Swart	Razor Hill (124)	H-4	Barracks
	Shikrik	Valley of Trials (136)	F-7	
Mulgore (58)	Narm Skychaser	Bloodhoof Village (102)	F-6	East tent
	Meela Dawnstrider	Camp Narache (105)	E-8	North tent
Orgrimmar (60)	Kandris Dreamseeker	Valley of Wisdom	D-4	Grommash Hold
	Sagorne Crestrider	Valley of Wisdom	D-4	Grommash Hold
	Sian'tsu	Valley of Wisdom	D-4	Grommash Hold
Swamp of Sorrows (76)	Haromm	Stonard (131)	F-6	Scaffolding just inside camp walls left of southern entrance
Thunder Bluff (84)	Beram Skychaser	Spirit Rise	B-2	Inside Hall of Spirits
	Slin Skychaser	Spirit Rise	B-2	Inside Hall of Spirits
	Tigor Skychaser	Spirit Rise	B-2	Inside Hall of Spirits

WARLOCK TRAINERS

REGION	NAME	MINI REGION	GRID LOC	NOTES
Dun Morogh (32)	Alamar Grimm	Coldridge Valley (107)	D-7	Anvilmar
	Gimrizz Shadowcog	Kharanos (116)	F-5	Gnomish camp on right of distillery
Durotar (34)	Dhugru Gorelust	Razor Hill (124)	H-4	Behind barracks
	Nartok	Valley of Trials (136)	F-7	Back of cave
Elwynn Forest (42)	Maximillian Crowe	Goldshire (114)	F-7	Basement of Lion's Pride Inn
	Drusilla La Salle	Northshire Valley (122)	G-4	Graveyard on right side of abbey
Ironforge (52)	Alexander Calder	The Forlorn Cavern	G-1	Building to the right of Traveling Fisherman
	Briarthorn	The Forlorn Cavern	G-1	Building to the right of Traveling Fisherman
	Thistleheart	The Forlorn Cavern	G-1	Building to the right of Traveling Fisherman
Orgrimmar (60)	Grol'dar	The Cleft of Shadow	E-5, F-5	Darkfire Enclave
	Mirket	The Cleft of Shadow	F-5	Darkfire Enclave
	Zevrost	The Cleft of Shadow	F-5	Darkfire Enclave
Stormwind (72)	Demisette Cloyce	Mage Quarter	D-8	The Slaughtered Lamb
	Sandahl	Mage Quarter	D-8	The Slaughtered Lamb
	Ursula Deline	Mage Quarter	D-8	The Slaughtered Lamb
Swamp of Sorrows (76)	Kartosh	Stonard (131)	F-5	Second floor of main hall
Tirisfal Glades (86)	Rupert Boch	Brill (104)	H-5	Second floor of Gallows' End Tavern
	Maximillion	Deathknell (109)	D-6	Church
Undercity (88)	Kaal Soulreaper	The Magic Quarter	L-2	Inside Skull Building
	Luther Pickman	The Magic Quarter	L-2	Inside Skull Building
	Richard Kerwin	The Magic Quarter	L:(1, 2)	Northeast corner of Skull Building

DEMON TRAINERS

REGION	NAME	MINI REGION	GRID LOC	NOTES
Dun Morogh (32)	Wren Darkspring	Coldridge Valley (107)	D-7	Anvilmar
	Dannie Fizzwizzle	Kharanos (116)	F-5	Gnomish camp on right of distillery
Durotar (34)	Kitha	Razor Hill (124)	H-4	Behind barracks
	Hraug	Valley of Trials (136)	F-7	Back of cave
Elwynn Forest (42)	Cylina Darkheart	Goldshire (114)	F-7	Basement of Lion's Pride Inn
	Dane Winslow	Northshire Valley (122)	G-4	Graveyard on right side of abbey
Ironforge (52)	Jubahl Corpseseeker	The Forlorn Cavern	G-1	First building on north from east entrance
Orgrimmar (60)	Kurgul	The Cleft of Shadow	E-5, F-5	Darkfire Enclave
Stormwind (72)	Spackle Thornberry	Mage Quarter	D-8	The Slaughtered Lamb
Swamp of Sorrows (76)	Greshka	Stonard (131)	F-5	Second floor of main hall
Tirisfal Glades (86)	Gina Lang	Brill (104)	H-5	Second floor of Gallows' End Tavern
	Kayla Smithe	Deathknell (109)	C-7	Church
Undercity (88)	Martha Strain	The Magic Quarter	L:(1, 2)	Inside Skull Building

WARRIOR TRAINERS

REGION	NAME	MINI REGION	GRID LOC	NOTES
Darnassus (26)	Arias'ta Bladesinger	Warrior's Terrace	H-3	Lower northwest platform
	Darnath Bladesinger	Warrior's Terrace	H-3	Lower northwest platform
	Sildanair	Warrior's Terrace	H-4	Middle of terrace
Dun Morogh (32)	Thran Khorman	Coldridge Valley (107)	D-7	Anvilmar
	Granis Swiftaxe	Kharanos (116)	F-5	Thunderbrew Distillery
Durotar (34)	Tarshaw Jaggedscar	Razor Hill (124)	H-4	Barracks
	Frang	Valley of Trials (136)	F-7	Structure to south
Dustwallow Marsh (38)	Captain Evencane	Theramore Isle (135)	I-5	2nd floor of Foothold Citadel
Elwynn Forest (42)	Lyria Du Lac	Goldshire (114)	E-7	Rear entrance of smith
	Llane Beshere	Northshire Valley (122)	G-4	Hall of Arms of abbey
Ironforge (52)	Bilban Tosslespanner	The Military Ward	I-9	Hall of Arms
	Kelstrum Stonebreaker	The Military Ward	I-9	Hall of Arms
	Kelv Sternhammer	The Military Ward	J-9	Hall of Arms
Mulgore (58)	Krang Stonehoof	Bloodhoof Village (102)	F-6	Combat ground east of village
	Harutt Thunderhorn	Camp Narache (105)	E-8	Main tent (north)
Orgrimmar (60)	Grezz Razorfist	Valley of Honor	J-3	Hall of the Brave
	Sorek	Valley of Honor	J-3	Hall of the Brave
	Zel'mak	Valley of Honor	J-3	Hall of the Brave
Stormwind (72)	Ander Germaine	Old Town	L-5	Command Center
	Ilsa Corbin	Old Town	L:(4, 5)	Command Center
	Wu Shen	Old Town	L:(4, 5)	Command Center
Swamp of Sorrows (76)	Malosh	Stonard (131)	F-5	First floor of inn
Teldrassil (80)	Kyra Windblade	Dolanaar (109)	G-6	Inn
	Alyissia	Shadowglen (127)	H-4	In northeast room inside main building
Thunder Bluff (84)	Ker Ragetotem	Hunter Rise	G-8	Inside Hunter's Hall
	Sark Ragetotem	Hunter Rise	G-9	Inside Hunter's Hall
	Torm Ragetotem	Hunter Rise	G-9	Inside Hunter's Hall
Tirisfal Glades (86)	Austil de Mon	Brill (104)	H-5	First floor of Gallows' End Tavern
	Dannal Stern	Deathknell (109)	D-6	First floor of second house on right side of road
Undercity (88)	Angela Curthas	The War Quarter	G-1	In Skull Building
	Baltus Fowler	The War Quarter	F-2	In Skull Building
	Christoph Walker	The War Quarter	F-2	In Skull Building

PROFESSION TRAINERS

ALCHEMY

TITLE/DESCRIPTION	REGION	NAME	MINI REGION	GRID LOC
Artisan Alchemist	Darnassus (26)	Ainethil	Craftsmen's Terrace	G-2
	Undercity (88)	Doctor Herbert Halsey	The Apothecarium	F-7
Expert Alchemist	Ashenvale (12)	Kylanna	Silverwind Refuge	G-6
	Darnassus (26)	Sylvanna Forestmoon	Craftsmen's Terrace	G-2
	Dustwallow Marsh (38)	Alchemist Narett	Theramore Isle (135)	H-5
	Hillsbrad Foothills (48)	Serge Hinott	Tarren Mill (133)	G-2
	Ironforge (52)	Tally Berryfizz	Tinker Town	I-5
	Orgrimmar (60)	Yelmak	The Drag	G-3
	Stormwind (72)	Lilyssia Nightbreeze	Mage Quarter	G-8
	Stranglethorn Vale (74)	Jaxin Chong	Booty Bay (103)	B-8
	Thunder Bluff (84)	Bena Winterhoof		E-3
	Undercity (88)	Doctor Marsh	The Apothecarium	G-7
Journeyman Alchemist	Darnassus (26)	Milla Fairancora	Craftsmen's Terrace	G-2
	Durotar (34)	Miao'zan	Sen'jin Village (126)	H-7
	Elwynn Forest (42)	Alchemist Mallory		E-5
	Ironforge (52)	Vosur Brakthel	Tinker Town	I-5
	Loch Modan (54)	Ghak Healtouch	Thelsamar (134)	E-5
	Orgrimmar (60)	Whuut	The Drag	G-3
	Stormwind (72)	Tel'Athir	Mage Quarter	G-8
	Teldrassil (80)	Cyndra Kindwhisper	Dolanaar (109)	G-6
	Thunder Bluff (84)	Kray		E-3
	Tirisfal Glades (86)	Carolai Anise	Brill (104)	H-5
	Undercity (88)	Doctor Martin Felben	The Apothecarium	F-7
Master Alchemist	Feralas (46)	Kylanna Windwhisper	Feathermoon Stronghold (111)	C-4
	Swamp of Sorrows (76)	Rogvar	Stonard (131)	F-5

BLACKSMITHING

TITLE/DESCRIPTION	NAME	REGION	MINI REGION	GRID LOC
Armorsmith	Okothos Ironrager	Orgrimmar (60)	Valley of Honor	J-2
Artisan Blacksmith	Bengus Deepforge	Ironforge (52)	The Great Forge	G-4
	Saru Steelfury	Orgrimmar (60)	Valley of Honor	J-2, K-2
Artisan Blacksmith of the Mithril Order	Galvan the Ancient	Stranglethorn Vale (74)		F-2
Expert Blacksmith	Traugh	Barrens (18)	The Crossroads (107)	F-3
	Clarise Gnarltree	Duskwood (36)	Darkshire (108)	J-5
	Rotgath Stonebeard	Ironforge (52)	The Great Forge	G-4
	Snarl	Orgrimmar (60)	Valley of Honor	J-2
	Therum Deepforge	Stormwind (72)	Dwarven District	H-2
	Karn Stonehoof	Thunder Bluff (84)		D-6
	James Van Brunt	Undercity (88)	The War Quarter	I-3
Journeyman Blacksmith	Delfrum Flintbeard	Darkshore (24)	Auberdine (101)	F-4
	Tognus Flintfire	Dun Morogh (32)	Kharanos (116)	F-5
	Dwukk	Durotar (34)	Razor Hill (124)	H-4
	Smith Argus	Elwynn Forest (42)	Goldshire (114)	E-6
	Groum Stonebeard	Ironforge (52)	The Great Forge	G-4
	Ug'thok	Orgrimmar (60)	Valley of Honor	J-2
	Guillaume Sorouy	Silverpine Forest (68)	The Sepulcher (127)	F-4
	Dane Lindgren	Stormwind (72)	Dwarven District	I-2, J-2
	Thrag Stonehoof	Thunder Bluff (84)		D-6
	Basil Frye	Undercity (88)	The War Quarter	H-3
Master Blacksmith	Brikk Keencraft	Stranglethorn Vale (74)	Booty Bay (103)	C-8
Weaponsmith	Borgosh Corebender	Orgrimmar (60)	Valley of Honor	J-2

ENCHANTING

TITLE/DESCRIPTION	NAME	REGION	MINI REGION	GRID LOC
Artisan Enchanter	Kitta Firewind	Elwynn Forest (42)	Tower of Azora	I-7
	Hgarth	Stonetalon Mountains (70)	Sun Rock Retreat (132)	F-6
Expert Enchanter	Taladan	Darnassus (26)	Craftsmen's Terrace	H-1
	Xylinnia Starshine	Feralas (46)	Feathermoon Stronghold (111)	C-4
	Gimble Thistlefuzz	Ironforge (52)	The Great Forge	H-4
	Godan	Orgrimmar (60)	The Drag	F-4
	Lucan Cordell	Stormwind (72)	The Canals	F-6
	Teg Dawnstrider	Thunder Bluff (84)		E-4
	Lavinia Crowe	Undercity (88)	The Apothecarium	I-6
Journeyman Enchanter	Lalina Summermoon	Darnassus (26)	Craftsmen's Terrace	H-1
	Thonys Pillarstone	Ironforge (52)	The Great Forge	H-4
	Jhag	Orgrimmar (60)	The Drag	F-4
	Betty Quin	Stormwind (72)	The Canals	F-6
	Alanna Raveneye	Teldrassil (80)	The Oracle Glade	D-3
	Mot Dawnstrider	Thunder Bluff (84)		E-4
	Vance Undergloom	Tirisfal Glades (86)	Brill (104)	H-5
	Malcomb Wynn	Undercity (88)	The Apothecarium	I-6
Master Enchanter	Annora	Badlands (16)	Uldaman	G-1

ENGINEERING

TITLE/DESCRIPTION	NAME	REGION	MINI REGION	GRID LOC
Artisan Engineer	Springspindle Fizzlegear	Ironforge (52)	Tinker Town	I-4
	Roxxik	Orgrimmar (60)	Valley of Honor	I-3, J-
Expert Engineer	Finbus Geargrind	Duskwood (36)	Darkshire (108)	K-5
	Trixie Quikswitch	Ironforge (52)	Tinker Town	I-4
	Nogg	Orgrimmar (60)	Valley of Honor	I-3, J-
	Lilliam Sparkspindle	Stormwind (72)	Dwarven District	H-1
	Franklin Lloyd	Undercity (88)	The Rogues' Quarter	K-7
Journeyman Engineer	Tinkerwiz	Barrens (18)	Ratchet (122)	H-4
	Jenna Lemkenilli	Darkshore (24)	Auberdine (101)	F-4
	Bronk Guzzlegear	Dun Morogh (32)	Steelgrill's Depot	G-5
	Mukdrak	Durotar (34)	Razor Hill (124)	H-4
	Jemma Quikswitch	Ironforge (52)	Tinker Town	I-4
	Deek Fizzlebizz	Loch Modan (54)	Stonewrought Dam	F-1
	Twizwick Sprocketgrind	Mulgore (58)		H-3
	Thund	Orgrimmar (60)	Valley of Honor	I-3, J-
	Sprite Jumpsprocket	Stormwind (72)	Dwarven District	H-1
	Graham Van Talen	Undercity (88)	The Rogues' Quarter	K-7
Master Engineer	Buzzek Bracketswing	Tanaris (78)	Gadgetzan (113)	H-3
Master Gnome Engineer	Tinkmaster Overspark	Ironforge (52)	Tinker Town	J-5
	Oglethorpe Obnoticus	Stranglethorn Vale (74)	Booty Bay (103)	B-8
	Vazario Linkgrease	Barrens (18)	Ratchet (122)	H-4
	Nixx Sprocketspring	Tanaris (78)	Gadgetzan (113)	H-3

HERBALISM

TITLE/DESCRIPTION	NAME	REGION	MINI REGION	GRID LOC
Apprentice Herbalist	Faruza	Tirisfal Glades (86)	Brill (104)	H-5
Herbalism Trainer	Firodren Mooncaller	Darnassus (26)	The Temple Gardens	F-7
	Herbalist Pomeroy	Elwynn Forest (42)		E-5
	Ruw	Feralas (46)	Camp Mojache (105)	I-4
	Reyna Stonebranch	Ironforge (52)	The Great Forge	G-6
	Jandi	Orgrimmar (60)	The Drag	F-4, G-4
	Alma Jainrose	Redridge Mountains (62)	Lakeshire (117)	B-4
	Shylamiir	Stormwind (72)	The Park	B-5
	Tannysa	Stormwind (72)	Mage Quarter	F-8, G-8
	Komin Winterhoof	Thunder Bluff (84)		F-4
	Martha Alliestar	Undercity (88)	The Apothecarium	H-5
	Telurinon Moonshadow	Wetlands (96)	Menethil Harbor (119)	A-6
Herbalist	Cylania Rootstalker	Ashenvale (12)	Silverwind Refuge	G-6
	Mishiki	Durotar (34)	Sen'jin Village (126)	H-7
	Brant Jasperbloom	Dustwallow Marsh (38)	Theramore Isle (135)	H-5
	Aranae Venomblood	Hillsbrad Foothills (48)	Tarren Mill (133)	G-2
	Kali Healtouch	Loch Modan (54)	Thelsamar (134)	D-5
	Malvor	Moonglade (56)	Nighthaven (121)	F-5
	Malorne Bladeleaf	Teldrassil (80)	Dolanaar (109)	G-6
Superior Herbalist	Angrun	Stranglethorn Vale (74)	Grom'gol Base Camp (114)	C-3
	Flora Silverwind	Stranglethorn Vale (74)	Booty Bay (103)	B-8

LEATHERWORKING

TITLE/DESCRIPTION	NAME	REGION	MINI REGION	GRID LOC
Artisan Leatherworker	Telonis	Darnassus (26)	Craftsmen's Terrace	I-2
	Una	Thunder Bluff (84)		D-4
Expert Leathercrafter	Narv Hidecrafter	Desolace (30)	Ghost Walker Post (113)	G-6
	Aayndia Floralwind	Ashenvale (12)	Astranaar (101)	E-5
	Krulmoo Fullmoon	Barrens (18)	Camp Taurajo (106)	F-6
	Faldron	Darnassus (26)	Craftsmen's Terrace	I-2
	Fimble Finespindle	Ironforge (52)	The Great Forge	E-3
	Karolek	Orgrimmar (60)	The Drag	H-4
	Simon Tanner	Stormwind (72)	Old Town	J-5
	Brawn	Stranglethorn Vale (74)	Grom'gol Base Camp (114)	C-3
	Tarn	Thunder Bluff (84)		E-4
	Arthur Moore	Undercity (88)	The Rogues' Quarter	I-6
Journeyman Leatherworker	Waldor	Barrens (18)	The Wailing Caverns	E-4
	Waldor	Barrens (18)	Wailing Caverns	E-4
	Darianna	Darnassus (26)	Craftsmen's Terrace	I-2
	Adele Fielder	Elwynn Forest (42)	Goldshire (114)	F-6
	Gretta Finespindle	Ironforge (52)	The Great Forge	E-3
	Chaw Stronghide	Mulgore (58)	Bloodhoof Village (102)	E-6
	Kamari	Orgrimmar (60)	The Drag	H-4
	Randal Worth	Stormwind (72)	Old Town	J-5
	Nadyia Maneweaver	Teldrassil (80)		
	Mak	Thunder Bluff (84)		D-4
	Shelene Rhobart	Tirisfal Glades (86)		I-6
	Dan Golthas	Undercity (88)	The Rogues' Quarter	I-6
Master Dragonscale	Peter Galen	Azshara (14)	Ruins of Eldarath	D-6
	Thorkaf Dragoneye	Badlands (16)		I-6
Master Elemental Leatherworker	Sarah Tanner	Searing Gorge (64)	Tanner Camp	H-7
Master Leatherworker	Hahrana Ironhide	Feralas (46)	Camp Mojache (105)	I-4
Master Leatherworking Trainer	Drakk Stonehand	The Hinterlands (50)	Aerie Peak (100)	B-4
Master Tribal Leatherworker	Se'Jib	Stranglethorn Vale (74)		D-4
Tribal Leatherworking Trainer	Caryssa Moonhunter	Feralas (46)	Thalanaar	K-5

MINING

TITLE/DESCRIPTION	REGION	NAME	MINI REGION	GRID LOC
Miner	Durotar (34)	Krunn	Razor Hill (124)	H-4
	Silverpine Forest (68)	Johan Focht	The Sepulcher (127)	F-4
	Tanaris (78)	Pikkle	Gadgetzan (113)	G-3
Mining Trainer	Darkshore (24)	Kurdram Stonehammer	Auberdine (101)	F-4
	Dun Morogh (32)	Dank Drizzlecut	Gol'Bolar Quarry	J-6
	Dun Morogh (32)	Yarr Hammerstone	Steelgrill's Depot	G-5
	Duskwood (36)	Matt Johnson	Darkshire (108)	J-5
	Ironforge (52)	Geofram Bouldertoe	The Great Forge	G-3
	Loch Modan (54)	Brock Stoneseeker	Thelsamar (134)	E-5
	Orgrimmar (60)	Makaru	Valley of Honor	I-3
	Stormwind (72)	Gelman Stonehand	Dwarven District	H-2
	Thunder Bluff (84)	Brek Stonehoof		C-6
	Undercity (88)	Brom Killian	The War Quarter	H-4

SKINNING

TITLE/DESCRIPTION	REGION	NAME	MINI REGION	GRID LOC
Skinner	Ashenvale (12)	Jayla	Silverwind Refuge	F-6
	Barrens (18)	Dranh	Camp Taurajo (106)	F-6
	Elwynn Forest (42)	Helene Peltskinner	Goldshire (114)	F-6
	Mulgore (58)	Yonn Deepcut	Bloodhoof Village (102)	E-6
	Teldrassil (80)	Radnaal Maneweaver		E-5
	Tirisfal Glades (86)	Rand Rhobart		I-6
Skinning Trainer	Darnassus (26)	Eladriel	Craftsmen's Terrace	I-2
	Desolace (30)	Malux	Shadowprey Village (128)	B-7
	Desolace (30)	Vark Battlescar	Shadowprey Village (128)	B-7
	Feralas (46)	Kulleg Stonehorn	Camp Mojache (105)	I-4
	Ironforge (52)	Balthus Stoneflayer	The Great Forge	E-3
	Orgrimmar (60)	Thuwd	The Drag	H-4
	Redridge Mountains (62)	Wilma Ranthal		L-7
	Stormwind (72)	Maris Granger	Old Town	J-5
	Thunder Bluff (84)	Mooranta		E-4
	Undercity (88)	Killian Hagey	The Rogues' Quarter	J-6

TAILORING

TITLE/DESCRIPTION	REGION	NAME	MINI REGION	GRID LOC
Artisan Tailor	Stormwind (72)	Georgio Bolero	Mage Quarter	G-7
	Undercity (88)	Josef Gregorian	The Magic Quarter	J-3
Expert Tailor	Barrens (18)	Mahani	Camp Taurajo (106)	F-6
	Darnassus (26)	Me'lynn	Craftsmen's Terrace	H-2
	Ironforge (52)	Jormund Stonebrow	The Great Forge	F-3
	Orgrimmar (60)	Magar	The Drag	H-5
	Stormwind (72)	Sellandus	Mage Quarter	F-8
	Stranglethorn Vale (74)	Grarnik Goodstitch	Booty Bay (103)	B-8
	Thunder Bluff (84)	Tepa		E-4
	Undercity (88)	Rhiannon Davis	The Magic Quarter	J-3
Journeyman Tailor	Barrens (18)	Kil'hala	The Crossroads (107)	F-3
	Darkshore (24)	Grondal Moonbreeze	Auberdine (101)	F-4
	Darnassus (26)	Trianna	Craftsmen's Terrace	I-2
	Elwynn Forest (42)	Eldrin	Eastvale Logging Camp	K-7
	Ironforge (52)	Uthrar Threx	The Great Forge	F-3
	Orgrimmar (60)	Snang	The Drag	H-5
	Stormwind (72)	Lawrence Schneider	Mage Quarter	G-7
	Thunder Bluff (84)	Vhan		E-4
	Tirisfal Glades (86)	Bowen Brisboise	Cold Hearth Manor	G-5
	Undercity (88)	Victor Ward	The Magic Quarter	J-3
Master Shadowweave Tailor	Stormwind (72)	Jalane Ayrole	Mage Quarter	D-8
	Undercity (88)	Josephine Lister	The Magic Quarter	L-2
Master Tailor	Dustwallow Marsh (38)	Timothy Worthington	Theramore Isle (135)	I-5
	Hillsbrad Foothills (48)	Daryl Stack	Tarren Mill (133)	H-2

SKINNING

Leather Type	Skinning Requirement
Light Leather	1-150
Light Hide	51-150
Medium Leather	65-225
Medium Hide	75-225
Heavy Leather	125-300
Heavy Hide	125-300
Thick Leather	175-300
Thick Hide	175-300
Rugged Leather	225-300
Rugged Hide	225-300

SKINNING—SPECIALTY

Specialty Leather Type	Skinning Requirement	Location(s)
Black Dragonscale	250-300	Skinning Level 50-60 Elite Whelps and Wyrmkin in Blackrock Spire and Burning Steppes
Black Whelp Scale	85-125	Skinning Level 17-25 Whelps in Redridge Mountains and Wetlands
Blue Dragonscale	250-300	Skinning Level 50-60 Elite Whelps and Wyrmkin in Azshara and Winterspring
Chimera Leather	250-275	Skinning Level 50-55 Chimeras in Winterspring
Core Leather	310 (Use Finkle's Skinner from Blackrock Spire)	Skinning Ancient Core Hounds in Molten Core (310 Skinning Req.)
Deviate Scale	75-110	Skinning and Looting Level 15-22 Beasts in and around Wailing Caverns (Barrens)
Devilsaur Leather	275-300	Skinning Level 55-60 Elite Devilsaurs in Un'Goro Crater
Enchanted Leather	Enchanter with 250 Skill	Created by Enchanters (Skill 250)
Frostsaber Leather	275-300	Skinning Level 55-60 Frostsabers in Winterspring
Green Dragonscale	200-300	Skinning Level 40-60 Elite Whelps and Wyrmkin in Swamp of Sorrows & Temple of Atal'Hakkar
Green Whelp Scale	170-180	Skinning Level 34-36 Whelps in Swamp of Sorrows
Heavy Scorpid Scale	250-275	Skinning Level 50-55 Scorpids in Blackrock Spire, Burning Steppes, and Silithus
Perfect Deviate Scale	75-110	Skinning and Looting Level 15-22 Beasts in and around Wailing Caverns (Barrens)
Red Dragonscale	250-300	Skinning Level 50-60 Elite Whelps and Wyrmkin in Blackrock Spire and Wetlands
Red Whelp Scale	120-135	Skinning Level 24-27 Whelps in Wetlands
Scorpid Scale	200-250	Skinning Level 40-50 Scorpids in Blasted Lands, Tanaris, and Uldaman
Shadowcat Hide	185-215	Skinning Level 37-43 Shadow Panthers in Stranglethorn Vale and Swamp of Sorrows
Slimy Murloc Scale	75-125	Looting Level 15-25 Murlocs (Many Locations)
Thick Murloc Scale	150-175	Looting Level 30-35 Murlocs in Dustwallow Marsh, Hillsbrad Foothills, and Stranglethorn Vale
Thick Wolfhide	200-250	Skinning Level 40-50 Wolves in Burning Steppes, Feralas, and Hinterlands
Thin Kodo Leather	50-100	Skinning Level 10-20 Kodos in Barrens and Mulgore
Turtle Scale	190-265	Skinning Level 38-53 Turtles in Dustwallow Marsh, Hinterlands and Tanaris
Warbear Leather	250-275	Skinning Level 50-55 Bears in Felwood, Western Plaguelands, and Winterspring
Worm Dragonscale	200-300	Skinning Level 40-60 Whelps/Wyrmkin in Azshara, Burning Steppes, Swamp of Sorrows, and Winterspring

RARE MOBS

ALTERAC MOUNTAINS, PAGE 8

ARAGA
Dalaran, Sofera's Naze, The Headland, D:(7, 8), E-9, Lvl 35 Average Rare; Roams small area around spawn point

CRANKY BENJ
Lordamere Lake, A-5, Lvl 32 Very Rare; Patrols eastern coast of lake

GRANDPA VISHAS
The Uplands, D-3, Lvl 34 Common; Inside house

GRAVIS SLIPKNOT
Strahnbrad, H-4, Lvl 36 Uncommon; Windmill on western side of town

JIMMY THE BLEEDER
Corrahn's Dagger, Sofera's Naze, F-8, H-7, Lvl 27 Average Rare; Roams around camp

LO'GROSH
Crushridge Hold, Slaughter Hollow, F-3, G-5, Lvl 39 Average Rare; Roams small area around spawn point

NARILLASANZ
Chillwind Point, J:(5, 6), K:(4-6), Lvl 44 Semi-Rare; Patrols area between lake and road

SKHOWL
Growless Cave, Ruins of Alterac, D:(5, 6), E-4, F-6, Lvl 36 Semi-Rare; Roams small area around spawn point

ARATHI HIGHLANDS, PAGE 10

DARBEL MONTROSE
Stromgarde Keep (127), C-7, D-6, Lvl 39 Semi-Rare; Roams with minion near spawn point

FOULBELLY
Stromgarde Keep (127), B-6, Lvl 42 Very Rare; Stands to the right of tower in ogre quarter of keep

KOVORK
Boulderfist Outpost, D-5, Lvl 36 Uncommon; Inside cave at Boulder'gor

MOLOK THE CRUSHER
Boulderfist Hall, G-8, Lvl 39 Semi-Rare; Westernmost point in cave

NIMAR THE SLAYER
Witherbark Village, I:(6, 7), J-6, Lvl 37 Uncommon; Roams in village

PRINCE NAZJAK
The Drowned Reef, C:(8, 9), Lvl 41 Very Rare; Roams in the reef

RUUL ONESTONE
The Tower of Arathor, B-7, Lvl 39 Average Rare; Roams the top floor of tower

SINGER
Northfold Manor, D-3, Lvl 34 Uncommon; Roams in farm

ZALAS WITHERBARK
Witherbark Village, J-8, Lvl 40 Uber-Rare; Cave south of village

ASHENVALE, PAGE 12

AKKRILUS
Fire Scar Shrine, C-6, D-6, Lvl 26 Average Rare; Close to northern entrance to Fire Scar Shrine

APOTHECARY FALTHIS
Bathran's Haunt, D-3, Lvl 22 Uncommon; Within haunt to the east

ECK'ALOM
Mystral Lake, F-7, G-7, Lvl 27 Average Rare; Spawns in areas around lake

LADY VESPIA
The Zoram Strand (131), B:(2-3), Lvl 22 Uncommon; Roams coastline

MIST HOWLER
C:(2-3), D-1, Lvl 22 Semi-Rare; Roams forest near spawn points

MUGGLEFIN
Lake Falathim, C-4, Lvl 23 Semi-Rare; Roams near spawn points

OAKPAW
Greenpaw Village, F-6, G-6, Lvl 27 Semi-Rare; Roams throughout village

PRINCE RAZE
Xavian, J:(4-5), Lvl 32 Uncommon; Can be found near delta, next to a totem in middle of camp, or next to Geltharis

RORGISH JOWL
Thistlefur Village, E-4, Lvl 25 Uncommon; Roams camp near spawn locations

TERROWULF PACKLORD
Howling Vale, G-4, Lvl 32 Average Rare; In front of structure

URSOL'LOK
Nightsong Woods, Satyrnaar, Warsong Lumber Camp, J-5, K-6, Lvl 31 Semi-Rare

AZSHARA, PAGE 14

ANTILOS
Legashi Encampment, A-5, I-2, Lvl 50 Very Rare; Roams south from first spawnpoint and around second

GATEKEEPER RAGEROAR
Timbermaw Hold, D-3, Lvl 49 Semi-Rare; Guards gate

GENERAL FANGFERROR
Temple of Zin-Malor, E-5, Lvl 50 Semi-Rare; Top of main temple

LADY SESSPIRA
Ruins of Eldarath, D-5, Lvl 51 Uncommon; Patrols the ruins

MAGISTER HAWKHELM
Thalassian Base Camp, G-3, Lvl 52 Average Rare; Roams close to spawn points

MASTER FEARDRED
Legash Encampment, H:(2-3), Lvl 51 Average Rare

MONNOS THE ELDER
Bitter Reaches, H-9, K-2, Lvl 54 Uber-Rare; Roams across northern and southern peninsulas

SCALEBEARD
Bay of Storms, G-5, Lvl 52 Uncommon; Spawns in Scalebeard's Cave and roams

THE EVALCHARR
Haldarr Encampment, A-5, B-6, Lvl 48 Very Rare; Roams area east of Southfury River

VARO'THEN'S GHOST
A:(7-8), B-7, Lvl 48 Uncommon; Roams area north of road among ruins

BADLANDS, PAGE 16

7:XT
Camp Boff, Camp Cagg, The Dustbowl, Mirage Flats, A-8, B-7, C-8, D:(5, 7), H-8, I-7, Lvl 41 Very Rare; Roams small area around spawn point

ANATHEMUS
C-7, Lvl 45 Uncommon; Patrols large radius around entire region

BARNABUS
Agmond's End, Badlands, Mirage Flats, F-7, G-7, H:(6, 7), Lvl 38 Average Rare; Roams small area around spawn point

BROKEN TOOTH
Angor Fortress, Dustwind Gulch, G-4, H-2, I-3, Lvl 37 Uncommon; Roams small area around spawn point

DIGMASTER SHOVELPHLANGE
Uldaman, G-1, Lvl 38 Semi-Rare

RUMBLER
Camp Cagg, A-8, B-9, Lvl 45 Uncommon; Roams small area around spawn point

SHADOWFORGE COMMANDER
Angor Fortress, F-3, Lvl 40 Semi-Rare; Patrols second floor of fortress

SIEGE GOLEM
Angor Fortress, F-4, Lvl 40 Average Rare; Patrols path to an area of Badlands just south of Kargath (A-6)

WAR GOLEM
Angor Fortress, Hammertoe's Digsite, The Maker's Terrace, G:(1, 3), H-3, Lvl 36 Semi-Rare; Roams small area around spawn point

ZARICOTL
The Dustbowl, Mirage Flats, E:(5, 6), H-6, Lvl 55 Uncommon; Roams small area around spawn point

BARRENS, PAGE 18

AMBASSADOR BLOODRAGE
Razorfen Downs, F-9, Lvl 36 Semi-Rare; Spawns in/near huts

AZZERE THE SKYBLADE
Southern Barrens, E-6, Lvl 25 Uncommon; Patrols area south of Camp Taurajo

BLIND HUNTER
Razorfen Kraul, E-9, Lvl 32 Rare

BROKESPEAR
The Stagnant Oasis, F:(4-5), G-4, Lvl 17 Uncommon; Stays near spawn points

BRONTUS
Blackthorn Ridge, E-8, Lvl 27 Average Rare; Spawns near center hut and roams ridge

CAPTAIN GEROGG HAMMERTOE
Bael'dun Keep, F-8, Lvl 27 Average Rare; Second floor of keep

DIGGER FLAMEFORGE
Bael Modan, E-8, Lvl 24 Uncommon; In excavation site tent

DISHU
F:(2-3), Lvl 13 Uncommon; Patrols close to spawn points

ELDER MYSTIC RAZORSNOUT
Thorn Hill, G:(2, 3), Lvl 15 Uncommon; Eastern Razormane camp

ENGINEER WHIRLEYGIG
The Sludge Fen, G-1, Lvl 19 Uncommon; Control room

FOREMAN GRILLS
The Sludge Fen, G-1, Lvl 19 Semi-Rare; Patrols derrick

GEOPRIEST GUKK'ROK
Agama'gor, E:(4-5), Lvl 19 Uncommon; Guards Bristleback den

GESHARAHAN
Lushwater Oasis, E-4, Lvl 20 Average Rare; Swims in the oasis

HAGG TAURENBANE
Blackthorn Ridge, D-8, E-8, Lvl 26 Uncommon

HEGGIN STONEWHISKER
Bael Modan, E-8, Lvl 24 Uncommon; Crane

RATHORIAN
Dreadmist Den, E-2, F-2, Lvl 15 Uncommon; In cave atop Dreadmist Peak

SLUDGE BEAST
The Sludge Fen, G-1, Lvl 19 Semi-Rare; In sludge

SNORT THE HECKLER
D-3, Lvl 17 Uncommon; Roams southwest of Forgotten Pools

STONEARM
E:(2-3), Lvl 15 Uncommon; Roams Kolkar villages around the pools

TAKK THE LEAPER
G-1, Lvl 19 Semi-Rare; Roams ridge southeast of Sludge Fen

THUNDERSTOMP
Southern Barrens, E-8, Lvl 24 Uncommon; Roams clearing near Dustwallow Marsh border

BLASTED LANDS, PAGE 20

AKUBAR THE SEER
Dark Portal, G-5, H-5, I-5, Lvl 54 Uncommon; Roams small area around spawn point

CLACK THE REAVER
Dreadmaul Post, G-4, Lvl 53 Semi-Rare; Patrols to tower ruins at the edge of Serpent's Coil (I-3)

DEATHEYE
Dreadmaul Hold, G:(2, 3), Lvl 49 Average Rare; Roams small area around spawn point

DREADSCORN
Altar of Storms, F-3, Lvl 57 Uncommon; Patrols to foot of hill in Blasted Lands (F-4)

GRUNTER
Serpent's Coil, H-3, I-3, Lvl 50 Very Rare; Roams small area around spawn point

MAGRONOS THE UNYIELDING
Dreadmaul Post, G-4, Lvl 56 Average Rare; Roam small area around spawn point

MOJO THE TWISTED
Dreadmaul Hold, F-1, G-2, Lvl 48 Uncommon; Roams small area around spawn point

RAVAGE
G-4, I-4, Lvl 51 Semi-Rare; Roams small area around spawn point

SPITEFLAYER
Dark Portal, I-5, Lvl 52 Semi-Rare; Patrols to tower ruins at the edge of Serpent's Coil (I-3)

BLACKROCK MOUNTAIN, PAGES 22 & 64

CRYSTAL FANG
Blackrock Spire, C-4/D-8, Lvl 60 Rare

GHOK BASHGUUD
Blackrock Spire, C-4/D-8, Lvl 59 Uncommon

JED RUNEWATCHER
Blackrock Spire, C-4/D-8, Lvl 59 Uncommon

LORD ROCCOR
Blackrock Depths, C-4/D-8, Lvl 51 Rare

PANZOR THE INVINCIBLE
Blackrock Depths, C-4/D-8, Lvl 57 Rare

QUARTERMASTER ZIGRIS
Blackrock Spire, C-4/D-8, Lvl 59 Uncommon

SPIRESTONE BATTLE LORD
Blackrock Spire, C-4/D-8, Lvl 58 Uncommon

Burning Steppes, Page 22

DEATHMAW
Dreadmaul Rock, Terror Wing Path, I-3, J-6, K:(3, Lvl 53 Uncommon; Roams small area around spaw point

GORGON'OCH
Dreadmaul Rock, J-4, Lvl 54 Average Rare

GRUKLASH
Altar of Storms, Blackrock Stronghold, A-3, E-5, Lvl 59 Uncommon

HAHK'ZOR
Dreadmaul Rock, J:(4, 5), K-4, Lvl 54 Semi-Rare; Roams small area around spawn point

HEMATOS
Blackrock Mountain, D-3, Lvl 60 Very Rare; Patrol circular path around Draco'dar

KROM'GRUL
Dreadmaul Rock, J:(4, 5), K:(4, 5), Lvl 54 Common Roams small area around spawn point

MALFUNCTIONING REAVER
Dreadmaul Rock, Terror Wing Path, J-3, K:(3, 6), L Lvl 56 Semi-Rare; Roams small area around spawn point

TERRORSPARK
E-4, F-4, G-4, H-4, I-3, Lvl 55 Average Rare; Roam small area around spawn point

THAURIS BALGARR
Ruins of Thaurissan, F-4, G-4, H-4, I-4, Lvl 57 Uncommon; Roams small area around spawn poin

VOLCHAN
Terror Wing Path, K-6, Lvl 60 Uncommon; Patrols circular path around Dreadmaul Rock to the east

DARKSHORE, PAGE 24

CARNIVOUS THE BREAKER
Twilight Vale, F-5, F-8, Lvl 16 Uncommon; Roams close to spawn point

FIRECALLER RADISON
The Master's Glaive, F-9, Lvl 19 Semi-Rare; Wand center isle

FLAGGLEMURK THE CRUEL
Mist's Edge, Twilight Shore, E:(6-7), G-2, Lvl 16 Uncommon; Roams the shore close to spawn poin

LADY VESPIRA
Ruins of Mathystra, I-2, Lvl 22 Semi-Rare; Roams throughout ruins

LICILLIN
Bashal'Aran, G-4, Lvl 14 Uncommon; Wanders through ruins

LORD SINSLAYER
Cliffspring Falls, H-3, Lvl 15 Uncommon; In caves

SHADOWCLAW
F-4, Lvl 13 Uncommon; Roams near Auberdine

DESOLACE, PAGE 30

ACCURSED SLITHERBLADE
Sar'theris Strand, C-2, D:(1-2), E-1, Lvl 35 Average Rare; Swims area between Ranzajar Isle and shore

IGGLER
Tethris Aran, F-1, G-1, H:(2-3), I:(2-3), Lvl 34 Semi-Rare; Roams near spawn points

ISSPERAK
Kodo Graveyard, E:(4-6), F-5, G-5, Lvl 37 Semi-Rare; Roams area northwest of the Kodo Graveyard

ASKK
Mannoroc Coven, F-7, G:(7-8), Lvl 40 Very Rare; Patrols spawn points

ESHLOK THE HARVESTER
Mauradon, D-5, Lvl 48 Rare

RINCE KELLEN
Sargeron, J-2, Lvl 33 Average Rare; Top of hill or east by hill

AVENCLAW REGENT
Sargeron, J-2, Lvl 22 Uncommon; Southwest of Nijel's Point

DUN MOROGH, PAGE 32

JARN
The Tundrid Hills, G-6, H-6, I-6, Lvl 12 Uncommon; Roams small area around spawn point

APTAIN BELD
Ironband's Compound, K-6, Lvl 11 Common; Basement of compound

DAN THE HOWLER
The Grizzled Den, E-5, F-5, Lvl 9 Uncommon; In cave

IBBLEWILT
Gnomeregan, C-4, Lvl 11 Uncommon; Roams small area around spawn point

REAT FATHER ARCTIKUS
Frostmane Hold, B-5, C-5, Lvl 11 Uncommon; Cave at Frostmane Hold

AMMERSPINE
Gol'Bolar Quarry, J-5, Lvl 12 Uncommon; Roams small area around spawn point

IMBER
Iceflow Lake, D-4, Lvl 10 Uncommon; Large island at center of lake

UROTAR, PAGE 34

APTAIN FLAT TUSK
Durotar, Razormane Grounds, F:(4, 5), G-5, Lvl 11 Uncommon; Near huts

EATH FLAYER
E-5, F-5, Lvl 11 Uncommon; Roams clearing south of road

EOLORD MOTTLE
Razormane Grounds, F-4, G-5, Lvl 9 Uncommon; Found near huts

ARLORD KOLKANIS
Kolkar Crag, F-8, Lvl 9 Uncommon; Outside hut (left as you enter, middle of chasm to right, or in the back)

ATCH COMMANDER ZALAPHIL
Tiragarde Keep, I-6, Lvl 9 Uncommon; Receiving room of castle

USKWOOD, PAGE 36

OMMANDER FELSTROM
Dawning Wood Catacombs, A-3, B-4, Lvl 32 Uncommon; Stands at spawn point

ENROS
Brightwood Grove, H-4, Lvl 32 Uncommon; Patrols to two additional worgen camps (I-6, H-3)

ORD MALATHROM
Dawning Wood Catacombs, C:(2, 3), Lvl 31 Uncommon; Roams small area around spawn point

UPOS
Brightwood Grove, The Darkened Bank, C-3, D-3, E-3, H-3, I-3, J-3, Lvl 23 Uncommon; Roams small area around spawn point

ARAXIS
L-5, Lvl 27 Uncommon; Cave

EFARU
Roland's Doom, I-8, J-8, Lvl 34 Uncommon; Roams small area around spawn point

USTWALLOW MARSH, PAGE 38

URGLE EYE
Dreadmurk Shore, H:(1-3), Lvl 38 Uncommon; Spawns on the five isles

ARKMIST WIDOW
Darkmist Cavern, D-2, Lvl 40 Uncommon; Back of cavern

DART
F-2, Lvl 38 Uncommon; Runs in a circle near spawn point

DROGOTH THE ROAMER
Bluefen, D-1, Lvl 37 Uncommon; Roams throughout Bluefen

LORD ANGLER
Tidefury Cove, G-6, Lvl 44 Average Rare; Roams the cove

OOZEWORM
The Den of Flame, The Dragonmurk, D:(6-7), E-6, Lvl 42 Very Rare; Roams spawn points

RIPSCALE
The Quagmire, E-5. F:(5-6), Lvl 39 Semi-Rare; Roams swamp

THE ROT
Beezil's Wreck, G-6, Lvl 43 Average Rare; Roams the area around the wreck

EASTERN PLAGUELANDS, PAGE 40

DEATHSPEAKER SELENDRE
The Fungal Vale, The Noxious Glade, E-5, K:(4, 5), Lvl 56 Uncommon; In camp

DUGGAN WILDHAMMER
The Undercroft, B-7, C-6, D-8, E-7, Lvl 55 Semi-Rare; Roams small area around spawn point

GISH THE UNMOVING
Pestilent Scar, F-4, J-6, Lvl 56 Average Rare; Patrols between its two spawn points

HEARTHSINGER FORRESTEN
Stratholme, D-2, Lvl 57 Rare

HED'MUSH THE ROTTING
Crown Guard Tower, Eastwall Tower, Northpass Tower, E-7, G-3, I-5, Lvl 57 Very Rare; Roams small area around spawn point

HIGH GENERAL ABBENDIS
Tyr's Hand, K-8, L-8, Lvl 59 Uncommon; Second floor of castle or in The Scarlet Basilica

LORD DARKSCYTHE
Plaguewood, D-3, E:(3, 4), F-3, Lvl 57 Average Rare; Roams small area around spawn point

RANGER LORD HAWKSPEAR
Quel'Lithien Lodge, G-2, Lvl 60 Uncommon; Patrols lodge

SKUL
Stratholme, D-2, Lvl 58 Rare

STONESPINE
Stratholme, D-2, Lvl 60 Rare

WARLORD THRESH'JIN
Mazra'Alor, Zul'Mashar, I-2, J-2, Lvl 58 Uncommon; Stands idle at spawn point

ZUL'BRIN WARPBRANCH
Mazra'Alor, Zul'Mashar, I-2, J-2, Lvl 59 Semi-Rare; Stands idle at spawn point

ELWYNN FOREST, PAGE 42

FEDFENNEL
Stone Cairn Lake, I-4, Lvl 12 Uncommon; Stands idle at spawn point

GRUFF SWIFTBITE
Forest's Edge, C-9, Lvl 12 Uncommon; Patrols small area around spawn point

MORGAINE THE SLY
Mirror Lake Orchard, D-6, Lvl 10 Uncommon; House next to lake

MOTHER FANG
Jasperlode Mine, H-5, Lvl 10 Uncommon; Roams in mine

NARG THE TASKMASTER
Fargodeep Mine, E-8, Lvl 10 Uncommon; Roams in mine

THUROS LIGHTFINGERS
Crystal Lake, Jerod's Landing, Mirror Lake, D-6, G:(6, 8), L-8, Lvl 11 Uncommon; Stands idle at spawn point

FELWOOD, PAGE 44

ALSHIRR BANEBREATH
Jadefire Glen, F-8, Lvl 54 Uncommon; Roams Jadefire Glen

DEATH HOWL
Felwood, Morlos'Aran, G:(7-8), H-9, Lvl 49 Average Rare; Roams near spawn points

DESSECUS
Irontree Cavern, H-2, Lvl 56 Semi-Rare; Bottom cave

IMMOLATUS
Shatter Scar Vale, F-4, Lvl 56 Semi-Rare; Roams eastern craters

MONGRESS
F:(7-8), Lvl 50 Very Rare; Roams near spawn points

OLM THE WISE
Irontree Woods, G:(2-3), H:(1-3), Lvl 52 Average Rare; Roams near spawn points

RAGEPAW
Deadwood Village, G-9, Lvl 51 Uncommon; Roams southern area of camp

THE ONGAR
Bloodvenom River, E-5, Lvl 51 Very Rare; Roams river near spawn point

FERALAS, PAGE 46

ARASH-ETHIS
The Twin Colossals, D-2, E-2, Lvl 49 Uncommon; Patrols area west of road near mountains

DIAMOND HEAD
Sardor Isle, A:(5-6), C:(5-6), Lvl 45 Semi-Rare; Seabed off coast of isle

GNARL LEAFBROTHER
The Writhing Deep, I-6, Lvl 44 Very Rare; Roams west to the Woodpaw Hills

LADY SZALLAH
Isle of Dread, B-7, Lvl 46 Uncommon; Roams various areas outside of Shalzaru's Lair

MUSHGOG
Dire Maul, G-4, Lvl 60 Rare

OLD GRIZZLEGUT
Lower Wilds, Ruins of Isildien, G-6, H-4, Lvl 43 Very Rare; Roams in a wide area

QIROT
The Writhing Deep, I-6, Lvl 47 Uncommon; In hive

SKARR THE UNBREAKABLE
Dire Maul, G-4, Lvl 58 Rare

SNARLER
Lariss Pavilion, I-4, Lvl 42 Uncommon; Spawns near delta and roams southeast

THE RAZZA
Dire Maul, The Maul, G-4, Lvl 60 Rare; In arena

TSU'ZEE
Dire Maul, G-4, Lvl 59 Rare

HILLSBRAD FOOTHILLS, PAGE 48

BIG SAMRAS
Durnholde Keep, I-3, K:(4, 5), Lvl 27 Semi-Rare; Roams small area around spawn point

CREEPTHESS
Azurelode Mine, B-5, C-6, D:(5, 6), Lvl 24 Semi-Rare; Roams small area around spawn point

LADY ZEPHRIS
Eastern Strand, H-9, Lvl 33 Uncommon; Patrols southeastern coastline

RO'BARK
Nethander Stead, H-6, Lvl 28 Uncommon; Patrols crop field

SCARGIL
Western Strand, B-7, C-7, Lvl 30 Uncommon

TAMRA STORMPIKE
Dun Garok, I-8, Lvl 28 Uncommon; Roams a small area around spawn point

HINTERLANDS, PAGE 50

GRIMUNGOUS
The Overlook Cliffs, K-5, Lvl 50 Very Rare; Patrols the southeastern ridgeline

IRONBACK
The Overlook Cliffs, L:(5, 6), Lvl 51 Semi-Rare; Roams small area around spawn point

JALINDE SUMMERDRAKE
Quel'Danil Lodge, D-5, E:(4, 5), Lvl 49 Uncommon; Roams small area around spawn point

MITH'RETHIS THE ENCHANTER
Jintha'Alor, I-8, J-8, Lvl 52 Average Rare; Roams from camp to camp

OLD CLIFF JUMPER
The Hinterlands, C:(5, 6), Lvl 42 Semi-Rare; Patrols small area around spawn point

RAZORTALON
Bogen's Ledge, D:(5, 7), E-5, F-5, Lvl 44 Average Rare; Roams small area around spawn point

RETHEROKK THE BERSERKER
The Altar of Zul, G:(6, 7), H-6, Lvl 48 Uncommon; Roams around base of altar

THE REAK
Agol'watha, Skulk Rock, The Creeping Ruin, G:(4, 5), I-4, Lvl 49 Very Rare; Roams small area around spawn point

WITHERHEART THE STALKER
Shadra'Alor, E-7, Lvl 45 Semi-Rare; Patrols while stealthed around small pond

ZUL'AREK HATEFOWLER
Hiri'Watha, Zun'Watha, D-6, E-6, Lvl 43 Uncommon; Roams small area around spawn point

LOCH MODAN, PAGE 54

BOSS GALGOSH
Ironband's Excavation Site, I-6, Lvl 22 Uncommon; On excavation platform with a Stonesplitter Geomancer and Berserk Trogg

GRIZLAK
Silver Stream Mine, D-3, Lvl 15 Uncommon; Roams small area around spawn point

LORD CONDAR
Ironband's Excavation Site, The Farstrider Lodge, H-8, J-7, K-7, Lvl 15 Semi-Rare; Roams small area around spawn point

MAGOSH
Ironband's Excavation Site, I-7, Lvl 21 Uncommon; With two Stonesplitter Diggers on hilltop in center excavation site

SHANDA THE SPINNER
K-5, Lvl 19 Semi-Rare; Roams small area around spawn point

MULGORE, PAGE 58

ENFORCER EMILGUND
D-2, Lvl 11 Uncommon; Venture Co. camp

GHOST HOWL
C-2, D:(1, 4), F-1, Lvl 12 Uncommon; Roams plains in multiple areas

SISTER HATELASH
D-1, Lvl 11 Uncommon; Northwest nest

SNAGGLESPEAR
F-7, Lvl 9 Uncommon; Camp

REDRIDGE MOUNTAINS, PAGE 62

BOULDERHEART
L-6, Lvl 25 Semi-Rare; Roams small area around spawn point

CHATTER
Alther's Mill, G-4, H-5, Lvl 23 Uncommon; Roams small area around spawn point

KAZON
Render's Camp, D-1, Lvl 27 Uncommon; Idle by hut

RIBCHASER
Lakeridge Highway, Three Corners, A-6, D-8, Lvl 17 Uncommon; Patrols around gnoll camp

ROHH THE SILENT
Galardell Valley, Stonewatch Falls, Tower of Ilgalar, J:(3, 4), K:(5, 6), Lvl 26 Semi-Rare; Stands idle at spawn point

SEEKER AQUALON
Lake Everstill, Stonewatch Falls, H-5, I-6, J-6, Lvl 21 Average Rare; Patrols the waterway connecting Lake Everstill with Stonewatch Falls

SNARLFLARE
Alther's Mill, D-6, E-3, F-3, Lvl 18 Uncommon; Roams small area around spawn point

SQUIDDIC
Lake Everstill, G-7, Lvl 19 Uncommon; Patrols back and forth just offshore by the murloc camp

SEARING GORGE, PAGE 64

FAULTY WAR GOLEM
The Sea of Cinders, C-6, D-5, E-4, F-7, G-6, Lvl 46 Semi-Rare; Roams small area around spawn point

HIGHLORD MASTROGONDE
Firewatch Ridge, A-4, C-3, Lvl 51 Uncommon; Roams small area around spawn point

REKK'TILAC
Tanner Camp, The Sea of Cinders, Thorium Point, C-7, D-3, F-7, G-3, H-7, I-7, Lvl 48 Average Rare; Stands idle at spawn point

SCALD
The Cauldron, D-5, G-4, Lvl 49 Average Rare; Patrols path near spawn point

SHLEIPNARR
H-4, Lvl 47 Very Rare; Patrols path near spawn point

SLAVE MASTER BLACKHEART
The Slag Pit, E:(2-4), Lvl 50 Uncommon; Roams small area around spawn point

SMOLDAR
C-6, Lvl 50 Semi-Rare; Patrols the northwestern portion of the zone

RARE MOBS

SILITHUS, PAGE 66

GRETHEER
Hive'Regal, E-2, F-3, G-4, Lvl 57 Very Rare; Roams close to spawn points

GRUBTHOR
E-4, Lvl 58 Semi-Rare; Roams close to spawn points

HURICANIAN
The Crystal Vale, D-1, Lvl 58 Uncommon; Roams vale

KRELLACK
Southwind Village, G-2, Lvl 56 Semi-Rare; Roams close to spawn points

LAPRESS
Hive'Regal, G-5, Lvl 60 Very Rare; Spawns in far southeast of hive and roams hive

REX ASHIL
Hive'Ashi, F-2, Lvl 57 Average Rare; Patrols above and within hive

SETIS
The Scarab Wall, E-5, Lvl 61 Uber-Rare; Spawns in front of the wall and roams the length of northern Silithus

TWILIGHT LORD EVERUN
Twilight Base Camp, Twilight Outpost, Twilight Post, D-5, E-2, F-3, Lvl 60 Uncommon; Roams respective camp

ZORA
Hive'Zora, D-4, Lvl 59 Average Rare; Roams hive

SILVERPINE FOREST, PAGE 68

DEATHSWORN CAPTAIN
Shadowfang Keep, F-7, Lvl 25 Rare

GOREFANG
Malden's Orchard, Silverpine Forest, G:(2, 3), H-2, I-1, Lvl 13 Uncommon; Roams small area around spawn point

KRETHIS SHADOWSPINNER
The Skittering Dark, E-1, Lvl 15 Uncommon; Roaming in or around cave

OLD VICEJAW
H:(5, 6), Lvl 14 Uncommon; Roams small area around spawn point

SNARLMANE
Fenris Keep, J:(2, 3), Lvl 23 Uncommon; Stands idle at spawn point

STONETALON MOUNTAINS, PAGE 70

FOREMAN RIGGER
Blackwolf River, Windshear Crag, H-5, I-5, Lvl 24 Uncommon; West end of the crag

PRIDEWING PATRIARCH
Mirkfallon Lake, F:(4-5), G-4, Lvl 25 Uncommon; Spawns in mountains east or south of Mirkfallon Lake

VENGEFUL ANCIENT
The Charred Vale, C-7, D-7, Lvl 29 Uncommon; Roams the vale

STORMWIND, PAGE 72

BRUEGAL IRONKNUCKLE
The Stockade, F-6, Lvl 26 Rare

STRANGLETHORN VALE, PAGE 74

GLUGGLE
Kal'ai Ruins, C-3, Lvl 37 Semi-Rare; Patrols between ruins and path heading north

HIGH PRIESTESS HAI'WATNA
Zul'Gurub, F-2, Lvl 57 Semi-Rare; Ruins just before the entrance to Zul'Gurub

KURMOKK
Ruins of Aboraz, D-6, Lvl 42 Very Rare; Patrols through Mistvale Valley toward the road heading into Booty Bay

LORD SAKRASIS
Nek'Mani Wellspring, B-6, Lvl 45 Uncommon; Far end of bridge in front of altar

RIPPA
Southern Savage Coast, B-6, Lvl 44 Very Rare; Patrols the cove on the northern side of The Cape of Stranglethorn

ROLOCH
Mizjah Ruins, D-3, Lvl 38 Average Rare; Patrols between ruins and the path to the north

SCALE BELLY
Crystalvein Mine, F-5, Lvl 45 Uncommon; Mine

VERIFONIX
The Cape of Stranglethorn, D-6, Lvl 42 Average Rare; Patrols a circular path around ridgeline stopping periodically to mine

SWAMP OF SORROWS, PAGE 76

FINGAT
Stagalbog Cave, H-8, Lvl 43 Semi-Rare; Patrols cave

GILMORIAN
The Forbidding Sea, J-9, Lvl 43 Average Rare; Patrols up and down the eastern coastline

JADE
Temple of Atal'Hakkar, I-5, Lvl 47 Very Rare; Entrance to the Temple of Atal'Hakkar

LORD CAPTAIN WYRMAK
H-4, Lvl 45 Uncommon; Patrols the upper right portion of swampland surrounding the Temple of Atal'Hakkar

LOST ONE CHIEFTAIN
Fallow Sanctuary, H-2, Lvl 39 Semi-Rare; Idle near huts in the northwest corner of camp

LOST ONE COOK
Fallow Sanctuary, H-2, Lvl 37 Uncommon; Idle by one of the two cauldrons in camp

MOLT THORN
The Shifting Mire, C-5, D-4, Lvl 42 Average Rare; Patrols back and forth between connecting bridges along the western waterways

VEYZHAK THE CANNIBAL
The Temple of Atal'Hakkar, I-5, Lvl 48 Uncommon

TANARIS, PAGE 78

CYCLOK THE MAD
Dunemaul Compound, Eastmoon Ruins, Southmoon Ruins, F:(5-7), G:(6, 7), Lvl 48 Very Rare; Spawns in ruins or compound and sticks close to spawn point

GREATER FIREBIRD
Abyssal Sands, F-4, Lvl 46 Average Rare; Flies throughout northern sands

HAARKA THE RAVENOUS
The Gaping Chasm, H-7, Lvl 50 Average Rare; Spawns in one of the chambers and sticks close to spawn point

KREGG KEELHAUL
Lost Rigger Cove, J-5, K-5, Lvl 47 Uncommon; In west building, ship being built, or far ship at dock

MURDEROUS BLISTERPAW
H-4, Lvl 43 Very Rare; Roams from one set of hills to the other

OMGORN THE LOST
Dunemaul Compound, Eastmoon Ruins, Southmoon Ruins, F:(6, 7), G:(6, 7), Lvl 50 Semi-Rare; Roams a wide path around spawn point

SORIID THE DEVOURER
The Noxious Lair, E:(4, 5), Lvl 50 Uncommon; Spawns in multiple chambers

TELDRASSIL, PAGE 80

BLACKMOSS THE FETID
Wellspring River, E:(3-4), Lvl 13 Uncommon; Patrols up and down river

DUSKSTALKER
F-8, G-8, Lvl 9 Uncommon; Patrols south of Lake Al'Ameth

FURY SHELDA
The Oracle Glade, D:(3-4), Lvl 8 Uncommon; Patrols near harpy camps west of road

GRIMMAW
Gnarlpine Hold, E-8, Lvl 11 Uncommon; Patrols Gnarlpine camps

THREGGIL
Fel Rock, G-5, Lvl 6 Uncommon; Runs around water in western section of cave

URUSON
Starbreeze Village, I-6, Lvl 7 Uncommon; Patrols road in village

THOUSAND NEEDLES, PAGE 82

ACHELLIOS THE BANISHED
Whitereach Post, B:(3-4), C-4, Lvl 31 Uncommon; Circles a couple plateaus in southwestern region

GIBBLESNIK
Windbreak Canyon, G:(4-5), H:(5-6), Lvl 28 Semi-Rare; Several spawn points around Windbreak Canyons

HARB FOULMOUNTAIN
Darkcloud Pinnacle, D-3, E-3, Lvl 27 Uncommon; Patrols across three small plateaus, north of pinnacle

TIRISFAL GLADES, PAGE 86

BAYNE
Stillwater Pond, E:(4, 5), F-5, G-4, Lvl 10 Uncommon; Roams small area around spawn point

DEEB
The North Coast, G-3, H-3, Lvl 12 Uncommon; Stands idle at spawn point

FARMER SOLLIDEN
Solliden Farmstead, D-5, E-5, Lvl 8 Uncommon; Stands idle at spawn point

FELLICENT'S SHADE
Balnir Farmstead, J-6, Lvl 12 Uncommon; Patrols a circular path around crop field

LOST SOUL
Agamand Mills (100), F-4, G-5, Lvl 6 Uncommon; Roams small area around spawn point

MUAD
Whispering Shore, D-4, Lvl 10 Uncommon; Patrols in and along shoreline

RESSAN THE NEEDLER
Nightmare Vale, E-7, F:(6, 7), G-6, Lvl 11 Uncommon; Roams a small area around spawn point

SRI'SKULK
Venomweb Vale, K-5, L:(4, 5), Lvl 13 Uncommon; Roams small area around spawn point

TORMENTED SPIRIT
Agamand Mills (100), E-3, Lvl 8 Uncommon; Patrols the northwestern edge of mill

UN'GORO CRATER, PAGE 90

CLUTCHMOTHER ZAVAS
The Slithering Scar, G-8, Lvl 54 Semi-Rare; Inside The Slighering Scar

UHK'LOC
Fungal Rock, I-2, Lvl 53 Uncommon; Northern section of cave

WESTERN PLAGUELANDS, PAGE 92

DREADWHISPER
Gahrron's Withering, H-6, Lvl 58 Semi-Rare; Roams small area around spawn point

FOREMAN JERRIS
Hearthglen, F:(1, 2), Lvl 62 Uncommon; Roams small area around spawn point

FOREMAN MARCRID
Northridge Lumber Camp, F-3, Lvl 58 Average Rare; Roams small area around spawn point

FOULMANE
Dalson's Tears, F-5, Lvl 52 Semi-Rare; Patrols around cauldron

LORD MALDAZZAR
Sorrow Hill, F-8, G:(7, 8), Lvl 56 Uncommon; Roams small area around spawn point

PUTRIDIUS
Ruins of Andorhal, F-7, Lvl 58 Uber-Rare; Roamd around city

SCARLET EXECUTIONER
Hearthglen, F-2, Lvl 60 Very Rare; Roams in tower on the southern end of city

SCARLET HIGH CLERIST
G-2, Lvl 63 Average Rare; Spawns inside or on top of tower south of Hearthglen

SCARLET INTERROGATOR
Hearthglen, F-1, Lvl 61 Uncommon; Spawns on the first or second floor of tower in the northeast corner of city

SCARLET JUDGE
Hearthglen, E-2, Lvl 60 Semi-Rare; Roams in town hall

SCARLET SMITH
Hearthglen, F-1, Lvl 58 Uncommon; Spawns in around to the right of smithy

THE HUSK
The Weeping Cave, H-4, I:(3, 4), Lvl 62 Very Rare; Roams small area around spawn point

WESTFALL, PAGE 94

BRACK
Longshore, C-8, Lvl 19 Uncommon; Runs entire Longshore coast

FOE REAPER 4000
Alexston Farmstead, The Dead Acre, Fulbrow's Pumpkin Farm, The Molsen Farm, Moonbrook, D-5, E-4, F-2, F-7, G-6, Lvl 20 Semi-Rare; Roams around spawn points

LEPRITHUS
The Dust Plains, D-3, G-8, Lvl 19 Uncommon; Appears near coffin/tombstones under tree

MASTER DIGGER
Jangolode Mine, E-2, Lvl 15 Uncommon; In back of mine

SERGEANT BRASHCLAW
D-3, Lvl 18 Uncommon; Guards gnoll camp in copse of trees

SLARK
Longshore, F-1, Lvl 15 Uncommon; Runs entire Longshore coast

VULTROS
The Dead Acre, The Dust Plains, Furlbrow's Pumpkin Farm, Stendel's Pond, Westfall, C-7, E-4, E-6, F-2, G-7, H-6, Lvl 26 Average Rare; Roams around spawn points

WETLANDS, PAGE 96

GARNEG CHARSKULL
Angerfang Encampment, E-5, F:(4, 5), Lvl 29 Uncommon; Spawns in a few different camps

GNAWBONE
Sundown Marsh, D-3, E-3, Lvl 24 Average Rare; Patrols mosside camps north of road across from excavation site

LEECH WIDOW
Thelgen Rock, G-6, Lvl 24 Uncommon; Patrols southwest area of cave

MA'RUK WYRMSCALE
Dun Algaz, G-7, Lvl 25 Uncommon; Patrols water south of windmill

MIRELOW
Bluegill Marsh, Sundown Marsh, B:(3, 4), C:(2-4), Lvl 25 Semi-Rare; Patrols water west and south of windmill and around bluegill camps

RAZORMAW MATRIARCH
Raptor Ridge, I-3, J-3, Lvl 31 Uncommon; Spawns western or northeastern chamber of cave

SLUDGINN
A-7, B-7, Lvl 30 Average Rare; South of Menethil Harbor, in hills across water

ZERILLIS
Zul'Farrak, E-1, Lvl 45 Rare

WINTERSPRING, PAGE 98

AZUROUS
Ice Thistle Hills, J-5, Lvl 59 Average Rare; Wanders hills east of road

GENERAL COLBATANN
Mazthoril, H-5, Lvl 57 Semi-Rare; Central cavern

GRIZZLE SNOWPAW
Winterfall Village, J-4, Lvl 59 Uncommon; Patrols village

KASHOCH THE REAVER
Frostwhisper Gorge, I-7, Lvl 60 Average Rare; Guards tower in gorge

LADY HEDERINE
Darkwhisper Gorge, H-8, Lvl 61 Very Rare; Deep within the gorge

MEZZIR THE HOWLER
Frostfire Hot Springs, E-4, Lvl 55 Uncommon; Roams to the west

RAK'SHIRI
Frostsaber Rock, G:(1, 2), H-1, Lvl 57 Semi-Rare; Roams base of rock

SKILL TRAINERS

COOKING

TITLE/DESCRIPTION	NAME	REGION	MINI REGION	GRID LOC
Butcher	Sherman Femmel	Redridge Mountains (62)	Lakeshire (117)	C-4
	Dirge Quickcleave	Tanaris (78)	Gadgetzan (113)	H-3
Cook	Duhng	Barrens (18)		G-3
	Tomas	Elwynn Forest (42)	Goldshire (114)	F-7
	Pyall Silentstride	Mulgore (58)	Bloodhoof Village (102)	E-6
	Zarrin	Teldrassil (80)	Dolanaar (109)	G-6
Cooking Trainer	Alegorn	Darnassus (26)	Craftsmen's Terrace	F-2
	Cook Ghilm	Dun Morogh (32)	Gol'Bolar Quarry	I-5
	Gremlock Pilsnor	Dun Morogh (32)	Kharanos (116)	F-5
	Daryl Riknussun	Ironforge (52)	The Great Forge	H-4
	Zamja	Orgrimmar (60)	The Drag	G-5
	Crystal Boughman	Redridge Mountains (62)	Lakeshire (117)	B-4
	Stephen Ryback	Stormwind (72)	Old Town	K-4
	Aska Mistrunner	Thunder Bluff (84)		F-5
	Eunice Burch	Undercity (88)	The Trade Quarter	H-4, I-4
Recipe Trainer	Henry Stern	Barrens (18)	Razorfen Downs	F-9
Superior Butcher	Slagg	Arathi Highlands (10)	Hammerfall (115)	J-3

FIRST AID

TITLE/DESCRIPTION	NAME	REGION	MINI REGION	GRID LOC
First Aid Trainer	Dannelor	Darnassus (26)	Craftsmen's Terrace	G-1
	Rawrk	Durotar (34)	Razor Hill (124)	H-4
	Nissa Firestone	Ironforge (52)	The Great Forge	G-6
	Vira Younghoof	Mulgore (58)	Bloodhoof Village (102)	E-6
	Arnok	Orgrimmar (60)	Valley of Spirit	C-8
	Shaina Fuller	Stormwind (72)	Cathedral Square	F-3
	Byancie	Teldrassil (80)	Dolanaar (109)	G-6
	Pand Stonebinder	Thunder Bluff (84)	Spirit Rise	C-2
	Nurse Neela	Tirisfal Glades (86)	Brill (104)	H-5
	Mary Edras	Undercity (88)	The Rogues' Quarter	J-5
	Fremal Doohickey	Wetlands (96)	Deepwater Tavern	A-6
Physician	Thamner Pol	Dun Morogh (32)	Kharanos (116)	F-5
	Michelle Belle	Elwynn Forest (42)	Goldshire (114)	F-7
Trauma Surgeon (First Aid)	Doctor Gregory Victor	Arathi Highlands (10)	Hammerfall (115)	J-4
	Doctor Gustaf VanHowzen	Dustwallow Marsh (38)	Theramore Isle (135)	I-5

FISHING

TITLE/DESCRIPTION	NAME	REGION	MINI REGION	GRID LOC
Artisan Fisherman	Nat Pagle	Dustwallow Marsh (38)	Tidefury Cove	H-6
Butcher	Sherman Femmel	Redridge Mountains (62)	Lakeshire (117)	C-4
Fisherman	Kil'Hiwana	Ashenvale (12)	Zoram'gar Outpost (137)	B-4
	Kilxx	Barrens (18)	Ratchet (122)	H-4
	Zizzek	Barrens (18)	Ratchet (122)	H-4
	Heldan Galesong	Darkshore (24)	Twilight Shore	E-6
	Lui'Mala	Desolace (30)	Shadowprey Village (128)	B-7
	Paxton Ganter	Dun Morogh (32)	Iceflow Lake	E-4
	Lau'Tiki	Durotar (34)	Darkspear Strand	H-8
	Lee Brown	Elwynn Forest (42)	Crystal Lake	F-6
	Brannock	Feralas (46)	Feathermoon Stronghold (111)	C-4
	Donald Rabonne	Hillsbrad Foothills (48)	Southshore (129)	F-6
	Warg Deepwater	Loch Modan (54)	The Loch	E-4
	Uthan Stillwater	Mulgore (58)	Stonebull Lake	E-6
	Androl Oakhand	Teldrassil (80)	Rut'theran Village (125)	G-9
	Clyde Kellen	Tirisfal Glades (86)	Brightwater Lake	I-5
Fishing Trainer	Astaia	Darnassus (26)	Tradesmen's Terrace	F-5
	Grimnur Stonebrand	Ironforge (52)	The Forlorn Cavern	F-1
	Lumak	Orgrimmar (60)	Valley of Honor	I-3
	Matthew Hooper	Redridge Mountains (62)	Lakeshire (117)	C-5
	Arnold Leland	Stormwind (72)	The Canals	G-6
	Kah Mistrunner	Thunder Bluff (84)		F-5
	Armand Cromwell	Undercity (88)	The Magic Quarter	K-3
	Harold Riggs	Wetlands (96)	Menethil Harbor (119)	A-6
Superior Fisherman	Myizz Luckycatch	Stranglethorn Vale (74)	Booty Bay (103)	B-8

SPECIALTY VENDORS

ARCANE TRINKETS VENDOR
Stormwind (72), Mage Quarter, E-8, Charys Yserian, Ancient Curios

BAEL'DUN MORALE OFFICER
Barrens (18), Bael'dun Keep, F-8, Malgin Barleybrew, Back of right wing

BLUE MOON ODDS AND ENDS
Undercity (88), The Apothecarium, H-5, Allesandro Luca,

BOY WITH KITTENS
Stormwind (72), Cathedral Square, The Canals, Lil Timmy, Roams Cathedral Square and The Canals

COCKROACH VENDOR
Undercity (88), The Trade Quarter, I:(4, 5), Jeremiah Payson, Under Bridge in Trade Quarter

CRAZY CAT LADY
Elwynn Forest (42), F-5, Donni Anthania, House southwest of Northshire Valley

FIREWORKS MERCHANT
Stranglethorn Vale (74), Booty Bay (103), B-8, Crazk Sparks, Shop on the back side of building near the overturned boat and hanging shark on the eastern side of bay

FIREWORKS VENDOR
Stormwind (72), Mage Quarter, D-7, Darian Singh, Pyrotechnics

FIREWORKS VENDOR
Ironforge (52), Tinker Town, J-5, Fizzlebang Booms, Things That Go Boom

FREEWHEELING MERCHANT
Westfall (94), Moonbrook, E-7, Defias Profiteer, Top floor of Moonbrook inn

FREEWHEELING TRADESWOMAN
Hillsbrad Foothills (48), Durnholde Keep, J-4, Kris Legace, Just below rear of ruins in the upper level of keep

GUILD TABARD VENDOR
Ironforge (52), The Commons, D-8, Lyesa Steelbrow, Ironforge Visitor's Center

HORSE BREEDER
Dustwallow Marsh (38), Theramore Isle (135), I-5, Gregor MacVince, Stables to southwest

HORSE BREEDER
Elwynn Forest (42), Eastvale Logging Camp, L-6, Katie Hunter, Corale

HORSE BREEDER
Hillsbrad Foothills (48), Southshore (129), F-6, Merideth Carlson, Stable

HORSE BREEDER
Wetlands (96), Menethil Harbor (117), A-5, Unger Statforth, Outside stables

ICE CREAM VENDOR
Thousand Needles (82), Mirage Raceway (119), J-8, Brivelthwerp, Next to building west of racetrack

KODO MOUNTS
Mulgore (58), Bloodhoof Village (102), E-6, Harb Clawhoof, Northern clearing

MASTER OF COOKING RECIPES
Stormwind (72), Old Town, J-5, Kendor Kabonka, Pig and Whistle Tavern

MECHANOSTRIDER MERCHANT
Dun Morogh (32), Steelgrill's Depot, G-5, Milli Featherwhistle, By mechanostrider's outside of depot

MERCHANT SUPREME
Hillsbrad Foothills (48), G-3, Zixil, Patrols with Overwatch Mark I between Tarren Mill and Southshore

OWL TRAINER
Darnassus (26), Warrior's Terrace, K-4, Shylenai, South of path just after entrance to city

PET VENDOR
Dun Morogh (32), Amberstill Ranch, I-5, Yarlyn Amberstill, Patrols circular path around ranch

PIRATE SUPPLIES
Stranglethorn Vale (74), Booty Bay (103), B-8, Narkk, Nautical Needs (shop) on the northern side of The Old Port Authority

POTIONS & HERBS
Wetlands (96), G-4, Kixxle, Next to road to Dun Modr, by bridge

POTIONS, SCROLLS AND REAGENTS
Dustwallow Marsh (38), Brackenwall Village (104), D-3, Balai Lok'Wein, Northern part of village

QUARTERMASTER
Westfall (94), Sentinel Tower, G-5, Quartermaster Lewis, Sentinel Tower

RAM BREEDER
Dun Morogh (32), Amberstill Ranch, I-5, Veron Amberstill, By carriage in front of corral

RAPTOR HANDLER
Durotar (34), Sen'jin Village (126), H-7, Zjolnir, Among raptors south of village

RARE GOODS
Duskwood (36), K-2, Kzixx, By carriage

REWARDS VENDOR
Alterac Mountains (8), I-6, Jekyll Flandring, Left camp outside Alterac Valley (Horde)

REWARDS VENDOR
Alterac Mountains (8), The Headland, E-8, Thanthaldis Snowgleam, Camp outside Alterac Valley

RIDING WOLF (KENNEL MASTER)
Orgrimmar (60), Valley of Honor, I-1, Ogunaro Wolfrunner, Outside of Hunter's Hall

SABER HANDLER
Darnassus (26), Cenarion Enclave, E-1, Lelanai, Intersection of paths

SCROLLS AND POTIONS
Arathi Highlands (10), Stromgarde Keep (132), C-6, Deneb Walker, Well near church

SHADY DEALER
Stormwind (72), Old Town, L-6, Jasper Fel, SI:7

SHADY DEALER
Wetlands (96), Deepwater Tavern, A-6, Samor Festivus, Northwest, upstairs room

SHADY DEALER
Ironforge (52), The Forlorn Cavern, G-1, Tynnus Venomsprout, Top of steps, just inside east entrance

SHADY GOODS
Stranglethorn Vale (74), Booty Bay (103), B-8, Sly Garrett, Outside of fireworks shop on the eastern side of bay

SILVERWING SUPPLY OFFICER
Ashenvale (12), Silverwing Grove, H-8, Illiyana Moonblaze, In tent to the right of ramp

SMOKYWOOD PASTURES
Barrens (18), Mor'shan Base Camp, E-1, Hecht Copperpinch, Outside entrance to Warsong Gulch

SNAKE VENDOR
Orgrimmar (60), Valley of Spirit, A-6, C-8, Xan'tis, Roams Valley of Spirits

SPECIAL GOODS DEALER
Wetlands (96), Sundown Marsh, C-3, Wenna Silkbeard, Building next to windmill

SPECIAL WEAPON CRAFTER
Ironforge (52), The Great Forge, G-5, H-5, Ironus Coldsteel, The Great Anvil

SPECIALIST LEATHERWORKING SUPPLIES
Barrens (18), Wailing Caverns, E-4, Kaldan Felmoon,

SPECIALIST LEATHERWORKING SUPPLIES
Barrens (18), The Wailing Caverns, E-4, Kalldan Felmoon, Right eye of cave above entrance

SPECIALIST TAILORING SUPPLIES
Redridge Mountains (62), Render's Valley, J-8, Captured Servant of Azora, By cages in camp

SPECIALITY DRESS MAKER
Moonglade (56), Nighthaven (121), G-3, Geenia Sunshadow, First floor of northeast building

SPECIALITY ENGINEER
Hillsbrad Foothills (48), , K-2, Zan Shivsproket, Basement of Chateau Ravenholdt

SPECIALITY TAILORING SUPPLIES
Ironforge (52), The Great Forge, F-3, Outfitter Eric, Stonebrow's Clothier

SPECIALTY GOODS
Wetlands (96), Dun Modr, F-2, Dark Iron Entrepreneur, Behind bar in southern building

STYLISH CLOTHIER
Barrens (18), E-4, Kiknikle, Near mountains west of oasis

SWEET TREATS
Orgrimmar (60), Valley of Strength, E-7, Alowicious Czervik,

TABARD VENDOR
Orgrimmar (60), Valley of Strength, E-7, Garyl, Horde Embassy

TABARD VENDOR
Undercity (88), The Trade Quarter, J-4, Merill Pleasance, East spoke from bank

TABARD VENDOR
Stormwind (72), Trade District, H-7, I-7, Rebecca Laughlin, Stormwind Visitor's Center

TABARD VENDOR
Darnassus (26), Craftsmen's Terrace, I-2, Shalumon, Southeast building, second floor

TABARD VENDOR
Thunder Bluff (84), D-6, Thrumn, Lower rise, in front of Thunder Bluff Civic Information tent

UNDEAD HORSE MERCHANT
Tirisfal Glades (86), Brill (104), H-5, Zachariah Post, Stable

WAR HARNESS MAKER
Orgrimmar (60), Valley of Honor, I-4, Kiro, Kiro's Harnesses

WAR HARNESS VENDOR
Thunder Bluff (84), F-5, Sura Wildmane, High rise, between Ragetotem Arms and Aska's Kitchen

WARSONG SUPPLY OFFICER
Barrens (18), Mor'shan Base Camp, E-1, Kelm Hargunth, Outside entrance to Warsong Gulch

World of WarCraft

ATLAS

LEGAL

ISBN: 978-0-7440-1047-3

Printing Code: The rightmost double-digit number is the year of the book's printing; the rightmost single-digit number is the number of the book's printing. For example, 05-1 shows that the first printing of the book occurred in 2005.

11 10 09 08   4 3 2 1

Printed by Mondadori Printing, Verona, Italy

BRADYGAMES STAFF

Publisher
David Waybright

Licensing Manager
Mike Degler

Director of Marketing
Debby Neubauer

Editor-In-Chief
H. Leigh Davis

Marketing Coordinator
Autumne Bruce

Team Coordinator
Stacey Beheler

CREDITS

Development Editor
Brian Shotton

Lead Designer
Dan Caparo

Designer
Areva

Brady Census Takers
Jennifer Sims
Kenny Sims

Cartography: Town & Encampment Maps
Argosy Publishing

ACKNOWLEDGMENTS

This project is a collaboration of so many talented people that we feel it's important to recognize them all.

From Blizzard
First off, we have to thank everyone at Blizzard (especially the QA teams) for their hospitality. Specifically, we'd like to thank Shane Cargilo for his help compiling data, Ben George for just being a fantastic front man, and Ben Brode for keeping us up and running and for providing that little application that made things so much easier. A very special thank you goes to Gina Pippin for handling such a massive project with style, and Tim Daniels for helping to whip us through the approvals. Finally, this book would be nothing without the guidance and assistance from Chris Metzen. Just working with this team was an honor.

From BradyGames
A bunch of people pitched in to help out on a project simply because of their knowledge of, and enthusiasm for, the **World of Warcraft**. Jennifer and Kenny Sims were an eternal source of information and just about everyone else mentioned in the staff/credits went beyond their normal duties to help on this project. Special thanks to Areva for putting up with me. Thanks to you all for helping to create such a wonderful product.